Contents

Denmark

The Netherlands

Belgium

Luxembourg

Germany

Switzerland

Austria

Poland

Czech Republic

Hungary

Slovenia

Croatia

Albania

Greece

United Kingdom

Ireland

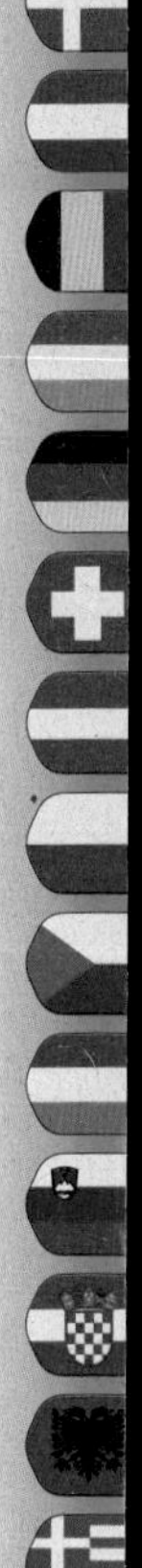

CampingCard ACSI's basic rules

CampingCard ACSI is an ideal product for a very cheap camping holiday in the off season. The clear basic rules that apply to all participants make it easy to use.

Let us go through the rules with you one by one

The CampingCard ACSI discount card is valid for one calendar year and is person specific. The discount card included in part one of this guide must be completed and be signed. The campsite owner may ask you for proof of identity. Discount cards from previous years are not accepted by campsites.

Only valid at participating campsites

You will only receive a discount on your overnight stay at campsites listed in this guide. These campsites can be recognised by the blue CC logo. See also 'only campsites with the CC logo' on page 11.

Only valid during acceptance dates

The information in this guide is only valid for 2024. Each calendar year, new campsites can register or cancel, and the participation tariff may change. A campsite also sets the acceptance dates for the validity of the CampingCard ACSI rate each year. This means you can only use your CampingCard ACSI discount card during the acceptance periods that are listed in the guide for a specific campsite. Should a campsite want to make a change after the guide has gone to press, this will be listed at campingcard.co.uk/modifications.

Excluding additional costs

For a set fee, you can stay at a participating campsite for a complete overnight stay. Which parts are included in this amount can be found in the chapter 'Rate per overnight stay'. It may occur that you will have to pay extra costs, such as government levies. The extras for which a campsite may charge you are listed in the chapter 'Not included in the overnight rate'.

Restricted number of standard pitches available

Your CampingCard ACSI discount card entitles you to an overnight stay at a standard pitch. Comfort pitches, pitches with their own water connections or pitches that are close to the sea may be excluded. A participating campsite is free to decide which pitches are for CampingCard ACSI campers. It is therefore possible that you cannot stay at a campsite even though the campsite has pitches that are available.

Reserving beforehand with CampingCard ACSI possible

In general, it is quieter in the low season than in the high season. Most campsites will have pitches available. A reservation is usually not necessary and, at some campsites, not even possible. Campsites that do accept reservations with CampingCard ACSI can be found listed under the campsite information, amenities, point 6A. In some cases, you can also book a CampingCard ACSI pitch via ACSI. You can find these campsites by filtering for 'Campsites bookable through ACSI'.

About ACSI

Did you know that ACSI has been around since 1965? What started out as stenciled campsite booklets has grown into convenient campsite apps. You can also easily book a motorhome pitch, mobile home or glamping tent through ACSI. What does ACSI have to offer campers?

How it all began

It was the summer of 1964. Ed van Reine, a teacher at the time, was driving his car and trailer from the Betuwe region in the Netherlands via Belgian and French roads, making his way to the Spanish sun. Finally, a holiday. Going out camping with the whole family again. They were full of anticipation: a carefree couple of weeks outdoors. But once they arrived, there was disappointment... 'Completo'. Most campsites were already full.

There had to be another way, Ed thought to himself. He started to muse about a European reservation system. And on that very spot, he conceived a tool that would help campers avoid facing locked gates. With his colleagues in the education sector, he put together his first campsite guide, containing the telephone numbers and other important details on the most popular campsites in Europe. This stencilled booklet was the prelude to what was to become the comprehensive guide you now have before you. And the start of ACSI: Auto Camper Service International. And by 2024, ACSI evolved into an internationally operating publisher and tour operator for camping holidays.

Reliable and objective information

Anyone can collect and compile information. That is why we have been doing things differently right from the start. Our 355 inspectors visit all the ACSI campsites every year. This is important, because things can change from one year to the next. After a training course, the inspectors head off. They check the campsites for more than 220 facilities, but of course also for quality. They get a taste of the atmosphere and talk to the campers and the campsite owners.

The inspectors then select the best campsites, which in turn are allowed to display the well-known ACSI logo. And that is what the campsites want. Because ACSI stands for quality and reliable information. The ACSI mission: to get campers to the campsites that are right for them. From luxury holiday parks to small natural campsites.

CampingCard ACSI

In 1993, Ramon van Reine took over the management of the company from his father.

He started working on professionalisation and digitalisation and began offering guides in several languages. In the meantime, new challenges had emerged. Campsites were looking for guests in the early and late seasons and campers were looking for discounted pitches. This is how CampingCard ACSI came to be. Within ten years, this discount system grew to become the biggest success story in the ACSI range. Over 770,000 campers travel throughout Europe every year with this discount card in their pockets.

Booking online

Ramon's father's idea – a booking system – has since become a reality. You can now easily book a camping pitch or accommodation through the ACSI websites and apps. And the developments are far from over. In this way we offer an online location where campsite visitors can search and book and find information and inspiration. A single location where you can find out everything about the campsites, regions and excursions in the area.

ACSI Awards

Which campsite has the best swimming pool, the best pitches for camper vans or the best restaurant? Every year, campers can vote for their favourite campsites. And there are no fewer than nine categories per country. All the campsites that have won awards can be found at eurocampings.co.uk/winners.

Camping guides

Leafing through a camping guide the old-fashioned way, at home or on the road. A lot of campers still like doing that. The guide with the CampingCard ACSI discount card is still a bestseller in our webshop.

Websites

The convenient filters on our websites make it easy for you to find your ideal campsite. And there are several campsites where you can book your pitch or accommodation directly. You can also find more camping inspirations and handy tips in our blog eurocampings.co.uk/blog.

Apps

Want to search for campsites and motorhome sites conveniently on your smartphone or tablet? This is possible at home and on the road with our handy apps. They help you quickly find a campsite nearby. You can also use the apps without an internet connection.

Your passport safe and sound

ACSI Club ID can be used as an alternative proof of identity at almost 8,100 campsites. This means you no longer have to hand in your passport or ID card at the campsite. As an added bonus, ACSI Club ID members receive a discount on the products in our webshop.

Suncamp

When booking a camping holiday with Suncamp, you are booking at one of the top campsites in Europe. You can choose from pitches, mobile homes, bungalow tents and luxurious glamping accommodations, such as the comfortable SunLodges.

More information can be found at acsi.eu.

How to find a campsite?

This CampingCard ACSI guide consists of two parts. Participating CampingCard ACSI campsites are described one by one in an 'editorial entry', which includes a description of the rate, the acceptance periods and the amenities.

In this guide campsites have been arranged alphabetically by place name per country. An example: Zaton Holiday Resort in Zaton/Nin (Zadar) in Croatia can be found under Z for Zaton/Nin (Zadar).

Exceptions to this are the Netherlands, Germany, France, Spain and Italy. These countries are divided up into regions. Within a region you will find the campsite by place name.
In the contents page of this guide and in the accompanying mini-atlas you will also see that the Netherlands, Germany, France, Spain and Italy are divided up into regions.

Using the general maps which precede the country information you will easily be able to find a campsite in your favourite holiday area!

How to find a participating campsite

There are several possibilities:

In this campsite guide:

- Search for a campsite by place name. Use the register at the back of the guide or the mini-atlas for this purpose.
- Search the country or region where you want to camp. For this you can use the table of contents in the front of the guide. Or use the mini-atlas. The CampingCard ACSI campsites are indicated by a blue logo, together with a number. The numbers in the guide go upwards, so you can easily find the corresponding editorial entry and you will find the information for the campsite you are looking for.
- You can also search for a particular amenity. Using the fold-out cover at the front of this book, you can easily see if the campsite offers the facilities that are important to you.

On the website:
Website campingcard.com.
Here, you can choose different ways to find a campsite. You can filter by holiday period, for example, or the availability of certain facilities, or by theme such as 'suitable for disabled people', 'naturist campsites' or 'winter sports'.

In the app:
The special CampingCard ACSI app. See also page 24.

In the mini-atlas:
Enclosed in this guide you will find a mini-atlas showing all the participating CampingCard ACSI campsites in Europe. In the mini-atlas you will see blue logos showing a number which corresponds to the blue logo and number in the editorial entry for each campsite.
The register in the mini-atlas is composed as follows: campsite number, campsite name, place name in alphabetical order, page number and sub-area on the page. In the Netherlands, Germany, France, Spain and Italy the campsites have been arranged in alphabetical place name order by region.

Your off-season discount card

It couldn't be easier. Using your discount card you can enjoy bargain holidays in low season at top-quality campsites throughout Europe. And all that for just one of eight fixed rates: 13, 15, 17, 19, 21, 23, 25 or 27 euros per night.

The rates

The fixed rates of 13, 15, 17, 19, 21, 23, 25 and 27 euros are lower than the minimum prices charged by the participating campsites in the low season. You can therefore be certain of big discounts on the overnight price up to as much as 60%. Some campsites offer an extra discount if you stay for a longer period. Campsites are just as attractive in the low season as in the high season; the owners guarantee the same standards of facilities and service and the main facilities are also available in the low season; you just pay less. You can therefore avoid the busy period and take advantage of your discount in early and late season!

What do you have to do to enjoy your discount?

It couldn't be easier - take the CampingCard ACSI with you and present it to the receptionist when you arrive at one of the participating campsites and take advantage of our preferential rates!
Show your discount card again at the reception when you pay and you will be charged the advantageous CampingCard ACSI rate. You can see what is included in the rate in the 'Rate per overnight stay' section on page 20 of this guide, and you can see any supplementary charges there may be in the 'Not included in the overnight rate' section on page 21.

Payment conditions

CampingCard ACSI may look like a credit or debit card but it is actually a discount card.
You show your CampingCard ACSI and you can stay on selected sites at advantageous rates. You don't usually have to pay in advance for a fixed number of nights; just pay when you depart.

However, ultimately the payment method is determined by the rules of the campsite, and that includes when you need to pay or provide a deposit. If for example you announce that you will be staying for just one night or want to reserve, the campsite may ask you to pay in advance or pay a deposit. The campsite reception will inform you of their policy in this matter.

Reservation with CampingCard ACSI

On some campsites you can reserve in advance with CampingCard ACSI. A campsite has then indicated facility 6A 'Reservation with CampingCard ACSI possible' in the campsite's information. A reservation with your CampingCard ACSI is in fact considered a normal reservation, only the overnight rate is lower. In some cases you will have to pay a reservation charge and a deposit may be required. A reservation made well in advance by a CampingCard holder can cause problems for campsites. In such cases a campsite may have a policy not to accept your reservation.
There are also some sites where reservation is never possible.

It is important when making a reservation to mention that you are a CampingCard holder. If you fail to do this there is a chance that you will have to pay the regular rate.

Only campsites with the CC-logo

Every year, ACSI inspects nearly 10,000 campsites across Europe. Of the campsites approved by ACSI, approximately 30% participate in the CampingCard ACSI discount system. The CampinqCard ACSI rate only applies for a stay at those campsites. In our ACSI products, you can recognise these campsites by the blue CC logo printed next to the campsite information. When you arrive at the campsite you will also notice the large CC flag or the CC sticker at reception. If you use the CampingCard ACSI guide or campingcard.com, you can be certain that all the campsites shown are members of CampingCard ACSI. Please check carefully whether the discount card will actually be accepted in the period that you want to stay at the campsite you have chosen. These periods differ from campsite to campsite.

355 inspectors

Inspectors set off every year throughout Europe to visit campsites for the renowned ACSI campsite guides. This is how ACSI has been collecting the most reliable campsite information for the past 59 years. In 2023, 355 inspectors visited the campsites.
They inspect the campsites using a more than 220 point checklist and also pay attention to details that cannot easily be rated, such as surroundings, recreational facilities and the friendliness of the staff, etc.

The opinion of the campers themselves is of course of the utmost importance, so our inspection teams regularly ask campsite guests for their opinions of the campsite. You can let your opinion count after visiting a CampingCard site. See page 27 for more information.

Probably the biggest advantage of camping in low season…

CampingCard ACSI is first and foremost a discount card for the low season. With it, you will pay a lower overnight rate.
Another advantage of camping outside the high season – and for some the biggest reason – is relaxation. You avoid congested roads, the sites are quieter, you rarely need to reserve a pitch and the staff have much more time and attention for you. Additionally, the local sights around your campsite are less busy.

In other words: everything you need for a relaxing and carefree holiday awaits you.
We hope you will make the most of it!

Instructions for use

Below is an example of a campsite listing as used in the CampingCard ACSI guide. This is a section with all the information about a campsite. This manual tells you what the numbers and symbols in the editorial listing mean. Page 9 explains how you can use this guide to search for a campsite.

1. Place name - Postal code - Region

4. Campsite name and star ratings

5. Address

6. Telephone

7. Opening period

8. E-mail address

9. Facilities (see fold-out flap)

Facilities open throughout the campsite's entire opening period

Roggel, NL-6088 NT / Limburg

Recreatiepark De Leistert*****
Heldensedijk 5
+31 4 75 49 30 30
1/1 - 31/12
info@leistert.nl

100ha 594**T**(90-130m²) 10-16A CEE

1 ACD**I**KLMNOQRS
2 ASTWXYZ
3 ABCD**G**HIKMNOP**RST**UWZ
4 (C 17/5-1/9)(F+H)IJKM (Q+S+T+U+V+X+Y+Z)
5 **AB**CDEFGIJKLMNOPR**T**UWXYZ
6 ACDFGH**K**LM(N 1km) OPSUV

Lovely campsite with spacious pitches, lo of the beautiful Leudal valley. There is a le campsite. Plenty of good cycle trips in the are ACSI campers are on a comfort pitch.

The campsite is on the N562, Helden-Rc 1 km from Roggel.

CC € 27 *1/1-29/3 12/4-26/4 13/5-17/5 21/5-5/7 24/8-31/12*

10. Surface area of the campsite in hectares (1 ha = 10,000 m² (square metres) or approximately 2.5 acres)
11. Number of touring pitches (size of the pitches is shown in brackets)
12. Maximum loading available for electrical connections
13. Three pin Euro adaptor required (CEE)
14. Rate and (possible) extra discount
15. Acceptance period
16. Description
17. Route description

2. Three children up to and including the age of 5 included
- ACSI Award 2023
- Honourable mention
- Dogs not permitted
- Campsite totally suitable for naturists
- Campsite partially suitable for naturists
- Winter sports campsite
- Amenities suitable for the disabled
- Wifi zone on the campsite
- Wifi coverage on at least 80% of the campsite
- Recognised by the environmental organisation in that particular country
- ACSI Club ID accepted as an identity card

3. 358 Campsite number

18. Sectional map with the exact position of the campsite

19. GPS coordinates

1. Place name, postal code and region

The place name and postal code of the campsite and the region in which it is located.

2. Three children up to and including the age of 5 included (possible)

You will find 383 campsites in this guide where (maximum) three children up to and including the age of 5 are included in the CampingCard ACSI rate. The symbol is shown in the editorial entry for these campsites. Take note: where a campsite displays this symbol they may still require you to pay tourist tax for children. Items such as shower tokens for children are not included either.

Dogs not allowed

The stay of one dog is included in the CampingCard ACSI rate, assuming dogs are allowed on the campsite. If you are bringing more dogs, it is possible that an extra payment will be required. At some campsites there is a limit to the number of dogs per guest and/or some breeds are not permitted. You can find the number of dogs you are allowed to bring with you on the campsite on the campsite page on campingcard.com. If you are in doubt if your dogs are permitted or not, please contact the campsite.At campsites with the above symbol, dogs are not permitted at all.

Wifi zone and/or wifi 80-100% coverage 

If you see this symbol: (wifi zone) in the editorial entry for a campsite, then there is a location on the campsite where you can access wireless internet.
If you see this symbol: (80-100% wifi coverage) in the editorial entry of a campsite, then you can access wireless internet on most of the campsite.

ACSI Club ID

On many campsites you can use the ACSI Club ID Card, this is a substitute identity card. When you can use the ACSI Club ID at a campsite, this is indicated in the facilities with the symbol iD. You will find more explanation of this Camping Carnet on page 28 of this guide.

3. Campsite number 

The number in the blue CC logo refers to the number in the mini-atlas, included with this guide, which gives a good overview of where the campsite is located. See also: 'In the mini-atlas' on page 9.

4. Campsite name and star ratings

Here you can see the campsite name and possibly the number of stars. ACSI does not give stars or other classifications to campsites. Star ratings or other types of classification are awarded to the campsite by local or national organisations and are shown after the campsite name. Stars do not always indicate the quality but more often the comfort that a campsite offers. The more stars there are, the more amenities.

5. Address

The postal address of the campsite. You will find the postal address including the post code in the uppermost block of the editorial entry. Sometimes, in France and Italy for example, you will see that there is no postal address. You will discover that you will usually be able to find the campsite yourself once you have arrived in the town. To make it easier to find the campsite we have included a route description and the GPS coordinates in the editorial entry.

6. Telephone

The telephone numbers in this guide are preceded by a + sign. The + is the international access code (00 in the United Kingdom). The digits after the + denote the country where the campsite is located.

7. Opening period

The periods advised by the campsite management during which the site will be open in 2024. Take note: campsites do not offer the CampingCard ACSI discount for the entire period that they are open. For dates when the CampingCard ACSI discount is available you will need to refer to the acceptance periods in the lower block of the campsite's editorial entry. See also: 'Acceptance period' on page 17.

The opening and acceptance data have been compiled with the greatest care. It is possible that circumstances may cause these dates to change after publication of this guide. Go to campingcard.com/modifications before heading out to see whether there have been changes at your chosen campsite.

8. E-mail address @

The campsite's e-mail address. The e-mail address is especially useful to make a reservation or enquiries in the low season, when the reception may be staffed less frequently.

9. Facilities

CampingCard ACSI is a discount card for the low season. Participating campsites will ensure that the most important facilities will also be available and functioning in the acceptance period of the discount card.
You will find a complete summary of all the facilities that are included in this guide in the fold-out cover at the front of the guide. If you leave the cover folded out you can see precisely which facilities are available at each campsite. By the numbers 1 to 6 you will find six categories with facilities:

1 Regulations
2 Location, ground and shade
3 Sports and play
4 Water recreation / Shops and restaurants
5 Washing up, laundry and cooking / Washing and toilet facilities
6 Miscellaneous

The letters after the numbers relate to the facilities in each category. Some facilities have a period shown in brackets, showing the day and month. These are the dates that you can expect these facilities to be available.
If a small key is shown, this facility can be used during the entire opening period of the campsite.

Take note:

- These are the facilities that are present at the campsite. This does not mean that all these facilities are available on standard pitches and can be used by CampingCard ACSI guests. For

example, when there is a mention of facility 6S, this means that the campsite offers pitches with radio/tv access. In most cases, these pitches will be comfort pitches, which are not meant for CampingCard ACSI guests.
- If a swimming pool or other facility is right next to the campsite, and campsite guests are allowed to use those facilities, the letters of those facilities are also shown in the campsite information.
- Some facilities on the fold-out cover have a *. Facilities with a * that are in bold script in the campsite information are not included in the overnight rate at that campsite. There are two exceptions for CampingCard ACSI guests: in the CampingCard ACSI rate, one dog (assuming they are allowed on the campsite) and one warm shower per person per overnight stay are included, even if the facility is printed in bold and therefore belongs to the facilities at the campsite that require payment. Facilities without a * are never in bold, but this does not mean they are free of charge.

10. Surface area of the campsite

The surface area of the campsite is given in hectares. 1 ha = 10,000 m^2 (square metres) or approximately 2.5 acres).

11. Number of touring pitches

As a camper on the move, it is interesting to know how many overnight pitches a site offers. The size of the pitches is shown in brackets, in m^2. If it says > 100 m^2, then the pitches are larger than 100 m^2. < 100 m^2 means smaller than 100 m^2. Every campsite makes some of these touring pitches available for campers with CampingCard ACSI. A standard pitch is included in the CampingCard rate. See page 20 for more explanation.

12. Maximum loading available for electrical connections

With your CampingCard ACSI a connection with maximum 6A or power consumption to a maximum of 4 kWh per day, including the connection fee, is included in the overnight rate.

If you use more, for example 5 kWh it is quite likely you have to pay a surcharge. You will find the minimum and maximum amperage available for the electrical connection for each campsite in the block with facilities. When the campsite information mentions 6-10A, this means that at this campsite there are pitches with an amperage of minimum 6 and maximum 10. This does not mean that 10A is included in the CampingCard ACSI rate.
State clearly on arrival at the campsite if you want a higher amperage than the included 6A, but be aware that you may have to pay a surcharge. Only when there is no lower amperage than 10A available at the campsite, you will not have to pay extra. Take note: on a connection that allows maximum 6A you cannot connect devices with a combined power consumption of more than 1380 Watt.

13. CEE

This indication means that you will need a three pin euro-adapter.

14. Rate and extra discount

A rate of 13, 15, 17, 19, 21, 23, 25 or 237 euros is shown for each campsite. The rates offered by CampingCard ACSI are already low but could be even lower. Some campsites give an extra discount if you stay longer.
If, for example a campsite is showing '7=6' this means that you pay only 6 nights at the CampingCard ACSI rate for a 7 night stay. Be sure to indicate the number of nights you wish to stay when arriving or reserving. The campsite will make one booking for the entire period and will apply the discount. The discount may not apply if you decide to stay longer during your stay and thereby reach the required number of days.
Take note! If a campsite has several of these discounts you only have the right to one of these offers. For example: the special offers are 4=3, 7=6 and 14=12. If you stay for 13 nights you only have the right to one 7=6 discount and not to multiples of 4=3 or a combination of 4=3 and 7=6.

15. Acceptance period

Each campsite decides its own acceptance period and so defines its own low season.
For dates when the CampingCard ACSI discount is available you will need to look at the acceptance periods in the lower blue block of the editorial entry for the campsite. The last date specified in a period is the date on which the discount is no longer valid. An acceptance period of 1/1 - 30/6 means that the first night you are entitled to a discount is the night from 1 January to 2 January, and the last night you are entitled to a discount is the night from 29 June to 30 June. So, on the night from 30 June to 1 July, you will pay the normal rate.

The opening and acceptance periods are compiled with the greatest care.
It is possible that circumstances may cause these dates to change after publication of this guide. Check campingcard.com/modifications to see whether we have been informed of any changes at the campsite of your choice.

16. Description

In this section you will get an idea of the layout of the campsite and its characteristics. Some examples: on the coast, by a lake, quiet family campsite, high specification of facilities, pleasant views, plenty of shade, privacy, pitches separated by shrubbery, stony ground, grass, terraced, etc.

17. Route description

The written directions in this route description will assist you in finding your way for the last few miles to the campsite entrance and will advise you which motorway exit to take and which signs to follow.

18. Sectional map

The sectional map shows where the campsite is located in its immediate surroundings. The precise location of the campsite is shown with the blue CampingCard ACSI logo.

19. GPS coordinates

If you make use of a navigation system the GPS coordinates are almost indispensable. ACSI has therefore noted the GPS coordinates in this guide. Our inspectors have measured the coordinates right next to the campsite barrier, so nothing can go wrong. Take care: not all navigation systems are configured for cars with a caravan so always read the route description that is included with each campsite and don't forget to watch out for the signs. The shortest route is, after all, not always the easiest one. The GPS coordinates are shown in degrees, minutes and seconds. Check when you enter the data into your navigation system that it is also configured in degrees, minutes and seconds. The letter N is shown by the first number. By the second number there is a letter E or W (east or west of the Greenwich meridian).

Rate per overnight stay

There are eight CampingCard ACSI rates:

At campsites in countries which use currencies other than the euro, you will normally pay in that country's currency. In this case, the CampingCard ACSI rate is converted to that currency using the daily exchange rate that is valid at that moment (average of highest and lowest rate of that day). Please take into account that exchange rates can be subject to large changes.

Inclusive

Participating campsites offer the following in the CampingCard ACSI rate on touring pitches:

- A camping pitch.*
- Overnight stay for 2 adults.
- Car & caravan & awning, or car & folding caravan, or car & tent, or motor home & awning.
- Electricity. A connection of maximum 6A or a consumption of maximum 4 kWh per day is included in the CampingCard ACSI rate. When a campsite only has pitches with a lower amperage, this lower amperage will apply. If you use excess, for example 5 kWh, it is possible that you might have to pay extra. See also 'Maximum loading available for electrical connections' on page 16.
- Hot showers. In campsites where showers are operated by tokens, CampingCard ACSI holders are entitled to one token per adult per overnight stay.**
- Maximum one dog staying on campsites which accept dogs. For a second (or additional) dog you might have to pay extra.
- VAT.

* Some campsites make a distinction between standard, luxury or comfort pitches. Luxury or comfort pitches are in general larger and equipped with their own water supply and drainage. CampingCard ACSI gives you the right to a standard pitch but it may occur that you are able to have a more expensive pitch at the CampingCard ACSI rate. The campsite has the right to decide this; you can never insist on a luxury or comfort pitch.
Be aware also that some campsites have a different policy with regard to twin-axled caravans and mobile homes which are so large that they will not fit on a standard pitch.

** As stipulated in the CampingCard ACSI terms and conditions, the campsite must allow the CampingCard ACSI holder one free shower per overnight stay. That means every CampingCard ACSI holder has a right to one shower token per person per night. If the campsite has a different 'shower system' , such as small change, a key or a sep-key, then the campsite must ensure that the charge for the CampingCard holder is reimbursed.
Hot water in washing up sinks is not included in the price. Unused shower tokens cannot be exchanged for money.

Not included in the overnight rate

In general the CampingCard ACSI rate is sufficient to pay for the overnight charge. The campsite may however make extra charges for a number of items:

- Tourist taxes, environmental taxes, waste disposal charges or local authority requirements are not included in the CampingCard ACSI rate. These taxes can differ greatly by country and region. In Switzerland and Austria in particular, and also in the Netherlands, you should be prepared for high charges for some of these taxes.
- Reservation and administration charges are not included in the CampingCard ACSI rate. You can read more about reserving with CampingCard ACSI on page 10.
- A campsite may make a surcharge for a luxury or comfort pitch (unless the campsite only has comfort pitches).
- Campsites make pitches available for two adults. The campsite may decide if more guests may stay on these pitches, apart from the two adults who can stay for the CampingCard ACSI rate (for example the guests' children or more adults), for payment of the regular rate per guest. If this is not allowed, then the camping group will be directed to pitches that are not meant for CampingCard ACSI users and for which the regular low season rates must be paid. However, at campsites which display the following symbol , (a maximum of) three children up to and including the age of 5 are included in the CampingCard ACSI rate. Items such as shower coins and tourist tax (if applicable) for these children are not included.
- Extra services such as facilities for which the campsite makes a charge, such as a tennis court, can be charged to you at the applicable low season rate.
- Electricity, if more is consumed than is specified on page 20. See also 'Maximum loading available for electrical connections' on page 16.

ACSI Awards

ACSI Awards are presented annually to the best campsites per camping country. ACSI will be putting campsites in the spotlight in 2024 as well with this coveted award. Campers from all over Europe can vote for their favourite campsite in different categories.

Your vote counts

What is the best campsite in France? Or the campsite with the best campsite swimming pool Germany? And which campsites are ideal if you go on holiday with your dog? The campsites that win an ACSI Award are decided by you!

You can vote for your favourite campsites again this year. You not only put these campsites in the spotlight, but you also have a chance to win great prizes yourself. More than a hundred prizes will be raffled off among all of those who vote. Follow our Facebook and Instagram accounts, websites and newsletters to know when you can vote.

Appreciation of campers

An ACSI Award is a reward for the hard work a campsite has done. It is a prize awarded by the public, based on the opinion of real campers. Running a successful campsite demands a lot. With an ACSI Award, campsites can show that they can vouch for a wonderful holiday.

Festive moment

Receiving an ACSI Award is a special event for a campsite. During the annual inspection, the ACSI inspectors present the crystal awards and corresponding certificates personally to the winning campsites. A festive and special moment for many campsite owners.

Check out the winners

Are you curious as to which campsites won an ACSI Award in 2023? This guide provides

a per-country overview of the winners. This overview can also be found at eurocampings.co.uk/winners. Campsites that were not awarded a prize but did receive a lot of votes were given an honourable mention from ACSI. These campsites can be recognised in the guide, on the website and in the app by this logo/icon:

- ACSI Award 2023 (guide)
- ACSI Award 2023 (website and app)
- Honourable mention

The ACSI Awards in 2024

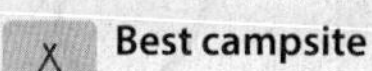

Best campsite
The best campsite in a country has the most votes in all categories and excels in amenities, location and general satisfaction of campsite visitors.

Nicest campsite for children
Children will have the time of their lives at this campsite because of the play facilities and the fantastic entertainment.

Most dog-friendly campsite
Your faithful four-footer is more than welcome at this campsite. It's a holiday for the dog, too.

Best campsite swimming pool
You and your children would love to spend the whole day in this beautiful swimming pool. Which campsite will receive your vote?

Best location for a campsite
This campsite is located in a beautiful spot, close to the water, the city, in the woods or the mountains. The location is perfect!

Best hiking campsite
This best hiking campsite is ideally located in the centre of breathtaking walking paths, surrounded by the lushness of nature and panoramic views..

Best campsite for cycling
The best campsite for cycling offers a perfect location with direct access to extensive cycle routes, allowing you to enjoy beautiful landscapes and picturesque villages.

Best campsite restaurant
You will want to eat every evening in this restaurant. The food is delicious and the service is super.

Best motorhome pitches
This campsite has everything you and your motorhome may need. The best pitches and all amenities are close at hand.

Campsite with the best sanitary facilities
The sanitary facilities at this campsite really stand out – they are clean and modern.

CampingCard ACSI app

With the CampingCard ACSI app you have all campsite information at your fingertips! The app, which can also be used without an internet connection, includes all CampingCard ACSI campsites and has many handy functionalities and search filters.

The campsite information in the CampingCard ACSI app is updated several times a year. The app is suitable for smartphones and tablets (Android 9 and higher, iOS 12 and higher)*.

Are you going on holiday with a motorhome? You can now purchase information in the app about more than 9,000 motorhome pitches in Europe!

Our clients awarded a rating of 8.3 to the CampingCard ACSI app

- **Search by name**

You can search by country, region, place, campsite number or campsite name. Fill in a search term and see where you can spend the night nearby on a map. The database is very extensive and contains more than 500,000 search terms!

- **Search in the area**

Is location awareness activated on your device? If so the app will identify your location and show the CampingCard ACSI campsites (and motorhome pitches if you have purchased the motorhome information for the app) that are close to you. If you prefer to search for a specific place on the map you can set your location on the map manually. Perfect if you're looking for a place to stay overnight.

- **Search filters**

The app contains really useful search filters. You can filter by more than 150 amenities, the CampingCard ACSI rates, periods of stay and stopover campsites.

- **View the campsite**

You will find comprehensive information about the grounds and the amenities for each campsite. Check if it's suitable by looking at the photos, map resources and campsite reviews from other campers.

- **Favourites**

Have you found your perfect spot? Then add it to your list of favourites so you can quickly find it later. You'll also be able to find your favourites on the map.

- **Booking a campsite**

There are more and more campsites in the app that have made it possible to see whether there is any availability and to make your booking directly.

- **Use on multiple devices**

You can use the app on three devices at once. To do this, log in with your My ACSI account and the app will be unlocked.

Attention:
To benefit from the low fixed rates, you must always show a valid discount card to the reception. Go to campingcard.com/app for more information and an explanation on how to purchase access to the app.

** System requirements subject to change*

Your unique purchase code

Access to the CampingCard ACSI app requires a unique purchase code. This code allows us to verify that you have a valid CampingCard ACSI discount card. The code can be found on your discount card, as pictured below:

All CampingCard ACSI campsites in one handy app

- Search and book quickly and easily
- Can be used without an internet connection
- Can be expanded to include 9,000 motorhome pitches

From just €3.99**

*** Prices subject to change*

The digital discount card

The CampingCard ACSI discount card is now also available in digital form. This means that both the discount card and all campsite (and possibly motorhome) information is available digitally in the CampingCard ACSI app. The campsite can scan the QR code of the digital discount card, which means that checking in is very quick. Would you like a digital discount card starting next year? Go to campingcard.com/digital to convert your subscription and for more information.

Comparison of ACSI apps

	ACSI Campsites Europe app	CampingCard ACSI app	ACSI Great Little Campsites app
Price	App with information about campsites and motorhome pitches: starting at €1.99*	App with campsite information: €3.99*	App with campsite information: €3.49*
Number of campsites	More than 9,300	3,000	1,900
Type of campsite	All campsites in the ACSI Campinggids Europa and ACSI Klein & Fijn Kamperen guide	All campsites that accept CampingCard ACSI	All campsites in the ACSI Klein & Fijn Kamperen guide
Information about more than 9,000 motorhome pitches	The purchase of this app includes the information about motorhome pitches	Can only be purchased in combination with campsite information	Can only be purchased in combination with campsite information
Digital CampingCard ACSIDigital		Optional	
Suitable for	Smartphone and tablet	Smartphone and tablet	Smartphone and tablet
Can be used on three devices at the same time	✓	✓	✓
Free updates	✓	✓	✓
Can be used offline	✓	✓	✓
Search by country, region, town or campsite name	✓	✓	✓
Search on map/GPS	✓	✓	✓
Search by CC rate and CC acceptance period		✓	
Total search filters	250	150	250
Book directly via the app	✓	✓	✓
Read and submit campsite reviews	✓	✓	✓
Plan route	✓	✓	✓
More information	**eurocampings.co.uk/app**	**campingcard.com/app**	**greatlittlecampsites.co.uk/app**

** Prices subject to change*

Win an iPad with your campsite review

Go to campingcard.com/ipad and find your campsite.

Add your review and enter your promotion code IPAD-2024-CCA.

You will automatically be eligible to win a free iPad. We will send an email to the winner.

ACSI Club ID

With a subscription to ACSI Club ID you can always keep your passport safe. Nearly 8,100 campsites in Europe accept the card as a replacement proof of identity. It also provides liability insurance. And that's not all: ACSI Club ID members also benefit from special discounts in our webshop.

The advantages of an ACSI Club ID subscription:

✔ Replacement ID

You can use your ACSI Club ID at almost 8,100 campsites across Europe as a replacement ID instead of your passport or ID card. That means you can leave your ID safely stowed away in your pocket when you're on holiday.

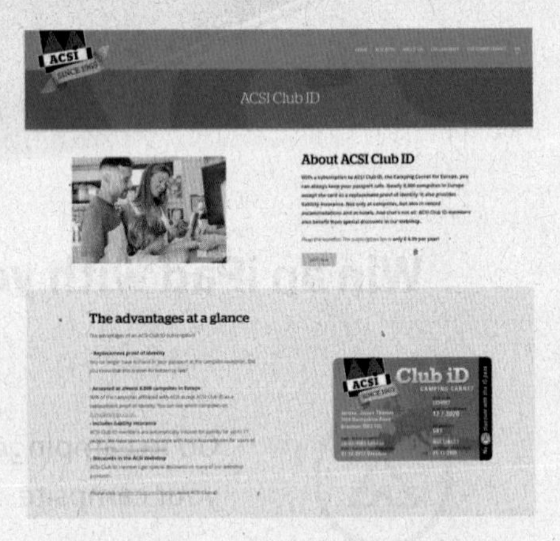

✔ Liability insurance

You can be sure of a carefree holiday if you travel with your ACSI Club ID. This card offers you and up to 11 people travelling with you liability insurance during your camping holiday, but also if you stay in a holiday home or a hotel!

✔ Discounts in the ACSI Webshop

You'll always pay a special, reduced price for ACSI products.

Order your ACSI Club ID now and pay just €5.95 a year! For more information please visit: acsi.eu/clubid

Differences between ACSI Club ID and CampingCard ACSI

ACSI Club ID is a card from ACSI, just like CampingCard ACSI. To clear up any confusion, we've compiled an overview of the differences.

	ACSI Club ID	CampingCard ACSI
What	Replacement ID for use at the campsite	Discount card for camping in the low season
Accepted for	Accepted as replacement ID at almost 8,100 campsites in 33 countries	Spend the night at 3,000 campsites in 23 countries at a fixed reduced rate
Extras	Liability insurance, membership discounts in the ACSI Webshop	With a guide or app that contains all information about the CampingCard ACSI campsites
Purchase	Membership, you can purchase it on the ACSI Webshop	Subscribe via the ACSI Webshop. Or make a one-time purchase of the discount card + campsite guide in a bookshop, camping shop or in the ACSI webshop.
Available digitally	No	Yes. For more information, consult campingcard.com/digital
Validity	1 year, until the expiry date (is automatically renewed every year)	1 calendar year (discount card + campsite guide) or valid for 1 year (CampingCard ACSI Digital)
Costs	€5.95 per year	From €16.95 per year
More information	www.acsi.eu/clubid	www.campingcard.com

Book your pitch via ACSI

Are you looking for a good campsite for a spring holiday in the sun? Or for a nice place to stay overnight en route? You will find your ideal campsite on our websites and apps. You can book your pitch immediately at more and more campsites. So convenient!

Booking a pitch

If you can book the campsite online, the pitches that are available will be listed on the website or app. Booking is easy to do.

- Enter the number of people and the duration of the stay.
- You will now see the price for your stay. The CampingCard ACSI rate will be displayed.
- Enter the names and addresses of your travel group.
- Choose your payment method.
- After confirmation of your payment method, the booking is finalised.
- If you book directly with the campsite, the booking and cancellation conditions of the campsite apply. These conditions can be read before you complete the booking.

Reserving at the CampingCard ACSI rate

If you are booking via the website or app of CampingCard ACSI, the CampingCard ACSI discount will immediately be included in the price. This also applies if you book for a period that falls partially in and partially outside of the acceptance period. In addition to the nightly rate, you also pay a small amount for a reservation fee. You will still be required to show your CampingCard ACSI discount card when you arrive at the campsite.

The benefits of booking online with ACSI

- You are sure of a pitch. The anticipation begins.
- For last-minute bookings as well. Book en route via your smartphone or tablet.
- All expenses clearly indicated.
- Safe and secure payment.

Growing number of campsites

More and more campsites can be booked immediately via ACSI. For more information and a handy overview of all bookable CampingCard ACSI campsites, go to campingcard.com/bookonline or look in the CampingCard ACSI app.

Sample

Speed limits (km/h) car

Country	Outside built-up areas	Dual carriage-way	Motor-way	Explanation
Albania	80	90	110	
Austria	100	-	130	-
Belgium	70 / 90*	-	120	* In Flanders 70 km/h (43 mph), in Wallonia and Brussels 90 km/h (56 mph).
Croatia	90 (80*)	110 (100*)	130 (120*)	*The lower speed limits apply to drivers under the age of 25.
Czech Republic	90	110	130	-
Denmark	80/90*	-	110/130	*The maximum speed is sometimes increased locally to 90 km/h (56 mph).
Finland	80/100*	-	100/120*	*The higher speed is always indicated with signs; in the winter, the lower speed always applies.
France	80/90***	110* (100**)	130 (110**)	*Non-toll dual carriageways. **During rain and for drivers who have held a driving licence for less than 3 years. ***There may apply an increased speed limit of 90 km/h.
Germany	100	130	130*	*130 km/h (81 mph) is not a maximum speed but a guide speed.
Greece	90/110	-	130	-
Hungary	90	110	130	-
Ireland	80/100	-	120	-
Italy	90	110	130*	*On some stretches of motorway, a speed limit of 150 km/h (93 mph) may apply. If there is precipitation or if you have held your driving licence for less than 3 years, the speed limit is 90 km/h (56 mph) on dual carriageways and 110 km/h (68 mph) on motorways.
Luxembourg	90	-	130*	*In the event of rain or other precipitation, a maximum speed of 110 km/h (68 mph) applies.
The Netherlands	80	100	130*(100)	*Between 6am and 7pm: 100 km/h (62 mph).
Norway	80	90/100*	90/100*	*The maximum speed can also be 110 km/h (68 mph).
Poland	90	100*	140	*On dual carriageways with four lanes, the maximum speed is 120 km/h (75 mph).
Portugal	90	100	120	-
Slovenia	90	110	130	-
Spain	90	100*	120**	*Roads with a physical separation between carriageways, such as a median strip. **Motorways and 'autovia'.
Sweden	60-100*	-	90-120	*If there is no sign, the maximum speed is 70 km/h (43 mph).
Switzerland	80	100	120	-
United Kingdom	60 mph (96 km/h)	70* mph (112 km/h)	70 mph (112 km/h)	*A road with four lanes where the two directions are separated.

Speed limits (km/h) car with trailer

Country	Outside built-up areas	Dual carriage-way	Motor-way	Explanation
Albania	70	70	80	-
Austria	70/80*(**)	-	80/100*(**)	*With a <0.75 tonnes trailer, you can drive 100 km/h (62 mph) on the motorway and outside built-up areas. **The higher speed limit only applies if the trailer is not heavier than the car and the car-trailer combination is less than 3.5 tonnes.
Belgium	70 / 90*	-	90**	*In Flanders 70 km/h (43 mph), in Wallonia and Brussels 90 km/h (56 mph). **Combination < 3.5 tonnes may travel 120 km/h on motorway
Croatia	80	80	90	-
Czech Republic	80	80	80	-
Denmark	70	-	80	-
Finland	80*	-	80*	*With an unbraked trailer, the maximum speed is 60 km/h.
France	80***	90*(**)	90**	*Non-toll dual carriageways. **Combination < 3.5 tonnes may keep the speed limit of a car ***An increased speed limit of 90 km/h may apply.
Germany	80	80	80*	*With a German Tempo 100 exemption you may drive 100 km/h (62 mph). To get this, your vehicle/caravan combination must be inspected first. See: tuev-nord.de (search for 'Tempo-100 Zulassung').
Greece	80	-	80	-
Hungary	70	70	80	-
Ireland	60/80	-	80	-
Italy	70	70	80	-
Luxembourg	75	-	90	-
The Netherlands	80	90*	90*	*Combination >3.5 tonnes: maximum speed is 80 km/h (50 mph).
Norway	80*	80*	80*	*Trailer >300 kg that does not have brakes: maximum speed is 60 km/h (37 mph).
Poland	70	80	80	-
Portugal	70	80	100	-
Slovenia	90*	100*	100*	*Car-caravan combinations of more than 3.5 tonnes: speed limit is 80 km/h (50 mph).
Spain	70	80***	90*(**)	*80 km/h (50 mph) for a car with a trailer of > 0.75 tonnes. **Motorways and 'autovia'. ***Roads with a physical separation between carriageways.
Sweden	60-80*	-	80	*If there is no sign, the maximum speed is 70 km/h (43 mph).
Switzerland	80	80*	80*	*You may drive 100 km/h on motorways and highways with a trailer or caravan with a maximum authorised mass < 3.5 tonnes provided the towing vehicle, trailer and wheels are approved for this speed.
United Kingdom	50 mph (80 km/h)	60* mph (96 km/h)	60 mph (96 km/h)	*A road with four lanes where the two directions are separated.

Speed limits (km/h) motorhome < 3.5 tonnes

Country	Outside built-up areas	Dual carriage-way	Motor-way	Explanation
Albania	70	70	80	-
Austria	100	-	130	-
Belgium	70 / 90*	-	120	*In Flanders 70 km/h (43 mph), in Wallonia and Brussels 90 km/h (56 mph).
Croatia	90 (80*)	110 (100*)	130 (120*)	*The lower speed limits apply to drivers under the age of 25.
Czech Republic	90	110	130	-
Denmark	80/90*	-	110/130	*The maximum speed is sometimes increased locally to 90 km/h (56 mph).
Finland	80(/100*)**	-	80(/100*)**	*The higher speed is always indicated with signs; in the winter, the lower speed always applies. **Only 100 km/h for motorhomes manufactured after 1994 with an empty weight up to 1875 kg and motorhomes up to 3.5 tonnes that have ABS, an airbag and seat belts for all seats and are approved by the manufacturer for 100 km/h.
France	80***	110* (100**)	130 (110**)	*Non-toll dual carriageways **During rain and for drivers who have held a driving licence for less than 3 years. ***An increased speed limit of 90 km/h may apply.
Germany	100	130	130*	*130 km/h (81 mph) is not a maximum speed but a guide speed.
Greece	90/110*	-	130*	-
Hungary	90	110	130	-
Ireland	80/100	-	120	-
Italy	90	110	130*	*On some stretches of motorway, a speed limit of 150 km/h (93 mph) may apply. If there is precipitation or if you have held your driving licence for less than 3 years, the speed limit is 90 km/h (56 mph) on dual carriageways and 110 km/h (68 mph) on motorways.
Luxembourg	90	-	130*	*In the event of rain or other precipitation, a maximum speed of 110 km/h (68 mph) applies.
The Netherlands	80	100	130*(100)	*Between 6am and 7pm: 100 km/h (62 mph).
Norway	80	90/100*	90/100*	*The maximum speed also can be 110 km/h (68 mph).
Poland	90	100*	140	*On dual carriageways with four lanes, the maximum speed is 120 km/h (75 mph).
Portugal	90	100	120	-
Slovenia	90	110	130	-
Spain	80	90*	100**	*Roads with a physical separation between carriageways, such as a median strip. **Motorways and 'autovia'.
Sweden	60-100*	-	90-120	* If there is no sign, the maximum speed is 70 km/h (43 mph).
Switzerland	80	100	120	-
United Kingdom	60 mph (96 km/h)	70* mph (112 km/h)	70 mph (112 km/h)	*A road with four lanes where the two directions are separated.

Speed limits (km/h) motorhome > 3.5 tonnes

Country	Outside built-up areas	Dual carriage-way	Motor-way	Explanation
Albania	70	70	80	
Austria	70	-	80	-
Belgium	70 / 90*	-	90	*In Flanders 70 km/h (43 mph), in Wallonia and Brussels 90 km/h (56 mph).
Croatia	80	80	90	-
Czech Republic	80	80	80	-
Denmark	80	-	100	-
Finland	80	-	80	-
France	80**	100*	110	*Non-toll dual carriageways. **An increased speed limit of 90 km/h may apply.
Germany	80	100	100	-
Greece	80	-	80	-
Hungary	70	70	80	-
Ireland	80	-	80	-
Italy	80	80	100	-
Luxembourg	75	-	90	-
The Netherlands	80	80	80	-
Norway	80	80	80	-
Poland	70	80	80	-
Portugal	70	90	110	-
Slovenia	80	80	80	-
Spain	80	80*	90**	*Roads with a physical separation between carriageways, such as a median strip. **Motorways and 'autovia'.
Sweden	60-100*(**)	-	90-120**	*If there is no sign, the maximum speed is 70 km/h (43 mph). **For a motorhome > 3.5 tonnes registered as a commercial vehicle, the speed limit is 80 km/h outside built-up areas and 90 km/h on motorways.
Switzerland	80	100	100	-
United Kingdom	50 mph (80 km/h)	60* mph (96 km/h)	70 mph (112 km/h)	*A road with four lanes where the two directions are separated.

Norway

Capital: Oslo
Currency: Norwegian krone
Time zone: UTC +1, UTC +2 (March to October)
Language: Norwegian
International dialling code: +47
Alcohol limit: 0.2‰
Emergency number: police: 112, fire: 110, ambulance: 113
Tap water: safe to drink

Norway:
magically beautiful

Fjords to fall in love with, landscapes from a book of fairy-tales and charming Scandinavian cities and villages. In Norway, you discover a wealth of natural beauty and fun activities. From walking, cruising and fishing to skiing, cross-country skiing and admiring the Northern Lights. Norway is magically beautiful!

The beautiful north: Lofoten, Tromsø and North Cape

Several world-famous Norwegian sights are located in the Arctic North above the Arctic Circle. The Lofoten archipelago is a stunning example. With deep fjords, impressive mountains and long sandy beaches this region is unbelievably beautiful. It's a great place for walks and winter sports. You can also discover picturesque fishing villages. At a campsite in Tromsø, you will be in the perfect spot to see the Northern Lights in autumn or winter.
And there is plenty more to do! Go on a whale safari, ride on a snow scooter and meet reindeer and huskies. For an unforgettable experience, go to North Cape. It is as if you are standing at the edge of the

world. Enjoy the peace and an endless view over the Arctic Ocean.

Rich culture in Oslo and the charming Bergen

Norway is also the place to be for a city break. The capital of Oslo is rich in art and history. Sights such as Akershus Festning (fortress) and the royal palace are certainly worth visiting.
The city of Bergen is on the west coast and stands out due to its charming atmosphere and typical wooden houses. Here, you can stroll over the fish market and walk through the exceptional district of Bryggen. For a fantastic view over the city and surroundings, take the Ulriken or Fløibanen funicular railway.

Midnight sun

In Norway, the midnight sun provides very long days in summer. Above the Arctic Circle, the sun doesn't even set for a few weeks. It is one of the most special experiences when you are camping in Norway. The days are exceptionally short in winter.

En route

Filling up

Lead-free petrol (Blyfri 95 and 98) and diesel are widely available. Do keep in mind that the fuel prices in Northern Norway are considerably higher. LPG is more widely available in the south around Oslo than in the north. The bayonet connector is used to refill with LPG and some fuelling stations use the Italian connector (Dish).
Fuelling stations are usually open between 7 am and 10 pm. Fuelling stations at large shopping centres and supermarkets are usually stay open for longer. Fuelling stations in and around major cities are often open day and night.
You can usually refuel using a fuel dispensing machine after closing time. Tip! In more rural areas, refuel at every fuelling station you come across because the distances between fuelling stations in Norway can be vast. It is usually forbidden to take fuel with you in a reserve tank.

Charging

The charging station network in Norway has been extended but most charging points are in the south and in Oslo.

Mountain roads

The mountain roads are narrow and winding, sometimes with steep slopes. Due to the snow, they are only accessible from mid-June to mid-October. Various roads could be closed in winter. Before travelling, check whether the mountain passes are closed.
More information: alpenpaesse.de (in German).

Ferry services

You can travel over land from Sweden to Norway via the Øresund Bridge (oeresundsbron.com) from Copenhagen (Denmark) to Malmö, but there is also the option of travelling to Norway by ferry boat, for example via Hirtshals (Denmark). Information about sailing times, departure times and fares can be found on the shipping operator's sites, such as colorline.com and fjordline.com. Fares depend on the season and departure times, among other things. It is advisable to book in advance. Ask the shipping operator beforehand whether you can take gas bottles on the boat. It is usually forbidden to take fuel in a reserve tank on the boat. Please note: the Norwegian police conduct strict checks of vehicles coming on the ferry between Hirtshals and Kristiansand (Norway).

"The peace, the space, the overwhelming countryside and the obscure Norwegian rock bands, fabulous!"

Mr B. Brink, inspector 700

Traffic regulations

Dipped headlights (or daytime running lights) are mandatory during the day. At an uncontrolled intersection, traffic from the right has priority. Traffic on a roundabout has priority. Trams always have priority. On mountain roads, the driver that can move over the easiest or reverse usually gives priority. You may not have telephone in your hand behind the wheel, not even when stopped (you can call hands free).
Children under 1.50 metres in height must be in a child's car seat. Winter tyres are only compulsory for vehicles with a maximum permissible mass of over 3.5 tonnes. You must use snow chains (or winter tyres) on roads covered with snow or ice.

Special regulations

On main roads in some major cities, the sign 'All stans forbudt' indicates you are not allowed to stop. In winter, summer tyres must also have a minimum tread depth of three millimetres. On narrow roads, the driver driving on the side nearest to the closest lay-by must give way. When overtaking cyclists, you must maintain a lateral distance of at least 1.5 metres. Parking is not allowed on roads with a broken white line. Cyclists may overtake vehicles other than bikes on the right.

Mandatory equipment

You must have a warning triangle and safety vest in the car. A fire extinguisher is only mandatory in a car-caravan combination with a Norwegian number plate, but everyone is advised to have a fire extinguisher with them. You are also advised to take a first aid kit.

Caravan and motorhome

A motorhome or car-caravan combination can be a maximum of 4 metres in height, 2.55 metres wide and 19.5 metres long, the caravan itself can be up to 12 metres long. If the caravan is over 2.3 metres in width and 50 centimetres wider than the car (excluding mirrors), you must put white reflectors on the back of the mirrors. On a few smaller roads, the maximum length could be 15 metres or 12.4 metres; this is indicated by signs. For motorhomes weighing over 3.5 tonnes, winter tyres are mandatory from mid-November to end-March.

Cycling

Bicycle helmets are not mandatory. Only children under 10 years may be transported on a bike.

Tolls

In Norway you pay a toll on many roads. You can do that in various ways:

- Visitor's Payment: register online in advance. More information: autopass.no/visitors-payment.
- AutoPASS box: if you are planning on staying in Norway for longer than two months. More information: autopass.no.
- None of the above, you simply drive onto the toll road and your number plate will be registered by cameras. You will receive the bill at home within a few months.

Please note! For a small number of routes, you must pay in cash at the toll gate. So make sure you have enough cash with you.

"The fjords, mountains, plateaus, peace, emptiness and a new surprise around every bend."

Mr H. Sybesma, inspector 342

Environmental zones

With serious smog, the centres of Oslo and Bergen could be closed for certain vehicles. The rules differ per location.
More information: oslo.kommune.no/english and bergen.kommune.no.

Breakdown and accident

Place your warning triangle at least 150 metres behind the car if it forms a hazard to other traffic. The driver must put on a safety vest. If you breakdown, call the emergency number of your breakdown assistance insurer. You can also call the Norwegian breakdown assistance service (NAF) on +47 2321 3100. You must call the police if you collide with an animal.

Camping

There is an abundance of nature, Norway is perfectly suited to walking, mountain climbing and fishing. The toilet and washing facilities are generally good. Demarcated pitches are rare. Wild camping outside recognised campsites is generally allowed. On cultivated land (such as mowing land, meadows, newly planted woods) you need the landowner's permission.
When you go camping in Norway there is a chance you will need a special card that you must present at reception. You can buy this card at the campsite in question. You usually pay per pitch, not per person. The range of groceries, amenities and recreational options is sparse compared to popular camping countries. Most campsites do have kitchens with cooking equipment for communal use. Open fires are not allowed from 15 April to 15 September. Please note: there are very few possibilities for filling propane bottles. You are therefore advised to travel with enough gas. Keep in mind that driving with a caravan or motorhome in the Fjord region and in the mountains can be problematic. A good towing vehicle is highly recommended. You are not allowed to dispose of wastewater at the side of the road. There are plenty of service stations on the major routes.

Practical

Inland in Norway, you could be plagued by mosquitoes near lakes and rivers.

Ballangen, N-8540 / Nordland

1

Ballangen Camping****
Stor Ballangen E6 160
+47 76 92 76 90
1/1 - 31/12
post@ballangencamping.com

9ha 130**T**(90-100m²) 16A CEE

1 ACDIKLMNOQS
2 ADHJNQSTUVWXY
3 CIKLP**R**SUWY
4 (**C** 10/6-20/8)(**H** 1/7-20/8) J**N**(Q+R 1/6-1/9) (T+U+V+Y+Z)
5 **AB**CDEFGHIJKLMNOPQRSUWXZ
6 CEFGHKLM(N 4km)P

Lovely campsite close to the sea, Lofoten, Senja and North Cape. Own swimming pool in the summer. Family friendly. Restaurant in the season. Three km from town. Summer and winter sports options. Many boat and hire facilities. Good public transport. Cycling, walking and mountain sport friendly.

From Ballangen take E6 direction Narvik. After 4 km, you'll see the fjord and campsite on the left, it is indicated by a large blue sign at the entrance gate.

CC € 27 *1/1-1/6 1/9-31/12*

N 68°20'20'' E 16°51'30''

Fåberg, N-2625 / Oppland

2

Hunderfossen Camping***
Fossekrovegen 90
+47 41 22 23 33
1/1 - 31/12
camping@hunderfossen.no

18ha 450**T**(80-100m²) 16A

1 ACDIKLMNOQ**RS**
2 DJNSUVXY
3 C**GRUW**
5 **AB**DFGIJK**L**MNO**PQR**UWZ
6 CFG(N 3km)V

Wonderfully situated family campsite near a popular fairytale park. The park has an authentic, traditional Norwegian set up. Hunderfossen dam at walking distance, where Norway's largest trout jump out of the water.

From the E6 take exit 'Hunderfossen Family Park', over the bridge in Øyer. Well signposted in both directions.

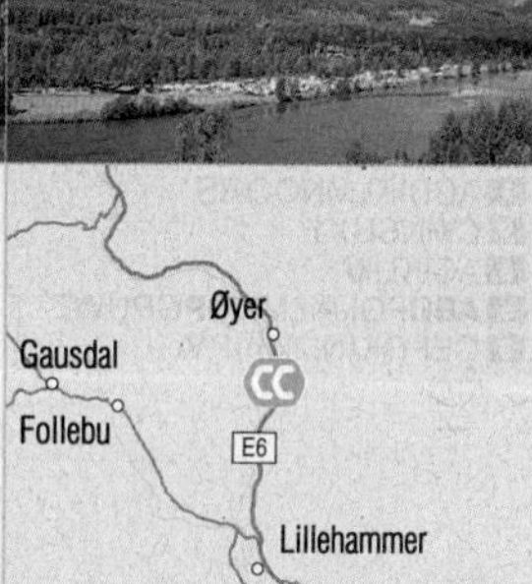

CC € 27 *13/4-28/6 19/8-30/9*

N 61°13'20'' E 10°26'19''

Kabelvåg, N-8310 / Nordland

3

Sandvika Camping
Ørsvågveien 45
+47 76 07 45 00
1/1 - 31/12
post@lofotferie.no

12ha 150**T** 16A

1 ACDEIKLMNOQRS
2 AGNOQRSTUVX
3 AIKLMUWY
5 **AB**CDFGIJKLMNO**P**UWZ
6 CEFGHK(N 3km)PQT

Campsite in a wonderful location with panoramic views of the mountains, sandy beach and sea. Fishing and walking options. Bike and boat hire. Excellent toilet and washing facilities. Green Key label campsite.

Continue in a southerly direction from Svolvær on the Lofoten road E10. The campsite is signposted near to Kabelvåg.

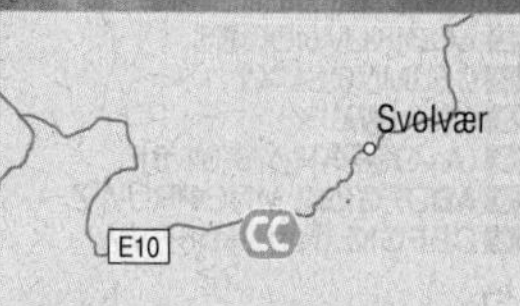

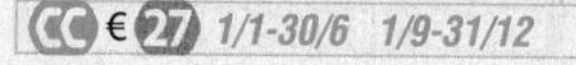

CC € 27 *1/1-30/6 1/9-31/12*

N 68°12'24'' E 14°25'35''

Lærdal, N-6887 / Romsdal-Sognefjord

4

Lærdal Ferie og Fritidspark****
Grandavegen 5
+47 57 66 66 95
14/1 - 14/12
info@laerdalferiepark.com

2ha 100T(80-120m²) 16A

1 ACDEIKLMNOQRS
2 AGJQRSWXY
3 ACIKMPUWY
4 (R 15/5-15/9)(V 1/5-15/9)
(Y 16/4-15/10)(Z 1/5-15/9)
5 **AB**DFGIJKLMNO**P**UWZ
6 FGHK(N 0,4km)PTV

Well maintained campsite. Unique and central on the Sognefjord. Excellent toilet facilities. Salmon centre within walking distance. Ideal for an active holiday with walking, cycling, climbing, glacier tours, fishing and sailing. The area is perfect for painting, drawing and photography and for anyone who loves nature or just wants to enjoy the relaxation.

From the E16 take route 5. Campsite located near the centre of Lærdal and close to the beach and playpark.

Amla
Naddvik
Lærdalsøyri
Ljøsne
E16

CC € 27 *2/4-7/5 12/5-15/5 20/5-12/6 16/6-19/6 25/8-25/9 29/9-19/10* ***7=6, 14=11***

N 61°06'02" E 07°28'13"

Loen, N-6789 / Romsdal-Sognefjord

5

Tjugen Camping***
Lodalsvegen 198
+47 57 87 76 17
1/5 - 1/10
camping@tjugen.no

2ha 60T(40-100m²) 10-16A

1 ACDIKLMNOQRS
2 CMNSUXY
3 ACIKU**W**
5 **AB**DFGIJKLMNO**P**QRUWZ
6 CEFGK(N 2km)PV

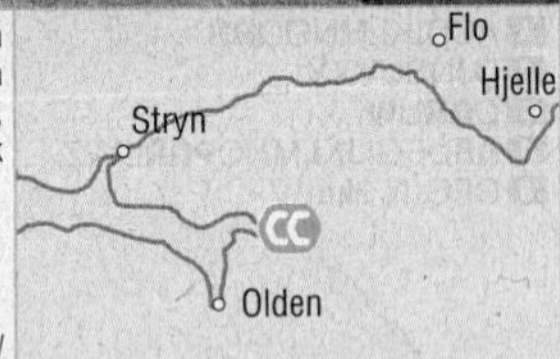

Beautiful view from the campsite to the lively Loelva river and snowy mountain tops. Welcoming reception by a kind married couple. Recommended: cycling, Loen skylift, Via Ferrata, glacier visit Bødalsbreen, Kjenndalen and walk to Skålatoren (1848 m).

In the centre of Loen follow road FV723 to Lodalen/ Kjendal. Campsite indicated 2 km further on the left side. This road starts at the Alexandra Hotel.

Flo
Hjelle
Stryn
Olden

CC € 25 *1/5-15/5 20/5-20/6 18/8-20/9*

N 61°52'05" E 06°52'36"

Olden, N-6788 / Romsdal-Sognefjord

6

Camping Oldevatn****
Oldedalsvergen 1015
+47 57 87 59 15
1/5 - 30/9
post@oldevatn.com

2,2ha 43T(40-100m²) 16A

1 ACDIKLMNOQ**R**S
2 CEJMNQSUXY
3 CIMU**WZ**
4 (**A**+Q)(R 1/6-31/8)
5 **AB**DFGIJKLMNO**P**RUWZ
6 CEFGKL(N 9,9km)PVW

A fairytale! Campsite is in an idyllic location, on the lake with mountains all around, and you can even see the ends of the glaciers. Beautiful Norwegian buildings at the campsite, you'll feel right at home here!

From route 60 in Olden take the FV724 in the direction of Briksdal. After 10 km the campsite is located near the bridge.

Innvik
Olden
Sanddal

CC € 27 *9/5-15/6 19/8-30/9*

N 61°45'31" E 06°48'45"

Olden, N-6788 / Romsdal-Sognefjord

7

- Gryta-Camping***
- Oldedalsvegen 1272
- +47 57 87 59 50
- 1/5 - 1/10
- @ gryta@gryta.no

1,5ha 140T 10-16A

1 AODIKLMNOQRS
2 CEJMNPQSTUVXY
3 ACEIMPUWZ
4 (**A** 15/5-15/9)(Q+R+Z)
5 **AB**DFGIJKLMNO**P**RUWZ
6 CEFGHKLPV

Uniquely situated on the Olden Lake with a view of the Briksdal glacier. A few pitches have shade. Free use of boat for fishing in the lake. The famous Briksdal Glacier is only 10 minutes from the campsite. Great walking and hiking in the mountains. Glaciers are visible from the campsite. You can see and hear the melting water flowing into the lake.

In Olden take route FV 724 dir. Briksal. Campsite after 12 km, 1st campsite left of the road after tunnel.

Olden
Sanddal

CC € 27 *1/5-15/6 19/8-30/9*

N 61°44'27" E 06°47'27"

Olden, N-6788 / Romsdal-Sognefjord

8

- Olden Camping***
- Oldedalsvegen 1296
- +47 48 22 69 70
- 1/5 - 30/9
- @ post@oldencamping.com

1ha 65T 16A CEE

1 ACDIKLMNOQ**RS**
2 CEJMNPQSTUXY
3 ACIMP**WZ**
4 (Q+R)
5 **AB**DFGIJKLMNO**PQ**RUW
6 EFGKLPW

A peaceful campsite with views of the lake and the Melkevoll Glacier. The famous Briksdal Glacier is about 10 km away. The campsite is in a very quiet location, free use of WiFi.

In Olden FV724 towards Briksdal, campsite is on the left 13 km further on. Take note, Olden Camping Gytri is the second site after the tunnel.

CC € 27 *9/5-15/6 19/8-30/9*

N 61°44'20" E 06°47'22"

Rjukan/Miland, N-3658 / Telemark-Buskerud

9

- Rjukan Hytte og Caravan Park
- Gaustavegen 78
- +47 35 09 63 53
- 1/1 - 15/10
- @ post@rjukanhytte.com

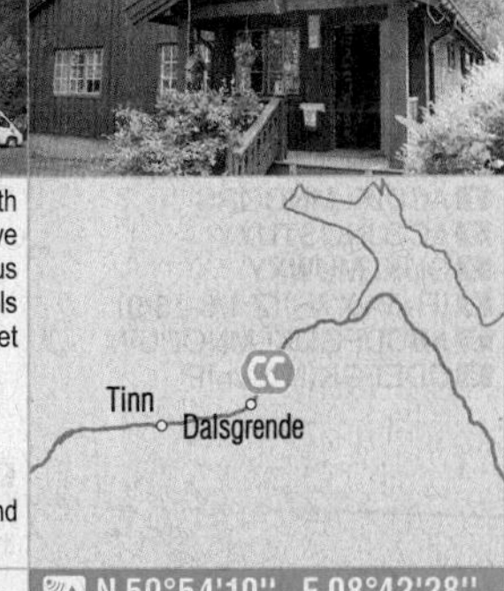

2ha 120T(90m²) 10-18A

1 ACD**I**KLMNO**RS**
2 BCJNSTUXY
3 A**G**IKX
4 (R)
5 **AB**DFGIJKMNO**P**UW
6 EFKL(N 5km)PU

Located between the hills and the mountains in the north of the Telemark province. A perfect base for a sportive/active holiday. Panoramic view of the 'Gaustatoppen'. The spacious pitches are on a large field surrounded by old stone walls and provide a real Norwegian camping feeling. Two toilet and washing blocks and good Wi-Fi.

Campsite located on route 37 between Rjukan and Miland and is well signposted.

CC € 27 *1/1-23/6 1/9-15/10 7=6*

N 59°54'10" E 08°42'28"

Sandsletta/Laukvik, N-8315 / Nordland

10

Sandsletta Camping***
Midnattsolveien 993
+47 90 91 52 30
1/1 - 31/12
sandsletta@camping-lofoten.com

3ha 100T(70-180m²) 10-16A

1 ACDEIKLMNOQ**R**S
2 GMNPSTUVWXYZ
3 ACIJKLUWY
4 **LN**(Q+R+U+V+Y+Z)
5 **AB**CDGHIJKLMNO**P**UW
6 CEFGJL(N 9km)PQV

This unique campsite located in Lofoten offers a pleasant stay for young and old. Key words are: fishing, walking, swimming, kayakking, sauna, massage, good restaurant, superb countryside and mountains.

Indicated on E10, 15 km north of Svolvær. Then 10 km in the direction of Laukvik.

Higrav
E10
Vinje
E10

CC € 27 *1/1-9/6 1/9-31/12*

N 68°20'10'' E 14°29'56''

Seljord, N-3840 / Telemark-Buskerud

11

Seljord Camping****
Manheimstrondi 61
+47 97 69 14 44
25/3 - 1/10
post@seljordcamping.no

3ha 180T(90m²) 16A

1 ACDIKLMNORS
2 AEJMNSTUXY
3 BDHIKSU**W**Z
4 M(Q+R 21/6-18/8)
5 **AB**DFGIJKLMNOPUW
6 EFGJ(N 1km)**P**V

Campsite situated by a lake with a sandy, pebble and rocky beach. You can do many different types of water sports. It's also great for children.

E134, exit RV36 direction Seljord/Bø/Skien. The campsite is about 500 metres on the right.

CC € 25 *25/3-15/5 22/5-20/6 18/8-9/9 16/9-30/9*

N 59°29'13'' E 08°39'13''

Sjøvegan, N-9350 / Finnmark-Troms

12

Elvelund Camping
Elvelund
+47 77 17 18 88
15/5 - 15/9
post@elvelund-camping.no

7ha 80T 16A

1 ACDIKLMNOQRS
2 ACGJNQSTUXY
3 CIJKLMU**W**XY
4 (R+V+X)(Z 1/6-15/9)
5 **AB**CDFGIJKLMNOPUW
6 CDEFGK(N 1km)P

A campsite that deserves to be found, situated right by a river and a fjord. The Sagelvas caves and island of Senja are worth visiting. There is a small restaurant at the campsite. Many types of water recreation and mountain sports possible here.

From the south, follow E6 to ca. 9 km before Setermoen. Then turn left, follow road 851. Campsite is signposted on the left 1 km after Sjøvegan.

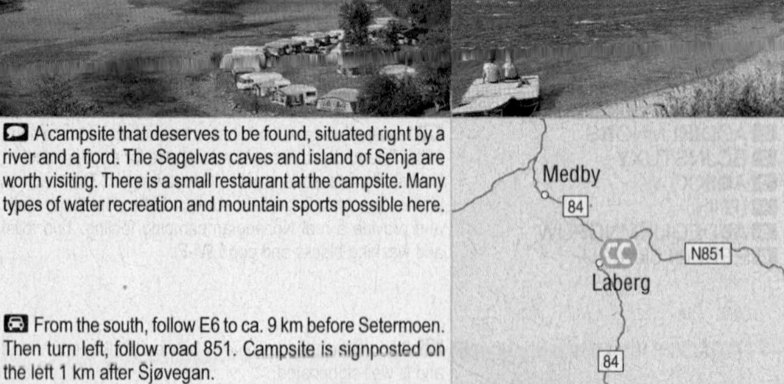

CC € 19 *15/5-1/7 1/9-15/9*

N 68°51'57'' E 17°51'41''

Tresfjord/Vikebukt, N-6392 / Romsdal-Sognefjord

13

Fagervik Camping
Daugstadvegen 630
+47 99 29 07 22
15/5 - 1/10
info@fagervikcamping.no

3ha 50T(40-100m²) 8-16A

1 CDIKLMNOQRS
2 BCGMNPQSVXY
3 AHIMWY
5 **AB**DFGIJMNOPQRUW
6 DEFGJ(N 2km)P

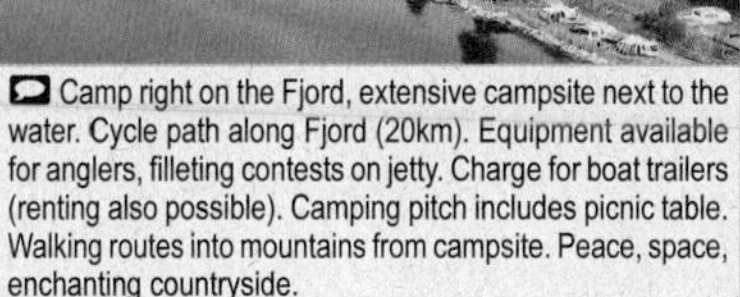

Camp right on the Fjord, extensive campsite next to the water. Cycle path along Fjord (20km). Equipment available for anglers, filleting contests on jetty. Charge for boat trailers (renting also possible). Camping pitch includes picnic table. Walking routes into mountains from campsite. Peace, space, enchanting countryside.

From Vikebukt head left before the new toll bridge to Tresfjord. From Vestnes head right before the new toll bridge and drive past Tresfjord.

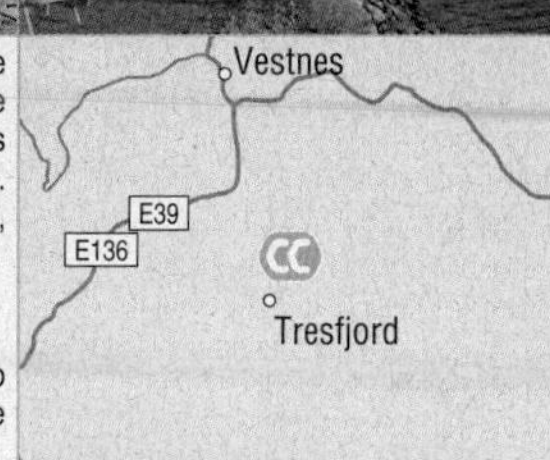

CC € 23 *15/5-30/6 18/8-20/9*

N 62°32'31" E 07°08'58"

Vågå, N-2680 / Oppland

14

Randsverk Camping
Fjellvegen 1972
+47 97 50 30 81
27/4 - 6/10
post@randsverk.no

3ha 110T(80-100m²) 16A

1 ACDIKLMNOQRUV
2 JMNSTUVX
3 AIKNPU**W**
4 (Q+R+U+V+W+X+Z)
5 **AB**DFGIJMNO**PQR**UW
6 CEFKL(N 6km)OPTV

Open terraced campsite with vast views and sunny pitches by the beautiful, touristic RV51, near Jotunheimen. Well-maintained, modern toilet and washing facilities. Family showers and a living room/kitchen with a great view for campsite guests. Good cafe. Departure point for mountain walks and cycling tours in the surrounding countryside.

On the RV51 directly on the T-junction with the 257, 27 km south of Vågåmo.

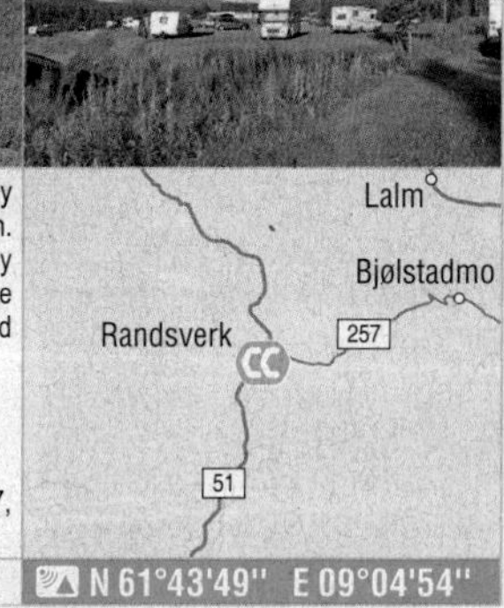

CC € 27 *27/4-20/6 20/9-6/10*

N 61°43'49" E 09°04'54"

Sweden

Sweden: natural beauty and fabulous cities

When you think of Sweden, you think of unspoiled countryside with countless forests and lakes. In this Scandinavian country, you can relax and unwind or have an active holiday amid the nature. But there is also plenty for culture enthusiasts to do too: from the metropolitan Stockholm to the modern and trendy Malmö.

Capital: Stockholm
Currency: Swedish krona
Time zone: UTC +1, UTC +2 (March to October)
Language: Swedish
International dialling code: +46
Alcohol limit: 0.2‰
Emergency number: police, fire and ambulance: 112
Tap water: safe to drink

The biggest attraction in Sweden is Mother Nature

Even just driving around in Sweden is a worthwhile trip. The country is characterised by many forests, lakes and typical red wooden houses with white window frames. Take in the natural beauty throughout your trip and don't be surprised if you have to stop and wait for a moose to cross the road. Some regions are particularly beautiful, including Dalarna and Värmland. These centrally located nature areas are great for walking and cycling. The Höga Kusten (High Coast), the island of Gotland and Kosterhavet National Park are also stunning. Wherever you camp in Sweden, there is always a lovely bit of countryside nearby.

Take in some culture in historic and trendy cities

Sweden offers much more than just calming forest and lakes. With the royal palace, the Vasa Museum and the island of Djurgarden, the capital of Stockholm also has plenty to offer.
And make sure to take a walk through the medieval town Gamla Stan, it is like travelling back in time.
The modern Malmö shows you another side of Sweden. Here, you can go shopping to your heart's content in trendy shops or enjoy culture in the Konsthall (art gallery). In the heart of the city, you can relax alongside the Swedish population in one of the many bars and restaurants. And don't forget Gothenburg. Visit the archipelago, wander through the vibrant district of Haga and go on a cruise on the city canals.

En route

Filling up

Euro 95 E10 lead free (Blyfri 95/ Bensin 95 E10) and Superplus 98 E5 (Blyfri 98/ Bensin 98 E5) are widely available. If your car is not suitable for E10, take note of the fuel's E label. Be careful that you do not accidently use E85 or B100, because those fuels can damage a standard car engine. There is

Winner in Sweden

Best location for a campsite
Kronocamping Lidköping

Winner: Kronocamping Lidköping

limited availability of LPG in the south and it's hardly available in the north. The Italian connector (Dish) is used to refuel with LPG. You are not allowed to use your own nipple reducer.
There are not many fuelling stations in the middle and north of Sweden, so you are advised to always fill up whenever you come across a station. Fuelling stations are open between 7 am and 9 pm and they usually work in automatic mode at night. Most fuelling stations in the major cities and on motorways are open day and night.

Charging

There are charging options present, most are in the south and in and around the large cities. There are fewer charging stations in the north. So plan your trip well!

Ferry services

You can travel over land to Sweden via the Øresund Bridge (oeresundsbron.com) from Copenhagen (Denmark) to Malmö, but there is also the option of travelling to Sweden by ferry boat, for example via Frederikshavn (Denmark), Rostock (Germany) or Sassnitz (Germany). Information about sailing times, departure times and fares can be found on the shipping operator's sites, such as scandlines.com, stenaline.com and ferries.nl. Fares depend on the season and departure times, among other things. Ask the shipping operator beforehand whether you can take gas bottles on the boat.

"With its stunning countryside, Sweden offers space and tranquillity in a friendly atmosphere!"
Mrs R. Kok, inspector 898

Traffic regulations

Dipped headlights (or daytime running lights) are mandatory during the day. At an uncontrolled intersection, traffic from the right has priority. Traffic on a roundabout has priority when indicated by traffic signs. You are only allowed to call hands free, and you are not allowed to operate communication or navigation devices while driving. Children under 1.35 metres in height must be in a child's car seat. Winter tyres are compulsory from 1 December to 31 March in wintry conditions.

Special regulations

At an intersection, if you see 'Flervägsväjning' (all-roads give way) under a stop sign or priority sign, drivers must give priority through mutual consideration (usually by order of arrival). As the slip roads are often short, drivers generally assume other drivers will give them space. Slower traffic usually gives way by moving to the hard shoulder to allow faster traffic to pass. There is a high probability of a colliding with large wild animals, such as reindeer or moose. So take note of the yellow warning signs.

Mandatory equipment

You must have a warning triangle in a car with a Swedish number plate. You are advised to have two warning triangles, a first aid kit, a fire extinguisher, tow rope, jumper cable, safety vests for all occupants and spare bulbs. In wintry conditions you must have a snow shovel in the car.

Caravan and motorhome

A motorhome or car-caravan combination can be a maximum of 4.5 metres in height, 2.6 metres wide and 24 metres long.

Cycling

Bicycle helmets are mandatory for children up to 15 years. Children up to 10 years old can only be transported on a bike by someone who is at least 15.

Toll

There are no toll roads in Sweden. However, you do have to pay a toll on the Øresund Bridge between Denmark and Sweden. You can pay at the bridge. Tip! You get a discount if you use a BroPas. More information: oeresundsbron.com.

Environmental zones

So far, only Sweden and Gothenburg have introduced environmental zones. You have to pay a congestion tax to enter these zones. It is very easy to pay: your number plate is registered by cameras and the bill is automatically sent to your home address. The amounts can vary, but they are no more than SEK 60 (Gothenburg) or SEK 135 (Stockholm) per day. With hire cars, the tax is usually included in the hire price. Ask the care hire firm about it.
More information: transportstyrelsen.se and epass24.com.

> *"Camping in Sweden means enjoying the countryside, the land and the language."*
>
> Mrs G. Faber, inspector 561

Breakdown and accident

On a motorway, place your warning triangle at least 100 metres (elsewhere at 50 metres) behind the car if you are somewhere where you are not allowed to

stop. All occupants are advised to put on a safety vest. If you breakdown, call the emergency number of your breakdown assistance insurer. You can also call the Swedish breakdown assistance service (Assistancekåren): +46 8 627 57 57. Towing is allowed on the motorway up to the first exit. If you have hit a reindeer, moose or other large animal, you must call the police immediately.

Camping

In Sweden, when it comes to wild camping the so-called 'Right of Public Access' applies. If you want to go wild camping, you need to ask for permission from the landowner and act according to the principle of 'don't disturb, don't destroy'. The Right of Public Access does not apply in nature reserves or other protected nature areas.

When you go camping in Sweden there is a chance you will need a special card that you must present at reception. You can buy this card at the campsite in question. You usually pay per pitch, not per person. The range of groceries, amenities and recreational options is sparse compared to popular camping countries. Most campsites do have kitchens with cooking equipment for communal use. Take note! There are very few possibilities for filling propane bottles. You are therefore advised to travel with enough gas. You cannot get butane gas at all.

Älmhult, S-34338 / Jönköping

15

First Camp Sjöstugan***
Bökhult 27
+46 47 67 16 00
1/1 - 31/12
sjostugan@firstcamp.se

1,6ha 100T(50-80m²) 10A

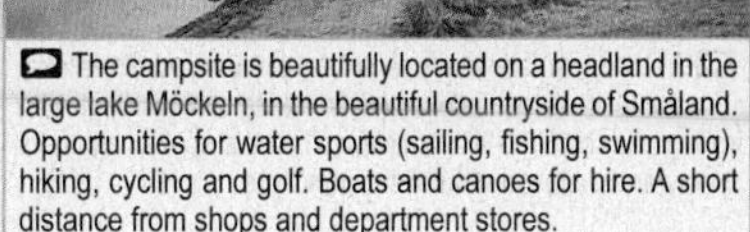

1 BCIKLMNOQ**RS**
2 ABELNSUXYZ
3 A**G**HM**R**U**W**Z
4 **KN**
(Q+R+U+W+X+Z 1/5-30/9)
5 **AB**CDEFGHIJKLMNO**P**UWZ
6 ACDEFHK(N 2km)TV

The campsite is beautifully located on a headland in the large lake Möckeln, in the beautiful countryside of Småland. Opportunities for water sports (sailing, fishing, swimming), hiking, cycling and golf. Boats and canoes for hire. A short distance from shops and department stores.

The campsite is signposted on route 23. On the E4 near Traryd take route 120 towards Älmhult.

Diö
Bråthult
120
Älmhult
23
Killeberg
121

CC € 23 *1/1-1/6 1/9-31/12*

N 56°34'07'' E 14°07'55''

Asarum/Karlshamn, S-37491 / Blekinge-Kalmar län

16

Långasjönäs Camping & Stugby***
Långasjönäsvägen 49
+46 4 54 32 06 91
1/1 - 31/12
info@langasjonas.com

11ha 115T(80-120m²) 10A CEE

1 ACDIKLMNOQRS
2 ABEILNORSTVWXYZ
3 BC**G**IKLMN**RUW**Z
4 **N**(Q 18/5-15/9)(R 1/6-1/9)
(V 7/6-1/9)(Z)
5 **AB**CDFGHIJKLMNO**P**RUWZ
6 ABCDEFGHKL(N 5km)PV

A beautifully located campsite in the middle of the Långasjönäs reserve. A campsite with beautiful views of the lake, located in an oasis of peace. Family friendly and with a lovely beach. It has the warmest beach in the whole of Blekinge.

From E22 exit 52 Karlshamn centre and follow camping signs from there. From route 29 exit Asarum then follow camping signs.

126
29
Mörrum
E22
15
E22
Karlshamn

CC € 25 *1/1-19/6 19/8-31/12* ***7=6, 14=11***

N 56°13'55'' E 14°51'11''

Båstad, S-26943 / Skåne

17

Båstad Camping
Norra Vägen 128
+46 43 17 55 11
22/3 - 29/9
info@bastadcamping.se

8,2ha 292T(110-120m²) 10A CEE

1 ACDIKLMNOQRS
2 ABIJSWXY
3 AC**G**HIKM**R**S
4 (Q+R+T+U+V+X+Z)
5 **AB**CDFGHIJKLMNO**PQ**RUWZ
6 CDEFGHK(N 3km)PTUV

A large campsite, within walking distance of a beautiful sandy beach.

From the E6/E20 follow direction Båstad. The campsite is clearly signposted from there on.

CC € 27 *2/4-8/5 13/5-6/6 9/6-20/6 19/8-29/9*

N 56°26'20'' E 12°55'05''

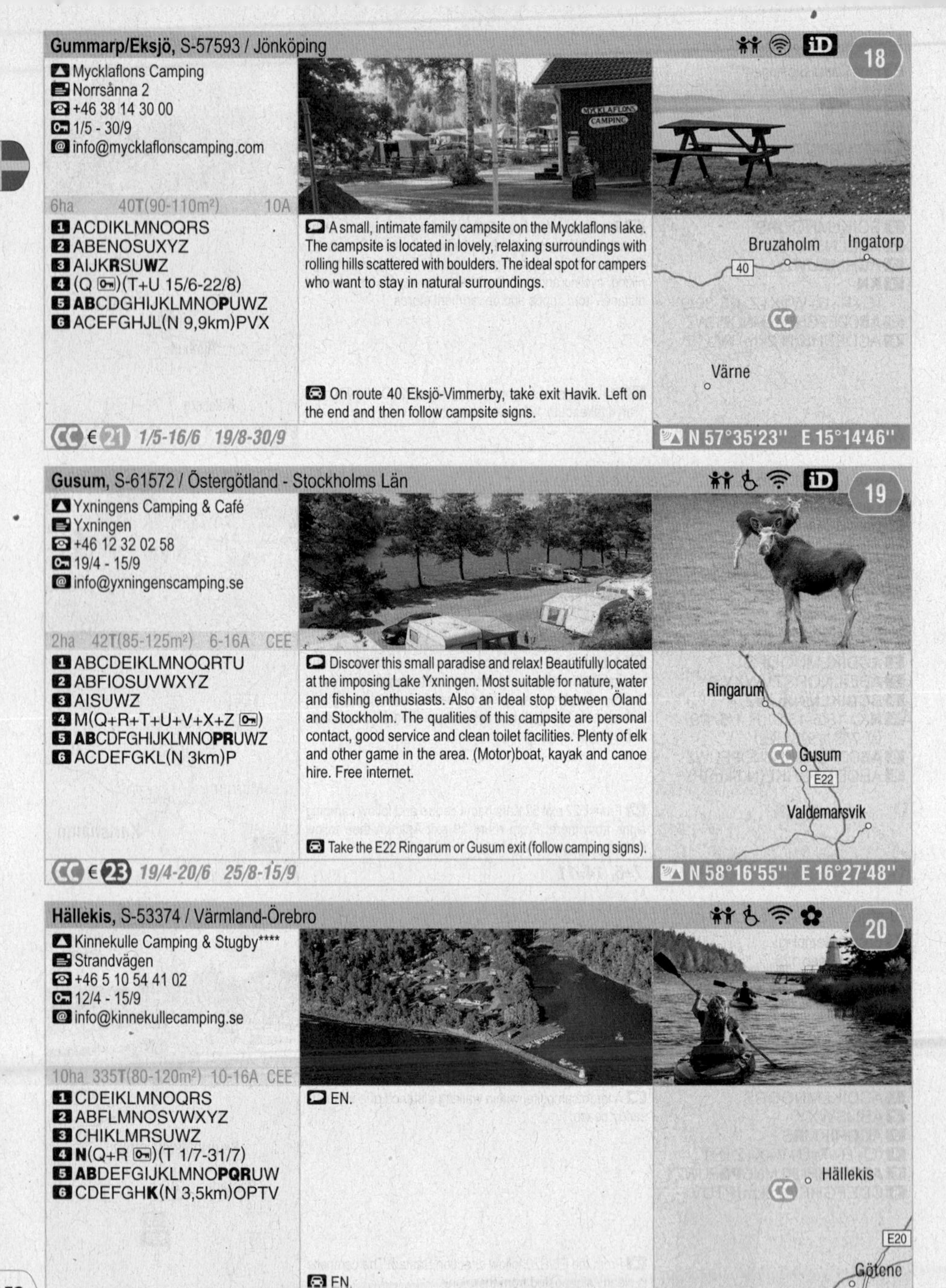

Gummarp/Eksjö, S-57593 / Jönköping

18

Mycklaflons Camping
Norrsånna 2
+46 38 14 30 00
1/5 - 30/9
info@mycklaflonscamping.com

6ha 40**T**(90-110m²) 10A

1 ACDIKLMNOQRS
2 ABENOSUXYZ
3 AIJK**R**SU**W**Z
4 (Q)(T+U 15/6-22/8)
5 **AB**CDGHIJKLMNO**P**UWZ
6 ACEFGHJL(N 9,9km)PVX

A small, intimate family campsite on the Mycklaflons lake. The campsite is located in lovely, relaxing surroundings with rolling hills scattered with boulders. The ideal spot for campers who want to stay in natural surroundings.

On route 40 Eksjö-Vimmerby, take exit Havik. Left on the end and then follow campsite signs.

CC € 21 *1/5-16/6 19/8-30/9*

N 57°35'23'' E 15°14'46''

Gusum, S-61572 / Östergötland - Stockholms Län

19

Yxningens Camping & Café
Yxningen
+46 12 32 02 58
19/4 - 15/9
info@yxningenscamping.se

2ha 42**T**(85-125m²) 6-16A CEE

1 ABCDEIKLMNOQRTU
2 ABFIOSUVWXYZ
3 AISUWZ
4 M(Q+R+T+U+V+X+Z)
5 **AB**CDFGHIJKLMNO**PR**UWZ
6 ACDEFGKL(N 3km)P

Discover this small paradise and relax! Beautifully located at the imposing Lake Yxningen. Most suitable for nature, water and fishing enthusiasts. Also an ideal stop between Öland and Stockholm. The qualities of this campsite are personal contact, good service and clean toilet facilities. Plenty of elk and other game in the area. (Motor)boat, kayak and canoe hire. Free internet.

Take the E22 Ringarum or Gusum exit (follow camping signs).

CC € 23 *19/4-20/6 25/8-15/9*

N 58°16'55'' E 16°27'48''

Hällekis, S-53374 / Värmland-Örebro

20

Kinnekulle Camping & Stugby****
Strandvägen
+46 5 10 54 41 02
12/4 - 15/9
info@kinnekullecamping.se

10ha 335**T**(80-120m²) 10-16A CEE

1 CDEIKLMNOQRS
2 ABFLMNOSVWXYZ
3 CHIKLMRSUWZ
4 **N**(Q+R)(T 1/7-31/7)
5 **AB**DEFGIJKLMNO**PQR**UW
6 CDEFGH**K**(N 3,5km)OPTV

EN.

EN.

CC € 23 *12/4-8/5 11/5-16/5 20/5-19/6 23/6-28/6 19/8-15/9*

N 58°37'24'' E 13°23'05''

Haverdal, S-30571 / Halland-Bohuslän

21

Haverdals Camping****
Haverdalsvägen 62
+46 3 55 23 10
28/3 - 24/11
info@haverdalscamping.se

5ha 230**T**(100-140m²) 10-16A CEE

1 ABCDIKLMNOQS
2 AHIJSWXY
3 AC**G**HIKMP**R**SU
4 (Q+R)
5 **AB**DFGIJKLMNO**P**QRUWXYZ
6 CDEFGHK(N 0,2km)O**P**TU

Anna-Lenna and Stefan guarantee a relaxing stay on their child-friendly campsite. The wide sandy beach and dunes which stretch for miles just 600m from the campsite, border a nature reserve with plenty of walking and cycling opportunities. The campsite has spacious pitches and modern toilet facilities. You have the use of a large communal kitchen next to the dining room.

E6, exit 46 Haverdal. Continue towards Haverdal.

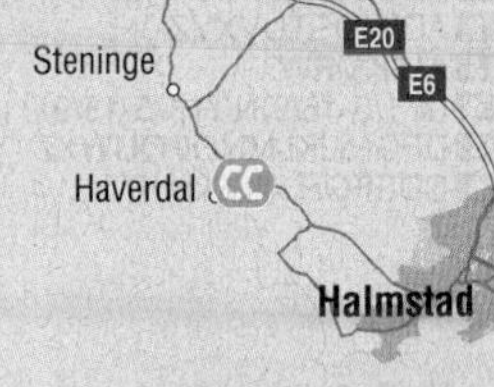

CC € 25 *1/4-7/5 12/5-18/6 23/6-28/6 18/8-24/9* ***30=25***

N 56°43'39'' E 12°40'25''

Hova/Otterberget, S-54891 / Värmland-Örebro

22

Otterbergets Bad & Camping***
Otterbergetscamping 1
+46 50 63 31 27
12/4 - 4/11
info@otterbergetscamping.se

3,2ha 77**T**(100-120m²) 10A

1 CDEIKLMNOQRS
2 ABEIOSTWXYZ
3 ACHIKP**R**SU**W**Z
4 N(Q+R)
5 **AB**CDFGHIJKLMNO**PQ**RUWZ
6 ACEFGH**K**(N 8km)PV

A very peaceful campsite on Lake Skagern with a kilometre-long beautiful sandy beach. Walking and cycling possible in the countryside of Tiveden.

On the E20 between Mariestad and Laxå, 5 km north of Hova. Turn off towards Otterberget. Campsite signposted here. Follow signs (3 km).

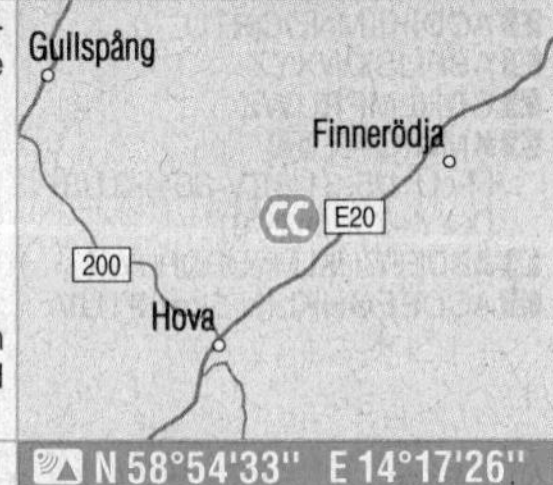

CC € 19 *12/4-15/5 19/5-10/6 19/8-11/9 15/9-4/11*

N 58°54'33'' E 14°17'26''

Johannisholm/Mora, S-79292 / Dalarnas-Uppsala län

23

Steiner's Camping & Lodge
Johannisholm 3
+46 7 36 23 26 99
1/4 - 31/10
info@steinerslodge.com

2,8ha 95**T**(100m²) 16A CEE

1 ACDIKLMNOQ**R**S
2 ABCFIJLNOSUXYZ
3 AU**W**Z
4 (Q+U+Y+Z 1/6-15/9)
5 **AB**CDFGHIJKLMNO**P**UW
6 CFJ

On Lake Örklingen, next to the E45, you will find this well-equipped campsite with very good restaurant. Many tourist attractions in the vicinity. The campsite offers a choice of sunny and shady pitches.

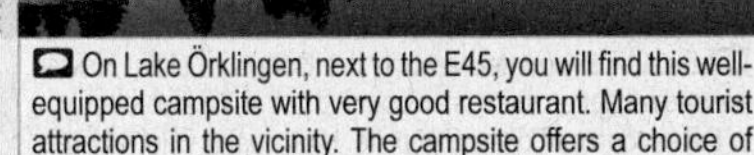

Campsite is located at junction of Malung-Mora and Vansbro-Mora roads 45 and 26. Site is signposted on all access roads.

E45
26
Kättbo
CC
E45
Johannisholm
26

CC € 23 *1/4-15/6 1/9-31/10* ***7=6***

N 60°49'35'' E 14°07'36''

Kapellskär, S-76015 / Östergötland - Stockholms Län

24

Kapellskär Camping***
Fiskarängsvägen 8
+46 17 64 42 33
25/4 - 15/9
info@kapellskarscamping.se

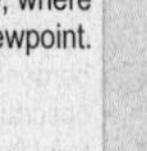

3,5ha 102T(70-120m²) 10A CEE

1 ABCDEIKLMNOQRS
2 ABIMOSTUVXYZ
3 AHIKM**R**W
4 (**A** 1/5-15/9)N(R 1/5-15/9)
5 DFGHIJKLMNOPQUWXZ
6 CDEFGHJ(N 6km)PT

This campsite with good facilities is located near the port of Kapellskär in the Riddarholm nature reserve, where there are marked hiking trails to a marina and a viewpoint. The campsite has a large separate field for tents.

At the end of road E18, at Kapellskär harbour, turn right into a dirt road. Follow signs for 600 metres.

E18 — Kapellskär

CC € 25 *25/4-8/5 11/5-20/6 18/8-15/9*

N 59°43'22'' E 19°03'00''

Karlstad, S-65346 / Värmland-Örebro

25

Karlstad Swecamp Bomstad Baden****
Bomstadsvägen 640
+46 54 53 50 68
1/1 - 31/12
info@bomstadbaden.se

9ha 160T(80-130m²) 10A CEE

1 ACDIKLMNOQ**R**TU
2 ABFIJSTWXYZ
3 C**G**HLMP**R**UWZ
4 **KMN**(Q+R)
(T+U 1/5-31/8)(V 30/4-31/8)
(X+Y+Z 1/5-31/8)
5 **AB**DEFGIJKLMNOPQRUWX
6 ACDEFGHKL(N 5km)**P**TUV

Beautifully located site on north side of Lake Vänern. Excellent base for walks and excursions in the recreational area. Trips out and activities can be combined with sunny beach days. Day trips through Värmland or to the Bergvik shopping centre 4 km from site. Public transport from campsite. Restaurant (May-Aug).

Campsite signposted from the E18, west of Karlstad (Skutberget/Bomstad exit).

CC € 25 *1/1-28/5 10/6-18/6 24/8-31/12*

N 59°21'44'' E 13°21'33''

Kungshamn, S-45634 / Halland-Bohuslän

26

Johannesvik Camping & Stugby****
Vägga Nordgård 1
+46 52 33 23 87
1/1 - 31/12

25ha 410T(80-120m²) 10A CEE

1 CDIKLMNOQRTU
2 GJLNOQRSWXY
3 C**G**IKLMP**R**UWY
4 **KN**(Q+R)
(S+T+V+Y+Z 15/6-15/8)
5 **AB**DEFGIJKLMNO**PQ**RUWZ
6 ACDEFGHKL(N 2km)**P**TV

Beautifully located among the Bohuslän cliffs. Having passed reception there is an opening in the cliff that takes you to the second part of the campsite. High quality toilet facilities. Many options for activities on as well as off the campsite. Kungshamn and the picturesque peninsula of Smögen are nearby and are definitely worth a visit.

From E6 route 171 to Askum. Dir. Kungshamn. Through Hovenäset, over bridge. After ± 1 km entrance of campsite on right.

CC € 23 *1/1-16/6 19/8-31/12*

N 58°22'01'' E 11°16'51''

Leksand, S-79390 / Dalarnas-Uppsala län

27

Leksand Strand Camping & Resort*****
Siljansvägen 61
+46 24 71 38 00
1/5 - 30/9
bokning@leksandresort.se

12ha 640**T**(100-120m²) 10-16A CEE

1 ACDIKLMNOQ**RS**
2 AFIJLMNSTUVWXY
3 CD**G**IKMP**RU**W**Z**
4 (C+**H** 11/6-13/8)**IJN** (Q+S+U+V+W+Y +Z 11/6-13/8)
5 **AB**CDEFGHIJKLMNOPQRUWXYZ
6 CDEFGHKL(N 2km)**P**TUV

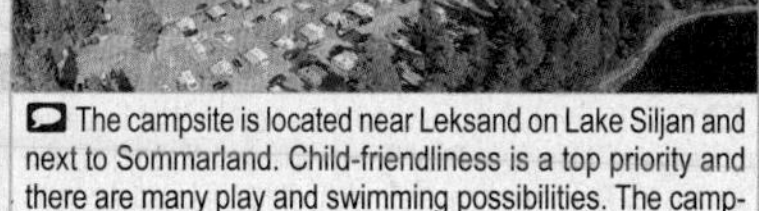

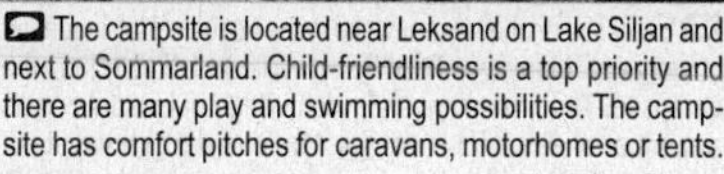

The campsite is located near Leksand on Lake Siljan and next to Sommarland. Child-friendliness is a top priority and there are many play and swimming possibilities. The campsite has comfort pitches for caravans, motorhomes or tents.

From road 70 Borlänge-Rattvik in centre of Leksand follow exit Tällberg. Follow the sings after 2 km.

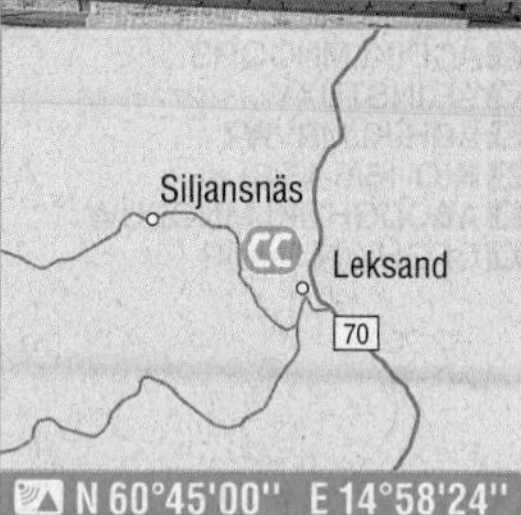

CC € 23 *1/5-9/6 19/8-30/9*

N 60°45'00'' E 14°58'24''

Leksand, S-79392 / Dalarnas-Uppsala län

28

Västanviksbadets Camping Leksand****
Västanviksiljansnäsvägen 130
+46 7 68 12 85 10
1/5 - 19/9
info@vbcl.se

4ha 100**T**(100m²) 10A

1 ACDIKLMNOQS
2 AFJLMNSTUXY
3 **G**IKU**WZ**
4 (Q 14/6-11/8)
5 **AB**DGIJNPUW
6 CEFG**K**(N 4km)PV

Charming, friendly campsite by Lake Siljan, run by enthusiastic owners. The service exceeds all expectations! Experience the countryside in this lovely area with plenty of walking and cycling opportunities. The tourist attractions in Siljan are quick to reach. Reservations are mandatory in September!

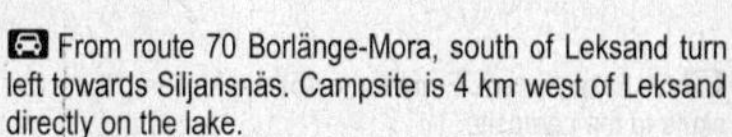

From route 70 Borlänge-Mora, south of Leksand turn left towards Siljansnäs. Campsite is 4 km west of Leksand directly on the lake.

CC € 21 *2/5-14/6 1/9-19/9*

N 60°43'49'' E 14°57'07''

Lidköping, S-53161 / Värmland-Örebro

29

Kronocamping Lidköping*****
Läckögatan 22
+46 51 02 68 04
1/1 - 31/12
info@kronocamping.com

5ha 493**T**(70-140m²) 10A CEE

1 CDEIKLMNOQRS
2 ABFJNOSTVWXYZ
3 ACD**G**HMP**R**SUVWZ
4 (C+H 1/6-31/8)**KN**(Q+R) (T+U+V+Y 1/4-31/8) (Z 1/6-1/9)
5 **AB**DEFGIJKLMNOPQRUWXYZ
6 CDEFGHKLM(N 1,5km) **P**STV

Large, luxury and very clean campsite by Lake Vänern. Modern toilet and washing facilities and child-friendly swimming beach. Free use of adjacent heated outdoor swimming pool. Rörstrand porcelain museum and Skara Sommarland water park are worth visiting.

Drive via Skara on route 184 to Lidköping. In the town follow the signs to the campsite.

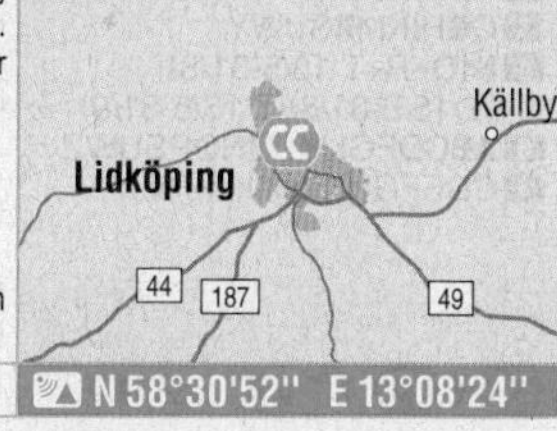

CC € 23 *1/1-27/3 2/4-7/5 13/5-19/6 24/6-29/6 2/9-31/12*

N 58°30'52'' E 13°08'24''

Ljusdal, S-82730 / Gävleborg-Västernorrland

30

Ljusdals Camping***
Ramsjövägen 56
+46 65 11 29 58
15/4 - 30/9
info@ljusdalscamping.se

4,5ha 95T(100-120m²) 10A

1 ACDIKLMNOQRS
2 AFJNSTUXY
3 A**G**HIKLM**R**V**WZ**
4 **N**(Q 15/6-15/8)
5 **AB**CDGHIJKLMNOPUW
6 CFGHK(N 3km)P

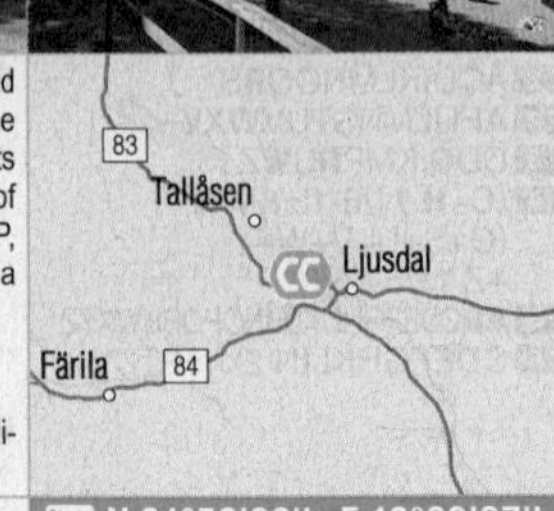

Campsite on the Växnan Lake in the beautiful Hälsingerland countryside. Many woodland hiking trails start directly from the campsite. The charming, shop-rich village of Ljusdal boasts a number of beautiful buildings. You can eat in a variety of restaurants. You can do your daily shopping at the COOP, Lidl or ICA. Thanks to the friendly Dutch management a pleasant stay is guaranteed.

3 km from the village of Ljusdal on road 83 in the direction of Ånge.

83 Tallåsen Ljusdal Färila 84

CC € 21 *15/4-14/6 20/8-30/9 7=6*

N 61°50'20'' E 16°02'27''

Mellerud, S-46421 / Halland-Bohuslän

31

Mellerud Swe-Camp Vita Sandar****
+46 53 01 22 60
1/1 - 31/12
mail@vitasandarscamping.se

14ha 210T(100-120m²) 10A

1 CDIKLMNOQRTU
2 AFSWXY
3 AC**G**IKM**O**P**R**UWZ
4 (**C** 1/6-31/8)**N** (Q+S+T+U+W+X +Z 1/6-31/8)
5 **AB**DFGIJKLMNO**P**QRUWZ
6 ACDFGHK(N 4km)**P**TV

Situated on the so-called Dalsland Riviera. Associations with summer, sunshine and swimming. Kilometres of long sandy beaches, rowing boats, canoes, outdoor pool, tennis, mini golf and football are all options for relaxation. There's even a shop and a restaurant (01/06-31/08).

On Lake Vänern. From route 45 near Mellerud there are signs to the campsite.

CC € 23 *1/1-16/6 19/8-31/12*

N 58°41'22'' E 12°31'01''

Sandarne, S-82673 / Gävleborg-Västernorrland

32

Stenö Havsbad & Camping****
Stenövägen 130
+46 27 07 51 50
1/1 - 31/12
stenocamping@soderhamn.se

5ha 191T(100-120m²) 16A CEE

1 ABCDIKLMNOQRS
2 ABHIJOSTUVWXYZ
3 C**G**HIKM**R**SUWY
4 **N**(Q+R+T 15/5-31/8) (Y 15/6-31/8)(Z 15/5-31/8)
5 **AB**CDFGIJKLMNOPSUWZ
6 CDEFGHK(N 3km)PV

Large campsite at the point of the peninsula. Large sandy beach. Suitable for families with children. In the direct vicinity of good fishing, walking and cycling options. Dog showers provided at the campsite. Card payments only. You can go ice skating and cross country skiing here during the winter.

From E4 Gävle-Söderhamn, 11 km southeast of Söderhamn. Eastern exit to Sandarne. Then follow signs for 'Stenocamping'.

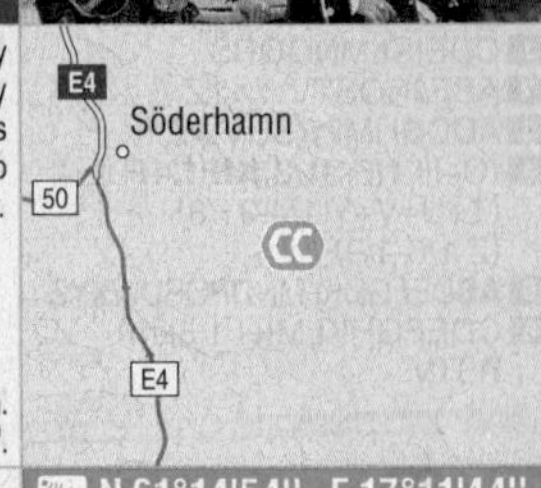

CC € 15 *1/1-6/6 6/9-31/12*

N 61°14'54'' E 17°11'44''

Sjötorp, S-54266 / Värmland-Örebro

33

Askeviks Camping & Stugor
Askevik 62
+46 7 68 14 14 09
1/1 - 31/12
info@askevik.nu

9ha 90T(80-140m²) 10A CEE

1 ACDEIKLMNOQRS
2 AEJMNPSUWXY
3 AC**G**HKSWZ
4 **N**(Q 16/6-12/8)
5 **AB**GIJKLMN**P**UWXY
6 ACEFGH**K**TV

Campsite is situated by the water and is ideal for water sports. Nearby are the locks of the Göta Canal. The surroundings invite you to go hiking or cycling. Campers can also relax on the sandy beach. Due to its location, it is virtually mosquito-free.

From Mariestad, drive north on E20. Left after 6 km E26 direction Mora. After 13 km pass Göta Canal. After 7 km left to Askeviks Camping & Stugor.

CC € 21 1/1-14/6 18/8-31/12

N 58°53'20'' E 14°00'49''

Sollerön, S-79290 / Dalarnas-Uppsala län

34

Sollerö Camping***
Soldvägen 149
+46 25 02 22 30
1/1 - 31/12
info@sollerocamping.se

0,7ha 133T(90-135m²) 16A CEE

1 ACDIKLMNOQS
2 AFIJLMNOSTUVWXY
3 ACD**G**HIKM**R**SU**W**Z
4 N(Q+V+X)
5 **AB**CDFGHIJKLMNOPRUW
6 CDEFGHK(N 3km)OPV

A large, charming campsite. Beautifully located on Sollerön island in the Siljan lake. A good base for visiting the sights around the Siljan lake. Plenty of walking and cycling opportunities. Golf course next to the campsite.

From Mora route 45, left at Sollerön exit. Left in Gesunda and follow signs.

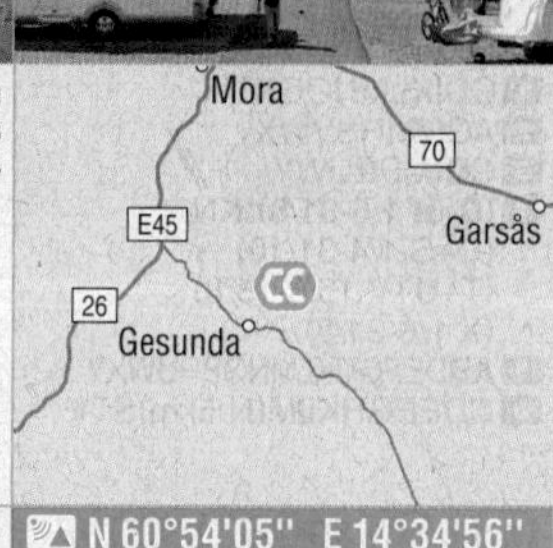

CC € 21 1/1-16/6 26/8-31/12 7=6

N 60°54'05'' E 14°34'56''

Sölvesborg, S-29477 / Skåne

35

Valjevikens Camping
Valjeallen 20
+46 45 61 40 90
1/3 - 30/9
valjevikens.camping@gmail.com

3ha 110T(80-100m²) 10A

1 CDEIKLMNOQRS
2 ABHIJNOSXYZ
3 ABIK**R**UW
4 (Q+R+U)
5 **AB**FGHIJKLMNOPQUWXYZ
6 CEFGJ(N 3km)OPUV

Campsite with a friendly ambience, by the sea and in Valje nature reserve with lovely walking and cycling paths. Good possibilities for sporting activities, recreation and excursions. Two kilometres from Sölvesborg with shops and restaurants.

From Malmö, follow E22, exit 45. Follow Sölvesborg and you will see the sign for Valjevikens Camping.

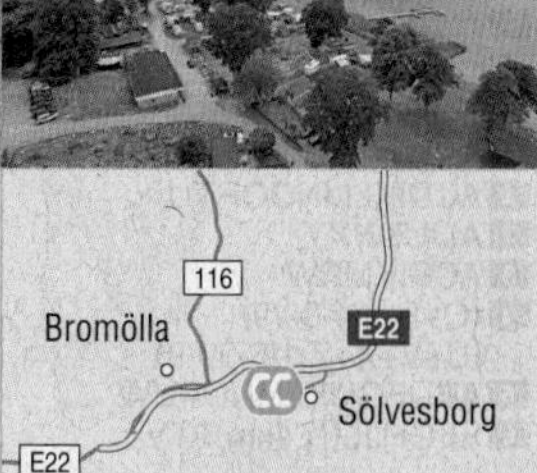

CC € 23 22/3-14/6 1/9-30/9 7=6

N 56°03'29'' E 14°33'04''

Stöllet, S-68051 / Värmland-Örebro

36

Alevi Camping
Fastnäs 53
+46 7 38 32 01 56
1/5 - 30/9
info@alevi-camping.com

4,1ha 60**T**(120-180m²) 4-16A CEE

1 ABCDIJKLMNOQ**R**TU
2 DJOSTWXY
3 AIKLPSU**W**X
4 (**A** 9/7-19/8)(Q)
(R+T+U 1/6-31/8)(Z)
5 **AB**DFGIJKLMNOPQRUWZ
6 ACEFGKLPV

A friendly campsite right on the bend of the River Klarälven. Rafting and canoeing, fishing and swimming. Basic meals in the restaurant and fresh bread each morning. Small camp shop, clean toilet facilities and free showers. You will arrive as a guest and leave as a friend!

On route 62, 18 km south of the intersection with the 45 (Stöllet). Turn left immediately after the bridge over the Klarälven as signposted. Coming from Karlstad 14 km north of Ekshärad.

CC € 23 *1/5-5/7*

N 60°17'07'' E 13°24'25''

Strömstad, S-45297 / Halland-Bohuslän

37

Camping Daftö Resort*****
Dafter 1
+46 52 62 60 40
8/1 - 20/12
info@dafto.se

11,8ha 469**T**(80-120m²) 10A CEE

1 CDIKLMNOQ**R**TU
2 AGIJMRSVWX
3 C**G**IMP**R**UWY
4 (**C+H** 1/6-31/8)**IK**N
(Q+S 1/4-31/10)
(T+U+V 15/6-15/8)
(X 1/6-31/8)
5 **AB**DEFGIJKLMNOPRUWXY
6 CDEFGHKLM(N 5km)STV

A luxury 5-star campsite directly on the reefs of Bohuslän. Little shade but excellent amenities such as a heated swimming pool, the famous outdoor play centre Daftöland, excellent toilet facilities, kayaks, pedalos, bikes, 100% (free) wifi, walking routes and 18 hole golf course close by.

Coming from the south follow the E6 as far as exit Sandfjord/ Strömstad (route 176) near the Hydro-service station. After 6.5 km the campsite is located on the left of the road.

Strömstad
Skee
CC
E6
164
176
Lur

CC € 25 *8/1-1/6 1/9-20/12*

N 58°54'15'' E 11°12'05''

Strömstad, S-45290 / Halland-Bohuslän

38

Seläter Camping***
Seläter
+46 52 61 22 90
1/1 - 31/12
info@selater.se

7ha 337**T**(100-120m²) 10A

1 ACDIKLMNOQRTU
2 AIJLSWXY
3 AC**G**IKM**R**W
4 (Q+R 1/4-30/9)
(U+V+X+Z 1/5-30/9)
5 **AB**DFGIJKLMNO**P**UW
6 EFGHJL(N 4km)**P**TV

Campsite Seläter is located in a rural area north-west of Strömstad, near the Capri beach. Free wifi at the new reception. It is possible to cycle to the centre of Strömstad and to use the ferry (special pass at reception). Bus stop at campsite. Walking route 1.5 km around the campsite.

Take E6 from south dir. exit Strömstad N. Right on 1st roundabout. Campsite is on the road to Seläter.

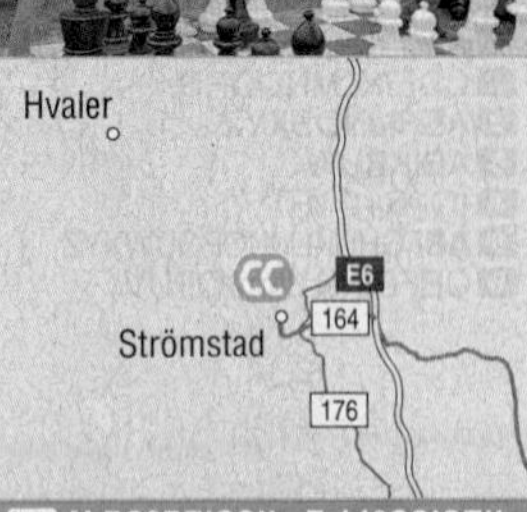

CC € 21 *2/4-20/6 18/8-30/9*

N 58°57'23'' E 11°09'27''

Tranås, S-57393 / Jönköping

39

Hätte Camping****
Badvägen 2
+46 14 01 74 82
1/1 - 31/12
info@hattecamping.se

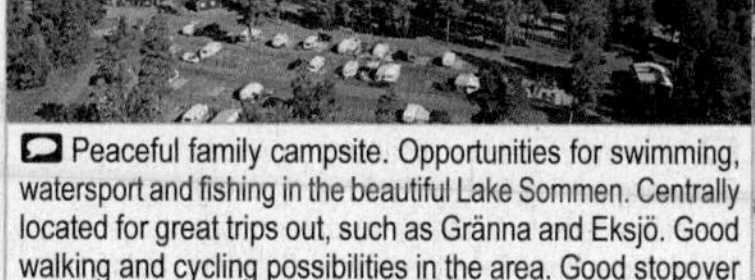

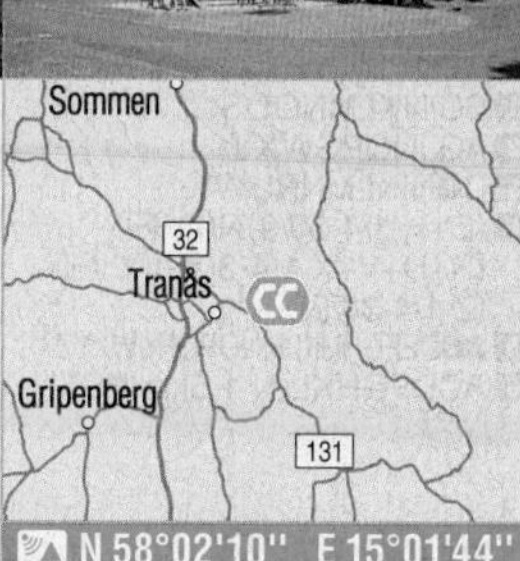

4ha 129T(80-100m²) 10-16A CEE

1 ABCDEIKLMNOQRS
2 ABEOSVWXYZ
3 A**G**IKLM**R**SU**W**Z
4 M(Q 20/6-15/8)(R ⊶)
(U 1/5-31/8)(V ⊶)
(X+Y 1/5-31/8)
5 **AB**DFGIJKLMNOPUWZ
6 ACEFGHKL(N 4km)PV

Peaceful family campsite. Opportunities for swimming, watersport and fishing in the beautiful Lake Sommen. Centrally located for great trips out, such as Gränna and Eksjö. Good walking and cycling possibilities in the area. Good stopover location for trips to Stockholm and the Arctic Circle.

Campsite located 3 km east of Tranås and signposted from route 131 (in the direction of Hätte). On route 32 take Tranås Sud exit, dir centre and the campsite is signposted.

CC € 21 *1/1-14/6 25/8-31/12*

N 58°02'10'' E 15°01'44''

Uddevalla/Hafsten, S-45196 / Halland-Bohuslän

40

Camping Hafsten Resort*****
Hafsten 120
+46 5 22 64 41 17
1/1 - 31/12
info@hafsten.se

17ha 383T(80-120m²) 10A CEE

1 CDIKLMNOQ**R**TU
2 AHLMNRSTWXY
3 CD**G**HIN**O**P**R**U**V**WY
4 (A 1/7-15/8)(C+H 1/5-6/11)
JKLM**NP**(Q+R ⊶)
(S 1/6-31/8)(T+U ⊶)
(V 1/6-31/8)(X+Y+Z ⊶)
5 **AB**DFGIJKLMNO**P**UWXYZ
6 CDFGHK(N 6km)OPSTV

Five-star, well-equipped campsite with spacious pitches and lovely sea views. Sandy beach, wellness, boat hire, tennis court, jeu de boules, go-karts/handcarts and climbing park, among others. Hiking routes in the Hafsten Fjord nature area. Beautiful, new, heated pool (open from 1/5 to 6/11).

From E6 take 161 to Lysekil as far as 160. Left to Orust. Left after 2 km then another 4 km (follow signs). Site clearly marked, is in Hafstensfjord (nature reserve).

CC € 27 *1/1-28/3 1/4-8/5 12/5-5/6 26/8-27/10 3/11-31/12*

N 58°18'52'' E 11°43'23''

Valdemarsvik, S-61533 / Östergötland - Stockholms Län

41

Grännäs Camping och Stugby****
Festplatsvägen 1
+46 12 35 14 44
26/4 - 15/9
info@grannascamping.se

10ha 66T(80-120m²) 10A CEE

1 ABCDEIKLMNQRS
2 ABHIMNOSWXYZ
3 AIL**O**P**R**SUWY
4 (Q ⊶)
5 **AB**CDFGHIJKLMNOPRUWZ
6 ACDEFGK(N 3km)PTV

Beautiful campsite in park-like surroundings, located directly on the only fjord of the Swedish eastern coast. The welcoming harbour town of Valdemarsvik with various restaurants is at walking distance (1.5 km). This campsite is on your way if you are driving to Stockholm from mainland Europe. You are very welcome.

From south take E22 exit Kårtorp/Gållósa and from here follow signs to Grännäs. From the north exit Valdemarsvik, then follow Grännäs.

CC € 23 *26/4-20/6 25/8-15/9*

N 58°11'39'' E 16°37'01''

Varberg, S-43253 / Halland-Bohuslän

42

Destination Apelviken*****
Sanatorievägen 4
+46 3 40 64 13 00
1/1 - 31/12
info@apelviken.se

6ha 308T(100-120m²) 10-16A CEE

1 BCDIKLMNOQS
2 AGJNQRSWXY
3 C**G**HIKLMN**R**UWY
4 (C+H 1/4-30/9)N(Q ⊶)
(R+U+V+X 1/4-30/9)(Y ⊶)
(Z 1/4-30/9)
5 **AB**DEFGHIJKLMNOPQRUWXYZ
6 ACDFGHKL(N 1,5km)**P**ST

Stunningly located on headland on Sweden's west coast. Swimming, surfing, SUP, golf (18 holes), walking, cycling (over the promenade to Varberg). estaurant open at weekends March-November. Take the train to Göteborg, Halmstad or beyond. 30 km from the site you will find Sweden's largest shopping centre: Gekås in Ullared.

E6, exit 53 to 55, depending on your direction. Keep on towards Varberg Centre, then follow the 'Apelviken' signs and the signs to the campsite.

CC € 27 *1/1-27/3 1/4-7/5 12/5-4/6 9/6-14/6 1/9-31/12*

N 57°05'17'' E 12°14'51''

Värnamo, S-33131 / Jönköping

43

Värnamo Camping***
Prostgårdsvägen
+46 37 01 66 60
1/5 - 12/9
info@varnamocamping.se

3ha 70T(100m²) 10A CEE

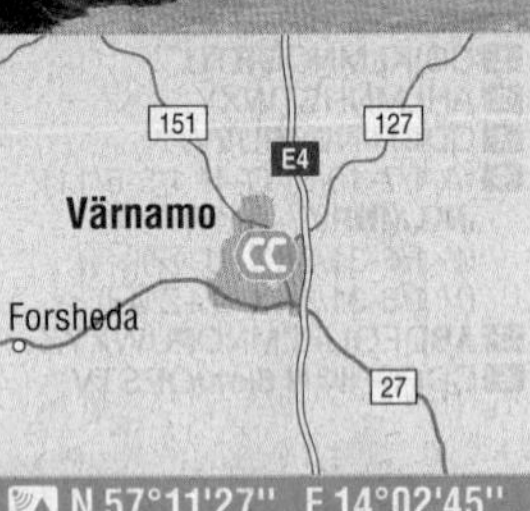

1 ABCDIKLMNOQRS
2 BCEJOSZ
3 C**G**HIKOP**R**U**W**Z
4 (Q 7/6-15/8)(R ⊶)
5 **AB**DEFGIJKLMNOPUW
6 AEFGHK(N 0,5km)PTV

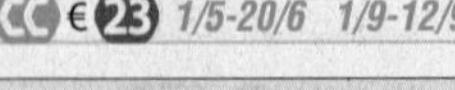

Shaded campsite a short walk from a lake, forest and the centre. National Park 15 km away.

E4, exit 85 Värnamo S, then follow camping signs. Also signposted on road 27.

CC € 23 *1/5-20/6 1/9-12/9*

N 57°11'27'' E 14°02'45''

Finland

Capital: Helsinki
Currency: euro
Time zone: UTC +2, UTC +3 (March to October)
Language: Finnish and Swedish Sámi languages have an official status regionally
International dialling code: +358
Alcohol limit: 0.5‰
Emergency number: police, fire brigade and ambulance: 112
Tap water: safe to drink

Finland: the country of 1000 lakes

A camping holiday in Finland is the perfect way to really relax. A Finnish campsite gives you the sensation of infinite space and nature in its purest form. Finland has 1.2 million acres of protected nature reserves. Truly a place to find yourself.

Midnight sun

Finland is a true water labyrinth with its countless lakes, island, rivers and rapids. The nickname 'country of a thousand lakes' is not an exaggeration: there are actually more than 180,000! After the long winter, the Finns enjoy the clear and warm summer days to the fullest. While camping in Finland, experience the endless summer evenings where it barely becomes night and possibly even remains twilight. See how the sun is almost continuously in the sky above your campsite in Finland. During Finnish summers, there are endless parties around a campfire to enjoy this.

A cultural visit or a visit to the sauna

With regard to the cultural aspect, there is no shortage of culture during a camping holiday in

Finland because the Finnish cultural summer buzzes with festivals. A great outing from your campsite in Finland would be a boat trip – available from all larger cities and lakes. Many campsites can also be accessed by boat or canoe.
Many Finnish campsites offer the opportunity to sweat out your fatigue in a healthy way: after all, the Finns invented the sauna. What you might not know: Finland is a must for those who love architecture and contemporary design. There is almost nowhere else on earth where modern buildings form such a harmonious whole with nature.

En route

Filling up

Petrol (95 E5, 95 E10 and 98 E5) and diesel are readily available (if you want to fill up with E10, check the filler cap, the owner's manual or at your car dealership to see if your car can run on it). LPG is not available.
Finland has more unmanned than manned petrol stations. Manned petrol stations are usually open from 7:00 to 21:00 but are often open for shorter periods on weekends. Along the motorways the opening hours are longer.
Do keep in mind that there are less petrol stations in the thinly populated north. Ferries do not usually allow fuel to be carried in a reserve tank.

Charging

Most of the charging points are in the south. There are plenty of them around Helsinki and Turku. If you will be travelling outside of the urban areas, it is wise to plan your journey well.

Ferry services

Information on schedules, departures and fares can be found at ferry companies such as eckerolinjen.se, finnlines.com, moby.it, tallink.com, stpeterline.com, sales.vikingline.com and wasaline.com. Fares vary according to factors such as the season and departure time. It is advisable to book in time.
Be sure to ask the ferry company in advance if you can take gas cylinders on board. Taking extra fuel along in a reserve tank is usually not allowed.

"In Finland, you can really go camping: freedom, nature and especially no mass tourism."
Mr Y. Bergman, inspector 1109

Traffic regulations

Dipped headlights (or daylight running lights) are mandatory during the daytime. Traffic coming from the right has right of way at equal intersections. Traffic on the roundabout almost always has right of way (unless there is no right-of-way sign). Trams always have right of way. Drivers are only allowed to use mobile phones in hands-free mode. Children shorter than 1.35 meters must be in a child seat. Winter tyres are mandatory from December to March.

Special regulations

Pedestrians walking in the dark or under poor visibility conditions must wear a reflector or a safety vest.

Mandatory equipment

A warning triangle in your car is mandatory. It is recommended that you have a safety vest for all passengers.

Caravan and motorhome

A motorhome or car-caravan combination may not be more than 4.40 metres high, 2.60 metres wide and 18.75 metres long (the caravan itself may not be more than 12 metres long).

Cycling

A bicycle helmet is compulsory. You are not allowed to talk or communicate by app/SMS on the phone while cycling. Children must be transported in a seat on the back of the bicycle. Children up to 9 years old may only go behind someone who is at least 15 years old. Children up to 12 years old may cycle on the pavement.

Breakdown and accident

Place your warning triangle between 100 and 200 metres behind the car if it endangers other traffic. All occupants are required to put on safety vests. In the event of a breakdown, call the emergency number of your breakdown assistance provider. You can also call Finnish roadside assistance (Autoliitto) at (+358) 200 8080. Towing on the motorway is permitted until the first exit. If you have hit a reindeer, moose or other large wild animal, call the police immediately.

Camping

Finnish campsites vary from simple sites with basic facilities to comfortable campsites with all amenities. Many of the Finnish campsites are located next to water. Between mid-June and mid-August, the water reaches a surprisingly high temperature of almost 20 degrees Celsius.

If you are going camping in Finland, there is a good possibility that you need a special card that you must present to the reception. This card can be purchased at the relevant campsite. The opportunities for filling propane gas bottles are very limited. It is best to begin your journey with enough gas. Almost every campsite has a communal kitchen that you can use. Most campsites also have a communal sauna, which is included in the price. Staying overnight along the public road in a caravan, motorhome or car is only permitted in case of an emergency.

Practical information

During the summer, the mosquitoes can be very troublesome, particularly in the north of Finland and by the lakes.

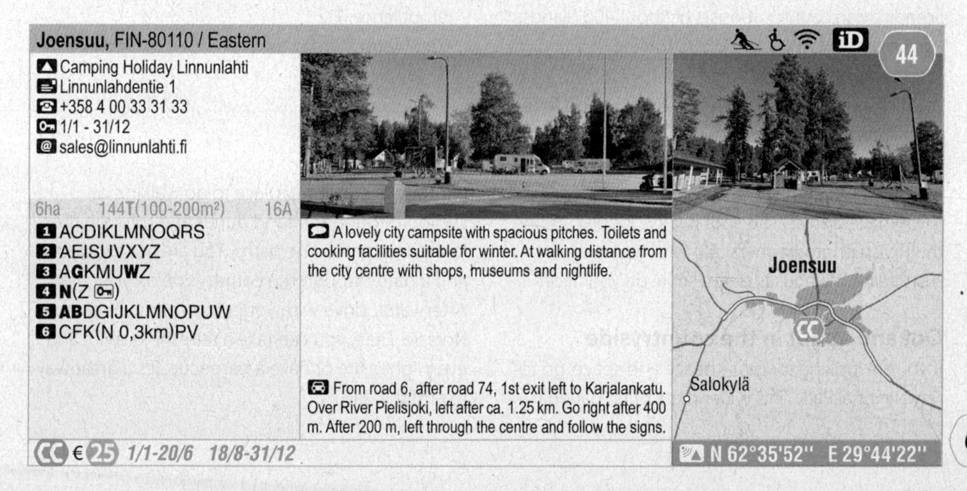

Joensuu, FIN-80110 / Eastern

44

Camping Holiday Linnunlahti
Linnunlahdentie 1
+358 4 00 33 31 33
1/1 - 31/12
sales@linnunlahti.fi

6ha 144T(100-200m²) 16A

1 ACDIKLMNOQRS
2 AEISUVXYZ
3 A**G**KMU**W**Z
4 **N**(Z)
5 **AB**DGIJKLMNOPUW
6 CFK(N 0,3km)PV

A lovely city campsite with spacious pitches. Toilets and cooking facilities suitable for winter. At walking distance from the city centre with shops, museums and nightlife.

From road 6, after road 74, 1st exit left to Karjalankatu. Over River Pielisjoki, left after ca. 1.25 km. Go right after 400 m. After 200 m, left through the centre and follow the signs.

CC € 25 *1/1-20/6 18/8-31/12*

N 62°35'52'' E 29°44'22''

Denmark

Capital: Copenhagen
Currency: Danish krone
Time zone: UTC +1, UTC +2 (March to October)
Language: Danish
International dialling code: +45
Alcohol limit: 0.5‰
Emergency number: police, fire and ambulance: 112
Tap water: safe to drink

Denmark: Cultural day trips and exceptional countryside

Denmark is the country of hygge: a mood of cosiness and comfortable conviviality. The southern Scandinavian country consists of about 400 islands. You will find exceptional cities, stunning countryside and plenty of culture.
To catch a glimpse of a fairy-tale, you must go to the capital. You can admire Hans Christian Andersen's The Little Mermaid in Copenhagen.
And don't forget the cheerfully coloured houses in the Nyhavn district. This spot is very popular among (hobbyist) photographers and with good reason. Just seeing the houses puts a smile on your face!

Out and about in the countryside

If you are looking for more peace and space, go to Thy National Park. This is Denmark's first national park and a wonderful place to go walking or cycling through the sand dunes and through the forest. Do stay on the paths. You are not allowed to find a path through the countryside on your own. Afterwards, drive with your motorhome or car to Nors Sø. Here, you can take a refreshing swim and even light a fire or have a barbecue. It's a great way to end the day.

Fun and culture

Of course, we can't forget LEGOLAND. You can play to your heart's content among the LEGO bricks. This park is also fun if you like amusement parks. It has various attractions, such as roller coasters.
If you are more of a culture enthusiast, go to Aarhus. The city was the European Capital of Culture in 2017. You will find various museums, such as the ARoS Art Museum and Den Gamle By. Den Gamle By is an open-air museum with 75-century-old houses from across Denmark.

"The peace, space, culture, countryside, inhabitants and varied landscape continue to thrill."

Mr P. Geelen, inspector 1195

Enjoy the mild weather

The summers are generally mild, so you can enjoy the sun without it getting excessively hot. As such, 30 degrees is exceptional across most of Denmark. If you want warmer weather, you have to the south of Jutland. Yet, Denmark is not the country for real sun worshippers. It can rain a lot. So don't forget to take your rainwear on holiday.

En route

Filling up

Lead-free petrol and diesel are widely available. LPG is hardly available. Many fuelling stations are open 24 hours a day in Denmark. There are also many unmanned fuelling stations.

Charging

The charging station network has been expanded but does not yet cover the entire country. So plan your trip well!

Ferry services

You can find information on sailing times, departure times and fares from the shipping operators such as bornholmslinjen.com, polferries.com, scandlines.de and ferries.nl. Fares depend on the season and departure times, among other things. It is advisable to book in advance. Ask the shipping operator beforehand whether you can take gas bottles on the boat.

Traffic regulations

Low beam headlights are mandatory during the day. At equivalent crossings, traffic from the right has right of way. As a rule, traffic on a roundabout

Winners in Denmark

84	***Best campsite***	Ribe Camping
86	***Most dog-friendly campsite***	Ringkøbing Camping
56	***Best location for a campsite***	Blushøj Camping - Ebeltoft
66	***Best motorhome pitches***	Gudhjem Camping

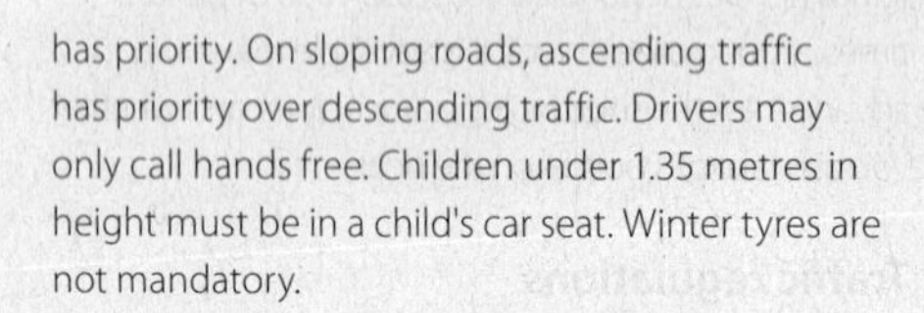

has priority. On sloping roads, ascending traffic has priority over descending traffic. Drivers may only call hands free. Children under 1.35 metres in height must be in a child's car seat. Winter tyres are not mandatory.

Special regulations

On motorways, you must alert other road users of a traffic jam or accident using your hazard warning lights. Parking is not allowed within 10 metres of a crossing.

Mandatory equipment

You must have a warning triangle in the car. You are advised to also have safety vests, a first aid kit, a fire extinguisher and spare bulbs.

Caravan and motorhome

A motorhome or car-caravan combination can be a maximum of 4 metres in height, 2.55 metres wide and 18.75 metres long (the caravan itself can be up to 12 metres long).

Cycling

Bicycle helmets are not mandatory. Calling or texting while cycling is prohibited. You may not transport a passenger on the rear bike rack (you can transport a child in a child's seat).

Toll

There are no toll roads in Denmark. However, you do have to pay a toll on The Great Belt Bridge and the Øresund Bridge. You can pay in various ways. More information: storebaelt.dk and oresundsbron. com.

Environmental zones

Environmental zones have been introduced in Aarhus, Aalborg, Odense, Copenhagen and Frederiksberg. Heavy diesel vehicles require an environmental vignette (sticker) to drive in these environmental zones. No environmental zones apply to standard passenger cars.
More information: ecosticker.dk.

Breakdown and accident

On a motorway, place your warning triangle at least 100 metres (elsewhere at 50 metres) behind the car if it forms a hazard to other traffic. All occupants are advised to wear a safety vest. If you breakdown, call the emergency number of your breakdown assistance insurer. You can also call the Danish breakdown assistance service: +45 70 10 20 30 (Falck) or +45 70 10 80 90 (SOS/Dansk Autohjaelp). You are not allowed to tow vehicles on the motorway.

"The space, quiet and the stunning countryside are overwhelming each and every time."

Mr W. Koster, inspector 1007

Camping

Free camping (outside of campsites) is generally not allowed. It is only allowed if the landowner has granted permission.
For campers who arrive late, the quick stop service is gaining in popularity: you have access for an overnight stay from 8 pm to 10 am the next morning, often outside the ordinary campsite.
Take note! There are very few options for filling propane bottles. You are therefore advised to travel with enough gas.
Since a decision by the Danish competition authority in 2017, there is no longer a national obligation to purchase a camping card from Camping Key Europe (CKE) at Danish campsites. You can now use your ACSI Club ID at many Danish campsites. And yet, you may still come across campsites that do require the CKE card. If that is the case, you can buy it on the spot.

Allingåbro, DK-8961

45

Dalgård Camping***
Nordkystvejen 65
+45 86 31 70 13
23/3 - 15/9
info@dalgaardcamping.dk

5ha 125T(80-100m²) 1-16A

1 ABCDHKLNOQRS
2 AGJMSTWY
3 CGHIKPRUWY
4 (Q+S)
5 ABDEFGHIJKLMNOPQRUWZ
6 CEFGHKLM(N 3km)OPV

Pleasant campsite with warm welcome by Arne and Diana. Spacious pitches, good, modern toilet facilities. The fine sandy beach is a short walk away over a path framed by wild roses. Good options for anglers. Lovely wooded area. Cycling or walking possible from campsite.

Situated on route 547. About 4 km to the west of Fjellerup. Campsite located on the right of the road.

CC € 21 23/3-16/5 20/5-23/6 18/8-14/9

N 56°30'33'' E 10°32'45''

Arrild/Toftlund, DK-6520

46

Arrild-Ferieby-Camping***
Arrild Ferieby 5
+45 20 48 37 34
1/1 - 31/12
info@arrildcamping.dk

8ha 250T(100-140m²) 16A CEE

1 ACDIKLMNOQRTU
2 BEJSXYZ
3 ACGHIOPQRSUW
4 J(S+T+U+W+Y)
5 ABDEFGIJKLMNOPQRUWXZ
6 CEFGJ(N 0,1km)OP

A peaceful family campsite in wooded surroundings. Spacious pitches sheltered from the wind. Beautiful heated indoor swimming pool (entry fee applies). Marked walking routes and cycling in surroundings. 18 hole golf course close by. The old towns of Ribe and Tønder are about 30 km away. Rømø island with beautiful beaches is 20 min away.

From the A7/E45 exit 73 route 175 towards Rømø. Follow the road at Toftlünd, campsite is indicated at the Arrild turning.

CC € 21 1/1-27/3 2/4-6/5 21/5-23/6 19/8-31/12 14=12

N 55°09'12'' E 08°57'24''

Assens, DK-5610

47

CityCamp Assens Strand
Næsvej 15
+45 63 60 63 62
1/1 - 31/12
info@assensstrand.dk

6,3ha 170T(100-120m²) 10A CEE

1 ACDIKLMNOQRS
2 AHJQSTWXYZ
3 CGKPRUWY
4 (Q+R)
5 ABDEFGIJKLMNOPRUWZ
6 CEFGHK(N 0,3km)OPTV

A park-like campsite located between Lille Belt and the harbour of Assens, close to the sea, the marina and the city. Lots of fun, situated on a beautiful beach. The reception is closed during the winter period (Christmas through to March). Checking in is possible at the entry post next to the reception. Please announce your arrival in advance.

Route 313 Nörre-Åby - Assens. Follow signs to harbour and Industrial area near Assens. Follow signs by sugar factory.

CC € 27 1/1-8/5 21/5-1/7 18/8-31/12

N 55°15'56'' E 09°53'02''

Augustenborg, DK-6440

48

Hertugbyens Camping**
Ny Stavensbøl 1
+45 74 47 16 39
1/4 - 30/9
hertugbyenscamping@mail.dk

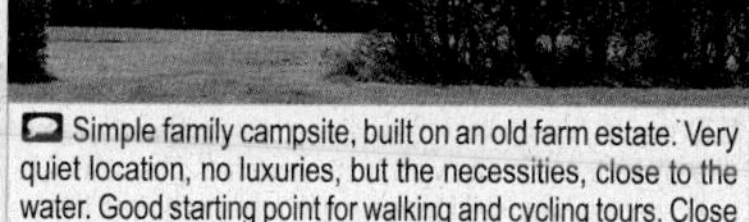

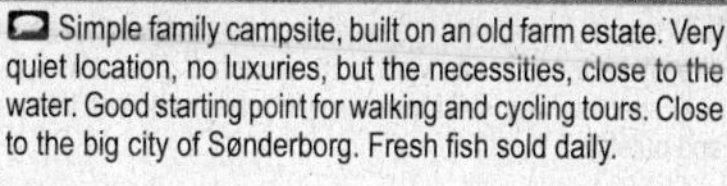

2,6ha 200T(100-150m²) 16A CEE

1 ACDIKLMNOQRS
2 AGILNQSUXY
3 AGIKMWY
5 **AB**DEFGIJKLMNO**P**QRUWZ
6 ACEFGK(N 1km)P

Simple family campsite, built on an old farm estate. Very quiet location, no luxuries, but the necessities, close to the water. Good starting point for walking and cycling tours. Close to the big city of Sønderborg. Fresh fish sold daily.

Main route 8, beyond Sønderborg take Augustenborg exit on the right. Turn left in centre. Follow signs. Turn first right before the hospital, then left and follow the road to the beach.

Augustenborg
41
481
Sønderborg
8

CC € 21 *1/4 11/7 31/8-29/9*

N 54°56'49'' E 09°51'15''

Ballum/Bredebro, DK-6261

49

Ballum Camping***
Kystvej 37
+45 74 71 62 63
22/3 - 18/10
info@ballumcamping.eu

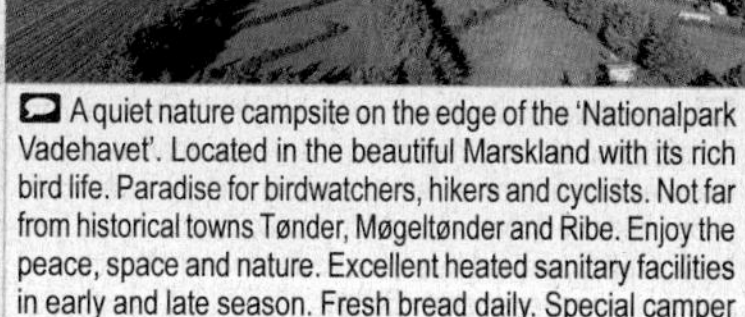

6,7ha 160T(100-240m²) 10A CEE

1 ACD**I**KLMNORS
2 JSXYZ
3 CIKMNP**R**U
4 (Q+R+U)
5 **AB**DEFGHIJKLMNO**P**QRUWZ
6 ACDEFGH**K**(N 1,5km)PT

A quiet nature campsite on the edge of the 'Nationalpark Vadehavet'. Located in the beautiful Marskland with its rich bird life. Paradise for birdwatchers, hikers and cyclists. Not far from historical towns Tønder, Møgeltønder and Ribe. Enjoy the peace, space and nature. Excellent heated sanitary facilities in early and late season. Fresh bread daily. Special camper pitches. Dutch owners.

Coast road 419 from Tønder to Ballum. Campsite sign-posted just before Ballum.

CC € 25 *22/3-27/6 22/8-18/10*

N 55°04'08'' E 08°39'38''

Bogense, DK-5400

50

First Camp Bogense City - Fyn*****
Vestre Engvej 11
+45 64 81 35 08
1/1 - 31/12
bogense@firstcamp.dk

11ha 425T(80-200m²) 13A CEE

1 ACD**I**KLMNORS
2 AJPSWXYZ
3 C**G**HIKM**OPR**SUVY
4 (**C** 15/6-31/8)(**F**+**H**)JN
5 ABDEFGIJKLMNOPQRUWXYZ
6 CDEFGHK(N 0,25km)O**P**SV

Bogense Beach Campsite with outdoor and indoor pools, is just 5 minutes from the centre of Bogense, the port and the beach. The campsite is ideally located for a walk in the woods, a journey through the beautiful landscapes, or swimming in the sea. Suitable for both nature lovers and city people, as Odense is also nearby.

From Odense direction Havn, follow signs.

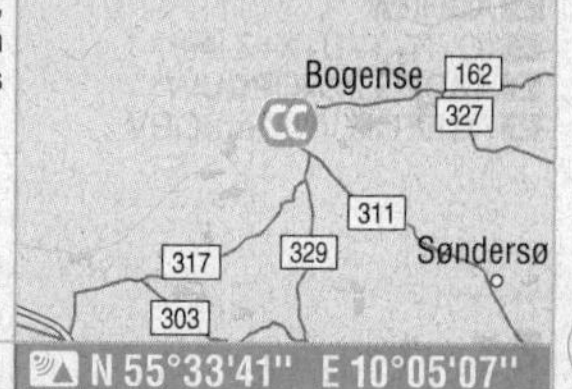

CC € 27 *1/1-27/3 2/4-7/5 13/5-16/5 21/5-19/6 1/9-22/12*

N 55°33'41'' E 10°05'07''

Bøjden/Faaborg, DK-5600

51

CampOne Bøjden Strand*****
Bøjden Landevej 12
+45 63 60 63 60
1/4 - 22/10
bojden@campone.dk

6,5ha 308T(80-140m²) 10A CEE

1 ACDFIKLMNOQRS
2 AGJMNSWXYZ
3 ACDGHIKMPRSUWY
4 (C 1/6-15/9)(F+H)IJKMN (Q+S+T+U+X+Y+Z)
5 ABDEFGIJKLMNOPQRSUWXYZ
6 CDEFGHKL(N 3km)OPTV

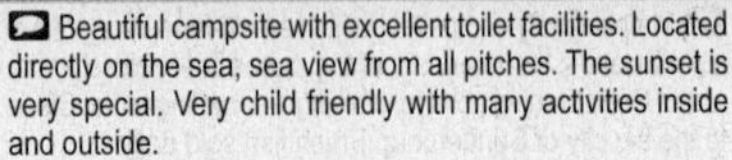

Beautiful campsite with excellent toilet facilities. Located directly on the sea, sea view from all pitches. The sunset is very special. Very child friendly with many activities inside and outside.

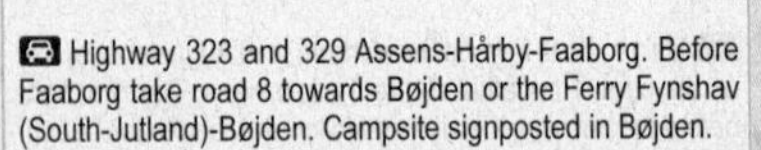

Highway 323 and 329 Assens-Hårby-Faaborg. Before Faaborg take road 8 towards Bøjden or the Ferry Fynshav (South-Jutland)-Bøjden. Campsite signposted in Bøjden.

CC € 25 *2/4-7/5 13/5-16/5 21/5-19/6 1/9-22/10*

N 55°06'20'' E 10°06'28''

Bork Havn/Hemmet, DK-6893

52

Bork Havn Camping***
Kirkehøjvej 9A
+45 75 28 00 37
20/3 - 20/10
mail@borkhavncamping.dk

4,5ha 115T(100-120m²) 6-10A CEE

1 ACDIKLMNORS
2 AESVWXYZ
3 CHIKMPRUW
5 ABDEFGIJKLMNOPRUWZ
6 CEFGHKTV

A very well maintained campsite with heated sanitary facilities and all amenities. There is a supermarket next to the site. The attractive fishing harbour with its restaurant, shops and snack bar is just 100m away. The enclosed fjord lends itself to wind or kite surfing and to fishing. Walking and cycling in the area is sheer delight.

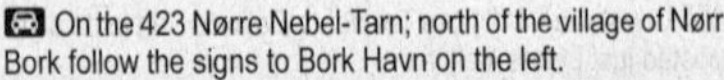

On the 423 Nørre Nebel-Tarn; north of the village of Nørr Bork follow the signs to Bork Havn on the left.

CC € 25 *2/4-8/5 21/5-21/6 20/8-20/10*

N 55°50'54'' E 08°17'00''

Bramming, DK-6740

53

Darum Camping***
Alsædvej 24
+45 75 17 91 16
23/3 - 29/9
info@darumcamping.dk

4,4ha 50T(100-140m²) 10-16A CEE

1 ACDIJKLMNOQRS
2 BCIJSTXYZ
3 AGHUW
4 (Q+R+T+U+X+Z)
5 ABDFGJMNOPQUW
6 ACEFGHJ(N 7km)OPV

An idyllic and scenic campsite halfway between Ribe and Esbjerg, good shelter, large units and new service building. A peaceful place for adults who love nature, cycling along the Wadden Sea National Park. Discover Sneum sluice and a rich bird life. Dinner can be enjoyed in the café.

From the south follow route 11-24 exit St. Darum. Follow campsite signs. From the north route 24.

CC € 25 *23/3-6/7 23/8-29/9*

N 55°26'03'' E 08°38'28''

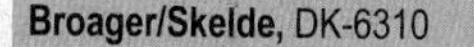

Broager/Skelde, DK-6310

54

- Broager Strand Camping***
- Skeldebro 32
- +45 74 44 14 18
- 1/1 - 31/12
- post@broagerstrandcamping.dk

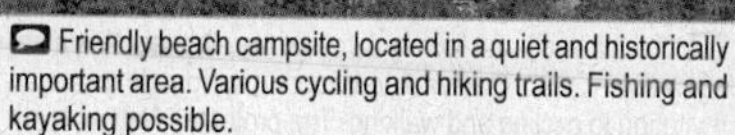

5,8ha 140T(80-125m²) 13-16A CEE

1. ACD**I**JKLMNOQRS
2. AGINPSTUWXYZ
3. A**G**HIKUWY
4. (Q+R+Z)
5. **AB**CDFGHIJKLMNOP**QR**UWXYZ
6. ABCDEFGHK(N 7km)OPUV

Friendly beach campsite, located in a quiet and historically important area. Various cycling and hiking trails. Fishing and kayaking possible.

From E45 motorway exit 73 dir. Sønderborg. Follow route 8 to Nybol then towards Broager to 1st traffic lights left. After traffic lights in Broager 1st right dir. Skelde. After 3.5 km straight ahead in Dynt. From there signposted.

CC € 25 1/1-22/3 1/4-8/5 21/5-30/6 31/8-31/12

N 54°52'04'' E 09°44'39''

Bryrup/Silkeborg, DK-8654

55

- Bryrup Camping****
- Hovedgaden 58
- +45 75 75 67 80
- 22/3 - 15/9
- info@bryrupcamping.dk

2,4ha 241T(80-130m²) 13A CEE

1. ACD**I**KLMNORS
2. CEJMSTXY
3. CIKP**R**SU**W**
4. (C 15/5-31/8)(H 15/5-1/9)J (Q 1/7-12/8)(Z)
5. **AB**DEFGIJKLMNOPQRUWXY
6. CEFGH**K**(N 0,4km)O**P**QV

A campsite close to a forest and lakes with a free swimming pool and water slides. Excellent walking and cycling opportunities in the hilly landscape. Excellent options for fishing.

After Vejle take road 13 to the north as far as Silkeborg. Turn right here onto the 453. Campsite on the left about 10 km further in Bryrup.

CC € 27 6/5-8/5 12/5-17/5 20/5-30/6 18/8-14/9

N 56°01'21'' E 09°30'32''

Ebeltoft, DK-8400

56

- Blushøj Camping - Ebeltoft***
- Elsegårdevej 55
- +45 86 34 12 38
- 22/3 - 29/9
- info@blushoj.com

6,5ha 270T 10A CEE

1. ABCDIKLMNORS
2. HJLMNPQSTXYZ
3. C**G**IKM**R**SU**W**Y
4. (C+H 1/6-15/8)J(Q+R)
5. **AB**DEFGIJKLMNO**PQR**UWZ
6. CEFGKL(N 5km)O**P**V

You are warmly welcome at this lovely family campsite close to the charming and attractive village of Ebeltoft with views over the Kattegat. Peace, countryside, fresh sea air. Spacious pitches with plenty of privacy. The reception can give you information (also in English and German) about the many walking and cycling routes. Opportunity for golf in the neighbourhood.

Drive from Ebeltoft to Elsegårde (4 m). Left towards the site at the junction by the pond.

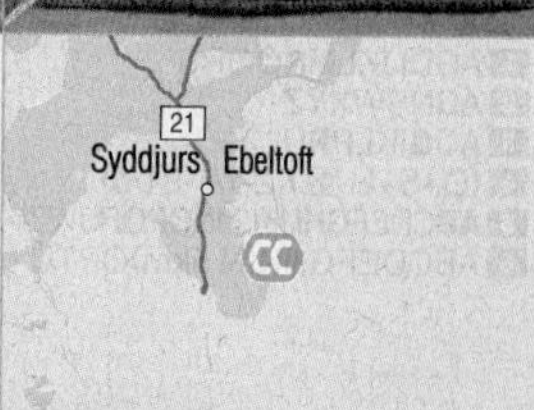

CC € 25 22/3-9/5 20/5-30/6 18/8-29/9

N 56°10'04'' E 10°43'49''

Ebeltoft, DK-8400

iD 57

Elsegårde Camping
Kristoffervejen 1
+45 86 34 12 83
1/1 - 31/12
info@egcamp.dk

1,9ha 60T(70-120m²) 13A CEE

1 ABCDHKLMNORS
2 GOPQWXY
3 C**G**K**R**U**W**Y
5 **AB**FGIJKLMNOPQUW
6 EFGHK(N 5km)OV

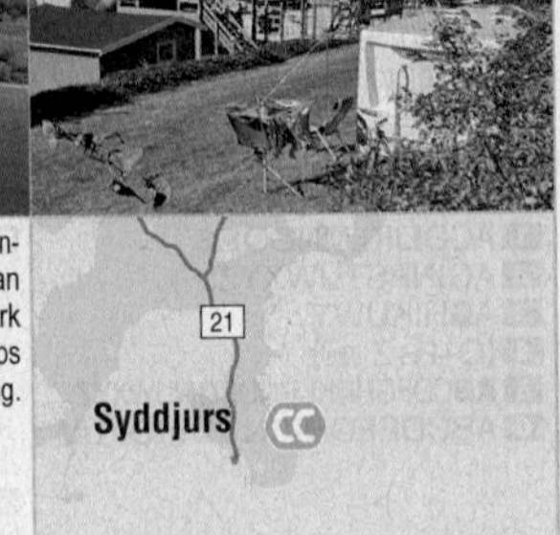

Quiet, friendly and flowery campsite near the sea. New management in 2022. The rural and wooded surroundings are an invitation to cycling and walking. The protected Nationalpark Mols Bjerge and the cosy town Ebeltoft with terraces and shops are only a few kilometres away to complete your holiday feeling.

Drive from Ebeltoft to Elsegårde (4 km). The campsite is located at the fork from the lake.

CC € 21 *1/3-30/6 18/8-1/10*

N 56°10'06'' E 10°43'23''

Ebeltoft/Krakær, DK-8400

iD 58

Krakær Camping***
Gl. Kærvej 18
+45 86 36 21 18
1/1 - 31/12
info@krakaer.dk

8ha 227T(70-130m²) 10-16A CEE

1 ACDIKLMNOQRS
2 BMSTWXY
3 C**G**HIKLP**QR**SU
4 (C+H 15/5-1/9)(Q 23/6-13/8)
(S+T+U 25/6-15/8)
(X 29/6-9/8)(Z 25/6-15/8)
5 **AB**DEFGIJKLMNO**PQR**UWZ
6 ACEFGH**K**LM(N 8km)O**P**RV

Krakær is a pearl in one of Denmark's loveliest areas of natural beauty. The terraced campsite with its marked out pitches is located in a hilly wooded area with natural protection from the wind. Restaurant open at weekends in low season. Lovely walking and cycling trips from the campsite.

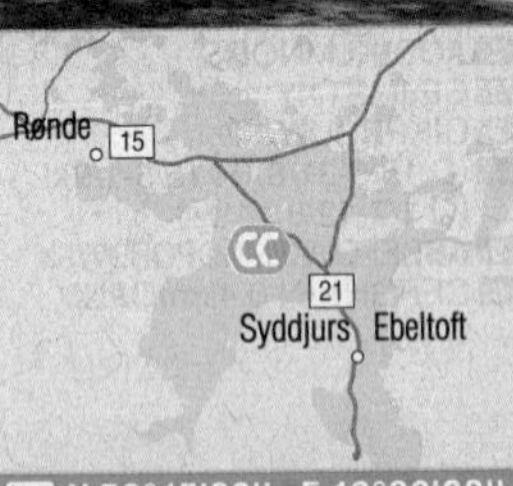

Via road 15 and 21 direction Ebeltoft. About 8 km before you reach Ebeltoft turn right direction Krakær. The campsite is signposted. For SatNav, use address: Gammell Kærvej 18.

CC € 27 *24/3-16/6 30/8-20/10*

N 56°15'08'' E 10°36'09''

Ejstrup Strand/Brovst, DK-9460

iD 59

Tranum Klit Camping
Sandmosevej 525
+45 98 23 52 82
22/3 - 1/10
info@tranumklitcamping.dk

13,5ha 220T(100-200m²) 10A CEE

1 ACDIJKLMNOQRS
2 ABNSWXYZ
3 AC**G**IKLP**R**U
4 (Q+S+U)(Z 1/7-31/8)
5 **AB**CDEFGHIJKLMNOPQRUWZ
6 ABCDEFGHK(N 5km)OPTU

A site that gives the feeling of being 'one with nature'. The forest provides good shelter from the wind while also allowing sunshine in. An atmosphere characterized by tranquility and hospitality. Beautiful, hidden pitches. The site is not far from the sea with a beautiful sandy beach. New on the site is a delimited naturist area with 12 pitches and private toilets.

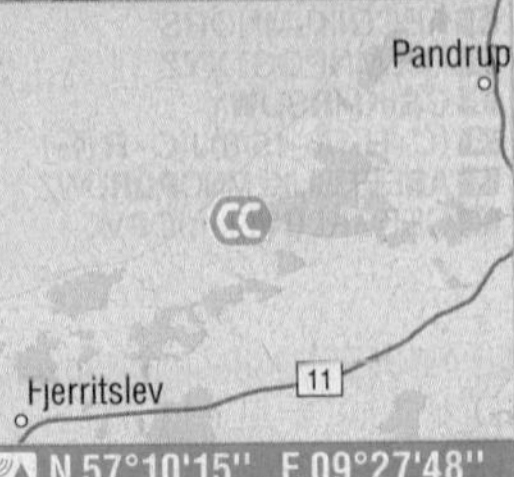

From route 11, by Brovst via Tranum to Tranum Klit or from Fjerritslev via Slettestrand and Fosdalen.

CC € 27 *22/3-23/6 18/8-1/10*

N 57°10'15'' E 09°27'48''

Fjand, DK-6990

60

Nissum Fjord Camping***
Klitvej 16
+45 97 49 60 11
1/1 - 31/12
kontakt@nissumfjordcamping.dk

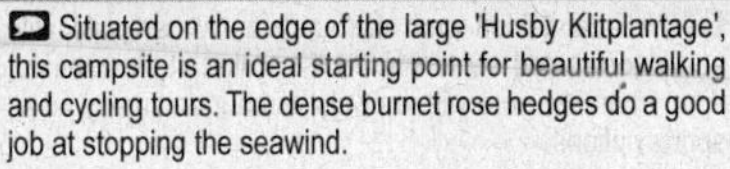

4,5ha 200T(80-120m²) 13-16A CEE

1 ACD**I**KLMNOQRS
2 EJSTUVWXY
3 CHIKLMP**R**UW
4 (C 15/6-15/8)(Q+R 1/4-30/9) (U+Y+Z 1/5-30/9)
5 **AB**DFGIJMNOPQRUW
6 CDEFGKL(N 3km)O**P**TUV

Situated on the edge of the large 'Husby Klitplantage', this campsite is an ideal starting point for beautiful walking and cycling tours. The dense burnet rose hedges do a good job at stopping the seawind.

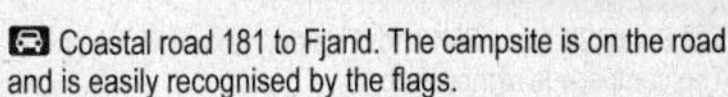

Coastal road 181 to Fjand. The campsite is on the road and is easily recognised by the flags.

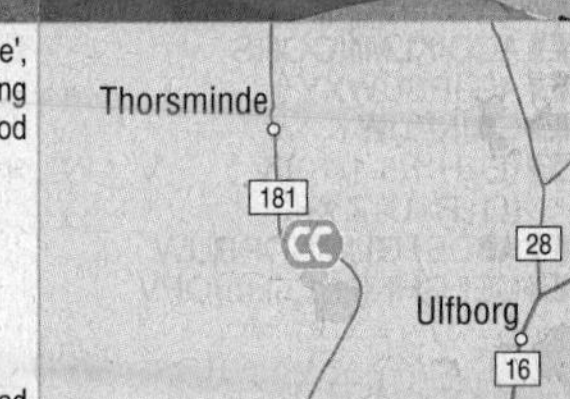

CC € 21 *13/4-14/6 18/8-27/10*

N 56°19'10'' E 08°08'59''

Fredericia, DK-7000

61

Dancamps Trelde Næs***
Trelde Næsvej 297
+45 75 95 71 83
1/1 - 31/12
info@dancamps.dk

10ha 475T 10A CEE

1 ACD**I**KLMNOQRS
2 ABGJNSWXY
3 CIP**R**SUWY
4 (A 1/7-31/8)(**B**+**G** 15/5-15/9) IJ**KLN**(Q+S) (T+U+X 1/7-31/8)(Z)
5 **AB**FGIJKLMNOPQ**R**UWXY
6 ACEFGHK(N 4km)OPSTV

Large campsite, no shade, beautifully located on the coast.

Route 28 (Vejle-Fredericia). From Vejle take Egeskov exit, then Trelde and Trelde-Næs. From Fredericia to Trelde, then Trelde Næs.

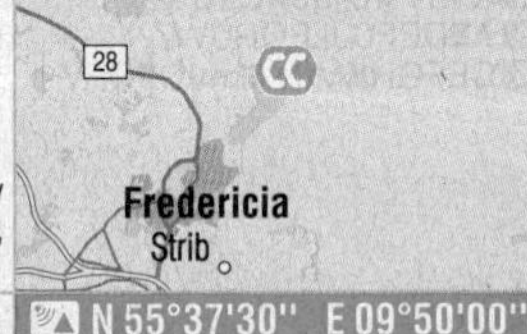

CC € 27 *1/1-8/5 12/5-16/5 20/5-3/7 20/8-31/12*

N 55°37'30'' E 09°50'00''

Frørup, DK-5871

62

Kongshøj Strandcamping***
Kongshøjvej 5
+45 65 37 12 88
1/1 - 31/12
info@kongshojcamping.dk

6ha 120T(80-150m²) 16A CEE

1 ACD**I**KLMNOQRS
2 AGQSWXYZ
3 CE**G**IKOP**R**SUW**Y**
4 (Q+R 1/4-1/10)
5 **AB**DEFGIJKLMNO**PQR**UW
6 CDEFGHK(N 9km)OPTUV

Quiet family campsite, child friendly, close to a beach with clean water (blue flag). Also suitable for taking walks over the pebble and sandy beach and in the woods. Great starting point for trips to the cities of Odense and Nyborg.

Route 163 Nyborg-Svendborg, take second exit to Tårup after about 11 km and follow Kongshøj-Strand camping signs.

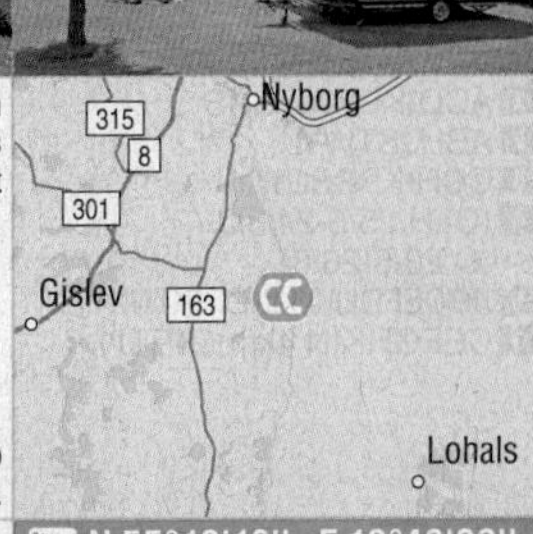

CC € 23 *1/1-24/6 28/8-31/12*

N 55°13'18'' E 10°48'22''

Glyngøre, DK-7870

63

Glyngøre Camping***
Sundhøj 20A
+45 97 73 17 88
1/1 - 31/12
info@glyngore-camping.dk

9ha 232T(80-120m²) 10A CEE

1 ACDIKLMNOQRS
2 AGJPSUWXY
3 CGIKPUWY
4 (E+H 1/5-1/10)**K**
(Q+R+U+Z)
5 **AB**DEFGIJMNOPRUW
6 CEFGHK(N 1,5km)OPV

Well-maintained and sheltered family campsite with an indoor heated swimming pool. Located at the Limfjord, 2 km from Glyngøre with a lovely harbour and many water sports options.

Road 26 from Skive to Thisted. Take exit Glyngøre. The campsite is signposted.

CC € 25 *1/1-30/6 18/8-31/12*

N 56°44'32" E 08°52'06"

Grenå, DK-8500

64

Fornaes Camping***
Stensmarkvej 36
+45 40 18 76 78
23/3 - 19/10
info@fornaescamping.dk

9,2ha 293T(100-140m²) 10-16A

1 ACD**I**KLNORS
2 HLMNPQSTUXYZ
3 AC**G**HKMP**R**SU**W**Y
4 (C+H 1/6-1/9)(Q+S)
5 **AB**DEFGJLPQRUWZ
6 CEFGH**K**M(N 6km)O**P**QRV

A family campsite located right by the sea. Lovely swimming pool and plenty of playing options for children. The camping pitches are spacious and the rolling campsite grounds provide beautiful sea views. Walking and cycling in the surrounding area.

Via route 15 or 16 to the ferry port and Grenå. Turn left, follow signs for another 5 km.

CC € 25 *23/3-29/6 18/8-19/10*

N 56°27'14" E 10°56'28"

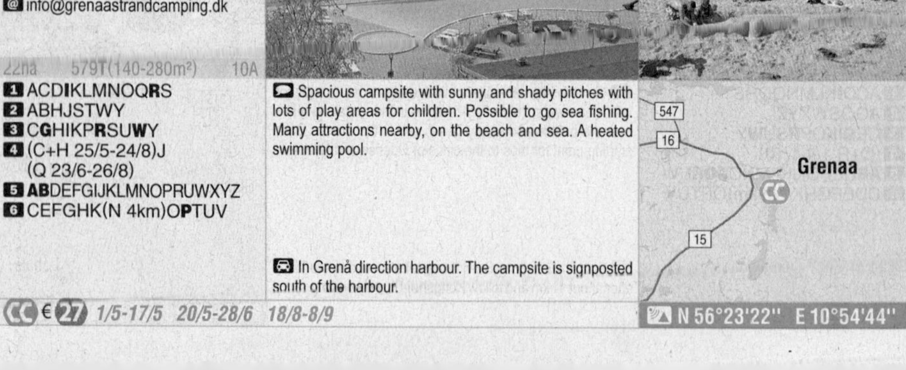

Grenå, DK-8500

65

Grenå Strand Camping*****
Fuglsangvej 58
+45 86 32 17 18
22/3 - 8/9
info@grenaastrandcamping.dk

22ha 579T(140-280m²) 10A

1 ACD**I**KLMNOQ**R**S
2 ABHJSTWY
3 C**G**HIKP**R**SU**W**Y
4 (C+H 25/5-24/8)J
(Q 23/6-26/8)
5 **AB**DEFGIJKLMNOPRUWXYZ
6 CEFGHK(N 4km)O**P**TUV

Spacious campsite with sunny and shady pitches with lots of play areas for children. Possible to go sea fishing. Many attractions nearby, on the beach and sea. A heated swimming pool.

In Grenå direction harbour. The campsite is signposted south of the harbour.

CC € 27 *1/5-17/5 20/5-28/6 18/8-8/9*

N 56°23'22" E 10°54'44"

Gudhjem, DK-3760

66

Gudhjem Camping***
Melsted Langgade 45
+45 42 41 58 15
15/3 - 23/10
mail@gudhjemcamping.dk

ACSI AWARDS WINNER

5ha 150T(80-100m²) 16A CEE

1 ACDIKLMNOQRS
2 HJLMNQRSTUXY
3 GIKWY
4 (Q)
5 ABGIJKLMNOPQUWZ
6 ABCEFGK(N 0,4km)OPT

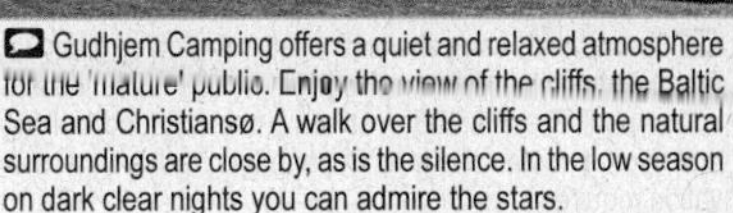

Gudhjem Camping offers a quiet and relaxed atmosphere for the 'mature' public. Enjoy the view of the cliffs, the Baltic Sea and Christiansø. A walk over the cliffs and the natural surroundings are close by, as is the silence. In the low season on dark clear nights you can admire the stars.

The campsite is on Gudhjem's eastern outskirts, close to the supermarket on the Allinge-Svaneke road and is signposted.

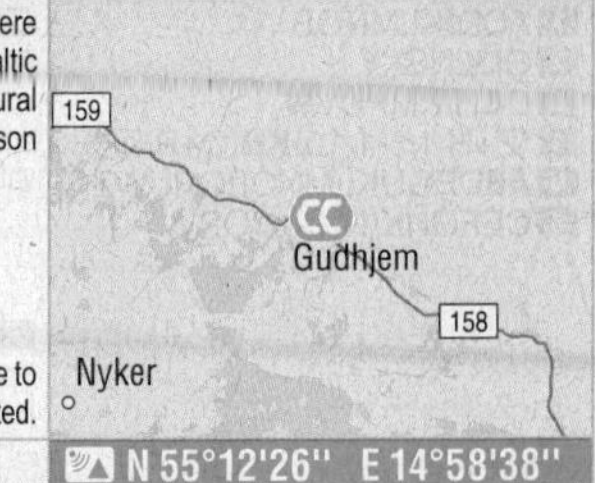

€27 1/5-2/6 1/9-30/9

N 55°12'26'' E 14°58'38''

Haderslev/Diernæs, DK-6100

67

Vikær Strand Camping***
Dundelum 29
+45 74 57 54 64
22/3 - 22/9
info@vikaercamp.dk

12ha 390T(100-140m²) 13A CEE

1 ACDIJKLMNOQRS
2 AGJLMNSTUWXY
3 CGIKPRSUWY
4 (Q+R+V+Z)
5 ABDEFGHIJKLMNOPQRUWXYZ
6 CDEFGHKM(N 5km)OPSV

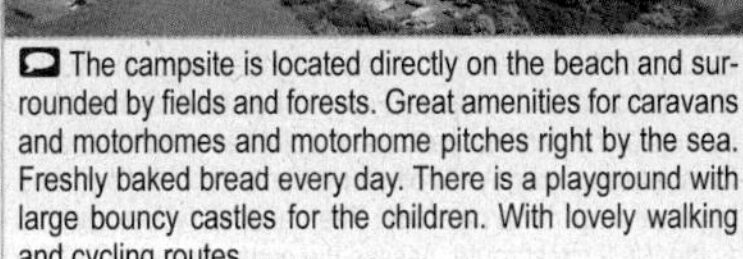

The campsite is located directly on the beach and surrounded by fields and forests. Great amenities for caravans and motorhomes and motorhome pitches right by the sea. Freshly baked bread every day. There is a playground with large bouncy castles for the children. With lovely walking and cycling routes.

In Aabenraa follow route 170 direction Kolding until Holtrup, turn right towards Diernaes. Follow signposts.

Vojens Starup 435 E45 170 24 429 Rødekro

€27 1/4-8/5 12/5-17/5 20/5-28/6 18/8-22/9

N 55°09'00'' E 09°29'40''

Hesselager, DK-5874

68

First Camp Bøsøre Strand - Fyn*****
Bøsørevej 16
+45 62 25 11 45
23/3 - 20/10
bosore@firstcamp.dk

23,6ha 350T(100-150m²) 10A CEE

1 ACDIKLMNOQRS
2 AGJQSWXYZ
3 CDGHIKPRSUWY
4 (F+H)IKMNP (Q+S+T+U)(X 20/6-14/8) (Z)
5 ABCDEFGIJKLMNOPQRUWXYZ
6 CDEFGHKL(N 7km)OPSTV

Bøsøre Strand Feriepark is located between the woods and the sea in the fairytale countryside of Fyn. The site is set around a beautiful Manor House and accompanying farm buildings which are 200 years old.

E20, exit 45 to route 163 Nyborg-Svendborg. Take Vormark/Bøsøre exit at Langå and follow Bøsøre campsite signs.

301 8 163 Lundeborg Lohals

€27 2/4-7/5 13/5-16/5 21/5-19/6 1/9-20/10

N 55°11'36'' E 10°48'23''

Holbæk, DK-4300

CampOne Holbaek Fjord***
Sofiesminde Allé 1
+45 63 60 63 63
1/1 - 31/12
holbaek@campone.dk

5ha 225T(80-120m²) 10-16A CEE

1 ACD**I**KLMNOS
2 GIJLNSXY
3 C**G**HIKMPUV**W**
4 (E+H 1/5-1/10)**KN**(Q+R)
5 **AB**DFGIJKLMNOPQRUWZ
6 CEFGHK(N 1km)OPV

Sunny family campsite on the sea with sloping grounds. Among other things it has a playground, wellness centre and indoor pool. Fresh bread every day, free wifi, and walking and cycling routes. Near to Copenhagen. Advance reservation required.

Route 21 exit 15 coming from Copenhagen, direction Holbæk at the roundabout (10 km). Turn right as you enter Holbæk. Follow signs.

CC € 25 *1/4-7/4 15/4-5/5 13/5-18/5 21/5-14/6 17/6-30/6 18/8-20/10*

N 55°43'05" E 11°45'40"

69

Hvide Sande, DK-6960

Dancamps Holmsland***
Tingodden 141
+45 97 31 13 09
27/3 - 22/9
info@dancamps.dk

2,5ha 92T(85-105m²) 10A CEE

1 ACD**I**KLMNORS
2 AGJNSTWX
3 A**G**IKUWY
4 (Q+R)
5 **AB**DFGIJKLMNOPRUW
6 CEFGK(N 4km)O**P**V

A small but friendly campsite right among a beautiful dune landscape on the west coast of Jutland. Surrounded by dunes you will find peace and quiet here. An ideal area for a relaxing holiday. Stroll along the wide white beaches together or go for a bike ride. The national cycle route, Nr. 1, the West coast route, passes the campsite.

Via coastal road 181, take the 'Søholmvej' road about 5 km south of Hvide Sande. The campsite is at the end of this road.

CC € 25 *27/3-8/5 12/5-16/5 20/5-3/7 20/8-22/9*

N 55°57'45" E 08°08'31"

70

Hvide Sande, DK-6960

Dancamps Nordsø***
Tingodden 3, Årgab
+45 96 59 17 22
22/3 - 27/10
info@dancamps.dk

12,5ha 299T(40-100m²) 10A CEE

1 ACD**I**KLMNORS
2 AGJSTUWX
3 C**G**IK**R**UWY
4 (**F+H**)J**LN**(Q+R)
(T+U+W+Z 1/7-1/9)
5 **AB**DEFGIJKLMNOPRUWXYZ
6 ACDEFGHKL(N 6km)O**P**SV

In the middle of the rugged countryside on the west coast of Jutland. It is a couple of kilometres from the Hvide Sande harbour town. The site is separated from the sea by a line of dunes. Lovely views from the dunes across the Ringkøbing Fjord and the North Sea. Indoor pool with slide, sauna and Turkish bath.

From Esbjerg to Varde, then take coastal road 181 north towards Hvide Sande. A little past Haurvig Kirke, campsite on the left, with swimming pool and green slide.

CC € 27 *22/3-8/5 12/5-16/5 20/5-3/7 20/8-22/9*

N 55°56'58" E 08°09'01"

71

Kalundborg/Saltbæk, DK-4400

72

Kalundborg Camping**
Saltbækvej 88
+45 93 88 79 00
1/1 - 31/12
info@kcamping.dk

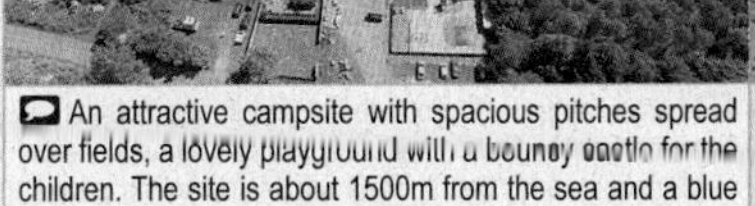

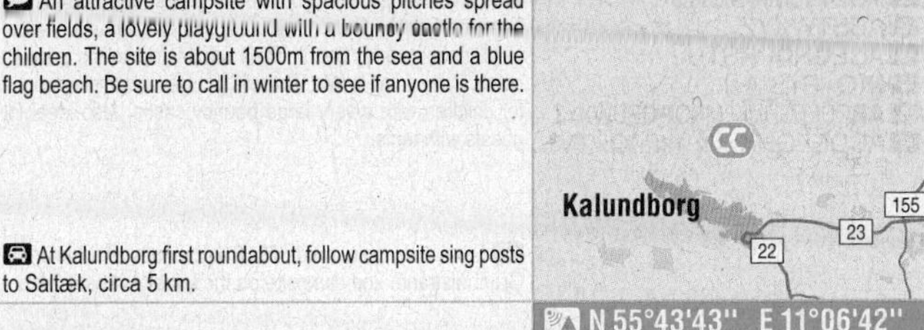

3,5ha 118T(120-180m²) 10-16A CEE

1 AODIKLMNOQRS
2 BQSTUXYZ
3 AC**G**HIKP**R**SU
4 (Q+R+T+U+Z 1/4-24/9)
5 **AB**DGI**J**KLMNP**Q**RUW
6 EFGHK(N 6km)O**P**T

An attractive campsite with spacious pitches spread over fields, a lovely playground with a bouncy castle for the children. The site is about 1500m from the sea and a blue flag beach. Be sure to call in winter to see if anyone is there.

At Kalundborg first roundabout, follow campsite sing posts to Saltæk, circa 5 km.

CC € 25 *1/1-1/7 18/8-31/12*

N 55°43'43" E 11°06'42"

Kruså/Kollund, DK-6340

73

First Camp Frigård - Flensborg Fjord****
Kummelefort 14
+45 74 67 88 30
1/1 - 31/12
frigaard@firstcamp.dk

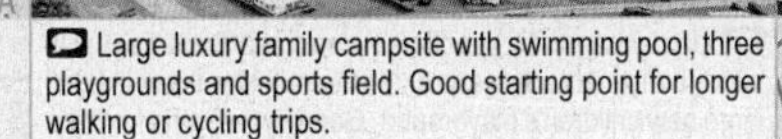

15ha 741T(80-120m²) 10A

1 ACD**I**KLMNOQRS
2 AGIJLSUWXYZ
3 CD**G**HIKMP**R**SUWY
4 (C+H 15/5-15/9)**KLN** (Q+R+S+T+U+Y+Z)
5 **AB**DEFGHIJKLMNOPQRUWXYZ
6 CDEFGHK(N 4km)O**P**TUV

Large luxury family campsite with swimming pool, three playgrounds and sports field. Good starting point for longer walking or cycling trips.

Take the Kollund road in Kruså. Located about 800 metres from the Kollund-Sønderhav road from Kollund direction Sønderhav.

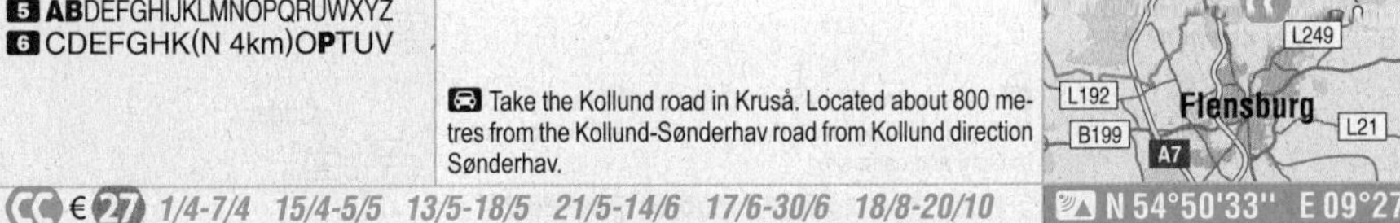

CC € 27 *1/4-7/4 15/4-5/5 13/5-18/5 21/5-14/6 17/6-30/6 18/8-20/10*

N 54°50'33" E 09°27'33"

Lisbjerg/Århus-N, DK-8200

74

First Camp Aarhus***
Randersvej 400
+45 86 23 11 33
1/1 - 31/12
aarhus@firstcamp.dk

6,9ha 190T(80-150m²) 16A CEE

1 ACD**I**KLMNOQRS
2 BIJSTXYZ
3 AB**GR**U
4 (C+H 15/6-15/8)K (Q+R+T+U+V+X)
5 **AB**DEFGIJLMNO**PQ**RUWZ
6 ACDEFG**K**L(N 4km)O**P**V

The site has all the information for visiting Århus, Denmark's second city with its museums and parks. You can relax in the jacuzzi near the refurbished pool from mid-June to mid-August. Plenty of greenery at the well-equipped site with spacious level pitches. English spoken at reception. Daily menu with Danish specialities in the new restaurant.

E45, exit 46 Arhus-N dir. Lisbjerg right, first traffic light left, then follow the campsite signs for another 2 km.

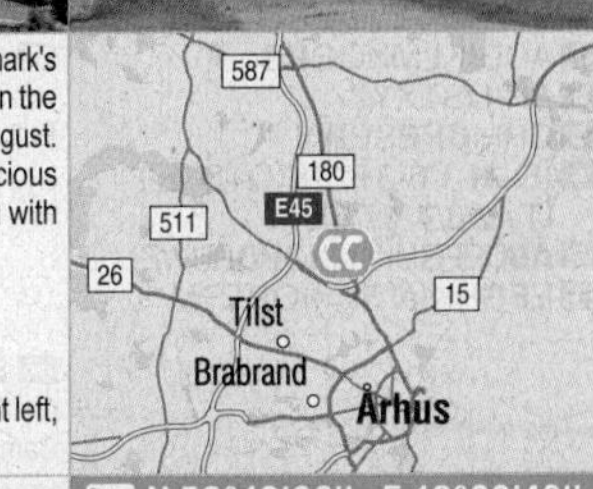

CC € 27 *1/1-27/3 2/4-7/5 13/5-16/5 21/5-19/6 1/9-22/12*

N 56°13'36" E 10°09'49"

Løkken/Ingstrup, DK-9480

75

Grønhøj Strand Camping***
Kettrupvej 125
+45 98 88 44 33
22/3 - 15/9
info@gronhoj-strand-camping.dk

14ha 516T(100-150m²) 13A

1 ACDIKLMNOQRS
2 ABSTWXYZ
3 ACE**G**H**O**P**R**STU
4 **N**(Q+R+S)
5 **AB**CDEFGHIJKLMNO**PQ**RUWXYZ
6 ACDEFGHKL(N 1km)OPTV

Large campsite, surrounded by forest and 700 metres from the beach. Good sheltered pitches. Beautiful, wide, child-friendly sandy beach. Free wifi. Motorcyclists are welcome. Pony riding is free. There is a large fenced playground for children with a very large bouncy castle. Also ideal for guests with tents.

From the main road 55, 6 km south of Løkken to Grønhøjstrand. 2nd campsite on the left after about 2 km.

CC € 21 *31/3-30/6 19/8-15/9*

N 57°19'15'' E 09°40'38''

Malling, DK-8340

76

CampOne Ajstrup Strand***
Ajstrup Strandvej 81
+45 63 60 63 64
1/1 - 31/12
ajstrup@campone.dk

9,2ha 396T(60-150m²) 10A CEE

1 ACD**I**KLMNOQ**R**S
2 AHJOPSTWXYZ
3 C**G**IKL**R**SU**W**Y
4 (**E**+**H** 10/4-16/10)
(Q 4/4-20/10)(R 4/4-22/10)
5 **AB**DEFGIJKLMNOPQRUWZ
6 ACEFGHK(N 4km)OPTV

Luxury campsite directly on clean sea (blue flag) with sandy beach. Attractive and extensive toilet facilities. In 2018 large new children's playground. Good cycle paths from the campsite. Visit Aarhuus, Denmark's second city with a lot of culture. Advance reservation required for arrivals after 24/10/21.

Leave route 451 between Odder and Århus at the exit to Malling. In Malling follow the signs in the direction of Ajstrup (beach) and campsite.

CC € 25 *1/4-7/4 15/4-5/5 13/5-18/5 21/5-14/6 17/6-30/6 18/8-20/10*

N 56°02'29'' E 10°15'52''

Middelfart, DK-5500

77

Vejlby Fed Strand Camping****
Rigelvej 1
+45 28 94 02 89
22/3 - 22/9
mail@vejlbyfed.dk

55,7ha 251T(100-140m²) 10A CEE

1 ACD**I**KLMNOQ**R**S
2 AHIOSTXYZ
3 CHM**OPR**SU**WY**
4 (C+**H** 1/6-31/8)**N**(Q+S)
(T+V 8/4-17/8)
5 **AB**DEFGIJKLMNO**PQ**RUWZ
6 EFGHK(N 5km)OPQTV

On the island of Funen. A quiet, friendly campsite with extensive amenities close to the beach and the 'Lillebæltsbroen'(Little Belt Bridge) with opportunities for fishing.

E20 exit 58 towards route 317 Bogense (Drive 3/4 around the 1st roundabout, at 2nd roundabout go straight ahead). Campsite signposted from Bogensevej.

CC € 25 *22/3-7/5 12/5-16/5 20/5-6/6 9/6-23/6 20/8-21/9*

N 55°31'11'' E 09°51'00''

Nordborg/Augustenhof, DK-6430

78

Augustenhof Strand Camping***
Augustenhofvej 30
+45 74 45 03 04
1/1 - 31/12
mail@augustenhof-camping.dk

4ha 252T(100-120m²) 16A CEE

1 ACDIKLMNOQRS
2 AGNQSUWXY
3 CGIKPRUWY
4 (Q+S+T+U+Z)
5 ABDEFGIJKLMNOPQRUWZ
6 CEFGHKM(N 4km)OP

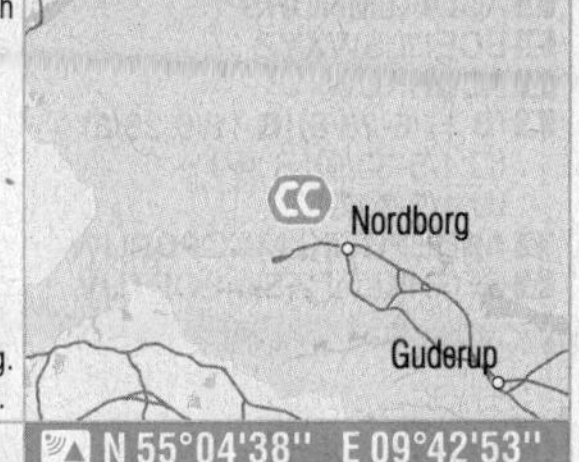

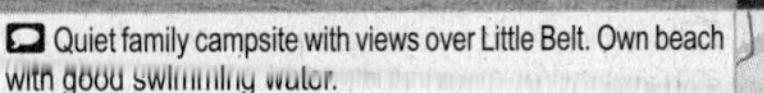

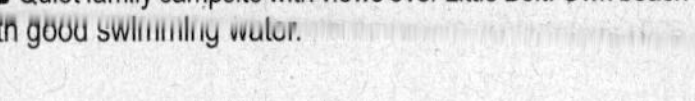

Quiet family campsite with views over Little Belt. Own beach with good swimming water.

Left on road Sønderborg-Fynshav, direction Nordborg. Then continue in direction Købingsmark and Augustenhof.

€25 *1/5-7/5 23/5-23/6 1/9-31/12*

N 55°04'38'' E 09°42'53''

Nørre Nebel, DK-6830

79

Houstrup Camping ApS***
Houstrupvej 90
+45 75 28 83 40
21/3 - 19/10
houstrup@houstrupcamping.dk

6ha 220T(120-170m²) 13A CEE

1 ACDIKLMNOQRS
2 ASVWXYZ
3 CGHOPRSU
4 (C+H 1/6-31/8)(Q+S+T)
5 ABDEFGIJKLMNOPRUWXZ
6 CDEFGKM(N 1km)OPTV

Houstrup campsite, located on the edge of the large 'Blåbjerg Klitplantage' dune and woodland. This beautiful 'West Jutland' area stretches right down to the North Sea with its wide beaches. It lends itself ideally to cycling and walking tours. Beautifully sheltered pitches and mini market with fresh bread baked all day. The 'OceWoot' sports centre with a tropical leisure pool is located 1500 metres away.

Route 181 Nørre Nebel direction Nymindegab, exit Lønne. Follow signs.

€25 *21/3-27/6 19/8-19/10*

N 55°46'28'' E 08°14'18''

Odder/Boulstrup, DK-8300

80

Hygge Strand Camping***
Toldvejen 50
+45 88 44 83 83
22/3 - 17/9
info@hyggestrandcamping.dk

5ha 120T(100-110m²) 10A CEE

1 ACDIKLMNOQRS
2 AGQSWY
3 CGHPWY
4 (Q+R)
5 ABDEFGIJKLMNOPQRUW
6 CDEFGHKM(N 9,9km)OPT

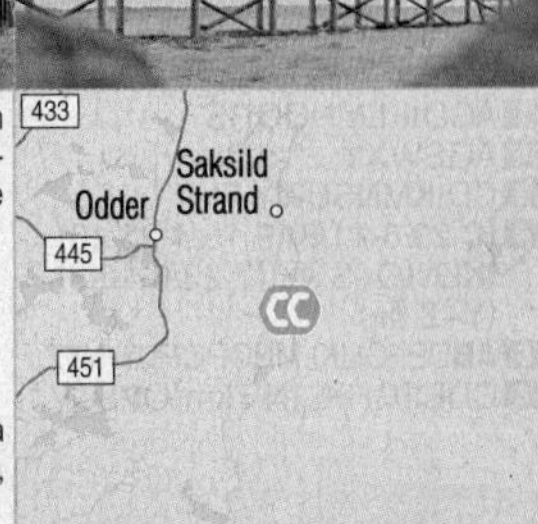

Beautifully appointed, park-like campsite, quiet location with little shade. Odder Strand Camping is located 50 metres from the sea. The beach has been certified with the eco-label 'Blue Flag'.

Route 451 Horsens-Odder. In Ørting direction Gylling, a bit further on Gosmer and Hou. From Halling direction Hou, then Spøttrup. Follow camping signs from here.

€25 *22/3-7/5 12/5-16/5 20/5-26/6 23/8-15/9*

N 55°56'04'' E 10°15'23''

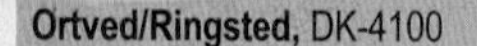

Ortved/Ringsted, DK-4100

Skovly Camping***
Nebs Møllevej 65
+45 57 52 82 61
1/4 - 30/9
info@skovlycamping.dk

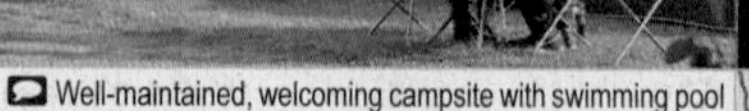

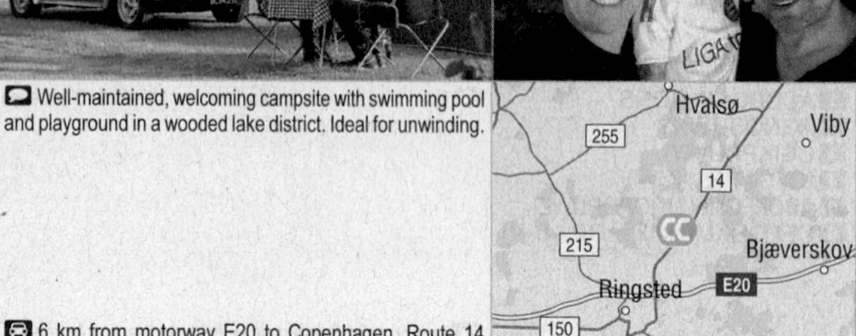

5,7ha 150T(80-120m²) 13A CEE

1 ACD**I**KLMNORS
2 BCEIJLSWXYZ
3 AC**G**HKUW
4 (**B** 17/6-28/8)(**G** 10/6-28/8) (Q 1/5-30/9)(R) (U 1/5-30/9)
5 **AB**DEFGIJKLMNO**PQR**UW
6 EFGHKL(N 2,5km)OPTUV

Well-maintained, welcoming campsite with swimming pool and playground in a wooded lake district. Ideal for unwinding.

6 km from motorway E20 to Copenhagen. Route 14 Ringsted-Roskilde. In Ortved follow campsite sign posts to the left.

CC € 27 *1/4-8/5 12/5-16/5 20/5-30/6 18/8-30/9*

N 55°29'48'' E 11°51'28''

81

Øster Hurup/Hadsund, DK-9560

Kattegat Strand Camping*****
Dokkedalvej 100
+45 98 58 80 32
22/3 - 15/9
info@922.dk

20ha 580T(100-140m²) 10-16A CEE

1 ACDE**I**KLMNOQRS
2 ACHJNSTWXY
3 ACDEHIKMNOP**R**SUV**W**Y
4 (C+H 9/5-31/8)**KN** (Q 1/7-18/8)(S) (T+U+V+X+Y+Z 1/7-18/8)
5 **AB**CDEFGHIJKLMNOPQR**S**UWXYZ
6 CDEFGHKL(N 2,5km) OPSUV

Beautiful family campsite by the beach with views of the sea and nature area. Indoor sports hall, water sport options, free wifi, pizzeria. Heated outdoor swimming pool (water is 26°C). Note: CampingCard rate is for a standard pitch.

Located on the coast road 541, 2 km north of Øster Hurup village.

CC € 27 *22/3-30/6 18/8-15/9* ***7=6***

N 56°49'32'' E 10°16'08''

82

Otterup, DK-5450

First Camp Hasmark Strand - Fyn***
Strandvejen 205
+45 64 82 62 06
1/1 - 31/12
hasmark@firstcamp.dk

12ha 550T(100-150m²) 10A CEE

1 ACD**I**KLMNOQRS
2 AGSWXY
3 CDIKMNSU**W**Y
4 (**C** 23/6-11/8)(**F** 15/4-23/10) **I**KLN(Q+S)(T 23/6-12/8) (Y+Z)
5 **AB**DEFGIJKLMNOPQRUWXYZ
6 CDEFGHKL(N 7km)O**P**STV

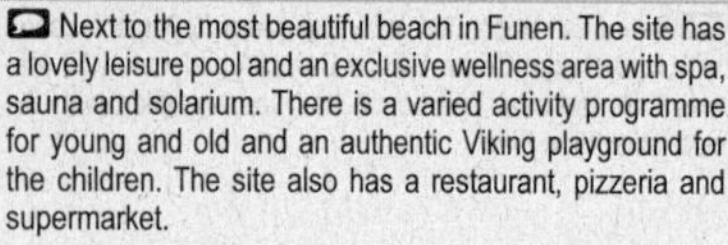

Next to the most beautiful beach in Funen. The site has a lovely leisure pool and an exclusive wellness area with spa, sauna and solarium. There is a varied activity programme for young and old and an authentic Viking playground for the children. The site also has a restaurant, pizzeria and supermarket.

Take direction Hasmark at the traffic lights in Otterup; continue to end of the road 300 metres before the beach. Campsite on the right side of the road.

CC € 27 *1/1-27/3 2/4-7/5 13/5-16/5 21/5-19/6 1/9-22/12*

N 55°33'45'' E 10°27'16''

83

Ribe, DK-6760

Ribe Camping****
Farupvej 2
+45 75 41 07 77
1/1 - 31/12
info@ribecamping.dk

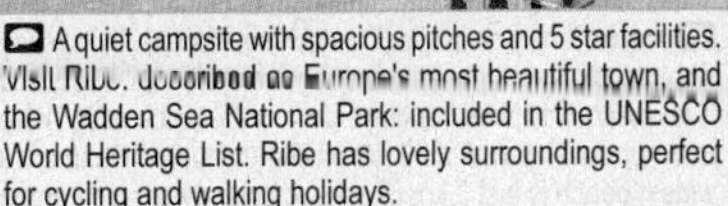

9ha 485T(100-200m²) 10-16A

1 ACDIKLMNOQRS
2 BSTVWXYZ
3 CE**G**IJKPSU
4 (C+H 1/6-31/8)(Q+R)
(T+X 25/6-18/8)
5 **AB**DEFGIJKLMNO**PQR**UWXYZ
6 ACDEFGH**K**(N 1km)
OPSTUV

A quiet campsite with spacious pitches and 5 star facilities. Visit Ribe, described as Europe's most beautiful town, and the Wadden Sea National Park: included in the UNESCO World Heritage List. Ribe has lovely surroundings, perfect for cycling and walking holidays.

Route 11 Tønder-Ribe. Dir. Varde/Esbjerg west of the town Ribe, until campsite is signposted. Turn right from the north of the town. From the south stay on route 11 Ribe Nord. Left at 1st traffic light.

€27 *1/1-22/3 2/4-8/5 21/5-21/6 8/9-31/12* ***14=12***

N 55°20'27'' E 08°46'00''

Riis/Give, DK-7323

Riis Feriepark****
Østerhovedvej 43
+45 75 73 14 33
20/3 - 15/9
info@riisferiepark.dk

10ha 184T(90-140m²) 13A CEE

1 ACD**I**KLMNOQRS
2 BISTY
3 ACE**GR**UV
4 (C+H 18/5-1/9)J**K**
(Q R T Z)
5 **AB**DEFGIJKLMNOPQRUWXY
6 CDEFGJ**K**(N 2km)OPTV

Large campsite in beautiful nature of Jutland. Modern facilities and an outdoor swimming pool. Visit the stunning architecture of Vejle, the fjord, the pedestrian area, the shopping centre and the vibrant city. Short distance to LEGOLAND, Givskud Zoo, WOW Park, LEGO House and Kongernes Jelling (museum). 5 min from the Midtjyske motorway

At road 442 in the village of Riis, well signposted. Then approx. 2 km. From road 441 between Give and Bredsten Riis, follow Givskud.

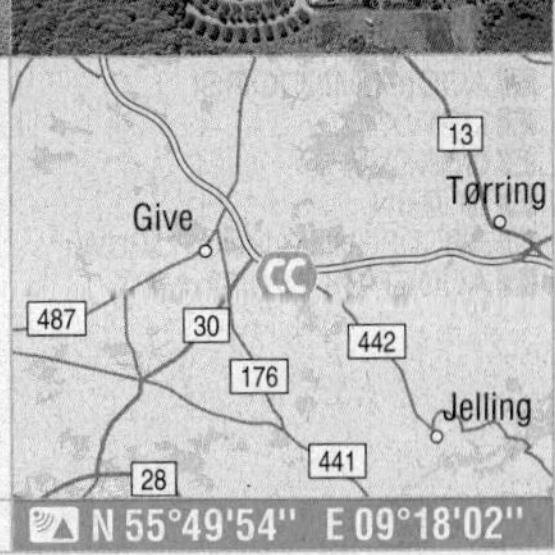

€27 *20/3-30/6 18/8-15/9*

N 55°49'54'' E 09°18'02''

Ringkøbing, DK-6950

Ringkøbing Camping***
Herningvej 105
+45 97 32 04 20
22/3 - 29/9
info@ringkobingcamping.dk

7,5ha 110T(36-140m²) 10A CEE

1 A**I**KLMNOQRS
2 BSTUWXYZ
3 AC**G**HIKPRS
5 **AB**DFGIJK**L**MNO**PR**UWZ
6 CEFGHJ(N 2,5km)O**P**RU

This quiet campsite has large sunny pitches with shade. With excellent shelter from the wind. Many walking and cycling possibilities from the campsite. Danish / German / English and Dutch spoken.

The campsite is on route 15, 4 km from Ringkøbing, towards Herning. The campsite is signposted.

€25 *22/3-5/5 24/5-30/6 26/8-29/9*

N 56°05'18'' E 08°19'00''

Rømø, DK-6792

87

Rømø Familiecamping***
Vestervej 13
+45 74 75 51 54
28/3 - 30/9
romo@romocamping.dk

10ha 345T(100-120m²) 10A CEE

1 ACIKLNOQRS
2 STWXY
3 CIPRU**W**
4 (Q+R)
5 **AB**EFGIJKLMNOPRUW
6 CEFGJ(N 4,5km)OPRSV

A quiet family campsite. The island of Rømø with its many sights lends itself perfectly to walking and cycle trips. The island is abundant with birds, making it ideal for the enthusiast. There is an unusual 'safari' minigolf on the campsite. Denmark's widest beach is just 3 km (5 mins. by car) away and can be driven on with a car or motorhome.

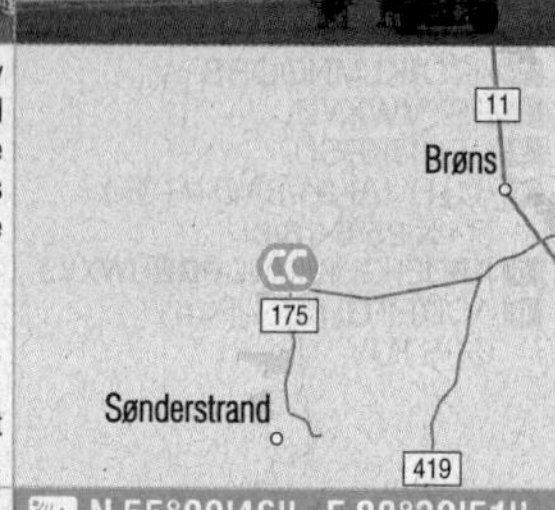

At Skaerbaek follow the 175 to Rømø. Turn right at first traffic lights in Rømø. Campsite signposted 2.5 km further on.

CC €27 *28/3-8/5 13/5-17/5 21/5-21/6 25/8-30/9* ***14=11***

N 55°09'46'' E 08°32'51''

Sakskøbing, DK-4990

88

Sakskøbing Camping***
Saxes Allé 15
+45 54 70 45 66
29/3 - 6/10
camping@saxsport.dk

2,5ha 71T(80-144m²) 10-16A CEE

1 ACDIKLMNOQRS
2 IJSWXYZ
3 **GOR**SV**W**
4 (**F**)N
5 **AB**CDFGHIJKLMNOPQRUW
6 ACDEFGK(N 0,3km)PT

A warm welcome to this small, peaceful campsite, located close to the centre of Sakskøbing and a forest. A short footpath beside the campsite leads to the fjord. A fine stop-over campsite on the route from or to the Puttgarden-Rødby ferry.

Exit 46 from E47, approx. 25 km from Rødby. Campsite is located near the centre of Sakskøbing and is signposted.

CC €23 *29/3-15/7 1/9-6/10*

289 E47 9 153 Sundby (Nykøbing Falster) 283 297

N 54°47'54'' E 11°38'28''

Silkeborg, DK-8600

89

Sejs Bakker Camping***
Borgdalsvej 15-17
+45 86 84 63 83
27/3 - 15/9
mail@sejs-bakker-camping.dk

4ha 170T(80-100m²) 10A

1 ACDIKLMNORS
2 IJSTYZ
3 AC**G**HIKLM**O**P**R**SU
4 (Q+R)
5 **AB**FGI**JKL**MN**P**RUW
6 ACEFG**K**(N 1km)O**P**V

Quiet family campsite amid woods and heaths, 5 km from Silkeborg and 800 m from the lakes where the famous 'Hjejlen' river boat sails. Ideal for walking, fishing and cycling.

At Skanderborg via exit 52, over route 445 to Ry. Follow Silkeborg. Campsite is indicated in Sejs. Or: highway in the direction of Hårup exit 26 Sejs-Svejbaek.

CC €25 *1/5-8/5 13/5-17/5 21/5-20/6 24/6-30/6 28/7-11/8 1/9-15/9*

N 56°08'25'' E 09°37'14''

Sindal, DK-9870

90

A35 Sindal Camping Danmark & Kanoudlejning****
Hjørringvej 125
+45 98 93 65 30
1/1 - 31/12
info@sindal-camping.dk

4,6ha 175T(100-150m²) 13-16A CEE

1 ACDIKLMNOQRS
2 BCIJOSTWXYZ
3 CGHIJKLMOPRSUW
4 (A 1/7-15/8)(C+H 1/6-15/8) (Q+R 1/4-20/9)
5 ABDEFGHIJKLMNOPQRUWYZ
6 ACDEFGHK(N 0,5km)OPTU

This well equipped family campsite is located in the heart of the top part of northern Denmark. Good starting point for exploring the countryside and surrounding towns. Campsite offers excellent facilities including a heated swimming pool. Camping before 1 April and after 15 September is possible on request. Midday break 13h-15h.

Approaching from the south via E39 exit 3 direction Sindal, route 35. Campsite located on the right after ± 6 km and ± 1 km before Sindal.

CC € 25 *1/1-29/6 18/8-31/12*

N 57°28'02'' E 10°10'43''

Skagen, DK-9990

91

CampOne Grenen Strand***
Fyr vej 16
+45 63 60 63 61
1/4 - 23/10
grenen@campone.dk

5,5ha 270T(80-110m²) 10A CEE

1 ACDIKLMNORS
2 AGJTXYZ
3 CMPSU
4 (Q+R)
5 ABCDEFGHIJMNOPQRUW
6 CEFK(N 1,5km)PTUV

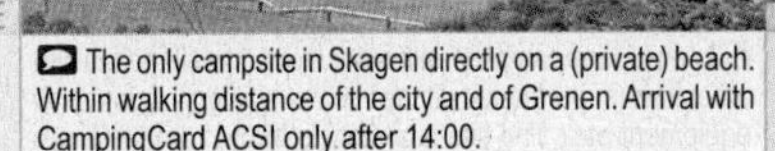

The only campsite in Skagen directly on a (private) beach. Within walking distance of the city and of Grenen. Arrival with CampingCard ACSI only after 14:00.

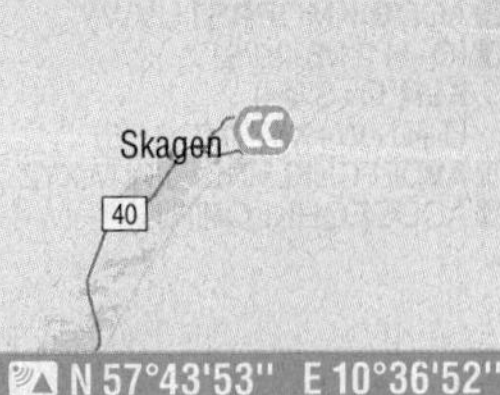

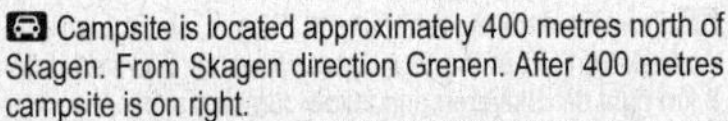

Campsite is located approximately 400 metres north of Skagen. From Skagen direction Grenen. After 400 metres campsite is on right.

CC € 25 *1/4-7/4 15/4-5/5 13/5-18/5 21/5-14/6 17/6-30/6 18/8-20/10*

N 57°43'53'' E 10°36'52''

Skagen, DK-9990

92

First Camp Råbjerg Mile - Skagen***
Kandestedvej 55
+45 98 48 75 00
1/1 - 31/12
raabjerg@firstcamp.dk

20ha 446T(80-150m²) 10A CEE

1 ACDIKLMNOQRS
2 AJSTUWXY
3 ACGHIJKMOPRSUW
4 (C 15/6-15/8)(F) (H 15/6-15/8)KN(Q+S) (T+U+V 1/7-15/8)
5 ABCDEFGHIJKLMNOPQRUWZ
6 CEFGHKL(N 8km)OPTUV

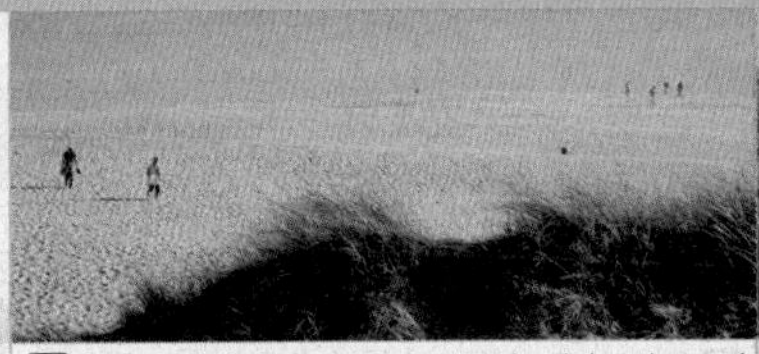

Close to idyllic Skagen between two lovely beaches and beautiful countryside. Cycling and walking to Skagen and Råbjerg Mile. Several playgrounds, outdoor and indoor pool, family-friendly. Good family toilet facilities.

Site is about 8 km north of Ålbæk. From route 40 direction Råbjerg Mile. Site 400m on the left.

CC € 23 *1/1-27/3 2/4-7/5 13/5-16/5 21/5-19/6 1/9-22/12*

N 57°39'19'' E 10°27'01''

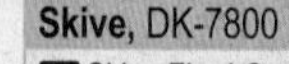

Skive, DK-7800

93

Skive Fjord Camping***
Marienlyst Strand 15
+45 97 51 44 55
24/3 - 15/9
info@skivefjordcamping.dk

12ha 198**T**(100-120m²) 10-16A CEE

1 ACD**I**JKLMNOQRS
2 AGJLMNOPQSUWXY
3 C**G**KP**R**SUWYZ
4 (C+H 1/6-31/8)(Q)
5 **AB**DEFGIJKLMNOPQRUW
6 CEFGHJ(N 1,9km)OPV

Modern, spacious terraced campsite with panoramic views of the Limfjord and a lovely, heated swimming pool. Walking/ cycling path along the fjord to Skive 4 km away.

From Skive route 26 (bypass) direction Nykøbing. Then route 551 direction Fur. The campsite is signposted from there.

CC € 25 *24/3-30/6 18/8-15/9*

N 56°35'53'' E 09°02'17''

Skiveren/Aalbæk, DK-9982

94

Skiveren Camping****
Niels Skiverens Vej 5-7
+45 98 93 22 00
15/3 - 22/10
info@skiveren.dk

18,4ha 595**T**(60-140m²) 10-16A CEE

1 ACD**I**KLMNOQRS
2 AGJNSVWXYZ
3 ACD**G**IKMOP**R**STU**V**WY
4 (C+H 21/5-29/8)
KLN(Q+S)
(T+U+W+X+Z 1/7-31/8)
5 **AB**DEFGIJKLMNOPQRUWXYZ
6 ACDEFGHKLO**P**TUV

A luxurious campsite with extensive and well-maintained amenities (supermarket, fitness centre, minigolf, indoor play equipment etc.) The site is a stone's throw from the North Sea in the middle of a protected natural area.

From Frederikshaven route 40 Skagen, about 1 km after Aalbæk turn left at the roundabout towards Tversted. After 8 km right dir. Skiveren and follow camping signs.

CC € 27 *15/3-6/7 24/8-20/10*

N 57°36'58'' E 10°16'50''

Smidstrup, DK-3230

95

Kongernes Feriepark - Gilleleje****
Helsingevej 44
+45 48 31 84 48
1/1 - 31/12
info@kongernesferiepark.dk

6,5ha 113**T**(110-150m²) 10-13A CEE

1 ABCDE**I**JKLMNOQRS
2 JSWXY
3 C**G**HIKMP**R**SU
4 (C+H 1/5-30/9)**K**(Q 1/4-1/10)
(S+T+U+W+X+Z)
5 **AB**DEFGI**JKL**MNO**P**RUWZ
6 ACDEFGHKL(N 1km)OPTV

Slightly sloping campsite, with reception in the centre. Well-equipped shop and beautiful pool.

Highway 237 Gilleleje-Rågeleje, take exit in Smidstrup, 2 km dir. Blistrup. Clearly indicated from then on.

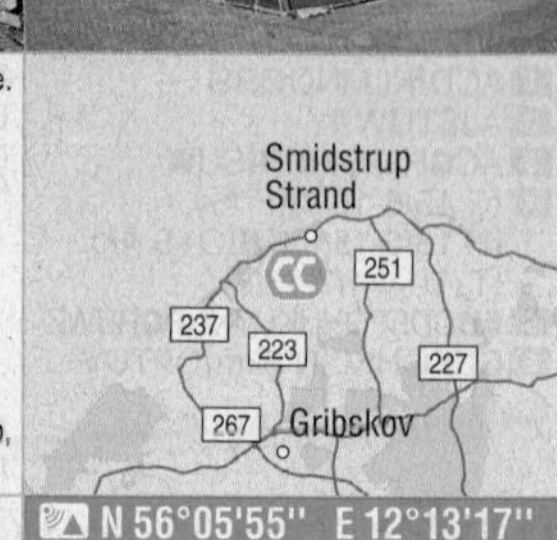

CC € 27 *1/1-14/6 1/9-31/12*

N 56°05'55'' E 12°13'17''

Stouby, DK-7140

96

Rosenvold Strand Camping***
Rosenvoldvej 19
+45 75 69 14 15
22/3 - 29/9
info@rosenvoldcamping.dk

11,5ha 265T(100-150m²) 10A CEE

1 ACDIKLMNOQRS
2 ABGNSWXYZ
3 ACEHIJKP**R**SU**W**Y
4 (Q+R+T+U+V)
5 **AB**DEFGIJKLMNOP**QR**UWX
6 CEFGHJ**K**(N 3,2km)OPUV

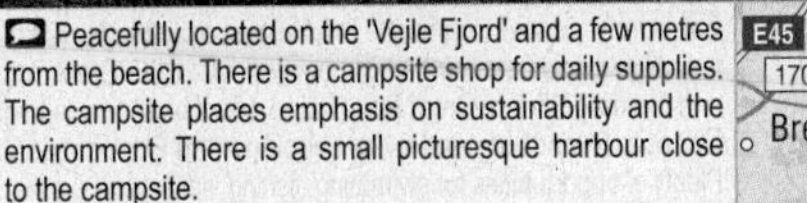

Peacefully located on the 'Vejle Fjord' and a few metres from the beach. There is a campsite shop for daily supplies. The campsite places emphasis on sustainability and the environment. There is a small picturesque harbour close to the campsite.

Route 23 Vejle-Juelsminde. In Stouby turn right, follow camping sign.

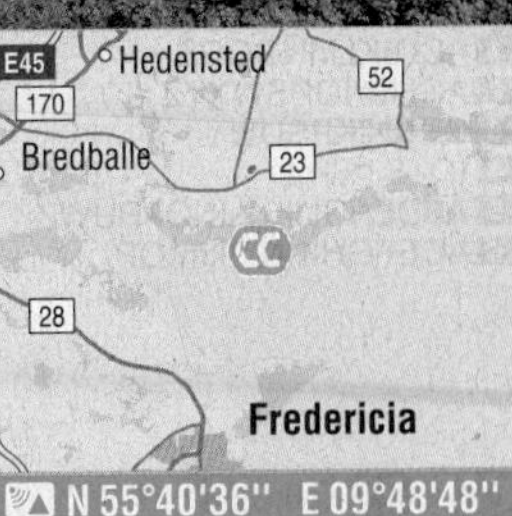

N 55°40'36" E 09°48'48"

CC € 27 *22/3-7/5 12/5-16/5 20/5-28/6 18/8-29/9*

Struer, DK-7600

97

Toftum Bjerge Camping***
Gl. Landevej 4
+45 97 86 13 30
1/1 - 31/12
info@toftum-bjerge.dk

5ha 250T(90-150m²) 10-13A CEE

1 ACDIKLMNORS
2 AGJLQSTUVWXYZ
3 ACE**G**HIKP**R**UWY
4 (Q+R 15/3-20/10)
(U+X 1/7-31/8)
(Z 15/3-20/10)
5 **AB**DEFGHIJKLMNOPRUWZ
6 CEFGHK(N 1km)OPUV

The campsite is located on the Toftum Bjerge, with the Limfjord and the Remmerstrand at its foot. Some camping pitches have stunning views over the surrounding area. The centrally located bar and restaurant are very hospitable. Make sure to visit the town of Struer and the Remmerstrand.

You reach the campsite via route 11. 5 km north of Struer, at the exit Humlum, the campsite is signposted. Just outside Humlum along route 565 the campsite is located on the right.

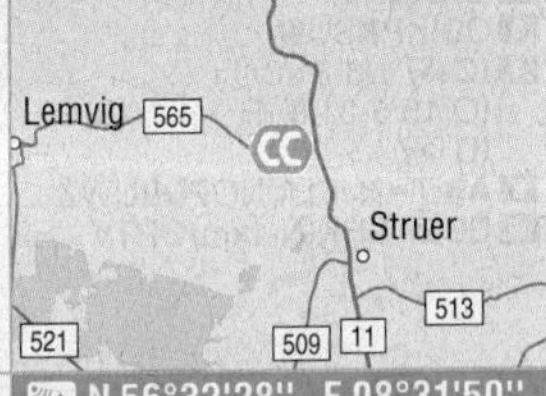

N 56°32'28" E 08°31'50"

CC € 25 *1/1-15/7 1/9-31/12*

Svendborg/Thurø, DK-5700

98

Thurø Strand Camping***
Smørmosevej 7
+45 51 18 52 54
21/3 - 15/9
info@thuroecamping.dk

6,5ha 243T(100-140m²) 13A CEE

1 ACD**I**KLMNORS
2 AGIJOSWXYZ
3 ACD**G**HIKP**R**SUV**W**Y
4 (A 22/6-12/8)(Q+R)
(T 22/6-12/8)
5 **AB**DFGIJK**L**MNO**PQ**RUWXZ
6 ADEFGH**K**(N 2,5km)O**P**TV

Thurø Strand Camping is 5 km from Svendborg, close to the sea and a good child-friendly beach. Quiet and relaxing, with new modern toilet and washing facilities. Good cycling and walking in the area. Good fishing in the sea.

From Svendborg over the bridge in direction Grasten, take 2nd left. At end of road follow the bend to the right. Then follow signs.

N 55°02'36" E 10°42'36"

CC € 21 *22/3-9/5 20/5-28/6 26/8-15/9*

Tårup/Frørup, DK-5871

99

Tårup Strand Camping
Lersey Alle 25
+45 65 37 11 99
5/4 - 22/9
mail@taarupstrandcamping.dk

11ha 140**T**(80-120m²) 10A CEE

1 ACD**I**KLMNOQRS
2 AGLMNOPSWXYZ
3 CE**G**HIKPSU**W**Y
4 (Q+S)
5 **AB**DEFGIJKLMNO**P**RUWZ
6 ACEFGHK(N 9km)OP

Lovely, peaceful campsite in natural surroundings, 10 km from Nyborg and the motorway. Lovely views of the Great Belt and the magnificent Great Belt Bridge. Ideal base for visiting Odense, Svendborg and even Legoland and Copenhagen. Plenty of opportunities for swimming, fishing, sailing and cycling.

From route Nyborg- Svendborg, after 10 km take the first left to Tårup, follow Tårup beach camping signs.

CC € 23 *5/4-30/6 19/9-22/9*

N 55°14'14" E 10°48'28"

Tønder, DK-6270

100

Møgeltønder Camping
Sønderstrengvej 2
+45 74 73 84 60
1/1 - 31/12
info@mogeltondercamping.dk

5ha 204**T**(80-120m²) 10A CEE

1 ACD**I**KLMNOQRS
2 EJSTXYZ
3 C**G**IKP**R**SU**W**
4 (C+H 1/6-31/8)J
(Q 15/6-31/8)(R 1/4-1/10)
(U)
5 **AB**DFGIJKLMNO**PQR**UWZ
6 BCEFGHK(N 1km)OPTV

Beautiful campsite in a quiet area with excellent facilities. Swimming pool and large playground. There are plenty of cycling and walking possibilities. Town of Tønder is 3 km away, a nice bike ride. Village has old-English atmosphere with boutiques, restaurants and cafes. Castle Schackenborg plus park are worth a visit.

From road 11 exit to 419 dir. Højer. Second exit to Møgeltønder. Site is well signposted from then on.

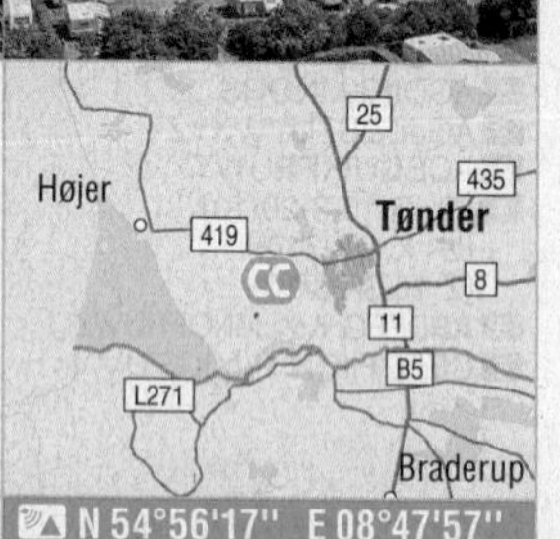

CC € 23 *1/1-30/6 1/9-31/12* ***7=6, 14=12***

N 54°56'17" E 08°47'57"

Tønder, DK-6270

101

Tønder Camping***
Sønderport 4
+45 74 92 80 00
1/1 - 31/12
booking@danhostel-tonder.dk

2ha 84**T**(80-130m²) 10-16A

1 ACIKLMNRS
2 CSWXYZ
3 C**G**HKM**O**PSU**VW**X
4 (F+H)**JLN**(Q)
5 **AB**DEFGIJKLMNOPRUWX
6 ACEFGK(N 1km)PQTV

A peaceful campsite in one of Denmark's oldest towns. The lively centre of Tønder is a 10 minute walk away. The pitches are well sheltered. Large sports field. An indoor swimming pool with fitness centre is right next to the campsite. Surroundings are excellent for walking and cycling trips. 40 newly constructed motorhome pitches with complete service.

Road 11 from the south. From the east take road 8 direction Tønder. Campsite located on east side of the village.

CC € 25 *1/1-30/6 1/9-31/12* ***7=6, 14=12***

N 54°56'04" E 08°52'36"

Tversted, DK-9881

102

Aabo Camping***
Aabovej 18
+45 98 93 12 34
9/3 - 8/9
info@aabo-camping.dk

14ha 500**T**(100-120m²) 13A CEE

1 ACD**I**KLMNOQRS
2 ACIJSTWXY
3 C**G**HIKMOP**R**SUW
4 (C+H 1/6-29/8)JK
(Q 20/6-15/8)(S 30/6-15/8)
(T 23/6-15/8)(U 1/7-15/8)
(V+W 30/6-15/8)
(Z 22/6-15/8)
5 **AB**CDEFGHIJKLMNO**PQ**RUWXYZ
6 CEFGHKL(N 0,3km)O**P**TV

Beautifully located on hilly ground and has access to the north to a large protected area where you can walk through the dunes to the beach. The campsite has all you could wish for. Centrally located for excursions to the whole of Jutland. Great campsite to continue by ferry from Hirtshals, to Iceland and Norway.

Route 597 Hirtshals-Skagen. Turn right at the Tversted/ Bindslev exit towards beach/Tversted. Turn left after 450m.

Tversted
Hirtshals
55
597
E39
190

CC € 27 *9/3-1/7 17/8-31/8*

N 57°35'06'' E 10°11'06''

Vejers Strand, DK-6853

103

Vejers Familie Camping***
Vejers Havvej 15
+45 75 27 70 36
1/1 - 31/12
info@vejersfamiliecamping.dk

4,2ha 156**T**(80-100m²) 16A CEE

1 AC**I**KLMNRS
2 AJSXYZ
3 C**GR**SU**W**
4 (C 26/5-27/8)(H 26/5-28/8)
(Q+R 23/3-9/9)
5 **AB**DEFGIJKLMNO**PQ**RUW
6 AEFG**K**(N 0,2km)OPTV

A quiet campsite by the North Sea. Beach accessible by car. Deer sometimes visit the site. Fishing is possible in Graerup lake and the North Sea. A lovely area for cycling, walking and relaxing. There are several boutiques in the village including an art gallery. Free admission to the 'Sportspark Blåvandshuk' water park in Oksbøl.

Via Oksbol 431 follow direction Vejers. Campsite at entrance to village. Signposted.

Vejers Strand
463
Blåvand

CC € 23 *1/1-8/4 21/5-5/7 22/8-31/12* ***7=6***

N 55°37'09'' E 08°08'11''

Vesløs, DK-7742

104

Bygholm Camping - Thy***
Bygholmvej 27, Øsløs
+45 26 20 97 90
1/1 - 31/12
info@bygholmcamping.dk

5ha 147**T**(95-125m²) 6A CEE

1 ACDIKLMNOQRS
2 AJSTUWXYZ
3 CDHKP**RU**W**Y**
4 (B 1/6-1/9)(Q+U+Z)
5 **AB**DEFGIJKLMNOPQRUWZ
6 CDEFGHK(N 2km)OPV

The province of Thy is in North Jutland, between the North Sea and Limfjord and has a few large nature parks. Bygholm camping is in the Vejlerne nature preserve, the largest bird reserve in Northern Europe. The campsite is the ideal starting point for travelling around this region by foot, bike or car. The friendly campsite has an outdoor pool, playground and a café.

On route 11 between Thisted and Fjerritslev. In Øsløs, follow the campsite sign.

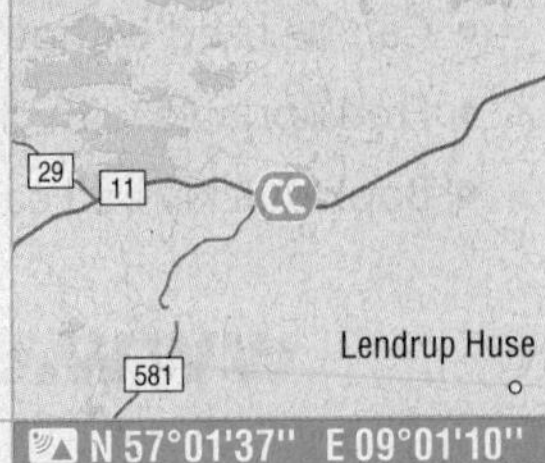

CC € 23 *1/1-30/6 18/8-31/12* ***7=6***

N 57°01'37'' E 09°01'10''

Vig, DK-4560

Kongsøre Camping***
Egebjergvej 342
+45 59 32 90 80
1/1 - 31/12
kontakt@kongsoerecamping.dk

4ha 115T(90-135m²) 10-16A CEE

1 ACD**I**JKLMNOQS
2 LNSTWXYZ
3 AC**G**IKP**R**SU
4 (**B** 1/6-1/9)(Q+R+U)
5 **AB**DFGIJKLMNO**PQR**UWZ
6 CEFGH**K**OPTU

Dorte and Henrik welcome you to their peacefully located campsite. Almost all the spacious tourist pitches have panoramic views. The campsite exudes a relaxed atmosphere.

Holbaek towards Vig (21) exit Asnaes/Grevinge/Gunderstup. Follow the road towards Egebjerg. The campsite is signposted further along.

CC € 25 *1/1-27/3 2/4-8/5 21/5-30/6 18/8-31/12*

N 55°49'26'' E 11°40'04''

The Netherlands

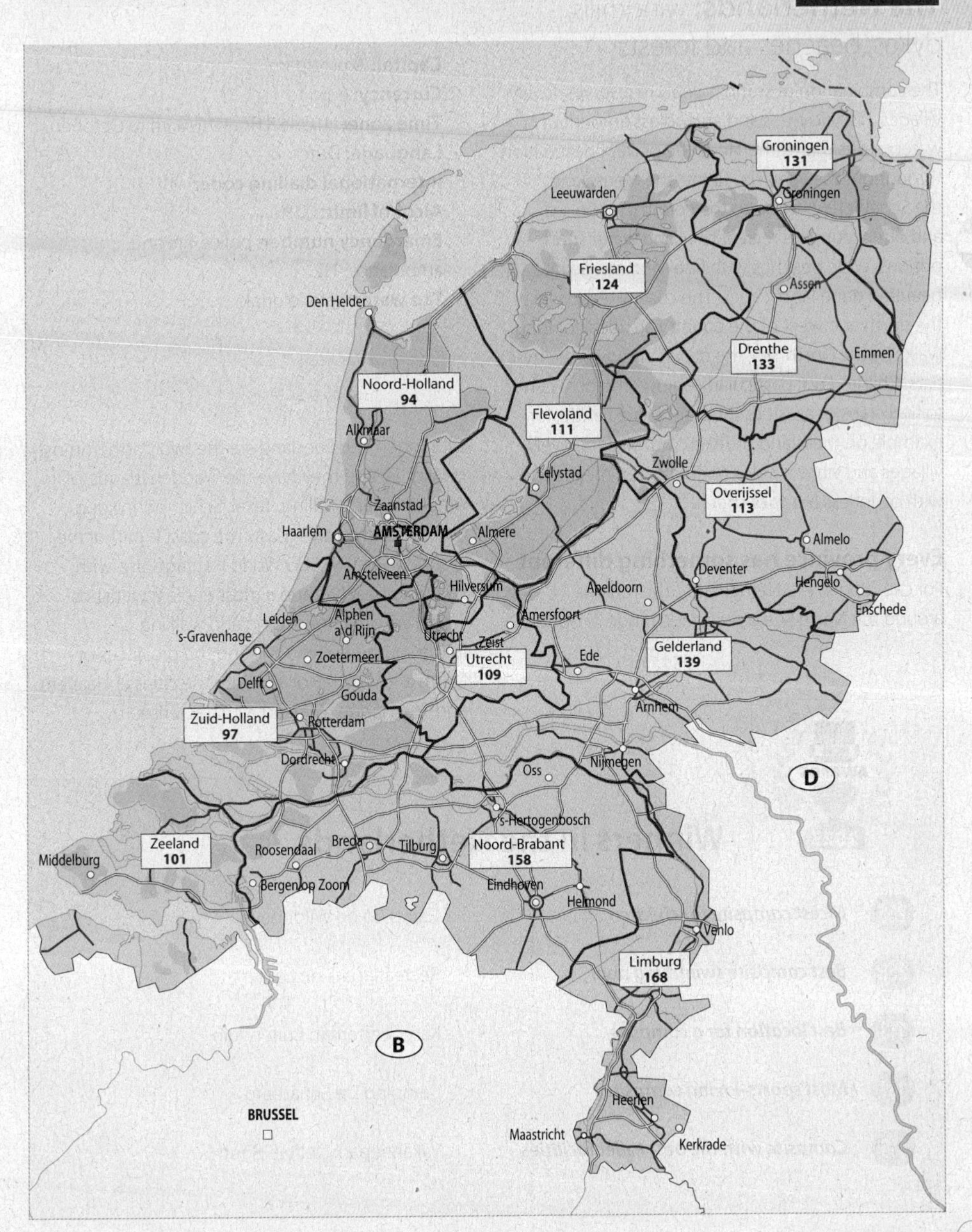

The Netherlands: windmills, dykes, beaches and forests

The combination of stunning nature reserves, lovely villages, historic cities and an endless amount of water makes the Netherlands the perfect destination throughout the year. The Rhine, the Meuse and the Scheldt flow through the country to the sea and offer countless recreational and water sports options. Wide beaches with fine sand merge into beautiful dune landscapes. The coastal resorts in the north and west of the country are ideal for long walks by the North Sea, the dunes and over the mud flats. Children will particularly enjoy a trip on a cutter to find crabs or a visit to the seal rescue centre, for example on the island of Texel. You will find lovely villages and vibrant cities behind green meadows with countless herds of sheep.

Capital: Amsterdam
Currency: euro
Time zone: UTC +1, UTC +2 (March to October)
Language: Dutch
International dialling code: +31
Alcohol limit: 0.5‰
Emergency number: police, fire and ambulance: 112
Tap water: safe to drink

Every province has something different

For camping in the Netherlands, the regions around the North Sea offer a wide range of options. Groningen and Friesland are the two northernmost provinces, and they have the Wadden Islands, of Ameland, Terschelling, Texel, Schiermonnikoog and Vlieland off the coast. The coast is part of the Wadden Sea UNESCO World Heritage Site, with stunning,beaches and almost endless wetlands which are great for cycling and walking.
In the southwest, you will find the provinces of North and South Holland with the cities of Haarlem and The Hague. Zeeland is characterised by

Winners in the Netherlands

255	***Nicest campsite for children***	Camping de Wildhoeve
358	***Best campsite swimming pool***	Recreatiepark de Leistert
113	***Best location for a campsite***	Kampeerterrein Buitenduin
361	***Most sports-loving campsite***	Camping De Schatberg
116	***Campsite with the best toilet facilities***	Vakantiepark Delftse Hout

various islands and peninsulas, most of which are interconnected by bridges and dams. Water sports enthusiasts, beach lovers, cyclists and hikers can indulge themselves to the full here.
No less enjoyable is Flevoland on Lake IJssel, the country's largest lake. But camping enthusiasts can also find interesting places inland, for example in Overijssel, where you can camp in wooded surroundings. In Drenthe, you can enjoy a holiday surrounded by pristine heathland. In the province of Limburg, you'll will have an enjoyable time in the many restaurants and outdoor cafes, and the province also has an exceptional landscape for Dutch standards - it has many hills.

From cheese to poffertjes

The Netherlands is famous for its cheese far beyond its borders. Goudse cheese, from the city of Gouda, is the most popular type of cheese. The famous fries are also one of the most well-known dishes from the Dutch cuisine, alongside 'kroketten' (croquettes), 'frikandellen speciaal' (minced-meat sausage with peanut sauce and mayo) and 'kibbeling' (deep-fried white fish).

The Netherlands also scores points for its sweet delicacies, the famous 'poffertjes' are available in many variaties. Poffertjes are a miniature version of pancakes.

En route

Filling up

Petrol (Euro 95, E10 and Superplus 98) is widely available (if you want to fill up with E10, check the fuel cap opening, the manual or your car brand dealership if you can drive on it). Diesel and LPG are also widely available. The bayonet connector is used to refill with LPG. Fuelling stations are usually open between 7 am and 8 pm. In larger cities and on motorways fuelling stations are generally open 24 hours a day. There are also many that work in automatic mode at night and unstaffed fuelling stations in the Netherlands.

Charging

There are many charging options in the Netherlands; there is always a charging station nearby.

Traffic regulations

Dipped headlights are compulsory during poor visibility, in the dark and in tunnels. At an uncontrolled intersection, traffic from the right has priority. Trams always have priority. Traffic on a roundabout has priority if indicated with traffic signs. If there are no signs, traffic from the right has priority.
Drivers are only allowed to call hands free. Children under 1.35 metres in height must be in a child's car seat. You are allowed to use your navigation software to notify you of speed cameras and trajectory speed controls. Winter tyres are not compulsory.

Special regulations

A green central line indicates that the maximum speed for passenger vehicles on that road is 100 kilometres per hour, for car-caravan combinations it is 90 kilometres per hour and for motorhomes over 3.5 tonnes it is 80 km per hour. Cyclists may overtake vehicles other than bikes on the right.
A pedestrian traffic lights that is flashing yellow (sometimes a triangle containing an exclamation mark) indicates that pedestrians may cross if there is no oncoming traffic.
Parking is not allowed next to a yellow line on the side of the road, among others.

"Fall in love with the Dutch campsite quality!"
Mr G. Peelen, inspector 625

Compulsory equipment

You do not have to have specific equipment in the car in the Netherlands. You are advised to take a warning triangle, safety vests and spare bulbs.

Caravans and motorhomes

A motorhome or car-caravan combination can be a maximum of 4 metres in height, 2.55 metres wide and 18 metres long (the caravan itself can be up to 12 metres long). On unpaved roads, the maximum width is 2.2 metres. With a car-caravan combination of over seven metres you may only drive on the two right-most lanes on motorways with three or more lanes, unless you want to turn left.

Bikes

Bicycle helmets are not compulsory. You may not call or text while on a bike. You may transport a passenger aged eight or over on the rear bike rack. Younger children must be in a child's seat. Cyclists are allowed to cycle in pairs next to each other.

Tolls

There are no toll roads in the Netherlands, but you do have to pay tolls for the Westerschelde Tunnel (N217) and the Kil Tunnel (N26) by Dordrecht. More information: westerscheldetunnel.nl and kiltunnel.nl.

"Dutch campsites often have beautiful and luxurious facilities."

Mr C. Iking, inspector 72

Environmental zones

A growing number of Dutch cities have environmental zones, including Amsterdam, Arnhem and Utrecht. The rules vary per location.

Breakdowns and accidents

On a motorway, place your warning triangle at least 100 metres (elsewhere at 30 metres) behind the car if the hazard warning lights are not working and the car forms an obstacle to other traffic. All occupants are advised to put on a safety vest.
If you breakdown, call the emergency number of your breakdown assistance insurer. You can also call the Dutch breakdown assistance service: +31 88 269 28 88 (ANWB).

Camping

Dutch campsites are among the best in Europe. Campsites are well organised and there is plenty of greenery. Cars often have to be parked outside the campsite, bringing more peace and quiet to the campsite. In the school holidays and weekends there is extensive entertainment for children and the amenities (such as indoor playgrounds and football pitches) are innovative.
Many Dutch campsites have a so-called family rate for four, five or more people, including electricity. This means that two people often pay the same rate as an entire family. Additional charges for items such as tourist taxes and environmental charges are sometimes quite high. You are not allowed to stay overnight on public roads in your caravan, motorhome or car.

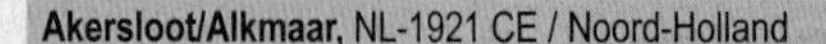

Akersloot/Alkmaar, NL-1921 CE / Noord-Holland

106

Camping De Boekel
Boekel 22
+31 7 25 33 01 09
1/1 - 31/12
info@deboekel.nl

2ha 40T(125-200m²) 16A CEE

1 ADIKLMNOPRS
2 IJNSVWXY
3 ABEGHIKMNPSUW
4 (Q+R)
5 ABCDFGHIJKLMNOPRSUWZ
6 ABCDEFGHK(N 2km)PTV

Small, car-free, child friendly campsite with spacious camping pitches and a recreation area. Situated on the Noordhollands Canal. Good fishing opportunities. Starting point for lovely cycle trips. You can take a sightseeing boat from the campsite to the cheese market. Campsite open all year.

A9 Amstelveen-Alkmaar, exit 11 direction Akersloot. In Akersloot straight on to ferry. From ferry another 1.5 km direction Alkmaar.

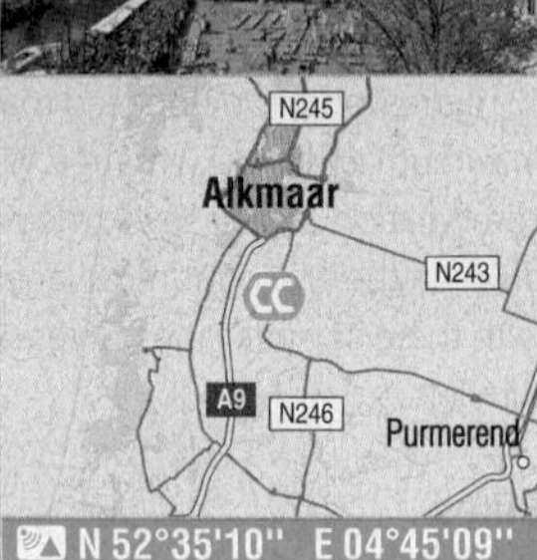

CC € 23 *1/1-19/4 20/5-4/6 15/6-12/7 1/9-31/12*

N 52°35'10'' E 04°45'09''

Amsterdam, NL-1026 CP / Noord-Holland

107

Camping de Badhoeve
Uitdammerdijk 10
+31 2 04 90 42 94
28/3 - 30/9
info@campingdebadhoeve.com

5ha 100T(15-50m²) 8A CEE

1 ABCDEIKLNPRTU
2 FINOSVWX
3 CGIKMPUWZ
4 (Q+R+T+U+X+Y+Z)
5 DGIJKLMPUWZ
6 ABCDEFGK(N 2km)PTV

Campsite located in the meadow and nature area "Waterland" on Lake Kinsel between Amsterdam (10 minutes) and picturesque Marken. Ideal starting point for cycling, hiking and fishing. The site has hardened pitches for motorhomes and caravans, well-maintained toilet facilities and free wifi.

A10 north, exit S115. Direction Durgerdam at traffic lights. Direction Durgerdam at roundabout. Straight on past Durgerdam. Campsite 500m. Follow signs.

CC € 25 *28/3-7/5 21/5-5/7 30/8-30/9*

N 52°23'04'' E 05°00'47''

Amsterdam, NL-1108 AZ / Noord-Holland

108

Gaasper Camping Amsterdam***
Loosdrechtdreef 7
+31 2 06 96 73 26
1/1 - 31/12
info@gaaspercamping.nl

5,5ha 360T(20-100m²) 10A CEE

1 ABCDHKLMNORS
2 IJSVWXY
3 AGIKMSW
4 (Q+S 1/4-1/11)
(T+U+V+X+Z 1/7-31/8)
5 ABDFGIJKLMNOPUWXYZ
6 BCDEFGHK(N 2,5km)OPT

The well-maintained campsite is located at 750 m from a large recreational lake with a beach. There is a park between the lake and the campsite. The Gaasperplas metro station is at walking distance. You can get to the centre of Amsterdam in 15 mins. The campsite has a bistro with take-away meals and a well stocked, small supermarket. Free Wi-Fi.

From A1 to A9 exit S113. Towards N236, follow the campsite signs. From A2 to A9 exit S112. Towards N236, Gaasperplas Noord.

CC € 27 *22/5-26/5 3/6-1/7 1/9-30/9*

N 52°18'45'' E 04°59'25''

Callantsoog, NL-1759 NX / Noord-Holland

109

Vakantiepark Callassande****
Voorweg 5a
+31 2 24 58 16 63
22/3 - 3/11
receptie.callassande@roompot.nl

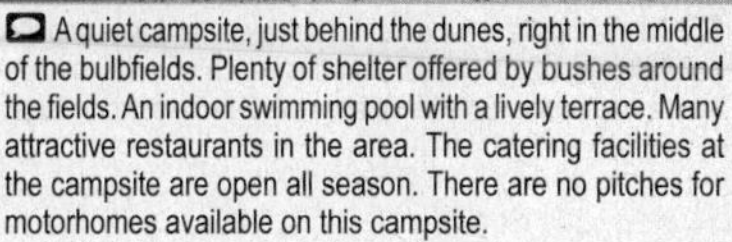

12,5ha 383T(60-120m²) 10A CEE

1 ACDIKLMNOQRS
2 AJSTWXY
3 BCGHIKMNOPSUW
4 (E+H)J (Q+S+T+U+V+X+Y+Z)
5 ABCDEFGHIJKLMNOPUWXYZ
6 ACEFGHKL(N 3km)PSTV

A quiet campsite, just behind the dunes, right in the middle of the bulbfields. Plenty of shelter offered by bushes around the fields. An indoor swimming pool with a lively terrace. Many attractive restaurants in the area. The catering facilities at the campsite are open all season. There are no pitches for motorhomes available on this campsite.

N9 exit 't Zand, direction Groote Keeten. Follow the camping signs.

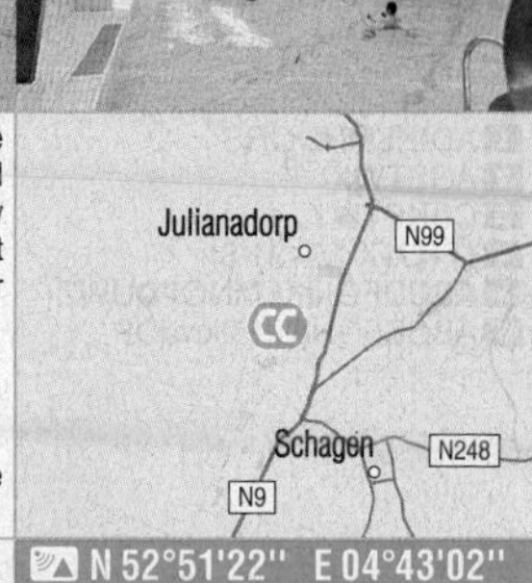

CC € 17 *12/4-25/4 13/5-17/5 21/5-29/5 3/6-28/6 30/8-3/11*

N 52°51'22'' E 04°43'02''

Edam, NL-1135 PZ / Noord-Holland

110

Camping Strandbad Edam***
Zeevangszeedijk 7A
+31 2 99 37 19 94
29/3 - 1/10
info@campingstrandbad.nl

4,5ha 70T(60-80m²) 16A CEE

1 ABCDEGKLMNRUV
2 FNOSVWXY
3 ABCGIJKMPSWZ
4 (G)J(Q+T+U+X+Y+Z)
5 ABCDEFGHIJKLMNOPQRUWZ
6 ABCDEFGHK(N 1,2km)P

Discover North Holland from Edam! The leading campsite at Edam, world famous for its cheese, has extensive views over the IJsselmeer. A good base for visiting Marken and Volendam. Amsterdam is only 20 minutes away by regular public transport. Marked out cycle routes through the centuries old polders and meadows of North Holland.

N247 Amsterdam-Volendam-Hoorn. Exit Edam-Noord and follow camping signs. Switch off SatNav.

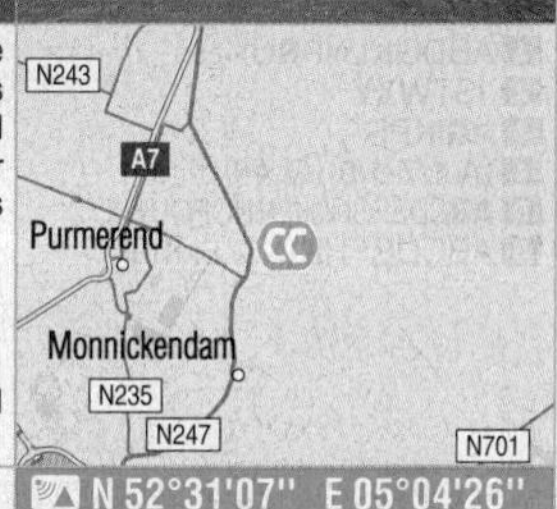

CC € 25 *8/4-5/5 27/5-30/6 1/9-30/9*

N 52°31'07'' E 05°04'26''

Hoorn/Berkhout, NL-1647 DR / Noord-Holland

111

Camping 't Venhop***
De Hulk 6a
+31 2 29 55 13 71
1/1 - 31/12
info@venhop.nl

8,5ha 61T(80-100m²) 10A CEE

1 ABCDEIKLMNPRTU
2 ISWXYZ
3 ABGIJKMNSUW
4 (Q+R) (T+U+X+Y+Z 1/4-1/10)
5 ABDGIJKLMNOPUXYZ
6 ABCDEFGHJ(N 3km)PSV

On good fishing and sailing water. The fields are surrounded by trees and shrubs. Starting point for canoe trips. Canoes and sups for rent at campsite. Centrally located for trips to Amsterdam and places like Hoorn/Medemblik/Enkhuizen and Marken/Edam/Volendam.

A7 Purmerend-Hoorn exit 7 Hoorn-West. Or A7 Hoorn-Purmerend, exit 7 Avenhorn. At the traffic lights turn left to Hoorn-West. At the next traffic lights follow Hoorn-West. After 350m turn right. Then follow signs.

CC € 23 *1/1-8/5 21/5-8/7 2/9-31/12*

N 52°37'55'' E 05°00'42''

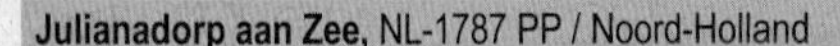

Julianadorp aan Zee, NL-1787 PP / Noord-Holland

112

- Camping De Zwaluw***
- Zanddijk 259
- +31 2 23 64 14 92
- 1/4 - 31/10
- campingdezwaluw@quicknet.nl

2ha 68**T**(50-100m²) 10-16A CEE

1. AD**I**KLMNOQRS
2. AGSTWX
3. C**G**KPT**W**Y
4. (T+U+X 1/7-31/8)
5. **AB**CDFGI**JKL**MNO**PQ**UWZ
6. ABCEFGH**K**(N 2km)OP

The campsite is sandwiched between the dunes and the bulbfields just 200 metres from the beach and 500 metres from a water park. Excellent places to eat in the surroundings.

From Alkmaar (N9) 1st exit Julianadorp (Zuid). From Den Helder (N9) 2nd exit Julianadorp (Zuid). Follow signs to Kustrecreatie. Turn right at the dunes. 1st campsite by the sea to your right in Julianadorp aan Zee.

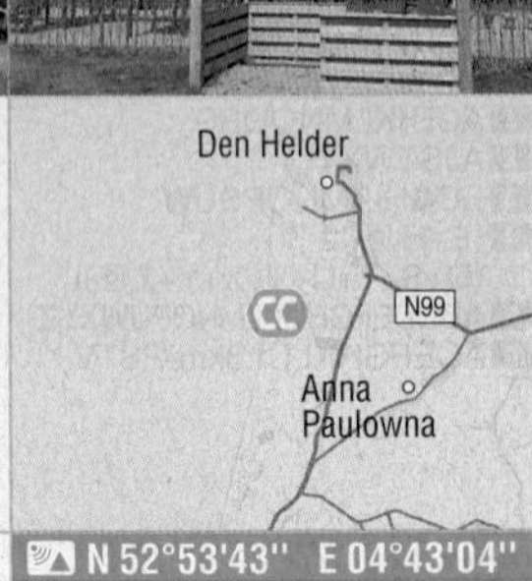

CC € 25 *1/4-8/5 20/5-30/6 30/8-30/10*

N 52°53'43'' E 04°43'04''

Schoorl, NL-1871 CD / Noord-Holland

113

- Kampeerterrein Buitenduin***
- Molenweg 15
- +31 7 25 09 18 20
- 22/3 - 3/11
- info@kampeerterreinbuitenduin.nl

ACSI AWARDS WINNER

1,2ha 44**T**(70-90m²) 10A CEE

1. ABDGKLNP**R**UV
2. JSTWXY
3. A**G**IKPS
4. (A 1/7-1/9)(Q)
5. **AB**CDEFGHIJKLMNOPQUWXYZ
6. ABCDEFH**K**(N 0,6km)PT

Quiet campsite in a wooded area within walking distance of the village centre and dunes. The friendly restaurant has a limited menu. Good starting point for walking and cycling trips. Campsite is suitable for young children. 'Kijkduin' corn mill is next to the campsite.

N9 Alkmaar-Den Helder, exit Schoorl, direction Schoorl. Turn right just before the traffic lights at the pedestrian crossing. Before the mill to the right.

N248 N9 N245 Heerhugowaard Alkmaar

CC € 27 *22/3-20/4 27/5-29/6 2/9-2/11*

N 52°42'12'' E 04°41'59''

Warmenhuizen, NL-1749 VW / Noord-Holland

114

- Landschapscamping de Kolibrie
- De Groet 2
- +31 2 26 39 45 39
- 29/3 - 1/10
- info@dekolibrie.eu

4ha 100T(150-280m²) 6-10A CEE

1. ABDE**I**KLMNP**R**U
2. NSWXY
3. ABE**G**IKNP**Q**SU
4. (Q)
5. **AB**CDFGHIJKLMNO**P**UWXYZ
6. ABCDEFGK(N 2km)P

Landscaped campsite with a central location in the rural part of Noord-Holland, 5 km from the lovely Schoorl wood and dunes area. Only 1500m from the Geestmerambacht recreation area. Spacious pitches, relaxed ambiance, peaceful surroundings. Lovely cycle and walking routes for the active holidaymaker.

N245 Alkmaar-Schagen, exit N504 Schoorl/Koedijk. Drive up to canal, then right. 1st road right. Right at fork in road (Diepsmeerweg). Follow road to campsite.

CC € 25 *29/3-26/4 21/5-4/7 30/8-1/10*

N 52°41'58'' E 04°44'46''

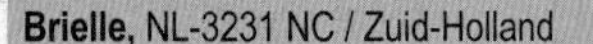

Brielle, NL-3231 NC / Zuid-Holland

115

- Camping De Krabbeplaat****
- Oude Veerdam 4
- +31 1 81 41 23 63
- 22/3 - 28/9
- @ info@krabbeplaat.nl

18ha 68T(81-120m²) 10A CEE

1 ACDIKLMNQRS
2 ADEISWY
3 CEGIKMNOPSUWZ
4 (G)M(Q+S+T+U)
(V 1/7-28/8)(X 1/7-26/8)
(Z 1/7-28/8)
5 ABCFGIJKLMNOPUWZ
6 CDEFGHJKL(N 7km)
OPSTV

The campsite has his own marina and beach with marked-out water for swimming on the 'Brielse meer' lake.

Motorway A16 Breda-Rotterdam, exit Europoort. Follow this road until you reach the town of Brielle. Just before Brielle follow the signs (exit Brielse Maas-Noord).

CC € 21 *22/3-27/4 20/5-13/7 1/9-28/9*

N 51°54'36'' E 04°11'05''

Delft, NL-2616 LJ / Zuid-Holland

116

- Vakantiepark Delftse Hout****
- Korftlaan 5
- +31 1 52 13 00 40
- 22/3 - 3/11
- @ info@delftsehout.nl

6ha 160T(100-120m²) 6-16A CEE

1 ACDHKLNORS
2 IJSWXY
3 CGIKMPSUWZ
4 (A 1/4-31/10)
(C+H 15/5-15/9)(Q 1/4-1/10)
(R)(T+U+Z 1/4-1/10)
5 ABDEFGIJKLMNPQUWXYZ
6 BCDEFGHKL(N 2km)
OPSTV

A modern campsite located in a nature reserve within walking distance of the picturesque centre. Countless opportunities for day trips in the 'randstad' urban area. This campsite has marked out pitches in secluded grounds.

Motorway A13. Exit 9 Delft, and from here on the campsite is signposted.

CC € 27 *22/3-29/3 2/4-26/4 21/5-5/7 26/8-3/11*

N 52°01'05'' E 04°22'45''

Den Haag, NL-2555 NW / Zuid-Holland

117

- Roompot Vakantiepark Kijkduin***
- Machiel Vrijenhoeklaan 450
- +31 7 04 48 21 00
- 1/1 - 31/12
- @ info@kijkduinpark.nl

29ha 350T(80-120m²) 10A CEE

1 ACIKLMNOQRS
2 AHIJSTWY
3 ABCDGHIKMNOPRSUWY
4 (F+H)K
(Q+S+T+U+V+X+Y+Z)
5 ABDEFGIJKLMNOPQRUWXYZ
6 CDFGHKL(N 1,5km)OPSTU
VX

Modern four-star camping site on the SW point of The Hague. Located in the dunes with its own access to the beach. Pitches with shadow available, as well as walking and cycling possibilities. The CampingCar ACSI rate only applies to comfort pitches. Free wifi on the entire campsite.

Located at Kijkduin (SW-point of The Hague). Enter The Hague (Den Haag) via the A12 motorway. Then head towards Kijkduin. Then follow campsite signs.

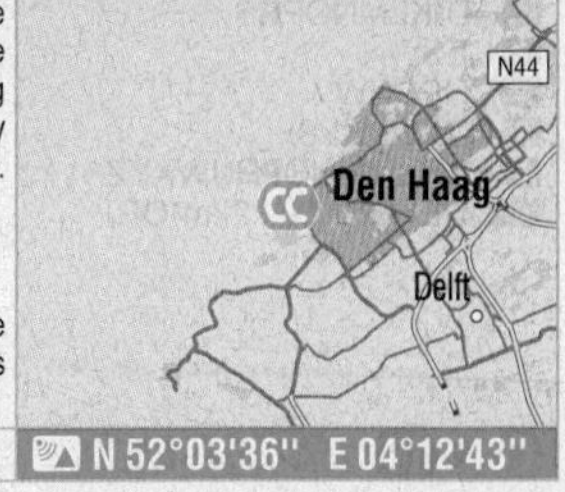

CC € 25 *12/4-25/4 13/5-17/5 21/5-29/5 3/6-28/6 30/8-3/11*

N 52°03'36'' E 04°12'43''

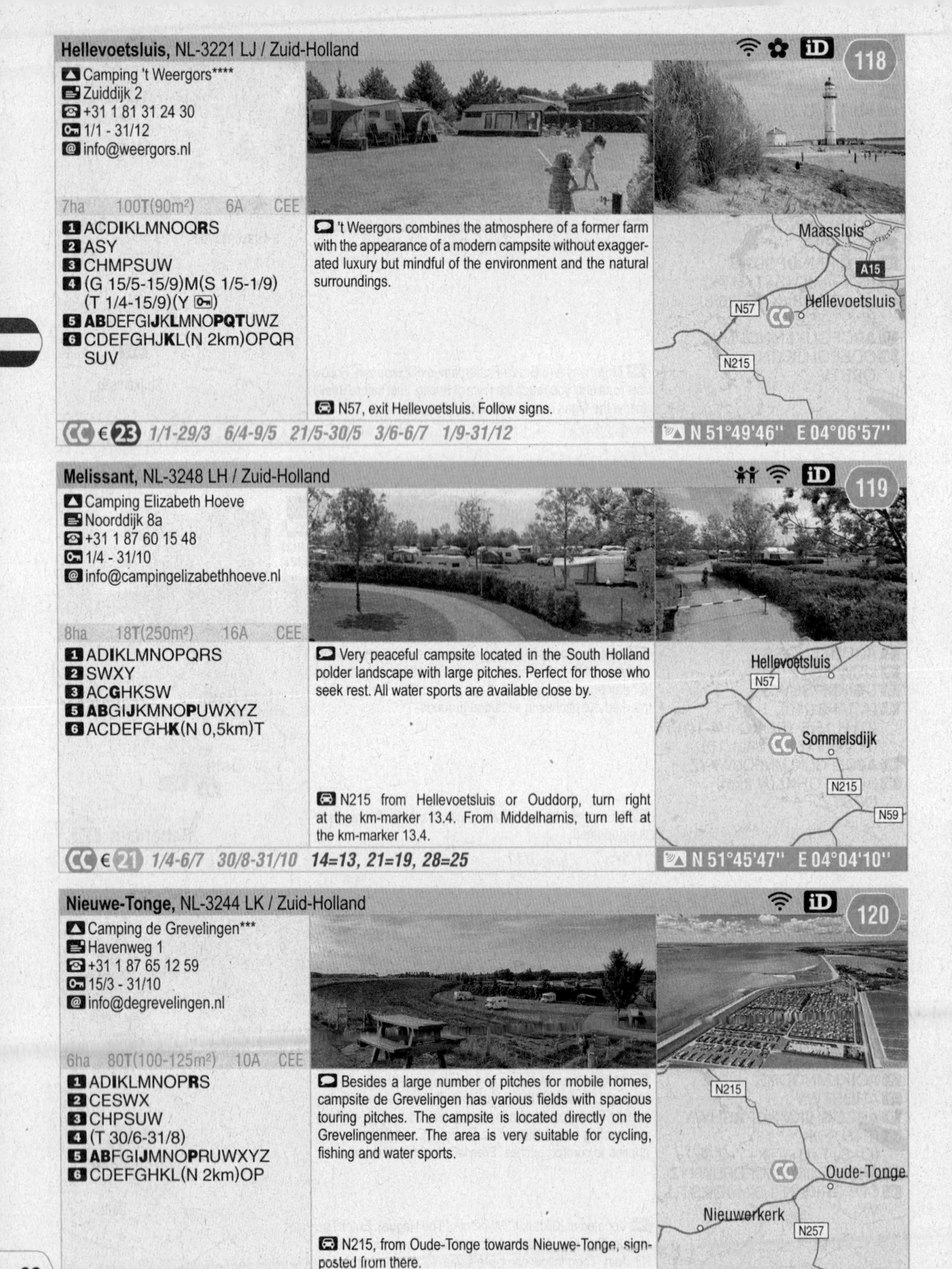

Hellevoetsluis, NL-3221 LJ / Zuid-Holland

118

Camping 't Weergors****
Zuiddijk 2
+31 1 81 31 24 30
1/1 - 31/12
info@weergors.nl

7ha 100**T**(90m²) 6A CEE

1 ACD**I**KLMNOQ**R**S
2 ASY
3 CHMPSUW
4 (G 15/5-15/9)M(S 1/5-1/9) (T 1/4-15/9)(Y)
5 **AB**DEFGI**JK**L**M**NO**PQT**UWZ
6 CDEFGHJ**K**L(N 2km)OPQR SUV

't Weergors combines the atmosphere of a former farm with the appearance of a modern campsite without exaggerated luxury but mindful of the environment and the natural surroundings.

N57, exit Hellevoetsluis. Follow signs.

CC € 23 *1/1-29/3 6/4-9/5 21/5-30/5 3/6-6/7 1/9-31/12*

N 51°49'46'' E 04°06'57''

Melissant, NL-3248 LH / Zuid-Holland

119

Camping Elizabeth Hoeve
Noorddijk 8a
+31 1 87 60 15 48
1/4 - 31/10
info@campingelizabethhoeve.nl

8ha 18**T**(250m²) 16A CEE

1 AD**I**KLMNOPQRS
2 SWXY
3 AC**G**HKSW
5 **AB**GI**J**KMNO**P**UWXYZ
6 ACDEFGH**K**(N 0,5km)T

Very peaceful campsite located in the South Holland polder landscape with large pitches. Perfect for those who seek rest. All water sports are available close by.

N215 from Hellevoetsluis or Ouddorp, turn right at the km-marker 13.4. From Middelharnis, turn left at the km-marker 13.4.

CC € 21 *1/4-6/7 30/8-31/10* ***14=13, 21=19, 28=25***

N 51°45'47'' E 04°04'10''

Nieuwe-Tonge, NL-3244 LK / Zuid-Holland

120

Camping de Grevelingen***
Havenweg 1
+31 1 87 65 12 59
15/3 - 31/10
info@degrevelingen.nl

6ha 80**T**(100-125m²) 10A CEE

1 AD**I**KLMNOP**R**S
2 CESWX
3 CHPSUW
4 (T 30/6-31/8)
5 **AB**FGI**J**MNO**P**RUWXYZ
6 CDEFGHKL(N 2km)OP

Besides a large number of pitches for mobile homes, campsite de Grevelingen has various fields with spacious touring pitches. The campsite is located directly on the Grevelingenmeer. The area is very suitable for cycling, fishing and water sports.

N215, from Oude-Tonge towards Nieuwe-Tonge, signposted from there.

CC € 19 *15/3-25/4 6/5-16/5 27/5-1/7 26/8-31/10*

N 51°42'20'' E 04°08'10''

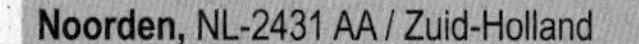

Noorden, NL-2431 AA / Zuid-Holland

121

- Koole Kampeerhoeve
- Hogedijk 6
- +31 1 72 40 82 06
- 1/4 - 1/10
- info@kampeerhoevekoole.nl

1ha 40**T**(40-100m²) 6A CEE

- **1** A**I**KLMNOP**R**S
- **2** JSY
- **3** CKMNP**W**
- **5** **A**DGIJKLMNO**P**UZ
- **6** CDEFGK(N 0,4km)

A campsite located in rural settings with countryside, peace and space. The site is located close to the Nieuwkoopse Plassen lakes where you can go canoeing and sailing on a 'whisper boat'. There are plenty of lovely cycle routes.

A2 exit 5 direction Kockengen (N401). Turn right at roundabout beyond Kockengen (N212), stay on first road to the left dir. Woerdens Verlaat/Noorden. The campsite is signposted past the church in Noorden with its own bill-board.

N201, N231, Mijdrecht, N207, A2, Alphen aan den Rijn, Nieuwkoop, N212, N11, N458

CC € 21 *1/4-5/5 24/5-30/6 1/9-30/9*

N 52°09'52'' E 04°49'08''

Noordwijk, NL-2204 AS / Zuid-Holland

122

- Camping De Duinpan***
- Duindamseweg 6
- +31 2 52 37 17 26
- 1/1 - 31/12
- contact@campingdeduinpan.com

3,5ha 81**T**(100-140m²) 16A CEE

- **1** ACD**I**KLMNPRS
- **2** ISUWXY
- **3** A**G**KLMN
- **4** (Q+U+Y+Z)
- **5** **AB**GI**J**MNOPUWXYZ
- **6** ABCEFGHKL(N 3km)OST

Camping De Duinpan is a friendly, well-equipped site with attractively landscaped grounds and clean toilet facilities. Rurally located near woods and dunes. Beautiful beach with the international Ecolabel. Good base for cycling and walking tours. Totally new restaurant with south-facing terrace.

A44 exit 3 Sassenheim/Noordwijkerhout, dir. Noordwijkerhout. At roundabout (Congrescentrum) turn right (Gooweg). Next roundabout turn left (Schulpweg) turns into Duindamseweg.

N208, Noordwijk, Voorhout, A4

CC € 23 *1/1-29/3 1/4-17/4 20/5-13/7 1/9-31/12*

N 52°16'06'' E 04°28'11''

Noordwijkerhout, NL-2211 XR / Zuid-Holland

123

- Camping Op Hoop van Zegen***
- Westeinde 76
- +31 2 52 37 54 91
- 15/3 - 14/10
- info@campingophoopvanzegen.nl

1,8ha 140**T**(80-100m²) 6-12A CEE

- **1** ACDGKLMNRTU
- **2** ISXY
- **3** ACDEIKLMPS
- **4** (Q 15/3-14/10)
- **5** **AB**CDEFGI**J**MN**PQ**UWZ
- **6** ABCDEFGHKL(N 2km)O**P**

Family campsite located between Noordwijk and Noordwijkerhout and situated in a 125-year-old cheese farm. Surrounded by bulb fields and woods, yet only 2.5 km from Noordwijk beach. Lovely cycling and walking routes. Completely smoking-free campsite.

A44 direction Sassenheim/Noordwijkerhout, direction Noordwijkerhout. Continue straight at roundabout 'congres-centrum'. Turn left at T-junction.

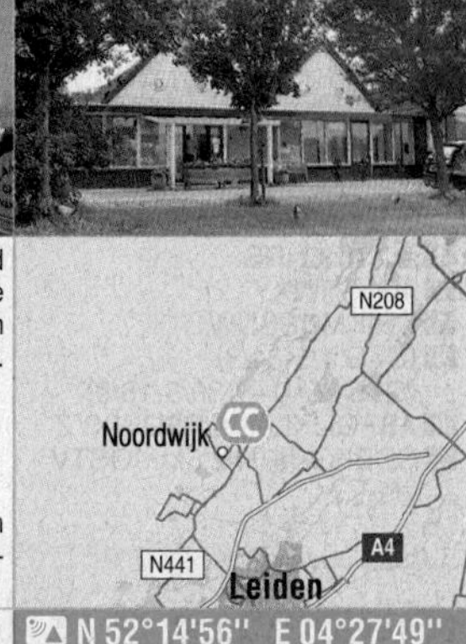

CC € 17 *15/3-28/3 22/4-7/5 20/5-4/7 2/9-13/10*

N 52°14'56'' E 04°27'49''

Rijnsburg, NL-2231 NW / Zuid-Holland

124

Vakantiepark Koningshof****
Elsgeesterweg 8
+31 7 14 02 60 51
23/3 - 27/10
info@koningshofholland.nl

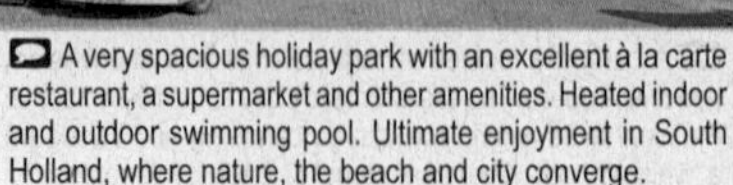

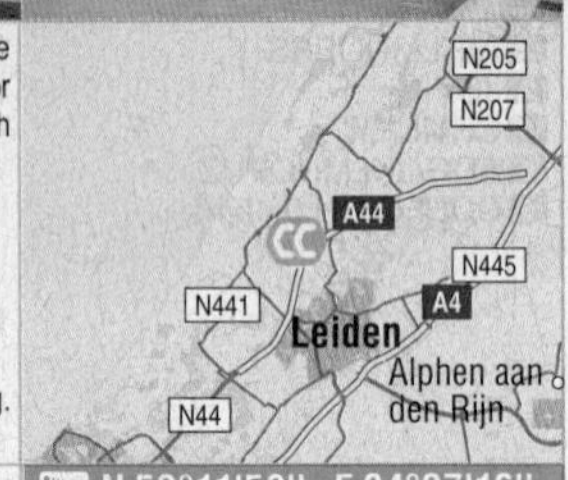

8,7ha 110T(90-110m²) 10A CEE

1 ACD**H**KLMNOQRS
2 ISUVWY
3 CD**G**KMNPSUW
4 (C 15/5-15/9)(F 15/4-27/10) (H)J(Q+S+T+U+Y+Z)
5 **AB**DEFGHIJKLMNOPQ**T**UWXYZ
6 BCDEFGHKL(N 2km) O**P**STVX

A very spacious holiday park with an excellent à la carte restaurant, a supermarket and other amenities. Heated indoor and outdoor swimming pool. Ultimate enjoyment in South Holland, where nature, the beach and city converge.

A44, exit 7 Oegstgeest/Rijnsburg, towards Rijnsburg. In Rijnsburg follow the signs to the campsite.

CC € 25 *23/3-29/3 20/5-6/7 25/8-27/10*

N 52°11'58'' E 04°27'16''

Rockanje, NL-3235 LL / Zuid-Holland

125

Midicamping Van der Burgh
Voet- of Kraagweg 9
+31 1 81 40 41 79
1/1 - 31/12
info@midicamping.nl

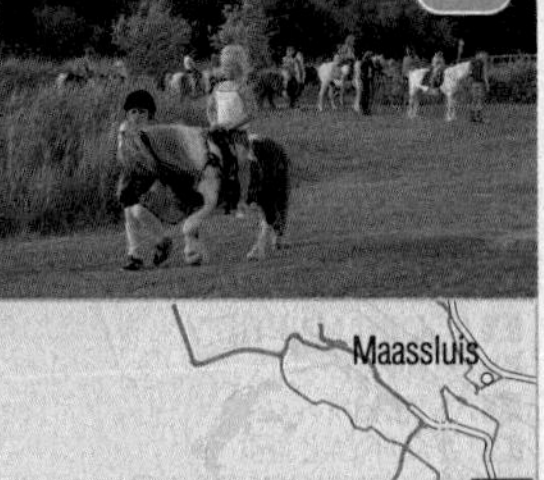

5ha 85T(150m²) 10A CEE

1 AD**I**KLMNOPQRS
2 SXY
3 CEKMS
4 (Q 1/7-31/8)
5 **AB**CDGI**J**MNO**PQT**UWXYZ
6 ACDEFGH**K**LOP

The campsite is located on the islands of South-Holland, close to the beach, dunes and fishing water. A medium-sized campsite with a new toilet pavilion and large pitches.

Rotterdam-Europoort A15, exit 12 direction Brielle. N57 Rockanje then N496, signposted in Rockanje.

CC € 21 *1/1-25/4 21/5-29/5 3/6-30/6 1/9-31/12*

N 51°51'23'' E 04°05'36''

Rockanje, NL-3235 LA / Zuid-Holland

126

Molecaten Park Rondeweibos****
Schapengorsedijk 19
+31 1 81 40 19 44
22/3 - 1/11
rondeweibos@molecaten.nl

32ha 122T(80m²) 10A CEE

1 ACD**I**KLNRS
2 AGJSTWXY
3 CHIKM**O**PSUW
4 (C+G 1/5-31/8) (Q+S+T+U+Y 30/3-15/9)
5 **AB**FGIJKLMNOP**S**UWXYZ
6 CDEFGH**K**(N 2,5km)OSTV

The campsite is a 10-minute walk from the beach. There is a very large playground. Beautiful, historic fortified towns in the area.

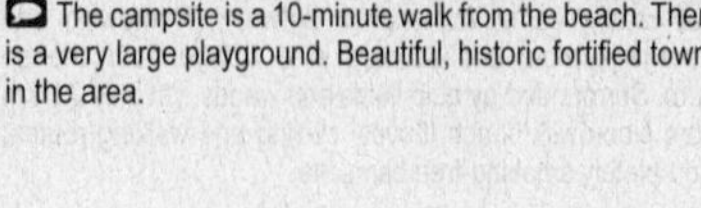

A15/N57. Exit Rockanje. Follow the Rondeweibos signs.

N15
Hellevoetsluis
N57
Middelharnis

CC € 21 *22/3-25/4 6/5-8/5 13/5-16/5 21/5-28/5 3/6-11/7 30/8-30/10*

N 51°51'25'' E 04°05'04''

Rockanje, NL-3235 CC / Zuid-Holland

127

Molecaten Park Waterbos****
Duinrand 11
+31 1 81 40 19 00
22/3 - 1/11
waterbos@molecaten.nl

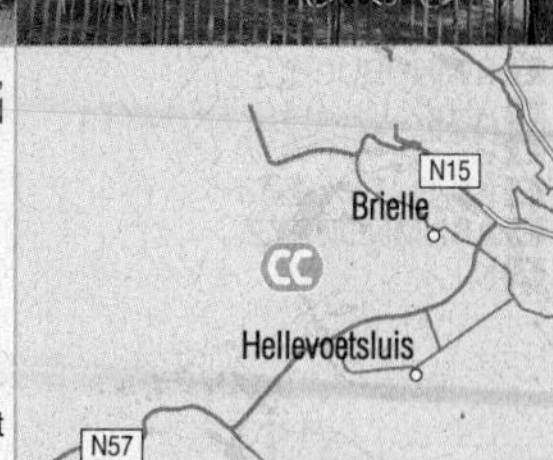

7,5ha 118T(100m²) 10A CEE

1 ACDGKLNRS
2 STWXYZ
3 CHKMPSUW
4 (C+H 30/4-1/9)(Q+R)
(T+X 15/6-15/9)
5 **AB**DFGJLMNO**PT**UWZ
6 CDEFGH**K**(N 1km)SV

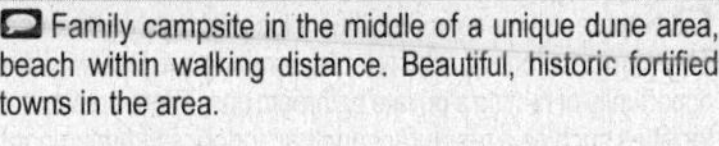

Family campsite in the middle of a unique dune area, beach within walking distance. Beautiful, historic fortified towns in the area.

A15, exit Europoort drive towards Hellevoetsluis, exit Rockanje, and then follow the signs.

CC € 21 *22/3-25/4 6/5-8/5 13/5-16/5 21/5-28/5 3/6-11/7 30/8-30/10*

N 51°52'48'' E 04°03'15''

Zevenhuizen, NL-2761 ED / Zuid-Holland

128

Recreatiepark De Koornmolen***
Tweemanspolder 6A
+31 1 80 63 16 54
29/3 - 29/9
info@koornmolen.nl

6ha 88T(90-140m²) 6A CEE

1 ACDE**I**KLMNOPQ**R**S
2 CEISVXYZ
3 CE**G**IKMPSU**VW**Z
4 (A 25/6-25/8)(F+Q)
(T+U 26/4-12/5,12/7-25/8)
(X+Y)
5 **AB**DFGIJKLMNP**T**UWZ
6 ABCDEFGHKL(N 2km)
OPTV

A friendly family campsite, part of 'De Koornmolen' recreation park on the edge of the Rottemeren (lakes). Tourist pitches and motorhome pitches surrounded by greenery and separated from the residential pitches. Cycling and walking options in the immediate vicinity.

A12 exit 9 Zevenhuizen-Waddinxveen; on the A20 exit 17 Nieuwerkerk a/d IJssel-Zevenhuizen. Then direction Zevenhuizen. Left at fire station to Tweemans Polder. Entrance to De Koornmolen about 1 km on the right.

A4 Zoetermeer N207 N470 A13 A20 N471 Rotterdam

CC € 21 *29/3-26/4 21/5-5/7 26/8-29/9*

N 52°00'32'' E 04°33'54''

Baarland, NL-4435 NR / Zeeland

129

Ardoer comfortcamping
Scheldeoord*****
Landingsweg 1
+31 1 13 63 99 00
22/3 - 3/11
scheldeoord@ardoer.com

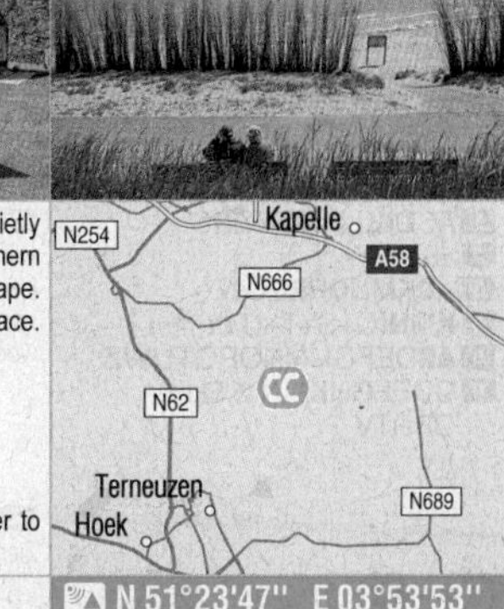

17ha 230T(120m²) 16-20A CEE

1 CD**I**KLMNOPQRS
2 AGJNSWY
3 C**D**HKM**O**PSUWY
4 (A 8/7-23/7)
(C 21/4-10/9)(F+H)J**N**
(Q+S+T+U+X+Z)
5 **AB**DEFGIJKLMNOPR**ST**UXYZ
6 BCDEFGH**K**L(N 2km)
O**P**RSTV

An active family campsite providing all amenities. Quietly located near the Westerschelde sea defences in Southern Beveland, a lovely area classified as a National Landscape. Plenty of space for being active but still having some peace. Walking, cycling, fishing? It's up to you!

A58 exit 's-Gravenpolder (35). Via 's-Gravenpolder to Hoedekenskerke. Follow 'Scheldeoord' signs.

CC € 27 *22/3-26/4 21/5-29/5 3/6-4/7 24/8-3/11*

N 51°23'47'' E 03°53'53''

Breskens, NL-4511 RT / Zeeland

130

Molecaten Park Waterdunen
Waterdunen 1
+31 1 17 79 20 11
22/3 - 3/11
waterdunen@molecaten.nl

14ha 222T(150-200m²) 10A

1 **I**LMNPRU
2 AHVX
3 U
4 (Q+R+T+X)
5 **AB**IJMNOPXYZ
6 K

Napoleon Hoeve is beautifully located right by the sea. The campsite offers comfortable camping pitches with the opportunity of renting a private bathroom unit. There are various facilities such as a restaurant and bar, indoor swimming pool, indoor playground, supermarket, tennis courts and bike hire.

Via Terneuzen (toll) towards Breskens, then via Schoondijke. At roundabout continue straight ahead, take the first exit to the right. Turn left under the viaduct. Follow signs.

Middelburg
Vlissingen
N676
N61

CC € 27 *22/3-25/4 6/5-8/5 13/5-16/5 21/5-28/5 3/6-11/7 1/9-30/10*

N 51°24'11" E 03°30'30"

Brouwershaven, NL-4318 TV / Zeeland

131

Camping Den Osse****
Blankersweg 4
+31 1 11 69 15 13
22/3 - 3/11
info@campingdenosse.nl

8,5ha 80T(80-120m²) 6-16A CEE

1 ACD**I**KLMNOPQRS
2 SWXYZ
3 CEHIK**O**PSUW
4 (C 18/5-15/9)(H 18/5-15/8) (Q+R+T+X)
5 **AB**DEFGIJMNOPQ**T**UWXY
6 ABCDEFGH**K**L(N 0,2km) PSTUV

A lively family campsite a stone's throw from the Grevelingenmeer and the Brouwersdam. Ideal for diving or if you enjoy rest, space, watersports, sun, sea and the beach. Heated swimming pool and entertainment in the summer.

N59 towards Zierikzee. In Zierikzee drive in the direction of Brouwershaven. In Brouwershaven the campsite is signposted.

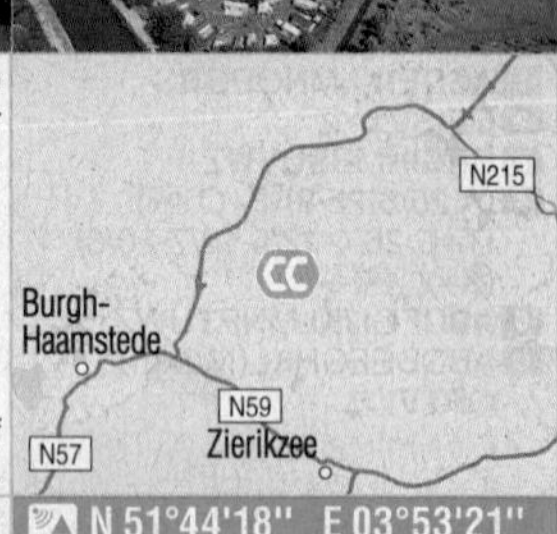

CC € 23 *22/3-28/3 8/4-7/5 20/5-24/5 3/6-26/6 26/8-3/11* ***7=6***

N 51°44'18" E 03°53'21"

Burgh-Haamstede, NL-4328 GR / Zeeland

132

Camping De Duinhoeve B.V.****
Maireweg 7
+31 1 11 65 15 62
21/3 - 3/11
info@deduinhoeve.nl

47,5ha 790T(100-110m²) 10A CEE

1 ACD**I**KLMNOPQ**RS**
2 JSTWY
3 A**D**KMN**O**P**R**SUW
4 **KMN**(Q+S+T+U+Y)
5 **AB**DEFGIJMNOPQ**T**UWZ
6 CDEFGHKL(N 2,5km) OPRTV

Luxury, or simply basic, young or not so young, you will always feel at home here! Camping De Duinhoeve is located in the middle of a lovely nature reserve on the Kop van Schouwen. The campsite is close to the beach and the woods. There are sheltered pitches with or without facilities.

A29 Dinteloord-Rotterdam. From Hellegatsplein towards Zierikzee. Then direction Renesse/Haamstede. Follow Route 107.

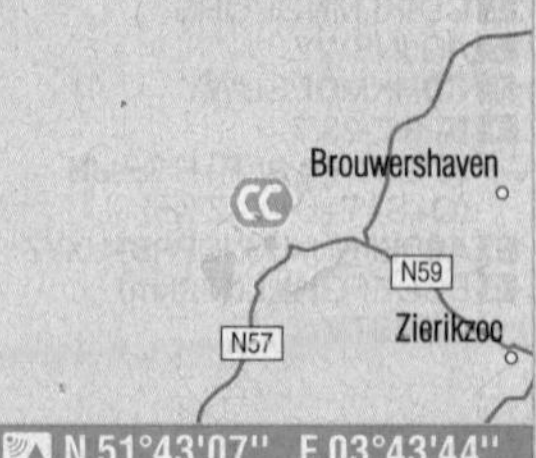

CC € 23 *21/3-8/5 20/5-29/5 2/6-27/6 30/6-5/7 1/9-3/11*

N 51°43'07" E 03°43'44"

Burgh-Haamstede, NL-4328 GV / Zeeland

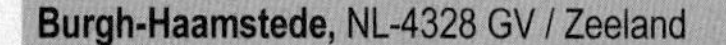

133

Camping Groenewoud****
Groenewoudswegje 11
+31 1 11 65 14 10
23/3 - 27/10
info@campinggroenewoud.nl

17ha 62**T**(100-125m²) 10A CEE

1 AGKLMNQRS
2 ESTWXY
3 CIKMNPSUVWZ
4 (C+H 15/5-15/9)
(Q+T+U+X+Y)
5 **AB**DFGIJKLMNO**PQ**UWY
6 ACDEFGH**K**L(N 0,2km)OSV

Located in a beautiful 17 hect. natural area, this site is recommended for rest and nature. Lovely outdoor pool with cafe serving bar meals, 2 ponds, luxurious new toilets with underfloor heating make your holiday complete. Pitches 100-125 m². Cable TV (free) and wireless internet available.

From Burgh-Haamstede drive towards 'vuurtoren' (lighthouse). After the traffic lights turn left down the fourth road and then after 200 metres the campsite is located on the left.

CC € 21 *23/3-8/5 12/5-17/5 20/5-13/7 31/8-27/10*

N 51°42'29'' E 03°43'18''

Cadzand, NL-4506 HK / Zeeland

134

Camping Wulpen***
Vierhonderdpolderdijk 1
+31 1 17 39 12 26
26/3 - 27/10
info@campingwulpen.nl

4,7ha 135**T**(100-130m²) 10A CEE

1 ADF**I**KLMNPQRS
2 JSWXY
3 AC**G**HKMNPSU
4 (Q+R+Z)
5 **AB**DEFGIJKLMNOPUWXYZ
6 ABCDEFGHKL(N 1,5km)
OPVX

A very well maintained family campsite with lots of privacy, sheltered pitches and a cozy living room with TV. The campsite is located directly on the cycle route junction system.

When entering Cadzand turn right at the mill and then take the first road to the right.

CC € 21 *26/3-29/3 2/4-9/5 13/5-17/5 21/5-6/7 24/8-27/10*

N 51°22'12'' E 03°25'00''

Dishoek/Koudekerke, NL-4371 NT / Zeeland

135

Camping Dishoek***
Dishoek 2
+31 1 18 55 13 48
22/3 - 3/11
info@roompot.nl

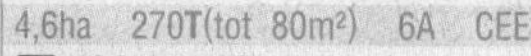

4,6ha 270**T**(tot 80m²) 6A CEE

1 ACD**I**KLMNPQRS
2 AGISTWXY
3 ACMPSUWY
4 (S+T+U+V+X+Z)
5 **AB**DFGIJKLMNOPUWXY
6 CDEFGH**K**LM(N 4km)
OPSTV

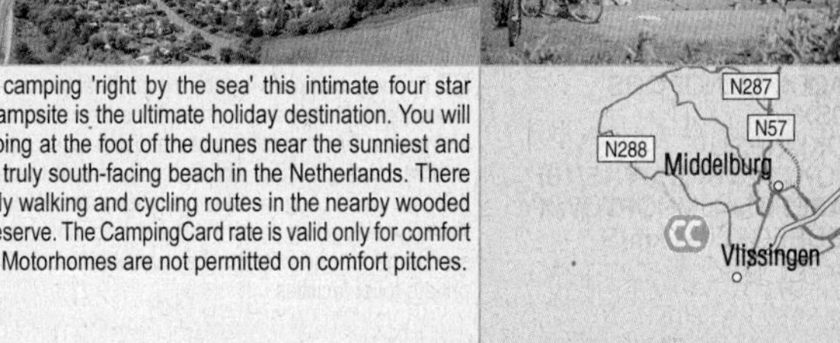

For camping 'right by the sea' this intimate four star family campsite is the ultimate holiday destination. You will be camping at the foot of the dunes near the sunniest and the only truly south-facing beach in the Netherlands. There are lovely walking and cycling routes in the nearby wooded nature reserve. The CampingCard rate is valid only for comfort pitches. Motorhomes are not permitted on comfort pitches.

A58 as far as Vlissingen, exit Dishoek. Follow signs.

CC € 23 *12/4-25/4 13/5-17/5 21/5-29/5 3/6-28/6 2/9-3/11*

N 51°28'08'' E 03°31'25''

Domburg, NL-4357 NM / Zeeland

136

Ardoer camping Westhove*****
Zuiverseweg 20
+31 1 18 58 18 09
22/3 - 27/10
info@westhove.nl

13,9ha 261T(80-120m²) 6-10A CEE

1 ADHKLMNOPRS
2 SVWXY
3 BCDGHKMPSUV
4 (F+H)N(Q+S+T+Y)
5 ABDEFGIJLMNOPQRTUWXYZ
6 ABCDEFGHKLM(N 1,5km)
OPSTV

Westhove campsite is located just 1500 metres from the resort of Domburg. Lovely spacious pitches, indoor swimming pool on the site, indoor playground and a bathhouse in Ancient Greek style.

Follow signs to Domburg from Middelburg. Signposted before Domburg.

CC € 23 22/3-28/3 2/4-18/4 21/5-28/5 3/6-4/7 26/8-26/10

N 51°33'21'' E 03°30'52''

Domburg, NL-4357 RD / Zeeland

137

Vakantiepark Hof Domburg****
Schelpweg 7
+31 1 18 58 82 00
1/1 - 31/12
info@roompot.nl

20ha 473T(80m²) 6A CEE

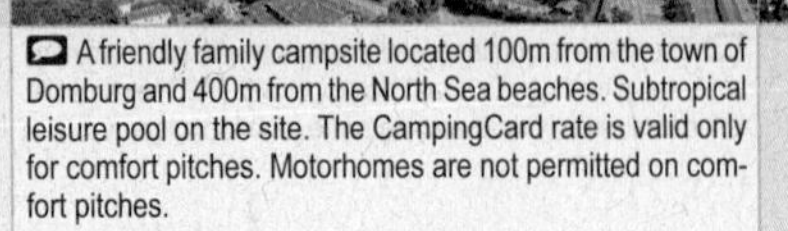

1 ACDEIKLMNPQRS
2 GJSWXYZ
3 ABCDFGKMNOPRSTUWY
4 (C 28/4-31/10)
(F+H)IJLNP
(Q+S+T+U+V+X+Y+Z)
5 ABDFGHJLMNPTUWXYZ
6 EFGHKL(N 0,5km)OPRSTX

A friendly family campsite located 100m from the town of Domburg and 400m from the North Sea beaches. Subtropical leisure pool on the site. The CampingCard rate is valid only for comfort pitches. Motorhomes are not permitted on comfort pitches.

Motorway A58 Bergen op Zoom-Vlissingen, Exit Middelburg. Follow the signs to Domburg. In Domburg the campsite is signposted.

CC € 27 12/4-25/4 13/5-17/5 21/5-29/5 3/6-28/6 2/9-3/11

N 51°33'33'' E 03°29'13''

Ellemeet, NL-4323 LC / Zeeland

138

Camping Klaverweide
Kuijerdamseweg 56
+31 1 11 67 18 59
15/3 - 27/10
info@klaverweide.com

4ha 76T(100-120m²) 16A CEE

1 ACDIKLMNOPQRS
2 JSX
3 CKMNPSU
4 (Q 1/7-25/8)(S 1/4-15/10)
5 ABEFGIJKLMNOPTUWXY
6 CDEFGKL(N 3km)S

Friendly campsite by the North Sea beach and lake Grevelingen. Many water sports options. Spacious pitches with 16A power, TV connection, water and drainage. Supermarket with fresh bread on Sat. and Sun. in early and late seasons, daily in July and August. Clean, modern toilets. Nice villages, walking and cycling paths through the countryside. Euro10 surcharge for caravans as they are always on a pitch with private toilet facilities.

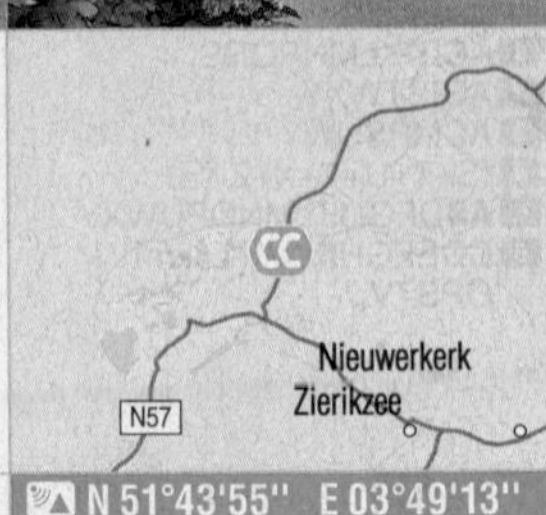

N57 Brouwersdam-Serooskerke, exit Ellemeet.

CC € 23 15/3-27/3 2/4-7/5 21/5-28/5 2/6-26/6 1/9-27/10

N 51°43'55'' E 03°49'13''

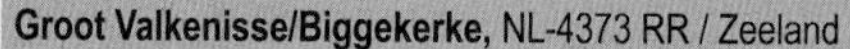

Groot Valkenisse/Biggekerke, NL-4373 RR / Zeeland

139

Strandcamping Valkenisse bv****
Valkenisseweg 64
+31 1 18 56 13 14
22/3 - 4/11
info@campingvalkenisse.nl

10,2ha 150T(100m²) 10-16A CEE

1 ADGKLNQRS
2 AGISWXY
3 ADMPSUWY
4 (Q+S+T+U+X+Y)
5 **AB**DEFGIJKLMNOP**T**UXY
6 ACEFGHKLM(N 2km)O**P**SV

Ideal holiday destination. Sunbathing on the beach, swimming and fishing; watching the sun go down, getting a breath of fresh air and enjoying the wild waves as they break on the shore; walking over the highest dunes in the Netherlands with lovely panoramic views of the passing ships; an ideally situated starting point for walking and cycling trips.

Vlissingen-Koudekerke, take the direction of Zoutelande, exit Groot Valkenisse.

CC € 21 *22/3-29/3 5/4-8/5 13/5-17/5 21/5-29/5 3/6-15/6 31/8-4/11*

N 51°29'32'' E 03°30'24''

Hoek, NL-4542 PN / Zeeland

140

Oostappen Vakantiepark Marina Beach*****
Middenweg 1
+31 1 15 48 17 30
22/3 - 3/11
info@vakantieparkmarinabeach.nl

212ha 475T(100-110m²) 4-6A CEE

1 D**I**KLMNOQRS
2 AEJNSTWXYZ
3 C**D**HKMPRSUWZ
4 (A 1/7-31/8)(Q+S+T+U+X+Y +Z 18/4-12/10)
5 **AB**DEFGIJKLMNO**PQ**UWXYZ
6 CDEFG(N 3,5km)STUV

A park with plenty of facilities located right by the water. Various indoor and outdoor sports activities. It has all the ingredients of a wonderful (family) holiday. Includes use Aquadome Scheldorado in Terneuzen.

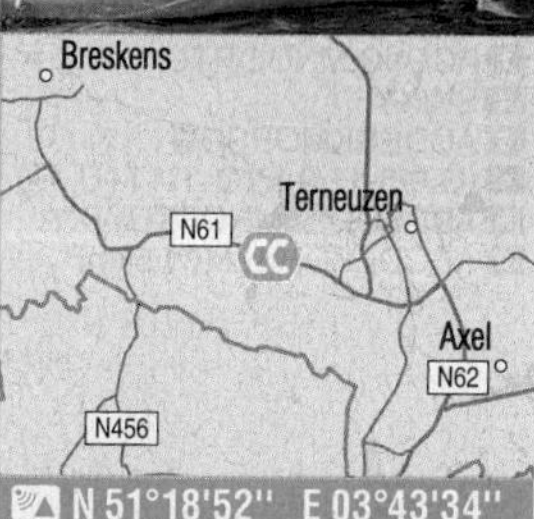

On route N61, 4 km west of Hoek.

CC € 19 *22/3-29/3 2/4-26/4 13/5-17/5 24/5-8/7 25/8-18/10*

N 51°18'52'' E 03°43'34''

Kamperland, NL-4493 CX / Zeeland

141

RCN de Schotsman****
Schotsmanweg 1
+31 8 50 40 07 00
29/3 - 3/11
schotsman@rcn.nl

30ha 668T(100m²) 10-16A CEE

1 ACD**H**KLMNPRS
2 FSTY
3 BCDKLMN**O**PU**VW**Z
4 (C 1/5-17/9)(F+H)J (Q+R+T+U+X+Y)
5 **AB**DFGIJKLMNOPQR**T**UWXYZ
6 ACDEFGHKL(N 2km)OS

RCN de Schotsman campsite is positioned right by the water on the Veerse Meer lake and next to an extensive wood for walking. The North Sea beaches are about 2 km away.

A58 Bergen op Zoom-Vlissingen, exit Zierikzee. Before the Zeeland Bridge direction Kamperland. Signposted in Kamperland.

CC € 21 *29/3-7/5 13/5-16/5 21/5-29/5 3/6-4/7 26/8-3/11*

N 51°34'06'' E 03°39'48''

Kortgene, NL-4484 NT / Zeeland

142

Ardoer vakantiepark de Paardekreek*****
Havenweg 1
+31 1 13 30 20 51
22/3 - 3/11
info@depaardekreek.nl

10ha 120T(80-120m²) 10A CEE

1 ADIKLMNOQRS
2 EJSWY
3 BCDHIKLMNPSUWZ
4 (C+F)JKMN (Q+S+T+V+Y)
5 ABDEFGIJMNOPQTUWXY
6 BCDEFGHKLM(N 0,5km)OP STUVX

Campsite de Paardekreek is located directly on the Veere Lake, so ideal for a wonderful water sports holiday. There is a large recreation hall and an indoor children's pool on the campsite. There is also a new outdoor pool.

Motorway A58 Bergen op Zoom-Vlissingen take exit Zierikzee. In the direction of Zierikzee, take exit Kortgene. Signposted from here.

CC € 25 *22/3-29/3 2/4-22/4 13/5-17/5 21/5-29/5 2/6-28/6 1/9-2/11*

N 51°33'04'' E 03°48'28''

Nieuwvliet, NL-4504 AA / Zeeland

143

Ardoer camping International****
St. Bavodijk 2D
+31 1 17 37 12 33
22/3 - 3/11
international@ardoer.com

8ha 107T(80-140m²) 6-10A CEE

1 ACDIKLMNOQRTU
2 SWXY
3 ACDEGKMOPSUW
4 (G 9/5-15/9)M(Q+R+T+U)
5 ABDFGIJKLMNOPTUWXY
6 ABCDEFGHKLM(N 5km) OPST

Peaceful campsite with views of rustic windmills, located directly on the cross-border cycle route network. Comfort pitches with CampingCard ACSI have every convenience.

Via Terneuzen (Toll) direction Breskens. Before Breskens, direction Goede and drive to Nieuwvliet. At roundabout R102 turn right. Campsite situated 700 metres further on.

CC € 19 *7/4-26/4 21/5-29/5 3/6-7/7 31/8-3/11*

N 51°22'28'' E 03°28'10''

Ouwerkerk, NL-4305 RE / Zeeland

144

Camping de Kreekoever***
Baalpapenweg 1
+31 1 11 64 14 54
29/3 - 21/10
info@dekreekoever.nl

7,5ha 49T(80-110m²) 6-10A CEE

1 ADIKLMNOQRTU
2 JSUWXYZ
3 AGIKPSUWY
4 (Q 15/4-31/8)(R)
5 ABCDEFGHIJKLMNOPUWXYZ
6 ABCDEFGHK(N 4km)OPST

Is a quiet and pleasant family campsite located on the creek district of Ouwerkerk and within cycling distance of the Oosterschelde and Zierikzee waters. You can fish, cycle, dive, swim etc. Campsite shop on site. Dogs allowed.

Via N59, exit Ouwerkerk. In Ouwerkerk, follow the campsite signs.

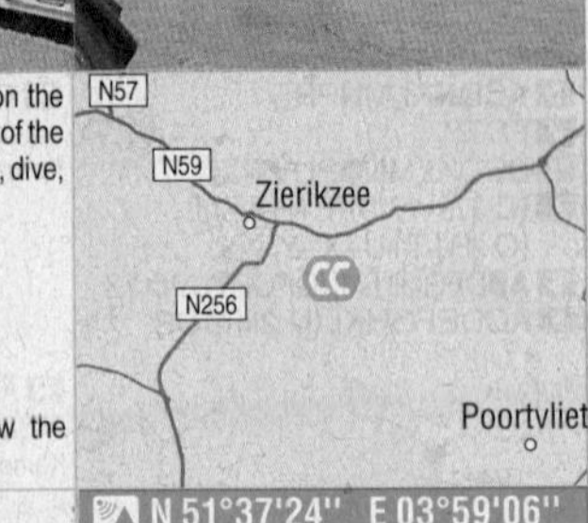

CC € 19 *31/3-7/5 21/5-4/7 23/8-21/10* ***7=6, 14=12, 21=18***

N 51°37'24'' E 03°59'06''

Renesse, NL-4325 CP / Zeeland

145

Molecaten Park Wijde Blick*****
Lagezoom 23
+31 1 11 46 88 88
22/3 - 1/11
wijdeblick@molecaten.nl

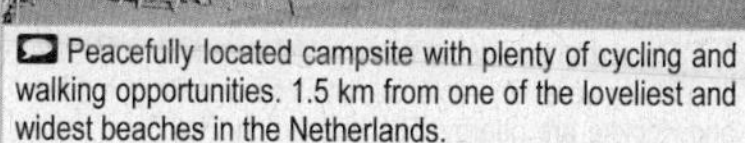

8ha 218**T**(90-120m²) 10-16A CEE

1 ACD**I**KLMNOPQRS
2 JSTY
3 CHKMP**Q**SU
4 (F+H+Q+S+T+U+X)
5 **AB**EFGIJKLMNOP**T**UWXYZ
6 ACDEFGHKL(N 1,5km) O**P**STV

Peacefully located campsite with plenty of cycling and walking opportunities. 1.5 km from one of the loveliest and widest beaches in the Netherlands.

From before Renesse continue on route R106. Signposted from here.

CC € 27 *22/3-25/4 13/5-16/5 21/5-28/5 3/6-26/6 1/7-11/7 30/8-30/10*

N 51°43'07'' E 03°46'05''

Retranchement/Cadzand, NL-4525 LW / Zeeland

146

Camping Cassandria-Bad***
Strengweg 4
+31 1 17 39 23 00
29/3 - 31/10
info@cassandriabad.nl

5,5ha 88**T**(80-100m²) 10A CEE

1 AD**H**KLMNOPQRS
2 SWXYZ
3 ACD**G**KMNPSUW
4 (Q+T+U+Z)
5 **AB**CDFGHIJMNPUWXY
6 ABCDEFGH**K**(N 1,7km) OPSV

Campsite in rural area with personal attention. Sheltered pitches, well-maintained toilet facilities. 100% wifi for small fee. Starting point for walks and cycling trips through the dunes. Sluis, Damme and Bruges are easily reached by bike.

Via Terneuzen (toll) as far as Schoondijke, then dir. Oostburg to Cadzand and Retranchement. Turn right and follow signs. Or N49 Antwerpen-Knokke exit Sluis. Left after 1 km (Retranchement). Through village then turn left and follow signs.

CC € 23 *29/3-8/5 12/5-16/5 20/5-8/7 25/8-30/10*

N 51°21'57'' E 03°23'11''

Retranchement/Cadzand, NL-4525 LW / Zeeland

147

Camping Den Molinshoeve***
Strengweg 2
+31 1 17 39 16 74
29/3 - 13/10
info@molinshoeve.nl

5,2ha 39**T**(160-190m²) 10A CEE

1 AD**I**KLMNRS
2 NSWXY
3 AC**G**HKSU**W**
4 (Q 1/7-31/8)
5 **AB**DFGHIJKLMNOPQ**T**UWXYZ
6 ABCDEFGHK(N 1,5km)P

Charming cp at Zeeland farm. Heated luxury toilet facilities. Spacious pitches, free wifi. Bicycles can be stored inside. Pitches with panoramic view of the polder at an additional charge in off-season. Near beach. Many walking/cycling possibilities. Good base for trips over the border.

Terneuzen (toll) up to Schoondijke. dir Cadzand. Retranchement, turn right. Follow signs. Or N49 Antwerpen-Knokke, Sluis. Left after 1 km to Retranchement. Through village, turn left.

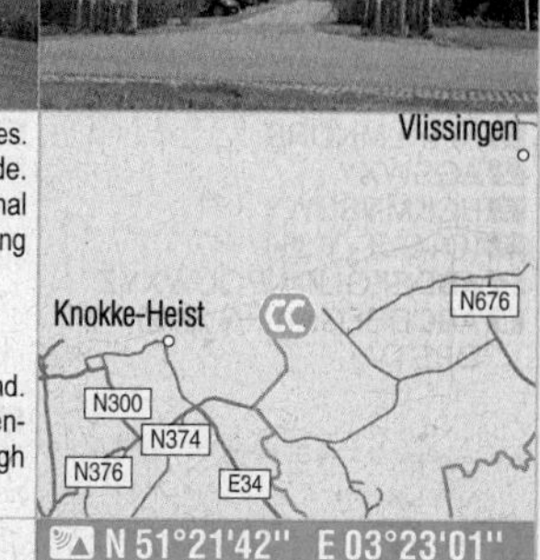

CC € 23 *29/3-8/5 12/5-17/5 20/5-6/7 25/8-13/10*

N 51°21'42'' E 03°23'01''

Sluis, NL-4524 LA / Zeeland

148

- Camping De Meidoorn***
- Hoogstraat 68
- +31 1 17 46 16 62
- 29/3 - 13/10
- info@campingdemeidoornsluis.nl

5,5ha 95T(80-120m²) 6A CEE

- 1 AD**I**KLMNOQ**R**S
- 2 JSWYZ
- 3 CHK**O**PSU
- 4 (U+V+Z)
- 5 **AB**DFGIJKLMOPUW
- 6 ACDEFGHK(N 0,5km)OPTV

Situated on the edge of the beautiful town of Sluis, between the old city walls. Characteristic cities such as Bruges, Ghent and Knokke are nearby. The beach and 'Het Zwin' nature reserve are just a few kilometres away. There is a choice of different tours in the West Zeeuws-Vlaanderen region for cyclists and walkers.

Campsite entrance via the Zuiddijkstraat. Enter no. 102 in the GPS. First Hoogstraat, turn into Sint Pieterstraat and turn left onto the Zuiddijkstraat.

CC € 23 *29/3-27/4 21/5-29/5 3/6-4/7 2/9-13/10*

N 51°18'45'' E 03°23'33''

St. Kruis/Oostburg, NL-4528 KG / Zeeland

149

- Camping Bonte Hoeve****
- Eiland 4
- +31 1 17 45 22 70
- 29/3 - 20/10
- info@bontehoeve.nl

9ha 50T(100-130m²) 10A CEE

- 1 AD**H**KLMNOQRS
- 2 JSWYZ
- 3 CD**G**HKPSUW
- 4 (Q)(R+T+Z 1/7-31/8)
- 5 **AB**FGI**JK**L**M**N**P**UWXYZ
- 6 ADEFGHK(N 3km)OPSTV

Enjoy peace, space and freedom. A lively family campsite with bar and snack bar with playground on terrace. Spacious pitches, separated by hedges, with 10A, water and TV connection, wireless internet. Excellent private bathroom possible with typical Zealandic design. Golf course and beach close by. Great cycling. Near Bruges and Ghent, plenty of opportunities for trips. Ideal base for a varied holiday in Zeelandic Flanders.

Located on the road Oostburg-St.Margriete (B).

CC € 25 *29/3-8/5 18/5-5/7 24/8-20/10*

N 51°18'06'' E 03°30'35''

Vrouwenpolder, NL-4354 NN / Zeeland

150

- Camping De Zandput***
- Vroondijk 9
- +31 1 18 59 72 10
- 22/3 - 3/11
- info@roompot.nl

12ha 238T(70-110m²) 10-16A CEE

- 1 AF**I**KLMNORS
- 2 AGSWXY
- 3 BCKMNSUWY
- 4 (Q+S+T+Y)
- 5 **AB**DEFGIJMNPQUWXYZ
- 6 ABCDEFGHKL(N 2km) OPSTV

Enjoy the peace, space and freedom to the full. A friendly family campsite with a bar, snackbar and playground by the terrace. The ideal base for a holiday with variety at Walcheren.

Motorway A58 Bergen op Zoom-Vlissingen, take exit Middelburg, Oostkapelle-Vrouwenpolder. In the village there are signs to the campsite.

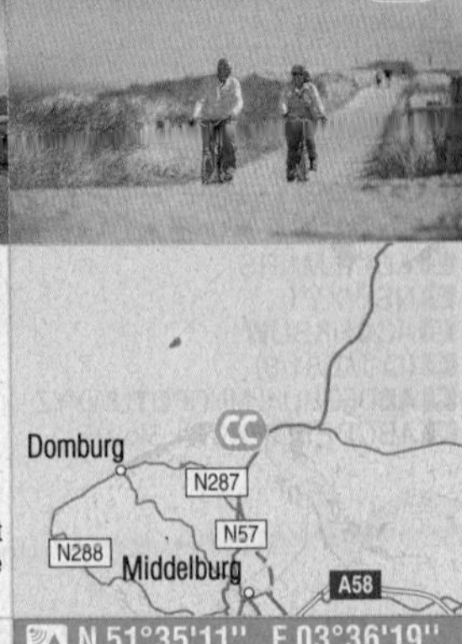

CC € 19 *12/4-25/4 13/5-17/5 21/5-29/5 3/6-28/6 2/9-3/11*

N 51°35'11'' E 03°36'19''

Doorn, NL-3941 ZK / Utrecht

151

RCN het Grote Bos****
Hydeparklaan 24
+31 8 50 40 07 00
29/3 - 3/11
reserveringen@rcn.nl

80ha 350**T**(75-150m²) 10A CEE

1 ACDF**I**KLMNOPQRUV
2 BIJSTUWXYZ
3 C**G**HIKLMN**O**P**Q**S**T**U
4 (**A**+C+H)IJM
(Q+S+T+U+V+X+Y+Z)
5 **AB**CDEFGHIJKLMNOPQR**T**U
WXYZ
6 ABCDEFGHKL(N 1,5km)
OSTV

A complete holiday resort, with attractive fields or real woodland pitches, in a beautiful nature reserve on the southern edge of the Utrechtse Heuvelrug (Utrecht Hill Ridge).

A12 Utrecht-Arnhem, exit Driebergen. Enter village and follow signs. Campsite located in the Doorn-Driebergen-Maarn triangle.

CC € 21 *29/3-7/5 13/5-16/5 21/5-4/7 26/8-3/11*

N 52°03'22'' E 05°18'49''

Doorn, NL-3941 XR / Utrecht

152

Vakantiepark De Maarnse Berg***
Maarnse Bergweg 1
+31 3 43 44 12 84
29/3 - 29/9
info@maarnseberg.nl

20ha 75**T**(100-225m²) 16A CEE

1 ADEFGKLMNOQ**R**UV
2 BISWXYZ
3 ABC**G**HIKLP**R**STUZ
4 (Q 8/5-31/8)(X+Y+Z)
5 **AB**CDGHIJKLMNPQUWXYZ
6 ABCDEFGHKL(N 2,5km)OP

Wonderfully located campsite in the woods of Utrechtse Heuvelrug National Park. The campsite has natural swimming water with a beach, miniature golf, restaurant, bread service (high season) and various playing options. Many cycling and walking opportunities.

Campsite sign on the A12 from Utrecht at Maarn/Doorn exit, twice to the right under the exit. A12 from Arnhem, exit Maarsbergen. Through centre of Maarn. Follow the signs on the N227.

CC € 23 *29/3-8/5 21/5-1/7 19/8-29/9*

N 52°03'48'' E 05°21'06''

Leersum, NL-3956 KD / Utrecht

153

Molecaten Park Landgoed Ginkelduin****
Scherpenzeelseweg 53
+31 3 43 48 99 99
22/3 - 1/11
landgoedginkelduin@molecaten.nl

95ha 220**T**(80-110m²) 10A CEE

1 ACDEFGKLMNOPQRS
2 BISTWXYZ
3 ABCDE**G**HIJKLMNOP**QR**S**T**U
4 (A 1/5-31/5,1/7-31/8)
(C 15/5-15/9)(F+H)**JKLN**
(Q+S+T+U+X+Y+Z)
5 **AB**CDEFGHIJKLMNOPQR**T**U
WXYZ
6 ABCDEFGH**K**M(N 3km)
OPSTVX

Situated in the middle of the Utrechtse Heuvelrug National Park; close to 'the quietest spot in the Netherlands'. Spacious camping fields with comfort (plus) pitches are encircled by beautiful trees. The campsite offers an indoor swimming pool, outdoor pool, tennis courts, restaurant, shop and bike hire. There are several lovely walking and cycle routes to be enjoyed close by.

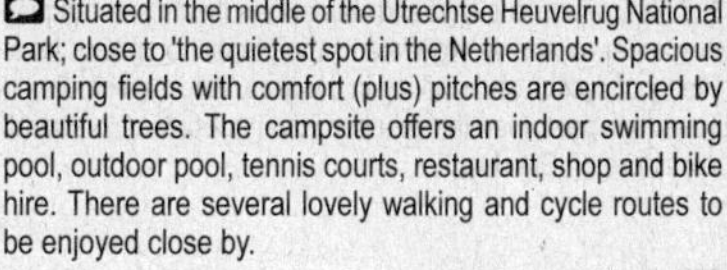

N225. In the centre of the town of Leersum signs are posted near the church.

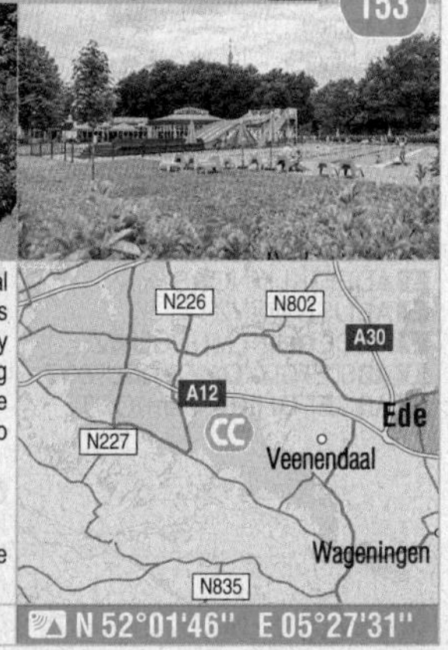

CC € 21 *22/3-25/4 6/5-8/5 13/5-16/5 21/5-11/7 30/8-30/10*

N 52°01'46'' E 05°27'31''

Renswoude, NL-3927 CJ / Utrecht

154

Camping de Grebbelinie***
Ubbeschoterweg 12
+31 3 18 59 10 73
28/3 - 1/10
info@campingdegrebbelinie.nl

6,5ha 135**T**(105-140m²) 6-10A CEE

1 AD**I**JKLMNO**R**TU
2 AEINSXY
3 ACEHIJKMNSUZ
4 (Q+R 🔑)
5 **AB**CDEFGIJMNOPQR**T**UWXY
6 ABCDEFGHK(N 2km)PST

De Grebbelinie is a unique campsite centrally located in the Netherlands between the Utrechtse Heuvelrug and the Veluwe. On the Grebbelinie (defence line) with Fort Daatselaar. Various walking and cycling routes start from the camp site through varied countryside.

From the A30 Scherpenzeel exit. Straight ahead at roundabout dir. Renswoude (follow camping signs). From the A12 exit 23 Renswoude/Veenendaal. Follow signs to Renswoude. Then follow camping signs.

€23 *28/3-25/4 22/5-9/7 26/8-30/9*

N 52°05'05'' E 05°33'04''

Woerden, NL-3443 AP / Utrecht

155

Camping Batenstein***
van Helvoortlaan 36
+31 3 48 42 13 20
1/4 - 31/10
info@camping-batenstein.nl

1,6ha 40**T**(60-100m²) 6A CEE

1 ACD**I**KLNP**R**TU
2 ISVWXY
3 BCHIKS**TVW**
4 **(F+H** 🔑**)IJN**(Q 27/3-25/10)
5 **AB**EFGI**J**K**L**MNO**P**UWYZ
6 ACDEFG**K**(N 1,5km)O**P**

A pleasant campsite in green surroundings on the edge of Woerden. Excellent, well maintained sanitary facilities. The whole site is surrounded by water. There is a modern leisure pool and fitness centre right next to the site.

On the A2 you follow exit 5 towards Kockengen. Then, the N212 to Woerden. In Woerden, the campsite is signposted. Or A12, exit 14, then follow signposts.

€23 *1/4-8/5 21/5-6/7 26/8-1/10*

N 52°05'34'' E 04°53'06''

Woudenberg, NL-3931 MK / Utrecht

156

Camping 't Boerenerf
De Heygraeff 15
+31 3 32 86 14 24
28/3 - 28/9
info@campingboerenerf.nl

4,5ha 50**T**(80-100m²) 6-16A CEE

1 ADEF**I**KLMNO**R**S
2 AEIJSUWXYZ
3 ABCE**G**HIKLMNPSU**W**Z
5 **AB**CDEFGI**J**K**L**MNO**PQR**UWXYZ
6 ABCEFGH**K**(N 3km)OPT

An environment, child and animal friendly site and camping farm near extensive woods and the Henschotermeer lake. Plenty of cycling and walking in the area. Rucksack route on Tuesdays past open farmhouses is very popular. No arrival/departure on Sunday.

A28 exit 5, Maarn-Amersfoort Zuid; A12, exit Maarn-Doorn towards Amersfoort. N224 in the direction of Woudenberg; turn right at the 1st road, Henschotermeer. Turn left after 50 metres and then turn right immediately.

€19 *28/3-8/5 21/5-6/7 24/8-28/9*

N 52°04'51'' E 05°23'12''

Woudenberg, NL-3931 ML / Utrecht

157

Vakantiepark De Heigraaf****
De Heygraeff 9
+31 3 32 86 50 66
27/3 - 2/11
info@heigraaf.nl

16ha 250**T**(100-250m²) 4-16A CEE

1 ADEFGKLMN**R**S
2 AEIJOSWXYZ
3 ABCDE**G**HIKLMNP**Q**SU**W**Z
4 M(Q 1/4-28/9)(S 1/4-29/8) (T 30/3-24/9)(U) (Y 24/4-30/8)
5 **AB**CDEFGHIJKLMNO**PQRT**U WXYZ
6 ABCDEFGH**K**LM(N 2,5km) O**P**ST

Beautiful holiday park on the Utrechtse Heuvelrug/Gelderse Valley. Perfect for cycling, woods, heathland, meadows. 150m from the Henschoten (swimming) lake. Spacious touring pitches and (early and late) seasonal pitches. English double-decker bus serving snacks, 'Eeterij' (Eatery), supermarket. Entertainment programme, play equipment, bouncy castles. Plenty of atmosphere. No arrival on Sunday.

Via the A12 or A28, exit Maarn, then indicated.

CC € 21 *27/3-26/4 21/5-12/7 29/8-2/11*

N 52°04'47'' E 05°22'54''

Biddinghuizen, NL-8256 RZ / Flevoland

158

Molecaten Park Flevostrand****
Strandweg 1
+31 3 20 28 84 80
22/3 - 1/11
flevostrand@molecaten.nl

49ha 392**T**(80-120m²) 10-20A CEE

1 ABCD**I**KLMNOPQRS
2 AEIJNSTWXY
3 ABCD**G**HIKMN**O**P**R**SU**W**Z
4 (A 1/4-31/8) (C 27/4-1/9)(**F**+H) IJ(Q+S+T 1/4-31/10) (U+V 1/7-31/8)(Y+Z)
5 **AB**DEFGIJK**L**MNOPQRUWXYZ
6 ABCEFGH**K**(N 3,5km) OPSTV

Located on the shores of lake Veluwemeer. An excellent location for watersports enthusiasts. Many cycling and walking opportunities in the surrounding area. Camping Flevostrand has spacious camping pitches by the water or behind the dikes. Activity complex including a restaurant and bar, indoor swimming pool, supermarket and boat and bike hire.

A28 exit 13, direction Lelystad. Follow Walibi signs. Located between the N306 and the Veluwemeer. Signposted.

CC € 21 *22/3-25/4 6/5-8/5 13/5-16/5 21/5-28/5 3/6-11/7 30/8-30/10*

N 52°23'07'' E 05°37'45''

Dronten, NL-8251 PX / Flevoland

159

Camping De Ruimte***
Stobbenweg 23
+31 3 21 31 64 42
22/3 - 29/9
info@campingderuimte.nl

6ha 94**T**(80-120m²) 6A CEE

1 AD**I**KLMNOPQRS
2 BSTWXYZ
3 A**G**IKMNPSU
4 (H 1/7-31/8)M (Q+R+T+U+V+Y+Z)
5 **AB**CDEFGHIJKLMNOPQRUWXYZ
6 ACDEFGK(N 7km)OPV

De Ruimte is a natural campsite with atmosphere in the middle of a wood. There are quiet pitches hidden away in the trees but also pitches on fields with playground equipment. Excellent amenities, also for disabled people. The site is located close to the Veluwe lake with its fine beaches. The lovely towns of Kampen and Elburg are within cycling distance.

A28 exit 16, past Elburg to Dronten. Bridge over Veluwemeer at the traffic lights towards Kampen. Campsite signposted.

CC € 23 *22/3-8/5 13/5-16/5 21/5-9/7 26/8-29/9*

N 52°29'48'' E 05°50'15''

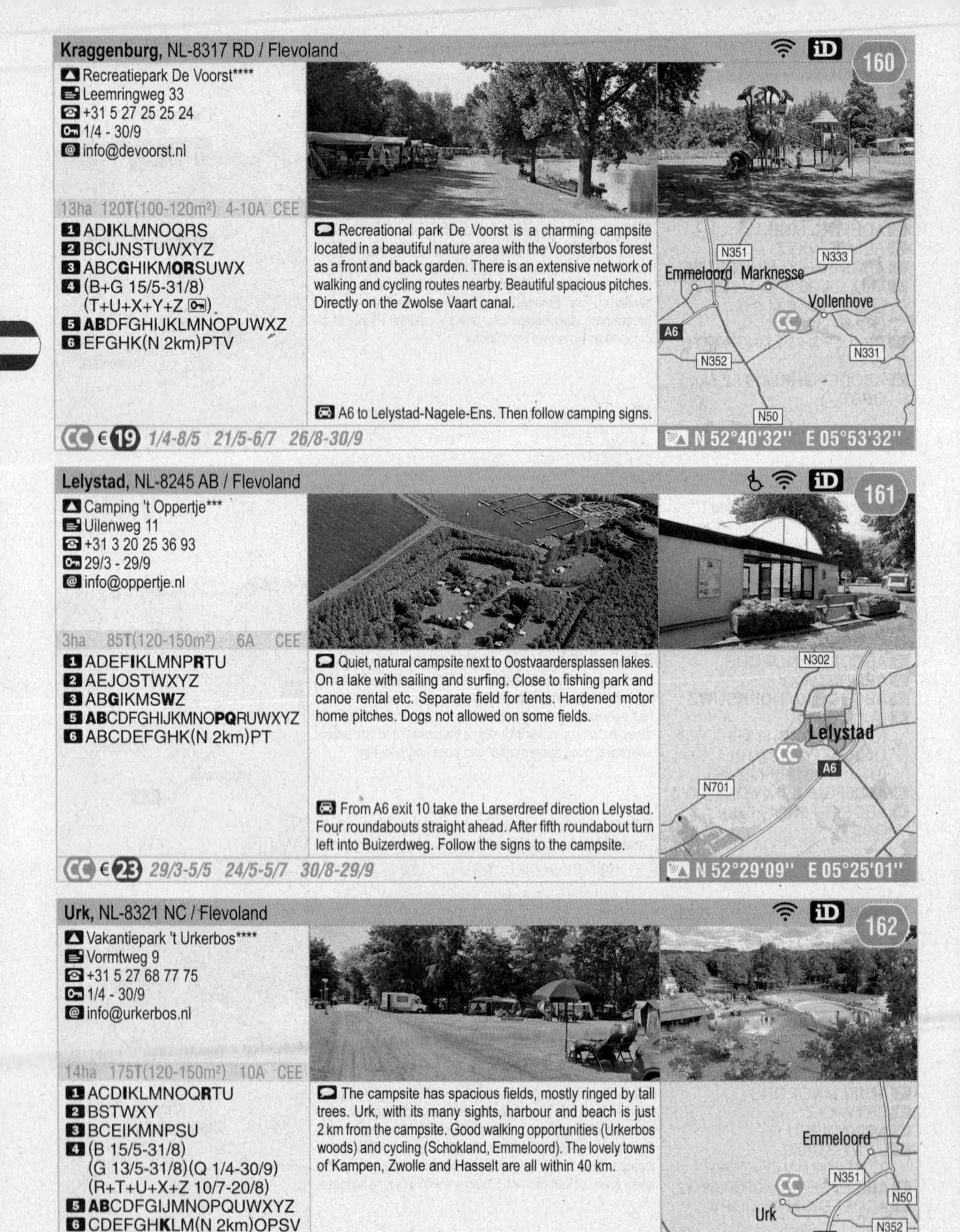

Kraggenburg, NL-8317 RD / Flevoland

160

- Recreatiepark De Voorst****
- Leemringweg 33
- +31 5 27 25 25 24
- 1/4 - 30/9
- info@devoorst.nl

13ha 120T(100-120m²) 4-10A CEE

1. ADIKLMNOQRS
2. BCIJNSTUWXYZ
3. ABCGHIKMORSUWX
4. (B+G 15/5-31/8) (T+U+X+Y+Z)
5. ABDFGHIJKLMNOPUWXZ
6. EFGHK(N 2km)PTV

Recreational park De Voorst is a charming campsite located in a beautiful nature area with the Voorsterbos forest as a front and back garden. There is an extensive network of walking and cycling routes nearby. Beautiful spacious pitches. Directly on the Zwolse Vaart canal.

A6 to Lelystad-Nagele-Ens. Then follow camping signs.

CC € 19 *1/4-8/5 21/5-6/7 26/8-30/9*

N 52°40'32'' E 05°53'32''

Lelystad, NL-8245 AB / Flevoland

161

- Camping 't Oppertje***
- Uilenweg 11
- +31 3 20 25 36 93
- 29/3 - 29/9
- info@oppertje.nl

3ha 85T(120-150m²) 6A CEE

1. ADEFIKLMNPRTU
2. AEJOSTWXYZ
3. ABGIKMSWZ
5. ABCDFGHIJKMNOPQRUWXYZ
6. ABCDEFGHK(N 2km)PT

Quiet, natural campsite next to Oostvaardersplassen lakes. On a lake with sailing and surfing. Close to fishing park and canoe rental etc. Separate field for tents. Hardened motor home pitches. Dogs not allowed on some fields.

From A6 exit 10 take the Larserdreef direction Lelystad. Four roundabouts straight ahead. After fifth roundabout turn left into Buizerdweg. Follow the signs to the campsite.

CC € 23 *29/3-5/5 24/5-5/7 30/8-29/9*

N 52°29'09'' E 05°25'01''

Urk, NL-8321 NC / Flevoland

162

- Vakantiepark 't Urkerbos****
- Vormtweg 9
- +31 5 27 68 77 75
- 1/4 - 30/9
- info@urkerbos.nl

14ha 175T(120-150m²) 10A CEE

1. ACDIKLMNOQRTU
2. BSTWXY
3. BCEIKMNPSU
4. (B 15/5-31/8) (G 13/5-31/8)(Q 1/4-30/9) (R+T+U+X+Z 10/7-20/8)
5. ABCDFGIJMNOPQUWXYZ
6. CDEFGHKLM(N 2km)OPSV

The campsite has spacious fields, mostly ringed by tall trees. Urk, with its many sights, harbour and beach is just 2 km from the campsite. Good walking opportunities (Urkerbos woods) and cycling (Schokland, Emmeloord). The lovely towns of Kampen, Zwolle and Hasselt are all within 40 km.

A6 exit 13 to Urk. Follow road right through Urk, turn left at 3rd roundabout (signposted). Campsite 1.5 km on the right.

CC € 21 *1/4-7/5 21/5-12/7 2/9-30/9*

N 52°40'45'' E 05°36'35''

Zeewolde, NL-3896 LS / Flevoland

163

Camping het Groene Bos***
Groenewoudse Weg 98
+31 3 65 23 63 66
1/4 - 14/10
info@hetgroenebos.nl

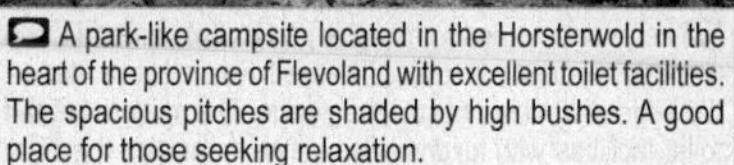

4ha 50T(85-225m²) 6-10A CEE

1 ABCD**I**KLMNQ**R**S
2 BSTWXY
3 BCE**G**HKMNSU
4 (Q 1/7-31/8)(Z)
5 **AB**CDFGHIJKLMNPUWXYZ
6 ACEFGH**K**L(N 4km)PV

A park-like campsite located in the Horsterwold in the heart of the province of Flevoland with excellent toilet facilities. The spacious pitches are shaded by high bushes. A good place for those seeking relaxation.

A28 exit 9 direction Zeewolde. Campsite is located west of Zeewolde and is signposted.

€19 *1/4-3/5 21/5-5/7 2/9-10/10*

N 52°20'24'' E 05°30'20''

Zeewolde, NL-3896 LT / Flevoland

164

RCN Zeewolde****
Dasselaarweg 1
+31 8 50 40 07 00
29/3 - 3/11
reserveringen@rcn.nl

43ha 170T(80-100m²) 10A CEE

1 ACD**I**KLMNOPQRS
2 AENOSTWXY
3 ABCE**G**HIKMNOPSU**W**Z
4 (F+H)M(Q+S+T+U)
(X 27/3-24/10)(Y)
5 **AB**DEFGIJKLMNPUWXYZ
6 CDEFGHKLM(N 1,5km)OPV

A large campsite with separate spacious grounds surrounded by two meters high bushes, located on the Wolderwijd lake area with many leisure activities. Part of the site is beyond the dike on the waterfront. Good toilet facilities.

A28 exit 9, direction Zeewolde. Campsite is on the south side, 1 km outside Zeewolde and is signposted.

€19 *29/3-7/5 13/5-16/5 21/5-9/7 26/8-3/11*

N 52°18'42'' E 05°32'37''

Balkbrug, NL-7707 PK / Overijssel

165

Camping Si Es An****
De Haar 7
+31 5 23 65 65 34
15/3 - 27/10
info@si-es-an.nl

9,5ha 69T(100-120m²) 10-16A CEE

1 ACD**I**KLMNOQRS
2 STXYZ
3 ABC**G**IJKMNPSUW
4 (**A** 1/7-31/8)M**N**
(Q+T+U+V+X+Y+Z)
5 **AB**DFGIJKLMNPQR**T**UWXY
6 ABCDEFGHKL(N 2km)
OPTV

Located in natural area Het Reestdal. A beautiful place for walking and cycling on the border between Overijssel and Drente. Spacious pitches in the middle of nature. Enjoy the tranquility and the space.

In Balkbrug head in direction De Wijk. Then follow the brown campsite signs. Avoid the sandy road!

€21 *15/3-8/5 21/5-6/7 2/9-27/10*

N 52°36'35'' E 06°22'19''

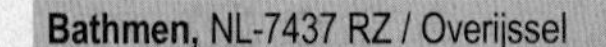

Bathmen, NL-7437 RZ / Overijssel

166

Camping de Flierweide
Traasterdijk 16
+31 5 70 54 14 78
15/3 - 1/11
info@flierweide.nl

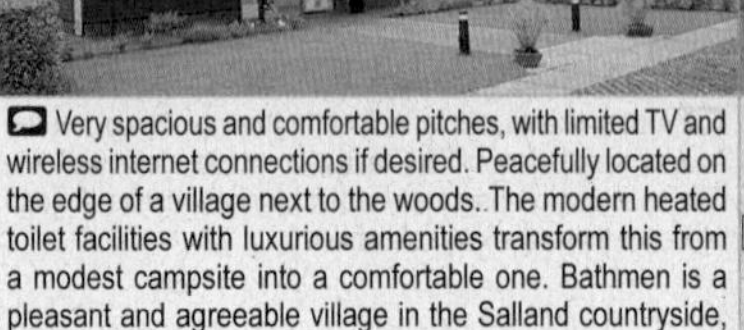

2ha 60**T**(120-140m²) 4-16A CEE

1 A**I**KLMNOP**R**S
2 IJSUVWXYZ
3 AB**G**HIKU
5 **AB**DEFGHIJKLMNPQUWXY
6 ACDEFG**KL**(N 1km)PSV

Very spacious and comfortable pitches, with limited TV and wireless internet connections if desired. Peacefully located on the edge of a village next to the woods. The modern heated toilet facilities with luxurious amenities transform this from a modest campsite into a comfortable one. Bathmen is a pleasant and agreeable village in the Salland countryside, located between Deventer and the Holterberg.

A1 exit 25 Bathmen. Follow camping signs (dir. Flierweide).

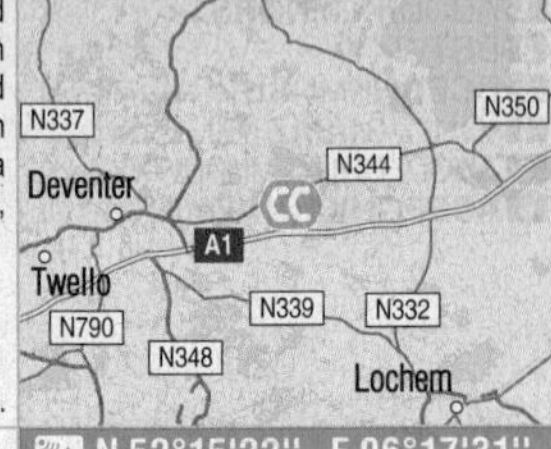

CC € 19 *15/3-8/5 21/5-5/7 2/9-1/11*

N 52°15'22'' E 06°17'31''

Beerze/Ommen, NL-7736 PJ / Overijssel

167

Camping Huttopia De Roos***
Beerzerweg 10
+31 5 23 25 12 34
28/3 - 27/10
deroos@huttopia.com

27ha 211**T**(120-150m²) 6A CEE

1 ACD**H**KLMNP**R**TU
2 ACSTWXYZ
3 AC**G**IKMNPSUWX
4 (A 7/7-26/8)(G)
(Q+S+U+V+X+Z 1/5-1/9)
5 **AB**DEFGHIJKLMNOPUWZ
6 CEFGHJL(N 7km)OPT

Attractive and spacious natural campsite, beautifully situated in a gently sloping landscape of rivers and dunes on the Vecht river. A side arm of the river runs across the playful and child-friendly campsite. The unique location, the beautiful countryside, the spaciousness, the harmonious atmosphere and the great facilities make camping at De Roos a lovely experience.

Left of the route Ommen-Beerze (R103). Next to de Vecht on the southern side.

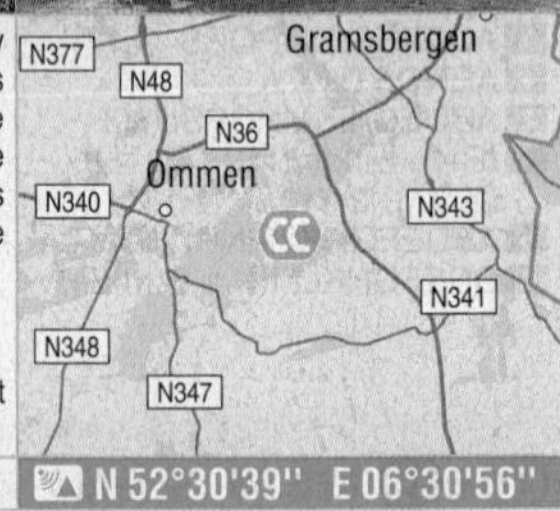

CC € 19 *28/3-26/4 12/5-17/5 20/5-30/6 25/8-27/10*

N 52°30'39'' E 06°30'56''

Belt-Schutsloot, NL-8066 PT / Overijssel

168

Camping Kleine Belterwijde***
Vaste Belterweg 3
+31 3 83 86 67 95
29/3 - 31/10
camping@kleinebelterwijde.nl

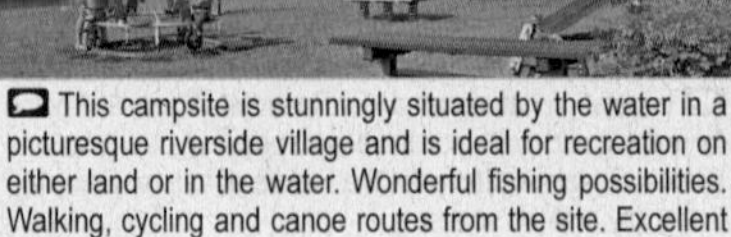

3,5ha 60**T**(70-100m²) 6A CEE

1 AD**I**KLMNOPQ**R**S
2 AFNOSTVWXYZ
3 ACHIKMNOPSUWZ
4 (G)JM(Q+R 29/3-31/10)
(Z 27/4-1/10)
5 **AB**DEFGI**JKL**MNO**P**QRUWXYZ
6 ADEFGKOPT

This campsite is stunningly situated by the water in a picturesque riverside village and is ideal for recreation on either land or in the water. Wonderful fishing possibilities. Walking, cycling and canoe routes from the site. Excellent toilet facilities.

N334 direction Giethoorn exit Belt-Schutsloot. Campsite signposted in village.

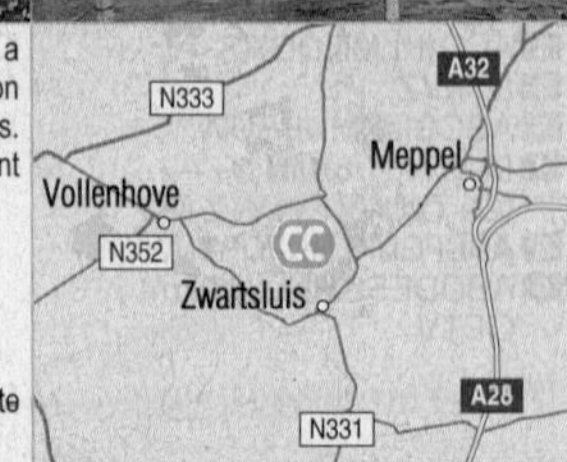

CC € 19 *29/3-3/5 24/5-12/7 2/9-31/10*

N 52°40'15'' E 06°03'38''

Blokzijl, NL-8356 VZ / Overijssel

169

- Watersportcamping 'Tussen de Diepen'***
- Duinigermeerweg 1A
- +31 5 27 29 15 65
- 1/4 - 31/10
- camping@tussendediepen.nl

5,2ha 60**T**(60-80m²) 10A CEE

1 ACD**I**KLMNOPQ**R**S
2 CNSWXY
3 AIKMNPSUW
4 (C 1/5-15/9) (Q+T+U+V+X+Y+Z)
5 **AB**CFGIJKLMNO**P**UWZ
6 ABCDEFGHKL(N 1km)OPV

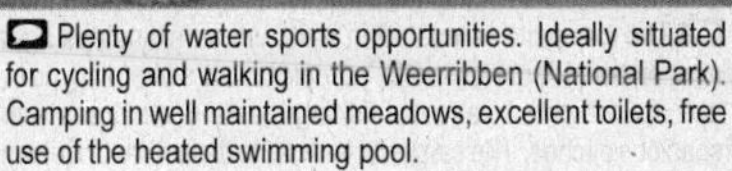

Plenty of water sports opportunities. Ideally situated for cycling and walking in the Weerribben (National Park). Camping in well maintained meadows, excellent toilets, free use of the heated swimming pool.

From Zwolle direction Hasselt-Zwartsluis-Vollenhove. Right along the sea wall at the roundabout to Blokzijl. Follow the camping signs.

CC € 25 *1/4-2/5 22/5-12/7 29/8-31/10*

N 52°43'44'' E 05°58'13''

Dalfsen, NL-7722 KG / Overijssel

170

- Camping Starnbosch***
- Sterrebosweg 4
- +31 5 29 43 15 71
- 1/1 - 31/12
- info@starnbosch.nl

8ha 248**T**(100-140m²) 6-10A CEE

1 ADIKLMNOPQRS
2 BSWXYZ
3 ACKMNPSU
4 (C+E+H 1/4-1/11)**N** (Q+R+S+T+U+Y+Z)
5 **AB**CDEFGHI**J**K**L**MNO**PQ**R**T**U WXYZ
6 ACDEFGHJ**K**M(N 4,5km) OTV

Starnbosch campsite is set among villas, country estates and castles and is the greenest campsite in the Vecht valley. A really hospitable site, noted for its relaxed and peaceful atmosphere, where people of all ages can enjoy their holiday.

A28 Zwolle-Meppel-Hoogeveen, exit 21 Dalfsen (N340). Follow the signs.

CC € 21 *1/5-16/5 22/5-25/5 30/5-6/7 28/8-31/12*

N 52°28'31'' E 06°15'47''

De Lutte, NL-7587 LH / Overijssel

171

- Landgoedcamping Het Meuleman***
- Lutterzandweg 16A
- +31 5 41 55 12 89
- 29/3 - 30/9
- info@camping-meuleman.nl

7ha 111**T**(100-300m²) 6-10A CEE

1 AD**I**KLMNPQRTU
2 ABEILTYZ
3 AB**G**HIJKLM**R**SUZ
4 (A+Q+U+X+Y)
5 **AB**DEFGIJKLMNOPQRUWXZ
6 ABEFJL(N 3km)OP

The campsite is an ideal base for cycle and walking tours in the surprisingly beautiful Twente region. Where the river Dinkel meanders through the landscape, on the estate 'Het Meuleman', you will find this camping with recreation pond. There are unique, green pitches almost all with partial shade on sandy soil. Here you will experience peace, space and nature.

A1 Hengelo-Oldenzaal exit De Lutte. Drive through De Lutte towards Beuningen, and follow the signs to the campsite.

CC € 23 *29/3-8/5 21/5-5/7 2/9-30/9*

N 52°20'01'' E 07°01'46''

Delden, NL-7491 DZ / Overijssel

172

Park Camping Mooi Delden***
De Mors 6
+31 7 43 76 19 22
29/3 - 1/11
info@mooidelden.nl

3ha 85**T**(100-130m²) 10A CEE

1 ADIKLMNORS
2 ISTWXYZ
3 AE**FG**IKOP**R**SU**V**W
4 (C+H 1/5-15/9)J**KLN** (Q+R+T+U+V+Z)
5 **AB**DEFGIJKLMNOPQRUWXYZ
6 ACEFGHK(N 1km)PV

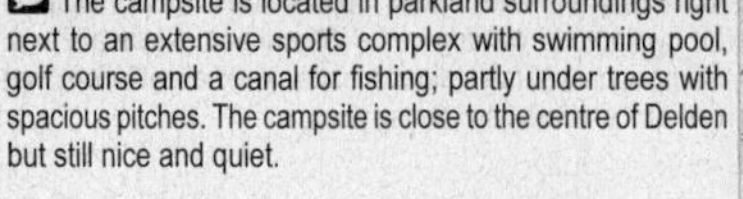

The campsite is located in parkland surroundings right next to an extensive sports complex with swimming pool, golf course and a canal for fishing; partly under trees with spacious pitches. The campsite is close to the centre of Delden but still nice and quiet.

The campsite is clearly signposted in and around Delden. Follow the signs.

CC € 21 *29/3-8/5 21/5-5/7 1/9-31/10*

N 52°15'16'' E 06°43'37''

Denekamp, NL-7591 NH / Overijssel

173

Papillon Country Resort*****
Kanaalweg 30
+31 5 41 35 16 70
22/3 - 27/10
info@papilloncountryresort.com

16,5ha 143**T**(110-140m²) 6-10A CEE

1 ACD**I**KLMNOPQRU
2 AEOSTWXYZ
3 ABCDE**G**HIKLMNPSUVWZ
4 (**A**+E+H)JM (Q+R+T+U+V+X+Y+Z)
5 **AB**CDEFGIJKLMNPQR**T**UWXYZ
6 ABCDEFGHKL(N 1,5km)OP STUVX

Situated in the cosy Twente, you'll find Papillon Country Resort close to Germany. This 5-star location is wonderfully situated in the nature and offers a lot of peace and quiet and space for nature lovers. The camping spots are spacious and some of them are situated at the cosy fishpond. Furthermore, the sanitary building is heated and luxuriously furnished and you can enjoy a delicious meal or a drink in the restaurant.

Follow the signs on the road N342 Denekamp-Nordhorn.

CC € 23 *2/4-26/4 29/4-8/5 1/6-5/7 30/8-27/10*

N 52°23'32'' E 07°02'55''

Diffelen/Hardenberg, NL-7795 DA / Overijssel

174

Camping de Vechtvallei****
Rheezerweg 76
+31 5 23 25 18 00
1/4 - 30/10
info@devechtvallei.nl

7,8ha 51**T**(100-120m²) 16A CEE

1 ADIKLMN**RS**
2 JSTWXYZ
3 ABCIJKLMNPSU
4 (A+E)(G 1/5-30/8) (Q+S+T+U+V+X+Z)
5 **AB**DEFGI**J**K**L**MNO**PT**UWXYZ
6 ABCEFGH**K**L(N 4,5km)OPV

The campsite is located in a wooded surroundigs and is quietly situated in the midst of nature. The facilities are good and from the campsite you can make nice bike and walking tours. Nice fishing possibilities at the campsite. Electric bicycles for rent on request. Indoor heated swimming pool.

Hardenberg-Rheeze. Through Rheeze, direction Diffelen On left of road after about 2 km.

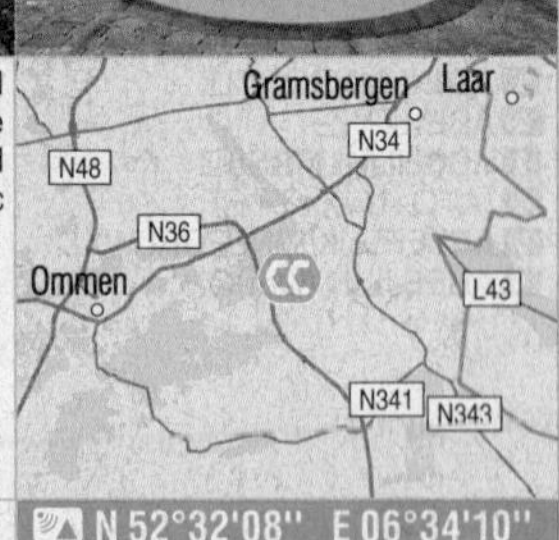

CC € 19 *1/4-25/4 21/5-1/7 31/8-30/10*

N 52°32'08'' E 06°34'10''

Haaksbergen (Twente), NL-7481 VP / Overijssel

175

Camping Scholtenhagen B.V.***
Scholtenhagenweg 30
+31 5 35 72 23 84
22/3 - 1/11
campingscholtenhagen@planet.nl

9,3ha 80T(100-110m²) 10A CEE

1 ACDIKLMNOQRS
2 ISTWXY
3 ABCGHIKMNOPSUW
4 (F+H)IJ
(Q+T+U+X 15/7-26/8)(Z)
5 ABDFGIJMNOPQTUWXYZ
6 ACDEFGK(N 1,5km)OPSUV

Relax in inviting surroundings for walking and/or cycling. The subtropical swimming pool 'De Wilder' is next to the campsite. It has an 80-metre slide, sunbathing area and sunbed. You have free entry with a ticket from the campsite.

From the north: N18 exit Haaksbergen, from the south N18 exit Haaksbergen-Zuid. Then follow the campsite signs or sign to 'Zwembad De Wilder'.

CC €21

N 52°08'53'' E 06°43'23''

Hardenberg/Heemserveen, NL-7796 HT / Overijssel

176

Ardoer vakantiepark 't Rheezerwold*****
Larixweg 7
+31 5 23 26 45 95
29/3 - 30/9
rheezerwold@ardoer.com

11ha 110T(100-175m²) 8-10A CEE

1 ADIKLMNRTU
2 BSTWXYZ
3 ABCHKLMNOPSUW
4 (C 1/5-1/9)(F+H)JN
(Q+R+T+U+V+X+Y)
5 ABDEFGIJKLMNOPQRTUWXYZ
6 ABCDEFGHKL(N 4km)
OSTUV

The campsite is located in a natural area and is peacefully situated amid the greenery. The toilet facilities are modern. There is a lovely indoor swimming pool with a Finnish sauna, infrared sauna, an outdoor pool, play equipment on all fields, etc. Furthermore, there is a multifunctional sports square with an interactive football wall, panna field and tennis court, etc.

N343 exit Hardenberg/Slagharen, follow Slagharen and campsite signs, then turn left.

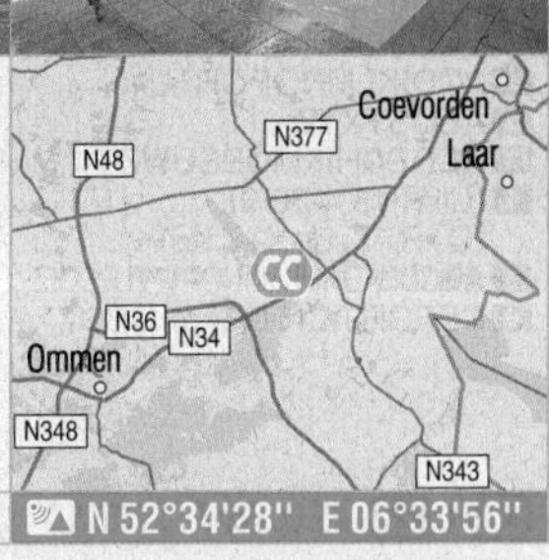

CC €19 *29/3-25/4 21/5-5/7 26/8-30/9*

N 52°34'28'' E 06°33'56''

Holten, NL-7451 HL / Overijssel

177

Ardoer camping De Holterberg****
Reebokkenweg 8
+31 5 48 36 15 24
1/3 - 3/11
holterberg@ardoer.com

6,5ha 125T(80-140m²) 6-16A CEE

1 ADIKLMNORS
2 BISUWXYZ
3 ABCDEHIKLMNPSU
4 (C+H 26/4-6/9)(Q 25/4-6/9)
(R)(T+U+Y+Z 29/3-15/9)
5 ABDEFGIJKLMNOPQRTUWXYZ
6 ACEFGHK(N 1km)OPV

Campsite against the southern slope of the Holterberg, the hilliest part of the 'Sallandse Heuvelrug' Nature Reserve. You can choose from fields, avenues and spacious, demarcated pitches around fields with many play and sports opportunities. Good toilet facilities and a tasty restaurant guarantee that you will want to stay for longer.

A1 Deventer-Hengelo, exit Holten. Just before Holten take the dir of Rijssen (Rd 350). Camping signs before you reach the roundabout.

CC €23 *1/3-25/4 21/5-5/7 2/9-3/11*

N 52°17'31'' E 06°26'06''

Holten, NL-7451 RG / Overijssel

178

Camping Ideaal
Schreursweg 5
+31 5 48 36 17 25
1/4 - 1/10
info@campingideaal.nl

2ha 50T(100-150m²) 6A CEE

1 ADGKLNRS
2 IJNSUVWXYZ
3 AHIKSU
5 **AB**EFGIJKLMNO**PQ**UWZ
6 ACDEFGK(N 0,3km)T

This small-scale campsite is in an undulating patchwork landscape within walking distance of Holten village. The spacious, bordered pitches are in sunny or shaded spots. Jeu de boules is played every evening. So, plenty of rest and relaxation. The campsite has a separate spacious motorhome site next to the campsite, with separate entrance with barrier.

On the A1 take exit 27 towards Holten then the 2nd exit on the right. The campsite is signposted.

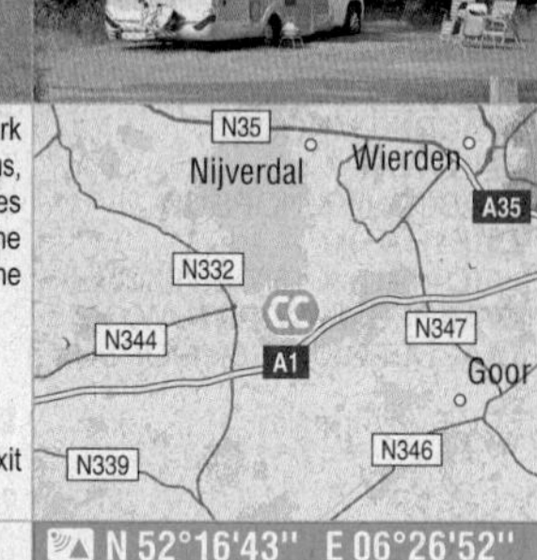

CC € 17 *1/4-8/5 21/5-5/7 26/8-1/10*

N 52°16'43'' E 06°26'52''

Lemelerveld, NL-8151 PP / Overijssel

179

Charmecamping Heidepark****
Verbindingsweg 2a
+31 5 72 37 15 25
29/3 - 1/10
info@campingheidepark.nl

5,5ha 100T(100-200m²) 6-10A CEE

1 ACD**I**KLMNOPQRTU
2 AEIJSTXYZ
3 BCDE**G**HIKM**O**PSU**WZ**
4 (C+H 15/4-30/9)
(Q+R+T+U+X+Z)
5 **AB**CDEFGHIJKLMNO**PQT**UWXYZ
6 CEFGHJ**K**(N 0,5km)OPST

Friendly family parkland campsite in wooded surroundings located in the Vecht valley on the border between the regions Salland and Twente. Play equipment in all fields. Child-friendly and traffic free.

A28 Amersfoort-Zwolle, exit 18 Zwolle-Zuid. Then N35 towards Almelo/Heino. At Raalte go towards Ommen. Exit Lemelerveld. Coming from the north, the campsite is located along the Hoogeveen-Raalte Road. Exit Lemelerveld.

CC € 23 *29/3-26/4 22/5-5/7 2/9-30/9*

N 52°26'26'' E 06°20'51''

Mander/Ootmarsum, NL-7663 TD / Overijssel

180

Camping Dal van de Mosbeek****
Uelserweg 153
+31 5 41 68 06 44
28/3 - 30/9
receptie@dalvandemosbeek.nl

6ha 128T(160-200m²) 10-16A CEE

1 AD**I**KLMNOPQRS
2 STWXY
3 ABCEHIKLPSU
4 (Q+T+Z)
5 **AB**CDEFGHIJKLMNO**PQ**RUWXYZ
6 ACEFGKL(N 1km)PSV

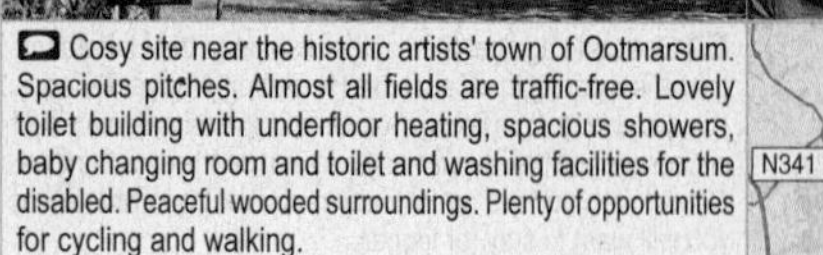

Cosy site near the historic artists' town of Ootmarsum. Spacious pitches. Almost all fields are traffic-free. Lovely toilet building with underfloor heating, spacious showers, baby changing room and toilet and washing facilities for the disabled. Peaceful wooded surroundings. Plenty of opportunities for cycling and walking.

A1 exit Almelo. Towards Tubbergen. Direction Uelsen. On Uelserweg 153, entrance Plasdijk to get to campsite.

CC € 23 *2/4-8/5 21/5-12/7 30/8-30/9*

N 52°26'40'' E 06°49'25''

Markelo, NL-7475 ST / Overijssel

181

Camping De Bovenberg***
Bovenbergweg 14
+31 5 47 36 17 81
29/3 - 7/10
info@debovenberg.nl

4,5ha 77T(100-200m²) 10A CEE

1 ADIKLMNOPRS
2 AEISTUWXYZ
3 ACDEHIKLPSUZ
4 (Q+R+T+V)
5 ABCDFGHIJKLMNOPQUWXYZ
6 ACDEFGHKL(N 4km)OPTV

De Bovenberg is located at the foot of the Friezenberg in rolling countryside, surrounded by fields, woods, heathland and historic burial mounds. You will camp on spacious, marked out pitches on a grassy field. The young landscaping means there are many sunny pitches. The new toilet building offers all modern comfort.

A1 Apeldoorn-Hengelo, exit 27. In Markelo take direction Rijssen, campsite signposted on the left before the roundabout about 3 km outside Markelo.

CC € 21 *29/3-27/4 21/5-6/7 31/8-7/10*

N 52°15'56" E 06°31'13"

Nieuw-Heeten, NL-8112 AE / Overijssel

182

Vakantiepark Sallandshoeve****
Holterweg 85
+31 5 72 32 13 42
23/3 - 15/10
info@sallandshoeve.nl

3ha 67T(100-150m²) 10A CEE

1 ACDHKLNRS
2 ISUWXY
3 ACIKMNPRSTU
4 (F)M
(Q+R+T+U+V+X+Y+Z)
5 ABDFGHIJMNOPUWXY
6 DEFGK(N 6km)PST

You will camp around a lake on spacious, bordered pitches. Most are sunny pitches, but there's shade towards the edge of the site. The campsite is located in an area a bit like a stage setting, bordering on the Sallandse Heuvelrug. Extensive walking and cycling options.

A1 motorway exit Holten, N332 direction Raalte. Turn right after 7 km (signposted).

CC € 23 *23/3-8/5 21/5-5/7 2/9-15/10*

N 52°19'15" E 06°20'35"

Nijverdal, NL-7441 DK / Overijssel

183

Ardoer camping De Noetselerberg*****
Holterweg 116
+31 5 48 61 26 65
28/3 - 3/11
noetselerberg@ardoer.com

11ha 210T(90-110m²) 10-16A CEE

1 ACDEHKLMNPRTU
2 STWXYZ
3 ABCDGIKLMNPSU
4 (B 1/5-1/9)(F+H)JM
(Q+R+T+U+V+Y)
5 ABDEFGIJKLMNOPQRTUWXYZ
6 ABCDEFGHKLM(N 1,5km)
OPRST

Pleasant family campsite, located at the foot of the hills of the 'Sallandse Heuvelrug'. Divided into several fields. Each field has its own play equipment. An attractive site for making the most of your discount card in early and late season. Perfect sanitary.

In Nijverdal follow the road to Rijssen. Follow the signs to campsite.

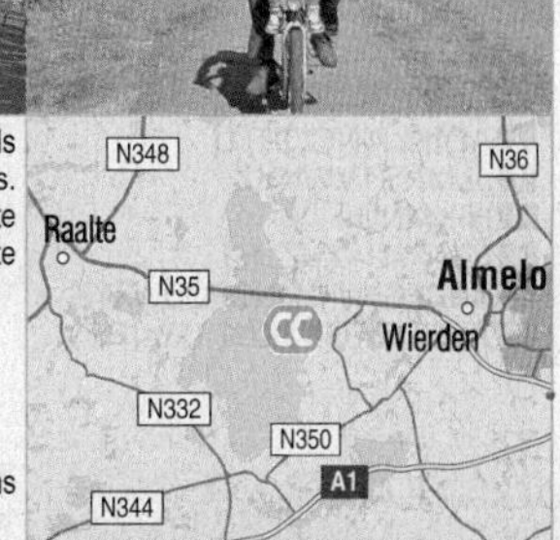

CC € 25 *8/4-19/4 13/5-17/5 21/5-6/7 2/9-18/10*

N 52°21'00" E 06°27'21"

Ommen, NL-7731 RC / Overijssel

184

Resort de Arendshorst****
Arendhorsterweg 3a
+31 5 29 45 32 48
29/3 - 30/9
info@arendshorst.nl

22ha 125T(150-250m²) 6-10A CEE

1 ADIKLMNOQRU
2 ABCISTWXYZ
3 CEGIKLMNPQRSUWX
4 (G 15/6-15/9)
(Q+R+T+U+V+Y+Z)
5 ABDFGIJKLMNOPQRUWXYZ
6 ADEFGK(N 3km)OPTV

Situated on the river Vecht, close to the lively town of Ommen. Spacious pitches on beautifully undulating grounds. Your discount card offers you value-for-money relaxation. CampingCard ACSI holders have a comfort pitch. When reserving (recommended) mention that you will be coming with CampingCard ACSI!

Campsite is signposted along the N340 Ommen-Zwolle. NOTE: take the parallel road.

N377 A28 N48 N36 N340 Ommen Dalfsen N35 N348 Vroomshoop Heino

CC € 21 *29/3-7/5 21/5-15/7 1/9-30/9*

N 52°31'10'' E 06°21'52''

Ootmarsum, NL-7638 PP / Overijssel

185

Camping Bij de Bronnen***
Wittebergweg 16-18
+31 5 41 29 15 70
1/1 - 31/12
info@campingbijdebronnen.nl

8ha 43T(70-120m²) 6A CEE

1 ADHKLMNOQRTU
2 BSTXYZ
3 CEHIKLMOPU
4 (T+U+X+Z)
5 ABCDEFGHIJKLMNOPTUXYZ
6 ABCDEFGHK(N 2,5km)OPV

A campsite located by a wood with attractive grounds and sunny pitches. There is excellent cycling and walking from here through surroundings that are so varied that you will be surprised time after time. Excellent 5 star toilet facilities with underfloor heating and every imaginable comfort make camping here a true delight. Private toilet possible when available.

The campsite is clearly indicated in Ootmarsum. Follow the signs.

Uelsen Neuenhaus N343 Nordhorn N349 Almelo N342

CC € 19 *1/1-8/5 21/5-15/7 2/9-31/12*

N 52°25'29'' E 06°53'23''

Ootmarsum, NL-7631 CJ / Overijssel

186

Camping De Kuiperberg***
Tichelwerk 4
+31 5 41 29 16 24
27/3 - 14/10
info@kuiperberg.nl

4ha 110T(100m²) 16A CEE

1 ADIKLMNOQRTU
2 JLMNSTVWXYZ
3 HIKMNU
4 (Q+T+U+X+Z)
5 ABDFGHIJKLMNOPQUWXYZ
6 ABCDEFGHJK(N 1km)PSV

Small natural site with unobstructed views over the rolling landscape. 700 meters from Ootmarsum. A "city campsite in the countryside". For active adults who want to walk, cycle or just enjoy the tranquility. Extensive and comfortable toilet facilities. No tokens or magnetic cards needed.

On route N349 from Ootmarsum to Almelo the campsite is clearly signposted.

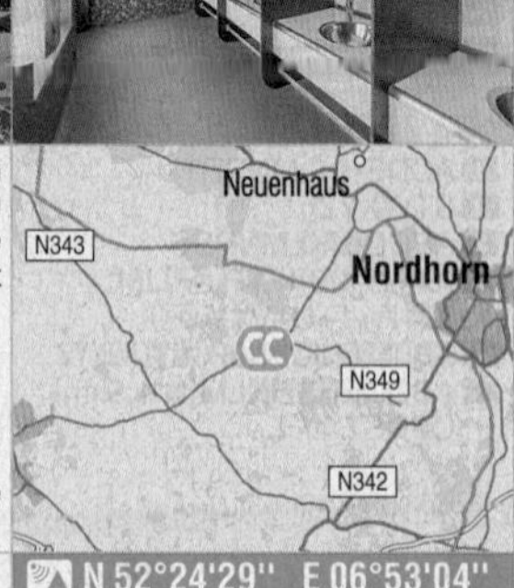

CC € 25 *2/4-26/4 29/4-7/5 23/5-21/6 5/9-14/10*

N 52°24'29'' E 06°53'04''

Ootmarsum, NL-7637 PM / Overijssel

187

- Camping De Witte Berg*****
- Wittebergweg 9
- +31 5 41 29 16 05
- 27/3 - 29/9
- info@dewitteberg.nl

6,5ha 141T(100-140m²) 6-10A CEE

1 AD**I**KLMNO**RU**
2 ABEOSTVWXYZ
3 ABCDHIKMNP**RST**WZ
4 (C+E+H)M (Q+R 27/3-29/9)(T+X+Y)
5 **AB**CDEFGI**JKL**O**PQ**R**T**UWXYZ
6 ABCEFGHKL(N 2,5km)OPX

This welcoming family campsite is situated on the edge of a beautiful nature reserve. You can enjoy the most delicious dishes in the restaurant, and the luxurious toilet facilities and the free wifi will make your stay a real pleasure.

Campsite well signposted in Ootmarsum. Follow the signs.

Uelsen, Neuenhaus, N343, Nordhorn, N349, N342

CC € 23 *27/3-8/5 21/5-5/7 23/8-29/9*

N 52°25'25'' E 06°53'35''

Ootmarsum/Agelo, NL-7636 PL / Overijssel

188

- Camping De Haer****
- Rossummerstraat 22
- +31 5 41 29 18 47
- 29/3 - 1/10
- info@dehaer.nl

5,5ha 130T(100-140m²) 6-10A CEE

1 AD**I**KLMNOQRS
2 BIJSTVWXYZ
3 ACIKMNPSU
4 (B 9/5-1/9)(Q+T+U+X+Z)
5 **AB**CDEFGHI**JKL**MNO**P**UWXY
6 ACDEFGK(N 1,5km)OPVX

The campsite is close to the attractive little town of Ootmarsum. Modern toilets with sepkey. Not for young single people. The surroundings are beautiful and suitable for walking and cycling. Television with digitenne (for rent). The campsite has existed for over 30 years and the young generation is enthusiastically working to make it even better for campers.

The campsite is located on the Ootmarsum to Oldenzaal road and is well signposted.

N343, Nordhorn, N349, N342, A30, Oldenzaal, A1, L42

CC € 21 *29/3-8/5 21/5-5/7 2/9-1/10*

N 52°23'25'' E 06°54'06''

Ootmarsum/Hezingen, NL-7662 PH / Overijssel

189

- Camping Hoeve Springendal***
- Brunninkhuisweg 3
- +31 5 41 29 15 30
- 29/3 - 1/11, 22/12 - 31/12
- info@hoevespringendal.nl

3ha 58T(120-200m²) 10A CEE

1 AD**I**KLMNOPQRS
2 BCNSTVWXYZ
3 AEHIKLMNUW
4 (**A**+Q+Z)
5 **AB**DFGI**J**MNO**PQ**RUWXYZ
6 ABEFGHKL(N 4,5km)PSV

A wonderfully quiet campsite located in the pretty Twente countryside. Close to a lovely stream, far away from the outside world. The site is run by an enthusiastic family who are there to help the camping guests with anything they need. Excellent walking and cycling options and also riding on horseback or with a wagon. Guided horse-drawn-carriage ride on Sundays.

Campsite well signposted in Ootmarsum, follow the signs.

CC € 25 *29/3-8/5 13/5-17/5 21/5-12/7 29/8-1/11 22/12-31/12*

N 52°26'30'' E 06°53'38''

Reutum, NL-7667 RR / Overijssel

190

Camping De Weuste****
Oldenzaalseweg 163
+31 5 41 66 21 59
29/3 - 30/9
info@deweuste.nl

9,5ha 91T(100-180m²) 10A CEE

1 ADIKLMNOQRTU
2 CIJSTWXYZ
3 ACE**G**HIJKMNPQSTUW
4 (C+H 1/5-15/9) (Q+R+T+U+X+Z)
5 **AB**CDEFGIJKLMNOPQRUWXYZ
6 ABCEFGHK(N 1,5km)PSV

Spacious comfort pitches with 10A electricity, luxury (children's) toilets, heated outdoor pool with free sun loungers, beautiful surroundings with various walking and cycle routes. Pure enjoyment for young and old at this friendly family campsite in the beautiful region of Twente. The restaurant is open at weekends in early and late season.

Campsite located on the N343 Oldenzaal-Tubbergen. Well signposted.

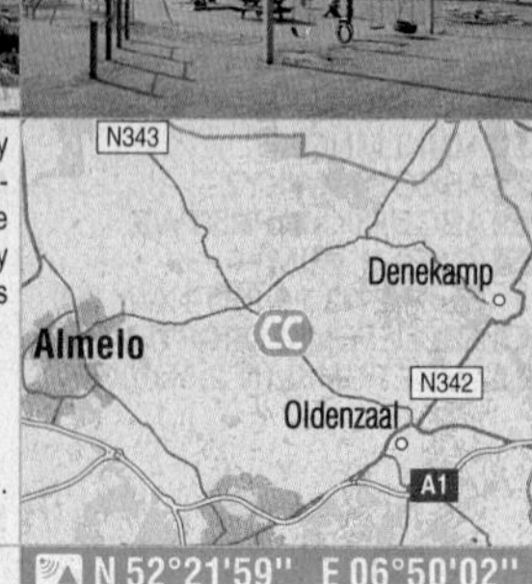

CC € 17 *29/3-5/7 1/9-29/9*

N 52°21'59'' E 06°50'02''

Reutum/Weerselo, NL-7667 RS / Overijssel

191

Camping De Molenhof*****
Kleijsenweg 7
+31 5 41 66 11 65
22/3 - 29/9
info@demolenhof.nl

16ha 500T(100-130m²) 10A CEE

1 ADIKLMNOPQRS
2 IJSTWXYZ
3 ABCD**G**IKMP**R**SUW
4 (C 27/4-1/9) (E 22/3-29/9)(H)IJM (Q+S+T+U+V+W+Z)
5 **AB**DEFGIJKLMNOPQRUWXYZ
6 BCEFGHKLM(N 1km) OPRSV

Large campsite run by a family. The site is well-designed and very spaciously appointed. It stands out for its excellent, very modern toilet facilities. Beautiful water plaza with swimming pools with water slide, separate toddler's pool, outdoor pool and play equipment. New PlonsPlas pond is a place for children to play with water and sand; they'll love it!

The site is signposted in Weerselo. It is on the road Weerselo-Tubbergen.

N343 N349 Denekamp Almelo N342 Oldenzaal A1 N734

CC € 21 *22/3-28/3 2/4-27/4 13/5-17/5 21/5-29/5 3/6-13/7 31/8-29/9*

N 52°21'57'' E 06°50'37''

St. Jansklooster, NL-8326 BG / Overijssel

192

Kampeer- & Chaletpark Heetveld
Heetveld 1
+31 5 27 24 62 43
1/4 - 30/9
info@campingheetveld.nl

5ha 51T(140-150m²) 6A CEE

1 ADIKLMNOPQRTU
2 JSUWXYZ
3 IKMN
4 (Q+U)(X 1/4-30/9)
5 **AB**CDGHI**J**LMNOPUWXYZ
6 ABEFG**K**(N 1,5km)PT

At the top of Overijssel, in the Weerribben-Wieden National Park, close to St. Jansklooster and the village of Heetveld. You can relax here in natural surroundings. All facilities are here to make your stay as enjoyable as possible.

On N331 Zwartsluis-Vollenhove direction St. Jansklooster when in Barsbook. Campsite in Heetveld indicated with blue signs.

CC € 17 *1/4-6/5 25/5-6/7 23/8-30/9*

N 52°40'05'' E 06°00'48''

Tubbergen, NL-7651 KP / Overijssel

193

Ardoer recreatiepark Kaps****
Tibsweg 2
+31 5 46 62 13 78
29/3 - 30/9
kaps@ardoer.com

10ha 89**T**(100-120m²) 6-10A CEE

1 AD**H**KLMNOPQRTU
2 STWXYZ
3 ACD**F**IKMNPSUW
4 (C+H 25/4-15/9)
(Q+R+T+U+X+Y+Z)
5 **AB**DFGIJKLMNPQRUWXYZ
6 ACEFGHKL(N 1,5km)OPS

This well-run campsite is located in the beautiful region of Twente. It offers a personal touch, well-maintained amenities, peace and quiet. There is excellent walking and cycling; free routes are available at reception.

Signposted from the Tubbergen ring road (N343). Follow campsite signs.

CC € 21 *29/3-27/4 21/5-13/7 30/8-30/9*

N 52°24'36" E 06°48'19"

Vollenhove, NL-8325 PP / Overijssel

194

Ardoer vakantiepark ´t Akkertien****
Noordwal 3
+31 5 27 24 13 78
1/1 - 31/12
akkertien@ardoer.com

11ha 150**T**(100-140m²) 6-10A CEE

1 AD**I**KLMNOQRTU
2 CJNSVWXY
3 ABCDEIKM**O**PRSUWX
4 (B)(E+H 1/4-30/9)J**N**
(Q+R)(T 26/3-30/9)(Z)
5 **AB**CDEFGHIJKLMNOPQRUWXYZ
6 ACDEFGHKL(N 0,8km)
OPSV

A friendly family campsite located near the Wieden and Weerribben nature reserves. Perfect for cyclists and walkers. Fishing and swimming opportunities. Spacious pitches and excellent toilet facilities. Within walking distance of the historic town of Vollenhove.

N331 direction Vollenhove then follow the signs. Do not go through the centre of Vollenhove.

CC € 19 *1/4-8/5 21/5-15/7 1/9-30/9*

N 52°40'32" E 05°56'22"

Zwolle, NL-8034 PJ / Overijssel

195

Molecaten Park De Agnietenberg***
Haersterveerweg 27
+31 3 84 53 15 30
22/3 - 1/10
deagnietenberg@molecaten.nl

14ha 63**T**(80-100m²) 10A CEE

1 ACD**I**KLMNPQRS
2 ABCEIOSWXYZ
3 AC**G**IKMPSU**W**XZ
4 (Q+T)
5 **AB**DFGIJKLMNOPUWXYZ
6 ACDEFGH**K**(N 3km)OSV

Family campsite located in a natural area on the outskirts of Zwolle. Plenty of opportunities for walking, cycling and water recreation.

A28 direction Leeuwarden/Groningen, below Zwolle-Noord exit turn right, then directly left. After 400 metres turn left at the traffic lights, and follow the road.

CC € 19 *22/3-25/4 6/5-8/5 13/5-16/5 21/5-11/7 30/8-30/9*

N 52°32'13" E 06°07'47"

Akkrum, NL-8491 CJ / Friesland

196

Camping Drijfveer***
Ulbe Twijnstrawei 31
+31 5 66 65 27 89
29/3 - 1/11
info@drijfveer.nl

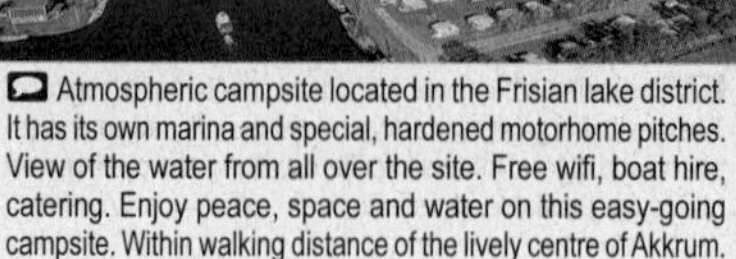

2,5ha 80**T**(72-100m²) 10A CEE

1 ADI**K**LMNOPQ**R**TU
2 CFIOSVXY
3 ACK**O**SUWXZ
4 (Q+Z 1/5-30/9)
5 **AB**DFGHIJKLMNOPQUWYZ
6 BCDEFGHKL(N 0,5km)PT

Atmospheric campsite located in the Frisian lake district. It has its own marina and special, hardened motorhome pitches. View of the water from all over the site. Free wifi, boat hire, catering. Enjoy peace, space and water on this easy-going campsite. Within walking distance of the lively centre of Akkrum.

Exit Akkrum from A32. Dir. Akkrum Oost. Follow signs 'Jachthaven Tusken de Marren'.

CC € 23 *29/3-7/5 21/5-4/6 10/6-5/7 2/9-31/10*

N 53°02'54'' E 05°49'33''

Anjum, NL-9133 DV / Friesland

197

Camping Landal Esonstad****
Skanserweí 28
+31 5 19 32 95 55
29/3 - 28/10
esonstad@landal.nl

5ha 129**T**(100-120m²) 16A CEE

1 BCD**I**KLMNOQRS
2 ACEJNOSVW
3 ABCD**F**HIJKMNOPSU**W**Z
4 (**A** 2/7-1/9)(F+H)KLMN (Q+S+T+U+V+X+Y+Z)
5 **A**BCDEFGHIJKLMNOP**T**UWXYZ
6 ACDEFGHKL(N 0,3km)PX

On the edge of Het Lauwersmeer National Park you will be camping right by the water. You can make use of the facilities of the bungalow park. Day trips out to Dokkum, Pieterburen and Schiermonnikoog.

From Leeuwarden N355 Dokkum direction Lauwersoog N361.

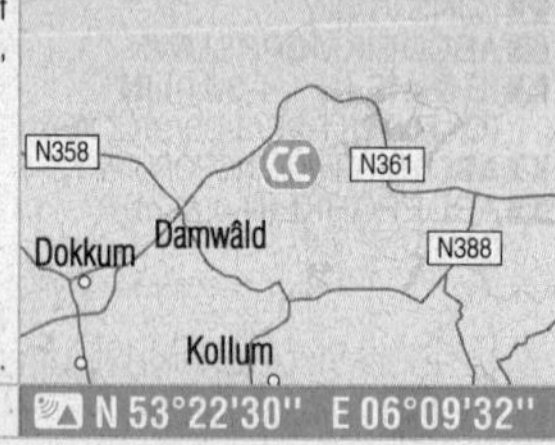

CC € 23 *29/3-29/3 5/4-26/4 24/5-5/7 30/8-28/10*

N 53°22'30'' E 06°09'32''

Appelscha, NL-8426 GK / Friesland

198

RCN de Roggeberg****
De Roggeberg 1
+31 8 50 40 07 00
29/3 - 3/11
reserveringen@rcn.nl

69ha 325**T**(100-120m²) 10A CEE

1 ACD**I**KLMNOPQRUV
2 BISTWXYZ
3 ABCD**G**HIKMN**O**P**R**SU
4 (A)(C+G 1/5-1/9)J (Q+R+T+U+X+Y+Z)
5 **AB**DEFGIJKLMNOPQR**T**UWXYZ
6 CDEFGHJ**K**LM(N 2,5km) OPSTUV

A well laid out campsite with spacious pitches in very attractive natural surroundings. Plenty of walking and cycling opportunities in the extensive Drents-Friese Wold national park.

This campsite is clearly signposted from the N381 near Appelscha.

N919
Oosterwolde
N373
N351
N381
N371
Beilen
N350
N855
A28

CC € 19 *29/3-7/5 13/5-16/5 21/5-9/7 26/8-3/11*

N 52°56'18'' E 06°20'30''

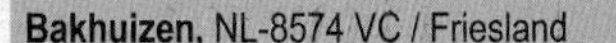

Bakhuizen, NL-8574 VC / Friesland

199

- Camping De Wite Burch***
- Wite Burch 7
- +31 5 14 58 13 82
- 15/3 - 31/10
- info@witeburch.nl

10ha 60**T**(80-100m²) 10A CEE

- **1** AD**I**JKLMNOQ**R**TU
- **2** STWXYZ
- **3** ACDE**G**KMNPSU
- **4** (Q+R+T+X+Z)
- **5** **AB**DEFGHI**J**MNO**P**UWXYZ
- **6** ACEFG**K**(N 0,6km)O**P**SV

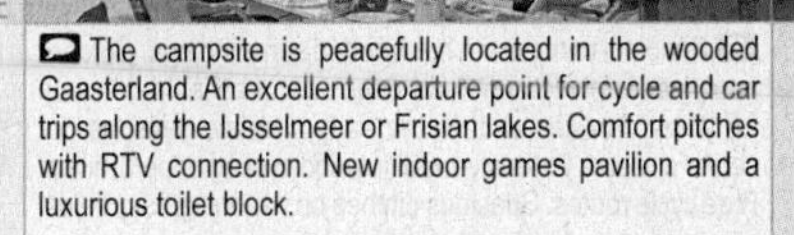

The campsite is peacefully located in the wooded Gaasterland. An excellent departure point for cycle and car trips along the IJsselmeer or Frisian lakes. Comfort pitches with RTV connection. New indoor games pavilion and a luxurious toilet block.

From Lemmer N359 direction Koudum. Exit Rijs to the left. Towards Bakhuizen at crossroads, follow camping signs. Campsite outside the village on the north side.

N359 · Tjerkgaast · CC

CC € 21 *15/3-8/5 21/5-5/7 26/8-31/10*

N 52°52'18'' E 05°28'08''

Bakkeveen, NL-9243 KA / Friesland

200

- Camping De Ikeleane****
- Duerswâldmerwei 19
- +31 5 16 54 12 83
- 1/4 - 30/9
- info@ikeleane.nl

9ha 86**T**(90-100m²) 6-16A CEE

- **1** AD**H**KLMNOPRS
- **2** IJNSTWXY
- **3** ABCDHIKMPSU
- **4** M(Q)(T 1/4-30/9) (U+V+X)(Z 1/4-30/9)
- **5** **AB**CDFGHIJKLMNO**PQRT**UWXYZ
- **6** ACDEFGHK(N 1,5km)OPSV

Peaceful campsite in Southeast Friesland with spacious natural comfort pitches and and a playpond with a beach. Modern luxury toilet facilities and the option to rent private toilet facilities. Excellent cycling possibilities.

From Heerenveen A7 to Drachten. At exit 31 direction Frieschepalen. In Frieschepalen direction Bakkeveen. In Bakkeveen direction Wijnjewoude. Campsite about 1.5 km on the left.

CC € 19 *1/4-7/5 21/5-8/7 26/8-30/9*

N 53°04'16'' E 06°14'34''

Bakkeveen, NL-9243 JZ / Friesland

201

- Camping De Wâldsang****
- Foarwurkerwei 2
- +31 5 16 54 12 55
- 22/3 - 28/10
- info@waldsang.nl

13ha 142**T**(100-120m²) 16A CEE

- **1** AD**I**KLMNOPQRS
- **2** BIJSTWXY
- **3** ABCDEHIKMPSU**V**W
- **4** (Q+T+U+V+X+Z)
- **5** **AB**DFGHIJKLMNOPQRUWXYZ
- **6** ACDEFGKL(N 0,5km) OPSTV

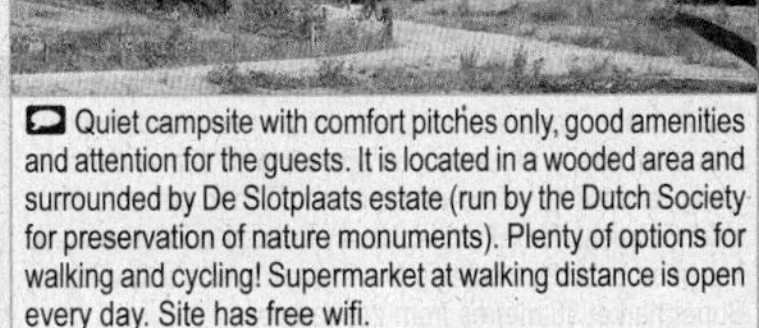

Quiet campsite with comfort pitches only, good amenities and attention for the guests. It is located in a wooded area and surrounded by De Slotplaats estate (run by the Dutch Society for preservation of nature monuments). Plenty of options for walking and cycling! Supermarket at walking distance is open every day. Site has free wifi.

A7 exit 31 (Frieschepalen). In Frieschepalen take direction Bakkeveen. Before Bakkeveen follow De Wâldsang campsite signs.

N369 · N358 · N980 · Leek · Roden · Drachten · A7 · N917 · CC · N381 · N919 · Gorredijk

CC € 25 *22/3-27/4 21/5-8/7 2/9-28/10*

N 53°05'08'' E 06°15'00''

Bakkeveen, NL-9243 KA / Friesland

202

Molecaten Park 't Hout****
Duerswâldmerwei 11
+31 5 16 54 12 87
22/3 - 1/10
thout@molecaten.nl

21,4ha 210T(100-120m²) 10A CEE

1 ADIKLMNPRUV
2 BIJSTWXYZ
3 ACDEIKMPSU
4 (C+H 17/5-1/9)JM (Q+T+U+V+X 29/4-7/5,8/7-3/9)
5 **AB**DEFGI**J**K**L**MNOPQUWXYZ
6 ACDEFGH**K**(N 0,3km) OPSTV

Peaceful campsite in the wooded surroundings. Outdoor pool, indoor playground and large sea of balls. Ideal camp for young families and, in the early and late seasons, for senior citizens. Extensive walking and cycling opportunities. Free cycle routes. Spacious pitches on various grassy fields, surrounded by trees and shrubbery.

A7 junction Oosterwolde, direction Oosterwolde. Exit Wijnjewoude/Bakkeveen. Or A7 Heerenveen-Groningen, exit 31 direction Bakkeveen. Follow signs.

N369 N358 N980 Leek Drachten A7 N917 N381 N919 Gorredijk

CC € 19 *22/3-25/4 6/5-8/5 13/5-16/5 21/5-11/7 30/8-30/9*

N 53°04'44'' E 06°15'11''

Dokkum, NL-9101 XA / Friesland

203

Camping Harddraverspark
Harddraversdijk 1a
+31 5 19 29 44 45
29/3 - 1/11
info@campingdokkum.nl

2,5ha 80T(100-120m²) 4-16A CEE

1 ABDIKLMNOQ**R**S
2 CJSTUVWXYZ
3 ACHIKMN**O**WX
5 **AB**CGI**J**KMNO**P**UWXYZ
6 ACDEFGHK(N 0,4km)OPT

A campsite set in parkland just a stone's throw from the historical town centre of Dokkum, with its ramparts, alleyways and small harbours.

From Leeuwarden direction Dokkum-Oost, follow signs. From Drachten direction Dokkum-Oost. Follow ring road (Lauwersseewei). From Groningen-Zoutkamp via N361 direction Dokkum. Follow the signs.

N357 Dokkum Kollum Buitenpost Bûtenpost N361 N355 N358

CC € 19 *1/4-6/5 21/5-5/7 9/9-31/10*

N 53°19'36'' E 06°00'17''

Franeker, NL-8801 PG / Friesland

204

Recreatiepark Bloemketerp bv***
Burg. J. Dijkstraweg 3
+31 5 17 39 50 99
1/1 - 31/12
info@bloemketerp.nl

5ha 85T(100m²) 10A CEE

1 ACD**I**KLMNOPQ**R**S
2 CIJSVXY
3 AC**D**IKMN**TV**W
4 (**F**+**G**)JN(S+T+U+Y+Z)
5 **AB**DFGI**J**MNO**P**UWXYZ
6 ACDEFGHKL(N 0,1km)PSV

A 4 star campsite and recreation park bordering the Franeker ramparts. Luxurious pitches with connections for water, electricity, waste water, cable TV and internet. Neat toilet facilities. Franeker is centrally located in Friesland and is a good base for visiting other Frysian towns and villages. Supermarket 50 metres from the campsite.

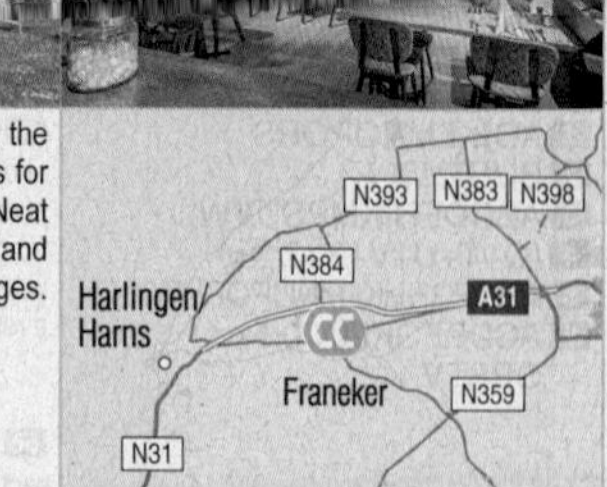

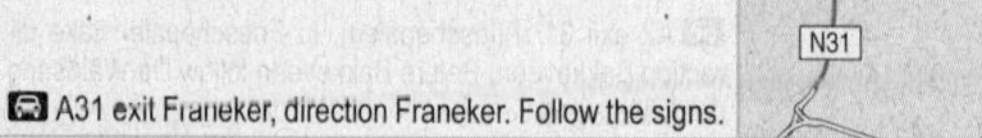

A31 exit Franeker, direction Franeker. Follow the signs.

CC € 21 *1/1-9/5 21/5-8/7 30/8-31/12*

N 53°11'22'' E 05°33'09''

Harlingen, NL-8862 PK / Friesland

205

Camping De Zeehoeve***
Westerzeedijk 45
+31 5 17 41 34 65
25/3 - 31/10
info@zeehoeve.nl

10ha 125**T** 16A CEE

1 ACD**I**KLMNOQ**R**S
2 AGISXY
3 ACKMNPSUWY
4 (Q)(T+U+Y+Z 8/4-30/9)
5 **AB**DFGI**J**K**L**MNO**PQ**RUWXYZ
6 CDEFGHKL(N 1km)OPV

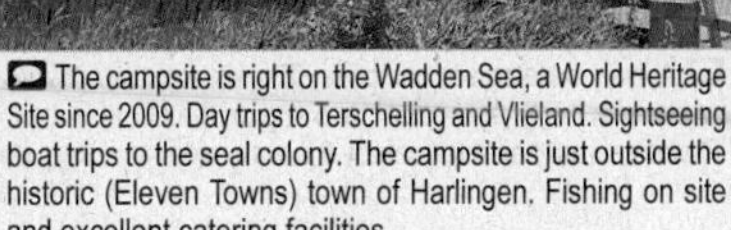

The campsite is right on the Wadden Sea, a World Heritage Site since 2009. Day trips to Terschelling and Vlieland. Sightseeing boat trips to the seal colony. The campsite is just outside the historic (Eleven Towns) town of Harlingen. Fishing on site and excellent catering facilities.

On the N31 Zurich-Harlingen, take Kimswerd exit. 3rd exit on roundabout and follow camping signs. Campsite located about 1 km on the right.

N393 A31 Franeker N384 CC N31 A7

CC € 21 *25/3-29/3 1/4-6/5 21/5-30/5 2/6-5/7 3/9-31/10*

N 53°09'44" E 05°25'01"

Kollum, NL-9291 MP / Friesland

206

Camping Bos en Pingo
Trekweg 9
+31 6 57 92 61 77
26/4 - 1/10
camping@depoelpleats.nl

13ha 127**T**(100-300m²) 6-10A

1 ADEF**I**KLMNOPQ**R**TU
2 BDNSXYZ
3 CEKRSUW
4 (T+Z 6/5-19/5,1/7-31/8)
5 **A**JNPUWXYZ
6 CDEFHJ

Natural recreation at its best. Fishing pond and separate swimming lake at the campsite. Near the village of Kollum.

From Buitenpost towards Lauwersoog, follow signs to Camping Bos en Pingo.

CC € 17 *21/5-1/7 31/8-30/9*

N 53°16'09" E 06°08'08"

Leeuwarden, NL-8926 XE / Friesland

207

Camping De Kleine Wielen***
De Groene Ster 14
+31 5 11 43 16 60
28/3 - 1/10
info@dekleinewielen.nl

15ha 200**T**(80-120m²) 4A CEE

1 ABCD**I**KLMNOQRS
2 AEIJSTWXYZ
3 ABC**F**IKP**R**SUWZ
4 (Q)(R 1/7-31/8)(X+Z)
5 **AB**DEFGIJKLMNOPUWZ
6 ACDEFGHKL(N 2km) OPTVX

Pleasant campsite in Friesland in the middle of nature reserve De Groene Ster, 5 km from the centre of Leeuwarden. The area has many hours' worth of walking and cycling routes. Visit theatre De Harmonie or De Oldehoeve, the leaning tower of Leeuwarden. A wonderful holiday destination for nature lovers, sports enthusiasts, peace seekers and culture spotters.

Along the N355 between Hardegarijp and Leeuwarden. It is sign posted. Exit De Kleine Wielen.

CC € 21 *28/3-30/6 1/9-1/10*

N 53°12'59" E 05°53'18"

Offingawier, NL-8626 GG / Friesland

208

RCN de Potten****
De Potten 2-38
+31 8 50 40 07 00
29/3 - 3/11
reserveringen@rcn.nl

3ha 164**T**(100m²) 10A CEE

1 CD**I**KLMNOPQRS
2 AEISWXY
3 ABCIKMN**O**P**R**SUWZ
4 (Q+R+T+U+Y+Z)
5 **AB**DEFGIJKLMNOPR**T**UWZ
6 ABCDEFGHKL(N 5km) OPTX

A lively watersports campsite. The site has two private marinas on the Sneekermeer lake and on the Grote Potten. The restaurant has a terrace by the waterside.

From the A7 direction Sneek, then follow the N7. Direction Sneekermeer. Follow campsite signs.

CC € 17 *29/3-7/5 13/5-16/5 21/5-29/5 3/6-9/7 26/8-3/11*

N 53°01'47'' E 05°43'28''

Oudega, NL-8614 JD / Friesland

209

Camping De Bearshoeke
Tsjerkewei 2a
+31 5 15 46 98 05
29/3 - 31/10
info@bearshoeke.nl

2ha 45**T**(100m²) 6-16A CEE

1 AD**I**KLMNPQ**R**S
2 AFJNOSWXYZ
3 ACIKMNSU**W**Z
5 **AB**DFGIJKLMNOPRUZ
6 ACDEFGHK(N 0,5km)UV

Attractively landscaped and well-maintained campsite by the water with new toilet and washing facilities (2021). The campsite is centrally located in Southwest Friesland. You can take wonderful cycling trips to the various 'Eleven Cities'. The village of Oudega is a 5-minute walk from the campsite.

Exit 18 from the A6. Follow N354 towards Sneek. Left in Hommerts towards Osingahuizen, follow road to Oudega. Follow camping signs.

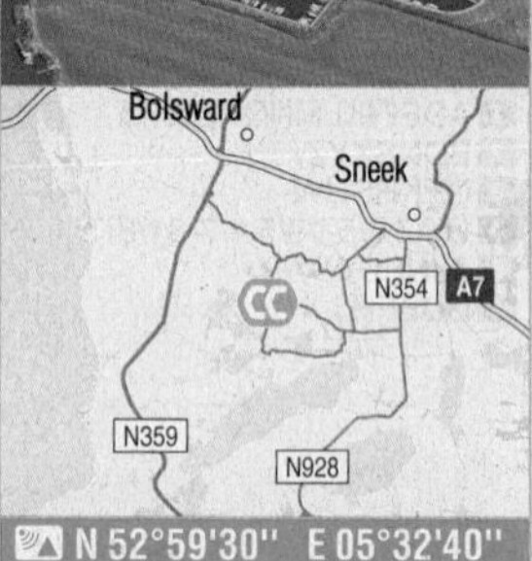

CC € 21 *29/3-8/5 21/5-6/7 1/9-31/10*

N 52°59'30'' E 05°32'40''

Reahûs, NL-8736 JB / Friesland

210

Camping De Finne
Sànleansterdyk 6
+31 5 15 33 12 19
22/3 - 13/10
info@campingdefinne.nl

2ha 50**T**(tot 140m²) 6A CEE

1 ADIKLMNOQRS
2 DIJNSTVWXY
3 ACKMSU**W**X
4 (Q 1/7-28/8)(R)
5 **AB**FGIJKLMNPUWZ
6 ABCDEFHK(N 3km)PV

Campsite De Finne is located 6 km east of Bolsward and about 4 km north of Sneek. The site has a large fishing pier and you can enjoy lovely sailing and cycling. The campsite has well-maintained toilet facilities, a recreation room with basic catering facilities and a terrace. An ideal place for peace and quiet.

From the Sneek roundabout direction Leeuwarden. Roundabout direction Scharnegoutum. Turn right to Wommels/ Oosterend, direction Roodhuis. Follow camping signs.

CC € 21 *22/3-8/5 21/5-8/7 25/8-13/10*

N 53°04'34'' E 05°37'58''

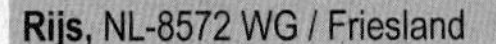

Rijs, NL-8572 WG / Friesland

211

Camping Rijsterbos***
Marderleane 4
+31 5 14 58 12 11
1/4 - 31/10
info@rijsterbos.nl

5ha 50T(100m²) 6-10A CEE

1 ADIKLMNOQRS
2 BIJSTYZ
3 CE**G**MNPSU
4 (C 1/5-1/9)(Q 1/5-30/9) (T+U+V+X+Z 1/5-15/9)
5 **AB**DFGI**J**K**L**MNOPQR**T**UWX
6 ACEFGHK(N 2km)OPSVX

Friendly family campsite located in Gaasterland between the IJsselmeer and the Fluessen. plenty of woodland and water. Ideal base for exploring Friesland on foot. Camping pitches surrounded by trees and bushes. Heated outdoor pool from late May.

A6, exit 17 Lemmer. Lemmer direction Balk. N359 Bolsward, exit Rijs. At the junction in Rijs turn left. The campsite is 100m on the right.

N354
Tjerkgaast
N359
Lemmer

CC € 21 *1/4-8/5 20/5-12/7 1/9-31/10*

N 52°51'44'' E 05°29'58''

Sloten, NL-8556 XC / Friesland

212

Recreatiepark De Jerden***
Lytse Jerden 1
+31 5 14 53 13 89
1/4 - 31/10
info@recreatieparkdejerden.nl

3,5ha 65T(120-150m²) 10-16A CEE

1 ACD**I**KLMNOQ**R**TU
2 CEIJSWXYZ
3 AC**G**HKMNPSUWZ
4 (Q+R)(U+Y 1/6-1/10)
5 **AB**CDFGHI**JKL**MNO**PQ**UWZ
6 ACDEFG**K**L(N 0,45km)OPV

A beautifully located campsite close to Sloten. Peace and privacy are the most important features. The campsite is located next to a waterway and is an excellent starting point for cycling and walking trips. Also an excellent spot for fishing.

From Emmeloord take A6 exit Oosterzee. N354 direction Sneek. At Spannenburg take direction Sloten.

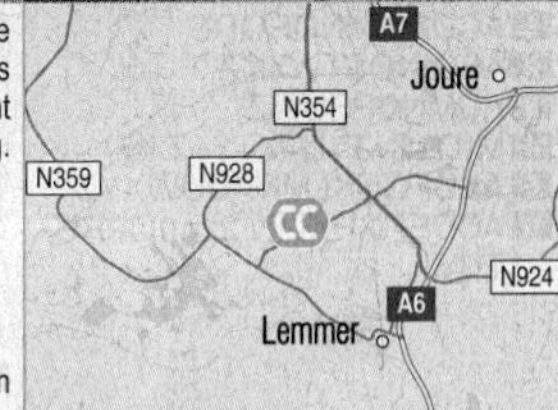

CC € 21 *1/4-8/5 21/5-2/7 8/9-31/10*

N 52°53'58'' E 05°38'32''

St. Nicolaasga, NL-8521 NE / Friesland

213

Landgoed Eysingastate****
Langwarderdijk 4
+31 5 13 43 13 61
29/3 - 31/10
info@eysingastate.nl

6ha 65T(80m²) 10A CEE

1 D**I**KLMNPQRS
2 AESTXY
3 ACE**G**IKMNPSUWZ
4 (Q+X+Z 15/7-18/8)
5 **AB**FGIJKLMNOPUXYZ
6 ACEFGH**K**L(N 1,5km)T

Atmospheric campsite in a green oasis, in the midst of woods, meadows and the Frisian lakes. There's walking, cycling and water sports in the surroundings and you can play golf in St. Nicolaasga. Own harbour with slipway.

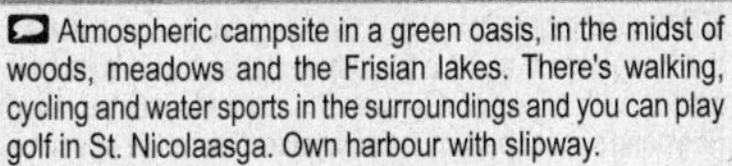

From A6 direction St. Nicolaasga. Through this village direction Joure. Exit direction Langweer. Campsite is located on the right of the road.

CC € 19 *29/3-7/5 22/5-5/7 24/8-31/10*

N 52°56'18'' E 05°45'00''

Witmarsum, NL-8748 DT / Friesland

214

- Camping Mounewetter****
- Mouneplein 1
- +31 5 17 53 19 67
- 1/4 - 13/10
- info@rcmounewetter.nl

4ha 33**T**(100m²) 10A CEE

1. ACD**I**KLMNOQRS
2. CIJSUWXY
3. ACHKMN**O**PSUW
4. (C+G 29/4-2/9)IJ (T+Z 1/6-1/9)
5. **AB**DEFGI**J**K**L**MN**PQ**RUWXYZ
6. ACDEFGI**K**L(N 1km)OPSV

A peaceful, excellently maintained campsite with large pitches sheltered by hedges. The site is situated on the Eleven Towns waterway for use by small boats. The toilet facilities are excellent and the welcome is very warm. Centrally located for discovering Friesland.

From the A7 direction Witmarsum. Follow the signs in the village through the residential area.

Harlingen
N31
CC
A7
Sneek
N359

CC € 21 *1/4-8/5 21/5-12/7 2/9-13/10*

N 53°05'56'' E 05°28'14''

Workum, NL-8711 GX / Friesland

215

- Soal Beach Resort****
- Suderséleane 29
- +31 5 15 54 14 43
- 22/3 - 4/11
- info@soalbeachresort.com

20ha 206**T**(60-100m²) 6-10A CEE

1. ACD**I**KLMNOPQRS
2. AFGINOSTWXYZ
3. ACMN**O**PSUWZ
4. M(Q+S+T+U+X+Y+Z 🔑)
5. **AB**DFGIJKLMN**PQ**UWXYZ
6. ACDEFGHKL(N 2km)O**P**RS TUV

An attractive 4 star campsite located right on the clear waters of the IJsselmeer, just beyond the historic town of Workum. A unique setting for sailing and surfers. Spacious pitches and good sanitary facilities. A superb base for exploring the province of Friesland. Your dog is only allowed to be at the touristic campsite field.

From A6 at Lemmer route N359 direction Balk/Bolsward, exit Workum, follow signs in the area.

Makkum
Bolsward
A7
CC
N359
N928

CC € 21 *22/3-28/3 2/4-8/5 3/6-29/6 31/8-4/11*

N 52°58'08'' E 05°24'52''

Woudsend, NL-8551 NW / Friesland

216

- Aquacamping De Rakken***
- Lynbaen 10
- +31 5 14 59 15 25
- 1/1 - 31/12
- info@derakken.nl

4ha 40**T**(80m²) 6-16A CEE

1. ACD**H**KLMNOPQRS
2. DEIJNSWXYZ
3. CE**G**HKMN**O**PSWZ
4. (**A** 16/7-28/8)
5. **AB**DFGI**J**K**L**MNOPUZ
6. ABCDEFGHIKLM(N 0,3km) PTUW

The campsite is located on the navigation course between the Heegermeer and the Slotermeer lakes and has its own marina with slipway. Woudsend is centrally located amid Friesland's most beautiful countryside. There are spacious pitches in sheltered fields. A good base for exploring Friesland.

A6 Lemmer-Joure, exit Oosterzee, direction Sneek. Exit N354 direction Woudsend. Campsite located at edge of village, signposted.

Sneek
N354
A7
Joure
CC
N928
N924
N359
A6

CC € 21 *1/1-3/5 20/5-29/5 3/6-1/7 1/9-31/12*

N 52°56'46'' E 05°37'40''

Bourtange, NL-9545 VJ / Groningen

217

Camping 't Plathuis***
Bourtangerkanaal Noord 1
+31 5 99 35 43 83
29/3 - 31/10
info@plathuis.nl

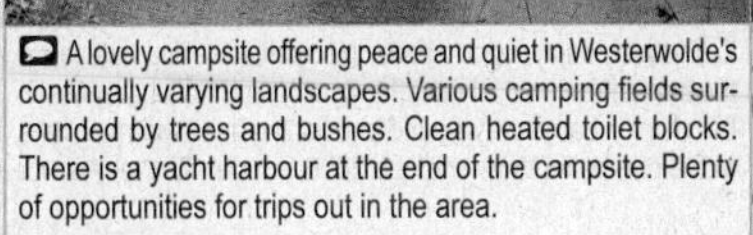

4ha 100**T**(100-150m²) 6-10A CEE

1 AD**I**KLMNOQRS
2 ACEIJSWXYZ
3 A**G**IKMNPSUWZ
4 (Q+T+Z 1/4-31/10)
5 **AB**DFGI**JKL**MNO**PQR**UWXYZ
6 ABCDEFGJ(N 6km)OP

A lovely campsite offering peace and quiet in Westerwolde's continually varying landscapes. Various camping fields surrounded by trees and bushes. Clean heated toilet blocks. There is a yacht harbour at the end of the campsite. Plenty of opportunities for trips out in the area.

Route Zwolle-Hoogeveen-Emmen-Ter Apel-Sellingen-Jipsinghuizen exit Bourtange. Follow the signs. Or autobahn 31 (Germany) exit 17, dir. Bourtange (7 km). Signposted in Bourtange.

CC € 21 *29/3-8/5 21/5-6/7 2/9-31/10* ***7=6***

N 53°00'34'' E 07°10'58''

Kropswolde, NL-9606 PR / Groningen

218

Siblu Camping Meerwijck*****
Strandweg 2
+31 5 98 32 36 59
29/3 - 4/11
meerwijck@siblu.nl

23ha 200**T**(100-120m²) 6A CEE

1 ACD**I**KLMNOQRTU
2 ABFISTVWXY
3 ABC**G**IJKMNPSU**WZ**
4 (F+H+Q+R)(T 29/4-4/9) (U+X+Y)(Z 29/4-4/9)
5 **AB**CDEFGHIJKLMNOPQRUWXYZ
6 BCDEFGHJ**K**L(N 4km) OPSTVX

Camping lies beautifully on the Zuidlaardermeer lake; sandy beach and a wood with play areas. Ideal for families, water sports lovers and fishing, walking and cycling enthusiasts. Meerwijck is a holiday where you can enjoy the countryside, the tranquillity and especially the friendliness.

From Groningen-Winschoten to Groningen-Nieuweschans exit Foxhol, exit 40 over railway, in Kropswolde follow signs. From Assen-Groningen exit Vries/Zuidlaren, exit 35 Hoogezand.

CC € 21 *29/3-8/5 21/5-6/7 1/9-4/11*

N 53°08'59'' E 06°41'35''

Leek, NL-9351 PG / Groningen

219

Landgoedcamping Nienoord***
Midwolderweg 19
+31 5 94 58 08 98
1/4 - 1/10
info@campingnienoord.nl

5,5ha 51**T**(120-140m²) 10A CEE

1 AD**I**KLMNOQRS
2 BIJSTVXYZ
3 ACPS
4 **I**(X+Y)
5 **AB**CDEFGHIJKLMNOPQRUWXYZ
6 CDEFGK(N 1km)OS

Family campsite on the Landgoed Nienoord. You can eat delicious pancakes and à la carte in the pancake farm right next to the campsite. Nienoord offers many possibilities for walking, cycling and entertainment.

A7 exit 34 Leek. Then follow sign posts immediately. Entrance to the campsite is on the dead-end parallel street.

CC € 19 *1/4-26/4 21/5-30/6 2/9-30/9*

N 53°10'17'' E 06°22'56''

Opende, NL-9865 XE / Groningen

220

Camping De Watermolen****
Openderweg 26
+31 5 94 65 91 44
12/4 - 15/9
info@campingdewatermolen.nl

12,5ha 85T(100-125m²) 6-16A CEE

1 ADIKLMNOPQRS
2 ABEINOSTVWXYZ
3 ABCIKMNSUWZ
4 M(Q+R)(T 18/5-30/8) (V 18/5-30/6,6/7-25/8) (X+Z)
5 ABDFGIJKLMNOPQUWXYZ
6 ABCDEFGKL(N 2,5km)PV

Actively enjoy peace, space, the countryside and water amid the beautiful scenic landscape. Cycling and walking routes in the vicinity. Large playground and fishing and swimming lake at the campsite. Winner of the 2016 Gouden Zoover Award.

From the A7 exit 32 Marum/Kornhorn dir Kornhorn. Turn left at the church in Noordwijk. After about 2 km turn into the Openderweg then turn right.

CC € 21 *12/4-7/5 13/5-16/5 21/5-4/7 23/8-15/9*

N 53°09'52'' E 06°13'22''

Sellingen, NL-9551 VT / Groningen

221

Camping De Bronzen Eik***
Zevenmeersveenweg 1
+31 5 99 32 20 06
1/1 - 31/12
info@debronzeneik.nl

4ha 136T(100-130m²) 6-16A CEE

1 ACDIKLMNOQRTU
2 BCSWXY
3 AGIJKLMNPW
4 (Y+Z)
5 ABDEFGIJKLMNPTUWXYZ
6 ABCEFGKLM(N 1km)P

Small-scale site in the wooded Sellingen nature reserve. Sellingen is within walking distance, only 2 km from Germany. Free entry to the heated municipal pool. The excellent De Ruiten Aa restaurant is next to the campsite. Starting point for cycle, mountainbike and walking routes. Footgolf course near the site.

Campsite clearly indicated in Sellingen. Turn left on the Ter Apel-Sellingen road just beyond the village. From Vlagtwedde turn right before the village.

CC € 19 *1/4-8/5 20/5-6/7 2/9-1/11*

N 52°57'16'' E 07°08'17''

Winsum, NL-9951 CG / Groningen

222

Camping Marenland***
Winsumerdiep 6
+31 5 95 44 27 50
1/4 - 30/9
info@marenland.nl

4ha 80T(80-100m²) 10-16A CEE

1 ACDIKLMNOPQRS
2 CJSVXYZ
3 CHIKMOSUWX
4 (C)J(Q+X+Y)
5 ABDEFGIJKLMNOPUWZ
6 BCDEFGHJL(N 0,3km)OPT

Nice, attractive canoe campsite near a municipal swimming pool and 300 m from the lovely village centre. Whisper boat hire. The campsite is located right on the Pieterpad (trail). Luxury restaurant at the campsite. Winsum has been named the most beautiful village in the Netherlands.

N361, in Winsum follow the signs for the campsite. Then from the swimming pool, follow the parallel road.

CC € 19 *1/4-26/4 21/5-5/7 2/9-30/9*

N 53°19'53'' E 06°30'38''

Amen, NL-9446 TE / Drenthe

223

Camping Diana Heide****
Amen 55
+31 5 92 38 92 97
1/4 - 1/10
dianaheide@ardoer.com

30ha 250**T**(100-200m²) 10A CEE

1 A**D**I**K**LMNOORTU
2 BESTWXYZ
3 AC**G**IKMNPSUWZ
4 (Q+R+T+Y+Z 🔑)
5 **AB**DEFGIJKLMNOPQUWXY
6 ACEFGHKL(N 4km)OPST

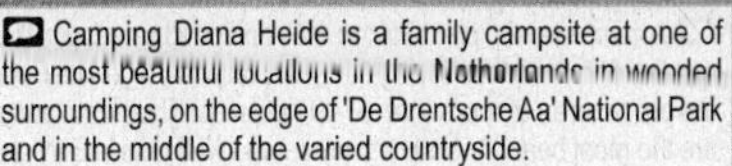

Camping Diana Heide is a family campsite at one of the most beautiful locations in the Netherlands in wooded surroundings, on the edge of 'De Drentsche Aa' National Park and in the middle of the varied countryside.

A28 Zwolle-Groningen exit 31A, direction Hooghalen. Exit Grolloo/Amen, follow sign posts.

CC € 21 *1/4-26/4 22/5-26/6 1/7-7/7 1/9-30/9*

N 52°55'57'' E 06°35'12''

Borger, NL-9531 TC / Drenthe

224

Bospark Lunsbergen****
Rolderstraat 11A
+31 5 99 23 65 65
22/3 - 3/11
info@bosparklunsbergen.nl

20ha 194**T**(100m²) 10A CEE

1 ACDE**I**KLMNOPQRS
2 BISTWXY
3 A**G**HIJKLMNP**R**SU
4 (F+H+Q+S+T+U+V+X +Y+Z 🔑)
5 **AB**DFGIJKLMNOPQUWXY
6 ACDEFGHKLM(N 3km) OSTUVX

Well-equipped family campsite, surrounded by a forest. With a heated indoor swimming pool and a recreation room. Very suitable for bicycle and/or hiking holidays.

A28, exit Assen-Zuid, take the N33 direction Veendam. Then exit Borger. About 2 km before you reach Borger, road signs leading to the campsite 'Euroase Borger' are posted.

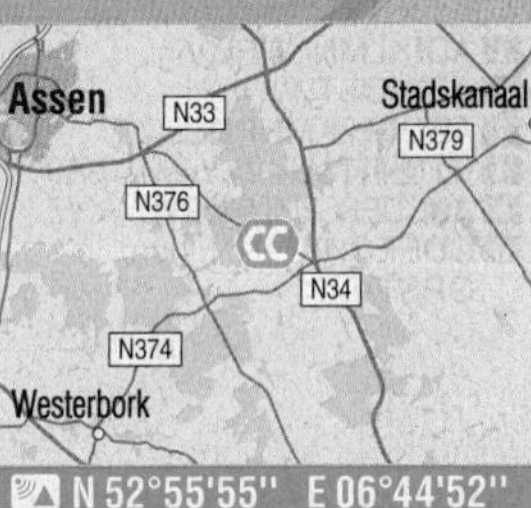

CC € 13 *22/3-12/7 30/8-3/11*

N 52°55'55'' E 06°44'52''

Borger, NL-9531 TK / Drenthe

225

Roompot Vakantiepark Hunzedal****
De Drift 3
+31 5 99 23 46 98
22/3 - 3/11
receptie.hunzedal@roompot.nl

30ha 346**T**(100m²) 6A CEE

1 ACDE**I**KLMNOPQRS
2 ABEIJSTWXYZ
3 ABCD**G**HIKLMN**O**P**R**S**T**U**W**Z
4 (C 1/4-31/10)(F+H 🔑)IJK**LN** (Q+S+T+U+V+X+Y+Z 🔑)
5 **AB**DEFGIJKLMNOPRUWXYZ
6 ACDEFGHKL(N 0,5km) O**P**STUX

This luxurious, all-round recreation park is located just outside Borger on the borders of the wooded Drentse Hondsrug. Excellent amenities for all weather conditions. The park is suitable as a family park and for people who appreciate the Drenthe countryside. There are no motorhome pitches available at this campsite.

From the N34 Groningen-Emmen direction Borger/ Stadskanaal, follow the signposts.

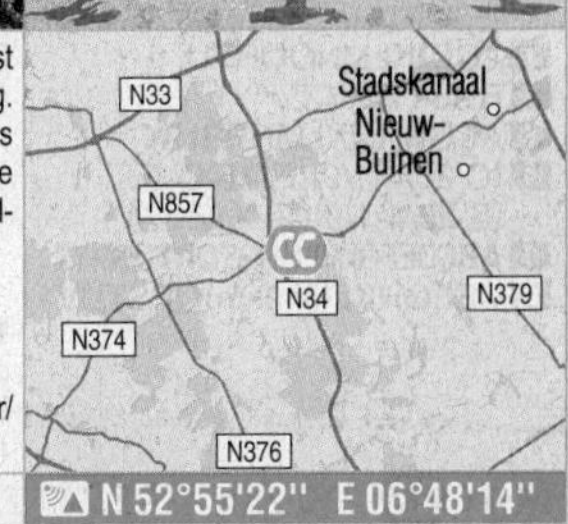

CC € 17 *22/3-29/3 2/4-25/4 13/5-17/5 21/5-28/6 30/8-3/11*

N 52°55'22'' E 06°48'14''

Dwingeloo, NL-7991 PB / Drenthe

226

RCN de Noordster***
De Noordster 105
+31 8 50 40 07 00
29/3 - 3/11
reserveringen@rcn.nl

42ha 329T(80-150m²) 10A CEE

1 ACDIKLMNOPQRS
2 BISTVXYZ
3 ABCDE**G**HIKMNOP**QR**SU
4 (A 4/7-30/8)(C+G 1/5-1/9)JM
(Q+R+T+U+V+X+Y+Z)
5 **AB**CDFGHIJKLMNOPQUWZ
6 ACDEFHKLM(N 2km)
OPSUVX

A campsite with plenty of facilities and good catering in the middle of the woods of Dwingelderveld National Park. The Park covers an area of more than 3700 hectares. The heathlands are the most beautiful and best preserved wetlands in Europe. A large flock of sheep contributes to nature conservation.

From Dieverbrug towards the centre of Dwingeloo. Through Dwingeloo to the five road junction by the woods. Follow signs on the woodland road.

CC € 19 *29/3-7/5 13/5-16/5 21/5-9/7 26/8-3/11*

N 52°48'48'' E 06°22'42''

Een (Gem. Noordenveld), NL-9342 TC / Drenthe

227

Ronostrand****
Amerika 16
+31 5 92 65 62 06
1/4 - 30/9
info@ronostrand.nl

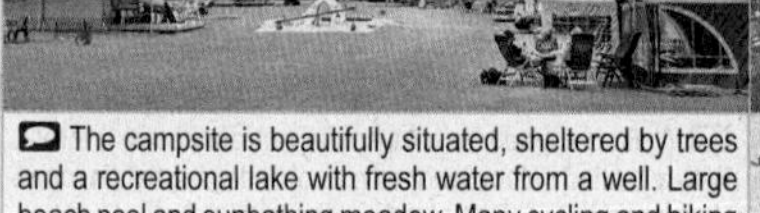

35ha 190T(80-120m²) 10-16A CEE

1 ADIKLMNOPRUV
2 AEINOSTWXYZ
3 ABC**G**HIKMNP**Q**SUZ
4 (Q)(T+U+V+Y 1/4-15/9)
5 **AB**CDEFGIJKLMOP**T**UWXYZ
6 CDEFGHKLM(N 4km)
OPSTV

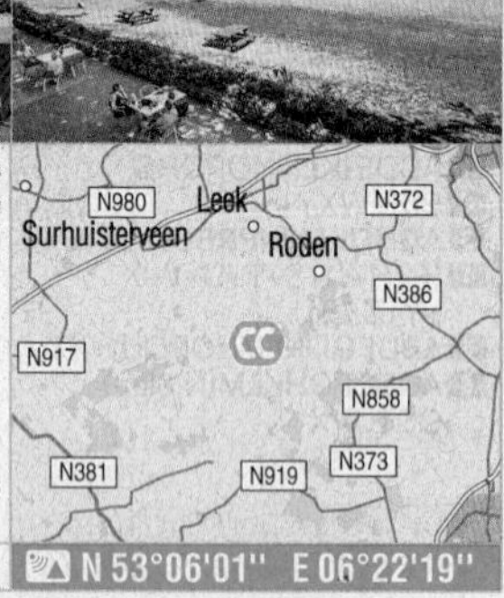

The campsite is beautifully situated, sheltered by trees and a recreational lake with fresh water from a well. Large beach pool and sunbathing meadow. Many cycling and hiking options. Extensive catering facilities right by the lake.

Road Roden-Norg. Beyond the cemetery and sport facilities turn right. Follow the signs.

CC € 21 *1/4-27/4 22/5-12/7 2/9-30/9*

N 53°06'01'' E 06°22'19''

Eext, NL-9463 TA / Drenthe

228

Camping De Hondsrug****
Annerweg 3
+31 5 92 27 12 92
29/3 - 30/9
info@hondsrug.nl

23ha 250T(75-150m²) 6-10A CEE

1 ACDIKLMNOQRTU
2 BIJSTWXYZ
3 ABC**G**HIJKLMNPSU**W**
4 (C 25/4-1/9)(F+H+Q)
(S 25/4-1/9)(T+X+Z)
5 **AB**CDEFGIJKLMNOPQR**T**UWXYZ
6 CEFGHKL(N 2km)OPSTUV

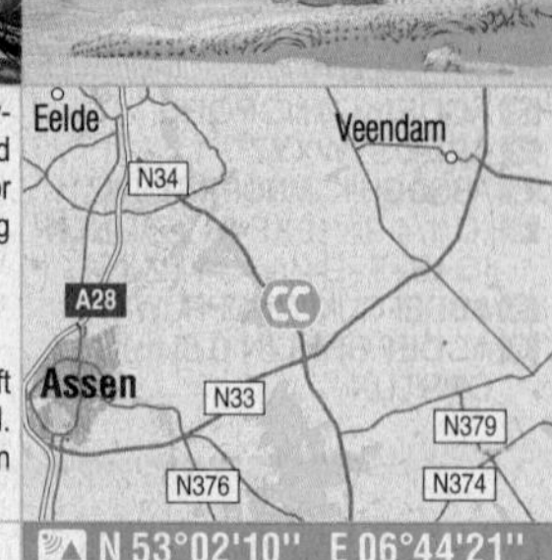

A vibrant campsite for young families with various playground equipment on the fields. There is also a large sand playground with climbing course. Heated indoor and outdoor swimming pool. Surrounded by woods with extensive cycling and walking opportunities.

N34 Groningen-Emmen exit Anloo/Annen, first left direction Annen, then turn right. Campsite is sign posted. N34 Emmen-Groningen, exit Anloo/Annen, turn right direction Annen, follow signs.

CC € 23 *29/3-26/4 22/5-7/7 2/9-30/9*

N 53°02'10'' E 06°44'21''

Exloo, NL-7875 TA / Drenthe

229

Camping Exloo
Valtherweg 37
+31 6 27 21 82 71
1/1 - 31/12
info@campingexloo.nl

3ha 60T(100-120m²) 6-10A CEE

1 ADEIKLMNOPQR3W
2 STWXYZ
3 GHIKUW
5 ABDGIJKLMNPUZ
6 ABCDEFGHK(N 2,5km)PU

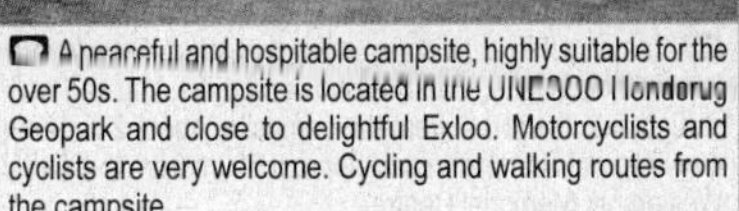

A peaceful and hospitable campsite, highly suitable for the over 50s. The campsite is located in the UNESCO Hondsrug Geopark and close to delightful Exloo. Motorcyclists and cyclists are very welcome. Cycling and walking routes from the campsite.

N34 direction Groningen, exit Exloo. Turn right at end of village towards Valthe. After 2 km campsite on the left.

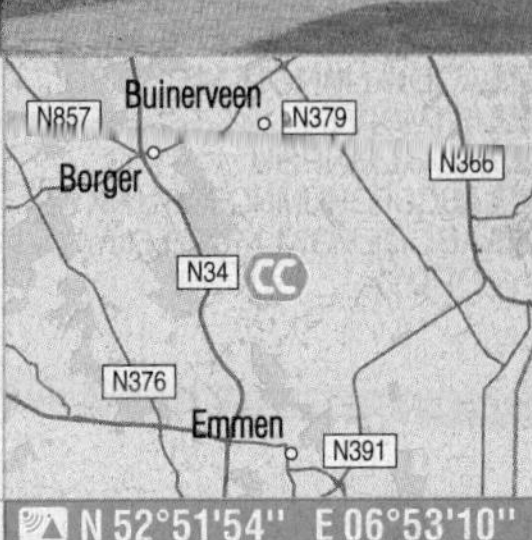

CC € 19 *1/1-8/5 21/5-15/7 1/9-31/12* ***14=12, 21=18***

N 52°51'54'' E 06°53'10''

Gasselte, NL-9462 TT / Drenthe

230

Camping Het Horstmannsbos****
Hoogte der Heide 8
+31 5 99 56 42 70
29/3 - 30/9
info@horstmannsbos.nl

6,5ha 106T(100-130m²) 10A CEE

1 ACDEIKLMNOPQRTU
2 BISTWXYZ
3 ABCGIKOPSWZ
4 M(Q+T+U+X+Z)
5 ABCDFGHIJKLMNOPQRUWZ
6 ABCEFGHJKL(N 3km) OPSTVX

A quiet spacious natural campsite located in woodland. It has a unique location right by Het Drouwenerzand nature area and has several grassy fields with spacious camping pitches as well as a woodland strip especially for nature lovers.

From the N34 Groningen-Emmen follow the road signs to the Gasselte exit. From here, follow the signs for Horstmannsbos (not your navigation system).

CC € 21 *29/3-8/5 19/5-6/7 25/8-30/9* ***7=6, 14=12, 21=18***

N 52°58'15'' E 06°48'26''

Gieten, NL-9461 AP / Drenthe

231

Boscamping-Zwanemeer
Voorste Land 1
+31 5 92 26 13 17
1/4 - 1/10
kamperen@zwanemeer.nl

6ha 160T(80-120m²) 6-10A CEE

1 ADEIKLMNOPQRTU
2 BIJSTXYZ
3 ABGIJKLMNPSUW
4 (A 1/7-31/8)(C+H 1/5-31/8)J (Q)(T+U+X+Z 1/7-31/8)
5 ABCDEFGHIJKLMNOPQRUWXYZ
6 AEFGHKL(N 0,8km)OPS

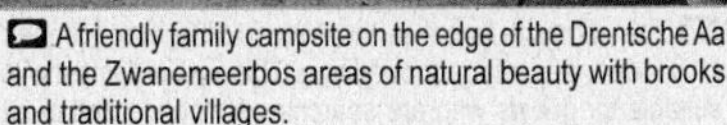

A friendly family campsite on the edge of the Drentsche Aa and the Zwanemeerbos areas of natural beauty with brooks and traditional villages.

Via the N33 Assen-Gieten, through the village of Gieten, follow the campsite signs (not your navigation system, you'll end up in the woods).

Veendam
A28
Assen
N33
Stadskanaal
N379
N376
N857
N34
N374

CC € 27 *1/4-9/5 21/5-6/7 2/9-30/9*

N 53°00'56'' E 06°46'00''

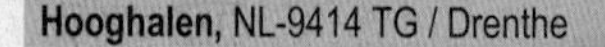

Hooghalen, NL-9414 TG / Drenthe

232

Camping Tikvah
Oosthalen 5
+31 5 93 59 20 97
1/4 - 1/11
info@campingtikvah.nl

1,5ha 53T(120-250m²) 6-16A CEE

1 ACDIKLMNOPQRS
2 ISTWXYZ
3 ACIKLMNPSU
5 ABCDFGHIJMNOPQRUWXYZ
6 ABCDEFGKLM(N 0,5km) OPUV

Camping Tikvah is surrounded by pine and deciduous forests, heathlands, marshes and sand drifts. You can walk straight into the forest from the campsite. About 2 km from the village of Hooghalen and approx. 500m from the Camp Westerbork Memorial Centre.

From A28 take exit Beilen-Noord/Emmen/Hooghalen. Follow signs to Hooghalen for ± 10 km. Just before Hooghalen follow the brown sign 'voormalig Kamp Westerbork'. Turn right before roundabout across railway, then 1.5 km.

CC €19 1/4-8/5 21/5-27/6 31/8-1/11

N 52°55'13'' E 06°33'33''

Meppen, NL-7855 TA / Drenthe

233

Camping De Bronzen Emmer****
Mepperstraat 41
+31 5 91 37 15 43
29/3 - 30/10
info@bronzenemmer.nl

20ha 230T(100-140m²) 4-10A CEE

1 ADHKLMNOPQRS
2 BISTWXYZ
3 ABEGHIKMOPQSU
4 (F+G 21/4-30/9)N(Q) (R+T+U+X+Z 28/4-20/5, 12/7-24/8)
5 ABDEFGIJKLMNPUWXYZ
6 ABCEFGHK(N 2km)OPSV

This lovely campsite is located in the wooded surroundings of the flatlands of Drenthe. Run by an enthusiastic family. Plenty of touring pitches with caravans and tents. Also car-free pitches. You will immediately feel at home here.

A37 Hoogeveen-Emmen, exit Oosterhesselen (N854) direction Meppen. Campsite signposted in Meppen in direction Meppen/Mantinge.

CC €21 29/3-8/5 21/5-11/7 28/8-30/10 7=6, 14=12, 21=18

N 52°46'44'' E 06°41'11''

Meppen, NL-7855 PV / Drenthe

234

Camping Erfgoed de Boemerang
Nijmaten 2
+31 5 91 37 21 18
1/4 - 1/10
info@erfgoeddeboemerang.nl

4ha 47T(100-200m²) 10A CEE

1 ADIKLMNPRSW
2 EISTVWXYZ
3 EGIKMU
5 ABCDGHIJMNOPTUWXYZ
6 ABDEFGK(N 2km)

The campsite is set in the historic village of Meppen in wooded, peaceful surroundings. This idyllic campsite is suitable for guests who are searching for peace and quiet and guests over 50 and is run by an enthusiastic couple who maintain an eye for detail on the site. The excellent toilet facilities are a sight to see.

A37 Hoogeveen-Emmen. Oosterhesselen exit (N854) towards Meppen. Then direction Mantinge. Follow the signs.

CC €21 1/4-6/5 24/5-7/7 24/8-30/9

N 52°46'49'' E 06°41'30''

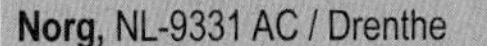

Norg, NL-9331 AC / Drenthe — 235

Bospark Langeloërduinen
Kerkpad 12
+31 5 92 61 27 70
1/4 - 30/9
info@bosparknorg.nl

7,5ha 100T(100-120m²) 10-12A CEE

1 ACD**I**KLMNOPQRS
2 BJSTXYZ
3 ACIKS
5 **AB**CDFGHIJKLMNOPQUWXYZ
6 EFGHK(N 0,7km)OS

At this campsite in Drenthe, you can enjoy the outdoor life in a tent, caravan, trailer tent or motorhome. You will find peace and space amid the forest and yet at walking distance from the lovely village of Norg. Many walking and cycling routes straight from the campsite.

From N371 direction Norg, follow signs in the centre via Kerkpad.

CC € 23 *1/4-8/5 21/5-5/7 2/9-30/9*

N 53°04'21'' E 06°27'25''

Norg, NL-9331 VA / Drenthe — 236

Camping De Norgerberg*****
Langeloërweg 63
+31 5 92 61 22 81
29/3 - 3/11
info@norgerberg.nl

20ha 170T(100-150m²) 10A CEE

1 AD**H**KLMNRS
2 BIJSUVWXYZ
3 AC**G**IJKMNOPSU
4 (A 30/4-16/5,9/7-28/8) (C+E+H 🔑)**KN** (Q+R+T+U+X+Y 🔑)
5 **AB**CDEFGHIJKLMNOPQR**T**U WXYZ
6 CEFGHKL(N 1km)OPSTV

Friendly family campsite, surrounded by woods and within walking distance of the village of Norg. Excellent base for visiting Groningen and Friesland. Centre of the cycle path network. Atmospheric restaurant in front of the campsite. Comfort and private sanitary pitches available at extra cost. Specific pitches available for CCA, can't be booked in advance. Modern luxury sanitary with wellness.

The campsite is located on the N373, 2 km north of Norg on the road Norg-Roden.

CC € 27 *2/4-25/4 21/5-4/7 31/8-2/11*

N 53°04'40'' E 06°26'55''

Ruinen, NL-7963 PX / Drenthe — 237

EuroParcs Ruinen****
Oude Benderseweg 11
+31 5 22 47 17 70
1/3 - 30/10
kcc@europarcs.nl

25ha 202T(110-150m²) 6A CEE

1 ACD**I**KLMNOPQRS
2 BIJSTWXYZ
3 BCE**G**HIKMS
4 (A 8/7-27/8) (F+H+Q+R+X 🔑)
5 **AB**DEFGIJKLMNOPQR**T**UWXYZ
6 CEFGK(N 1,5km)PSV

EuroParcs Ruinen is adjacent to the Dwingelderveld nature reserve. A naturally landscaped family campsite with lovely big pitches, suitable for the over 50s and families with children. Indoor pool, restaurant and a children's zoo. The campsite is right on beautiful cycling routes.

Ruinen direction Pesse. After 600 metres, the fourth street on the left. Campsite is signposted, also from Ruinen via Engeland.

CC € 27 *1/3-29/3 2/4-26/4 13/5-17/5 20/5-5/7 2/9-30/10*

N 52°46'31'' E 06°22'14''

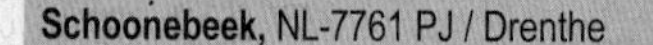

Schoonebeek, NL-7761 PJ / Drenthe

238

Camping Emmen
Bultweg 7
+31 5 24 53 21 94
29/3 - 29/9
info@campingemmen.nl

3,3ha 50T(100-120m²) 6-16A CEE

1 ADIJKLMNOPQRTU
2 EIJSWXYZ
3 ABCGIKMNUW
4 (C 9/5-15/9)
(Q 9/5-20/5,22/7-23/8)
(T+U+V+Y+Z)
5 ABDFGIJMNOPTUWZ
6 ABCDEFGJK(N 1km)PVX

A convenient campsite suitable for young and old. Suitable for a visit to the Wildlands Adventure Zoo in Emmen. The camping pitches are spacious. Heated swimming pool near reception. There are various fields with picnic tables. Many cycling routes from the campsite.

A37 exit 5 direction Schoonebeek. Campsite signposted from there. On the left just before Schoonebeek.

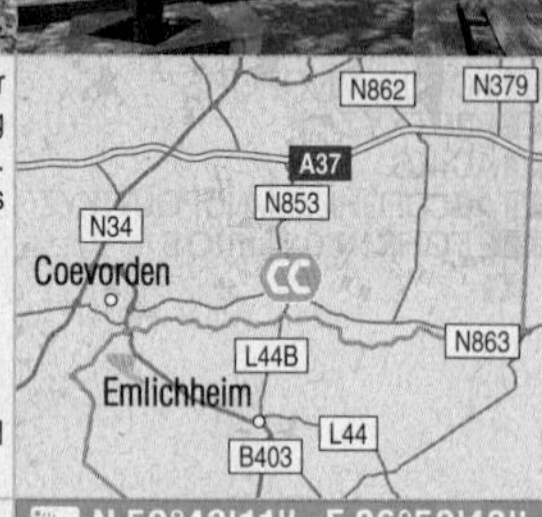

CC € 21 *29/3-8/5 1/6-1/7 1/9-29/9*

N 52°40'11'' E 06°52'43''

Wateren, NL-8438 SC / Drenthe

239

Molecaten Park Het Landschap****
Schurerslaan 4
+31 5 21 38 72 44
22/3 - 1/10
hetlandschap@molecaten.nl

16ha 205T(100-150m²) 6-10A CEE

1 ACDIKLMNORUV
2 AESTXYZ
3 ACHIKMNPQRSUWZ
4 (A 5/7-17/8)(F+H 1/5-30/9)
(Q+T+U+X+Z)
5 ABFGIJKLMNOPUWXYZ
6 EFGHK(N 6km)OPSTV

The campsite is located in the Drents Friese Wold (6000 hectare) national park by an idyllic lake which is suitable for swimming. Plenty of walking and cycling opportunities in the area. Spacious camping pitches.

From Diever drive towards Zorgvlied. The campsite is located just before Zorgvlied on the right side. Marked with signs.

CC € 19 *22/3-25/4 6/5-8/5 13/5-16/5 21/5-11/7 30/8-30/9*

N 52°55'19'' E 06°16'04''

Westerbork, NL-9431 GA / Drenthe

240

Camping Landgoed Börkerheide***
Beilerstraat 13a
+31 5 93 33 15 46
23/3 - 29/9
info@landgoedborkerheide.nl

15ha 88T(80-120m²) 6A CEE

1 ADEIKLMNOPQRTU
2 BIJSTVWXYZ
3 AGIKLSU
4 (C+H 15/4-1/9)
5 ABDEFGIJKLMNOPUWXZ
6 ACDEFGK(N 0,7km)U

Discover Drenthe's best secret. The peacefully located estate with its own woods, heath and marsh is 1 km from the very sociable Westerbork. There are lovely walking and cycling opportunities in the surrounding area. The toilet and washing facilities are good and guests can use the adjacent open-air swimming pool for free. The Wi-Fi is good and free.

A28 Zwolle-Hoogeveen-Groningen, exit 30 Beilen and follow signs Westerbork. The campsite is signposted.

Smilde, Borger, Grolloo, N371, Beilen, A28, CC, N376, N855, N381, N374, N375

CC € 19 *23/3-8/5 21/5-6/7 25/8-29/9*

N 52°51'10'' E 06°35'25''

Wezuperbrug, NL-7853 TA / Drenthe

241

Molecaten Park Kuierpad****
Oranjekanaal NZ 10
+31 5 91 38 14 15
22/3 - 1/11
kuierpad@molecaten.nl

55ha 550T(95-200m²) 6-10A CEE

1 ACD**I**KLMNOQRS
2 ABFISTWXY
3 ABC**G**HIJKLMNP**R**SUWZ
4 (C 1/5-1/9)(F+H+Q)
(S 25/3-31/10)(T)
(U 24/3-31/10)
(X+Y 1/4-1/11)
5 **AB**DEFGIJKLMNOPQRUWXYZ
6 ACEFGH**K**LM(N 2km)
OPSTVX

Located in remarkably beautiful countryside, ideal for cyclists, hikers and families with children.

N31 Beilen-Emmen exit Westerbork. Via Orvelte in the direction of Schoonoord.

CC € 19 *22/3-25/4 6/5-8/5 13/5-16/5 21/5-11/7 30/8-30/10*

N 52°50'26'' E 06°43'28''

Zweeloo, NL-7851 AA / Drenthe

242

Camping De Knieplanden***
Hoofdstraat 2
+31 5 91 37 15 99
29/3 - 30/9
info@campingknieplanden.nl

2,5ha 64T(90-110m²) 10A CEE

1 AD**I**KLMNOPQ**R**S
2 IJSTWXYZ
3 AC**G**HIKS
4 (**C**+**G** 6/5-31/8)J
(T+U 18/7-21/8)
5 **AB**DEFGIJMNPQRUWZ
6 ABEFGK(N 0,3km)**P**

Quiet campsite on the edge of the picturesque and atmospheric village green of Zweeloo. Wonderful hiking and cycling region. A paradise for everyone who loves peace, the countryside or an active holiday.

A37 Hoogeveen-Emmen, exit Oosterhesselen N854. Campsite clearly indicated in Zweeloo.

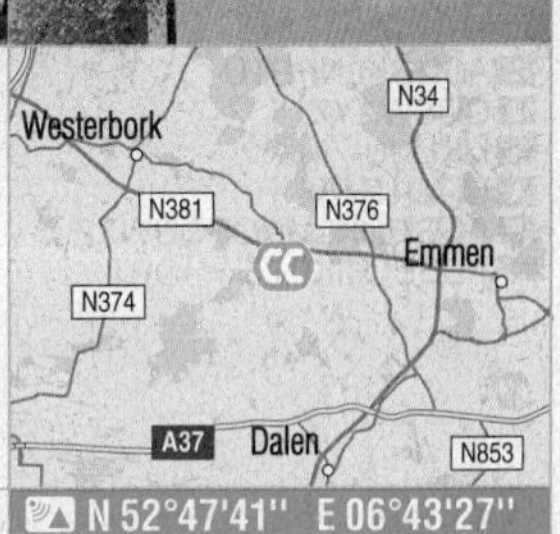

CC € 21 *29/3-8/5 21/5-7/7 24/8-30/9*

N 52°47'41'' E 06°43'27''

Aalten, NL-7122 PC / Gelderland

243

Camping Goorzicht****
Boterdijk 3
+31 5 43 46 13 39
25/3 - 29/9
info@goorzicht.nl

6,5ha 59T(70-100m²) 6A CEE

1 ACD**I**KLMNOQ**RS**
2 BISTXYZ
3 ACHIKMPSU
4 (**C**+G 1/5-31/8)M
(Q+T+Z 27/4-8/5,8/7-3/9)
5 **AB**DEFGI**JKL**MNO**PT**UXYZ
6 ABDEFGH**K**(N 3km)PV

On the edge of the beautiful nature reserve 'Het Goor'. Plenty of cycling and walking opportunities. Enjoy peace, space and rural life. The site stands out for its spacious comfort pitches with a choice of sunny pitches or more shade. Modern and heated toilet block. Comfort pitches with private toilet facilities for a surcharge.

A18, N318 direction Varsseveld-Aalten-Winterswijk, before Aalten follow the brown-white ANWB signs.

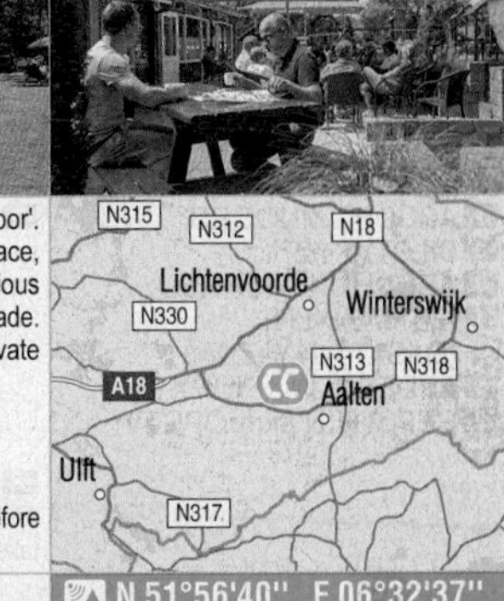

CC € 17 *25/3-7/5 22/5-29/5 3/6-12/7 29/8-29/9* ***7=6, 14=12, 21=18***

N 51°56'40'' E 06°32'37''

Aalten, NL-7121 LZ / Gelderland

244

Camping Lansbulten***
Eskesweg 1
+31 5 43 47 25 88
28/3 - 13/10
info@lansbulten.nl

10ha 55T(110-120m²) 6-16A CEE

1 ADIKLMNOQRS
2 BCSTXYZ
3 BCEIKPSWX
4 (C+H 16/5-14/9)
(Q 9/5-21/5,8/7-22/8)
5 ABDEFGIJMNOPUXYZ
6 ADEFGHKL(N 1,5km)P

Peaceful family campsite with plenty of greenery on the edge of Aalten. Very spacious pitches with water, electricity and drainage. Fishing possible in the adjacent stream (Keizersbeek). Wireless internet available. Good walking and cycling opportunities. Plenty of sports opportunities and a heated swimming pool for children.

N318 Varsseveld-Winterswijk. Follow brown and white signs at Bredevoort.

CC € 21 *28/3-26/4 6/5-9/5 21/5-29/5 3/6-13/7 2/9-13/10* ***14=12***

N 51°55'34'' E 06°36'15''

Aerdt, NL-6913 KH / Gelderland

245

Camping De Rijnstrangen
Beuningsestraat 4
+31 6 12 55 94 64
1/4 - 1/11
info@derijnstrangen.nl

0,6ha 30T(100m²) 6A CEE

1 ACDGKLNPRTU
2 CIJSWXYZ
3 IJKLMU
4 (A+Q+R)
5 ACGHIJKLMNOPQUWXZ
6 ABDEFHIK(N 3km)OPT

A well maintained campsite in Aerdt (close to Lobith) with underfloor heating in the toilet buildings, and located in 'de Gelderse Poort' nature reserve on the old course of the Rhine. Conveniently located for cycle trips through the polders and meadows but also for Montferland. Bed and breakfast available.

A12 exit 29, direction Lobith as far as Aerdt exit. Turn right onto the dike. Continue 1.5 km to church. Down to the left after 100 metres.

CC € 21 *2/4-26/4 21/5-6/7 23/8-1/11*

N 51°53'47'' E 06°04'13''

Arnhem, NL-6816 RW / Gelderland

246

Oostappen Vakantiepark Arnhem****
Kemperbergerweg 771
+31 2 64 43 16 00
22/3 - 3/11
info@vakantieparkarnhem.nl

36ha 455T(80-150m²) 10A CEE

1 ABCDIKLMNOQRS
2 BILSTVXYZ
3 ABCGHIJKLMOPRSU
4 (D+H)KLN
(Q+S+T+U+Y+Z)
5 ABDEFGIJMNPUWXY
6 CEFGHJ(N 8km)OPSTV

The perfect family campsite located in woodland close to the Hooge Veluwe National Park and Arnhem. Many facilities including an indoor swimming pool.

A12 (in both directions) and A50 from the south take exit Arnhem North. Then follow the signs. From Apeldoorn (A50), take exit Schaarsbergen.

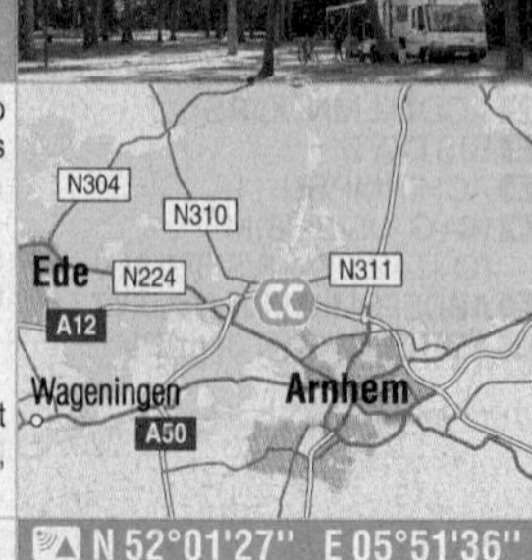

CC € 19 *22/3-29/3 2/4-26/4 13/5-17/5 24/5-8/7 25/8-18/10*

N 52°01'27'' E 05°51'36''

Beekbergen, NL-7361 TM / Gelderland

247

Camping Het Lierderholt****
Spoekweg 49
+31 5 55 06 14 58
1/1 - 31/12
info@lierderholt.nl

25ha 210**T**(100-150m²) 6-10A CEE

1 ACD**I**KLMNOPQRS
2 BISTWXYZ
3 ABC**G**HIJKLMN**O**P**R**SU
4 (A 22/4-7/5,8/7-3/9)
(C 1/5-30/9)(G 25/4-16/9)
IJM(Q)(R 1/4-31/10)
(T)(V 1/4-31/10)(Y+Z)
5 **AB**DEFGIJKLMNPQRT**U**WXYZ
6 ABCDEFGHKL(N 3,2km)
OPSTV

Cosy holiday park, beautifully situated in the middle of the Veluwe. Large open spaces with various height differences. The park has many facilities, including an attractive restaurant.

A50 from Arnhem, exit 22 Beekbergen or A50 from Zwolle, exit 22 Hoenderloo. Follow signs.

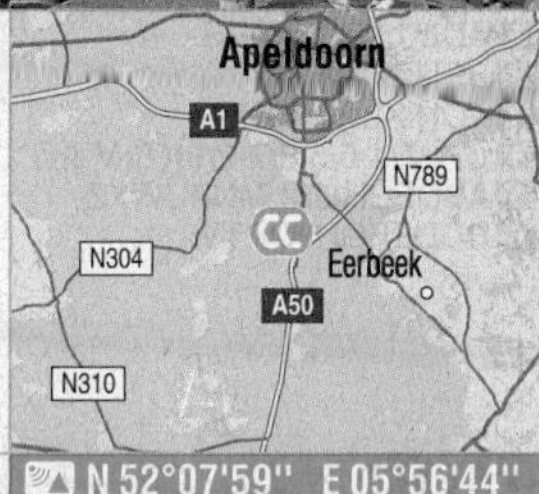

CC € 21 *1/1-8/5 21/5-6/7 30/8-31/12* ***14=12, 21=18***

N 52°07'59" E 05°56'44"

Beesd, NL-4153 XC / Gelderland

248

Camping Betuwestrand****
A. Kraalweg 40
+31 3 45 68 15 03
29/3 - 28/9
info@betuwestrand.nl

30ha 150**T**(80-100m²) 10A CEE

1 ADGKLMNRS
2 AEISWXY
3 BCHIJKOPSUWZ
4 J(Q+S+T+U+Y+Z)
5 **AB**CDFGHI**J**K**L**MNO**PQ**RUWXYZ
6 ABCDEFGHJ**K**M(N 2km)
O**P**TUV

For many years one of the loveliest and most hospitable campsites in the Netherlands, excellent amenities. Spaciously laid out, located by its own recreational lake with a sandy beach. In the fascinating Betuwe countryside, plenty of opportunities for cycling/walking. Connected to route.nl for the best regional cycling routes. Centrally positioned in the Netherlands between Utrecht and 's-Hertogenbosch (25 km).

A2 's-Hertogenbosch-Utrecht, exit 14 Beesd, thereafter signposted.

CC € 25 *29/3-9/5 21/5-13/7 31/8-28/9*

N 51°53'56" E 05°11'18"

Berg en Dal, NL-6571 CH / Gelderland

249

Nederrijkswald BV
Zevenheuvelenweg 47
+31 2 46 84 17 82
15/3 - 31/10
info@nederrijkswald.nl

1,5ha 52**T**(80-130m²) 6-16A CEE

1 ACD**I**KLMNPQ**R**TU
2 BJSTWXYZ
3 AE**FG**HIJKLMNPU
4 (**A**+Q)
5 **AB**CDFGHI**JKL**MNO**P**QUWXZ
6 ABCDEFGH**K**M(N 3km)
OPTV

Located near the Nederrijk estate on the edge of Berg en Dal en Groesbeek, and is surrounded on three sides by woods. You can enjoy to the full the beautiful nature, peace, space, places of interest, hospitality and the rural lifestyle. Spacious pitches and good toilet facilities.

A73, exit 3 Malden. N271 direction Groesbeek. Direction Berg en Dal at roundabout; left at T junction, 2nd road to the right N841 (at service station). After 750 metres on the left.

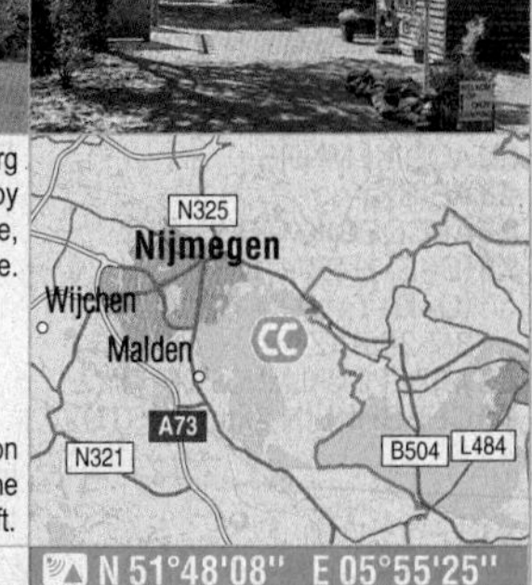

CC € 23 *15/3-25/4 21/5-6/7 25/8-31/10*

N 51°48'08" E 05°55'25"

Braamt, NL-7047 AP / Gelderland

250

Camping Recreatie Te Boomsgoed***
Langestraat 24
+31 3 14 65 18 90
1/1 - 31/12
info@teboomsgoed.nl

6ha 37T(100m²) 10-16A CEE

1 ADIKLMNOPQRS
2 BEIJSTWYZ
3 ACHIKLP**QR**SU
4 (Q 27/4-6/5,8/7-2/9)(T+V)
5 **AB**DFGHIJKLMN**P**UWXZ
6 BCDEFGHJOPTV

Located on the Pieterpad route in the Montferland. Camping pitches marked out by beech hedges. Meal delivery is possible. The site offers stables, a minigolf course and a recreation hall.

A18 exit 3 to Doetinchem/Zelhem/Zeddam. Turn left after the exit, left at second roundabout towards Braamt. Campsite 250 metres further on.

CC € 15 *1/1-25/4 21/5-5/7 1/9-31/12*

N 51°55'31'' E 06°15'42''

Doetinchem, NL-7004 HD / Gelderland

251

Camping De Wrange****
Rekhemseweg 144
+31 3 14 32 48 52
22/3 - 18/10
info@dewrange.nl

10ha 70T(90-110m²) 10A CEE

1 ACD**I**KLMPQ**R**S
2 BISTWXYZ
3 C**G**HJK**R**SU
4 (C+H 27/4-6/9)
(Q+S+T+U+X+Y+Z 1/4-4/10)
5 **AB**DFGI**J**K**L**MNO**P**UWXYZ
6 AEFGH**K**(N 3km)OPUV

Peaceful campsite in wooded surroundings, but not isolated. Spacious non fenced off pitches in grassy clearings in the woods.

From the A18, exit 4 Doetinchem-Oost. Turn left under the main road. Continue to the next traffic lights, then turn right and follow the signs (partially through a residential area).

CC € 19 *22/3-9/5 21/5-15/7 1/9-18/10* ***7=6, 14=11, 21=18***

N 51°56'47'' E 06°20'01''

Doornenburg, NL-6686 MC / Gelderland

252

Camping De Waay****
Rijndijk 67a
+31 4 81 42 12 56
29/3 - 30/9
info@de-waay.nl

19ha 140T(100-120m²) 10A CEE

1 ACDIKLMNRS
2 AEISXY
3 ABCDE**G**HKM**O**PSUWZ
4 (C+E+H 28/4-17/9)
(Q+R+T+U+X+Y 29/4-7/5,
8/7-26/8)(Z)
5 **AB**DEFGIJKLMNOPQRUWYZ
6 CEFGHKL(N 2km)OPSTUV

Pleasant campsite with modern sanitary facilities. Orchards all around. Separate fields for touring campers, and another for permanent pitches. Indoor swimming pool.

From A15 exit Bemmel/Gendt. Turn left in Gendt and follow the signs. Follow signs from Arnhem.

CC € 23 *29/3-6/5 21/5-8/7 26/8-30/9*

N 51°54'16'' E 05°59'08''

Eerbeek, NL-6961 LD / Gelderland

253

- Camping Landal Coldenhove****
- Boshoffweg 6
- +31 31 3- 65 91 01
- 15/3 - 4/11
- coldenhove@landal.nl

20ha 180T(100-120m²) 10A CEE

1. ACDIKLNRS
2. BILSTWYZ
3. ABCDGHIJKLMNPRSTU
4. (A+F+H)M (Q+S+T+V+X+Y+Z)
5. ABDEFGIJKLMNOPRUWXZ
6. ABCEFGHJL(N 3km) OPSTVX

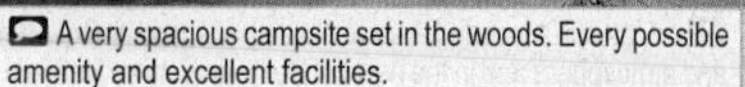

A very spacious campsite set in the woods. Every possible amenity and excellent facilities.

A50 exit Loenen/Eerbeek direction Loenen/Eerbeek. Then at the roundabout direction Dieren. Follow signs to Coldenhove.

CC € 23 15/3-29/3 2/4-26/4 21/5-5/7 2/9-1/11

N 52°05'31'' E 06°02'05''

Elburg, NL-8081 LB / Gelderland

254

- Natuurcamping Landgoed Old Putten
- Zuiderzeestraatweg Oost 65
- +31 5 25 68 19 38
- 15/4 - 15/9
- info@oldputten.nl

5ha 70T(100-120m²) 4A CEE

1. ADGJKLNPRTU
2. CIJSUXYZ
3. AIKMOUW
4. (A 30/5-10/6,22/7-16/8) (G)(Q 22/7-16/8)
5. AFGIJMNPUWZ
6. CEFGK(N 0,5km)PT

A peaceful family campsite, perfect for small children. Spacious pitches. Beautiful countryside and cycling area close to the fortified town of Elburg.

A28, exit 16 't Harde. N309 direction Elburg. Right opposite Elburg-Vesting exit on roundabout N309 entrance on left.

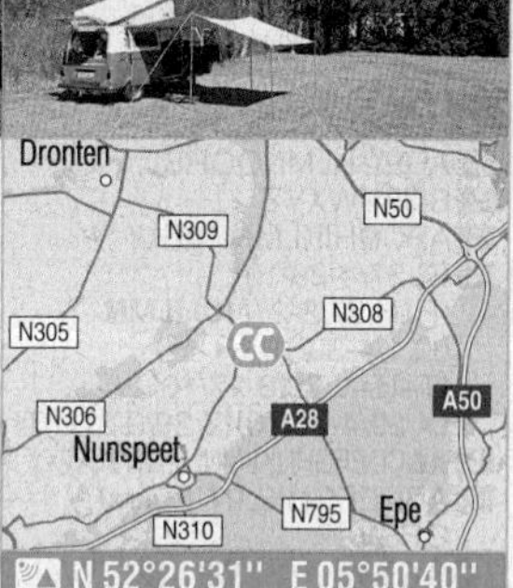

CC € 17 15/4-7/5 21/5-7/7 24/8-15/9

N 52°26'31'' E 05°50'40''

Emst, NL-8166 JJ / Gelderland

255

- Camping De Wildhoeve*****
- Hanendorperweg 102
- +31 5 78 66 13 24
- 29/3 - 30/9
- info@wildhoeve.nl

12ha 310T(80-120m²) 8-10A CEE

1. ACDGKLMNOPQRS
2. BISWXYZ
3. ABCHIJKMNOPSU
4. (A 29/4-7/5,8/7-1/9) (C 1/5-31/8)(F+H)JM (Q+S+T+Y)
5. ABDEFGIJKLMNOPQRTUWXYZ
6. BCDEFGHKL(N 3km) OPSTV

ACSI AWARDS WINNER

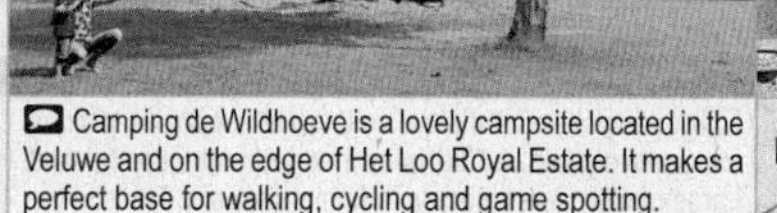

Camping de Wildhoeve is a lovely campsite located in the Veluwe and on the edge of Het Loo Royal Estate. It makes a perfect base for walking, cycling and game spotting.

A50 Arnhem-Zwolle, exit 26 Vaassen and then towards Emst. Follow the signs.

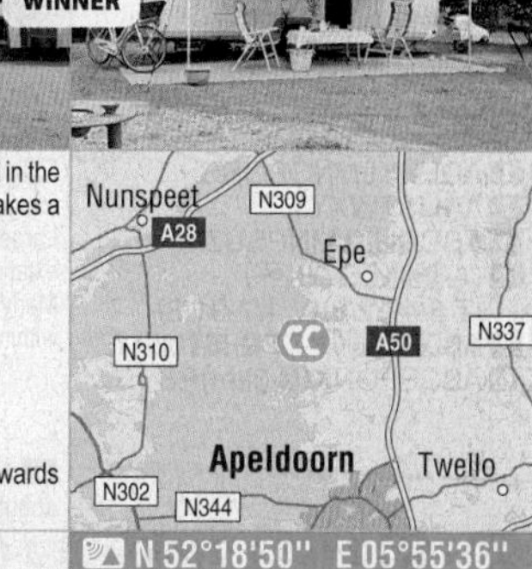

CC € 27 2/4-25/4 21/5-5/7 1/9-29/9

N 52°18'50'' E 05°55'36''

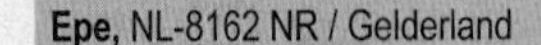

Epe, NL-8162 NR / Gelderland

256

RCN de Jagerstee****
Officiersweg 86
+31 8 50 40 07 00
29/3 - 3/11
reserveringen@rcn.nl

33ha 350T(100m²) 10-16A CEE

1 ACD**I**KLMNPRS
2 BISTXYZ
3 ABCDE**G**IKMNPRSU
4 (A)(C+H 24/4-15/9)M
(Q+S+T+U+X+Y+Z)
5 **AB**DEFGIJKLMNPQR**T**UWZ
6 CDEFGHKLM(N 3km)
OPSTV

Located in a wooded area with plenty of space, tranquillity and atmosphere and in the heart of De Hoge Veluwe National Park. An ideal area for walking and cycling. The campsite has an open-air theatre and a supermarket. Many attractive towns close by such as Apeldoorn and Zwolle. Comfort pitch Euro 3.00 extra.

A50 Apeldoorn-Zwolle, exit 27, follow the N309 towards Nunspeet, after the roundabout follow the 'Jagerstee' camping signs.

CC € 21 *29/3-7/5 13/5-16/5 21/5-4/7 26/8-3/11*

N 52°21'51'' E 05°57'32''

Ermelo, NL-3852 AM / Gelderland

257

Ardoer cp. & bungalowpark De Haeghehorst*****
Fazantlaan 4
+31 3 41 55 31 85
1/1 - 31/12
haeghehorst@ardoer.com

10ha 255T(75-160m²) 6-10A CEE

1 ADEGKLMNOQRS
2 BIJSTWXYZ
3 ABC**G**HIKLMNP**Q**SU
4 (C 27/4-28/10)
(F+H 27/3-27/10)J**LMN**
(Q 1/4-30/10)(R)
(T+U+V 29/3-27/10)
(X 29/4-27/10)(Z 29/3-27/10)
5 **AB**CDEFGHIJKLMNOPQR**T**UWXY
6 ABCEFGHKL(N 1,5km)
OPSV

The campsite is family-oriented and very well equipped, ideally located on the edge of Ermelo, close to the Veluwe woods in the direction of Harderwijk. Excellent toilet facilities. The campsite has an indoor and outdoor swimming pool.

A28, exit 12 direction Ermelo, then follow camping signs. Campsite is located on the north side of Ermelo.

CC € 27 *1/1-29/3 2/4-26/4 22/5-5/7 31/8-31/12*

N 52°18'47'' E 05°37'48''

Ermelo, NL-3852 MC / Gelderland

258

Kriemelberg BushCamp****
Drieërweg 104
+31 3 41 55 21 42
22/3 - 12/10
camping@kriemelberg.nl

10ha 109T(80-140m²) 6-10A CEE

1 ADE**H**KLMNOPQRS
2 ABIJSTWXYZ
3 ABC**G**IJKLMNPSUZ
4 (A)M(Q+R)
(T 3/4-12/9)(V 1/7-31/8)
5 **AB**DEFGI**J**KMNO**PQ**R**ST**UWXYZ
6 ABCEFGH**K**(N 3km)PS

A campsite in parkland setting with spacious pitches, imaginatively laid out between hedges and large bushes. Large modern toilet block with family showers. The site has extensive woods and the Ermelo Heath is slightly further away. Many tourist places (Ermelo, Putten, Garderen, Harderwijk) within easy reach.

A28 exit 12 (Ermelo) direction Ermelo. Left at 5th round about towards Drie. Campsite signposted.

CC € 19 *2/4-25/4 21/5-7/7 25/8-11/10*

N 52°17'12'' E 05°38'48''

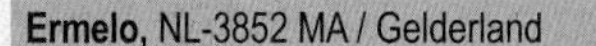

Ermelo, NL-3852 MA / Gelderland

259

- Recreatiepark De Paalberg*****
- Drieërweg 125
- +31 3 41 55 23 73
- 1/1 - 31/12
- info@paalberg.nl

30ha 163**T**(100-120m²) 6-10A CEE

1 ACDE**I**KLMNOPQRU
2 BIJSTWXYZ
3 ABC**G**HIJKLMNOP**R**SU
4 (C 1/5-30/9)(F+H)IJK**LMN** (Q+S+T+U+V+Y+Z)
5 **AB**CDFGHIJKLMNOPQUWXYZ
6 ABCDEFGHKL(N 3km) OPSTV

Stunning campsite, bordering the Heathlands of Ermelo. Walking and cycling opportunities. Close to the bordering lakes. Wonderfully designed leisure pool and toilet and washing facilities. Free Wi-Fi. Comfort pitches for 3 euro supplement.

A28 exit 12 dir. Ermelo. Turn left at the 6th roundabout (on the south side of Ermelo) dir. Drie. Campsite signposted.

Harderwijk
Zeewolde
A28
N705
CC
N310
Nijkerk
N303
N302
N301
A1

CC € 23 *1/1-27/4 21/5-6/7 24/8-31/12* ***7=6, 14=12, 21=18, 28=24***

N 52°17'16'' E 05°39'25''

Groesbeek, NL-6561 KR / Gelderland

260

- Vakantiepark De Oude Molen***
- Wylerbaan 2a
- +31 2 43 97 17 15
- 1/4 - 31/10
- vakantiepark@oudemolen.nl

6,5ha 140**T**(80-120m²) 4-16A CEE

1 AD**I**KLNORS
2 IJLSTWXY
3 ACE**G**HKMNPSU
4 (C+H 29/4-30/8)JN (T+U+X+Y+Z)
5 **AB**DEFGIJKLMNOPQRUWXY
6 ACEFGHKL(N 0km)OPTV

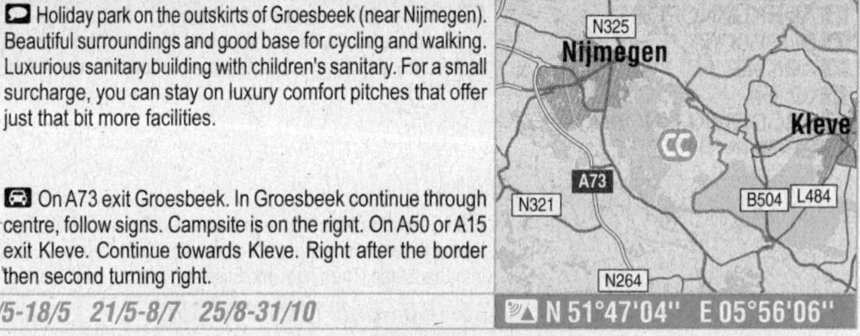

Holiday park on the outskirts of Groesbeek (near Nijmegen). Beautiful surroundings and good base for cycling and walking. Luxurious sanitary building with children's sanitary. For a small surcharge, you can stay on luxury comfort pitches that offer just that bit more facilities.

On A73 exit Groesbeek. In Groesbeek continue through centre, follow signs. Campsite is on the right. On A50 or A15 exit Kleve. Continue towards Kleve. Right after the border then second turning right.

CC € 19 *1/4-27/4 6/5-9/5 13/5-18/5 21/5-8/7 25/8-31/10*

N 51°47'04'' E 05°56'06''

Harfsen, NL-7217 MD / Gelderland

261

- Camping De Huurne
- Harfsensesteeg 15
- +31 5 73 45 90 26
- 30/3 - 1/10
- campingdehuurne@hotmail.com

1,5ha 65**T**(80-180m²) 16A

1 AD**I**KLMNOQ**R**S
2 SUWXYZ
3 CEKS
4 M
5 **A**BGHIJMNO**P**UWZ
6 CH**K**(N 3km)

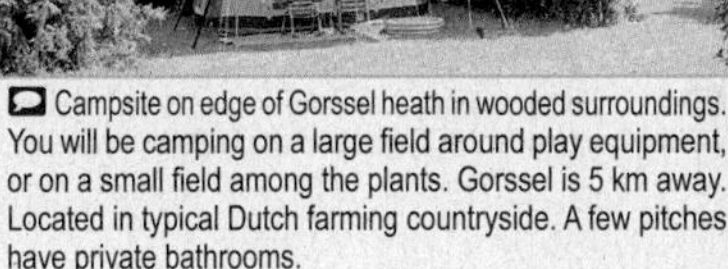

Campsite on edge of Gorssel heath in wooded surroundings. You will be camping on a large field around play equipment, or on a small field among the plants. Gorssel is 5 km away. Located in typical Dutch farming countryside. A few pitches have private bathrooms.

A1 exit 23 Deventer direction Eefde. Keep left around the church. After 2 km Harfsense Steeg. After 4 km campsite on the left. Some GPS navigation systems don't work here. If so enter coordinates.

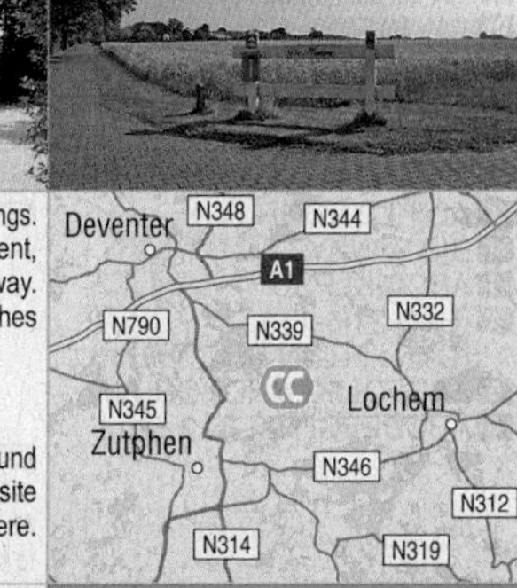

CC € 15 *1/4-8/5 21/5-30/6 2/9-1/10*

N 52°10'59'' E 06°16'34''

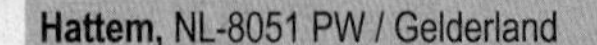

Hattem, NL-8051 PW / Gelderland

262

Molecaten Park De Leemkule****
Leemkuilen 6
+31 3 84 44 19 45
22/3 - 1/11
deleemkule@molecaten.nl

24ha 150**T**(100m²) 10A CEE

1 ACDGKLMNOPQRS
2 BISTUWXYZ
3 ACE**G**IKMN**O**P**R**SU
4 (A 10/7-20/8)(B 27/4-1/9) (F+H)K**LN** (Q+R+T+U+X+Y+Z)
5 **AB**DFGIJKLMNOPQUWXYZ
6 EFH**K**M(N 4km)OPSTV

Attractive holiday park in the Veluwe woods close to Hattem and the Molecaten Country Estate. Comfort pitches, indoor swimming pool, tennis courts, restaurant, shop and bike hire. Walking and cycling routes. Close to Apenheul, Het Loo Palace and the Dolfinarium.

A28 exit 17 Wezep, straight ahead at roundabout then at the next junction direction Heerde. Over the railway line after 3.5 km as far as Hattem Wapenveld exit. Turn left. Entrance to the park about 3 km on the left.

CC € 21 *22/3-25/4 6/5-8/5 13/5-16/5 21/5-11/7 30/8-30/10*

N 52°27'22'' E 06°02'11''

Hattem, NL-8051 PM / Gelderland

263

Molecaten Park Landgoed Molecaten***
Koeweg 1
+31 3 84 44 70 44
22/3 - 1/10
landgoedmolecaten@molecaten.nl

10ha 41**T**(100m²) 10A CEE

1 AD**H**KLMNOPQ**R**S
2 BIJSWXYZ
3 A**G**KMS
4 (Q)
5 **ABC**DCGI**JK**L**M**NO**PQ**UWXZ
6 EFG**K**(N 1km)OPTV

The campsite is situated in wooded surroundings but is also close to the lovely village of Hattem. You will find both sunny and shaded pitches in a number of small fields.

A50 exit Hattem. Via Hessenweg and Gelderse Dijk. Turn right at the end. Turn right on Nieuweweg into Stationstraat. Left into Stadslaan. Then right into Eliselaan and left into Koeweg.

CC € 17 *22/3-25/4 6/5-8/5 13/5-16/5 21/5-11/7 30/8-30/9*

N 52°27'59'' E 06°03'26''

Heerde, NL-8181 LP / Gelderland

264

Camping De Zandkuil***
Veldweg 25
+31 5 78 69 19 52
1/4 - 1/11
info@dezandkuil.nl

11,5ha 183**T**(90-100m²) 6-10A CEE

1 AD**I**KLMNOQRUV
2 BISTVWXYZ
3 ABC**G**IKLPSU
4 (B+G 21/5-1/9) (Q+R+T+U+V+X+Z)
5 **AB**DFGI**JKL**MNOPQRUWZ
6 ABCDEFGHJ**K**L(N 2,5km) OPST

A comfortable family campsite in the Noord Veluwe woods. CampingCard ACSI gives access to the luxury pitches.

A50 Apeldoorn-Zwolle, exit 29, Heerde. At 1st roundabout second exit (Molenweg), at second roundabout, first turn. At third roundabout second turn towards Wapenveld. Left to the Koerbergseweg. Follow signs.

CC € 17 *2/4-8/5 22/5-30/6 1/9-31/10* ***14=12***

N 52°24'38'' E 06°02'37''

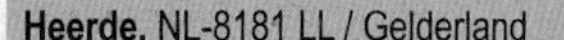

Heerde, NL-8181 LL / Gelderland

iD 265

- Molecaten Park De Koerberg****
- Koerbergseweg 4/1
- +31 5 78 69 98 10
- 22/3 - 1/11
- @ dekoerberg@molecaten.nl

22ha 150T(80-100m²) 16A CEE

1 ACD**H**KLMNOQRS
2 BILSTWXYZ
3 AC**G**IKMN**O**PS**T**U
4 (C+H 1/5-31/8) (Q+R+T+U+X+Y+Z)
5 **AB**DEFGHIJKLMNOPQRUWXY
6 ACDEFGHJ**K**(N 3km) OPSTX

The location of the Koerberg is fantastic. The Zwolsche Bos (woodland) and the beautiful heaths of the Veluwe are the greatest attractions.

A50 Apeldoorn/Zwolle, exit 29 Heerde/Wapenveld. Direction Heerde. 2nd exit at roundabout (Molenweg), next roundabout 3rd exit (Veldweg). At end of Veldweg left into Koerbergseweg, then immediately right.

CC € 19 *22/3-25/4 6/5-8/5 13/5-16/5 21/5-11/7 30/8-30/10*

N 52°24'34'' E 06°03'05''

Heteren, NL-6666 LA / Gelderland

iD 266

- Camping Overbetuwe
- Uilenburgsestraat 3
- +31 2 64 74 22 33
- 1/1 - 31/12
- @ info@campingoverbetuwe.nl

4,2ha 39T(100-200m²) 10A CEE

1 AIKLMNOP**RS**
2 IJSTWY
3 ACE**G**HIKPSUW
5 **AB**DFGI**J**MNO**P**UZ
6 ADEFGJ(N 3km)**P**TV

More than just a campsite. Centrally located, quiet and easily accessible via the A50. Pitches are marked out with bushes and there is plenty of shade. Ideally situated for trips (by bike) to the Veluwe and the Betuwe. There are play facilities for the little ones. The beautiful nature and the bird paradise (peacocks) are special at this campsite.

A50, exit 18 Heteren. Then follow camping signs.

CC € 17 *1/1-8/5 21/5-15/7 1/9-31/12*

N 51°56'55'' E 05°46'21''

Hoenderloo, NL-7351 TN / Gelderland

iD 267

- Camping De Pampel*****
- Woeste Hoefweg 35
- +31 5 53 78 17 60
- 1/1 - 31/12
- @ info@pampel.nl

14,5ha 278T(100-200m²) 6-16A CEE

1 ACDGKLNORS
2 BIJLSTWXYZ
3 ABCDEHIKMN**O**PSU
4 (C 15/5-31/8) (E 15/4-30/9,13/10-28/10) (H 1/5-30/9)IJM (Q+S 16/4-30/9) (T+U+V+Y 1/4-30/9)
5 **AB**CDEFGIJKLMNOPQR**T**UWXYZ
6 ABCEFGH**K**(N 1km)OPST

Beautiful 5 star campsite in wooded surroundings. Spacious pitches on a grassy field, or private pitches surrounded by trees and bushes. Underfloor heating and climate control in the toilet blocks make this an ideal winter location. Heated indoor swimming pool. Arrival after 13:00 and departure before 12:00.

A1 exit 19 Apeldoorn/Hoenderloo. In Hoenderloo continue in the direction of Loenen. Or take A50 Arnhem-Apeldoorn, exit 22 Hoenderloo. Follow the Hoenderloo signs.

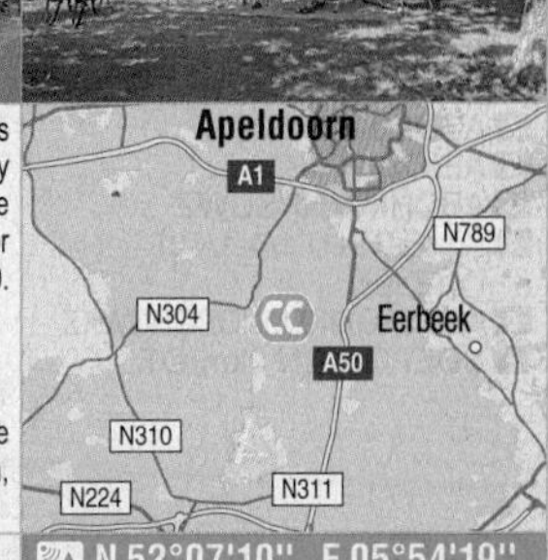

CC € 23 *1/1-26/4 21/5-6/7 24/8-31/12* ***7=6, 14=12, 21=18***

N 52°07'10'' E 05°54'19''

Hoenderloo, NL-7351 TM / Gelderland

268

Recreatiepark 't Veluws Hof
Krimweg 152-154
+31 5 53 78 17 77
23/3 - 26/10
info@veluwshof.nl

32ha 70T(100-130m²) 6A CEE

1 ADIKLNRS
2 BILSTWXYZ
3 ABCGHIKLMNOPRSTU
4 (A 1/7-1/9)(C+H 26/4-14/9)J (Q+S+T+U+Y+Z)
5 ABDFGIJMNOPQRUWXY
6 ABCEFGHKL(N 4km) OPSTV

Recreatiepark 't Veluws Hof is located close to the Hoge Veluwe National Park among woods where you can enjoy cycling and walking. All the pitches are spacious comfort pitches with every amenity. Maximum two pets allowed (first pet is free). There is a recreation team in high season.

A1, exit 19 Apeldoorn-Hoenderloo, in Hoenderloo follow camping signs or A50 Arnhem-Hoenderloo, exit 22 Hoenderloo, follow signs to Hoenderloo.

Apeldoorn, A1, N789, A50, N304, Eerbeek, N310, N224, N311

CC € 21 *23/3-7/5 21/5-5/7 24/8-25/10*

N 52°07'21" E 05°55'17"

Hoenderloo, NL-7351 BP / Gelderland

269

Veluwe camping 't Schinkel***
Miggelenbergweg 60
+31 5 53 78 13 67
29/3 - 31/10
info@hetschinkel.nl

7,5ha 200T(80-100m²) 6-16A CEE

1 ACDIKLMNOPRS
2 ILSTWXYZ
3 BCDHIKMNPSU
4 (C+H 22/4-15/9)J (Q+R+T+U+V)
5 ABDEFGIJKLMNOPQRUWXYZ
6 BCDEFGK(N 1km)OPST

Campsite is an oasis of peace and tranquillity in both early and late seasons. The site is located on the edge of a wood in a sunny and spacious setting. Its central position in the heart of the Veluwe makes the campsite the perfect base for cycling or walking in the endless Veluwe and for discovering the rich culture.

From Arnhem/Apeldoorn/Ede maintain direction Hoenderloo. Then follow the sign Beekbergen/Loenen direction Beekbergen and follow the camping signs.

Apeldoorn, A1, N789, N304, Eerbeek, A50, N310, N311

CC € 21 *29/3-26/4 21/5-13/7 31/8-1/10 7=6, 14=12, 21=18*

N 52°07'42" E 05°54'15"

Kesteren, NL-4041 AW / Gelderland

270

Camping "Betuwe"***
Hoge Dijkseweg 40
+31 4 88 48 14 77
15/3 - 15/10
info@campingbetuwe.nl

30ha 60T(90-110m²) 10A CEE

1 ACDIKLMNOQRU
2 AEIOSXY
3 ABCHIKMNPSUWZ
4 (Q)(T+U 1/4-1/10) (Y+Z)
5 ABDEFGIJKLMNOPQRUWXZ
6 CDEFGHK(N 2km)OT

A pond on the campsite can be used as a swimming pond.

A15, exit 35 Ochten/Kesteren. N320 direction Culemborg. Follow signs camping site. A12 exit Veenendaal/Rhenen. Over the Rijnbrug, exit Kesteren. Turn right at the bottom of the road, then 1st li.

CC € 23 *15/3-28/3 2/4-8/5 13/5-16/5 21/5-30/6 1/9-15/10*

N 51°56'15" E 05°32'46"

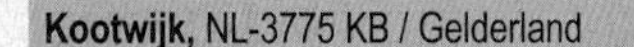

Kootwijk, NL-3775 KB / Gelderland

271

Camping Huttopia De Veluwe***
H. van 't Hoffweg 25
+31 3 18 45 62 72
28/3 - 27/10
develuwe@huttopia.com

16ha 200T(100-200m²) 6-10A CEE

1 ADIJKLMNPRUV
2 BIJSTXYZ
3 BCIJKLP
5 **AB**DEFGI**J**KMNO**PQ**UXYZ
6 BEFGHJ(N 2,5km)T

Perfectly located in a Dutch Forestry Commission (Staatsbosbeheer) nature reserve. Within walking distance of Kootwijker Zand and Radio Kootwijk in the heart of the Amersfoort-Apeldoorn-Arnhem triangle. An attractive, characteristic woodland campsite with a large variety of pitches; only touring pitches and no permanent pitches.

A1, exit 17 towards Harskamp, and then follow the signs.

CC € 19 *28/3-26/4 12/5-17/5 20/5-5/7 25/8-27/10*

N 52°09'01'' E 05°44'28''

Laag-Soeren, NL-6957 DP / Gelderland

272

Ardoer Vakantiedorp De Jutberg****
Jutberg 78
+31 3 13 61 92 20
1/1 - 31/12
info@jutberg.nl

18ha 152T(80-120m²) 6-10A CEE

1 ACD**I**KLMNQRS
2 BILSTWYZ
3 ABC**G**IKLMNPSU
4 (A 6/7-25/8)(E+H 1/4-31/10) J(Q+R+T+U+X+Z 1/4-31/10)
5 **AB**DEFGIJKLMNOPQR**T**UWXYZ
6 CEFGHKL(N 3km)OPSTV

A top class campsite which lives up to the expectations of all its campers.

A1 exit Apeldoorn-Zuid direction Dieren, follow the signs. From the A12 direction Zutphen-Dieren, Laag-Soeren then follow the signs.

CC € 25 *1/1-7/5 21/5-4/7 2/9-31/12* ***21=18***

N 52°04'05'' E 06°04'48''

Lieren/Beekbergen, NL-7364 CB / Gelderland

273

Ardoer comfortcamping De Bosgraaf****
Kanaal Zuid 444
+31 5 55 05 13 59
29/3 - 29/10
bosgraaf@ardoer.com

22ha 187T(100-144m²) 6-16A CEE

1 ACDGKLMNRS
2 BISTXYZ
3 ABCE**G**IJKLMN**O**PSU
4 (C+H 1/5-15/9)JM (Q+R+T+U+X+Z)
5 **AB**DFGIJKLMNOPQRUWXZ
6 ABEFGHKL(N 2,5km) OPSTV

A large but peaceful campsite outside the village next to a canal. Lovely pitches in open fields and in the woods.

A1 exit 20 Apeldoorn-Zuid/Beekbergen turn left after the exit and then follow the signs. Or A50 exit 23 Loenen, towards Loenen and then turn left towards Klarenbeek. Follow the signs.

CC € 21 *2/4-25/4 5/5-7/5 13/5-16/5 21/5-5/7 31/8-29/10*

N 52°08'39'' E 06°02'09''

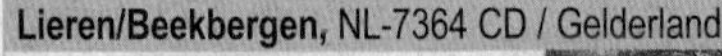

Lieren/Beekbergen, NL-7364 CD / Gelderland

274

Camping De Vinkenkamp***
Vinkenkamp 10
+31 5 55 05 12 53
1/1 - 31/12
info@vinkenkamp.nl

3,7ha 50T(80-130m²) 10-16A CEE

1 AD**I**KLMNPRS
2 ISTWXYZ
3 ABCE**G**HIKLMNSU
4 (C+H 15/5-15/9)(Q+R)
(T+U 8/7-3/9)(X)
(Z 8/7-3/9)
5 **AB**DFGIJKLMNPUWXYZ
6 BCDEFGKL(N 5km)T

Small-scale campsite close to Scherpenbergh golf course. Special grass pitches with paved surface for motorhomes. Excellent walking and cycling region.

A1, exit Apeldoorn-Zuid/Beekbergen, turn left after the exit then follow the signs. Or A50 exit 23 Loenen, towards Loenen, turn left to Klarenbeek. Follow the signs. Albaweg, follow signs to Scherpenbergh golf course

N344 · Apeldoorn · A1 · N790 · Zutphen · N304 · A50 · N786 · N348

CC € 19 *1/1-25/4 21/5-7/7 24/8-31/12*

N 52°09'02'' E 06°01'20''

Lunteren, NL-6741 KG / Gelderland

275

Camping De Rimboe***
Boslaan 129
+31 3 18 48 23 71
15/3 - 19/10
info@campingderimboe.com

12,2ha 140T(80-120m²) 6-10A CEE

1 ACD**H**KLMNOQRS
2 BILSTWXYZ
3 ABCHIKLMPSU
4 (A 1/7-1/9)
5 **AB**CDFGI**J**K**L**MNO**PR**UWXYZ
6 ABCEFGH**K**L(N 2,5km)
OPTV

A friendly and hospitable campsite for relaxing and cycling. Beautiful pitches in various fields (both sunny and shaded), or free camping in the wood. The campsite has excellent toilet facilities. Many cycling and walking opportunities. Lively tourist towns such as Lunteren, Ede and Barneveld. A short distance from an open air swimming pool.

A30, exit Lunteren. Follow ring road (so not into the centre) after which the campsite is signposted.

N301 · A1 · Barneveld · N310 · N304 · N802 · A30 · Veenendaal · Ede · N224 · A12

CC € 19 *15/3-5/5 21/5-5/7 1/9-19/10* ***21=18***

N 52°05'31'' E 05°39'47''

Lunteren, NL-6741 JP / Gelderland

276

Recreatiecentrum de Goudsberg***
Hessenweg 85
+31 3 18 48 23 86
1/1 - 31/12
info@goudsberg.nl

16ha 63T(80-120m²) 10-16A CEE

1 ACD**I**KLMNOQ**R**S
2 BIJLSTUYZ
3 CIJKL**O**P**R**SU
4 (B 1/5-30/9)(F+H 1/4-31/10)
(T 1/7-31/8)(Y)
(Z 1/7-31/8)
5 **AB**CDEFGIJMNPUXY
6 ABEFGHJ(N 1,5km)PT

Camping in the Veluwe, enjoy peace, quiet and greenery. Discover the comfort of both an outdoor and an indoor swimming pool. The park is located directly on a nature reserve where you can enjoy walking, cycling, mountain biking as well as horseback riding. With the centre of the Netherlands within walking distance and many fun activities nearby.

A30, exit 3 towards Lunteren, then follow the tourist information signs for De Goudsberg recreation centre.

CC € 23 *2/1-25/4 13/5-16/5 21/5-11/7 2/9-23/12 27/12-31/12* ***7=6, 14=12, 21=18***

N 52°05'54'' E 05°38'40''

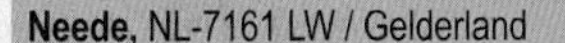

Neede, NL-7161 LW / Gelderland

277

- Camping Den Blanken****
- Diepenheimseweg 44
- +31 5 47 35 13 53
- 1/4 - 30/9
- info@campingdenblanken.nl

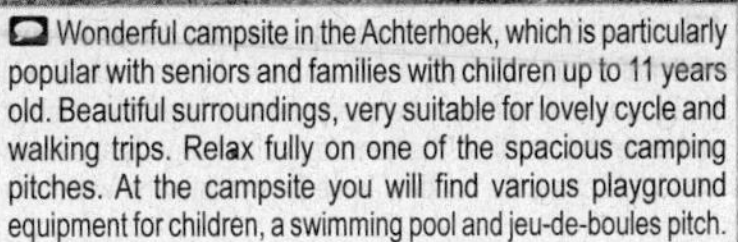

7,2ha 184**T**(100-150m²) 6-10A CEE

1 ADE**I**KLMNOQRTU
2 CSTWXYZ
3 ABCD**G**HIKMNOSU**W**X
4 (C+H 1/5-1/9)(Q 6/7-1/9) (R+T)
5 **AB**CDEFGI**JKL**MNO**P**QUWXYZ
6 ABCDEFGHKM(N 3km) OPTU

Wonderful campsite in the Achterhoek, which is particularly popular with seniors and families with children up to 11 years old. Beautiful surroundings, very suitable for lovely cycle and walking trips. Relax fully on one of the spacious camping pitches. At the campsite you will find various playground equipment for children, a swimming pool and jeu-de-boules pitch.

On the Diepenheim-Neede road. Campsite signposted.

CC € 19 *1/4-8/5 21/5-1/7 1/9-29/9*

N 52°10'49'' E 06°35'13''

Nunspeet, NL-8072 PK / Gelderland

278

- Camping De Witte Wieven***
- Wiltsangh 41
- +31 3 41 25 26 42
- 22/3 - 31/10
- info@wittewieven.nl

18,8ha 70T(100m²) 6-10A CEE

1 AD**I**KLMNOPQ**R**TU
2 BISXY
3 BCGKMN**Q**S
4 (B+G 1/6-1/9)(T+U+X+Z)
5 **AB**DFGIJMNO**P**UWZ
6 CEFGH**K**(N 1km)OPVX

Beautiful campsite in the Nunspeet woods. There is new play equipment for youngsters and pony riding is among the possibilities. You can also take your own horse/pony.

On A28 take exit 15 towards Nunspeet, 1st right after level crossing.

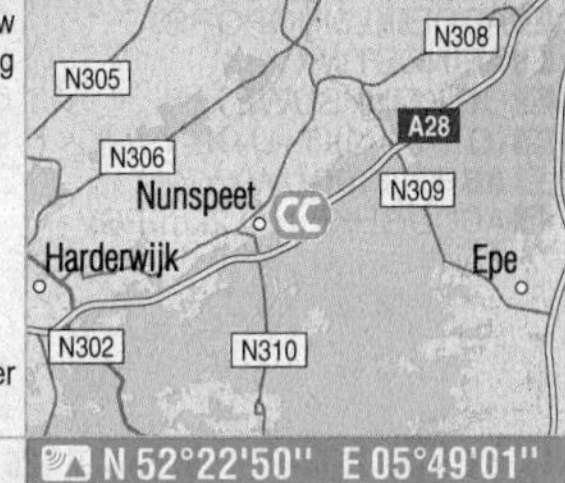

CC € 19 *22/3-8/5 21/5-5/7 30/8-31/10*

N 52°22'50'' E 05°49'01''

Otterlo, NL-6731 SN / Gelderland

279

- Camping Beek en Hei***
- Heideweg 4
- +31 3 18 59 14 83
- 1/1 - 31/12
- info@beekenhei.nl

5ha 128**T**(60-100m²) 4-6A CEE

1 ACD**I**KLMNP**R**UV
2 BIJSTVWXYZ
3 ACIKLMNSU
4 (Q 15/7-31/8)(R)
5 **AB**DFGIJKLMNO**P**RUWXY
6 ABCEFGHJ**K**(N 1km)PTV

Friendly campsite just outside Otterlo. Set in a beautiful area close to the Hoge Veluwe national park, the Kröller-Müller modern art museum, Planken Wambuis and Ginkelse Heide. A good base for cycling and walking.

A12 exit 23 Arnhem-Oosterbeek direction Arnhem. Then direction Otterlo and follow the campsite signs.

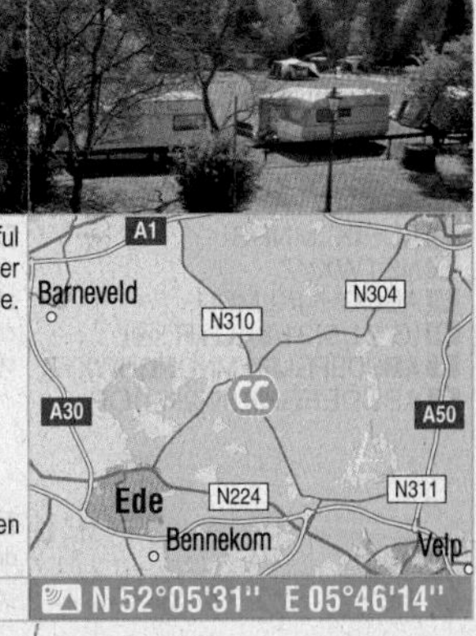

CC € 21 *3/1-21/4 22/5-3/7 3/9-20/12* ***7=6, 14=12, 21=18***

N 52°05'31'' E 05°46'14''

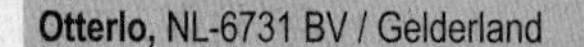

Otterlo, NL-6731 BV / Gelderland

280

EuroParcs De Wije Werelt****
Arnhemseweg 100-102
+31 8 80 70 81 70
29/3 - 1/11
kcc@europarcs.nl

12ha 150T(100-150m²) 10-16A CEE

1 ACD**I**KLMNORS
2 BIJSTVWXYZ
3 ABCDE**G**IJKLMNPSU
4 (**A** 1/4-1/9)(C+H 25/4-15/9)M (Q+S+T+Y+Z)
5 **AB**DEFGIJKLMNPQ**T**UWXY
6 ABCEFGHKL(N 2km)OSTX

A beautifully located campsite near the Hoge Veluwe National Park, adjoining the Wambuis Ginkel and Ginkel Heath nature reserves. The campsite has spacious pitches and excellent facilities. The beautiful Veluwe woods and fields make this campsite an ideal base for cyclists and walkers.

A12 exit 23 or 25. A1 exit 17 or 19. All exits signposted to Park Hoge Veluwe. In Otterlo follow signs.

CC € 27 *2/4-26/4 13/5-17/5 20/5-5/7 2/9-1/11*

N 52°05'12'' E 05°46'10''

Putten, NL-3882 RN / Gelderland

281

Strandparc Nulde****
Strandboulevard 27
+31 3 41 36 13 04
29/3 - 1/10
info@strandparcnulde.nl

15ha 30T(90-110m²) 10A CEE

1 ACDE**I**KLMNOPQRS
2 AFINOSTWXY
3 C**G**IKMNPSUWZ
4 (Q 1/7-1/9)(T+U+X+Y)
5 **AB**FGIJN**PQ**UWXYZ
6 ABCDGHKL(N 0,2km)PSV

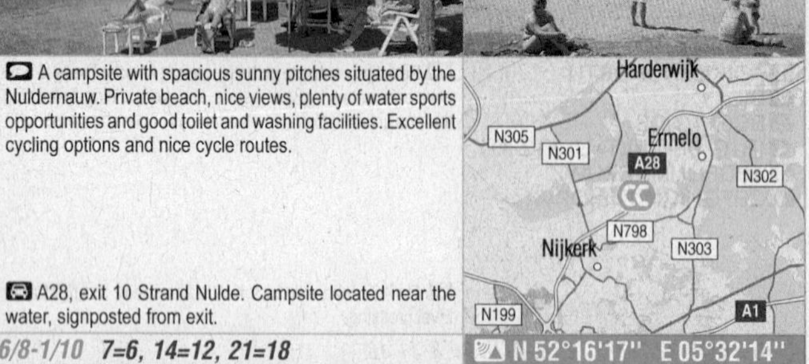

A campsite with spacious sunny pitches situated by the Nuldernauw. Private beach, nice views, plenty of water sports opportunities and good toilet and washing facilities. Excellent cycling options and nice cycle routes.

A28, exit 10 Strand Nulde. Campsite located near the water, signposted from exit.

CC € 19 *29/3-8/5 21/5-8/7 26/8-1/10* ***7=6, 14=12, 21=18***

N 52°16'17'' E 05°32'14''

Ruurlo, NL-7261 MR / Gelderland

282

Camping Tamaring***
Wildpad 3
+31 5 73 45 14 86
29/3 - 6/10
info@camping-tamaring.nl

3,5ha 108T(100-150m²) 10A CEE

1 ADF**I**KLMNRS
2 NSTWXYZ
3 ABC**G**HIJKLMSU
4 (G 21/5-31/8)(Q+R)
5 **AB**CDEFGI**JKL**MNO**PQ**UWXYZ
6 ABCDEFGHK(N 2km)OP

A wonderfully hospitable and friendly campsite, located right in the middle of the Achterhoek region. The site is suitable for those wanting to relax and for families with young children. Surrounded by various nature reserves. Ideal for cycling and walking.

Motorway A1, exit 26 when coming from the north. N332 direction Lochem-Barchem-Ruurlo. Follow signs.

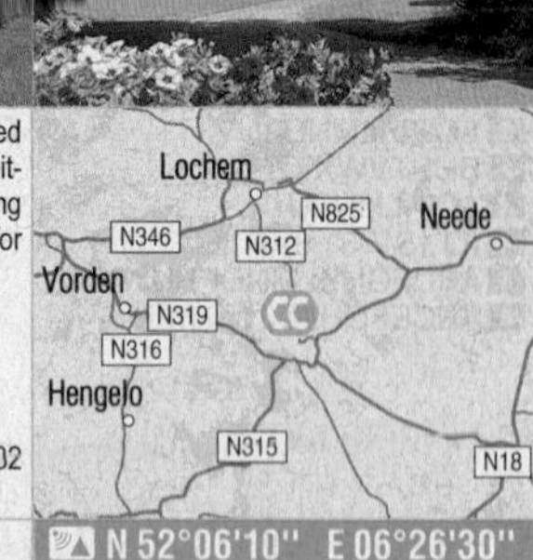

CC € 21 *29/3-7/5 21/5-8/7 25/8-4/10*

N 52°06'10'' E 06°26'30''

Stokkum, NL-7039 CW / Gelderland

283

Camping De Slangenbult
St. Isidorusstraat 12
+31 3 14 66 27 98
1/1 - 31/12
info@deslangenbult.nl

10ha 75T(100-140m²) 10-16A CEE

1 ADIKLMNOQRS
2 BIJLSTXY
3 ACEGHIKMNPS
5 ABCDFGIJKLMNOPUZ
6 ACEFGK(N 3km)PS

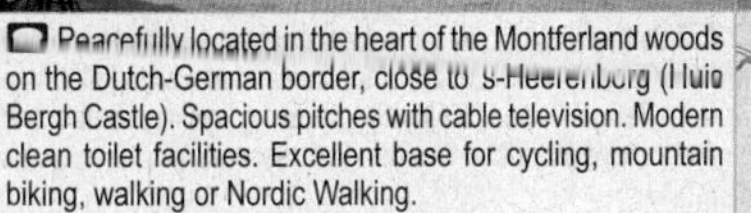

Peacefully located in the heart of the Montferland woods on the Dutch-German border, close to 's-Heerenberg (Huis Bergh Castle). Spacious pitches with cable television. Modern clean toilet facilities. Excellent base for cycling, mountain biking, walking or Nordic Walking.

A12 exit 30 to Beek, continue towards Beek. Turn right at 1st roundabout in Beek then immediately left, follow road for 3 km. 1st street on the right in Stokkum (long hedge). Follow camping signs.

N336
A10
N317
N335
B8
Emmerich am Rhein
A3
L8
Kleve

CC € 19 12/1-3/5 24/5-7/7 25/8-15/12

N 51°52'43'' E 06°12'53''

Stokkum, NL-7039 CV / Gelderland

284

Camping Landgoed Brockhausen
Eltenseweg 20
+31 3 14 66 12 12
29/3 - 1/10
campingbrockhausen@gmail.com

4ha 47T(100-160m²) 10A CEE

1 ADIKLMNOQRU
2 BISTXYZ
3 AGHIJK
4 (A+Q 🔑)
5 ABDEFGHIJKLMNOPQRUWXYZ
6 BCDEFGKT

Quality, peace and nature. Peaceful family campsite set in rural woodland. Spacious pitches in several grassy fields, surrounded by trees and shrubbery. Excellent toilet block with many facilities.

A12/A3 exit 's-Heerenberg, then direction Stokkum, then follow campsite signs.

N336
A12
A18
N317
N335
A12
Emmerich am Rhein
A3
B8
L8
Kleve

CC € 23 29/3-8/5 20/5-1/7 15/7-29/7 1/9-1/10

N 51°52'40'' E 06°12'39''

Stroe, NL-3776 PV / Gelderland

285

Camping Jacobus Hoeve***
Tolnegenweg 53
+31 3 42 44 13 19
29/3 - 31/10
info@jacobus-hoeve.nl

5ha 60T(100-150m²) 10-16A CEE

1 ACDEIKLMNOPQRS
2 ISTUVWXY
3 ABCHIKMNS
4 (A 30/4-30/8)M
(T+U+X+Z 🔑)
5 ABCDFGIJMNOPUWXY
6 ABDEFGHKLM(N 1km)OPS

Friendly family campsite surrounded by woods and drifting sand. Stunning location on the edge of the vast Veluwe. The restaurant is only open on Saturdays. The reception is closed on Sundays.

A1 exit 17 direction Stroe. Left at 1st roundabout, right before level crossing. Campsite 800m on the left of the road.

Putten
N302
A28
Nijkerk
N344
N301
A1
Barneveld
N310
N304
A30

CC € 17 29/3-8/5 21/5-1/7 19/8-31/10

N 52°11'38'' E 05°40'42''

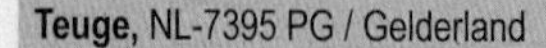

Teuge, NL-7395 PG / Gelderland

286

Camping de Weeltenkamp***
De Zanden 215
+31 5 52 00 02 04
15/3 - 1/10
info@deweeltenkamp.nl

4ha 104T(120-150m²) 6-10A CEE

1 ACD**I**JKLMNOP**R**S
2 INSUVWXYZ
3 ABCDE**G**HIKMPSUZ
4 (**A**)(B 1/4-1/10) M(Q 1/7-31/8) (T+U+V+X+Z)
5 **AB**CDEFGHIJK**L**MNOPQUWXYZ
6 CDEFGHKL(N 3km)PT

Lovely small-scale campsite between the Veluwerand and River Ijssel, with excellent amenities and at walking distance from Teuge Airport. Enjoy the stunning cycling routes and then a lovely drink in the friendly brasserie.

A50 exit 26 Terwolde/Vaassen, left at Terwolde, then direction Teuge. Campsite is signposted after 1.5 km.

CC € 21 *19/5-30/6 1/9-30/9*

N 52°14'56'' E 06°03'25''

Ugchelen, NL-7339 GG / Gelderland

287

Camping De Wapenberg***
Hoenderloseweg 187
+31 5 55 33 45 39
28/3 - 6/10
info@dewapenberg.nl

4ha 59T(80-140m²) 6-16A CEE

1 AD**I**KLMNRS
2 BILSTUWXYZ
3 AIKLMSU
4 M
5 **AB**DEFGIJKLMNO**P**UWXYZ
6 ABCEFG**K**(N 2km)PT

This attractive campsite is located in an extensive area of woodland, heathland, hills and by the source of several springs. You will be camping on the edge of a wood with unusually laid out individual pitches. Rest, nature, walking and cycling with the sights of Apeldoorn close by.

A1 exit 19 Hoenderloo dir. Ede/Hoenderloo. Follow camping signs. Via A50 exit 22. In Beekbergen left at first traffic lights. Follow road till campsite is signposted.

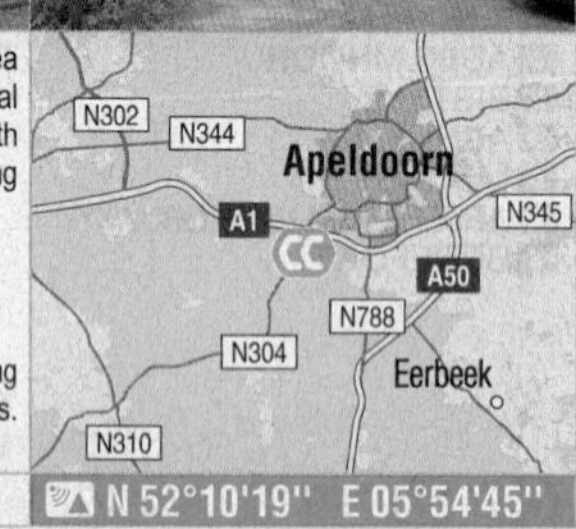

CC € 21 *28/3-26/4 21/5-1/7 1/9-6/10*

N 52°10'19'' E 05°54'45''

Vierhouten, NL-8076 PM / Gelderland

288

Recreatiepark Samoza****
Plaggeweg 90
+31 5 77 41 12 83
22/3 - 4/11
info@samoza.nl

70ha 329T(100-150m²) 4-10A CEE

1 ACDIKLMNOQRS
2 BISTUWXYZ
3 ABCDE**G**HIKMNP**Q**SU
4 (C 30/4-28/8)(F+H)JM (Q+S+T+X+Y+Z)
5 **AB**DEFGHIJKLMNOPQR**T**UXYZ
6 CFGHJL(N 2km)OPSTV

A family campsite, hidden in the woods. Extensive amenities such as a swimming pool, restaurant, riding stables and modern toilet facilities. The beautiful surroundings are an invitation to take endless walks and cycle trips.

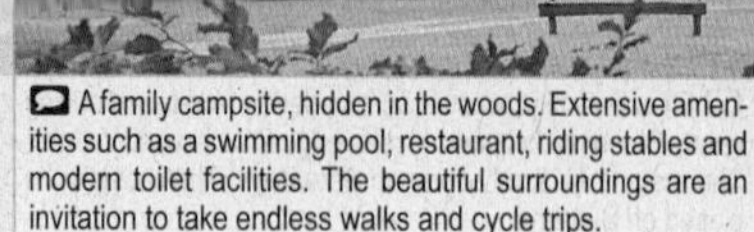

Motorway A28 Amersfoort-Zwolle, exit 14 Nunspeet/Elspeet. Then direction Vierhouten. Follow the signs.

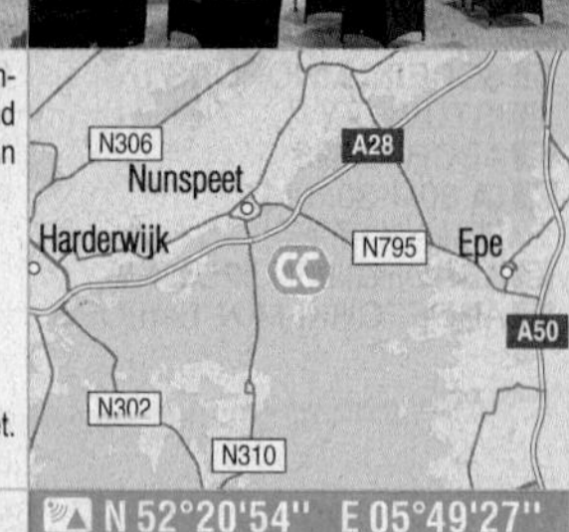

CC € 27 *22/3-28/3 2/4-25/4 21/5-4/7 2/9-3/11*

N 52°20'54'' E 05°49'27''

Voorthuizen, NL-3781 NJ / Gelderland

289

Ardoer Vakantiepark Ackersate*****
Harremaatweg 26
+31 3 42 47 12 74
23/3 - 2/11
receptie@ackersate.nl

23ha 194T(100-130m²) 10-16A CEE

1 ACDE**H**KLMNOPQRS
2 IJSTWXY
3 ABC**D**EHKMN**O**P**R**SU
4 (C 1/5-15/9)(F+H)IJKM (Q+S+T+U+V+Y+Z)
5 **AB**CDEFGIJKLMNOPQR**S**UWXY
6 ABCDEFGHKL(N 1,5km) OPSVX

A large campsite with spacious fields. The amenities are excellent, the swimming pool includes a 20 metre indoor pool and, since 2018, a heated outdoor pool. Voorthuizen has many tourist amenities. It is located between the woods of the Veluwe and the agricultural Gelderse Valley.

A1 exit 16. In Voorthuizen turn right onto N344 direction Garderen. Turn right just past Voorthuizen. Campsite signposted.

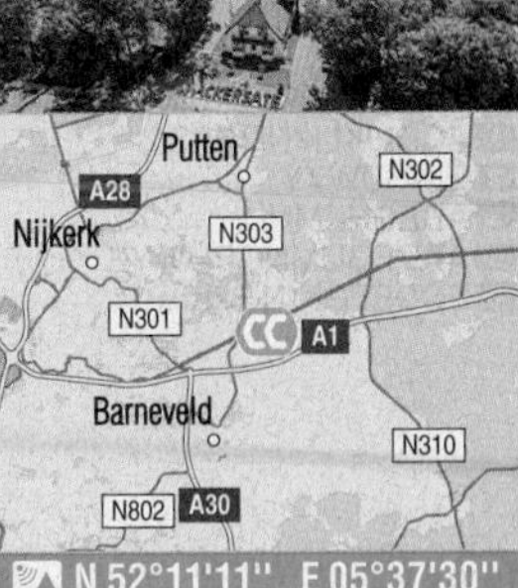

CC € 27 *23/3-29/3 1/4-26/4 20/5-6/7 31/8-2/11*

N 52°11'11'' E 05°37'30''

Voorthuizen, NL-3781 NG / Gelderland

290

Camping Beloofde Land****
Bosweg 17
+31 3 42 47 29 42
29/3 - 26/10
info@beloofdeland.nl

11ha 120T(80-150m²) 6-10A CEE

1 ADE**I**KLMNOPQRS
2 AIJSTWXY
3 ABCDEIKMPSU
4 (B+H 29/4-26/10)M (Q 1/7-31/8)(R) (T 1/7-31/8)(Y 1/6-26/10)
5 **AB**DEFGIJKLMNPQUWXYZ
6 DEFGKL(N 1,5km)OPV

Campsite with Christian values with modern facilities, opposite the forest. All pitches are car-free comfort pitches. There are also pitches with private toilet facilities. Campsite has a large new heated outdoor pool. Interesting places nearby and many notable 'Klompenpaden' (clog paths) on which you can enjoy hours of walking.

A1 exit 16. In Voorthuizen, turn right on N344 towards Garderen. Turn right just after Voorthuizen. The campsite is signposted.

CC € 23 *29/3-8/5 21/5-6/7 2/9-26/10* ***7=6, 14=12, 21=18***

N 52°11'14'' E 05°37'23''

Voorthuizen, NL-3781 NJ / Gelderland

291

Recreatiepark De Boshoek*****
Harremaatweg 34
+31 3 42 47 12 97
23/3 - 26/10
info@deboshoek.nl

4,5ha 116T(110-120m²) 10A CEE

1 ACDE**H**KLMNOPQRS
2 IJSTWXY
3 ABCHIKMNOPRS**T**U
4 (C 1/5-30/9) (**F**+**H**+Q+R+S+T+U+Y+Z)
5 **AB**DEFGIJKLMNPQR**T**UWXY
6 ABDEFGHKL(N 1,5km) OPSTVX

A new, modern campsite with spacious pitches, separated by hedges. Partly car-free. Swimming pool and catering at the bungalow park opposite the campsite. Lovely, large toilet block. Supplement for private toilet facilities. Enjoy yourself at the campsite and explore the area.

A1 exit 16 direction Voorthuizen, towards Garderen at the roundabout on the N344. Turn right just after Voorthuizen. Campsite signposted. Reception opposite the site entrance!

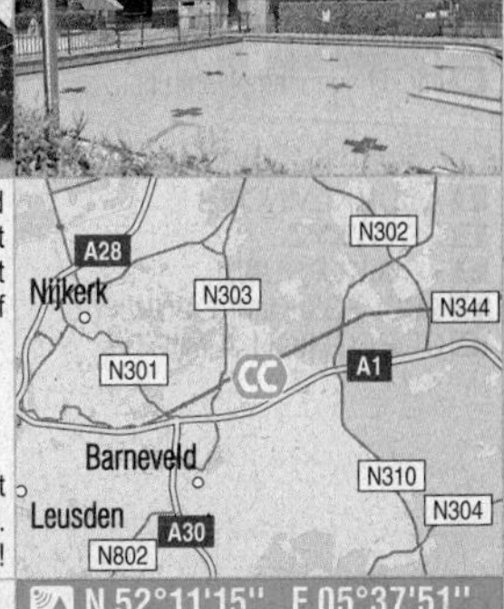

CC € 27 *23/3-28/3 2/4-8/5 13/5-16/5 21/5-9/7 26/8-26/10* ***7=6, 14=11***

N 52°11'15'' E 05°37'51''

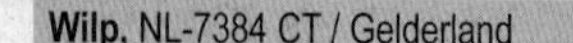

Wilp, NL-7384 CT / Gelderland

292

Kampeerhoeve Bussloo
Grotenhuisweg 50
+31 6 20 98 16 59
1/1 - 31/12
info@kampeerhoevebussloo.nl

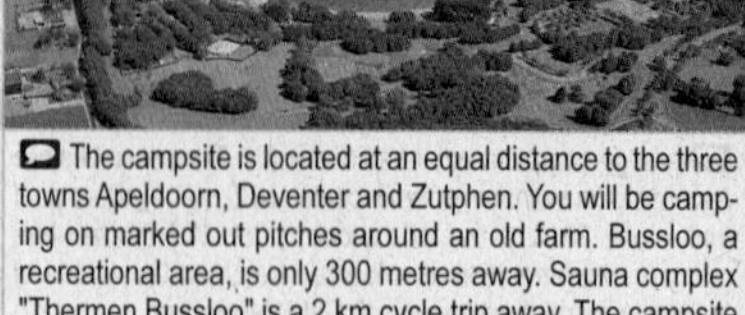

1ha 40**T**(144m²) 10A CEE

1 ACD**I**JKLMNOP**RS**
2 EINSUWXY
3 ABE**G**HKMNU
5 **AB**DFGIJMNOPUWYZ
6 ACDEFGK(N 3km)P

The campsite is located at an equal distance to the three towns Apeldoorn, Deventer and Zutphen. You will be camping on marked out pitches around an old farm. Bussloo, a recreational area, is only 300 metres away. Sauna complex "Thermen Bussloo" is a 2 km cycle trip away. The campsite is open all year round. Sunday (because of rest day) and Tuesday no arrivals.

A1 exit 22 Twello direction Wilp. After 200m turn right (Molenallee). Follow road until campsite (Grotenhuisweg).

CC € 21 *1/1-29/3 2/4-7/5 21/5-30/6 1/9-22/12*

N 52°12'33" E 06°06'33"

Winterswijk, NL-7115 AG / Gelderland

293

Camping Het Winkel****
De Slingeweg 20
+31 5 43 51 30 25
1/1 - 31/12
info@hetwinkel.nl

20ha 350**T**(90-200m²) 10-16A CEE

1 ABCD**H**KLMNOQRS
2 BSTWXY
3 ACDE**G**HIJKMN**O**PS**T**U
4 (C+H 27/4-1/9)J**N** (Q+R+T+U+V+X +Y+Z 1/3-3/11)
5 **AB**CDEFGIJKLMNOPQUWXZ
6 BDEFGH**K**L(N 3km)PV

A campsite with spacious pitches, a luxury swimming pool with water slide and a children's pool. Private toilet facilities are available. It is a good base for cycling and walking trips. CampingCard ACSI not valid during the weekend of 2, 3, and 4 October.

Winterswijk direction Borken. Campsite is signposted.

CC € 23 *1/1-23/3 8/4-26/4 21/5-29/5 3/6-5/7 26/8-31/12*

N 51°57'08" E 06°44'13"

Winterswijk, NL-7103 EA / Gelderland

294

Camping Klompenmakerij ten Hagen***
Waliënsestraat 139A
+31 5 43 53 15 03
1/1 - 31/12
info@hagencampklomp.nl

2ha 50**T**(100-150m²) 10-16A CEE

1 ACD**H**KLMNQ**R**S
2 ESTWXYZ
3 AC**G**IKLPSU**W**Z
5 **AB**CDFGI**J**K**L**MNO**P**UWXYZ
6 CDEFGHK(N 1km)**PT**

Situated on the banks of recreation lake 't Hilgelo. Various water sports such as surfing, swimming, diving. Cycling and walking routes. Also suitable for people with disabilities.

N319 Groenlo-Winterswijk. At roundabout on the Groenloseweg continue to of Winterswijk 't Hilgelo rccreational lake. Follow signs. Located about 1 km north

CC € 23 *1/1-28/3 2/4-8/5 13/5-17/5 21/5-29/5 3/6-12/7 1/9-31/12*

N 51°59'28" E 06°43'09"

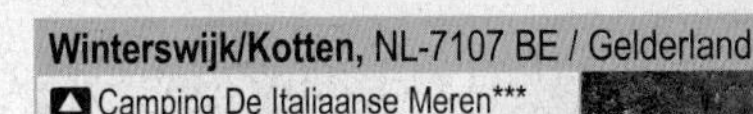

Winterswijk/Kotten, NL-7107 BE / Gelderland

295

- Camping De Italiaanse Meren***
- Buitinkweg 7
- +31 5 43 56 32 71
- 29/3 - 31/10
- info@italiaansemeren.nl

20,5ha 131**T**(120-200m²) 6-16A CEE

1. ACD**I**KLMNOQR
2. SXY
3. BC**FG**KLMN**ORW**
4. (Q 29/4-8/5,1/7-1/9)(R)
   (T+U+Y+Z 29/4-8/5,1/7-1/9)
5. **AB**IJKLMNOP**T**UZ
6. BCGHI**K**X

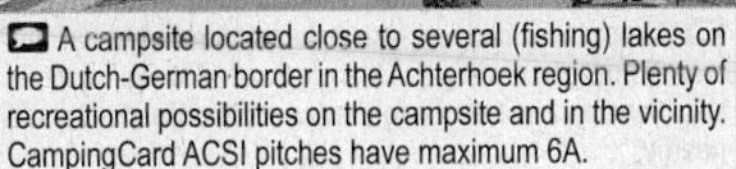

A campsite located close to several (fishing) lakes on the Dutch-German border in the Achterhoek region. Plenty of recreational possibilities on the campsite and in the vicinity. CampingCard ACSI pitches have maximum 6A.

N319 Winterswijk-Borken (D). Follow camping signs.

CC € 21 *29/3-26/4 6/5-9/5 21/5-29/5 3/6-24/6 1/9-31/10*

N 51°55'53'' E 06°46'54''

Winterswijk/Meddo, NL-7104 BG / Gelderland

296

- Camping Recreatiepark Sevink Molen****
- Hilgeloweg 7
- +31 5 43 55 12 25
- 1/1 - 31/12
- info@campingsevinkmolen.nl

7,5ha 73**T**(140m²) 10A CEE

1. CD**I**KLMNOQRS
2. AESTXYZ
3. CD**E**G**I**KMNWZ
4. (Q+T+U+W+X+Y)
5. **ABD**EFGIJKLMNOP**T**UWXYZ
6. CDEFGH**K**PS

Campsite holiday park Sevink Molen, located directly on the lake 't Hilgelo. Many amenities, including a very extensive restaurant, a brand new heated toilet block, themed indoor play hall and a historic mill that can be visited.

Coming from Aalten or Groenlo continue straight on. At the second roundabout follow signposts.

CC € 25 *8/1-29/3 3/4-26/4 21/5-29/5 3/6-5/7 2/9-2/10 7/10-31/12*

N 51°59'53'' E 06°43'10''

Winterswijk/Woold, NL-7108 AX / Gelderland

297

- Camping De Harmienehoeve
- Brandenweg 2
- +31 5 43 56 43 93
- 1/1 - 31/12
- info@campingdeharmienehoeve.nl

14ha 50**T**(100-180m²) 4-16A CEE

1. AD**I**KLMNOQ**R**S
2. BSUXYZ
3. C**F**IKU
4. (B+G 23/5-1/9)(Q+T)
   (Z 1/7-1/10)
5. **AB**DFGIJMNO**PQ**UWXYZ
6. AGH**K**(N 7km)PTV

The campsite is located in the 'Woold' neighbourhood of Winterswijk. A lovely area for cycling and walking. Heated toilet facilities, cafe and snack bar. A recharging point for electric bikes is provided.

N318 Aalten direction Winterswijk. At N319 roundabout, direction A31 (Rondweg Zuid). After 1,5 km roundabout direction Woold. Road splits after 700m, follow blue and white signs to Harmienehoeve. Drive another 7,5 km.

CC € 17 *1/3-27/3 3/4-28/5 4/6-5/7 22/7-29/7 3/9-31/10*

N 51°54'30'' E 06°43'31''

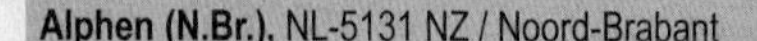

Alphen (N.Br.), NL-5131 NZ / Noord-Brabant

298

Recreatiepark 't Zand****
Maastrichtsebaan 1
+31 1 35 08 17 46
22/3 - 28/9
info@tzand.nl

40ha 125T(100-120m²) 10A CEE

1 ADHKLMNOPQRS
2 ABEIOSTWXYZ
3 ABCGHIJKLMOPSUZ
4 (A+Q+R 27/4-5/5,8/7-3/9) (T)(U 27/4-5/5,1/7-31/8) (V 26/4-5/5,1/7-5/9)(X) (Z 27/4-5/5,8/7-3/9)
5 ABDEFGIJKLMNOPQRUWXYZ
6 ACDEFGHKL(N 1,5km) OPSUV

Campsite located by a lake in the middle of a recreational area. Forms part of the green triangle Baarle-Tilburg-Turnhout. Woodland cycling area. Lovely towns such as Baarle-Nassau nearby.

A58 exit Gilze/Rijen, direction Baarle-Nassau. Follow signs in Alphen. Be sure to follow campsite signs, not the sign 'recreatiegebied'.

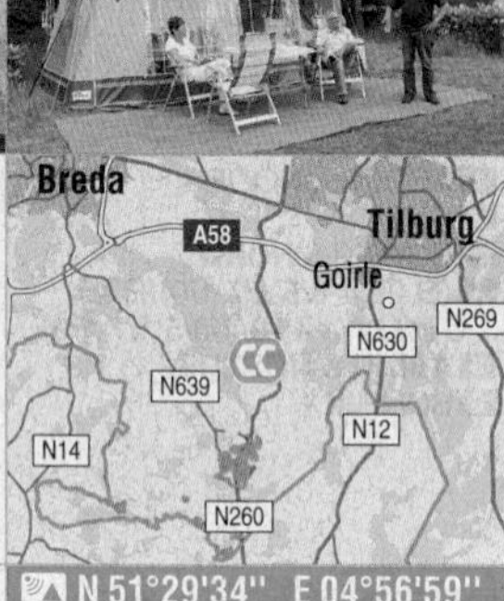

CC € 21 *22/3-28/3 2/4-19/4 13/5-16/5 21/5-5/7 26/8-28/9*

N 51°29'34'' E 04°56'59''

Asten/Heusden, NL-5725 TG / Noord-Brabant

299

Camping De Peel****
Behelp 13
+31 6 29 21 62 99
22/3 - 28/10
info@campingdepeel.nl

2,2ha 64T(90-110m²) 6A CEE

1 ADHKLMNOPQRTU
2 ISWXYZ
3 ABCEGIJKMNSUW
4 (B 1/6-31/8)(Q 10/7-25/8)
5 ABCDEFGIJMNOPUWZ
6 ABCEFGHK(N 1km)P

Small, friendly family campsite where 50-somethings will also feel at home. Explore the area of the bell-tower village of Asten and De Peel by bike, foot or the Peel Express. Modern, comfortable toilet block and free wifi. Brabant enjoyment and hospitality.

From A67 exit 36 towards Asten, then N279 towards Someren. Turn right after 2 km and left after 1 km towards Heusden. Follow signs in Heusden. From Someren direction Asten then follow signs.

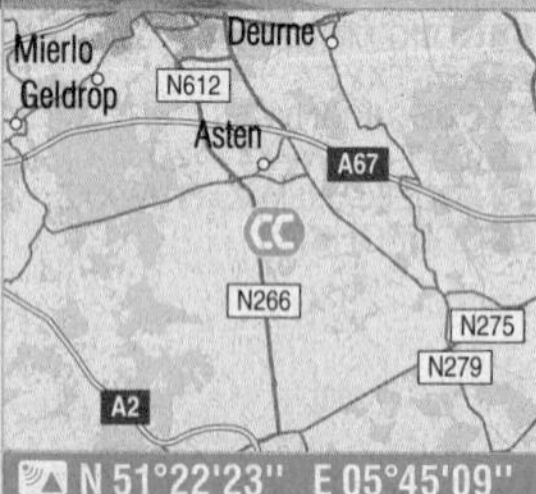

CC € 21 *22/3-8/5 21/5-5/7 23/8-28/10*

N 51°22'23'' E 05°45'09''

Asten/Ommel, NL-5724 PL / Noord-Brabant

300

Oostappen Vakantiepark Prinsenmeer*****
Beekstraat 31
+31 4 93 68 11 11
22/3 - 3/11
info@vakantieparkprinsenmeer.nl

50ha 200T(80-100m²) 6-10A CEE

1 ACDIKLMNQRUV
2 AFIOSWXY
3 ABCDGHIJKLMOPRSTUZ
4 (F+H)IJKLN (Q+S+T+U+V+Y+Z)
5 ABDEFGIJKLMNPQUWXY
6 BCFGHJM(N 3km)OPTU

The camping grounds are situated on a Plaza with countless amenities. There is a large recreational lake with slides and a sandy beach containing plenty of playground equipment. Fun in the water not only outside but also in the subtropical leisure pool.

A67 Eindhoven-Venlo, exit 36 Asten. Direction Ommel. Follow the signs.

CC € 19 *22/3-29/3 2/4-26/4 13/5-17/5 24/5-8/7 25/8-18/10*

N 51°25'21'' E 05°44'09''

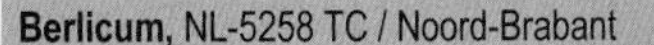

Berlicum, NL-5258 TC / Noord-Brabant

301

Camping De Hooghe Heide***
Werstkant 17
+31 7 35 03 15 22
22/3 - 30/9
info@hoogheheide.nl

1,8ha 69T(100m²) 10A CEE

1 ABDE**I**KLMNPRS
2 BISTWXYZ
3 BC**G**IJKMP**Q**RS
4 (B+H 1/5-31/8)M
(Q 15/7-27/8)(R+T+Y+Z)
5 **AB**DFGI**J**K**L**MNPQUWXYZ
6 CEFGHKL(N 2km)OPSTU

Quiet family campsite in the woods with comfort pitches (10A) and good amenities. Restaurant with lunch and dinner. Cable connection for HDTV and free wifi. The park is in a lovely nature area with walking and cycling routes. There are numerous cultural excursions and fun activities to do in the area. The vibrant city of 's-Hertogenbosch is within cycling distance.

A59, exit 48, towards Berlicum. Follow signs. Campsite is signposted.

N329
A59
's-Hertogenbosch
A50
N65
A2

CC € 19 *22/3-28/3 2/4-18/4 21/5-5/7 26/8-30/9*

N 51°41'38'' E 05°24'53''

Bladel, NL-5531 NA / Noord-Brabant

302

Recreatiepark De Achterste Hoef*****
Troprijt 10
+31 4 97 38 15 79
28/3 - 29/9
info@achterstehoef.nl

23ha 430T(100-160m²) 6-10A CEE

1 ACD**I**KLMNOQRTU
2 ABFIOSWXYZ
3 ABCDE**F**HIJKLMP**R**SUZ
4 (C+F+H)J
(Q+S+T+X+Y+Z)
5 **AB**CDEFGHIJKLMNOPQR**T**UWXY
6 ACGHKL(N 3km)O**P**SU

On the edge of an extensive wooded natural landscape, this campsite has lots of amenities. In particular, the restaurant with long opening hours, the covered pool, and the golf course spring to mind. Cycling area unparalleled for its beauty, with Eersel and the Abbey of Postel less than 10 km away.

A67 Eindhoven-Antwerpen exit 29 Hapert/Bladel. Follow signs to Bladel. In Bladel follow signs to the campsite.

N269
Veldhoven
Bladel
A67
N118
A21
E34
Retie
N69
N18
N746

CC € 27 *28/3-8/5 21/5-5/7 2/9-29/9*

N 51°20'36'' E 05°13'40''

Breda, NL-4838 GV / Noord-Brabant

303

Camping Liesbos***
Liesdreef 40
+31 7 65 14 35 14
1/4 - 1/10
info@camping-liesbos.nl

5ha 50T(100m²) 10-16A CEE

1 ACD**I**KLMNORS
2 ISTWY
3 C**G**HIKMN**O**PSU
4 (C+H 30/4-30/9)
(Q+R+T+U 1/4-30/9)
(V+Y+Z)
5 **AB**CFGI**J**MNO**P**UWX
6 ACDEFGHK(N 3km)O**P**STV

Excellently managed campsite with swimming pool and friendly owner. Close to Breda. Lovely cycle routes in the area (details available from reception). Early and late season: restaurant only open in the weekend.

Motorway A58 Breda-Roosendaal exit 18 Etten-Leur. Then follow camping signs.

CC € 21 *1/4-7/5 13/5-16/5 20/5-6/7 26/8-30/9*

N 51°33'54'' E 04°41'47''

Chaam, NL-4861 RC / Noord-Brabant — 304

RCN de Flaasbloem*****
Flaasdijk 1
+31 8 50 40 07 00
29/3 - 3/11
reserveringen@rcn.nl

100ha 446**T**(80-150m²) 10-16A CEE

1 ACD**I**KLMNOPQRS
2 ABEIOSTXYZ
3 ABCEGHIKMNOPSUWZ
4 (F 🔑)(H 1/5-1/9)JM
(Q+S+T+U+V+X+Y 🔑)
5 **AB**CDEFGIJKLMNOPQRUWZ
6 ACDEFGH**K**LM(N 2km)OPS

A large campsite with plenty of recreational opportunities. There is a fantastic water play park for the youngest ones. Indoor pool for family swimming. New in 2017: a 'smugglers beach' and a frisbee field.

A58 exit 14 Ulvenhout direction Chaam. From Chaam direction Alphen. Then follow the signs to campsite.

CC € 21 *29/3-7/5 13/5-16/5 21/5-4/7 26/8-3/11*

N 51°29'28'' E 04°53'47''

Chaam, NL-4861 RE / Noord-Brabant — 305

Recreatiepark Klein Paradijs
Schaanstraat 11
+31 1 61 49 14 46
22/3 - 3/11
info@campingkleinparadijs.nl

14ha 50**T**(100-150m²) 16A CEE

1 ABD**I**KLMNPRS
2 ISWXY
3 ACEIKPSU
4 (B+G 20/5-1/9)(T 🔑)
5 **AB**DFGHIJMNOPUXY
6 BDFGH**K**(N 2km)SV

Cosy family campsite in Chaam in Brabant. The spacious sunny campsite is located on the edge of a vast nature reserve with woods, streams and heathland.

A58 exit 14 direction Baarle Nassau via N639. From roundabout at the end of Chaam, follow N639 for another 800m. Then turn left. After 700m campsite on your left.

CC € 17 *22/3-28/3 2/4-26/4 6/5-7/5 13/5-16/5 21/5-4/7 2/9-3/11*

N 51°29'31'' E 04°53'03''

De Heen, NL-4655 AH / Noord-Brabant — 306

Camping De Uitwijk****
Dorpsweg 136
+31 1 67 56 00 00
29/3 - 29/9
info@de-uitwijk.nl

2,5ha 75**T**(100-150m²) 10A CEE

1 ACD**I**KLMNPQ**R**TU
2 CIJSWY
3 ACE**G**HIKMP**R**SU**W**X
4 (C+H 23/4-16/9)**N**
(Q+T+U+Y+Z 🔑)
5 **AB**CDEFGHIJKLMNOPRUWXYZ
6 ACDEFGH**K**(N 4km)
OPSTUV

Peaceful sheltered site with a beautiful authentic farmhouse with restaurant and close to a nature reserve and yacht harbour. Excellent toilet facilities. Heated swimming pool, toddlers' pool and sauna. Starting point for cycling and boat trips. Friendly and welcoming owner.

A4 exit 25 to Steenbergen. Then follow signs to 'De Heen'.

CC € 21 *1/4-26/4 21/5-5/7 26/8-29/9*

N 51°36'37'' E 04°16'22''

Eerde, NL-5466 PZ / Noord-Brabant

307

Camping Het Goeie Leven
Vlagheide 8b
+31 6 27 51 89 81
28/3 - 30/9
info@hetgoeieleven.nl

5ha 66T(100-200m²) 10A CEE

1 ADHKLMNPRS
2 IJSXYZ
3 ABCGHIJKLMNPSUW
4 (A 6/7-1/9)(B)(Q 6/7-1/9) (T+U+V+Y+Z)
5 ABCDEFGHIJKLMNPQTUWXYZ
6 ABCEFGHKL(N 1km)P

A naturally laid out campsite on the outskirts of the attractive village of Eerde. Partly surrounded by woods. Suitable for both families with children and those seeking relaxation though its diversity of camping pitches. Attractive bistro with woodland patio and extended opening times. Village shop in the windmill within walking distance. Very suitable for a visit to the city of 's-Hertogenbosch.

A50 exit 10 Veghel-Eerde. Continue towards Eerde and follow signs.

CC € 21 1/4-19/4 5/5-8/5 12/5-17/5 20/5-5/7 25/8-30/9

N 51°36'14'' E 05°29'13''

Eersel, NL-5521 RD / Noord-Brabant

308

Camping Recreatiepark TerSpegelt*****
Postelseweg 88
+31 4 97 51 20 16
22/3 - 4/11
info@terspegelt.nl

68ha 480T(80-160m²) 6-16A CEE

1 ACDGKLMNOPRS
2 AFIOSWXYZ
3 ABCDEGHIJKLMNOPRSUWZ
4 (F+H)IJKM (Q+S+T+U+V+X+Y+Z)
5 ABDEFGIJKLMNOPQTUWXYZ
6 BCFGHJKLM(N 3km)OPST

Five-star park with three recreational lakes and unique amenities such as leisure pool and playground. Special activities for the over-55s in spring and autumn. Cycling and walking possible. Camp quietly by the water or in a more lively ambiance on the fields. Luxury and comfort pitches at a supplement. Reservations with CampingCard only possible within 7 days before arrival.

Via A67 Eindhoven-Antwerpen, exit 30 Eersel. Follow signs.

N269 Veldhoven Eindhoven A67 N69 N284 Valkenswaard E34

CC € 27 22/3-28/3 2/4-19/4 13/5-17/5 3/6-1/7 1/9-4/11

N 51°20'16'' E 05°17'38''

Esbeek, NL-5085 NN / Noord-Brabant

309

Camping De Spaendershorst***
Spaaneindsestraat 12
+31 1 35 16 93 61
22/3 - 3/11
info@spaendershorst.nl

11ha 90T(80-130m²) 10A CEE

1 ABDIKLMNPQRS
2 JSTWXYZ
3 ACGHIKPSU
4 (C+H)(T+Z 1/4-1/10)
5 ABCDFGHIJKLMNOPUWXY
6 ABEFGHK(N 1,5km)P

A friendly and peaceful family campsite on the edge of extensive woodlands that continue into Belgium. Good, heated toilet facilities.

A58 exit 10 to N269 direction Reusel. Follow camping signs beyond Hilvarenbeek at Esbeek.

Tilburg A58 N269 Oirschot N260 N630 N395 N12 N118 Bladel

CC € 17 22/3-28/3 2/4-26/4 6/5-7/5 13/5-16/5 21/5-4/7 2/9-3/11

N 51°28'00'' E 05°07'37''

Hilvarenbeek, NL-5081 NJ / Noord-Brabant

310

Lake Resort Beekse Bergen****
Beekse Bergen 1
+31 1 35 49 11 00
29/3 - 3/11
info@beeksebergen.nl

75ha 236T(100m²) 10A CEE

1 ACD**H**KLMNRS
2 ACEISTWXYZ
3 ACD**G**KMNPWZ
4 (**A** 1/5-1/8)(F+H)J
(Q+S+T+U+V+X+Y+Z)
5 **AB**DEFGHIJKLMNOPUWXYZ
6 ABCEFGHK(N 4km)OSTU

A camping holiday at Lake Resort Beekse Bergen will feel like a holiday with a touch of Africa. The fields are named after African animals, which can be seen in the Beekse Bergen Safari Park next door, and countries. The site has modern toilet facilities which are partially heated.

N65 Den Bosch-Tilburg. A65 exit Beekse Bergen. A58 Breda-Eindhoven. Follow 'Beekse Bergen' signs.

CC € 17 *2/4-19/4 21/5-5/6 12/6-28/6 1/9-18/10*

N 51°31'42'' E 05°07'29''

Hoeven, NL-4741 SG / Noord-Brabant

311

Molecaten Park Bosbad Hoeven****
Oude Antwerpsepostbaan 81b
+31 1 65 50 25 70
22/3 - 1/11
bosbadhoeven@molecaten.nl

56ha 240T(110-160m²) 10A CEE

1 ACDGKLMNOQRTU
2 BEIJSTWXYZ
3 ABCDEHIKMN**O**RSUW
4 (C 27/4-1/9)IJM(Q+T+V)
(Y+Z 1/4-1/9,12/10-27/10)
5 **AB**DFGIJKLMNO**PQ**UWXY
6 ACEFGH**K**(N 2,5km)OPSTV

Wonderfully wooded campsite for the whole family! As campsite guest you have free entry to the 'Splesj' (Splash) water park (May to early September). Cycling and walking close by. The camping fields with comfort pitches are beautifully laid out and surrounded by trees. The site also has an tennis court, large playground and a restaurant.

A58 Roosendaal-Breda, exit 20 St. Willebrord (take note, SatNav may differ). Direction Hoeven. Follow signs.

CC € 21 *22/3-25/4 6/5-8/5 13/5-16/5 21/5-11/7 30/8-30/10*

N 51°34'10'' E 04°33'42''

Kaatsheuvel, NL-5171 RL / Noord-Brabant

312

Recreatiepark Brasserie Het Genieten***
Roestelbergseweg 3
+31 4 16 56 15 75
30/3 - 27/10
info@hetgenieten.nl

12,5ha 120T(100-120m²) 10A CEE

1 ACD**I**KLMNRS
2 ISTWXYZ
3 ABCD**G**HIJKLMNPSU
4 (F+G)M(Q 1/5-1/9)
(R+T+U+Y+Z)
5 **AB**DEFGIJKLMNOPUWXYZ
6 ABCEFGHK(N 3km)OPSVX

A friendly leisure park with indoor and outdoor water playground. Nice pavement cafe at the brasserie with the possibility to dine heartily. Located at the foot of the Loon and Drunen Dunes. From the campsite you can cycle or walk straight into the forest. Entertainment at Ascension and Whitsun.

A59 exit Waalwijk N261 direction Loonse- en Drunense Duinen. Follow the campsite signs.

CC € 25 *30/3-7/5 22/5-5/7 2/9-27/10*

N 51°39'27'' E 05°05'15''

Lierop/Someren, NL-5715 RE / Noord-Brabant

313

Camping De Somerense Vennen****
Philipsbosweg 7
+31 4 92 33 12 16
29/3 - 31/10
info@somerensevennen.nl

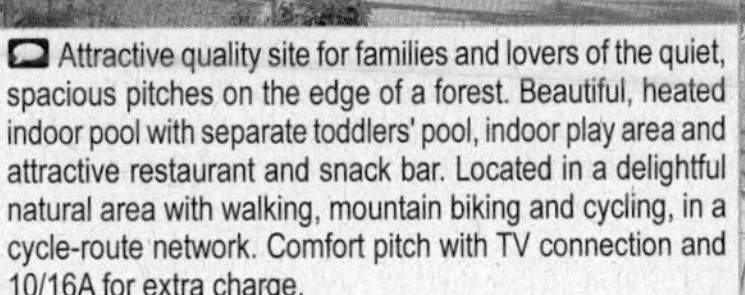

10ha 165T(80-150m²) 6-16A CEE

1 ADIKLMNORS
2 BISWXYZ
3 ABCDGHIJKLMNPSU
4 (F+H+T+Y+Z 22/4-1/9)
5 ABCDEFGHIJMNPUWXYZ
6 ABCEFGHKLM(N 2km)PS

Attractive quality site for families and lovers of the quiet, spacious pitches on the edge of a forest. Beautiful, heated indoor pool with separate toddlers' pool, indoor play area and attractive restaurant and snack bar. Located in a delightful natural area with walking, mountain biking and cycling, in a cycle-route network. Comfort pitch with TV connection and 10/16A for extra charge.

A67 Eindhoven-Venlo, exit 35 Someren. In Someren direction Lierop. Follow signs.

Helmond Eindhoven N270 N612 N279 A67 N266 A2

CC € 25 *29/3-26/4 21/5-5/7 22/8-31/10*

N 51°24'00'' E 05°40'35''

Mierlo, NL-5731 XN / Noord-Brabant

314

Boscamping 't Wolfsven****
Patrijslaan 4
+31 4 92 66 16 61
22/3 - 3/11
receptie.wolfsven@roompot.nl

67ha 167T(100m²) 6A CEE

1 ACDIKLMNOQRS
2 ABEIJOSWXYZ
3 CDGHIJKLMNPRSUWZ
4 (F+H)K
(Q+S+T+U+V+X+Y+Z)
5 ABDFGIJMNPQUWXY
6 ABCDFGHKLM(N 2km) OSUVX

Family campsite with comfortable pitches in the woods. Have fun in the natural pool and indoor swimming pool. Amenities open all season.

A2 to Eindhoven. Then A67 to Venlo. Exit 34 Geldrop, direction Geldrop, then Mierlo. In Mierlo signs Wolfsven are posted.

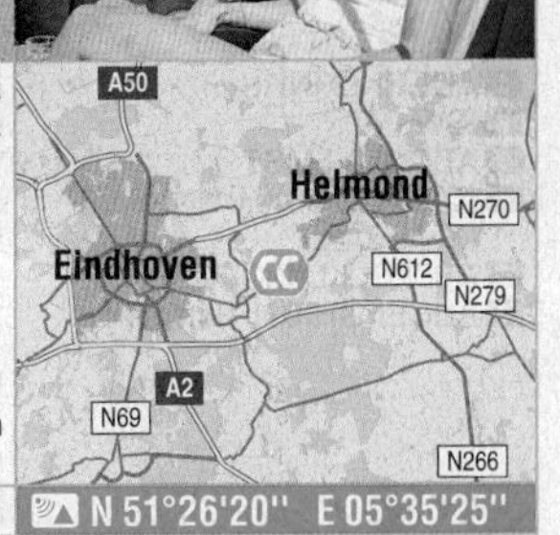

CC € 15 *22/3-29/3 2/4-25/4 13/5-17/5 21/5-28/6 30/8-3/11*

N 51°26'20'' E 05°35'25''

Netersel, NL-5534 AP / Noord-Brabant

315

Camping De Couwenberg***
De Ruttestraat 9A
+31 4 97 68 22 33
15/3 - 28/10
info@decouwenberg.nl

8ha 97T(80-120m²) 6-10A CEE

1 ADIKLMNOQRTU
2 ISWXYZ
3 CGHIJKPSUW
4 (C+H 1/5-15/9)
(Q+T+X+Z)
5 ABDEFGIJKLMNPUWXZ
6 AEFGHK(N 5km)OPV

Welcoming family campsite with heated outdoor pool. Surrounded by forests. Heath and fens in direct vicinity (the De Utrecht estate). Excellent for cycling and walking. 20 minutes (by car) from Safari and recreation park Beekse Bergen.

A58 exit 10 Hilvarenbeek, take the direction of Reusel. Reaching Lage Mierde, go to Netersel. Coming from A67 to Antwerpen, Belgium: exit 29 Hapert/Bladel, direction of Bladel. Then exit Bladel-Netersel. Follow the signs.

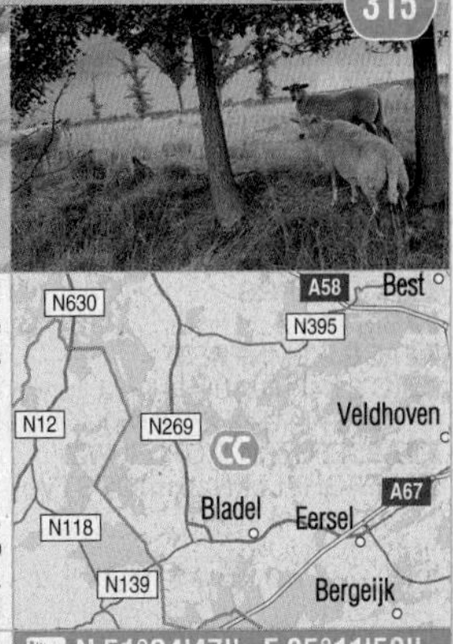

CC € 23 *15/3-8/5 21/5-5/7 22/8-26/10*

Nispen/Roosendaal, NL-4709 PB / Noord-Brabant

316

Camping Zonneland***
Turfvaartsestraat 4-6
+31 1 65 36 54 29
29/3 - 20/10
info@zonneland.nl

15ha 54**T**(100-130m²) 10A CEE

1 ACDGKLMNOQRS
2 BISTWYZ
3 CKPSUVW
4 (C 15/5-3/9)(R)
5 **AB**DEGI**JM**P**R**UXYZ
6 CEFGHK(N 3,5km)PTV

This campsite is close to the Dutch-Belgian border and has spacious pitches in the woods or on the field. From the campsite, you can take enjoyable trips out on foot or by bike in the woods or heathlands in the surrounding area.

A58 exit 24 Nispen. Follow N262 until sign posts.

CC € 21 *29/3-5/7 26/8-20/10*

N 51°29'40'' E 04°29'06''

Oirschot, NL-5688 MB / Noord-Brabant

317

Camping de Bocht*****
Oude Grintweg 69
+31 4 99 55 08 55
1/1 - 31/12
info@campingdebocht.nl

1,8ha 29**T**(100m²) 6-10A CEE

1 ADE**H**KLMNRS
2 ISWXYZ
3 ABC**G**IJKLMS**T**
4 (C 20/6-31/8)(H 16/6-31/8) (X+Y+Z)
5 **AB**DFGIJKLMNO**PQ**UWXYZ
6 ABCEFGHK(N 1km)OPS

Enjoy old-fashioned relaxation. Heathland, woods, fens, country estates. Close to historic Oirschot. Stunning surroundings with exquisite walking and cycling options. Spacious comfort pitches. Nice and comfortable toilet facilities. Restaurant with its own patio and bowling alley.

A58 exit 8 Oirschot dir Oirschot, turn right at 4th roundabout. On the left after 800m. Or A2 exit 26 dir Boxtel, over roundabout, left towards Oirschot. After 8 km on the right.

CC € 27 *1/1-8/5 21/5-5/7 26/8-31/12*

N 51°31'01'' E 05°18'28''

Oosterhout, NL-4904 SG / Noord-Brabant

318

Vakantiepark De Katjeskelder****
Katjeskelder 1
+31 1 62 45 35 39
22/3 - 3/11
receptie.katjeskelder@roompot.nl

28ha 95**T**(80m²) 5A CEE

1 ACD**I**KLPRS
2 BISTWYZ
3 AC**G**JKLMNP**RST**
4 (C 21/4-1/10)(F+H)J (Q+S+T+U+X+Y+Z)
5 **AB**DEFGIJKLMNOPQRUWZ
6 AEFGHKLM(N 3km)OPSTV

A friendly camping ground surrounded by woods. Own large recreation park, large playground and tropical leisure pool. Lovely surroundings for walking and cycling trips. Its location in a water catchment area means that motorhomes are not permitted.

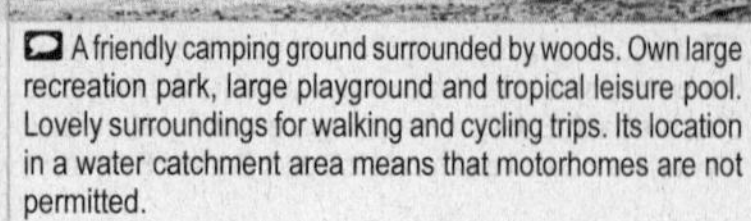

A27 exit 17 Oosterhout-Zuid. Follow signs to Katjeskelder.

CC € 17 *22/3-29/3 2/4-25/4 13/5-17/5 21/5-28/6 30/8-3/11*

N 51°37'45'' E 04°49'57''

Sint Anthonis, NL-5845 EB / Noord-Brabant

319

Ardoer vak.centrum De Ullingse Bergen****
Bosweg 36
+31 4 85 38 85 66
29/3 - 29/9
ullingsebergen@ardoer.com

11ha 108T(100-150m²) 10-16A CEE

1 ACDGKLMNORUV
2 BISTWXYZ
3 ACDHIJKMOSU
4 (C+H 29/4-10/9)J(Q+T)
(U 29/4-17/9)(Y)
5 **AB**DFGIJKLMNPUWXYZ
6 ABCEFGH**K**L(N 1,5km)
OPST

Take advantage of the peace and quiet of the countryside. There is extensive walking and cycling right from the campsite, over heathland and sand drifts. The perfect site for young families (with children up to about 10 years), senior citizens and nature lovers. Camp in a small field or in one of the quiet avenues. All pitches are separated by greenery.

A73 exit St. Anthonis. Follow the signs in St. Anthonis.

CC € 25 *19/4-26/4 13/5-17/5 21/5-7/7 24/8-29/9*

N 51°37'39'' E 05°51'42''

Sint Hubert, NL-5454 NA / Noord-Brabant

320

Camping Van Rossum's Troost***
Oude Wanroijseweg 24
+31 4 85 47 01 93
29/3 - 29/9
info@rossumstroost.nl

5,5ha 32T(90-120m²) 6A CEE

1 ABDE**I**KLMNP**R**TU
2 BIJSWXYZ
3 BCHIJKPSV
4 (A 9/5-20/5,20/7-17/8)
(G 30/7-27/8)(Z 22/7-20/8)
5 **AB**CEFGHI**J**MO**PQ**UXYZ
6 ABCEFGH**K**M(N 0,8km)
OPST

A welcoming family campsite located on the edge of the Molenheide nature reserve. 260 hectares with plenty of cycling and walking (free routes at the campsite). Spaciously laid out grounds with lovely touring and comfort pitches, clean toilet facilities with large showers and wireless internet.

A73 exit Haps direction Mill. After St. Hubert direction Wanroij. Follow signs.

CC € 21 *1/5-8/5 20/5-6/7 24/8-29/9* ***14=12***

N 51°40'09'' E 05°47'48''

Soerendonk, NL-6027 RD / Noord-Brabant

321

Oostappen Vakantiepark Slot Cranendonck****
Strijperdijk 9
+31 4 95 59 16 52
22/3 - 3/11
info@slotcranendonck.nl

17,8ha 208T(100m²) 6-10A CEE

1 AD**I**KLMNORUV
2 IJSXYZ
3 ABCD**G**HIJKLMOPRSW
4 (B 19/4-15/9)
(F+H)J(Q+S)
(T+Z 19/4-5/5,5/7-1/9)
5 **AB**DFGIJKLMNOPUWXY
6 ACFGHJ**K**M(N 5km)OPSX

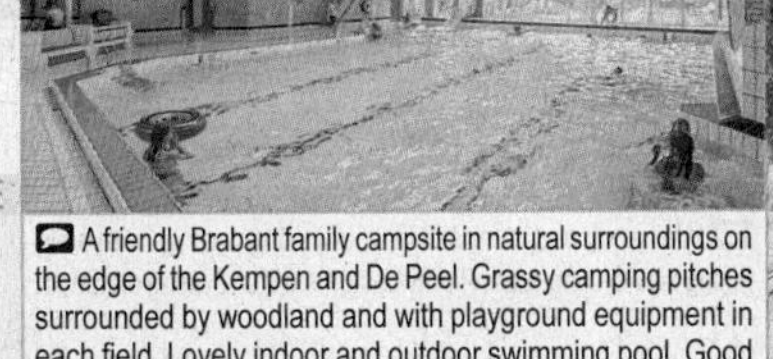

A friendly Brabant family campsite in natural surroundings on the edge of the Kempen and De Peel. Grassy camping pitches surrounded by woodland and with playground equipment in each field. Lovely indoor and outdoor swimming pool. Good restaurant with an attractive patio and extended opening times, also out of season.

Motorway A2 Eindhoven-Weert, exit Soerendonk. Direction Soerendonk. Follow signs.

CC € 17 *22/3-29/3 2/4-26/4 13/5-17/5 24/5-8/7 25/8-18/10*

N 51°19'11'' E 05°34'29''

Someren, NL-5712 PD / Noord-Brabant

322

Camping De Kuilen
Kuilvenweg 15
+31 4 93 49 45 82
1/3 - 31/10
info@campingdekuilen.nl

3ha 45T(120m²) 10A CEE

1 ADIKLMNORS
2 ISWXY
3 AFHIKLMNPSU
4 (B 1/6-31/8)(Z)
5 ABDGIJMNOPUWX
6 ACEFGHK(N 3km)PV

A small-scale and friendly family campsite. Unusually attractive and quiet location on the edge of an extensive nature reserve. Next to a golf course and 3 km from Someren with its shops. Pleasant cafe with terrace. Bike shed.

A67 exit 34 towards Heeze, then towards Someren. Take a right before Someren, signposted.

CC € 19 *1/3-8/5 21/5-1/7 18/8-31/10*

N 51°22'39'' E 05°40'19''

St. Oedenrode, NL-5491 TE / Noord-Brabant

323

Camping De Kienehoef***
Zwembadweg 37
+31 4 13 47 28 77
30/3 - 29/9
info@kienehoef.nl

15ha 160T(100m²) 4-10A CEE

1 ADIKLMNRS
2 AFIOSWXYZ
3 ABCGHIJKLMNPSWZ
4 (C+H 1/5-30/8)(Q)
(T+X+Z 13/7-17/8)
5 ABDFGHIJKLMNPQUWXYZ
6 ABCEFGHKLM(N 1km)P

Atmospheric and beautifully landscaped campsite, bordering an attractive recreational park with a restaurant and petting farm. Close to the characterful village of St. Oedenrode.

The campsite is accessible from the A2 (exit 27) and A50 (exit 9) St. Oedenrode. Towards Schijndel after the built-up area 1st left, then 2nd left. Campsite is signposted.

CC € 27 *30/3-8/5 13/5-17/5 25/5-6/7 24/8-29/9* ***7=6, 14=11, 21=17***

N 51°34'39'' E 05°26'46''

Valkenswaard, NL-5556 VB / Noord-Brabant

324

Oostappen Vakantiepark Brugse Heide***
Maastrichterweg 183
+31 4 02 01 83 04
22/3 - 3/11
info@vakantieparkbrugseheide.nl

7ha 82T(80-100m²) 6A CEE

1 ACDIKLMNORS
2 BISWXYZ
3 ABCDGHIJKLMPRSU
4 (B+G 8/5-2/9)
(Q+T+U+X+Y+Z 5/7-1/9)
5 ABDEFGIJKLMNPQUWXY
6 ACEFGHJ(N 1,5km)PS

Well equipped campsite in woody surroundings with a big hiking and cycling area. Plenty of sights within cycling distance.

Via A2 exit Valkenswaard to Achel. Follow the signs.

CC € 13 *22/3-29/3 2/4-26/4 13/5-17/5 24/5-8/7 25/8-18/10*

N 51°19'44'' E 05°27'45''

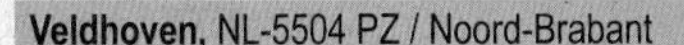

Veldhoven, NL-5504 PZ / Noord-Brabant

325

Vakantiepark Witven****
Witvenseweg 6
+31 4 02 30 00 43
28/3 - 22/9
info@witven.nl

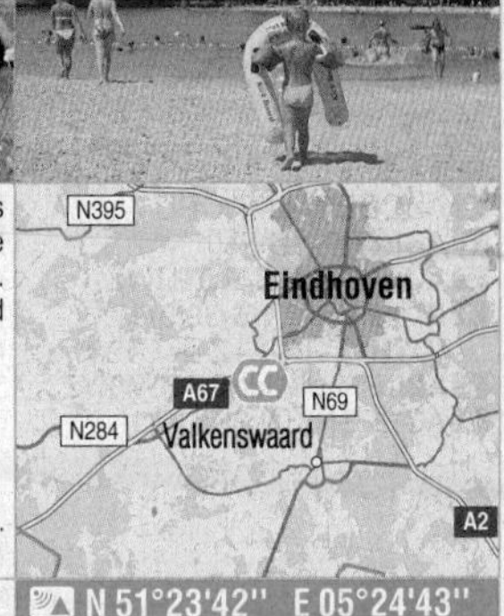

13,3ha 117T(80-120m²) 6-10A CEE

1 ACD**H**KLMNOPRS
2 AFIJOSWXYZ
3 ABCE**G**IJKLMP**R**SUWZ
4 (Q+R 🔑)(T+U 6/7-18/8) (Z 🔑)
5 **AB**DFGIJKLMNPQ**S**UWXYZ
6 ACDEFGHKL(N 3km)P

The campsite is situated near a recreational lake with lots of playing facilities just outside Veldhoven surrounded by the countryside. Also suitable for a trip to the city of Eindhoven. Private toilet and washing facilities for hire. Special hardened motorhome pitches, winter camping possible.

Randweg (Ring) Eindhoven N2 exit 32 direction Veldhoven. Then follow signs.

CC € 27 *28/3-6/5 13/5-16/5 21/5-13/6 17/6-20/6 24/6-5/7 22/8-22/9*

N 51°23'42'' E 05°24'43''

Veldhoven/Zandoerle, NL-5506 LA / Noord-Brabant

326

Vakantiepark Molenvelden***
Banstraat 25
+31 4 02 05 23 84
22/3 - 1/10
molenvelden@kempenrecreatie.nl

14ha 78T(80-120m²) 10A CEE

1 ABCDE**I**KLMNRS
2 ISWXYZ
3 ABC**G**HIJKLMNPS
4 (C+H 1/5-3/9)M (Q+T+U+X+Y+Z 🔑)
5 **AB**DEFGHI**J**KLMNOPQUWXY
6 ABEFGHJL(N 3km)S

A family campsite with nice, open pitches, located in woodland. Rural area with many walking and cycling opportunities. The restaurant and cafe with its lovely patio have extended opening hours, also in low season. Heated outdoor pool.

N2 ring road Eindhoven, exit number 31 Veldhoven. Follow signs.

CC € 27 *22/3-8/5 21/5-5/7 22/8-1/10*

N 51°24'30'' E 05°21'27''

Vessem, NL-5512 NW / Noord-Brabant

327

Eurocamping Vessem****
Zwembadweg 1
+31 4 97 59 12 14
23/3 - 1/10
info@eurocampingvessem.com

50ha 322T(100-200m²) 6-10A CEE

1 ADE**I**KLMNOQRS
2 BIJSXYZ
3 ABCE**G**IJKLMNOPRSUW
4 (C+G 15/5-1/9) (Q+R+T+Z 6/7-7/9)
5 **AB**CDFGIJMNO**PT**UWXYZ
6 ACDEFGHKLM(N 1,5km)

A unique campsite located in the heart of Brabant. Large wooded grounds with plenty of space and attractively laid out fields. Many cycling and walking opportunities. Large fishing lake surrounded by woods. Special motorhome pitches in front of the campsite.

A58 exit 8 Oirschot direction Middelbeers, then Vessem. Campsite signposted on Vessem-Hoogeloon road.

CC € 23 *23/3-8/5 13/5-17/5 21/5-5/7 26/8-1/10*

N 51°24'38'' E 05°16'35''

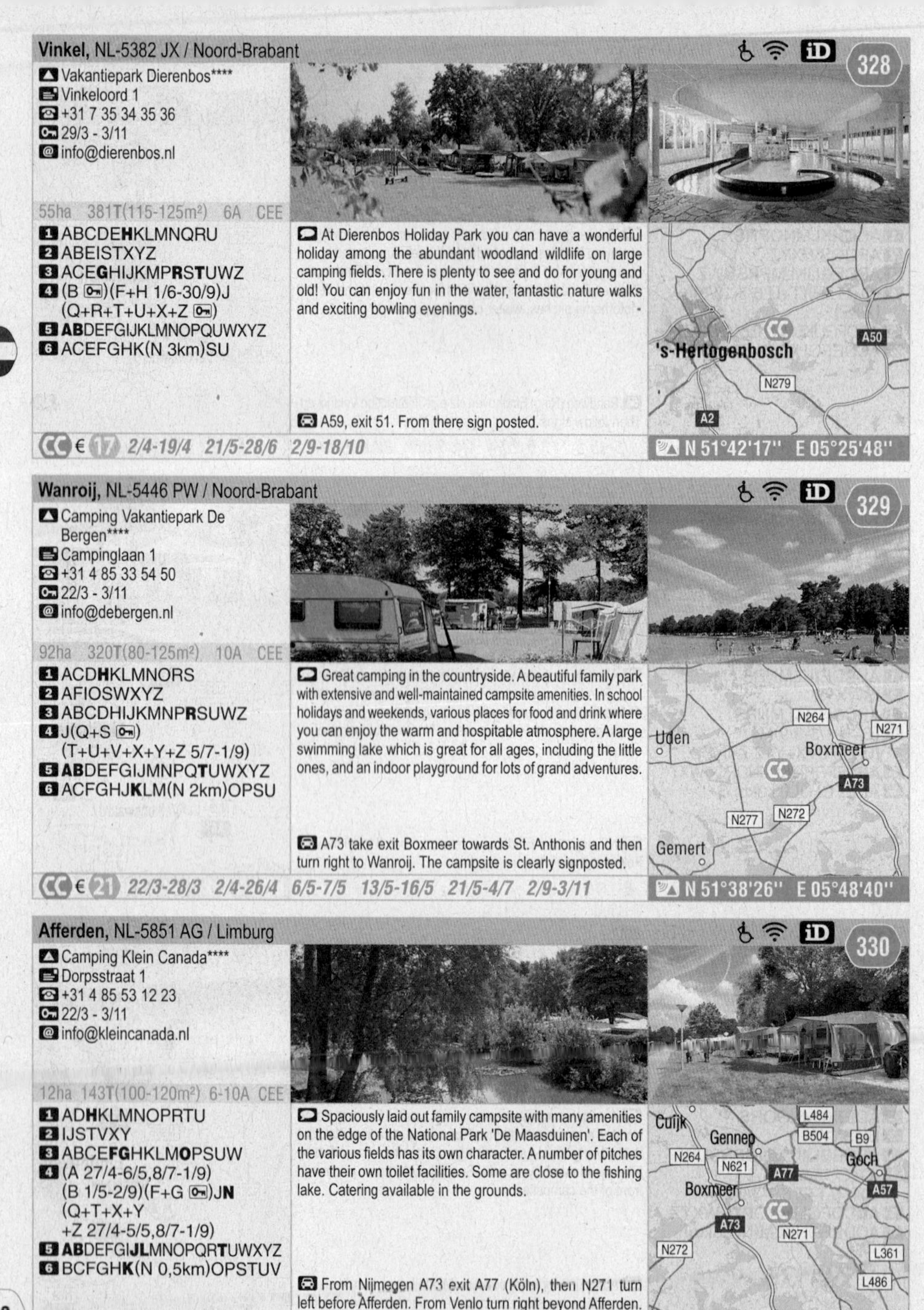

Vinkel, NL-5382 JX / Noord-Brabant

328

Vakantiepark Dierenbos****
Vinkeloord 1
+31 7 35 34 35 36
29/3 - 3/11
info@dierenbos.nl

55ha 381T(115-125m²) 6A CEE

1 ABCDE**H**KLMNQRU
2 ABEISTXYZ
3 ACE**G**HIJKMP**RST**UWZ
4 (B)(F+H 1/6-30/9)J (Q+R+T+U+X+Z)
5 **AB**DEFGIJKLMNOPQUWXYZ
6 ACEFGHK(N 3km)SU

At Dierenbos Holiday Park you can have a wonderful holiday among the abundant woodland wildlife on large camping fields. There is plenty to see and do for young and old! You can enjoy fun in the water, fantastic nature walks and exciting bowling evenings.

A59, exit 51. From there sign posted.

CC € 17 *2/4-19/4 21/5-28/6 2/9-18/10*

N 51°42'17'' E 05°25'48''

Wanroij, NL-5446 PW / Noord-Brabant

329

Camping Vakantiepark De Bergen****
Campinglaan 1
+31 4 85 33 54 50
22/3 - 3/11
info@debergen.nl

92ha 320T(80-125m²) 10A CEE

1 ACD**H**KLMNORS
2 AFIOSWXYZ
3 ABCDHIJKMNP**R**SUWZ
4 J(Q+S) (T+U+V+X+Y+Z 5/7-1/9)
5 **AB**DEFGIJMNPQ**T**UWXYZ
6 ACFGHJ**K**LM(N 2km)OPSU

Great camping in the countryside. A beautiful family park with extensive and well-maintained campsite amenities. In school holidays and weekends, various places for food and drink where you can enjoy the warm and hospitable atmosphere. A large swimming lake which is great for all ages, including the little ones, and an indoor playground for lots of grand adventures.

A73 take exit Boxmeer towards St. Anthonis and then turn right to Wanroij. The campsite is clearly signposted.

CC € 21 *22/3-28/3 2/4-26/4 6/5-7/5 13/5-16/5 21/5-4/7 2/9-3/11*

N 51°38'26'' E 05°48'40''

Afferden, NL-5851 AG / Limburg

330

Camping Klein Canada****
Dorpsstraat 1
+31 4 85 53 12 23
22/3 - 3/11
info@kleincanada.nl

12ha 143T(100-120m²) 6-10A CEE

1 AD**H**KLMNOPRTU
2 IJSTVXY
3 ABCE**FG**HKLM**O**PSUW
4 (A 27/4-6/5,8/7-1/9) (B 1/5-2/9)(F+G)J**N** (Q+T+X+Y +Z 27/4-5/5,8/7-1/9)
5 **AB**DEFGI**JL**MNOPQR**T**UWXYZ
6 BCFGH**K**(N 0,5km)OPSTUV

Spaciously laid out family campsite with many amenities on the edge of the National Park 'De Maasduinen'. Each of the various fields has its own character. A number of pitches have their own toilet facilities. Some are close to the fishing lake. Catering available in the grounds.

From Nijmegen A73 exit A77 (Köln), then N271 turn left before Afferden. From Venlo turn right beyond Afferden.

CC € 17 *22/3-28/3 2/4-26/4 6/5-7/5 13/5-16/5 21/5-4/7 2/9-3/11*

N 51°38'20'' E 06°00'15''

Afferden, NL-5851 EK / Limburg

331

Camping Roland****
Rimpelt 33
+31 4 85 53 14 31
1/1 - 31/12
info@campingroland.nl

11ha 85T(80-120m²) 6A CEE

1 ADIKLMNOPQRS
2 ISWY
3 CDGHIKMPRSUW
4 (C+H 27/4-20/9)J
(Q+R+S+T+U+Y
+Z 1/4-1/10)
5 ABDFGJLMNOPRUWXYZ
6 BCDEFGHKL(N 1km)
OPSTUV

A luxurious family campsite with a delightful location in the heart of the Maasduinen national park. You can walk or cycle to your heart's content around these beautiful woods, pastures and lakes which are located between the River Maas and the German border.

A73 (Nijmegen-Venlo), at the junction Rijkevoort drive via the A77 to exit 2, route N271 (Nieuw-Bergen/Afferden). After approximately 5 km, direction Venlo. Follow the signs.

CC € 23 *1/1-8/5 21/5-29/5 3/6-5/7 26/8-31/12*

N 51°38'04'' E 06°02'03''

Arcen, NL-5944 EX / Limburg

332

Vakantiepark Klein Vink****
Klein Vink 4
+31 7 74 73 25 25
1/1 - 31/12
receptie.kleinvink@roompot.nl

17ha 310T(80-90m²) 10A CEE

1 ABCDIKLMNOQRS
2 ABEIOSTWXYZ
3 ACDHIKMNOPRSUVWZ
4 (F+H ⊶)KLNOP
(Q+S+T+U+V+X+Y+Z ⊶)
5 ABCDFGHIJKLMNOPUWXYZ
6 ACDFGHKLM(N 0,1km)
OSTUV

A lovely campsite with a nice atmosphere. Very well taken care of. There are excellent thermal baths on the grounds. The recreational lake is wonderful for swimming. Separate grassy spots for motorhomes.

N271 Nijmegen-Venlo. Well signposted.

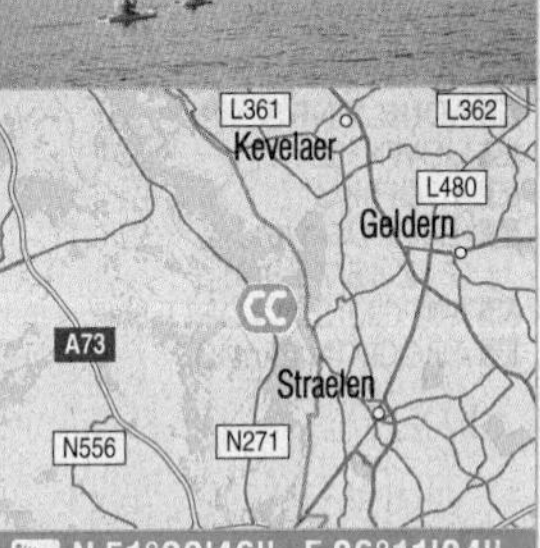

CC € 17 *2/1-22/3 12/4-25/4 13/5-17/5 21/5-29/5 3/6-28/6 30/8-20/12*

N 51°29'46'' E 06°11'04''

Baarlo, NL-5991 NV / Limburg

333

Oostappen Vakantiepark De Berckt
Napoleonsbaan Noord 4
+31 7 74 77 72 22
22/3 - 3/11
info@vakantieparkdeberckt.nl

40ha 257T(80-120m²) 10A CEE

1 ACDIKLMNOQRS
2 BIJSTXYZ
3 ACEFHIKMPRSU
4 (F+H ⊶)IJKLN
(Q+S+T+U+X+Y+Z ⊶)
5 ABDEFGIJKLMNOPQUWXYZ
6 CEFGHJKM(N 2km)STV

A cheerful family campsite set in woodland with a beautiful leisure pool in a fairytale setting. There is also a lovely play castle outside for your enjoyment!

A73 exit Baarlo (N273). The campsite is located on the west side of the N273 (Napoleonsbaan) between Blerick and Baarlo

CC € 19 *22/3-29/3 2/4-26/4 13/5-17/5 24/5-8/7 25/8-18/10*

N 51°20'46'' E 06°06'20''

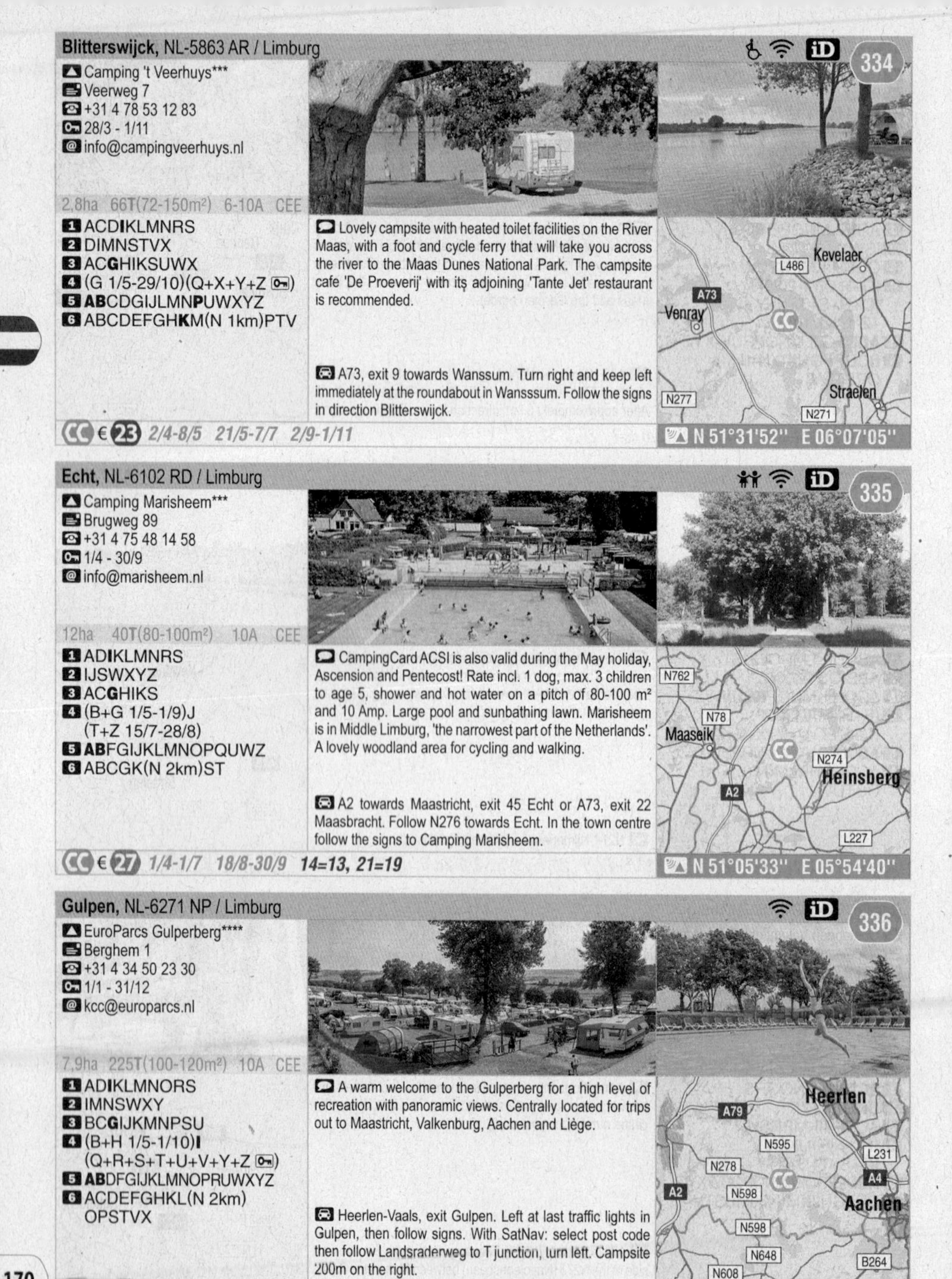

Blitterswijck, NL-5863 AR / Limburg

334

Camping 't Veerhuys***
Veerweg 7
+31 4 78 53 12 83
28/3 - 1/11
info@campingveerhuys.nl

2,8ha 66**T**(72-150m²) 6-10A CEE

1. ACD**I**KLMNRS
2. DIMNSTVX
3. AC**G**HIKSUWX
4. (G 1/5-29/10)(Q+X+Y+Z)
5. **AB**CDGIJLMN**P**UWXYZ
6. ABCDEFGH**K**M(N 1km)PTV

Lovely campsite with heated toilet facilities on the River Maas, with a foot and cycle ferry that will take you across the river to the Maas Dunes National Park. The campsite cafe 'De Proeverij' with its adjoining 'Tante Jet' restaurant is recommended.

A73, exit 9 towards Wanssum. Turn right and keep left immediately at the roundabout in Wansssum. Follow the signs in direction Blitterswijck.

CC € 23 *2/4-8/5 21/5-7/7 2/9-1/11*

N 51°31'52'' E 06°07'05''

Echt, NL-6102 RD / Limburg

335

Camping Marisheem***
Brugweg 89
+31 4 75 48 14 58
1/4 - 30/9
info@marisheem.nl

12ha 40**T**(80-100m²) 10A CEE

1. AD**I**KLMNRS
2. IJSWXYZ
3. AC**G**HIKS
4. (B+G 1/5-1/9)J (T+Z 15/7-28/8)
5. **AB**FGIJKLMNOPQUWZ
6. ABCGK(N 2km)ST

CampingCard ACSI is also valid during the May holiday, Ascension and Pentecost! Rate incl. 1 dog, max. 3 children to age 5, shower and hot water on a pitch of 80-100 m² and 10 Amp. Large pool and sunbathing lawn. Marisheem is in Middle Limburg, 'the narrowest part of the Netherlands'. A lovely woodland area for cycling and walking.

A2 towards Maastricht, exit 45 Echt or A73, exit 22 Maasbracht. Follow N276 towards Echt. In the town centre follow the signs to Camping Marisheem.

CC € 27 *1/4-1/7 18/8-30/9* ***14=13, 21=19***

N 51°05'33'' E 05°54'40''

Gulpen, NL-6271 NP / Limburg

336

EuroParcs Gulperberg****
Berghem 1
+31 4 34 50 23 30
1/1 - 31/12
kcc@europarcs.nl

7,9ha 225**T**(100-120m²) 10A CEE

1. AD**I**KLMNORS
2. IMNSWXY
3. BC**G**IJKMNPSU
4. (B+H 1/5-1/10)**I** (Q+R+S+T+U+V+Y+Z)
5. **AB**DFGIJKLMNOPRUWXYZ
6. ACDEFGHKL(N 2km) OPSTVX

A warm welcome to the Gulperberg for a high level of recreation with panoramic views. Centrally located for trips out to Maastricht, Valkenburg, Aachen and Liège.

Heerlen-Vaals, exit Gulpen. Left at last traffic lights in Gulpen, then follow signs. With SatNav: select post code then follow Landsraderweg to T junction, turn left. Campsite 200m on the right.

CC € 25 *1/1-29/3 2/4-12/4 16/4-26/4 13/5-17/5 20/5-5/7 2/9-31/12*

N 50°48'25'' E 05°53'40''

Gulpen, NL-6271 PP / Limburg

337

- Terrassencamping Osebos****
- Osebos 1
- +31 4 34 50 16 11
- 1/4 - 5/11
- info@osebos.nl

7ha 210T(100-120m²) 6-10A CEE

- **1** ABD**I**KLMNRTU
- **2** IJMNSUWXY
- **3** AC**G**IJKLPSU
- **4** (B+G 15/5-30/9) (Q+S+T+U+V+Y+Z)
- **5** **AB**DEFGIJKLMNPQUWXYZ
- **6** ABCEFGHKL(N 1,5km)OPS

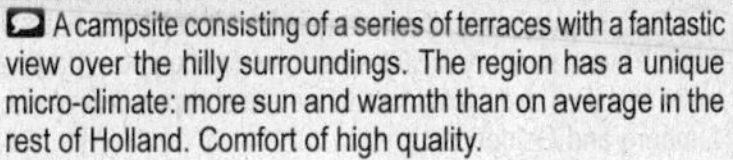

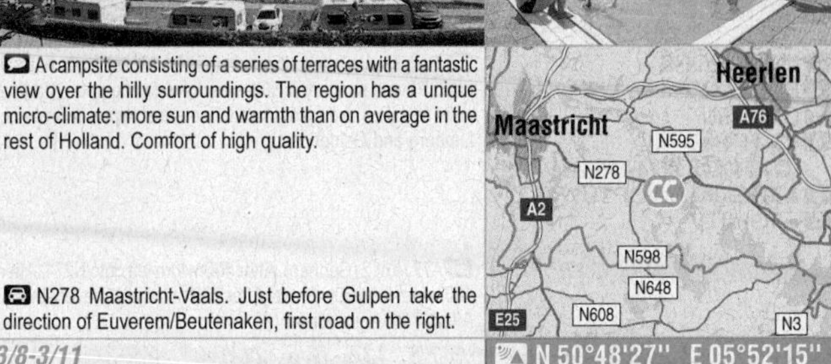

A campsite consisting of a series of terraces with a fantastic view over the hilly surroundings. The region has a unique micro-climate: more sun and warmth than on average in the rest of Holland. Comfort of high quality.

N278 Maastricht-Vaals. Just before Gulpen take the direction of Euverem/Beutenaken, first road on the right.

CC € 23 *1/4-26/4 20/5-6/7 23/8-3/11*

N 50°48'27'' E 05°52'15''

Heel, NL-6097 NL / Limburg

338

- Oostappen Vakantiepark Heelderpeel****
- De Peel 13
- +31 7 74 77 72 24
- 22/3 - 3/11
- receptie@vakantieparkheelderpeel.nl

55ha 160T(100m²) 10A CEE

- **1** ACD**I**KLMNOPQRS
- **2** AEISTWY
- **3** BCHIKMOPRSWZ
- **4** (C 15/5-15/9)(T 1/7-31/8) (X+Z)
- **5** **AB**DFGIJKLMNOPUWZ
- **6** AEFHJ(N 3km)SU

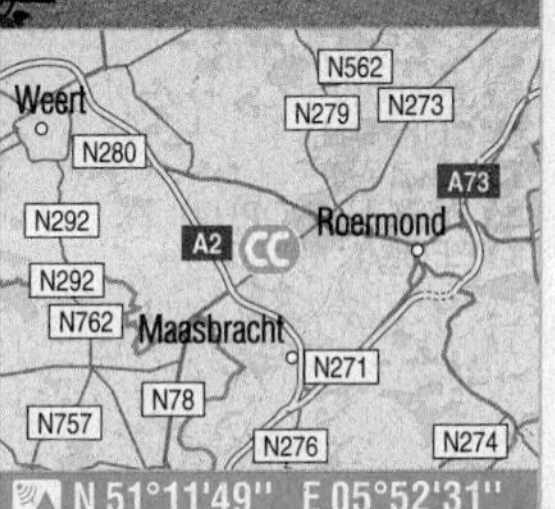

A family campsite in Central Limburg. Plenty of cycling and walking opportunities in the vicinity. There are also plenty of watersports possibilities close by.

From Eindhoven A2, exit 41. On the N273 take direction Venlo. The campsite is signposted after ± 3 km on the left.

CC € 17 *22/3-29/3 2/4-26/4 13/5-17/5 24/5-8/7 25/8-18/10*

N 51°11'49'' E 05°52'31''

Heerlen, NL-6413 TC / Limburg

339

- Camping Hitjesvijver***
- Willem Barentszweg 101
- +31 4 55 21 13 53
- 1/1 - 31/12
- info@hitjesvijver.nl

4,5ha 114T(90-100m²) 6-10A CEE

- **1** ACD**I**KLMNP**R**S
- **2** IJMOSVWXYZ
- **3** ACE**G**HIJKLMNPSU
- **4** (C+H 8/5-1/9)(Q 9/7-3/9) (R+T+U+Y+Z)
- **5** **AB**DFGHIJKLMNOPUWZ
- **6** ACDEFGJ**K**(N 0,6km)OPST

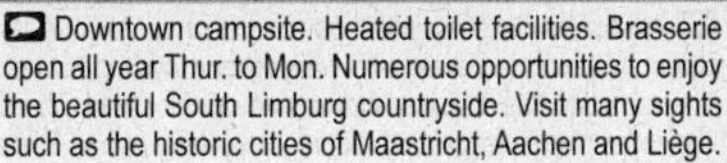

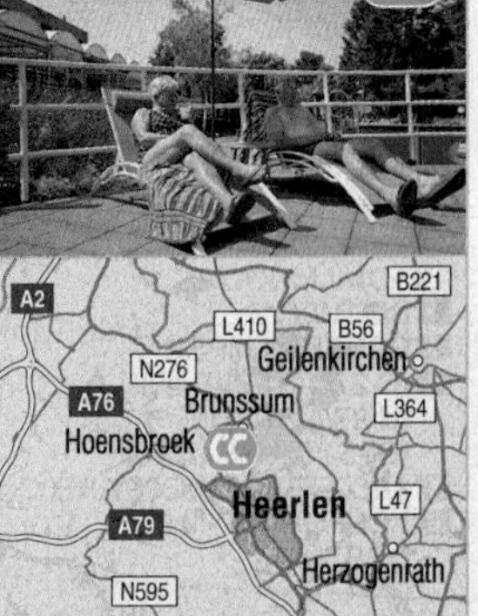

Downtown campsite. Heated toilet facilities. Brasserie open all year Thur. to Mon. Numerous opportunities to enjoy the beautiful South Limburg countryside. Visit many sights such as the historic cities of Maastricht, Aachen and Liège.

From Eindhoven follow signs A76 direction Heerlen, after Nuth take N281 to Heerlen exit Heerlen-Nrd. Left after exit, left at roundabout after McDonald's, then right at 1st roundabout. William Barentszweg. Site 800m on the left.

CC € 21 *1/1-11/4 15/4-7/5 28/5-4/7 1/9-31/12* ***7=6***

N 50°55'16'' E 05°57'26''

Heijen, NL-6598 MH / Limburg

340

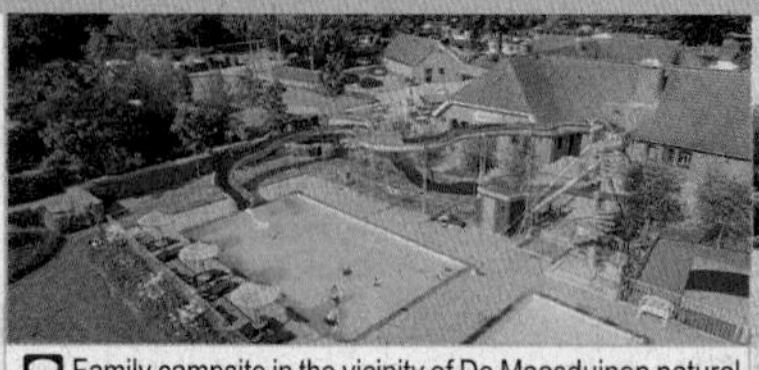

Camping Hoeve De Schaaf***
Brem 11
+31 4 85 53 12 42
22/3 - 3/11
info@campingdeschaaf.nl

10ha 43**T**(100-150m²)

1 **I**KLMNPQRS
2 BDOWXYZ
3 CHKPSU
4 (C+H)J
(Q+T+X+Z 26/4-6/5,22/7-1/9)
5 **AB**DGIJKLMNOP**T**UWXYZ
6 EFGH**J**TV

Family campsite in the vicinity of De Maasduinen natural park. Private sanitary facilities and swimming pool. Starting point for hikes and cycle tours to historical towns in Brabant, Limburg and Gelderland.

A77, exit 2 (Gennep). After 400m turn left onto N271. After 180m turn left to De Grens. After 700m to the Karrevenseweg. After 870m to the Brem.

CC € 17 22/3-28/3 2/4-26/4 6/5-7/5 13/5-16/5 21/5-4/7 2/9-3/11

N 51°39'51'' E 06°00'28''

Heijenrath/Slenaken, NL-6276 PD / Limburg

341

Camping Heyenrade
Heyenratherweg 13
+31 4 34 57 32 60
29/3 - 1/11
info@heyenrade.nl

4ha 120**T**(100m²) 10A CEE

1 ACDIKLMNORS
2 JSWXY
3 **G**IJKLMN
4 (Q+Z)
5 **AB**DGIJMNO**P**UW
6 EFGK(N 1km)OPX

Spacious campsite next to a hotel/restaurant. Lovely setting on the plateau between Epen and Slenaken. Toilet facilities fully renovated in 2022.

N278 Maastricht-Vaals. Past Margraten, towards Noorbeek. Hoogcruts signposted from the junction.

CC € 19 29/3-26/4 21/5-5/7 26/8-1/11

N 50°46'28'' E 05°52'23''

Helden, NL-5988 NH / Limburg

342

Ardoer Camping De Heldense Bossen*****
De Heldense Bossen 6
+31 7 73 07 24 76
29/3 - 3/11
info@deheldensebossen.nl

30ha 327**T**(80-225m²) 10-16A CEE

1 AD**I**KLMNOQRS
2 BISTWXYZ
3 BCE**G**HIKLMPSU
4 (C 27/4-31/8)(F)
(H 27/4-31/8)JM
(Q+S+T+U+Y+Z)
5 **AB**CDEFGHIJKLMNOPQ**T**UWXYZ
6 ACEFGHKLM(N 2km)
OPSTUV

Attractive campsite with spacious pitches. Unique location in a wooded area with walking and cycling routes. The campsite has a heated indoor and outdoor pool. There is also a unique playground, petting zoo, lake, sports fields and an open air theatre. With CampingCard ACSI, you camp on a Basic Plus pitch.

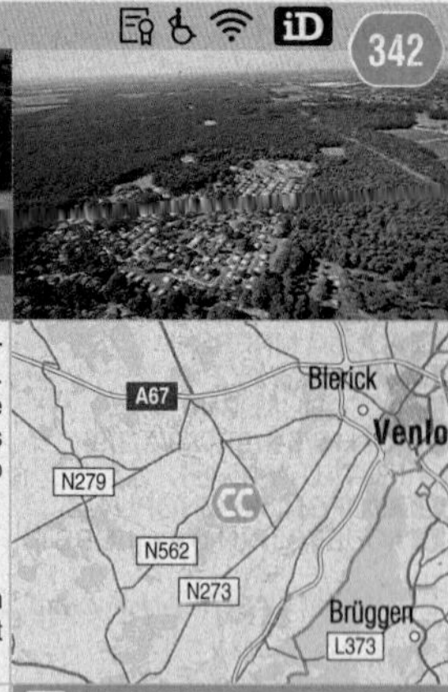

From N277, Middenpeelweg, take exit Helden. From Helden direction Kessel. Turn left after 1 km. Campsite about 1 km further on.

CC € 25 2/4-26/4 12/5-16/5 20/5-29/5 2/6-5/7 31/8-2/11

N 51°19'05'' E 06°01'25''

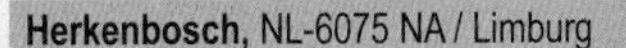

Herkenbosch, NL-6075 NA / Limburg

343

Huttopia De Meinweg
Meinweg 7
+31 4 75 74 55 82
28/3 - 27/10
demeinweg@huttopia.com

27ha 190**T**(90-130m²) 8-16A CEE

1 ABCDE**H**KLMNOQ**R**UV
2 BSTXYZ
3 C**G**HIJKLMNPSU
4 (**A** 8/7-31/8)(C 2/6-1/9) (E+H+Q+R)(V 8/7-31/8) (Z)
5 **AB**DFGIJKLMNOPUW
6 CDEFGHJL(N 3,5km)OPV

In the middle of the National Park the campsite welcomes you on an unspoiled nature plot with spacious pitches among the trees and two lovely heated swimming pools. The ideal base for visiting the south of the Netherlands.

Take A2 or A73 towards Roermond. In Roermond, follow the signs Roermond-East/Melick. Take the Herkenbosch exit and then follow the route " natuurpark Meinweg " until the Meinweg exit.

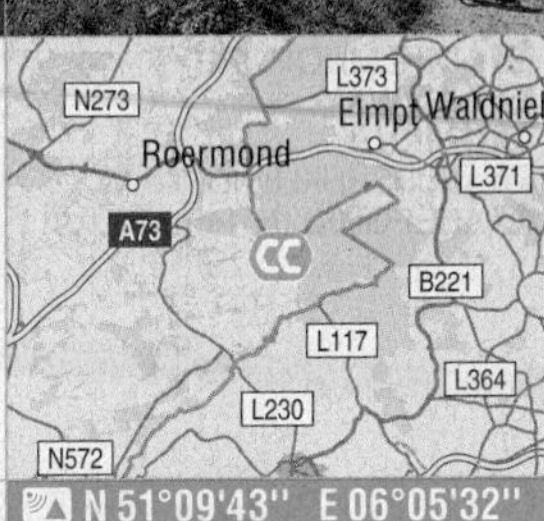

N 51°09'43'' E 06°05'32''

CC € 19 *28/3-26/4 12/5-17/5 20/5-5/7 25/8-27/10*

Hulsberg, NL-6336 AV / Limburg

344

Familiecamping & Recreatiepark 't Hemelke***
Klimmenerweg 10
+31 4 54 05 13 86
23/3 - 30/9
info@hemelke.nl

7ha 330**T**(110-150m²) 6-16A CEE

1 AD**I**KLNRS
2 IJLMSWXYZ
3 ACE**G**HIJKLP**R**SU**V**
4 (B+G 26/4-3/9)J(Q+R+ T+V 26/4-20/5,10/7-25/8) (Y 8/5-20/5,10/7-3/9) (Z 26/4-20/5,10/7-25/8)
5 **AB**EFGIJKLMNOPQ**T**UWZ
6 ACDEFGHK(N 0,2km) OPSTUV

A campsite with spacious pitches, where a long tourist tradition reflects itself in ambiance and hospitality.

From A2 exit A76 direction Heerlen. Exit Nuth. In Nuth direction Hulsberg. Campsite signposted in Hulsberg.

N 50°53'16'' E 05°51'46''

CC € 21 *23/3-26/4 21/5-5/7 1/9-30/9*

Kelpen-Oler, NL-6037 NR / Limburg

345

Camping Geelenhoof***
Grathemerweg 16
+31 4 95 65 18 58
18/3 - 18/10
info@geelenhoof.nl

5ha 57**T**(120-150m²) 6-10A CEE

1 AD**H**KLMNOP**R**S
2 IJSTWXY
3 BCDGHIKMNP**R**SUW
4 (C 1/5-30/9)(Q)
5 **AB**CDFGHIJKMNOPUWXYZ
6 ACDEFGHK(N 3km)PT

Quiet campsite with large car-free comfort pitches. Jeu de boules and fishing lake. Indoor bike shed, charging point for e-bikes. Recommended: Thorn, Roermond and nature parks.

From the north: A2, exit 40 Kelpen/Oler. On the N280, at the traffic lights, take exit Kelpen/Oler and follow the main road. From the south: A2 exit 41 towards Grathem. On the N273, follow the signs for the campsite. Traffic light, turn left to Grathem.

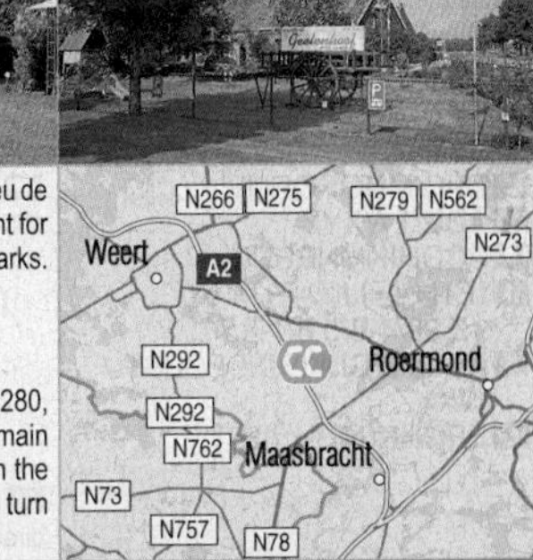

N 51°12'35'' E 05°49'47''

CC € 19 *18/3-8/5 21/5-5/7 1/9-18/10*

Kessel, NL-5995 RP / Limburg

346

Camping Oda Hoeve
Heldenseweg 10
+31 7 74 62 13 58
22/3 - 1/11
info@odahoeve.nl

3,5ha 124T(120-140m²) 6-10A CEE

1 ADIKLMNOPQRS
2 INSVWXY
3 GHIKU
5 ABCDGHIJKLMNOPTUWXY
6 ABEFGHKL(N 1km)PTUV

Hospitable campsite for those seeking space and peace on a lovely landscaped site with paved pitches. Located in a wooded area with many cycling and walking routes, at 1 km from the River Meuse. Owner organises activities on and from the campsite. Free wifi.

Via Napoleonsweg N273, drive to Kessel. At the traffic lights in Kessel, take dir. Helden. After 800 metres, the campsite is on your right.

CC € 21 *22/3-4/5 21/5-6/7 24/8-31/10*

N 51°17'54'' E 06°02'14''

Landgraaf, NL-6374 LE / Limburg

347

Camping De Watertoren****
Kerkveldweg 1
+31 4 55 32 17 47
5/4 - 30/9
info@dewatertoren.nl

5,3ha 116T(100-150m²) 6-10A CEE

1 ACDIKLMNRTU
2 BISUXYZ
3 ACGHIJKLMNPSU
4 (A 12/7-23/8)(C+H 15/5-1/9) (Q+R+T+U+Y+Z)
5 ABDEFGIJKLMNOPQRUWZ
6 ACEFGHKL(N 2km)OPSV

Ideal for young families and nature lovers. Close to a large woodland area. Restaurant. Heated outdoor swimming pool and heated toilet block with facilities for the disabled. Spacious pitches. Walking and cycling routes from campsite.

A2 exit 47 Born/Brunssum. Follow Brunssum. From Maastricht/Heerlen: exit Kerkrade-West (Beitel) or Park Gravenrode signs. Follow Hofstr., Einsteinstr., Dr.Calsstr., Torenstr. Left at Europaweg-Zuid roundabout.

CC € 21 *5/4-7/5 21/5-19/6 24/6-7/7 24/8-30/9*

N 50°54'38'' E 06°04'23''

Maasbree, NL-5993 PB / Limburg

348

Vakantiepark BreeBronne*****
Lange Heide 9
+31 7 74 65 23 60
22/3 - 1/11
info@breebronne.nl

12ha 315T(80-120m²) 16A CEE

1 DIKLMNOPQRUV
2 ABEITWXYZ
3 ACDHIKMNRSUZ
4 (F+H)J(Q+R+T+Y +Z 29/4-8/5,8/7-4/9)
5 ABCDEFGIJKLMNOPQRSTU WXYZ
6 EFGHK(N 3km)ST

Ideal campsite for all ages. Nature lovers and sun worshippers alike will have a great time.

A67, exit Zaarderheiken/Venlo-West/Zuid and N556 direction Maasbree. Follow campsite signs.

CC € 27 *22/3-29/3 2/4-9/5 13/5-17/5 21/5-29/5 4/6-1/7 2/9-19/10*

N 51°22'27'' E 06°03'41''

Meerssen, NL-6231 RV / Limburg

349

- Camping 't Geuldal***
- Gemeentebroek 15
- +31 4 36 04 04 37
- 29/3 - 23/12
- receptie@camping-geuldal.nl

9ha 190T(100-150m²) 6-10A CEE

1. ACDIKLMNOQRTU
2. BDISWXYZ
3. CDEGHIKMNPS
4. M(Q+T+V 14/6-2/9)(Y+Z)
5. ABDFGIJKLMNOPQUWXZ
6. ABCDEFGHKL(N 3km)OPX

Cozy campsite with indoor playground between marlstone walls and River Geul. Good for cycling and walking. Good toilet facilities and spacious pitches. Close to Maastricht and Valkenburg. ACSI Award 2022 for best campsite restaurant of the Netherlands.

A2 exit 51. 1st roundabout left, 2nd right, 3rd left. Over train track directly left. Right before left bend or via A79 to Heerlen exit 2 to Meerssen, left on roundab., left after track. Motorhomes higher than 2.8m: see website.

CC € 21 *1/4-12/4 14/4-26/4 20/5-5/7 1/9-23/12*

N 50°52'21'' E 05°46'17''

Meijel, NL-5768 PK / Limburg

350

- Camping Kampeerbos De Simonshoek***
- Steenoven 10
- +31 7 74 66 17 97
- 1/1 - 8/1, 1/3 - 31/12
- info@simonshoek.nl

8,5ha 75T(120-130m²) 6A CEE

1. ADIKLMNOQRS
2. BISTWXYZ
3. AGHIKMPS
4. (C+E+H 1/4-15/10) (Q 31/3-31/10)(Z)
5. ABDFGIJKLMNOPUWZ
6. ABCEFGHJ(N 1km)PTV

Kampeerbos De Simonshoek is centrally located in the 'Land van Peel en Maas' in Dutch Limburg, in large wooded surroundings close to the Groote Peel National Park. Quietly located with large camping pitches, good toilet facilities, and Simon's Swimming Arena offering fun every day. Lovely cycling and walking routes in the area.

From A67 Eindhoven-Venlo, take exit 36, Asten/Meijel, then N279 direction Meijel. Right after about 12 km. Campsite 700m on the right.

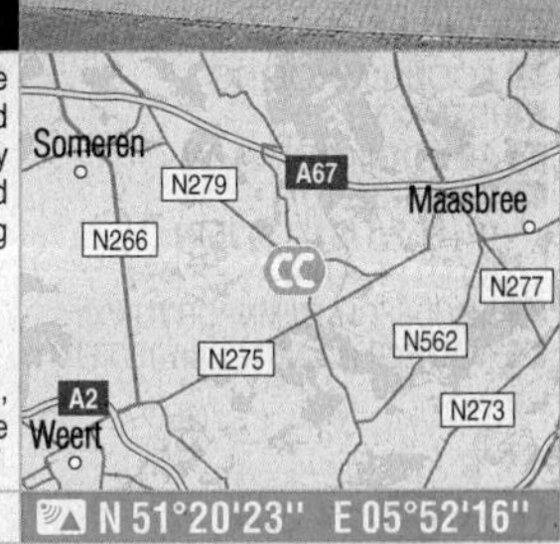

CC € 19 *1/1-8/1 1/3-5/5 25/5-6/7 23/8-31/12*

N 51°20'23'' E 05°52'16''

Melderslo, NL-5962 PA / Limburg

351

- Camping De Kasteelse Bossen***
- Nachtegaallaan 4
- +31 7 73 98 73 61
- 1/1 - 31/12
- info@dekasteelsebossen.nl

3ha 52T(80-140m²) 6-16A CEE

1. ABDIKLMNOPQRUV
2. ISTWXYZ
3. AHIKLPSU
4. (T+U+X+Z)
5. ABCDFGHIJKLMNPTUWZ
6. CEFGHK(N 1km)PSTV

Quiet and beautifully situated, well maintained campsite next to the forest, close to the village. Located in a beautiful cycling and walking area. Suitable for all ages. Enthusiastic owners who will do their utmost to make their guests feel welcome. Restaurant with limited choice. The sanitary facilities are heated. Private facilities are also available.

A73, exit 10 direction Horst-Noord. Turn left at the traffic lights, continue on this road, then follow the campsite signs.

Venray
L361
N270
A73
L480
N277
N271
L2
N556
Venlo
A67
Blerick
B221

CC € 21 *1/1-29/3 2/4-27/4 6/5-9/5 21/5-15/7 1/9-31/12* ***7=6, 14=12***

N 51°27'41'' E 06°04'20''

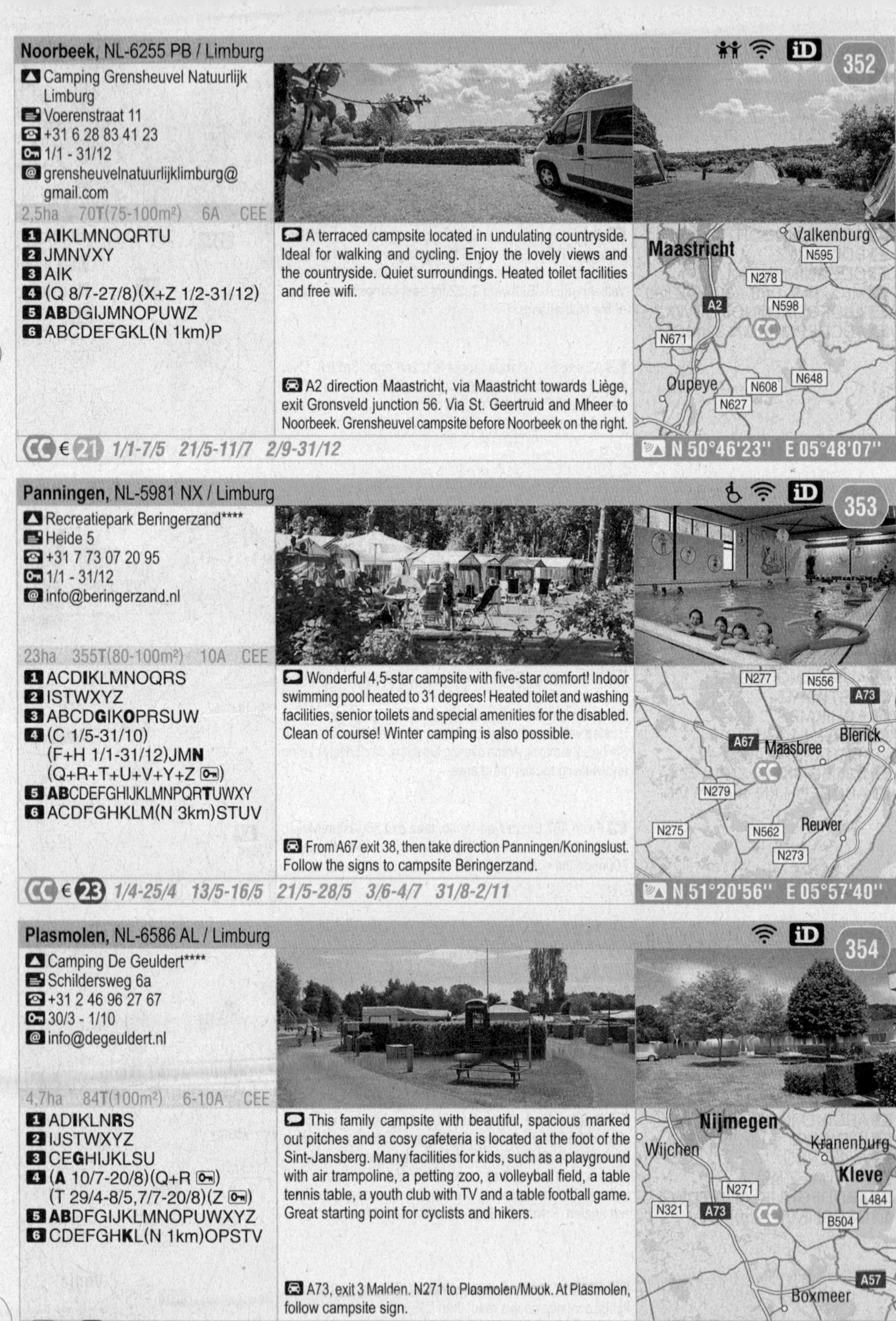

Noorbeek, NL-6255 PB / Limburg

352

Camping Grensheuvel Natuurlijk Limburg
Voerenstraat 11
+31 6 28 83 41 23
1/1 - 31/12
grensheuvelnatuurlijklimburg@gmail.com

2,5ha 70**T**(75-100m²) 6A CEE

1 A**I**KLMNOQRTU
2 JMNVXY
3 AIK
4 (Q 8/7-27/8)(X+Z 1/2-31/12)
5 **AB**DGIJMNOPUWZ
6 ABCDEFGKL(N 1km)P

A terraced campsite located in undulating countryside. Ideal for walking and cycling. Enjoy the lovely views and the countryside. Quiet surroundings. Heated toilet facilities and free wifi.

A2 direction Maastricht, via Maastricht towards Liège, exit Gronsveld junction 56. Via St. Geertruid and Mheer to Noorbeek. Grensheuvel campsite before Noorbeek on the right.

CC € 21 *1/1-7/5 21/5-11/7 2/9-31/12*

N 50°46'23'' E 05°48'07''

Panningen, NL-5981 NX / Limburg

353

Recreatiepark Beringerzand****
Heide 5
+31 7 73 07 20 95
1/1 - 31/12
info@beringerzand.nl

23ha 355**T**(80-100m²) 10A CEE

1 ACD**I**KLMNOQRS
2 ISTWXYZ
3 ABCD**G**IK**O**PRSUW
4 (C 1/5-31/10)
(F+H 1/1-31/12)JM**N**
(Q+R+T+U+V+Y+Z)
5 **AB**CDEFGHIJKLMNPQR**T**UWXY
6 ACDFGHKLM(N 3km)STUV

Wonderful 4,5-star campsite with five-star comfort! Indoor swimming pool heated to 31 degrees! Heated toilet and washing facilities, senior toilets and special amenities for the disabled. Clean of course! Winter camping is also possible.

From A67 exit 38, then take direction Panningen/Koningslust. Follow the signs to campsite Beringerzand.

CC € 23 *1/4-25/4 13/5-16/5 21/5-28/5 3/6-4/7 31/8-2/11*

N 51°20'56'' E 05°57'40''

Plasmolen, NL-6586 AL / Limburg

354

Camping De Geuldert****
Schildersweg 6a
+31 2 46 96 27 67
30/3 - 1/10
info@degeuldert.nl

4,7ha 84**T**(100m²) 6-10A CEE

1 AD**I**KLN**R**S
2 IJSTWXYZ
3 CE**G**HIJKLSU
4 (**A** 10/7-20/8)(Q+R)
(T 29/4-8/5,7/7-20/8)(Z)
5 **AB**DFGIJKLMNOPUWXYZ
6 CDEFGH**K**L(N 1km)OPSTV

This family campsite with beautiful, spacious marked out pitches and a cosy cafeteria is located at the foot of the Sint-Jansberg. Many facilities for kids, such as a playground with air trampoline, a petting zoo, a volleyball field, a table tennis table, a youth club with TV and a table football game. Great starting point for cyclists and hikers.

A73, exit 3 Malden. N271 to Plasmolen/Mook. At Plasmolen, follow campsite sign.

CC € 19 *30/3-27/4 21/5-7/7 24/8-1/10* ***14=12***

N 51°44'13'' E 05°55'47''

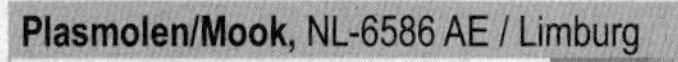

Plasmolen/Mook, NL-6586 AE / Limburg

355

Camping Eldorado***
Witteweg 18
+31 2 46 96 19 14
22/3 - 3/11
info@eldorado-mook.nl

6ha 140**T**(70-100m²) 16A CEE

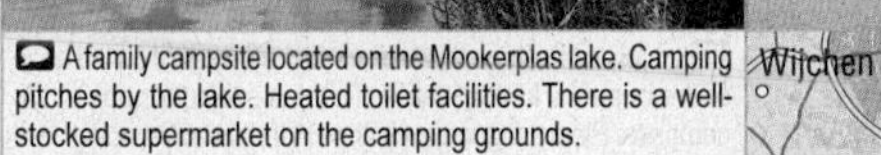

1 ADIKLMNOR
2 CFINSTXYZ
3 ABCHIKSUWZ
4 (**A** 22/7-20/8)(G 1/5-4/9)M (Q+S+T+X+Y+Z)
5 **AB**GIJMNO**P**UWXYZ
6 BCDH**K**(N 0km)OPSX

A family campsite located on the Mookerplas lake. Camping pitches by the lake. Heated toilet facilities. There is a well-stocked supermarket on the camping grounds.

A73 exit 3 Malden. Continue towards Malden. Right at traffic lights direction Mook. Right after about 7 km onto Witteweg and follow camping signs.

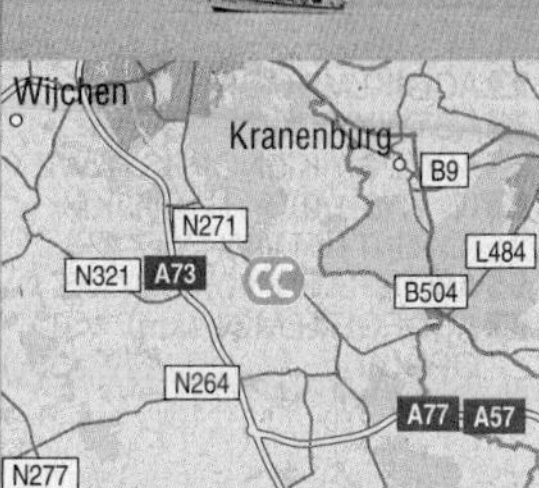

CC € 21 *22/3-28/3 2/4-26/4 6/5-7/5 13/5-16/5 21/5-4/7 2/9-3/11*

N 51°44'08'' E 05°55'01''

Reuver, NL-5953 HP / Limburg

356

Camping Natuurplezier
Keulseweg 200
+31 7 74 74 54 85
22/3 - 13/10
info@natuurplezier.nl

2ha 66**T**(120-135m²) 6A CEE

1 AE**I**KLMNOP**RS**
2 BSTWXYZ
3 AEHIKLS
5 **AB**CFGIJKLMNOPUWXYZ
6 ABCDEFG**K**(N 3km)

Camping Natuurplezier is next to the Brachter Wald forest and the Pieterpad walking trail. Lovely countryside with good walking and cycling options. Perfectly suited for those seeking space and peace. Note: CampingCard ACSI is even valid from 29/7 to 11/8!

From the north A73 exit 17. From the south A73 exit 18. Then on N271 Venlo-Roermond take exit where campsite is indicated in Reuver.

CC € 19 *22/3-26/4 21/5-30/6 29/7-12/8 1/9-13/10*

N 51°16'28'' E 06°07'23''

Roermond, NL-6041 TR / Limburg

357

Resort Marina Oolderhuuske****
Oolderhuuske 1
+31 4 75 58 86 86
28/3 - 3/11
info@oolderhuuske.nl

5,5ha 80**T**(80-200m²) 6-16A CEE

1 ACD**H**KLMNO**R**S
2 ACEINOSVWXY
3 ACHKMN**O**PS**VW**Z
4 (**F**+**H**)MN(Q+R 1/4-31/10) (T+V+Y+Z)
5 **AB**DFGIJKLMNOPQRUWXYZ
6 ACEFGHKL(N 5km)TU

Campsite located directly on the river Maas with watersports opportunities. The campsite has modern toilet facilities and has a sandy beach especially for campsite guests.

Take Hatenboer/de Weerd exit from the N280. Then immediately left and follow brown signs to Marina Oolderhuuske.

CC € 25 *2/4-26/4 13/5-17/5 21/5-29/5 3/6-22/6 19/8-11/10*

N 51°11'32'' E 05°56'58''

Roggel, NL-6088 NT / Limburg

358

- Recreatiepark De Leistert*****
- Heldensedijk 5
- +31 4 75 49 30 30
- 1/1 - 31/12
- info@leistert.nl

ACSI AWARDS WINNER

100ha 594**T**(90-130m²) 10-16A CEE

1. ACD**I**KLMNOQRS
2. ASTWXYZ
3. ABCD**G**HIKMNOP**RST**UWZ
4. (C 17/5-1/9)(F+H)IJKM (Q+S+T+U+V+X+Y+Z)
5. **AB**CDEFGIJKLMNOPR**T**UWXYZ
6. ACDFGH**K**LM(N 1km) OPSUV

Lovely campsite with spacious pitches, located on the edge of the beautiful Leudal valley. There is a leisure pool on the campsite. Plenty of good cycle trips in the area. CampingCard ACSI campers are on a comfort pitch.

The campsite is on the N562, Helden-Roggel road. About 1 km from Roggel.

CC € 27 *1/1-29/3 12/4-26/4 13/5-17/5 21/5-5/7 24/8-31/12*

N 51°16'27'' E 05°55'55''

Schimmert, NL-6333 BR / Limburg

359

- Camping Mareveld***
- Mareweg 23
- +31 4 54 04 12 69
- 29/3 - 30/9
- info@campingmareveld.nl

3,5ha 45**T**(80m²) 10A CEE

1. ACD**I**KLMNP**R**TU
2. IJNSXYZ
3. CEIJKP
4. (C 1/5-31/8)(X+Y+Z)
5. **AB**DFGIJMNOPUWXY
6. ABEFGH**K**(N 1km)PV

Rustic campsite with a very special brasserie with a unique atmosphere. Beautifully located in South Limburg. The campsite has a heated outdoor pool. Ideal starting point for cyclists and walkers.

A76 exit Spaubeek, turn right towards Schimmert. 2nd on the left in Schimmert. Campsite signposted.

CC € 19 *29/3-25/4 12/5-17/5 21/5-5/7 26/8-30/9*

N 50°54'26'' E 05°49'54''

Schin op Geul/Valkenburg, NL-6305 PM / Limburg

360

- Camping Vinkenhof/Keutenberg***
- Engwegen 2a
- +31 4 34 59 13 89
- 1/1 - 3/1, 15/3 - 31/12
- info@campingvinkenhof.nl

2,5ha 94**T**(80-100m²) 6-10A CEE

1. ACD**I**KLMNRS
2. CIJSUWXYZ
3. AC**G**HIJKLPSU
4. (C 1/5-15/9) (Q 27/4-21/5,2/7-26/8) (T+U+V+Y+Z 1/4-1/10)
5. **AB**CDFGIJKLMNO**PT**UWXYZ
6. ACEFGHKL(N 0,5km)PTV

Vinkenhof campsite is located in a unique spot in the South Limburg landscape at the foot of the Keutenberg and Sousberg hills. An ideal location for walks or trips out to Valkenburg, Maastricht, Aachen and Liége.

From A76 exit Nuth, via Hulsberg to Valkenburg and in Valkenburg drive towards Schin op Geul.

CC € 23 *15/3-28/3 1/4-10/4 15/4-25/4 20/5-4/7 24/8-14/11*

N 50°51'00'' E 05°52'23''

Sevenum, NL-5975 MZ / Limburg

361

Camping De Schatberg*****
Middenpeelweg 5
+31 7 74 67 77 77
1/1 - 31/12
info@schatberg.nl

96ha 450T(100-150m²) 10-16A CEE

1 ACD**I**KLMNOQRUV
2 ABEIOSWXYZ
3 ABCD**FG**HIKLMNP**R**S**T**U**W**Z
4 (B 1/5-1/9)(F)(H 1/5-1/9) IJKM(Q+S+T+U +V+W+X+Y+Z)
5 **AB**DEFGIJKLMNOPQR**T**UWXYZ
6 ACFGHKM(N 6km)OSTUV

Large family campsite in a unique location in the North Limburg Peel. Open all year. Plenty of indoor and outdoor amenities. Fun & Entertainment Center Sevenum within walking distance. Lovely cycling and walking routes. Reservation recommended for Ascension Day/Whitsun holidays. CampingCard ACSI holders camp in the Comfort zone.

From A67 Eindhoven-Venlo, take exit 38 Panningen and then follow the signs. Campsite is located along the N277, the Middenpeelweg.

ACSI AWARDS WINNER

€23 *1/1-27/4 13/5-17/5 21/5-6/7 24/8-31/12* ***14=11***

N 51°22'58'' E 05°58'34''

Vaals, NL-6291 NM / Limburg

362

Camping Hoeve de Gastmolen***
Lemierserberg 23
+31 4 33 06 57 55
22/3 - 31/10
info@gastmolen.nl

6ha 97T(100-140m²) 6-10A CEE

1 AD**I**KLMNPRS
2 CJLMNSUWXYZ
3 A**G**HIJKLSU
4 (Q)
5 **AB**DFGIJKLMNOPQUWXYZ
6 ACDEFJ(N 1,5km)OPV

Hoeve de Gastmolen used to be a courtyard farm of the province Limburg. The meadows which now form part of the camping grounds border onto the babbling Selzer brook. Modern sanitary facilities.

From A76 intersection Bocholtz dir. N281. At Nijswiller N278 dir. Vaals. Campsite signposted just before Vaals. Take note: GPS takes you not to main entrance but to the crossroads you need to take to the site.

€23 *22/3-26/4 21/5-5/7 1/9-31/10*

N 50°46'44'' E 06°00'17''

Valkenburg aan de Geul, NL-6325 AD / Limburg

363

Camping De Cauberg
Rijksweg 171
+31 4 36 01 23 44
22/3 - 23/10, 15/11 - 20/12
info@campingdecauberg.nl

1ha 55T(70-110m²) 6-16A CEE

1 AD**I**KLMNRS
2 IJMNSVXYZ
3 A**G**IJK
4 (Q+R+T+V+Z)
5 **AB**DFGIJMNPUWXZ
6 ABCDEFGK(N 1,5km)PS

A pleasant small-scale campsite on the highest point of Cauberg hill. Sunny and shaded pitches. Electricity at all pitches. Heated toilet block with good facilities. Plenty of wellness, cycling and walking opportunities in the immediate surroundings. Free wifi. Bus stop in 350m.

A2 exit 53 direction Berg en Terblijt/Valkenburg. Campsite is signposted after 5 km on the left of the road.

€23 *22/3-28/3 2/4-11/4 16/4-25/4 21/5-4/7 2/9-23/10*

N 50°51'24'' E 05°49'08''

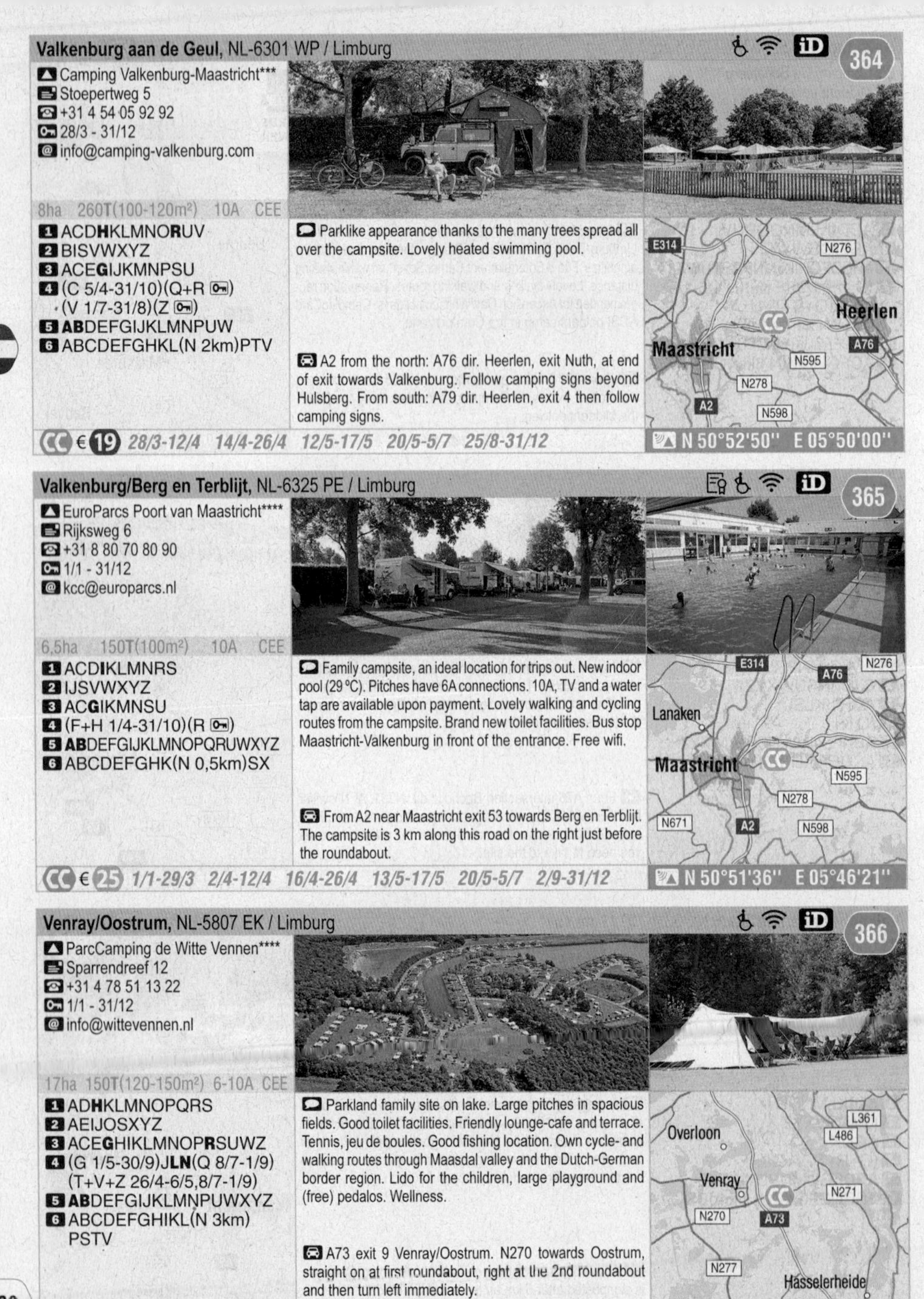

Valkenburg aan de Geul, NL-6301 WP / Limburg

364

Camping Valkenburg-Maastricht***
Stoepertweg 5
+31 4 54 05 92 92
28/3 - 31/12
info@camping-valkenburg.com

8ha 260T(100-120m²) 10A CEE

1 ACD**H**KLMNO**R**UV
2 BISVWXYZ
3 ACE**G**IJKMNPSU
4 (C 5/4-31/10)(Q+R 🔑)
(V 1/7-31/8)(Z 🔑)
5 **AB**DEFGIJKLMNPUW
6 ABCDEFGHKL(N 2km)PTV

Parklike appearance thanks to the many trees spread all over the campsite. Lovely heated swimming pool.

A2 from the north: A76 dir. Heerlen, exit Nuth, at end of exit towards Valkenburg. Follow camping signs beyond Hulsberg. From south: A79 dir. Heerlen, exit 4 then follow camping signs.

CC € 19 *28/3-12/4 14/4-26/4 12/5-17/5 20/5-5/7 25/8-31/12*

N 50°52'50'' E 05°50'00''

Valkenburg/Berg en Terblijt, NL-6325 PE / Limburg

365

EuroParcs Poort van Maastricht****
Rijksweg 6
+31 8 80 70 80 90
1/1 - 31/12
kcc@europarcs.nl

6,5ha 150T(100m²) 10A CEE

1 ACD**I**KLMNRS
2 IJSVWXYZ
3 AC**G**IKMNSU
4 (F+H 1/4-31/10)(R 🔑)
5 **AB**DEFGIJKLMNOPQRUWXYZ
6 ABCDEFGHK(N 0,5km)SX

Family campsite, an ideal location for trips out. New indoor pool (29 °C). Pitches have 6A connections. 10A, TV and a water tap are available upon payment. Lovely walking and cycling routes from the campsite. Brand new toilet facilities. Bus stop Maastricht-Valkenburg in front of the entrance. Free wifi.

From A2 near Maastricht exit 53 towards Berg en Terblijt. The campsite is 3 km along this road on the right just before the roundabout.

CC € 25 *1/1-29/3 2/4-12/4 16/4-26/4 13/5-17/5 20/5-5/7 2/9-31/12*

N 50°51'36'' E 05°46'21''

Venray/Oostrum, NL-5807 EK / Limburg

366

ParcCamping de Witte Vennen****
Sparrendreef 12
+31 4 78 51 13 22
1/1 - 31/12
info@wittevennen.nl

17ha 150T(120-150m²) 6-10A CEE

1 AD**H**KLMNOPQRS
2 AEIJOSXYZ
3 ACE**G**HIKLMNOP**R**SUWZ
4 (G 1/5-30/9)J**LN**(Q 8/7-1/9)
(T+V+Z 26/4-6/5,8/7-1/9)
5 **AB**DEFGIJKLMNPUWXYZ
6 ABCDEFGHIKL(N 3km)
PSTV

Parkland family site on lake. Large pitches in spacious fields. Good toilet facilities. Friendly lounge-cafe and terrace. Tennis, jeu de boules. Good fishing location. Own cycle- and walking routes through Maasdal valley and the Dutch-German border region. Lido for the children, large playground and (free) pedalos. Wellness.

A73 exit 9 Venray/Oostrum. N270 towards Oostrum, straight on at first roundabout, right at the 2nd roundabout and then turn left immediately.

CC € 21 *1/1-31/3 2/4-27/4 6/5-9/5 21/5-30/5 3/6-8/7 25/8-31/12*

N 51°31'25'' E 06°02'08''

Vijlen, NL-6294 NB / Limburg

367

Camping Rozenhof***
Camerig 12
+31 4 34 55 16 11
1/1 - 31/12
info@campingrozenhof.nl

2ha 58T(tot 110m²) 10A CEE

1 ACDIKLMNPRS
2 LMNSUXYZ
3 CGIJKLPSU
4 (C+H 15/5-15/9) (Q+S+T+Y)
5 ABDGIJKLMNOPUWXY
6 ABCDFGK(N 2km)OPV

A warm welcome to this beautifully appointed terraced campsite, with comfort pitches only (10 Amp). Panoramic views of Geul valley and Vijlener woods. A delight for walkers and cyclists. Maastricht, Valkenburg, Aachen and Liège are all within a reasonable distance.

From A75 intersection Bochholz direction N281. At Nijswiller 278 direction Vaals. Exit Vijlen. From Vijlen direction Epen. Left at fork in road. Signposted from here.

CC € 23 1/1-26/4 21/5-8/7 26/8-31/12

N 50°46'12'' E 05°55'45''

Voerendaal, NL-6367 HE / Limburg

368

Camping Colmont****
Colmont 2
+31 4 55 62 00 57
29/3 - 29/9
info@colmont.nl

4ha 150T(80-120m²) 6-10A CEE

1 ADEIKLMNRS
2 IJLMNSUVWXYZ
3 ACGIJKLMNPSU
4 (C+H 1/5-15/9)(Q+R) (T+U 8/5-19/5,13/7-23/8) (V)(X 8/5-19/5,13/7-23/8) (Z)
5 ABDEFGIJKLMNOPUWZ
6 ACDEFGHKL(N 3km) OPTVX

Panoramic campsite (180m above sea level) in the hills of the southern Netherlands. A rural yet central location between Maastricht and Heerlen. Heated outdoor pool. Both sunny and shady pitches and motorhome pitches. Well-maintained toilet facilities. Ideal base for cyclists, hikers and trips to Maastricht, Valkenburg, Aachen and Liege. Free wifi.

From A79 on junction Voerendaal direction Kunrade. In Kunrade direction Ubachsberg. Indicated from Ubachsberg centre.

CC € 21 29/3-6/7 23/8-29/9

N 50°51'08'' E 05°56'03''

Well, NL-5855 EG / Limburg

369

Camping Leukermeer*****
De Kamp 5
+31 4 78 50 24 44
31/3 - 30/10
vakantie@leukermeer.nl

14ha 239T(100m²) 10A CEE

1 ACDHKLMNOPQRS
2 ABEJNSTUWXYZ
3 CGHIKLMNOPQRSUVWZ
4 (C 26/4-15/9)(F+H)KMN (Q+S+T+U+V+X+Y+Z)
5 ABDEFGJKLMNPQRUWXYZ
6 BCEFGHJKLM(N 3km) STUVX

This campsite is located close to water. Ideal camping place for fans of water sport. Nature lovers can enjoy De Maasduinen national park on foot, or by bike.

Coming from Venlo, on reaching Well follow the signs 't Leukermeer. Coming from Nijmegen via Bergen en Aijen follow the signs 't Leukermeer. Or take the A73 exit 9 via the N270 direction Wanssum.

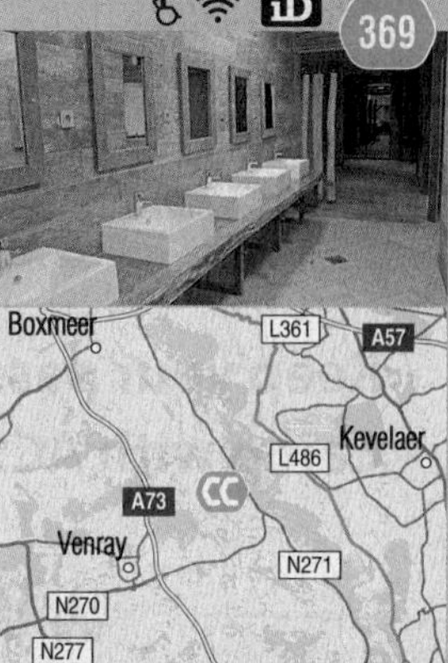

CC € 27 8/4-26/4 13/5-17/5 21/5-29/5 3/6-14/6 17/6-21/6 24/6-28/6 1/9-11/10

N 51°34'03'' E 06°03'38''

Wijlre, NL-6321 PK / Limburg

370

Camping De Gele Anemoon
Haasstad 4
+31 8 80 99 09 57
30/3 - 28/9
degeleanemoon@nivon.nl

1,1ha 51T(90-100m²) 6A CEE

1 ABCD**H**KLNPRS
2 CSXYZ
3 A**G**IJKLSU
4 (G)
5 **AB**CDEFGHIJKLMNOPUWZ
6 ADEFGHK(N 1,4km)OPV

A superbly located campsite in an old orchard next to the River Geul at the foot of the Keutenberg hill. Perfect departure point for cycling and walking tours and for trips out, for example to Maastricht, Valkenburg, Aachen and Liége.

A2 to Maastricht, then towards Vaals. In Gulpen, go towards Wijlre. Signposted in Wijlre. Situated on a narrow dead-end road, but with many passing places.

CC € 23 *30/3-8/5 21/5-5/7 31/8-28/9*

N 50°50'26'' E 05°52'46''

Wijlre, NL-6321 PK / Limburg

371

Camping De Gronselenput
Haasstad 3
+31 4 34 59 16 45
29/3 - 28/9
gronselenput@nivon.nl

2ha 58T(60-120m²) 10-16A CEE

1 ACD**H**KLNPRS
2 CSVWXY
3 AC**G**IJKLPSU
4 M(Q+R+V+Z)
5 **AB**DFGIJKLMNOPUWXY
6 ADEFGHK(N 3km)OPV

Nature campsite on the river Geul with an un-Dutch atmosphere right at the foot of the Keutenberg. Rest and nature are well catered for. Small campsite with manageable pitches, also ideal for families with small children.

A2 as far as Maastricht, then direction Vaals. In Gulpen direction Wijlre. Signposted in Wijlre. Located on a narrow dead-end road, but with plenty of room to manoeuvre.

CC € 21 *29/3-26/4 21/5-6/7 24/8-28/9*

N 50°50'31'' E 05°52'38''

Belgium

Belgium: camping near the nicest cities or in the middle of the Ardennes

It is no secret that you can enjoy a great holiday in Belgium. In Flanders, cities like Brussels, Antwerp, Ghent and Bruges are very popular. In Wallonia, the Ardennes are very popular, with the amazing vantage points as well as many beautiful towns like Durbuy and Huy, where you can enjoy architecture that is centuries old.

Capital: Brussels
Currency: the euro
Time zone: UTC +1, UTC +2 (March to October)
Language: Dutch and French
International dialling code: +32
Alcohol limit: 0.5‰
Emergency number: police, fire brigade and ambulance: 112
Tap water: safe to drink

Gastronomic enjoyment in Belgium

Belgium is known for its exuberant lifestyle. This becomes evident when you visit the most popular museums in Bruges. You go from the Frietmuseum (chips museum), past the Biermuseum (beer museum), straight on to the Chocolademuseum (chocolate museum). That is culinary enjoyment!
In Brussels and Antwerp, it is a pleasure to walk through the city centre. Both cities have a beautiful historic city centre with numerous top restaurants and delightful shops. Be sure to visit Manneken Pis (Little Man Pee) and the Grote Markt (Grand Place) in Brussels, where you can admire the old guildhalls. Did you know

Winners in Belgium

382	*Best campsite*	Camping Sandaya Parc la Clusure
398	*Nicest campsite for children*	Provinciaal Recreatiedomein Zilvermeer
400	*Best campsite swimming pool*	Recreatieoord Wilhelm Tell
403	*Best location for a campsite*	Camping Ile de Faigneul
384	*Most sports-loving campsite*	Camping Worriken
407	*Campsite with the best toilet facilities*	Camping de l'Eau Rouge

ACSI Awards

Winner: Camping Sandaya Parc la Clusure

that Manneken Pis even has a female counterpart, Jeanneke Pis? She is across the street from the Delirium Café, which has an extensive beer menu.

Nature in the Ardennes

In addition to all these amazing cities, the Ardennes have been popular with many tourists for decades. And rightly so. These beautiful woods allow you to enjoy cycling, hiking and other sports. The Ardennes are also famous for the many outdoor activities and survival excursions. Go abseiling, explore remarkable caves, such as the Caves of Han, or experience a survival day in the rugged countryside. In the winter, you can also enjoy (cross-country) skiing in the Ardennes, or simply enjoy the snow. In the east, close to the German border, there is also the Belgian Formula 1 circuit, Circuit de Spa-Francorchamps, where car enthusiasts and speed freaks can let themselves go.

En route

Filling up

Petrol (Euro 95, E10 and Superplus 98) is widely available (if you want to fill up with E10, check the mouth of your petrol tank, the manual or with your dealer as to whether your car can drive on this; otherwise, fill up with Superplus 98). Diesel and LPG are also widely available. When filling up with LPG, the European connection (acme) is used. Most petrol stations are usually open from 8:00 to 20:00 and the petrol stations along motorways are often open 24 hours. There are also many unmanned fuelling stations.

"Belgium is a small country, but there is something wonderful to discover everywhere in the countryside or in the culture."
Ms A. Cousin, inspector 821

Charging

There is a difference between the Walloon and Flemish sections of Belgium with regard to charging. Wallonia is not really set up for electric driving yet. This has in part to do with an antiquated energy network. The main routes in Flanders are well equipped with fast-chargers. There are also more public charging stations in Flanders than in Wallonia.

Traffic regulations

Low beam headlights are mandatory when it is dark, when visibility is poor, and in tunnels. At equivalent crossings, traffic from the right has right of way. Trams always have right of way. Traffic on the roundabout has right of way if so indicated by traffic signs. On sloping roads, ascending traffic has priority over descending traffic. Drivers may only call hands free. Children under 1.35 metres must be in a child's seat. Navigation software that warns of speed cameras or average speed checks is permitted. Winter tyres are not mandatory.

Special regulations

Smoking in the car is prohibited if a child is present. When merging, you could receive a fine if you merge too soon or do not give right of way to mergers. When passing cyclists (including those on a bicycle path), you are required to maintain a lateral distance of at least 1.50 metres. Leaving your engine idling is prohibited if you stand still for a longer period of time, such as at a crossing.

Mandatory equipment

A warning triangle and a safety vest are mandatory in the car. A first-aid box and fire extinguisher are only mandatory in cars with a Belgian registration number.

> *"The cycling and hiking junctions are fantastic, and I enjoy the delicious Belgian beer."*
>
> Mr J. Verrezen, inspector 140

Caravan and motorhome

A motorhome or car-caravan combination may be a maximum of 4 metres high, 2.55 metres wide and 18.75 metres long (the caravan itself may be a maximum of 12 metres long).

Cycling

A bicycle helmet is not mandatory. Calling or texting while cycling is prohibited. You may not transport a passenger on the rear bike rack (but may transport a child in a child's seat).

Toll

There is a toll for the Liefkenshoektunnel to the north of Antwerp.
For more information: liefkenshoektunnel.be.

Environmental zones

In Belgium, the cities Antwerp, Brussels and Ghent have a low-emission zone (LEZ). As from 2023, all of Wallonia will be a zone de basses émissions (ZBE) or a low-emission zone. Municipalities may introduce this earlier. Vehicles will be registered with cameras. If you enter an LEZ with a vehicle that is not

permitted, you risk a hefty fine.
For more information: lez.brussels, slimnaarantwerpen.be, stad.gent, vlaanderen.be/lage-emissiezones-lez and walloniebassesemissions.be.

Breakdown and accident

Position your warning triangle at least 100 metres behind the car if you have stopped where stopping is prohibited. The driver must wear a safety vest. If you have had a breakdown, call the alarm number of your breakdown assistance insurer. You can also call a Belgian breakdown service: +32 70 344 777 (Touring Belgium Go) or +32 70 344 666 (VAB). Towing is prohibited on motorways; you must engage a salvage service.

Camping

Belgian campsites are generally of reasonable to good quality. As a rule, Belgian campsites are child-friendly. There is often entertainment and usually many amenities such as playgrounds and sports fields. Free camping (outside of campsites) is allowed with permission from the police or the landowner. Free camping in Flanders and along the coast is not permitted.

Adinkerke/De Panne, B-8660 / West-Vlaanderen

372

Camping Kindervreugde**
Langgeleedstraat 1a
+32 4 68 04 08 95
30/3 - 30/9
info@kindervreugde.be

3ha 40T(95-130m²) 6A CEE

1 ABDHKLMNOQRTU
2 IJSWXYZ
3 AGIKW
4 (Q)
5 ABCFGIJMNPQUWXYZ
6 AEFGK(N 2,3km)PT

Camping Kindervreugde is a small, quiet campsite in the countryside. It is close to Plopsaland, nature reserves and the French border. Spacious pitches, well-kept toilet and washing facilities and good, free wifi. At 1.3 km from Adinkerke's train and tram station.

Coming from the E40 direction Adinkerke, take first road left behind the station. Keep driving until the T-junction. Here, go left after about 50 m. The campsite is on your right.

CC € 21 14/4-9/5 12/5-17/5 20/5-30/6 1/9-30/9

N 51°04'35" E 02°35'11"

Amel/Deidenberg, B-4770 / Liège

373

Camping Oos Heem BVBA***
Zum Schwarzenvenn 6
+32 80 34 97 41
1/1 - 31/12
info@campingoosheem.be

3,5ha 57T(100m²) 16A CEE

1 ADHKLMNOQRS
2 CINSWX
3 CEHIJKPS
4 (C+H 1/7-31/8)(Q)
(T+U+V+Y+Z 1/7-31/8)
5 ABDFGIJKMNPUWZ
6 DEFGHJL(N 3,5km)OPT

Campsite with a family atmosphere, near the High Fens Nature Park in the green, quiet East Cantons. Direct access form the campsite to the Ravel-Vennbahn cycle route. Ideal area for walking and climbing. Tasty, affordable cuisine with extensive menu. Swimming pool in July-August.

E42 Verviers-St. Vith exit 13. E42 St. Vith-Verviers, exit 13, direction Recht. Follow signs 'Camping Oos Heem' from there.

CC € 25 1/1-8/5 13/5-17/5 21/5-30/6 1/9-31/12

N 50°20'54" E 06°07'12"

Aywaille, B-4920 / Liège

374

Camping Domaine Château de Dieupart*
37 route de Dieupart
+32 43 84 44 30
1/1 - 31/12
info@dieupart.be

5ha 106T(80-120m²) 10A CEE

1 ACDIKLMNQRTU
2 BDIJSUVWXYZ
3 CHIJKLSWX
4 (A+T+U+X+Z)
5 ABCDEFGHIJKLMOPUWXYZ
6 ACDEFGHJ(N 0,1km)PRTV

Authentic castle grounds by the Amblève with lovely covered patio. Town centre accessible via a RAVel (public road) beside the Amblève (500m). Supermarket and hot bakery a stone's throw away, all pitches on a stable surface. In the vicinity of the Luik-Bastenaken-Luik route.

Leave E25 at exit 46 Remouchamps/Aywaille. Turn right at traffic lights dir. Aywaille, and right by the church. Immediate left and then right at Delhaize car park, take avenue up to the castle. Signposted.

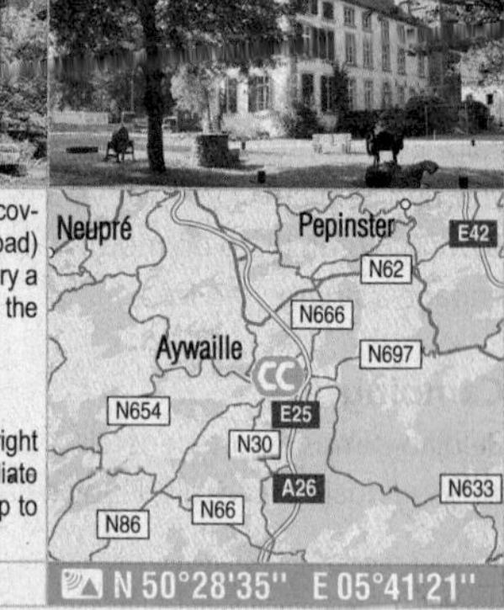

CC € 25 1/1-10/5 12/5-17/5 20/5-8/7 25/8-31/12

N 50°28'35" E 05°41'21"

Bastogne, B-6600 / Luxembourg

375

Camping de Renval***
rue de Marche 148
+32 61 21 29 85
1/3 - 1/12
info@campingderenval.eu

7ha 60T(100m²) 10A CEE

1 ACDHKLMNORS
2 DISUWX
3 AHIKLRSW
5 ABDFGIJKLMNOPUWZ
6 CDFGK(N 0,5km)P

Suitable as a stopover campsite. Near exit E25 and N4, and Bastogne centre with a war museum and monument. First part of campsite is for residential pitches. Behind that there is a part for touring pitches. Many sports facilities close to campsite. Free wifi. Automatic reception (24 hours a day).

From the centre of Bastogne drive towards Marche. The campsite is located to the right after 1.2 km. From E25 and N4 towards Bastogne, 500 m from the exit.

CC € 21 1/3-1/6 1/9-30/11

N 50°00'11'' E 05°41'44''

Bertrix, B-6880 / Luxembourg

376

Ardennen Camping Bertrix****
route de Mortehan
+32 61 41 22 81
22/3 - 4/11
info@campingbertrix.be

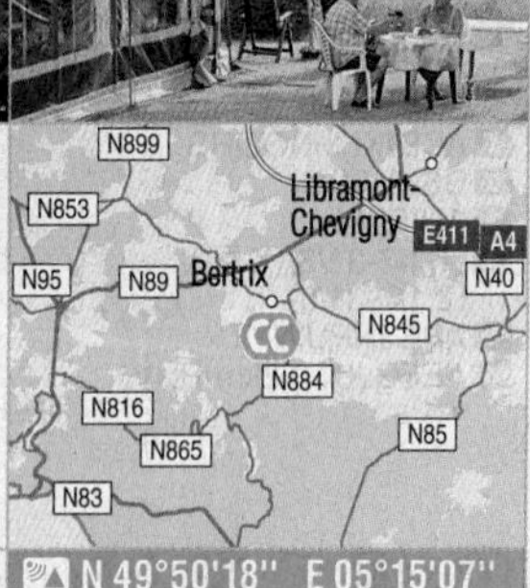

16ha 314T(80-120m²) 10A CEE

1 ACDIKLMNORS
2 BILMSUWXYZ
3 CHIKLOPSU
4 (A 1/7-31/8)(C+H 1/5-15/9)(Q+R+T+V+Y+Z)
5 ABDEFGIJKLMNOPRUWXZ
6 CDFGHJ(N 3km)OPTUV

A wonderful terraced campsite with a high level of service and first class amenities. Bordering immense forests with streams and game. Luxury camping in an oasis of peace and unspoiled countryside, ideal for a complete holiday or as a stopover campsite.

From E411 exit 25 Bertrix. Follow N89 as far as Bertrix exit. Take the N884 to the centre. Then follow camping signs.

CC € 23 22/3-7/7 24/8-3/11 7=6, 14=11

N 49°50'18'' E 05°15'07''

Blankenberge, B-8370 / West-Vlaanderen

377

Camping Bonanza 1***
Zeebruggelaan 137
+32 50 41 66 58
22/3 - 29/9
info@bonanza1.be

5ha 65T(80-100m²) 10A CEE

1 ACDHJKLMNORS
2 SUVXY
3 CHIKMS
4 (Q 1/7-31/8)
5 ABDFGIJKLMOPUX
6 ACDEFGHK(N 0,5km)OPSV

Bonanza 1 is a modern family campsite located within walking distance of the beach and the centre of Blankenberge town. An ideal base for visiting Bruges, Ostend, Knokke, Damme, Ghent and Sluis (NL). CampingCard ACSI users pay cash.

E40 direction Oostende, exit Brugge/Zeebrugge drive towards Blankenberge. In Blankenberge turn right at the 2nd traffic lights. The campsite is signposted.

CC € 21 22/3-7/5 12/5-16/5 20/5-5/7 22/8-29/9

N 51°18'42'' E 03°09'12''

Bocholt, B-3950 / Limburg

378

Camping Goolderheide****
Bosstraat 1
+32 89 46 96 40
29/3 - 30/9
info@goolderheide.be

45ha 190T(100-150m²) 6-16A CEE

1 ACDEIKLMNORTU
2 ABFJSTVWXYZ
3 BCEHIJKMNOPRSUWZ
4 (C+H 18/5-31/8)IJM(Q)
(S+T+U+V+Y 1/7-31/8)
(Z)
5 ABDEGIJKLMNOPQRTUWXYZ
6 ABCDEFGHJ(N 3km)PSTV

Large family campsite with children's farm in a wooded park close to the Dutch-Belgian border and just three kilometres from the centre of Bocholt. There is a swimming pool complex with water slide. The fishing lake is beautifully integrated into the surroundings and freely available for campers. There is also a restaurant.

Route Weert-Bocholt. In Kaulille drive towards Bocholt. Half way between Kaulille and Bocholt (3 km) the campsite is clearly signposted.

CC € 21 *29/3-8/7 26/8-30/9*

N 51°10'24'' E 05°32'21''

Bohan, B-5550 / Namur

379

La Douane**
26 rue de France
+32 61 50 04 08
15/3 - 13/10
info@campingladouane.be

1,5ha 75T 16A CEE

1 ACDIKLMNOQRS
2 DSUWXY
3 AHISWX
4 (T 1/7-31/8)(X)
(Z 1/7-31/8)
5 ABGJNPUWYZ
6 AEFGJ(N 0,2km)PUV

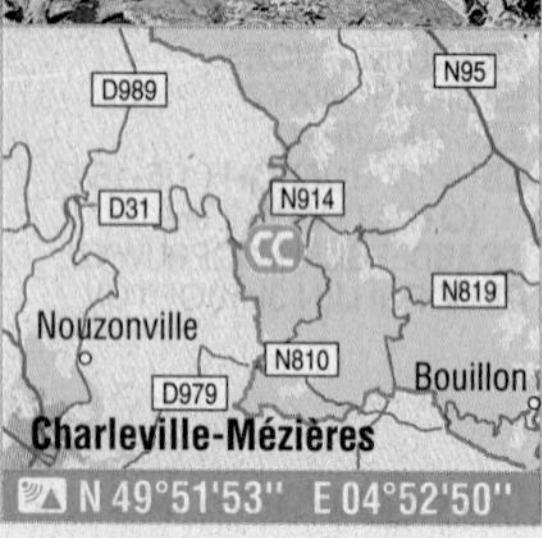

Cosy family campsite directly by the Semois. Authentic camping in the middle of nature. Campfire and barbecue allowed. You can swim and fish in the river. Quietly situated, within walking distance of the centre of Bohan. During the low season, the snack bar is only open on Friday and Saturday evening.

Via the N95 (Dinant-Bouillon) to Vresse-sur-Semois. Follow the signs to the town as well as the campsite signs. When in doubt, follow the signs to Monthermé (France).

CC € 23 *15/3-26/4 21/5-4/7 26/8-12/10*

N 49°51'53'' E 04°52'50''

Bohan-sur-Semois, B-5550 / Namur

380

Camping Confort****
rue Mont-les-Champs 214
+32 61 50 02 01
29/3 - 4/11
info@camping-confort.be

6ha 95T(100-130m²) 10A

1 ACDEIKLMNOQRS
2 DSUWX
3 CHIKLSUWX
4 (C 15/5-15/9)(Q+V 1/7-31/8)
(Y 10/6-3/9)(Z 1/7-31/8)
5 ABDFGIJKLMNPUWX
6 DEFGK(N 1km)OPTV

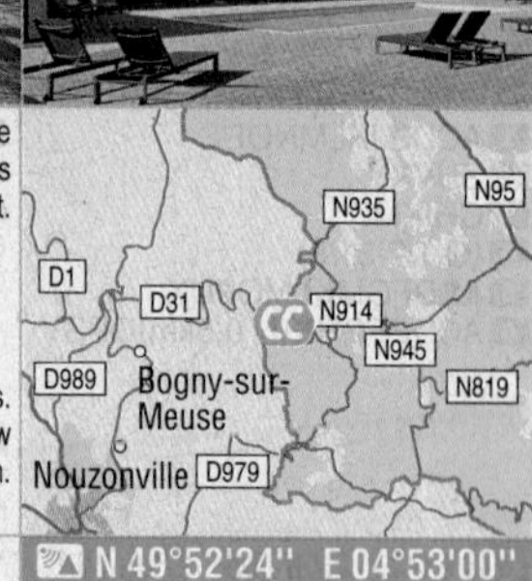

Holiday park with touring pitches on the banks of the Semois. Village centre walkable. Bar-restaurant 'Adagio' is closed on Tues. and/or Wed. apart from in July and August.

On the N95 (Dinant-Bouillon) direction Vresse-sur-Semois. Follow the town name and campsite signs. At the church follow the water. After the half bridge, continue for about 1.5 km. The campsite is on the left.

CC € 27 *14/4-28/4 12/5-16/5 20/5-30/6 1/9-3/11*

N 49°52'24'' E 04°53'00''

Bree, B-3960 / Limburg

381

Recreatieoord Kempenheuvel***
Heuvelstraat 8
+32 89 46 21 35
18/3 - 3/11
info@campingkempenheuvel.be

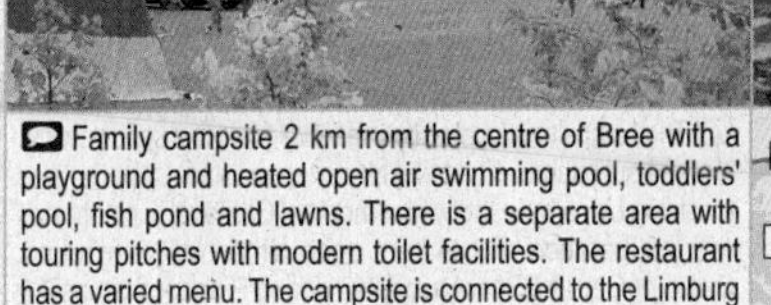

7,5ha 80**T**(80-140m²) 6A CEE

1 ACD**I**JKLMNOQ**R**TU
2 JSTVWXYZ
3 BCHIKMNPSUW
4 (C+H 15/5-15/9) (T+U+Y+Z 🔑)
5 **AB**DFGIJKLMNOPUWXYZ
6 ABCEFGH**K**(N 1km) OPTUVX

Family campsite 2 km from the centre of Bree with a playground and heated open air swimming pool, toddlers' pool, fish pond and lawns. There is a separate area with touring pitches with modern toilet facilities. The restaurant has a varied menu. The campsite is connected to the Limburg cycle route network.

Route Eindhoven-Hasselt. In Hechtel drive via Peer to Bree. The campsite is located 1 km before Bree at the left of the road and is signposted.

CC € 21 *18/3-4/7 21/8-3/11*

Bure/Tellin, B-6927 / Luxembourg

382

Camping Sandaya Parc la Clusure****
chemin de la Clusure 30
+32 84 36 00 50
27/3 - 28/9
parclaclusure@sandaya.be

ACSI AWARDS WINNER

15ha 235**T**(100m²) 16A CEE

1 ACD**H**KLMNOQRS
2 BCISUXYZ
3 ACHIKLNPSU**W**X
4 (A 🔑)(C 15/4-15/9)(E 🔑)IJK (Q+S+T+U+V+Y+Z 🔑)
5 **AB**CDEFGIJKLMNOPUWYZ
6 AFGH**K**LM(N 5km) O**P**RSTUVW

A charming campsite under Dutch management in the heart of the Ardennes, in a sheltered valley and on the banks of a river well stocked with fish. The lovely countryside offers unique walking opportunities. Clean toilet facilities and quality amenities guarantee a comfortable stay.

From Brussels A4/E411, exit 23a via Bure/Tellin or from Liége N63 Marche, Rochefort direction St. Hubert. From Luxembourg A4/E411, exit 24 past Bure/Tellin.

Rochefort N836 N4 N849 N889 N86 N835 Tellin E411 A4 N803 N89 N40 N848 Transinne N808

CC € 21 *27/3-5/7 31/8-28/9*

N 50°05'46'' E 05°17'09''

Burg-Reuland, B-4790 / Liège

383

Camping Hohenbusch*****
Hohenbusch, Grüfflingen 31
+32 80 22 75 23
29/3 - 3/11
info@hohenbusch.be

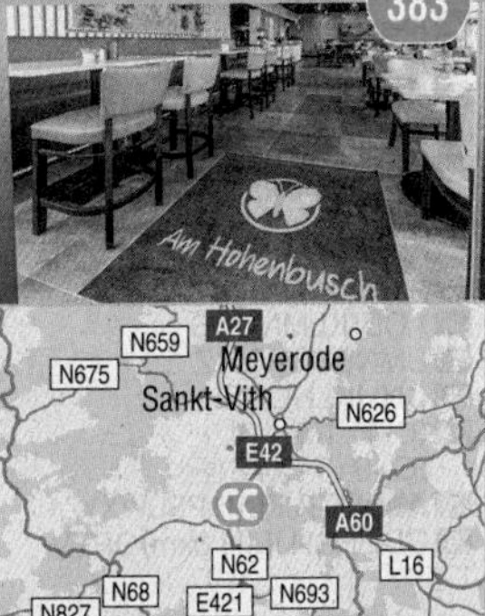

5ha 74**T**(100-175m²) 10-16A CEE

1 ACD**I**JKLMNQRTU
2 IJMNSWXY
3 CDEHILPS
4 (C+H 29/5-31/8) (Q+T+U+Y 🔑)
5 **AB**CDFGJLN**PQRT**UWXYZ
6 ACEFGKL(N 5km)PTU

Well-kept family campsite with excellent restaurant, clean toilets, wifi and electric charging stations. Near E42, Luxembourg and Germany. 6 km from Vennbahn cycle route. Heated swimming pool in the season with patio and sun loungers. Electricity, water supply and drainage at all pitches. Low season: cosy hospitality open Wed. to Sun.

E42/A27 exit 15 Sankt Vith. On road N62 Sankt Vith direction Luxembourg. Campsite after 3 km at the right. Use GPS coordinates.

CC € 25 *29/3-8/5 12/5-17/5 20/5-29/5 2/6-5/7 1/9-3/11*

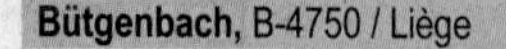

Bütgenbach, B-4750 / Liège

384

Camping Worriken*
Worriken 9
+32 80 44 69 61
1/1 - 31/12
info@worriken.be

ACSI AWARDS WINNER

16ha 45**T**(80-100m²) 10A CEE

1 ABCD**I**JKLMNQ**R**TUXY
2 AELMNOQSUWXY
3 ACHIKLN**O**PS**W**Z
4 (F 2/1-26/11,23/12-31/12) **N**(Q+T)
(U 2/1-20/11,26/12-31/12)
(W 1/1-20/11,16/12-24/12)
(X+Y 2/1-20/11,26/12-31/12)
(Z 2/1-20/11,23/12-31/12)
5 **AB**DGIJKMNPUXYZ
6 ABDEFGHJ(N 0,5km)P

The campsite is located by a reservoir next to a sports centre. Marked out pitches. The toilet blocks are heated. Opportunities for skiing close by in the winter months. Carnaval is celebrated with exuberance. Restaurant open almost all year round. CampingCard ACSI not accepted during Francorchamps F1.

E40/A3 exit 38 Eupen, direction Malmedy, follow the signs Worriken.

CC € 19 *1/1-30/6 1/9-31/12*

N 50°25'29'' E 06°13'19''

De Haan, B-8421 / West-Vlaanderen

385

Camping Ter Duinen
Wenduinesteenweg 143
+32 50 41 35 93
15/3 - 1/10
info@campingterduinen.be

12,5ha 214**T**(90-100m²) 16A CEE

1 ADE**I**JKLMNQRS
2 AGJSXY
3 A**G**HIKUY
4 (Q+R+T+V+Y+Z)
5 **AB**CDEFGHI**JKL**MNO**P**UZ
6 ACDEFGHJ**K**L(N 0,3km) OPSV

Campsite situated in the wooded dunes of De Haan, Belle Epoque town on the coast. Nice, well-maintained pitches. Lovely new restaurant. New shop with food vending machines.

E40 towards Ostend exit Jabbeke, towards De Haan, follow signs 'Ter Duinen'.

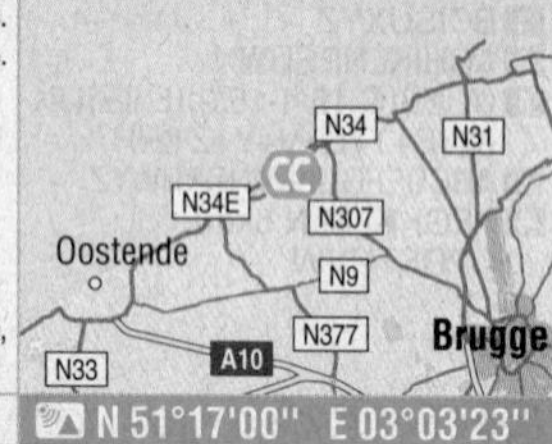

CC € 21 *15/3-7/7 24/8-22/9*

N 51°17'00'' E 03°03'23''

Dochamps, B-6960 / Luxembourg

386

ArdenParks Petite Suisse****
Al Bounire 27
+32 84 44 40 30
28/3 - 4/11
info@petitesuisse.be

7ha 145**T**(80-125m²) 10A CEE

1 ACD**I**KLMNO**R**S
2 BMNSUVWXYZ
3 CHIJKLNOPSU
4 (C+H 1/5-1/9) (Q+S+T+X+Z)
5 **AB**DEFGIJKLMNPRUWXYZ
6 CDEFGHJL(N 8km)OPTV

Terraced campsite in a wooded area with swimming pool and a varied recreational programme. Beautiful views of the surroundings, numerous hiking possibilities and mountain bike trails.

From Baraque Fraiture, exit 50 on the E25, via N89 direction La Roche. Right at Samree direction Dochamps via D841. Campsite at entrance to Dochamps. Signposted.

CC € 21 *28/3-7/5 13/5-16/5 21/5-30/6 1/9-4/11*

N 50°13'52'' E 05°37'54''

Grand-Halleux, B-6698 / Luxembourg

387

Camping Les Neufs Prés***
31 av. de la Resistance
+32 80 21 68 82
3/4 - 29/9
camping.les9pres@gmail.com

5ha 140T(80-100m²) 10A CEE

1 ACD**I**KLMNQRS
2 CJSXYZ
3 ACHIK**O**P**R**SU**W**
4 (**C**+Z 1/7-31/8)
5 **AB**DGIJKLMNO**P**U
6 ADEFGHJ(N 0,5km)PTV

Easily accessible, spacious campsite for all ages by River Salme. Walking routes in the stunning region. Large playground for children. Swimming pool in July and August. Bar.

The campsite is located on the N68 Vielsalm-Trois Ponts, 1 km from the centre.

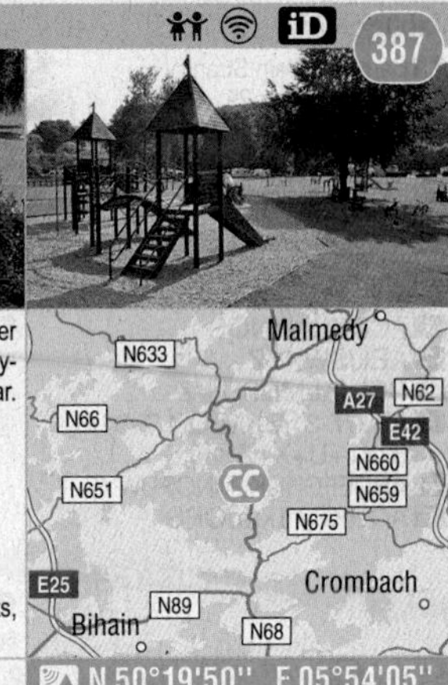

CC € 17 *1/5-7/7 24/8-28/9*

N 50°19'50'' E 05°54'05''

Houthalen, B-3530 / Limburg

388

Camping De Binnenvaart****
Binnenvaartstraat 49
+32 11 52 67 20
1/1 - 31/12
debinnenvaart@limburgcampings.be

6ha 200T(100-140m²) 6-16A CEE

1 AD**I**KLMNOQRTU
2 ABFINSTWXYZ
3 C**G**HIKOPSU**W**Z
4 **K**(Q+T+U+V+Y+Z)
5 **AB**DEFGI**JK**L**M**NO**PQRS**UWXYZ
6 ACDEFGK(N 2,5km)PSTV

Reasonably large campsite. Very large pitches for touring campers in the middle of the grounds. There is a lake next to the campsite. The site borders a large recreation park with a restaurant and fishing pond. There is also a snack bar on the site itself.

Follow Eindhoven-Hasselt as far as Houthalen. Then turn left towards 'Park Midden-Limburg'. At the second roundabout, near the furniture store, turn left towards the campsite and follow the signs.

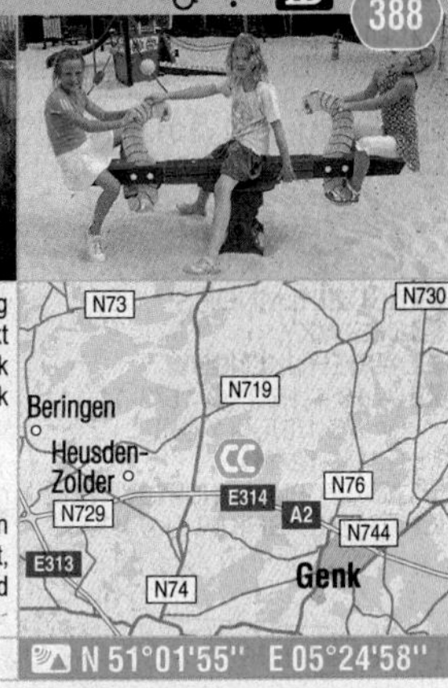

CC € 21 *1/1-14/5 21/5-1/7 28/8-31/12*

N 51°01'55'' E 05°24'58''

Houthalen/Helchteren, B-3530 / Limburg

389

Oostappen Vakantiepark Hengelhoef NV
Tulpenstraat 141
+32 89 38 25 00
22/3 - 3/11
info@vakantieparkhengelhoef.be

15ha 290T(80-120m²) 10A CEE

1 ABCDE**I**KLMNORS
2 ABEIJSTWXYZ
3 AD**G**HIKMOPRSU
4 (F+H 1/7-31/8)IJKLN
(Q+S+T+U 1/7-31/8)
(V 7/7-31/8)(Y+Z 1/7-31/8)
5 **AB**DFGIJKLMNOPUXYZ
6 ACEFGHJ(N 2km)STUV

Campsite in a recreation park that belongs to the 'Oostappen' group. It has excellent swimming facilities including a wave pool. The pool is only open on Friday, Saturday and Sunday outside the holiday period.

From Eindhoven in Houthalen keep following road as far as the E314. Cross bridge, take E314 and drive in the direction of Aachen (Aken). After approx. 5 km exit 30 'Park Midden Limburg'. Follow signs to Hengelhoef and campsite.

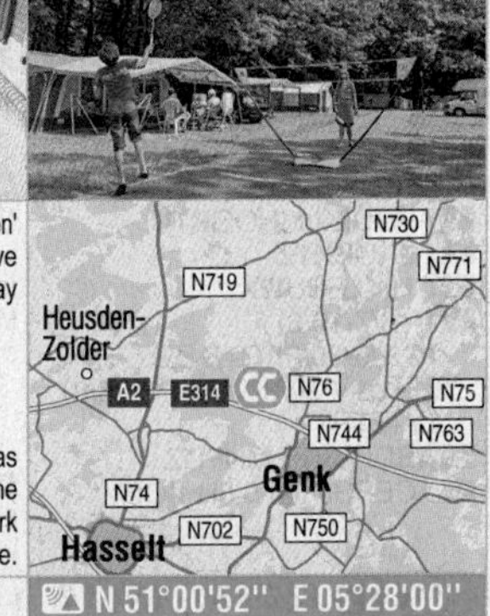

CC € 19 *22/3-29/3 2/4-26/4 13/5-17/5 24/5-8/7 25/8-18/10*

N 51°00'52'' E 05°28'00''

Jabbeke/Brugge, B-8490 / West-Vlaanderen

390

- Camping Klein Strand
- Varsenareweg 29
- +32 50 81 14 40
- 1/1 - 31/12
- info@kleinstrand.be

22ha 92T(100m²) 10A CEE

1. ACD**H**KLMNQS
2. AEIJSWXYZ
3. C**G**HIKLMNSU**WZ**
4. (G 1/7-31/8)**I**M(Q 1/7-31/8) (R+T+U+X+Z)
5. **AB**DEFGHIJKLMNO**P**UWYZ
6. ACGK(N 1km)OPS

Child-friendly campsite located by a lake with its own sandy beach. Fantastic leisure pool. Plenty of amenities and a good location between Bruges and the coast make this campsite unique.

Take exit 6 from the E40 Brussel-Oostende. Campsite signposted in the city centre of Jabbeke.

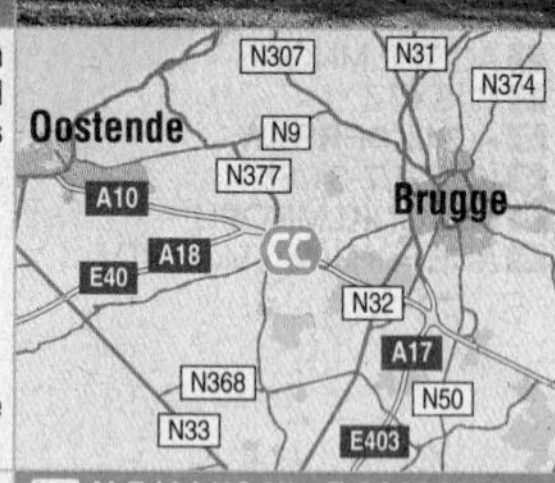

CC € 23 *1/1-29/3 15/4-8/5 22/5-6/7 29/8-31/12* ***7=6, 14=12, 21=18***

N 51°11'04'' E 03°06'18''

Kasterlee, B-2460 / Antwerpen

391

- Camping Houtum****
- Houtum 39
- +32 14 85 92 16
- 1/1 - 12/11, 13/12 - 31/12
- info@campinghoutum.be

9ha 39T(100-130m²) 10A CEE

1. ACDE**I**KLMNORS
2. CIJSWXY
3. AC**D**EHIJKLN**RUW**
4. (A 15/4-15/9)(Q 15/3-11/11) (V 1/5-1/9)(X+Y) (Z 1/4-12/11)
5. **AB**CDFGHI**JKL**MNO**PQR**UWXYZ
6. ABCDEFGHK(N 1km)PV

Campsite with various hospitality venues at the campsite or in the vicinity. In the area, you can find over 250km of hiking and cycling paths on junction route networks. Wonderful location for the touristic Kasterlee. Comfort pitches with supply and discharge (Euro4 supplement).

E34 exit 24 Kasterlee. Campsite signposted 500m past the village centre, near the windmill. Or E313, exit 23 Kasterlee/ Turnhout. Follow N19 (not N19-g). Turn right 1 km before village centre.

CC € 23 *1/1-8/5 20/5-16/6 25/6-1/7 26/8-12/11 13/12-31/12*

N 51°13'59'' E 04°58'40''

La Roche-en-Ardenne, B-6980 / Luxembourg

392

- Camping Club Benelux***
- 26 rue de Harzé
- +32 84 41 15 59
- 22/3 - 3/11
- stay@club-benelux.be

13ha 500T(100m²) 6-10A

1. ABCD**I**KLMNOQ**R**TU
2. DJNOSXYZ
3. CHIKLPSU**W**X
4. (A 6/7-16/8) (C 1/5-30/9)(Q+S) (T+U+V 30/3-14/4,1/7-25/8) (Y+Z)
5. **AB**DFGIJKLMNPUZ
6. ACEFGJL(N 0,5km)O**P**V

Family campsite located on the banks of the Ourthe, at walking distance from the lovely town of La Roche. Own restaurant with charming patio. Heated outdoor swimming pool. Many options for walking. The campsite's tourist train takes children to the entertainment, tours are also organised for adults.

Exit Baraque De Fraiture. From centre direction Marche. Follow camping signs at bridge over River Ourthe. Campsite located 500m from the centre.

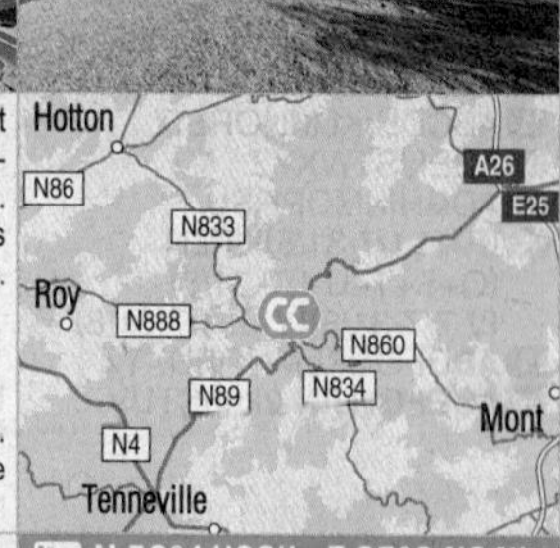

CC € 19 *22/3-28/3 15/4-7/5 13/5-16/5 21/5-5/7 22/8-3/11*

N 50°11'28'' E 05°34'24''

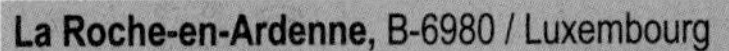

La Roche-en-Ardenne, B-6980 / Luxembourg

393

- Camping De l'Ourthe**
- 8 rue des Echavées
- +32 84 41 14 59
- 15/3 - 13/10
- info@campingdelourthe.be

4ha 150T(50-100m²) 10A

1. ABCD**I**KLMNQ**R**TU
2. BDOSUVXYZ
3. CHIKLSV**WX**
4. (Q+S)(T 15/7-15/8)(Z)
5. **AB**CDFGIJMOPUW
6. CDEFG**K**L(N 1,5km)**P**

Completely renovated campsite on the banks of the Ourthe, close to the touristic La Roche. Spacious pitches in natural surroundings. There are also pitches on the banks of the river. The sanitary facilities have been completely renovated.

From the town centre, follow signs for Marche, cross Ourthe bridge and turn right, and follow campsite signs (1.5 km from town centre).

N807, Malempré, N86, E25, N833, N888, Bande, N860, E46, N89, N4, N834, Mabompré, N889

CC € 19 *15/3-7/5 13/5-16/5 21/5-30/6 2/9-13/10*

N 50°11'19'' E 05°34'14''

Lille/Gierle, B-2275 / Antwerpen

394

- Camping De Lilse Bergen****
- Strandweg 6
- +32 14 55 79 01
- 1/1 - 31/12
- info@lilsebergen.be

60ha 214T(100m²) 10A CEE

1. ACD**I**KLMNOPRS
2. ABFISTWYZ
3. AC**F**HIKLMNOP**R**SZ
4. (G)JM(Q+R 1/4-15/9) (T+U+X+Z 1/6-15/9)
5. **AB**DEFGIJKLMNO**PQ**RUWXZ
6. CDEFGHKM(N 5km)OPTU

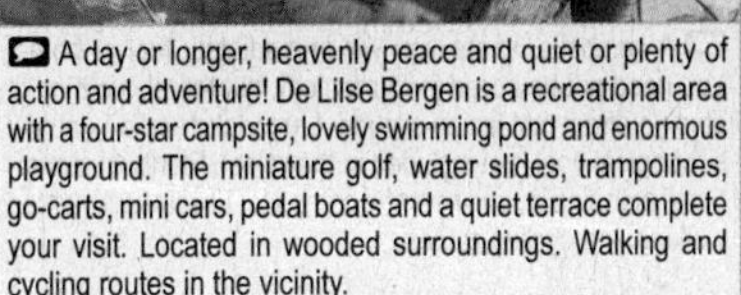

A day or longer, heavenly peace and quiet or plenty of action and adventure! De Lilse Bergen is a recreational area with a four-star campsite, lovely swimming pond and enormous playground. The miniature golf, water slides, trampolines, go-carts, mini cars, pedal boats and a quiet terrace complete your visit. Located in wooded surroundings. Walking and cycling routes in the vicinity.

Turn right before the motorway on to the road Beerse-Gierle. Follow signs. The campsite entrance is close to exit 22 of the E34.

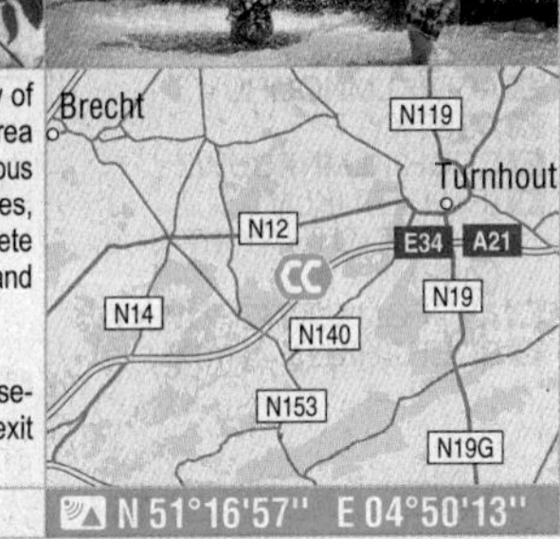

CC € 25 *15/4-7/5 22/5-30/6 1/9-15/11*

N 51°16'57'' E 04°50'13''

Lommel, B-3920 / Limburg

395

- Oostappen Park Blauwe Meer*****
- Kattenbos 169
- +32 11 54 45 23
- 22/3 - 3/11
- receptie@vakantieparkblauwemeer.be

27ha 480T(80-100m²) 10A CEE

1. ACD**I**KLMNOQR
2. ABEJSTWXYZ
3. ACD**G**IKLMPRSUW
4. (F+G 10/4-10/5,1/7-31/8) JKLMN(Q+S+T+U+Y+Z)
5. **AB**DFGIJKLMNOPUWYZ
6. ACFGHJM(N 5km)PSTUV

A large fishing pond and a covered beach and swimming pool with slide. Fun for all ages!

On the road from Leopoldsburg to Lommel, route 746, close to the German cemetery located to the right of the road.

N69, Lommel, Neerpelt, N71, Mol, N748, N746, N74, N18, Peer, N73, N141

CC € 17 *22/3-29/3 2/4-26/4 13/5-17/5 24/5-8/7 25/8-18/10*

N 51°11'39'' E 05°18'13''

Maasmechelen, B-3630 / Limburg

396

Recreatieoord Kikmolen****
Kikmolenstraat 3
+32 89 77 09 00
1/4 - 31/10
info@kikmolen.be

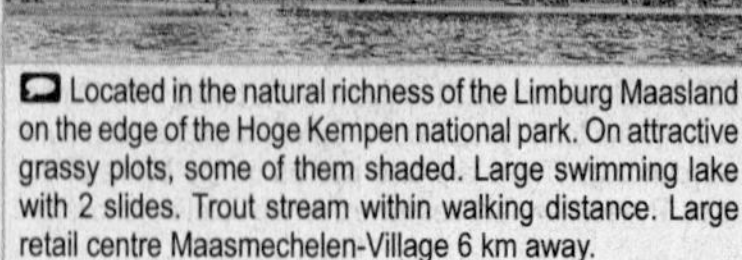

20ha 106T(80-100m²) 6-10A CEE

1 ABCDE**H**JKLMNOQ**R**TU
2 BDFIOSUWXYZ
3 CDEHIKLMNPU**W**Z
4 J(Q+S+T+U 1/5-15/9)
(Y+Z 1/4-30/9)
5 **AB**CDGHI**J**K**L**MN**P**QRSUWXYZ
6 ABCDEFGH**K**(N 1,5km)
TUVX

Located in the natural richness of the Limburg Maasland on the edge of the Hoge Kempen national park. On attractive grassy plots, some of them shaded. Large swimming lake with 2 slides. Trout stream within walking distance. Large retail centre Maasmechelen-Village 6 km away.

Leave the A2/E314 at exit 33 in the direction of Lanaken. At the roundabout go straight ahead and after 1 km turn right towards Zutendaal. Then follow the signs to the campsite.

N76 N75 A2 N744 N763 Geleen Genk E314 CC N750 Lanaken N2

CC € 23 *1/4-9/5 20/5-1/7 1/9-31/10*

N 50°57'14'' E 05°39'45''

Mol, B-2400 / Antwerpen

397

EuroParcs Zilverstrand
Kiezelweg 17
+31 8 80 70 80 90
1/1 - 31/12
kcc@europarcs.nl

26ha 66T(120m²) 10A CEE

1 ACD**I**KLMNOQRUV
2 AESTXY
3 CD**G**HIKLMN**R**SUWZ
4 (F+H key)IJKLN
(Q+R+T+U key)(Y 1/7-31/8)
(Z key)
5 **AB**DFGIJKLMNOPUWXY
6 BCEFGHKL(N 4km)X

A campsite where you will immediately feel at home! You need not be bored for a moment, but there's nothing to stop you from just lazing around. Large lake and a beautiful subtropical pool (not included in the price). Plenty of recreational activities in, and near the campsite. Lovely well marked walking and cycling routes.

Motorway Mol-Lommel, immediately left after second canal. Follow the signs 'Molse meren'. The campsite is located on the N712 between Mol and Lommel.

E34 Dessel Lommel N118 N18 CC N71 Mol N746 Geel N110 N126 N73

CC € 25 *1/1-29/3 2/4-26/4 13/5-17/5 20/5-5/7 2/9-31/12*

N 51°12'34'' E 05°10'20''

Mol, B-2400 / Antwerpen

398

Provinciaal Recreatiedomein Zilvermeer****
Postelsesteenweg 71
+32 14 82 95 00
1/1 - 11/11, 13/12 - 31/12
camping@zilvermeer.be

160ha 184T(98-184m²) 16A CEE

1 ACD**I**KLMNOPQRS
2 ABFJTVWYZ
3 ABC**G**HIJKLMOP**R**SUVWZ
4 JM
(Q+S 1/4-11/11,13/12-31/12)
(T 1/4-30/9)(X+Y+Z key)
5 **AB**DEFGHIJKLMNOPQUWZ
6 ACDEFGHK(N 5km)OPTU

A well-maintained campsite located on a large lake with a water playground and climbing course. Three restaurants with differing opening dates. Children's playground near to touristic sights. Water park and water sports. Themed walks.

E34 Antwerpen-Eindhoven, . exit 26 Retie/Arendonk and then follow the signs 'Molse Meren' or E313 Hasselt/ Antwerpen exit 23 Geel-West then via N19, R14, N71, N712, N136 to the campsite.

E34 A21 N123 N18 Lommel N118 CC N71 Mol Geel N746 N110 N126 Hechtel

CC € 21 *1/4-5/5 13/5-16/5 21/5-18/6 24/6-27/6 30/8-29/9*

N 51°13'09'' E 05°10'57''

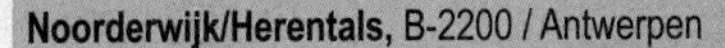

Noorderwijk/Herentals, B-2200 / Antwerpen

399

- Camping Domein De Schuur
- Pastoorsbos 35
- +32 14 26 16 52
- 29/3 - 4/11
- info@deschuur.be

7ha 26T(80-120m²) 10-16A

- **1** ACDIKLMNOP**R**S
- **2** IJSXYZ
- **3** ACE**G**HIKOPS**W**
- **4** (T 1/5-1/10)(U+X+Z)
- **5** **AB**DGHIJKLMNOPQ**T**UWYZ
- **6** ABCFGHK(N 0,1km)PSTUV

Small family campsite in the heart of the Antwerp Campine. In the area you can find over 250 km of hiking and cycling routes. Cycle junction 65 at your door. You can also enjoy a lovely regional beer/wine with a tasty snack at the outdoor cafe amid the greenery and the animals.

E313 exit 22 Olen, turn right at the traffic lights. At the second traffic lights, turn left towards Noorderwijk. Straight ahead for 3 km until you see the sign for 'Domein de Schuur' on your right.

CC € 23 *2/4-30/4 6/5-8/5 21/5-8/7 25/8-30/9*

N 51°07'56'' E 04°49'52''

Opglabbeek/Oudsbergen, B-3660 / Limburg

400

- Recreatieoord Wilhelm Tell*****
- Hoeververweg 87
- +32 89 81 00 10
- 1/1 - 31/12
- wilhelmtell@limburgcampings.be

6ha 75T(80-100m²) 16-20A CEE

- **1** ABD**I**KLMNOQRS
- **2** ISWXY
- **3** BCD**G**HIKMNSU
- **4** (C 1/7-31/8)(F) (H 1/7-31/8)IJKM (Q+R+T+U+V+Y+Z)
- **5** **AB**DEFGI**JKL**MN**PQRS**UWXYZ
- **6** BCDEFGKL(N 2km)**P**STUV

ACSI AWARDS WINNER

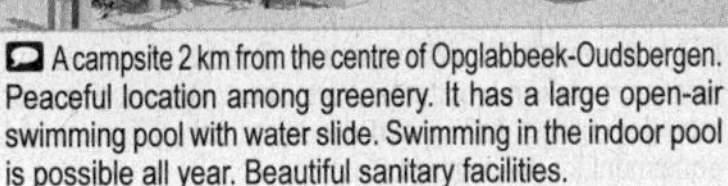

A campsite 2 km from the centre of Opglabbeek-Oudsbergen. Peaceful location among greenery. It has a large open-air swimming pool with water slide. Swimming in the indoor pool is possible all year. Beautiful sanitary facilities.

E314 Brussels-Aachen; exit 32. Continue on A2 in direction As. Just before As centre take exit towards Oudsbergen. Campsite signposted after about 5 km. Located about 1 km before centre Opglabbeek on right of road.

CC € 25 *1/1-1/7 28/8-31/12*

N 51°01'42'' E 05°35'52''

Opoeteren, B-3680 / Limburg

401

- Camping Zavelbos****
- Kattebeekstraat 1
- +32 89 75 81 46
- 1/1 - 31/12
- zavelbos@limburgcampings.be

6ha 50T(100-120m²) 16-20A CEE

- **1** ABD**I**KLMNORS
- **2** BJSUWXYZ
- **3** BC**G**HIKLMNSUW
- **4** **KP**(Q+T+U+Y+Z)
- **5** **AB**DEFGI**JKL**MN**PQRS**UWXY
- **6** ACDEFGKL(N 4km)**P**SV

Campsite with a fish pond in wooded surroundings. Excellent toilet facilities. Located on marked out footpaths, cycle paths and bridleways just 6 km from the 6000 hectare Hoge Kempen National Park.

A2 Eindhoven-Maastricht, exit Maaseik. Then via Neeroeteren to Opoeteren. The campsite is located on the right of the Opoeteren-Opglabbeek road.

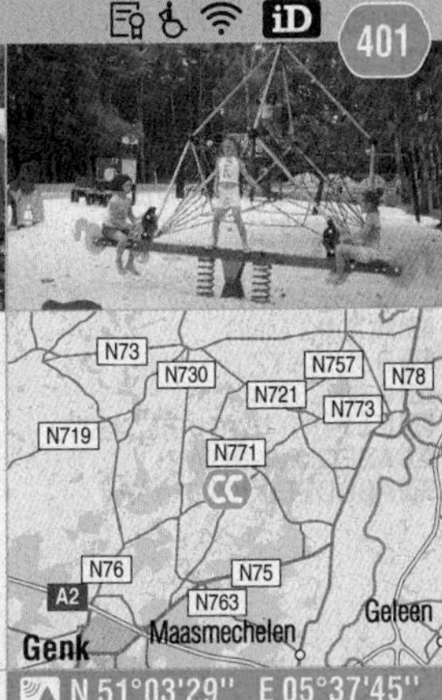

CC € 25 *1/1-1/7 28/8-31/12*

N 51°03'29'' E 05°37'45''

Overijse, B-3090 / Vlaams Brabant

402

Camping Druivenland***
Nijvelsebaan 80
+32 26 87 93 68
1/4 - 30/9
info@campingdruivenland.be

5ha 34T(150-200m²) 16A CEE

1 ABD**I**KLMNO**R**UV
2 IJNSTWXY
3 HIKS
4 (Q)
5 **AB**DEGIJKLMNO**P**UWXYZ
6 BCEFG**K**(N 2,4km)T

Overijse, home of the Belgian table grape, renowned for its grape festivals. From here you can visit the art cities of Brussels and Leuven. Waterloo, Walibi and the Afrikamuseum in Tervuren are nearby. The boat lifts are a Unesco heritage site and definitely worth a day's visit.

On the A4/E411, take exit 3 direction Overijse, then first right on the N218 (Nijvelsebaan) as far as the campsite.

€ 23 *1/4-30/6 1/9-30/9*

N 50°45'43'' E 04°32'50''

Poupehan, B-6830 / Luxembourg

403

Camping Ile de Faigneul***
54 rue de la Chérizelle
+32 4 78 96 12 40
1/4 - 30/9
info@iledefaigneul.com

3ha 130T(100m²) 6A CEE

1 ACD**I**KLNRS
2 BDSUWXYZ
3 CHIKLPSU**W**X
4 (Q+R+T+U+Z)
5 **AB**DFGIJKLMNPRUWZ
6 EFGHK(N 5km)PV

In the middle of unspoilt nature. Dozens of marked out walking routes in wooded surroundings. Opportunities for mountain biking, fishing and canoeing. Lovely playground equipment for the children.

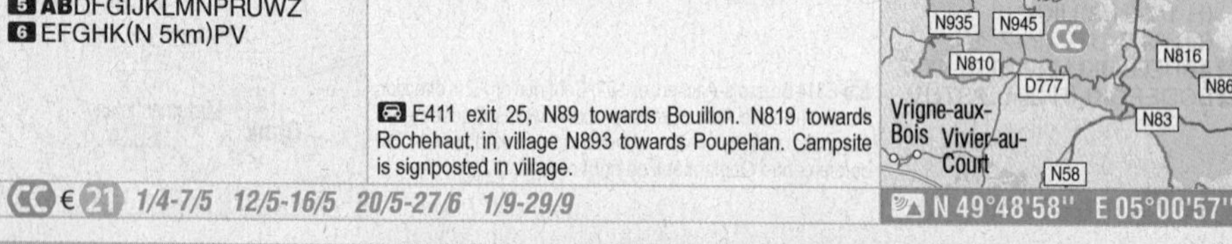

E411 exit 25, N89 towards Bouillon. N819 towards Rochehaut, in village N893 towards Poupehan. Campsite is signposted in village.

€ 21 *1/4-7/5 12/5-16/5 20/5-27/6 1/9-29/9*

N 49°48'58'' E 05°00'57''

Poupehan, B-6830 / Luxembourg

404

Camping Le Prahay***
rue de la Chérizelle 48
+32 4 76 83 84 00
29/3 - 3/11
info@camping-leprahay.com

5ha 168T(100-130m²) 6-16A

1 ACD**I**KLMNR
2 BDUWXYZ
3 CHIKLS**WX**
4 (Q)(T 1/7-31/8)(Z)
5 **AB**FGIJMN**P**UWZ
6 ABCDEFGJ(N 5km)PV

Camping on the banks of River Semois, amid the countryside of the Belgian Ardennes. Great walks from the campsite, as well as mountain bike trails for active cyclists. Enjoy the peace and quiet and all the wonderful things this region has to offer. Sitting at the friendly terrace by the water is highly enjoyable.

E411 exit 25, N89 in direction Bertrix/Bouillon. After Plainevaux direction Rochehaut via N019. Before Rochehaut, N093 dir. Poupehan, then follow campsite signs.

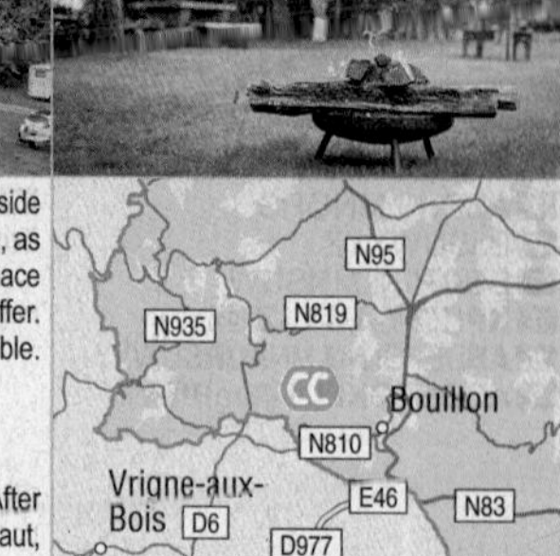

€ 21 *29/3-8/5 21/5-30/6 1/9-2/11* ***7=6, 14=11***

N 49°48'49'' E 05°00'53''

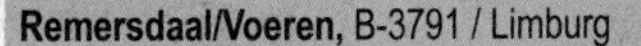

Remersdaal/Voeren, B-3791 / Limburg

405

Camping Natuurlijk Limburg***
Roodbos 3
+32 4 72 12 16 87
1/1 - 31/12
campingnatuurlijklimburg@gmail.com

6ha 70T(80-100m²) 6A CEE

1 ADIKLMNOPQRTU
2 JLSUVXYZ
3 CIKLPSU
4 (C 1/6-1/10)(Q 1/3-1/12)
(U+Y+Z 1/2-30/12)
5 **AB**DGI**J**K**L**MNOPQUWZ
6 ABCDEFGJL(N 2km)PV

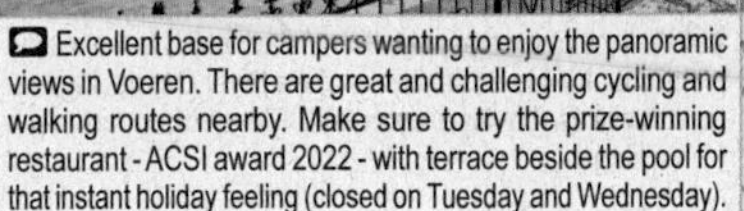

Excellent base for campers wanting to enjoy the panoramic views in Voeren. There are great and challenging cycling and walking routes nearby. Make sure to try the prize-winning restaurant - ACSI award 2022 - with terrace beside the pool for that instant holiday feeling (closed on Tuesday and Wednesday).

Leave the A2/E25 in Maastricht direction Aachen/Vaals. Right just before Margraten direction De Planck. Cross Belgian border (± 5 km) towards Aubel.

CC € 21 *1/1-8/5 21/5-28/6 1/9-31/12*

N 50°43'46'' E 05°51'53''

Retie, B-2470 / Antwerpen

406

Camping Berkenstrand****
Brand 78
+32 14 37 90 41
1/4 - 13/10
info@berkenstrand.be

10ha 33T(120-150m²) 10A CEE

1 ADIKLMNPQRS
2 ACFISTWXYZ
3 CHIJKLPSU**WZ**
4 (Q 1/7-31/8)
(R+T+U+V+X+Z)
5 **AB**DEFGI**JKL**MNO**P**UXYZ
6 ABCDEFGHJ**K**L(N 3,5km)
OPTUV

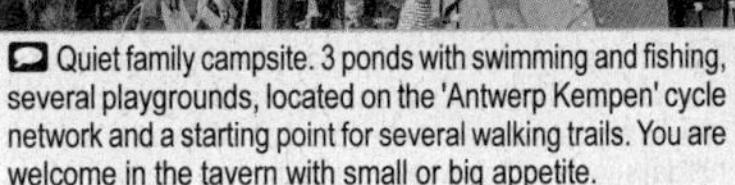

Quiet family campsite. 3 ponds with swimming and fishing, several playgrounds, located on the 'Antwerp Kempen' cycle network and a starting point for several walking trails. You are welcome in the tavern with small or big appetite.

E34 exit 26 direction Retie, left at traffic lights then 1st right towards Postel. Campsite signposted (SatNav: Postelsebaan 3).

CC € 21 *1/4-30/6 18/8-13/10*

N 51°16'32'' E 05°07'44''

Stavelot, B-4970 / Liège

407

Camping Domaine l'Eau Rouge
Cheneux 25
+32 80 86 30 75
29/3 - 30/10
info@eaurouge.nl

4ha 151T(100-120m²) 6-10A

1 ADIKLMN**R**TU
2 BDIJSUXYZ
3 BCIKLPSU**WX**
4 (C 1/5-30/9)
(Q 1/4-14/4,1/7-31/8)
(U 29/5-10/6,7/7-26/8)(X)
(Z 29/5-10/6,7/7-26/8)
5 **AB**CDEFGHIJKLMN**P**RUWXYZ
6 ACEFGHJL(N 1,5km)PTUV

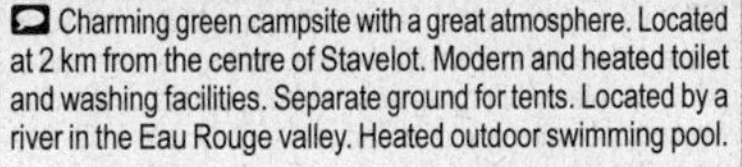

Charming green campsite with a great atmosphere. Located at 2 km from the centre of Stavelot. Modern and heated toilet and washing facilities. Separate ground for tents. Located by a river in the Eau Rouge valley. Heated outdoor swimming pool.

From the E42 take exit 11, roundabout dir. Stavelot (switch off SatNav), continue for ± 5 km as far as T-junction on right. Then 1st road on right, small road downhill.

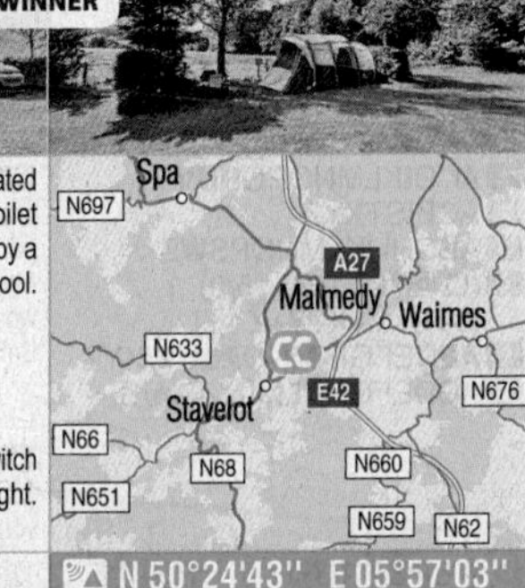

CC € 23 *27/5-28/6 26/8-30/9 7=6*

N 50°24'43'' E 05°57'03''

Tenneville, B-6970 / Luxembourg

408

Camping Pont de Berguème***
Berguème 9
+32 84 45 54 43
1/1 - 31/12
info@pontbergueme.be

3ha 100T(80-100m²) 6A CEE

1 ACD**I**KLMNOQRS
2 DSWXY
3 AHIKSU**WX**
4 (Z)
5 **AB**DGIJKLMNOPUZ
6 CDEFGJ(N 4km)**P**V

Well maintained peaceful campsite located in the middle of the countryside on the banks of the River Ourthe. Modern toilet facilities. Lovely playground. Plenty of opportunities for walking.

Via the N4, exit Berguème. Then follow the Berguème and campsite signs.

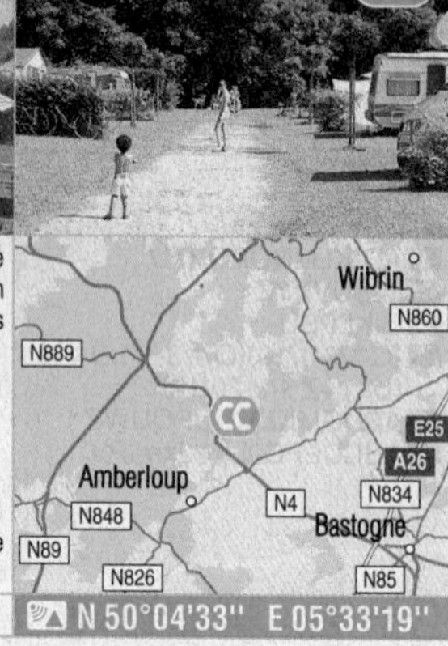

CC € 19 *1/1-8/5 20/5-5/7 22/8-31/12*

N 50°04'33" E 05°33'19"

Tintigny, B-6730 / Luxembourg

409

Camping de Chênefleur****
rue Norulle 16
+32 63 44 40 78
1/3 - 3/11
info@chenefleur.be

7,2ha 270T(100-125m²) 6A CEE

1 ACD**I**KLMNOQ**R**TU
2 DIJSWXYZ
3 CHIKLSU**WX**
4 (A 6/7-23/8)(C+H 20/5-6/9) KN(Q+R) (T+U+V+Y+Z 1/5-3/11)
5 **AB**DEFGIJKLMNOPUWXZ
6 DEFGJ**K**(N 2km)OPUV

This friendly campsite is situated by River Semois, which is filled with fish. There is a swimming pool and a dining cafe with snacks and take-away meals, open from May to the Autumn holidays (only during weekends in the low season). Many walking and cycling possibilities. Various cultural excursions are also possible.

From E411 exit 29 direction Etalle (N87). In Etalle go towards Florenville (N83). Follow camping signs in Tintigny village. Clearly signposted.

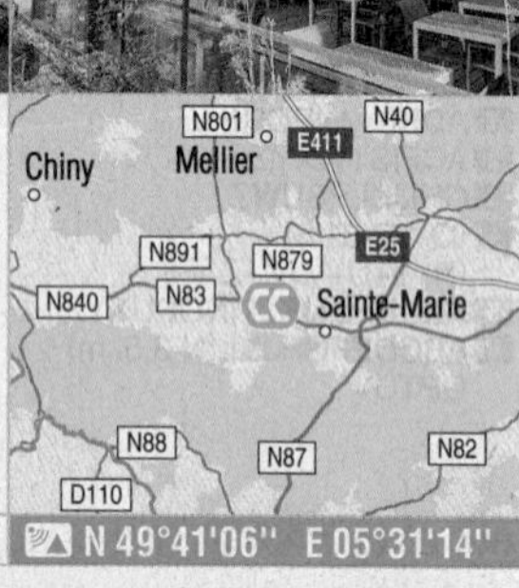

CC € 23 *1/3-14/7 31/8-3/11*

N 49°41'06" E 05°31'14"

Turnhout, B-2300 / Antwerpen

410

ArdenParks Baalse Hei****
Roodhuisstraat 10
+32 14 44 84 70
1/1 - 31/12
info@baalsehei.be

30ha 48T(100m²) 16A CEE

1 ACD**I**KLMNOPQ**R**UV
2 ACEISTXYZ
3 ABCHIJKLMNOPS**WZ**
4 (Q)(R 15/6-15/9) (T+U+V+X+Y+Z)
5 **AB**DEFGIKMNO**PQ**UWXYZ
6 ACDEFGHKLM(N 4km)S

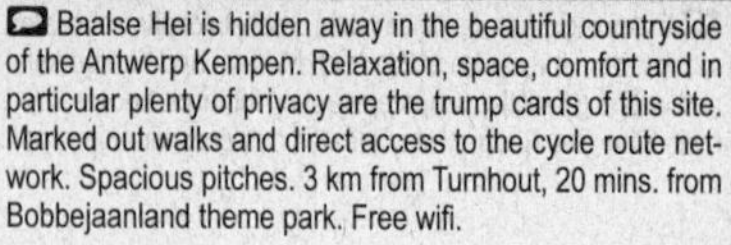

Baalse Hei is hidden away in the beautiful countryside of the Antwerp Kempen. Relaxation, space, comfort and in particular plenty of privacy are the trump cards of this site. Marked out walks and direct access to the cycle route network. Spacious pitches. 3 km from Turnhout, 20 mins. from Bobbejaanland theme park. Free wifi.

From the Netherlands: follow the Breda/Baarle-Nassau/ Turnhout road. Campsite signposted after 10 km. Don't follow your Satnav.

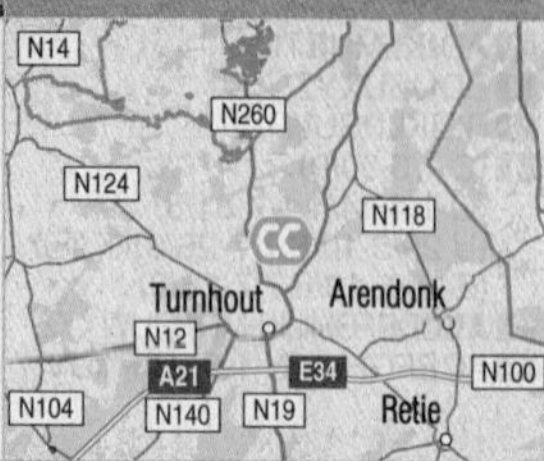

CC € 23 *1/3-31/3 15/4-5/5 27/5-30/6 1/9-31/10*

N 51°21'27" E 04°57'32"

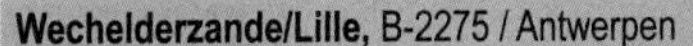

Wechelderzande/Lille, B-2275 / Antwerpen

411

Camping Siesta
Bersegembaan 36
+32 33 11 62 36
1/1 - 31/12
info@campingsiesta.be

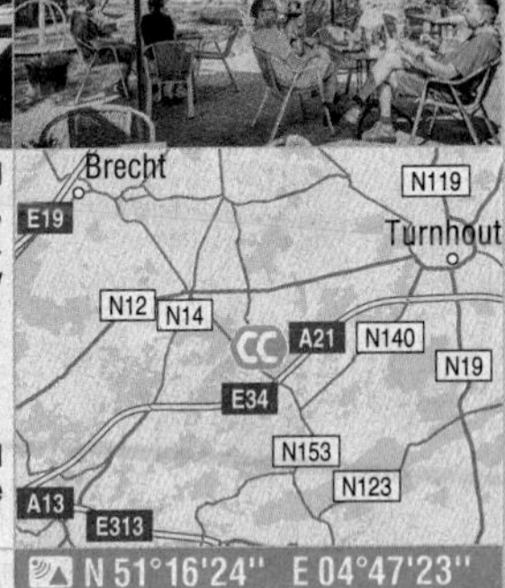

7ha 28T(80-120m²) 16A CEE

1 ACDHKLMNOQRUV
2 IJSWXYZ
3 AGIKLMNS
4 (G)(Q+X+Z 15/3-1/10)
5 **AB**DFGIJKLMOP**T**UWZ
6 CDEFHKM(N 1,5km)T

Camping Siesta is a charming campsite. The wooded surroundings of the Antwerp Campine invites you to go cycling, walking from the grounds or on a safari with a Siesta ranger. There are great touring pitches for an unforgettable holiday in wooded surroundings.

From the E34 motorway take exit 21 to Lille. At the end of the exit, follow the signs to Wechelderzande until you see the signs for Camping Siesta.

CC € 15 *1/3-31/3 15/4-30/4 13/5-16/6 1/9-31/12*

N 51°16'24'' E 04°47'23''

Westerlo/Heultje, B-2260 / Antwerpen

412

Camping Hof van Eeden***
Kempische Ardennen 8
+32 16 69 83 72
1/1 - 31/12
info@hofvaneeden.be

12ha 45T(100-150m²) 10-16A CEE

1 ACD**I**KLMNORS
2 ABEIJOSTVWXYZ
3 CHIKPSUWZ
4 (B+G 22/6-31/8) (T 15/3-31/10)(U 1/4-31/10) (X+Y 15/3-31/10)(Z)
5 **AB**CDGIJKLMNO**P**UXYZ
6 BCDEFGHK(N 2km)OPSTV

A quiet, hospitable campsite. Lovely walking and cycling around the Merode Castle and Merode woods. New toilet facilities and spacious comfort pitches, hardened motorhome pitches.

On E313 Herentals-oost, Olen, take exit 22, follow N152 until Zoerle-Parwijs, then towards Heultje. At the church there is a campsite sign to Hulshout-Heultje industrial area. Campsite sign along the industrial road.

CC € 23 *1/1-7/7 26/8-31/12*

N 51°05'17'' E 04°49'20''

Luxembourg

Capital: Luxembourg
Currency: euro
Time zone: UTC + 1, UTC +2 (March to October)
Language: Luxembourgish, French and German
International dialling number: +352
Alcohol limit: 0.5‰
Emergency number: police, fire brigade and ambulance: 112
Tap water: safe to drink

Luxembourg: a small country with a lot to offer

Luxembourg is one of the smallest countries in Europe. Its combination of beautiful nature and welcoming villages and towns make it a small but very varied country.

Walking

The best way to explore Luxembourg is on foot. The country's many forests and hilly areas are a feast for the eye. Discover them at your leisure on a walk. The most famous of Luxembourg's walking routes is the Mullerthal Trail. It is located in the east of the country, close to the German border, and is known tantalisingly as 'Little Switzerland'. Put on some good sturdy shoes and enjoy the spectacular rock formations, beautiful stream valleys and romantic fortresses you will come across as you walk along the trail.

A capital city with an international feel

Luxembourg is made up of a number of little villages and towns. The capital city of the same name is much bigger but still has less than 120,000 residents. A number of European organisations have offices there, which creates an international feel. The city is clean and its facilities are excellent.

A city walk is the perfect way to familiarise yourself with the city's many sights. Take a look in the Grand Ducal Palace, enjoy some downtime in the seventeenth-century cathedral or admire modern art in the Grand Duke Jean Museum of Modern Art. Last but not least, take a stroll around the Ville-Haute and Gare areas. Fashion lovers will enjoy the trendy little boutiques, luxury stores and chain stores there.

"Green and hilly, a lot to see and a big choice of camp sites and restaurants."
Mr. R. Wauters, Inspector 283

Luxembourg is a green and pleasant country

Luxembourg is known predominantly for its wealth of green space. The country's landscape consists largely of forests, hills and meadows and forms part of the Ardennes in the north. The three biggest rivers - the Moselle, the Our and the Sûre - flow peacefully through the country. Because mass tourism is rare in Luxembourg, you will find that you are able to enjoy its tranquillity and nature without being disturbed.

A camping holiday with castles

If you like castles, Luxembourg is definitely the destination for you. There are so many castles, fortresses and ruins that you will always find one near your camp site. A visit to Viandel Castle is a must during any camping holiday in Luxembourg. This imposing structure was built between the eleventh and fourteenth centuries and is great fun to visit with the children. If you can, see it at the end of July or the beginning of August when a big medieval-castle festival is organised. In the Eisch valley - an area in the south-west that is rich in forests and meadows - you will find no fewer than seven castles. Some are still intact, while others are just ruins.

En route

Filling up

Petrol (95 E10 and Super 98) is widely available (before buying E10, check your vehicle's filler neck, your car manual or contact your car dealer to see whether you can use it in your car; if not, use Super 98 instead). Diesel and LPG are widely available too. The European connection (acme) is used for LPG. Fuel is cheap in Luxembourg in comparison with other countries, because of which many drivers from other countries choose to fill up their vehicles here. So, service stations on the border and alongside major roads are often open 24 hours a day. Other service stations are often open from 08.00 to 20.00 hours.
Please note! You may not fill up or discharge fuel from an additional tank.

Winners in Luxembourg

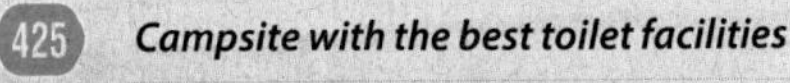

423	*Best campsite swimming pool*	Europacamping Nommerlayen
425	*Campsite with the best toilet facilities*	Camping du Barrage Rosport

Charging

Luxembourg still has just a limited network of public charging points so it is important to plan your trip carefully before you set off. Most charging points are located in the south of the country.

Traffic regulations

Dipped lights are mandatory when driving in the dark, in tunnels and if visibility is less than 100 metres.
Traffic from the right has priority at equal priority junctions. Trams have priority at all times. Traffic on roundabouts has priority if indicated by road signs. On mountain roads, ascending traffic has priority over descending traffic; if necessary, the smallest vehicle must reverse.
Drivers are only allowed to make calls hands-free. Children under the age of 18 and shorter than 1.50 metres must be strapped into a child seat. Winter tyres are mandatory in winter conditions.

Special regulations

In the event of a traffic jam, move as far to the right or left as possible, so that easy access (rettungsgasse) for emergency vehicles is created in the middle of the road.
It is compulsory to use your hazard lights when approaching a traffic jam.
If you are in a traffic jam in a tunnel, you must maintain a distance of 5 metres between yourself and the vehicle in front of you.
When parking, ensure you maintain a distance of at least 1 metre between you and other parked vehicles.

Mandatory equipment

You must have a warning triangle and safety vest in your car. It is recommended that you have enough safety vests for everyone. If you are driving a camper van with a maximum permissible mass of more than 3.5 tons, you must have a fire extinguisher and a warning triangle on board too.

Caravan and motorhome

A motorhome or car-caravan combination may be a maximum of 4 metres high, 2.55 metres wide and 18.75 metres long (the caravan itself may be a maximum of 12 metres long).
If you have a car-caravan combination of more than 7 metres in length (or > 3.5 tons), you must keep a distance of at least 50 metres between yourself and another car-caravan combination or lorry.

> *"Luxembourg: close by but still a world away."*
> Mr. K. Geeraert, Inspector 558

Cycling

Bicycle helmets are not mandatory. You may not make phone calls or use apps while using a bicycle. A child up to the age of 8 may only be transported on a bicycle by an adult and then only if seated in a bike seat. Children up to the age of 10 are only allowed to cycle on a public highway if supervised. Children up to the age of 12 are permitted to cycle on pavements.

Breakdown and accident

On a motorway, position your warning triangle at least 200 to 300 metres (100 metres elsewhere) behind your car if it is on the lane itself (only do this on a motorway if your hazard lights are not working). Everyone in the vehicle must put on a safety vest.
If you break down, call the emergency number provided by your breakdown insurer. Alternatively, call ACL, the Luxembourg breakdown assistance company, on +352 26 000.
Towing to the first exit is permitted on the motorway and to the first garage on a main highway.

Camping

Bathroom facilities are of an above average quality in Luxembourg. Entertainment and other facilities are available for children on many camp sites.
Free-camping outside camp sites is not permitted. You must have the permission of the land owner to camp on private land. Camping on a farm is permitted - with the permission of the farmer - provided there are no more than two adults and three children.
More than half of camp sites are classified via a star system: varying from one to five stars. This classification only applies for camp sites that voluntarily agree to participate. Some camp sites have chosen to continue to use the 'old' category-based classification. Please note: some high-quality camp sites have chosen not to be included in any classification system at all.

Berdorf, L-6551 / Mullerthal

413

- Belle-Vue 2000 Kat.I
- Rue de Consdorf 29
- +352 79 06 35
- 1/1 - 31/12
- campbv2000@gmail.com

5,5ha 161T(90-120m²) 6-16A CEE

- 1 ABCDEIKLMNOQRS
- 2 JSWXYZ
- 3 CIKLSU
- 4 (Q+R)(T 1/6-31/10)(U)
- 5 ABDGIJMNOPUWZ
- 6 ABEFGIK(N 0,35km)OP

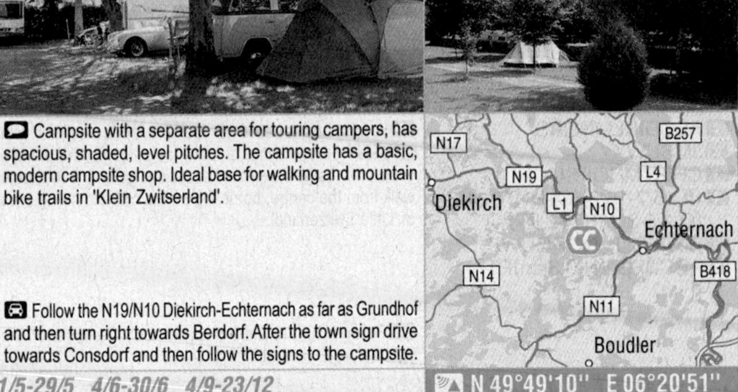

Campsite with a separate area for touring campers, has spacious, shaded, level pitches. The campsite has a basic, modern campsite shop. Ideal base for walking and mountain bike trails in 'Klein Zwitserland'.

Follow the N19/N10 Diekirch-Echternach as far as Grundhof and then turn right towards Berdorf. After the town sign drive towards Consdorf and then follow the signs to the campsite.

CC € 21 *2/1-7/5 13/5-16/5 21/5-29/5 4/6-30/6 4/9-23/12*

N 49°49'10'' E 06°20'51''

Consdorf, L-6211 / Mullerthal

414

- Camping La Pinède Kat.I/***
- 33 rue Burgkapp
- +352 79 02 71
- 15/3 - 15/11
- info@campinglapinede.lu

3ha 76T(100-140m²) 10A CEE

- 1 ABCDIKLMNOQRS
- 2 BJLMSWXYZ
- 3 CHIKLMNOPRSU
- 4 (Q)(R 1/4-30/10) (T+U+X+Y+Z)
- 5 ABDFGIJKLNOPUWZ
- 6 ABCDEFGHK(N 0,5km)P

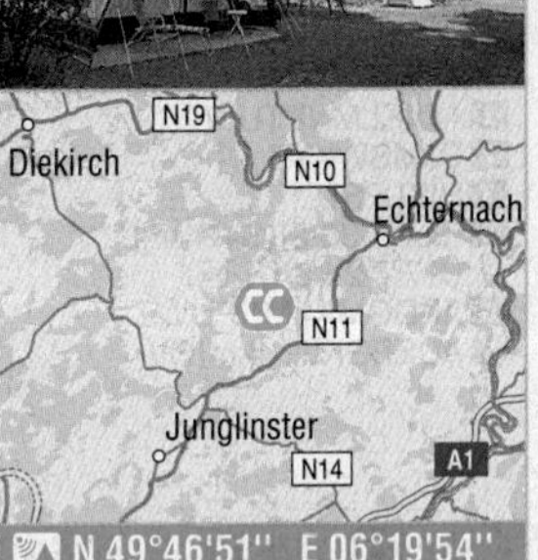

Beautiful and well-maintained quiet terraced campsite with marked out pitches. Located beside the forest with beautiful rocks in the heart of 'Little Switzerland'. Tennis and miniature golf course. New restaurant with bar and terrace. New toilet facilities.

Follow the N14 Diekirch-Larochette. In Larochette turn left towards Christnach/Consdorf. Follow the signs in Consdorf.

CC € 21 *15/3-29/3 1/4-9/5 12/5-17/5 20/5-12/7 1/9-15/11*

N 49°46'51'' E 06°19'54''

Diekirch, L-9234 / Ardennes

415

- Camping De la Sûre***
- route de Gilsdorf
- +352 8 08 78 07 01
- 29/3 - 6/10
- info@camping-diekirch.lu

5ha 196T(50-100m²) 10A CEE

- 1 ABCDHKLMNORS
- 2 CIJSTWXYZ
- 3 CHKMNPSUW
- 4 (Q+T+X+Z)
- 5 ABDEFGIJKLMNPUWXZ
- 6 ABCDEFGJ(N 0,5km)PV

A lovely level campsite situated on the banks of the River Sûre with sufficient shaded pitches, 5 minutes' walk from the centre of Diekirch. Indoor swimming pool close by.

In Diekirch drive towards Larochette. After the bridge over the Sûre turn left towards Gilsdorf. After 100 metres, 1st campsite.

L4 B50 N17 L3 Bastendorf Diekirch L1 N19 N15 N10 N14 Christnach N22 N7

CC € 21 *30/3-8/5 13/5-16/5 28/5-30/6 1/9-6/10*

N 49°51'57'' E 06°09'54''

Echternach, L-6430 / Mullerthal

416

Camping Officiel Wollefsschlucht
17 route de Diekirch
+352 72 02 72
1/1 - 31/12
camping@visitechternach.lu

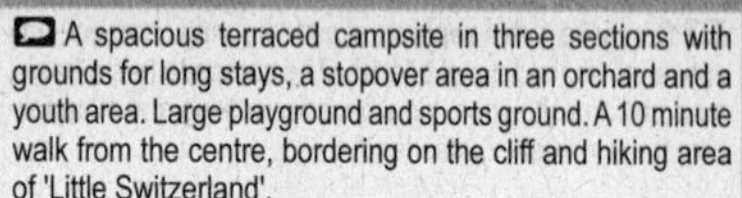

4ha 214T(80-120m²) 10-12A

1 ABCD**I**KLMNQ**R**S
2 JMSUWXY
3 CHIKLMNOPSU
4 (**A** 15/7-15/8)(C+H 1/7-31/8)
(Q 1/5-30/9)(T+Z 🔑)
5 **AB**DFGIJMNOPQUWZ
6 ABCDFGJ(N 0,3km)PT

A spacious terraced campsite in three sections with grounds for long stays, a stopover area in an orchard and a youth area. Large playground and sports ground. A 10 minute walk from the centre, bordering on the cliff and hiking area of 'Little Switzerland'.

Follow N10-N19 Diekirch-Echternach. Campsite on the right before Echternach.

CC € 23 *1/1-29/3 14/4-8/5 12/5-17/5 22/5-29/5 3/6-30/6 13/9-31/12*

N 49°49'01'' E 06°24'38''

Ermsdorf, L-9366 / Mullerthal

417

Camping Neumuhle Kat.I/****
27 Reisduerferstrooss
+352 87 93 91
15/4 - 15/9
info@camping-neumuhle.lu

3ha 105T(80-100m²) 6A CEE

1 AD**I**KLMN**R**TUW
2 DJMSWXYZ
3 HIKLPSU
4 (B 1/5-30/8)(Q+R 🔑)
(T 7/7-24/8)(X 🔑)
5 **AB**DGI**J**K**L**MNPUWZ
6 ACEFGK(N 4km)OV

A well maintained adult only terraced campsite on a hill with marked out pitches of maximum 100 m². Lovely views. A small swimming pool provides cool refreshment on hot days. A good base for countless trips out and walks. Free wifi. Dutch owners.

Follow the N14 Diekirch-Larochette as far as Medernach and then turn left towards Ermsdorf. In Ermsdorf continue driving for approx. 1 km towards Reisdorf as far as Hostellerie and campsite Neumühle.

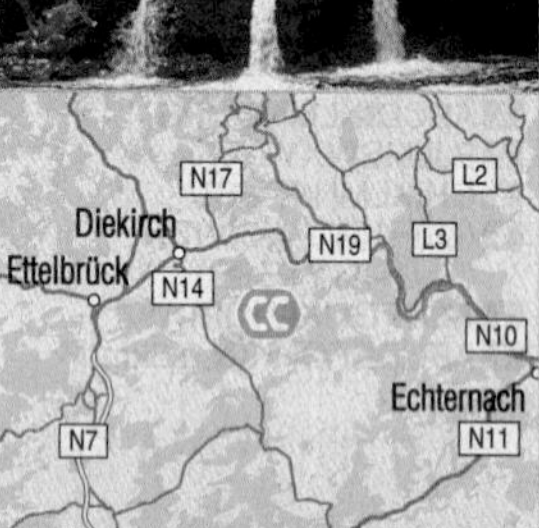

CC € 23 *15/4-5/7 30/8-15/9*

N 49°50'21'' E 06°13'31''

Esch-sur-Sûre, L-9650 / Ardennes

418

Camping Im Aal***
1 Am Aal
+352 83 95 14
23/2 - 8/12
info@campingaal.lu

2,5ha 150T(100m²) 10A CEE

1 ACDE**I**JKLMNOQRS
2 DJSWXYZ
3 CHIJKLPSU**WX**
4 (A 5/7-20/8)
(Q+R+Z 1/4-30/9)
5 **AB**DFGIJMNOPUWZ
6 ACEFGJ(N 7km)PTV

Located in wooded surroundings on the banks of the Sûre. Quiet, calm and laid out with respect for the country-side. Walking and various leisure opportunities in the vicinity. Reception closed between 12.30 pm and 1 pm.

Take Bastogne-Diekirch N15, exit Esch-sur-Sûre. Through the tunnel, campsite 150 further on by the river.

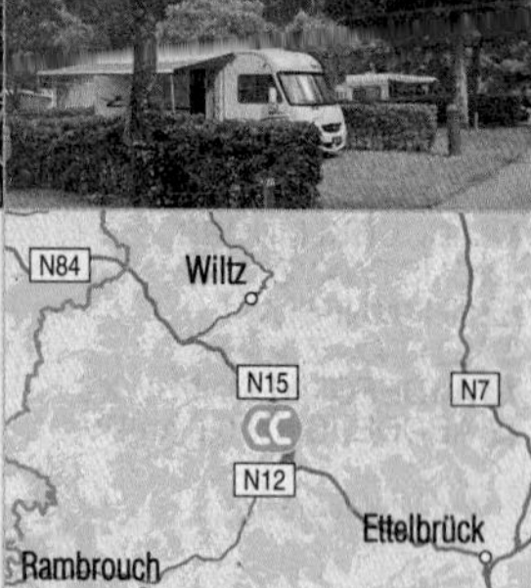

CC € 23 *23/2-28/3 1/4-7/5 20/5-30/6 25/8-7/12*

N 49°54'24'' E 05°56'34''

Ettelbruck, L-9022 / Ardennes

419

Camping Ettelbrück
88 chemin du Camping
+352 81 21 85
1/4 - 10/10
camping@ettelbruck.lu

3ha 100T(80-120m²) 16A CEE

1 ACDEIKLMNOQRS
2 IJMNSWXYZ
3 CHIKLMNSU
4 (A+Q+T+U+X+Z)
5 ABDFGIJKLMNOPUWZ
6 ACDEFHJ(N 1km)PUV

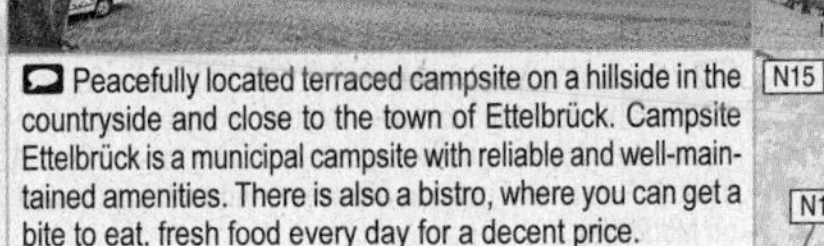

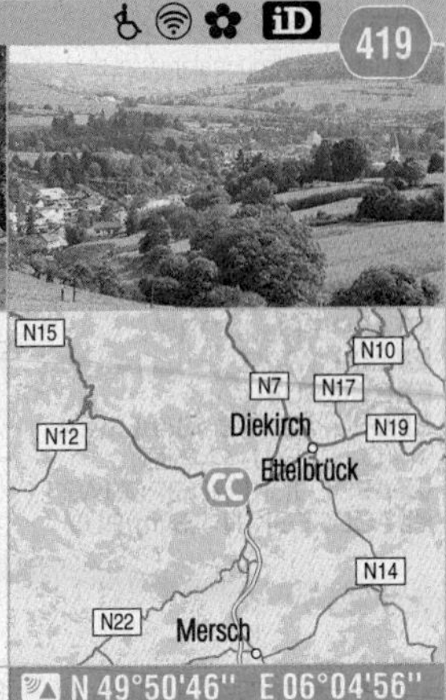

Peacefully located terraced campsite on a hillside in the countryside and close to the town of Ettelbrück. Campsite Ettelbrück is a municipal campsite with reliable and well-maintained amenities. There is also a bistro, where you can get a bite to eat, fresh food every day for a decent price.

In Ettelbrück town centre take the N15 to Wiltz/Bastogne. Follow the camping signs 300m on the left. Coming from Wiltz turn right before the centre.

CC € 21 *1/4-30/6 1/9-9/10*

N 49°50'46'' E 06°04'56''

Ingeldorf/Diekirch, L-9161 / Ardennes

420

Camping Gritt Kat.I/***
2, Um Gritt
+352 6 91 31 94 14
1/3 - 3/11
info@campinggritt.lu

3,5ha 137T(75-120m²) 10-16A CEE

1 ABCDIKLMNORS
2 DIJSWXY
3 CIKLW
4 (Q+R+T+U+X+Y+Z)
5 ABDEFGHIJMNOPQUWXYZ
6 ABCDEFGK(N 0,8km)V

Quiet, completely renovated campsite set in picturesque surroundings on the bank of the river Sûre. Spacious pitches with water and drainage. A friendly bar and restaurant with a terrace. The campsite is located within walking distance of the shopping centre and the town of Diekirch and Ettelbrück. Ideal for cycling tours.

Take the N7 Ettelbrück-Diekirch. After about 2 km take the direction of Ingeldorf. Then follow the signs.

CC € 23 *1/3-6/7 24/8-3/11 7=6*

N 49°51'02'' E 06°08'04''

Larochette, L-7633 / Mullerthal

421

hu Birkelt Village Kat.I/*****
1 Um Birkelt
+352 87 90 40
27/4 - 15/9
birkelt@huopenair.com

12ha 124T(80-100m²) 10-16A CEE

1 BCDIKLMNQRTU
2 BJLSWXYZ
3 ACDGIKLPS
4 (B+E+G)J
(Q+S+T+U+V+X+Y+Z)
5 ABDEFGIJKLMNOPQRUWXYZ
6 BCEFGHK(N 2,5km)SV

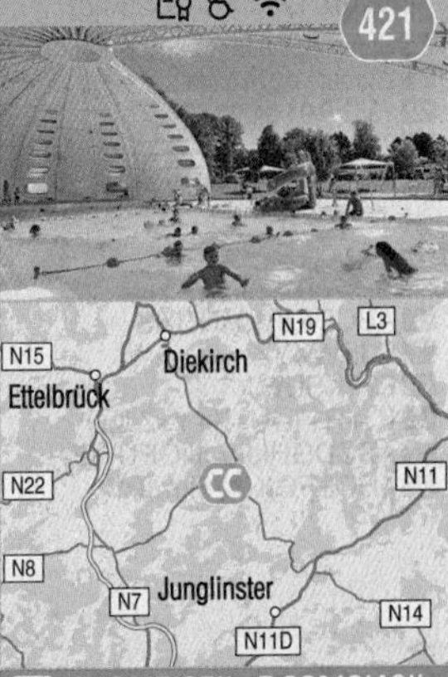

A modern, well maintained family campsite with spacious pitches with man-sized hedges. The campsite offers every comfort. Camp shop. Plenty of recreational opportunities including an all-weather swimming pool, new outdoor pool and entertainment in low and high season.

Follow the N14 Diekirch-Larochette. Turn right in the centre of Larochette and then follow the signs to the campsite.

CC C 23 *27/4-6/7 24/8-15/9*

N 49°47'05'' E 06°12'40''

Mersch, L-7572 / Centre

422

Camping Krounebierg*****
2 rue du Camping, BP 35
+352 32 97 56
29/3 - 31/10
contact@campingkrounebierg.lu

3ha 138T(60-200m²) 6-10A CEE

1 ACDEIKLMNORS
2 IMSUWXYZ
3 CHIKPUV
4 (F)(G 15/6-15/9)IJKLN
(Q+S+T+U+Y+Z)
5 ABDFGIJKLMNOPQUWZ
6 ACDEFGK(N 1,5km)PUV

1.5 km from Mersch. Marked-out pitches. Near N7 and A7, suitable as stopover site. Next to a water recreation centre (free for 2 hours a day when staying longer than 3 nights). Restaurant open in afternoon and evening (closed on Mondays).

From the north A7, exit Kopstal; dir. Mersch. Follow camping signs. Follow signs from the N7 in Mersch town centre. From the south A6 dir. Bruxelles; then exit 3 Bridel/ Kopstal. Dir. Mersch, then follow camping signs.

CC € 21 *1/4-26/4 21/5-11/7 25/8-31/10*

N 49°44'37'' E 06°05'23''

Nommern, L-7465 / Centre

423

Europacamping Nommerlayen Kat.I/*****
rue Nommerlayen
+352 87 80 78
22/3 - 2/11
info@nommerlayen-ec.lu

ACSI AWARDS WINNER

15ha 385T(70-130m²) 10-16A CEE

1 ABCDIKLMNOQRS
2 IMNSWXYZ
3 ABCGHIJKMNPSTUV
4 (A 6/7-1/9)(B 1/5-15/9)
(E 27/4-15/9)(H 1/5-15/9)MN
(Q+S+T+U+X+Y+Z)
5 ABCDEFGHIJKLMNOPSUWXYZ
6 BCDEFGHKL(N 8km)PTV

Luxury terraced campsite in walking area with spacious, marked out level pitches with water and drainage. Modern toilets including private bathrooms. Two open air pools, one with sliding roof. More expensive pitches (better location) also possible with CampingCard ACSI for extra fee.

N7 as far as Ettelbrück/Schieren and then exit 7, Cruchten, Colmarberg. At end of exit, after petrolstation, turn left towards Cruchten/Nommern. In Cruchten turn left and then follow signs.

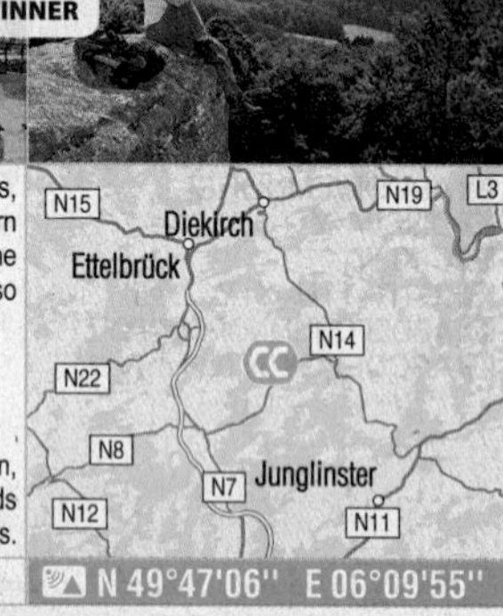

CC € 25 *1/4-26/4 30/5-5/7 1/9-2/11*

N 49°47'06'' E 06°09'55''

Reisdorf, L-9390 / Mullerthal

424

Camping De la Sûre Reisdorf Kat.I
23 route de la Sûre
+352 6 91 84 96 66
23/3 - 3/11
info@campingdelasure.lu

2,9ha 95T(100-150m²) 10-16A CEE

1 ABCDEIKLMNORS
2 CJSWXYZ
3 CHIKSUW
4 (Q+R+T+U+X+Y+Z)
5 ABCDGHIJLMNOPUWZ
6 ABCEFGK(N 5km)PV

Peaceful family campsite on the River Sûre in Reisdorf with lovely shaded pitches. Bar/restaurant with a large terrace. An excellent departure point for bike trips and walks. Second campsite on the left, past the bridge in Reisdorf.

Follow N10 Diekirch to Echternach. In Reisdorf the 2nd campsite after the bridge.

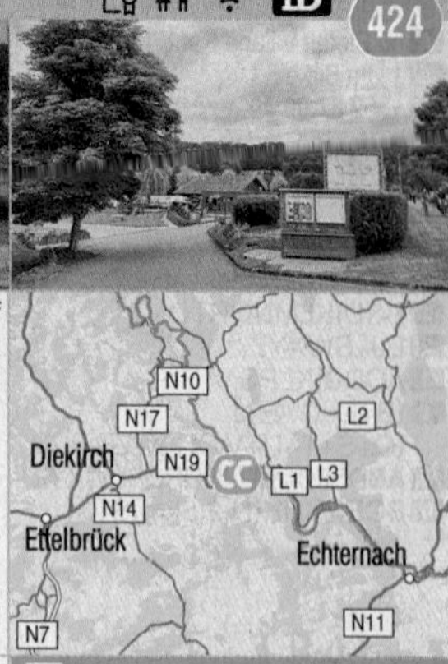

CC € 19 *23/3-6/7 24/8-3/11 7=6*

N 49°52'11'' E 06°16'03''

Rosport, L-6580 / Mullerthal

425

Camping Du Barrage Rosport Kat.I
1, rue du camping
+352 73 01 60
1/1 - 31/12
campingrosport@pt.lu

4,0ha 111**T**(100m^2) 12-16A CEE

1 ACD**I**KLMNORS
2 CJSTWXY
3 CHIKMNPS**W**
4 (C+H 15/6-15/9)
(Q 15/5-31/8)(U)
(Y 1/5-30/10)(Z)
5 **AB**DEFGIJKMNOPQUWZ
6 ABCDFGHK(N 0,5km)

A level family campsite located on the banks of the Sûre with spacious pitches. A paradise for cyclists and anglers (fishing season 15/6-28/2). New toilet facilities, bar-restaurant and an outdoor swimming pool. Good starting point for trips out in this cycling and walking region.

ACSI AWARDS WINNER

Follow route N10 Echternach-Wasserbillig as far as Rosport. Then follow the signs.

Welschbillig, Echternach, Trier, L2, B257, B422, N10, L4, B51, L42, B52, B418, N11, A64, L43

CC € 21 *1/1-30/6 1/9-31/12 7=6*

N 49°48'33'' E 06°30'12''

Simmerschmelz, L-8363 / Centre

426

Camping Simmerschmelz Kat.I
Simmerschmelz 2
+352 30 70 72
1/1 - 31/12
info@simmerschmelz.com

5ha 72**T**(80-120m^2) 6A CEE

1 ACDE**I**KLMNORU
2 BIJLSTWXYZ
3 CISU
4 M(Y+Z)
5 **AB**DEGIJMNPUWZ
6 DEFGHK(N 7km)PUV

Campsite, located in a wooded area: peace, enjoy the countryside, walking tours. Paved motorhome pitches with a grass area. Heated sanitary facilities. Lively cafe. Restaurant open in the evenings (closed on Tuesdays from early September to late June).

E25 exit 1 direction Steinfort. Straight on at roundabout direction Septfontaines. Right after 300 metres direction Goeblange. Right at end of road and immediately left towards Simmerschmelz. Campsite on right after 3 km.

CC € 19 *1/1-7/7 25/8-31/12*

N 49°41'34'' E 05°59'08''

Troisvierges, L-9912 / Ardennes

427

Camping Troisvierges Kat.I
rue de Binsfeld
+352 99 71 41
1/4 - 30/9
info@camping-troisvierges.lu

5ha 100**T**(80-120m^2) 10A

1 ABCDE**I**KLMNO**R**S
2 DJMSWXYZ
3 C**G**HIKLNOPSU
4 (A 6/7-14/8)(C+G 18/5-15/9)
J(Q+T+U+V+X+Z)
5 **AB**DFGJLMNPUWX
6 ACDEFGHK(N 0,2km)PUV

Relaxation for all ages in a nature park. Lovely walking and cycling area, including the Vennbahn. Located on the edge of the town. Many sports facilities. Plenty of playing options for children. The major asset is the lovely open-air swimming pool.

The campsite is located 300 metres from the centre of the small town Troisvierges, on the road to Binsfeld. In Troisvierges: follow the camping signs.

CC € 25 *1/4-26/4 21/5-5/7 1/9-29/9*

N 50°07'07'' E 06°00'04''

Walsdorf, L-9465 / Ardennes

428

Camping Vakantiepark Walsdorf****
Tandelerbach 1
+352 83 44 64
29/3 - 2/11
info@campingwalsdorf.com

6ha 93T(80-140m²) 4A CEE

1 ABCDEIKLMNQRTU
2 BCMSTVWXYZ
3 AILPSU
4 (Q+S+T)(U 4/5-5/7) (X+Y 6/7-24/8) (Z 27/4-4/5,6/7-24/8)
5 **AB**DEFGHIJKLMNOPUWZ
6 ABDEFGHJ**K**(N 9km)P

Beautifully situated campsite in peaceful natural surroundings. Plenty of amenities including modern sanitary facilities. Spacious pitches including some on the 'Tandelerbach' brook. The site is operated by 'Beter-uit'. Close to the historic towns of Vianden and Diekirch.

Take the N17 Diekirch-Vianden. Beyond Tandel turn left. Follow the signs. The campsite access road is very narrow.

€ 19 *29/3-27/4 4/5-6/7 31/8-26/10*

Germany

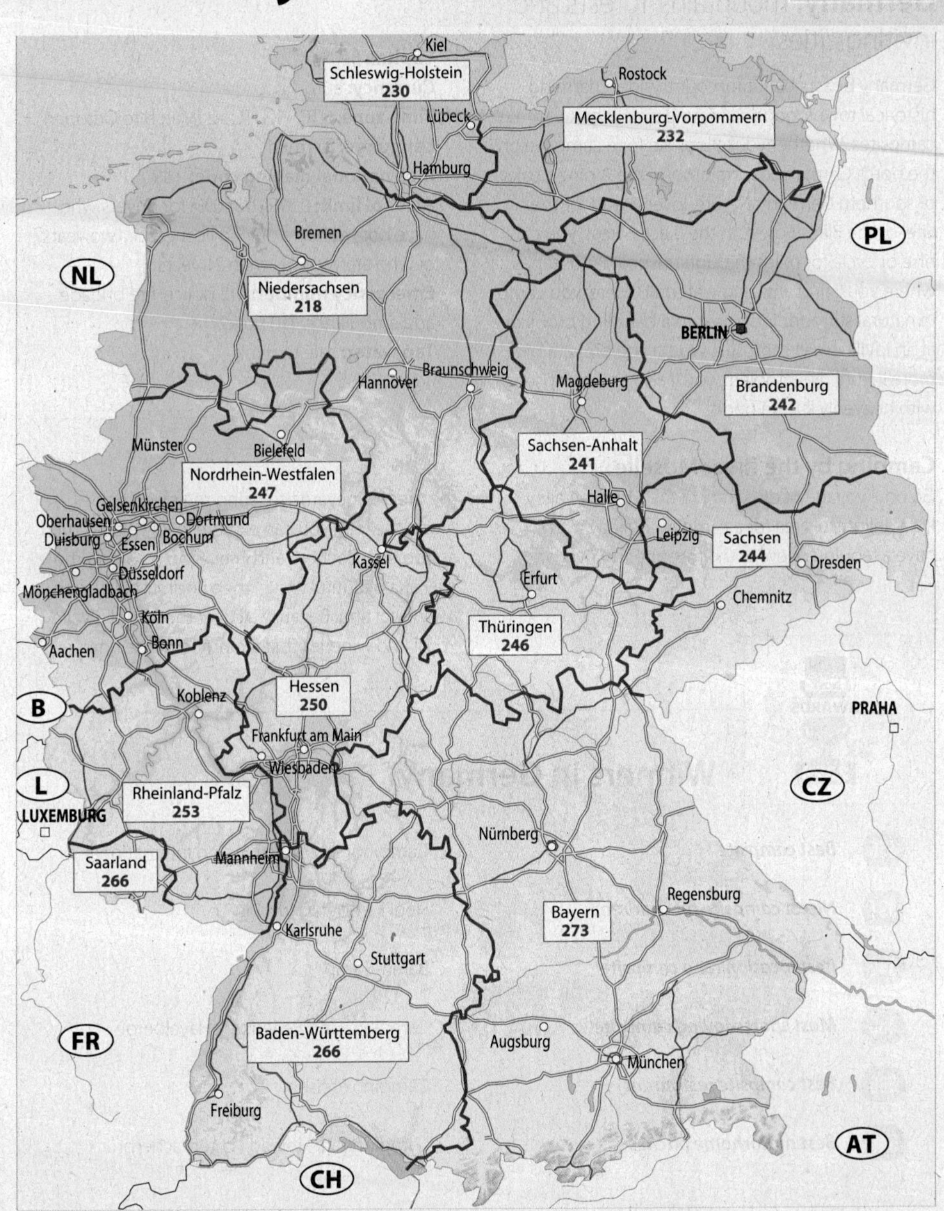

Kiel
Schleswig-Holstein
230
Rostock
Lübeck
Mecklenburg-Vorpommern
232
Hamburg
Bremen
PL
NL
Niedersachsen
218
BERLIN
Hannover
Braunschweig
Magdeburg
Brandenburg
242
Münster
Bielefeld
Sachsen-Anhalt
241
Nordrhein-Westfalen
247
Gelsenkirchen
Halle
Oberhausen
Dortmund
Duisburg
Essen
Bochum
Leipzig
Sachsen
244
Kassel
Dresden
Düsseldorf
Mönchengladbach
Erfurt
Chemnitz
Köln
Aachen
Bonn
Thüringen
246
Koblenz
Hessen
250
B
PRAHA
Frankfurt am Main
Wiesbaden
L
Rheinland-Pfalz
253
CZ
LUXEMBURG
Nürnberg
Saarland
266
Mannheim
Regensburg
Bayern
273
Karlsruhe
Stuttgart
Baden-Württemberg
266
Augsburg
FR
München
Freiburg
AT
CH

Germany: mountains, forests and inviting cities

Germany boasts beautiful countryside, charming historical towns, good roads and excellent campsites. Whether you're looking for a campsite on the north German coast or among the Alpine peaks of southern Germany. Nature-lovers head for the Eifel or the Black Forest. In the Black Forest, you can hike or cycle for miles through unspoilt landscapes, where you'll find amazing waterfalls. Here, you camp in natural surroundings, next to a babbling brook or at an idyllic small campsite. Would you prefer a bit more luxury? No problem, you'll also find campsites with heavenly leisure pools!

Capital: Berlin
Currency: euro
Time zone: UTC +1, UTC +2 (March to October)
Language: German
International dialling code: +49
Alcohol limit: 0.5‰, but 0‰ for drivers who have not yet had a driving licence for two years or who are younger than 21 years
Emergency number: 112 police, fire brigade and ambulance; 110 police
Tap water: safe to drink

Camping by the River Moselle

Go on a voyage of discovery in the Moselle Valley. It's a delightful area for a camping holiday. You'll have a fabulous view of the meandering river and the green vineyards covering the steep slopes. Along the way, you can explore lovely places such as Koblenz, Cochem and Trier. Stop off along the way at a beautiful castle, then finish the day with a wine-tasting. Because all over the Moselle Valley, you'll find wineries that are proud of their harvest.

Winners in Germany

456	***Best campsite***	Campingplatz Stover Strand International
591	***Nicest campsite for children***	Hegi Familien Camping
540	***Best location for a campsite***	Bären-Camp
480	***Most sports-loving campsite***	Camping- und Ferienpark Havelberge
600	***Best campsite restaurant***	Camping Preishof
545	***Best motorhome pitches***	Campingpark Freibad Echternacherbrück

Winner: Camping Preishof

Would you rather leave your caravan or tent in just one place? The Moselle Valley is also ideal as a base. Most campsites in the Moselle Valley are right by the river. Great for some quiet fishing or a refreshing swim in summer.

"ACSI campsites in Germany: for campers who deserve to find just the right campsite."
J. Urlings, inspector 933

Discover the Baltic Sea coast, islands and lakes of northern Germany

Northern Germany is an excellent choice for lovers of nature and culture. If you're a keen cyclist, we recommend the Baltic Sea Cycle Route. This cycle path runs along the German Baltic Sea coast from Flensburg to the island of Usedom. Along the way, you'll pass lovely cities such as Lübeck and Rostock, and extensive beaches with their typical wicker beach chairs. On the scenic islands such as Zingst and Rügen, you'll find attractive campsites in the middle of unique landscapes. If you love water sports, peace and quiet, or birds, the East German lakes of the Mecklenburgische Seenplatte (Mecklenburg Lake District) region are highly recommended. In a water-rich area of more than 100 lakes, you might be lucky and spot white-tailed eagles or ospreys. And in spring, countless cranes come here to breed.

From cathedrals to fine dining

In Germany, it's easy to combine your camping holiday with a city trip. You'll find a number of ACSI campsites near beautiful and lively cities such as Berlin, Dresden and Munich. Marvel at the history of centuries-old cathedrals and castles, and enjoy German hospitality with delicious food and drink.

En route

Filling up

Petrol (Super 95, Super 95 E10 and Super Plus 98) is widely available (if you want to fill up with E10, check the fuel tank opening, the manual or your car dealer to find out whether your car can run on this fuel). Diesel and LPG are also widely available. The European connector (ACME) is used for filling up with LPG. Most fuelling stations are open at least from 8:00 to 20:00 CET and those on motorways are often open day and night.There are also unmanned fuelling stations.

Charging

There are many charging points for electric cars, although there are also some areas with less comprehensive coverage. Please take note of the various charging rates. It's sometimes cheaper to charge your car at night. You'll find a list of the charging points on www.ladesaeulenregister.de.

Traffic regulations

Low beam headlights are mandatory in bad visibility, in the dark and in tunnels. At equivalent crossings, traffic from the right has right of way. Traffic on a roundabout has priority if this is indicated by a priority sign. On sloping roads, ascending traffic has priority over descending traffic (but on narrow mountain roads, the vehicle that can most easily move out of the way must give way).

Drivers may only call hands free. Children under the age of 12 years and under 1.50 metres in height must sit in a child car seat. Winter tyres are required in winter weather conditions.

Special regulations

If you're in a traffic jam, you must move as far as possible to the right or left, to create a free lane (Rettungsgasse) in the middle for emergency vehicles. When overtaking cyclists (including those on a cycle lane), you must maintain a lateral distance of at least 1.50 metres. In Germany, cars are not permitted on a dedicated 'bicycle road' (Fahrradstraße), unless indicated otherwise. Zig-zag lines on the road indicate that you're not permitted to stop or park there.

Mandatory equipment

It's mandatory to have a warning triangle, a high-visibility safety vest and a first-aid kit in your vehicle.

Caravan and motorhome

A motorhome or car-caravan combination may be a maximum of 4 metres high, 2.55 metres wide and 18 metres long (the caravan itself may be a maximum of 12 metres long). On motorways with three or more lanes, you may not drive with a caravan in the lane furthest to the left, unless you want to turn left. If you're towing a caravan weighing more than 750 kg, you must have two wheel chocks.

"Germany has something for everyone, including mountains and valleys, Bratwurst and Schnitzel."

G. Brink, inspector 609

Cycling

A cycle helmet is not mandatory. It's forbidden to telephone or message while cycling. Children must cycle on the pavement and cross roads on foot

until they're 8 years old. Cyclists must be aged 16 years or older before they're allowed to transport a child under 7 years in a child bicycle seat. Cycling side-by-side is only permitted on a cycle path that is separated from the road by a raised barrier or a grass strip.

Environmental zones

An environmental sticker or vignette ('Umweltplakette') is required in increasing numbers of German towns and cities. This also applies to foreign vehicles. The vignette may be yellow, green or red, depending on your vehicle's emissions. This vignette is not required on motorways. An environmental zone is indicated by signs for 'Umweltzone'. If you drive into such a zone without a vignette, you risk a fine. Some cities have a 'diesel ban', meaning that older diesel cars and cars without a catalytic converter are no longer permitted. The rules vary from one place to the other.
For more information, see: gis.uba.de/website/umweltzonen.

Breakdown and accident

Place your emergency triangle on the motorway at least 200 metres (on other roads 50-100 metres) behind the car. All people in the car are advised to put on a high-visibility safety vest. In the event of a breakdown, phone the emergency number of your roadside assistance insurer. You can also call a German breakdown service: +49 89 22 22 22 (ADAC) or +49 711 530 34 35 36 (ACE). And you can call for roadside assistance from an orange emergency telephone. You're advised not to repair your vehicle yourself on the side of the motorway. Towing on the motorway is permitted as far as the next exit.

Camping

German campsites are among the better-quality sites in Europe. Campsites are focusing increasingly on target groups such as families with children, hikers and cyclists, or wellness fans.

Free camping outside organised campsites is generally forbidden. It is only allowed if the landowner gives permission.

Practical information

Nearly all campsites have a midday rest time (usually from 13:00 to 15:00 CET), which must generally be strictly observed.

Altenau, D-38707 / Niedersachsen

429

Camping Polstertal***
Polstertal 1
+49 53 23 55 82
1/1 - 31/12
info@campingplatz-polstertal.de

1,8ha 80T(60-90m²) 10A CEE

1 ACDIKLNRS
2 BCLSUVWYZ
3 ACIKLSW
4 (Q+R+V)
5 ABDEFGIJKLMNOPQUWZ
6 EFGJ(N 4km)OP

An idyllic, small campsite with a pleasant atmosphere amid a forest. Extremely relaxing due to the stunning countryside. There is a forest lake you can swim in 200 m away. This charming family campsite in Upper Harz is an excellent holiday tip. The campsite is open all year. Cooking and heating with electricity is not allowed.

A7, exit 67 Seesen. Via Bad Grund, Clausthal and Zellerfeld, to Altenau.

CC € 23 8/1-15/3 8/4-26/4 6/5-9/5 13/5-16/5 21/5-21/6 6/9-30/9

N 51°47'58'' E 10°24'59''

Aschenbeck/Dötlingen, D-27801 / Niedersachsen

430

Camping Aschenbeck
Zum Sande 18
+49 44 33 96 88 47
1/1 - 31/12
aschenbeck.camping@web.de

16ha 65T(100m²) 16A

1 ACDIJKLMNOQRS
2 AEISUXYZ
3 AEGHKPRSUWZ
4 (Q+R 1/5-30/9)
(T+U 1/5-15/9)
5 ABCDGIJLNPUWZ
6 EFGJ(N 2km)OPU

Large campsite, partly located in an open part of a forest. Fishing and swimming options in a lake. Stopover campsite to Scandinavia. Great starting point for cycling and walking.

A1 Osnabrück-Bremen, exit Wildeshausen/Nord. Then direction Wildeshausen. At the traffic lights drive in the direction of Dötlingen. Signposted after Aschenstedt.

CC € 23 1/5-8/5 21/5-23/6 18/8-30/9

N 52°56'02'' E 08°24'13''

Bad Bentheim, D-48455 / Niedersachsen

431

Camping Am Berg
Suddendorferstraße 37
+49 59 22 99 04 61
4/3 - 1/11
info@campingplatzamberg.de

3ha 100T(100-120m²) 10A CEE

1 ADIJKLMNOQRTU
2 JSXYZ
3 GHIK
4 (Q 1/4-30/9)
5 ABDGJKNPTUWYZ
6 CEFGK(N 4km)P

You can camp at this site just outside the historic village in a meadow surrounded by trees or in a lovely 'avenue'. The surrounding area is excellent for walks and bike rides. You will be welcomed by the Dutch owners.

A1 Hengelo border direction Osnabrück (A30). Exit 3 direction Bad Bentheim. Follow road 403. Campsite signposted.

CC € 21 4/3-5/5 28/5-8/7 26/8-1/11

N 52°17'52'' E 07°11'30''

Bad Rothenfelde, D-49214 / Niedersachsen

432

- Camping Campotel*****
- Heidland 65
- +49 54 24 21 06 00
- 1/1 - 31/12
- info@campotel.de

13ha 140T(75-180m²) 16A CEE

1 ACDE**I**JKLMNOQ**R**S
2 AIOPSUVWXYZ
3 ADE**G**HIKMN**O**PSU**VW**
4 (Q+R)(T+U+X 18/3-3/11)
5 **AB**CDFGJKLNP**RS**UWXYZ
6 CDEFGHK(N 1,5km)OTU

Campsite with unusual features and with excellent toilet facilities. A great area for cycling, walking and inhaling the healthy air by the salt walls. The new thermal bath is recommended. The tourist card gives you nice discounts in the region.

A30 Enschede as far as Lotte Kreuz. Then drive towards Hannover. At Autobahnkreuz Osnabrück-Süd take the A33 towards Bielefeld/Bad Rothenfelde. Then exit 13 direction Bad Rothenfelde. Straight ahead at roundabout, then follow signs.

CC € 21 *8/1-15/3 7/4-8/5 21/5-29/5 2/6-21/6 19/8-11/10 3/11-20/12*

N 52°05'53'' E 08°10'22''

Bleckede, D-21354 / Niedersachsen

433

- Knaus Campingpark Bleckede/ Elbtalaue****
- Am Waldbad 23
- +49 5 85 43 11
- 1/3 - 3/11
- bleckede@knauscamp.de

6,5ha 142T(80-150m²) 10-16A CEE

1 ACD**I**JKLMNOQRUV
2 BCJSWXYZ
3 CHIKSU**W**
4 (C+H 1/5-15/9)J**N**(Q+R) (T 1/6-1/9)
5 **AB**DEFGHJLNPQUWZ
6 ACEFGK(N 6km)OPV

A beautifully laid out campsite in the 'Niedersächsische Elbtalaue' bio-reserve, a paradise for cyclists, watersports, walkers and anglers. Comfortable, easily accessible, modern, spacious toilet facilities. Located next to extensive woodland with unlimited entry.

A7 Hannover-Hamburg exit Soltau-Ost direction Lüneberg/ Dahlenburg. Left to Bleckede, then Hitzacker.

CC € 27 *1/3-30/6 19/7-2/8 1/9-3/11*

N 53°15'34'' E 10°48'20''

Bleckede (OT Radegast), D-21354 / Niedersachsen

434

- Camping Elbeling
- Hinter den Höfen 9a
- +49 5 85 75 55
- 1/4 - 1/10
- info@elbeling.de

3,8ha 100T(100-150m²) 16A CEE

1 AE**I**KLMNORS
2 ACJNOSXYZ
3 C**G**HIKSU**WX**
4 (G 1/5-1/10) (Q+T+U+V 1/4-1/10)(Y) (Z 1/4-1/10)
5 **AB**DEFGHIJLMNOPUWXZ
6 ACDEFGH**K**(N 5km)OPTV

A beautiful, well-kept and comfortable campsite with spacious pitches. Level and situated on the Elbe and recognized by UNESCO as a 'biosphären reservat' nature reserve. Unique surroundings for nature lovers with plenty of cycling and walking opportunities. The campsite was renovated and is Dutch-owned.

From Luneburg direction Bleckede, then towards Radegast. Campsite signposted in Radegast. Take side road at covered wagon. Entrance: Hinter den Höfen 9a.

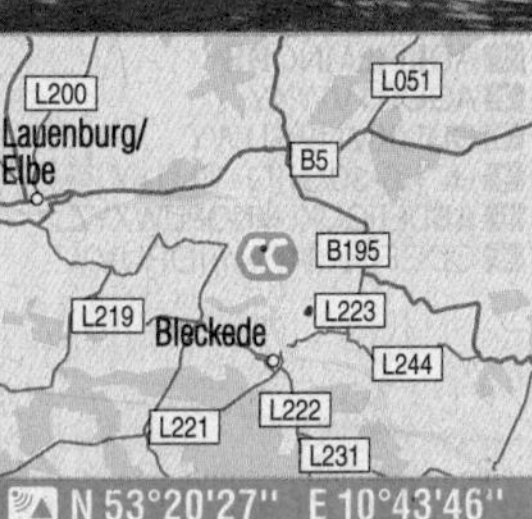

CC € 25 *1/5-7/7 28/8-30/9*

N 53°20'27'' E 10°43'46''

Clausthal-Zellerfeld, D-38678 / Niedersachsen

435

- Camping Prahljust***
- An den langen Brüchen 4
- +49 53 23 13 00
- 1/1 - 31/12
- camping@prahljust.de

13ha 250**T**(80-110m²) 16A CEE

- **1** ABCD**I**KLMNOQRS
- **2** BELPSUVXYZ
- **3** BCIKLSU**WZ**
- **4** **N**(Q+U+Y+Z)
- **5** **AB**DFGIJKLMNOPUWZ
- **6** CDEFGHKL(N 4km)OPU

A peaceful family campsite with plenty of trees and lakes in the immediate vicinity. Excellent walking and cycling. Opportunities for wintersports in the winter. The site has heated toilet facilities. Lovely villages such as Clausthal-Zellerfeld and Goslar nearby.

A7, exit 67 Seesen. To Bad Grund and Clausthal-Zellerfeld. Then on B242 direction Braunlage.

CC € 23 *8/1-8/5 22/5-21/6 1/9-15/12*

N 51°47'05'' E 10°21'01''

Dorum/Neufeld, D-27632 / Niedersachsen

436

- Knaus Campingpark Dorum***
- Am Kutterhafen
- +49 47 41 50 20
- 1/4 - 30/9
- dorum@knauscamp.de

8,5ha 120**T**(80-140m²) 16A CEE

- **1** ACDE**I**JKLMNQ**R**S
- **2** GIJNOSWX
- **3** ACKMN**W**Y
- **4** (C+F+H+Q+R) (T+V 20/4-30/9)(X+Y+Z)
- **5** **AB**GIJKLMNOPUWZ
- **6** ABCDEFGK(N 7km)O

The campsite is located on level grounds beyond the dike. Plenty of options for eating and drinking within 50m of the site. Lovely small harbour. The campsite is constructed in the early season and dismantled again in late season.

Motorway A27 Bremerhaven-Cuxhaven. Exit Neuenwalde. Head in the direction of Dorum, subsequently in the direction of Dorum/Neufeld-Kutterhafen. Drive for about 7 km up to the harbour. Turn to the right uphill and follow the signs to the campsite.

CC € 27 *1/4-8/5 12/5-17/5 22/5-28/5 3/6-21/6 3/9-30/9*

N 53°44'19'' E 08°31'03''

Eckwarderhörne, D-26969 / Niedersachsen

437

- Knaus Campingpark Eckwarderhörne****
- Zum Leuchtfeuer 116
- +49 47 36 13 00
- 1/1 - 31/12
- eckwarderhoerne@knauscamp.de

6ha 25**T**(80-130m²) 16A CEE

- **1** AD**I**JKLMNO**R**S
- **2** AGOSTVWXY
- **3** CHIJKMNPSUWY
- **4** (**A** 1/6-30/9)(Q+T+U+Y)
- **5** **AB**DEFGIJKLMNOPUWXYZ
- **6** CDEFGK(N 3km)OPUVX

A rural camp site on the Wadden Sea (UNESCO). Your pets are also welcome in specially designated areas. The cycle ferry will take you directly from Eckwarderhörne to the Helgoland Quay in Wilhelmshaven several times a week.

A7 Groningen-Leer. A28 at Oldenburg, exit 14 dir. Wilhelmshaven. A29 exit 8 Varel Exit Schwelburg B437 dir. Nordenham/Butjadingen/Eckwarden then dir. Burhave. Campsite signposted.

CC € 27 *1/1-8/5 12/5-17/5 22/5-28/5 3/6-21/6 3/9-30/12*

N 53°31'17'' E 08°14'06''

Essel/Engehausen, D-29690 / Niedersachsen

438

- Camping Aller-Leine-Tal
- Marschweg 1
- +49 50 71 51 15 49
- 15/3 - 27/10
- camping@camping-allerleinetal.de

5ha 80**T**(100-120m²) 10A

1 ACD**I**KLMNORUV
2 BCEISXYZ
3 CIKRS**W**XZ
4 (Q 15/3-15/10)(U+Y+Z)
5 **AB**DFGIJKLMNPUWZ
6 AEFGJ(N 7km)OPV

The campsite is located in woodland 100m from the Aller. Its location on the southern edge of the Lüneburger Heath makes it suitable for longer stays. The campsite is 800m from the A7 and is ideal as a stopover campsite. Friendly Dutch owners.

A7 Hannover-Bremen, exit 'Rasthof Allertal', direction Celle. Follow camping signs.

CC € 21 *15/3-30/6 18/8-27/10*

N 52°41'22" E 09°41'53"

Ganderkesee/Steinkimmen, D-27777 / Niedersachsen

439

- Camping & Ferienpark Falkensteinsee****
- Falkensteinsee 1
- +49 4 22 29 47 00 77
- 1/1 - 31/12
- camping@falkensteinsee.de

24ha 130**T**(100-150m²) 16A CEE

1 ACDE**I**KLMNOQ**RS**
2 ABFIOSWXYZ
3 AC**G**HIKP**R**SU**W**Z
4 (Q 1/4-31/10)(R 1/4-1/11) (T+U 1/4-31/10) (V 24/1-29/12) (Y+Z 1/4-31/10)
5 **AB**DEFGJLMN**PQR**UWXYZ
6 ACDEFGHK(N 6km)OPUV

Delightful countryside by the Falkenstein lake! Water, beach, fields, woods: everything! It offers one of the loveliest spots in North Germany, surrounded by the Hasbruch nature reserve and the Wildeshauser Geest, between Oldenburg and Bremen. Simply relax as a couple, as a family, as cyclists, relaxation-seekers, adventurists. Your dog is welcome.

Motorway Groningen-Leer-Oldenburg. Direction Bremen, exit 18 Hude direction Falkenburg. The campsite is signposted.

CC € 25 *12/5-17/5 20/5-29/5 1/6-21/6 1/9-30/9*

N 53°02'50" E 08°27'52"

Garlstorf, D-21376 / Niedersachsen

440

- Freizeit-Camp-Nordheide e.V.
- Egestorfer Landstraße 50
- +49 1 52 28 49 13 77
- 1/1 - 31/12
- freizeit-camp-nordheide@outlook.de

6ha 150**T**(80-140m²) 16A CEE

1 ACDE**I**JKLMNOQRS
2 BISUXYZ
3 ACIKPSU
5 **AB**DEGHIJKLMNOPUWZ
6 CEFGK(N 4km)O

A campsite in the middle of the Nordheide, just 4 km from the autobahn. Ideal as stopover campsite. Just 40 km from Hamburg. 4 km from the Wildpark Nindorf. Heideblütenfest. Luxurious toilet facilities. Club building open from Thursday to Saturday from 18.00-23.00.

A7 exit 40 Garlstorf. Then Hansteder-Landstrasse direction Garlstorf. Campsite signposted towards Egestorf.

CC € 23 *1/1-15/7 1/9-31/12*

N 53°13'30" E 10°05'16"

Hameln, D-31787 / Niedersachsen

441

Campingplatz Hameln an der Weser
Uferstraße 80
+49 5 15 16 74 89
1/3 - 4/11
info@campingplatz-hameln.de

2ha 115T(80-200m²) 16A CEE

1. ABFIKLMNOQRS
2. CJNSVXYZ
3. CGIKW
4. (Q+U+X+Y)
5. ABDEFGIJKLMNOPUWXZ
6. ACDEFGK(N 1km)P

The campsite is right by River Weser, 10 min, walk to the centre. Close to a wooded area with walking options. Artistically furnished toilet block. Eco and hygiene tax not included with CampingCard ACSI. Supplement for pitches on 1st row by the Weser.

From Paderborn: In Hameln, follow B1. Turn left before Weser Bridge, dir. Rinteln. CP is signposted. From Hildesheim: Turn right directly after Weser Bridge, then turn right. After 300m follow the signposts.

CC € 25 *1/3-28/3 2/4-8/5 13/5-17/5 3/6-30/6 1/9-4/11*

N 52°06'33'' E 09°20'52''

Hann. Münden, D-34346 / Niedersachsen

442

Spiegelburg Camping und Gasthaus
Zella 1-2
+49 55 41 90 47 11
28/3 - 31/10
info@gasthausspiegelburg.de

20ha 80T(100m²) 16A CEE

1. AIKLMNQRS
2. CIJNOSUWXY
3. AIKUWX
4. (Q+U+Y+Z)
5. GIJMNOPUWZ
6. EFGJ(N 5km)PV

Campsite located on the River Werra in wooded surroundings 5 kilometres from the half-timbered village of Hann. Münden. The cafe/restaurant and the recreation room are open for the whole camping period. The surroundings are perfect for walking, cycling and watersports. River is perfect for canoeing.

A7 Kassel-Göttingen, 2nd exit at roundabout B80 Hann. Münden then left at bridge over the Werra. Follow camping signs.

CC € 23 *28/3-8/5 20/5-29/5 2/6-7/7 1/9-30/10*

N 51°23'43'' E 09°43'31''

Haren/Ems, D-49733 / Niedersachsen

443

Knaus Campingpark Haren
Kirchstraße 52
+49 5 93 27 33 89 77
1/3 - 3/11
haren@knauscamp.de

5ha 150T(100-150m²) 16A CEE

1. ACDEIJKLMNQRUV
2. FIJOSWXYZ
3. AGKMNPSUW
4. (Q)
5. ABDFGJKLNPUWZ
6. CEFGJ(N 0,5km)

A pleasant campsite which has the facilities of a large site and the peace and quiet of a small site, thanks to its unique location on the edge of the small town of Haren.

A31 Meppen - Emden exit 9 to Haren (B408). Continue following 408 towards Haren Ost/Eurohafen. Then left towards Yachthafen. The campsite is on the left, indicated with signs.

CC € 27 *1/3-8/5 12/5-17/5 22/5-28/5 3/6-21/6 3/9-3/11*

N 52°47'10'' E 07°14'25''

Heinsen, D-37649 / Niedersachsen

444

Weserbergland Camping
Weserstraße 66
+49 55 35 87 33
15/4 - 15/10
info@weserbergland-camping.com

2,5ha 128T(120m²) 10A CEE

1 ADIKLMNORTU
2 CJOSVXY
3 ACGHIKPSWX
4 (C 1/5-15/10)(Q+Z)
5 ABCDGIJKLMNOPQUWX
6 ACEFGHK(N 2km)OPTV

A real family campsite in beautiful countryside and peacefully located on the Weser. Own slipway and an ideal base for walking and cycling trips. Fishing and canoeing possible. Swimming pool provided.

Via Hameln and Bodenwerder to Heinsen, B83. Follow signs.

CC € 25 15/4-5/7 22/8-15/10

N 51°53'07" E 09°26'33"

Hohegeiß/Braunlage (Harz), D-38700 / Niedersachsen

445

Camping Am Bärenbache****
Bärenbachweg 10
+49 55 83 13 06
1/1 - 31/12
info@campingplatz-hohegeiss.de

3ha 124T(80-100m²) 6-16A

1 ACDIKLMNOQRS
2 BMNSUVWXYZ
3 CIKLS
4 (A+Q+R)
5 ABDEFGIJKLMNOPUWZ
6 CDEFGK(N 0km)OP

Centrally located in the Harz. Conveniently situated for all the sights in the area. Plenty of walking and skiing opportunities. Close to a swimming pool located in the middle of the forest. Several restaurants in walking distance in the village. Various activities are organised during the holidays. Camping equipment available.

A7 Kassel-Hannover, exit 72 Göttingen. Via Herzberg and Walkenried (or Braunlage) to Hohegeiß.

CC € 21 1/1-5/5 21/5-21/6 1/9-31/12

N 51°39'25" E 10°40'04"

Lünne, D-48480 / Niedersachsen

446

Camping Blauer See
Moorlager Str. 4a
+49 5 90 69 33 04 12
12/4 - 1/11
info@campingplatz-blauer-see.de

2,3ha 30T(80-120m²) 10A CEE

1 AFHJKLMNPQR
2 AFSXYZ
3 BKMSZ
5 ABFGIJMPUWZ
6 CEFHK(N 2km)

At the entrance of the campsite is a large meadow for pitching tents. Along the hedge the pitches have electric hookup points and are numbered. The lake with beach is adjacent to the field. A beautiful area for cycling.

A30 Hengelo-Osnabrück, exit 7, turn left towards Lingen. Campsite is signposted before Lünne.

CC € 21 12/4-8/5 13/5-17/5 21/5-29/5 3/6-21/6 19/8-1/11

N 52°24'48" E 07°24'41"

Meppen, D-49716 / Niedersachsen

447

Knaus Campingpark Meppen
An der Bleiche 1a
+49 5 93 18 81 18 48
1/3 - 3/11
meppen@knauscamp.de

2,5ha 150T(100-150m²) 16A CEE

1 ACDE**I**JKLMNQ**R**UV
2 DIJSWXYZ
3 AKMN**W**X
5 **AB**DFGJKLNP**S**UWXY
6 FGJL(N 0,2km)

Campsite located on a tributary of the River Ems in the middle of a small town that is more than 1000 years old, but with the facilities of a larger town, which of course are available to campsite guests.

A31 Lingen- Emden exit 22 Meppen then 9 km to centre of Meppen. B70 from Lingen or Papenburg exit Freilichtbühne then turn left. Campsite on left on the other side of the Ems after 100 metres.

L61, B402, Meppen, A31, Haselünne, L47, L48, B213, B70

CC € 27 *1/3-8/5 12/5-17/5 22/5-28/5 3/6-21/6 19/7-2/8 3/9-3/11*

N 52°41'32'' E 07°17'11''

Müden/Örtze (Gem. Faßberg), D-29328 / Niedersachsen

448

Camping Sonnenberg
Sonnenberg 3
+49 50 53 98 71 74
15/4 - 15/10
info@campingsonnenberg.com

5ha 80T(150-350m²) 6-16A

1 AE**I**KLMNOQRS
2 BMNSWXYZ
3 ACIKLU
4 (Q 15/5-15/9)(T+V+X+Z)
5 **AB**DGIJKLMNOP**S**UWXYZ
6 ACEFGHJ(N 1,5km)OPTV

Peaceful campsite located in the middle of the Lüneburgerheide. An ideal base for walking and cycling trips and for enjoying the beautiful countryside. Free access to municipal swimming pool.

A7 Hannover-Hamburg exit Soltau-Ost, then on route B71 to Munster. After Munster exit Celle. In Müden follow camping signs.

CC € 21 *15/4-7/7 1/9-15/10*

N 52°53'16'' E 10°05'58''

Neustadt/Mardorf, D-31535 / Niedersachsen

449

Campingplatz Mardorf GmbH
Uferweg 68
+49 5 03 65 29
1/1 - 31/12
info@camping-steinhuder-meer.de

4,2ha 80T(70-110m²) 16A CEE

1 ABCD**I**JKLMNOQRS
2 BEJNSVWXYZ
3 **G**IKMN**W**Z
4 (Q+T 1/4-31/10)
5 **AB**DEFGIJMNO**P**UWXZ
6 ACDEFJ(N 1,5km)OPSU

Water sports campsite on the Steinhuder lake. Good cycling and walking possibilities. Excellent toilet facilities.

B6 Nienburg-Neustadt. In Neustadt dir Steinhuder Meer. In Mardorf follow campsite signs. SatNav: Entrance is on Weidebruchsweg.

CC € 27 *1/1-20/3 21/5-28/5 5/6-30/6 1/9-31/12*

N 52°29'30'' E 09°19'29''

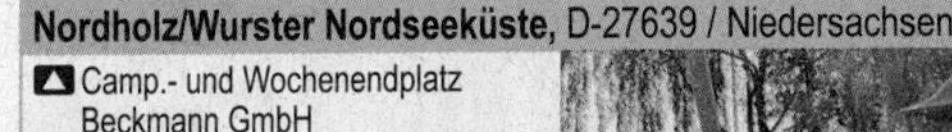

Nordholz/Wurster Nordseeküste, D-27639 / Niedersachsen

450

Camp.- und Wochenendplatz Beckmann GmbH
Wanhödenerstraße 28
+49 47 41 85 88
1/1 - 31/12
post@nordholz-camping.de

5,5ha 190T(80-160m²) 16A CEE

1 ACDEIJKLMNOQRS
2 BISWXYZ
3 ACIKMSU
4 (B+G 1/5-15/9) (Q+R+T+U+X+Z 1/4-15/9)
5 **AB**DGIJMNOPQUWXZ
6 BEFG**K**(N 3km)OPV

Campsite with friendly managers. Toilet block is very well-maintained. Naval airfield nearby with a museum on the development of private and naval aviation. Suitable as a stopover campsite.

A27, exit Nordholz, after about 1800m the campsite is on the left.

Wurster Nordseeküste, B73, A27, L135, L118, L129, L119

CC € 19 *1/1-8/5 22/5-23/6 21/8-31/12*

N 53°45'11'' E 08°38'22''

Osterode (Harz), D-37520 / Niedersachsen

451

Campingplatz Eulenburg****
Scheerenberger Straße 100
+49 55 22 66 11
1/1 - 31/12
ferien@eulenburg-camping.de

4,1ha 65T(80-200m²) 16A CEE

1 ACD**I**KLMNOQRS
2 BDIJSWXYZ
3 CIKL**O**PS**T**
4 (B+G 15/5-15/9) (Q+R+T+U+X+Z)
5 **AB**DEFGIJKLMNO**P**RUWZ
6 CDEFGKL(N 2km)OPUV

Campsite is on the edge of a forest and has demarcated and non-demarcated pitches. The campsite is surrounded by streams and is in a wooded area with romantic footpaths. TV reception available at many pitches using your own co-axial cable. There are two charging stations for electric cars.

Motorway A7 Kassel-Hannover, exit 67 Seesen. Drive towards Osterode (Sösestausee). Exit Osterode-Süd. Follow the signs to Sösestausee.

A7, B242, B498, Osterode am Harz, B241, B243, L521, L523, B247, B27

CC € 27 *2/1-24/3 2/4-5/5 21/5-20/6 1/9-21/12*

N 51°43'38'' E 10°16'59''

Ostrhauderfehn, D-26842 / Niedersachsen

452

Camping- u. Freizeitanlage Idasee
Idafehn-Nord 77B
+49 49 52 99 42 97
1/1 - 31/12
info@campingidasee.de

7,4ha 75T(100m²) 10A CEE

1 A**I**JKLMNOQRS
2 AFIJOSTUVWXYZ
3 ABCHKMNPSUWZ
4 **N**(Q+T+U+Z)
5 **AB**DEFGIJKLMNOP**Q**R**S**UWXYZ
6 ABCDEFG**K**L(N 2km)OSU

Located on the Idasee with many recreational possibilities: fishing, swimming and water skiing. One of the most beautiful cycling routes in Germany begins close to the campsite: the German Fehn route through the typical East Frisian landscape with its peat marshes, canals and rivers. Adventure playground for children.

Groningen-Leer, then B70 direction Lingen. In Folmhusen turn left B438 direction Ostrhauderfehn, then left B72. Follow signs.

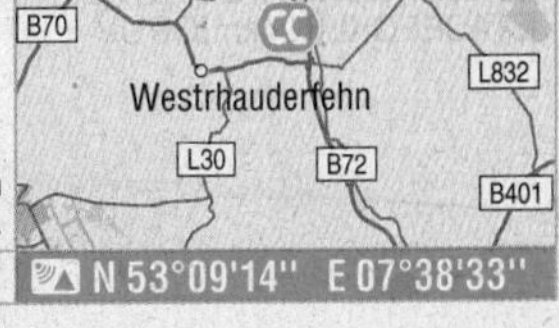

CC € 19 *1/1-27/3 2/4-7/5 21/5-28/5 3/6-24/6 25/8-30/9 7/10-31/12*

N 53°09'14'' E 07°38'33''

Oyten, D-28876 / Niedersachsen

453

Knaus Campingpark Oyten****
Oyter See 1
+49 42 07 28 78
1/3 - 3/11
oyten@knauscamp.de

3ha 101T(70-100m²) 16A CEE

1 ACD**I**JKLMNOQRS
2 AEIJOSXYZ
3 AC**G**KS**WZ**
4 **I**M(Q+T)
5 **AB**DEFGIJKLMNOPUWZ
6 ABCEFG**K**(N 2km)O

A lovely family campsite next to a lake. Being located on the A1 it is perfect as a stopover campsite en route to Scandinavia.

A1 Bremen-Hamburg, exit 52 direction Oyten. Left at Lidl, through Oyten then direction Oyter See and follow camping signs.

CC € 27 1/3-8/5 12/5-17/5 22/5-28/5 3/6-21/6 19/7-2/8 3/9-3/11

N 53°02'47'' E 09°00'24''

Schüttorf, D-48465 / Niedersachsen

454

Camping Quendorfer See
Weiße Riete 3
+49 59 23 90 29 39
22/3 - 3/11
info@camping-schuettorf.de

1,5ha 73T(100-120m²) 10A CEE

1 ACDE**I**JKLMNOQRTU
2 AEIJSVWXY
3 AIKSZ
4 (Q+R)
5 **AB**DEFGHJNP**T**UWXY
6 CDEFG**K**(N 2km)OPT

This rustic campsite is situated behind a row of old trees. Spacious pitches, open views, very well maintained toilet facilities. Within walking distance of a lovely lake for swimming, surfing and fishing.

A1/A30 exit 4 Schüttorf-Nord or A31 exit 28 Schüttorf-Ost towards town centre, follow camping signs.

CC € 25 22/5-24/5 2/6-1/7 1/9-1/10

N 52°20'19'' E 07°13'36''

Seeburg, D-37136 / Niedersachsen

455

Comfort-Camping Seeburger See
Seestraße 20
+49 55 07 13 19
27/3 - 29/10
info@campingseeburgersee.com

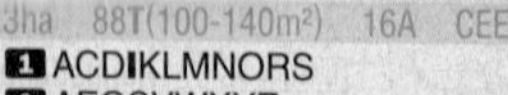

3ha 88T(100-140m²) 16A CEE

1 ACD**I**KLMNORS
2 AEOSVWXYZ
3 CE**G**HIJKL**O**P**QR**SWZ
4 (G 15/5-15/9)(Q+R+T+U)
5 **AB**DFGIJKLOPQUWXYZ
6 ACEFGKL(N 4km)OPUV

Well-maintained family campsite by Seeburger See. You can go swimming, hire a rowing boat or pedalo or go fishing in the lake. The campsite's location, amid stunning nature reserves, makes it an ideal base for hours of walking and cycling fun. Göttingen Forest is very popular with climbers. The German university city of Göttingen with its lovely churches is only 20 km away.

Motorway A7, exit 72 Göttingen Nord. Via the B27/B446 direction Duderstadt.

CC € 23 1/5-9/5 12/5-17/5 21/5-1/6 10/6-14/6 17/6-21/6 2/9-1/10

N 51°33'49'' E 10°09'13''

Stove/Hamburg, D-21423 / Niedersachsen

456

- Campingplatz Stover Strand International*****
- Stover Strand 10
- +49 4 17 74 30
- 1/1 - 31/12
- info@stover-strand.de

30ha 130T 16A CEE

1. ACD**I**JKLMNOQ**R**S
2. ACEIJOSVWXYZ
3. CD**G**HIKMNPSU**W**X
4. (**A** 1/5-1/10)**N** (Q+S+T+U+Y+Z)
5. **AB**DEFGJLN**PQ**RUWXYZ
6. ACDEFGHKLM(N 0km)O**P**Q TUVW

Modern five star campsite located on the Elbe. Ideal for visiting Hamburg. The campsite has its own restaurant, snack bar and market produce. Plenty of sports and recreational opportunities.

Motorway A7 Hannover-Hamburg, exit Maschener Kreuz direction Winsen/ Lüneburg. A39, then the B404 exit to Geesthacht. Exit in Rönne direction Stove. Continue to end of Stover Strand road. 2nd campsite at the end of the access road.

L314 · L219 · A25 · Geesthacht · B5 · B404 · L217 · Winsen (Luhe) · A250

CC € 27 *8/1-22/3 8/4-29/4 21/5-29/5 5/6-30/6 1/9-30/9 10/10-20/12*

N 53°25'27'' E 10°17'44''

Stuhr/Groß Mackenstedt, D-28816 / Niedersachsen

457

- Campingplatz Steller See
- Zum Steller See 15
- +49 42 06 64 90
- 1/4 - 30/9

9ha 60T(80-100m²) 16A CEE

1. ACDIKLMNOQ**R**S
2. AEISXY
3. BCKPSZ
4. (Q)(T 15/5-15/9) (U+Y 1/5-30/9)
5. **AB**DEFGIJKLMNO**P**UWZ
6. BCEFGH**J**(N 2km)OTU

This family campsite is located around a clear swimming lake no less than 60,000 m² in a nature reserve. Camping is located just a few minutes from the highway on the outskirts of Bremen. All types of watersports (without motor) in the swimming lake.

From the A1 take the Stuhr intersection (from Hamburg or Osnabrück), first exit 58, right at exit dir. Groß Mackenstedt. Enter village and turn right. Follow 'Steller See' signs.

CC € 23 *2/4-25/4 2/5-7/5 22/5-18/6 1/9-30/9*

N 53°00'25'' E 08°41'33''

Uetze, D-31311 / Niedersachsen

458

- Camping Irenensee****
- Fritz-Meinecke-Weg 2
- +49 5 17 39 81 20
- 1/1 - 31/12
- info@irenensee.de

45ha 110T(80-125m²) 6-10A CEE

1. ACD**I**JKLMNOQRS
2. AEJNSVWXY
3. ABC**G**HKMPS**W**Z
4. (Q+R 1/4-15/10)(T 4/7-14/8) (U 8/6-30/9)(Y 1/3-30/11)
5. **AB**DEFGI**J**KLMNO**PQR**UWXYZ
6. FGK(N 1km)O

Campsite with every amenity. Some toilet facilities have been renovated and look good. The rest will follow in steps. Situated by a natural lake with sandy beach. Plenty of water recreation for children.

Motorway A2 direction Celle, exit 49 Burgdorf. Then on to the B188 direction Gifhorn/Uetze.

CC € 19 *1/1-16/3 2/4-12/5 27/5-20/6 4/9-30/9 1/11-31/12*

N 52°27'56'' E 10°09'36''

Walkenried, D-37445 / Niedersachsen

459

Knaus Campingpark Walkenried****
Ellricherstraße 7
+49 5 52 57 78
1/1 - 3/11, 20/12 - 31/12
walkenried@knauscamp.de

5,5ha 110T(70-100m²) 16A CEE

1 ACDIJKLMNOQRS
2 BLSUVWYZ
3 CIKLMNPRS
4 (F)N (Q+R 1/1-3/11,20/12-31/12) (U+Y)
5 ABDEFGIJKLMNOPUWXYZ
6 CDEFGH(N 1km)OP

A lovely campsite with a fantastic and friendly couple running it. Extremely clean toilets and excellent service. CampingCard ACSI rate does not include entrance to indoor pool.

Motorway A7, exit 67 Seesen and via Herzberg and Bad Sachsa to Walkenried.

CC € 27 7/1-8/5 12/5-17/5 22/5-28/5 3/6-21/6 3/9-2/11

N 51°35'21'' E 10°37'28''

Werlte, D-49757 / Niedersachsen

460

Camping Hümmlinger Land****
Rastdorfer Straße 80
+49 59 51 53 53
1/1 - 31/12
info@huemmlingerland.de

1,8ha 59T(80-140m²) 16A CEE

1 ACDEIKLMNORS
2 STWXY
3 CIJKS
4 N(Q+R+U)
5 ABDFGHJLNPUW
6 CEFGK(N 3km)OS

A well-kept campsite with excellent toilet facilities just outside the town of Werlte. The municipality has an active tourism policy. Good cycling region, now with cycle junctions.

B233 Emmen-Meppen-Cloppenburg direction Werlte. Campsite signposted (direction Rastdorf).

CC € 23 2/1-6/5 23/5-28/6 26/8-27/12

N 52°52'12'' E 07°41'17''

Wiesmoor, D-26639 / Niedersachsen

461

Cp. & Bungalowpark Ottermeer*****
Am Ottermeer 52
+49 49 44 94 98 93
1/1 - 31/12
camping@wiesmoor.de

00ha 205T(90-120m²) 16A CEE

1 CDIKLMNOQRS
2 AEOSTVWXYZ
3 ABCGIKMPSWZ
4 J(Q+R+T+U 1/4-15/10)
5 ABDFGIJKLMNOPRUWXY
6 CDEFGHK(N 2km)OT

Comfortable campsite located on a beautiful natural lake. There are lovely cycle routes along the Fehn wetlands where peat is still collected. The floral town of Wiesmoor is 1.5 km from the campsite.

Motorway A31 Groningen-Leer. Exit 2 Leer-Ost towards Aurich B72/B436. Then take exit B436 Bagband towards Wiesmoor. In Wiesmoor the campsite is clearly signposted 'Ottermeer'.

CC € 23 1/1-27/3 2/4-7/5 21/5-28/5 3/6-24/6 25/8-30/9 7/10-31/12

N 53°24'56'' E 07°42'38''

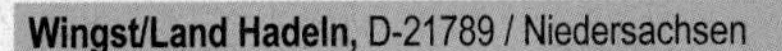

Wingst/Land Hadeln, D-21789 / Niedersachsen

462

- Knaus Campingpark Wingst****
- Schwimmbadallee 13
- +49 47 78 76 04
- 1/3 - 3/11
- wingst@knauscamp.de

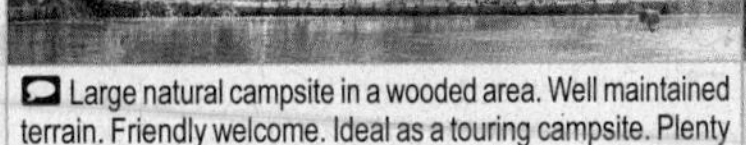

9ha 265**T**(100m²) 16A CEE

- **1** ACDE**I**JKLMNOQRS
- **2** BEJLMSUWXYZ
- **3** ACEHKMP**R**SU**W**
- **4** (B 1/5-15/9)(F+H)IJ (Q+R+U+V+X+Y)
- **5** **AB**DFGIJKLMNOP**QR**UWXZ
- **6** ACEFG**K**(N 3km)OPTUV

Large natural campsite in a wooded area. Well maintained terrain. Friendly welcome. Ideal as a touring campsite. Plenty of activities with 50 metres of the site.

Road B73 Cuxhaven-Stade exit Wingst Schwimmbad.

CC € 27 *1/3-30/6 19/7-2/8 1/9-2/11*

N 53°45'09'' E 09°05'00''

Winsen (Aller), D-29308 / Niedersachsen

463

- Camping Allerblick
- Auf der Hude 1
- +49 5 14 39 31 99
- 1/1 - 31/12
- info@camping-allerblick.de

13ha 215**T**(100-150m²) 16A CEE

- **1** ABCDE**I**KLMNOQ**R**S
- **2** ADJNOSVWXYZ
- **3** ACE**G**HIKP**Q**SW**X**
- **4** (Q+R)(T 1/4-31/10)(U) (Y 1/1-31/12)
- **5** **AB**DFGIJKLMNOPUWZ
- **6** ABCDEFG**K**(N 0,5km)OPUV

A pleasantly landscaped campsite. Some of the pitches are in a big field next to the Aller, some in a park-like grounds. The centre of Winsen is within walking distance.

A7 Hannover-Bremen, exit Allertal (petrol station) direction Celle. Signposted to the campsite in Winsen (turn right). Campsite near centre of Winsen.

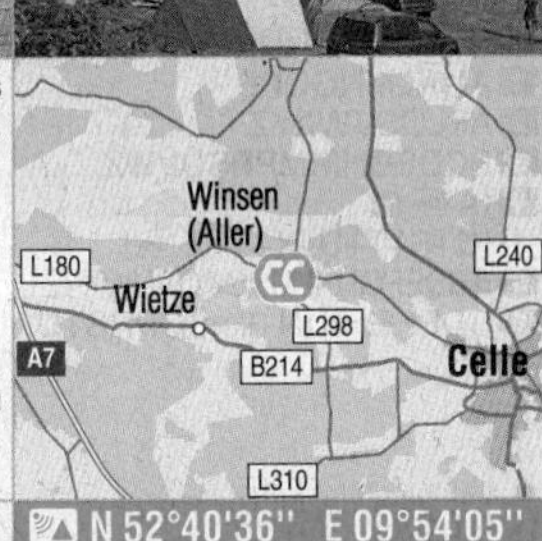

CC € 27 *1/1-7/5 27/5-23/6 18/8-2/10 21/10-31/12*

N 52°40'36'' E 09°54'05''

Wolfshagen (Harz), D-38685 / Niedersachsen

464

- Campingplatz Am Krähenberg***
- Am Mauerkamp 21
- +49 53 26 96 92 81
- 1/1 - 31/12
- post@campingplatz-wolfshagen.de

6,4ha 70**T**(70-100m²) 16A CEE

- **1** ACD**I**JKLMNRS
- **2** BJLNSUXY
- **3** CIKLSZ
- **4** (**B**+H 15/5-15/9)**N**(Q+R) (U+Y 1/1-31/10,1/12-31/12) (Z)
- **5** **AB**DFGIJKLMNOPUWZ
- **6** CDEFGK(N 1,5km)OPU

Camping 'Am Krähenberg' in the spa town Wolfshagen is in a romantic location in the middle of Harz Nature Park. The campsite is open all year round. There is a heated open-air swimming pool right next to the campsite in the forest. The restaurant has regional dishes and a children's playground, among other things, on the grounds.

Motorway A7 Hannover-Kassel, exit 66 Rhüden, then direction Goslar via the B82. At the end of Langelsheim, turn south, and continue for another 4 km.

CC € 21 *1/1-9/5 21/5-20/6 1/9-15/12*

N 51°54'04'' E 10°19'39''

Zetel/Astederfeld, D-26340 / Niedersachsen

465

Campingplatz am Königssee
Tarbarger Landstr. 30
+49 44 52 17 06
1/3 - 31/10
info@campingplatz-am-koenigssee.de

2,5ha 40T(100-150m²) 10-16A CEE

1 ADIKLMNOPQRUV
2 AEOSTX
3 ACGKPUZ
4 (Q)
5 ABDGIJKLMNPUWXY
6 EFGK(N 4km)OPU

Peacefully located campsite by a swimming lake in the middle of a nature reserve. Extensive cycle path network, not far from the coast and the German moor route.

A28 exit 6 Westerstede, L815 direction Zetel. After 14 km turn left towards Astederfeld. Campsite signposted.

CC € 23 1/3-4/4 20/4-8/5 21/5-30/6 1/9-31/10

N 53°21'19" E 07°55'46"

Augstfelde/Plön, D-24306 / Schleswig-Holstein

466

Camping Augstfelde-Vierer See****
Augstfelde 1
+49 45 22 81 28
28/3 - 20/10
info@augstfelde.de

20,6ha 255T(90-110m²) 16A CEE

1 AIJKLMNOQRS
2 AFLOSVWXYZ
3 BCDEGHIKMPRSUVWZ
4 (A)N
(Q+S+T+U+X+Y+Z)
5 ABDEFGIJKLMNOPQRUWXYZ
6 CDEFGHK(N 3km)OPRSTU

A lovely family campsite on the Vierermeer lake with a 1 km long private sandy beach. Clear swimming water. Close to the Plöner lake plateau.

From the A1 to Eutin, then towards Plön via the B76. Clearly indicated after Bösdorf exit.

CC € 19 28/3-8/5 21/5-6/7 1/9-20/10

N 54°07'43" E 10°27'18"

Glücksburg, D-24960 / Schleswig-Holstein

467

Ostseecamp Glücksburg-Holnis****
An der Promenade 1
+49 46 31 62 20 71
1/4 - 15/10
info@ostseecamp-holnis.de

0ha 125T(100m²) 6-16A CEE

1 ABCDHKLMNOQRS
2 AHJSTWXY
3 ACGHIKMPQSUWY
4 (Q)(R 1/7-31/8)
(T+U+X+Z)
5 ABDEFGIJKLMNOPQUWXYZ
6 CDEFGK(N 5km)PUV

A clean campsite with a lovely beach cafe/bistro along the east coast on one of the most beautiful sandy beaches of the Baltic Sea. Many options in the surrounding area. Cycling, walking and water sports.

From Glücksburg drive towards Holnis. Camp site well signposted.

CC € 25 1/5-8/5 27/5-21/6 1/9-30/9

N 54°51'26" E 09°35'29"

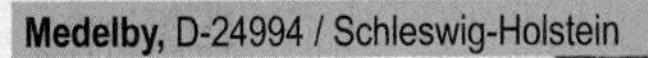

Medelby, D-24994 / Schleswig-Holstein

468

Camping Mitte
Sonnenhügel 1
+49 46 05 18 93 91
1/1 - 31/12
info@camping-mitte.de

5,2ha 154T(tot 120m²) 10-16A CEE

1 ACDHKLMNOQRS
2 SUWXY
3 ACDKSU
4 (B 1/5-31/8)(**F**+Q+R+T)
5 **AB**DEFGIJKLMNOPQRUWXYZ
6 CDEFGK(N 1km)OPT

A modern, quiet, open campsite in the middle of a nature area. Flexible in all kinds of ways to spend your time. Indoor swimming pool open from 15 June to 15 August.

A7 exit 2, road 199 direction Niebüll. Follow signs from Wallsbüll.

€ 27 *1/1-27/3 2/4-8/5 13/5-16/5 21/5-30/6 1/9-24/12*

N 54°48'54'' E 09°09'49''

Salem, D-23911 / Schleswig-Holstein

469

Naturcamping Salemer See
Seestr. 60
+49 4 54 18 25 54
28/3 - 31/10
info@camping-salem.de

25ha 150T(35-80m²) 16A CEE

1 ACD**I**KLMNOQ**R**S
2 ABFLMNOSTUWXYZ
3 CDIKP**R**SU**W**
4 (Q+U+X+Z)
5 **AB**DFGJMNOPUWXZ
6 ABCDEFJ(N 6km)O**P**

Forest campsite by a lake, ideal for canoeists and SUP enthusiasts. There are walking and cycling routes from the campsite. In addition to camping pitches directly by the lake, there are pitches on various higher terraces, one of which is specially designed for larger campers. There is also a beautiful playground on the upper grounds.

From A20, B207 towards Ratzeburg. In Ratzeburg B208/L203 towards Seedorf. After 4 km, exit Salem, follow campsite signs. Is well signposted.

€ 19 *1/4-30/6 1/9-31/10*

N 53°38'58'' E 10°50'07''

Scharbeutz, D-23683 / Schleswig-Holstein

470

Ostseecamp Lübecker Bucht Gmbh
Bormwiese 1
+49 1 52 04 14 13 45
1/4 - 31/10
info@ostseecamp-luebecker-bucht.de

5,5ha 85T(80-160m²) 16A CEE

1 ACD**I**JKLMNOPQRTU
2 IJMSWXYZ
3 ACMNS
4 **N**(Q+R+U+Y+Z)
5 **AB**FGHIJKLMNOPQUWXYZ
6 BCEFGHKL(N 1km)OP

Beautifully situated on the edge of a nature reserve. Close to the motorway and beach. Bicycle hire and a good restaurant.

Eutin, Neustadt in Holstein, L176, A1, L184, B432, L309, B76

A1 HH-Puttgarden/Fehmarn. Exit Haffkrug/Scharbeutz, B76 direction Eutin, near the motorway.

€ 21 *20/4-3/5 12/5-19/6 10/9-1/10*

N 54°03'18'' E 10°43'49''

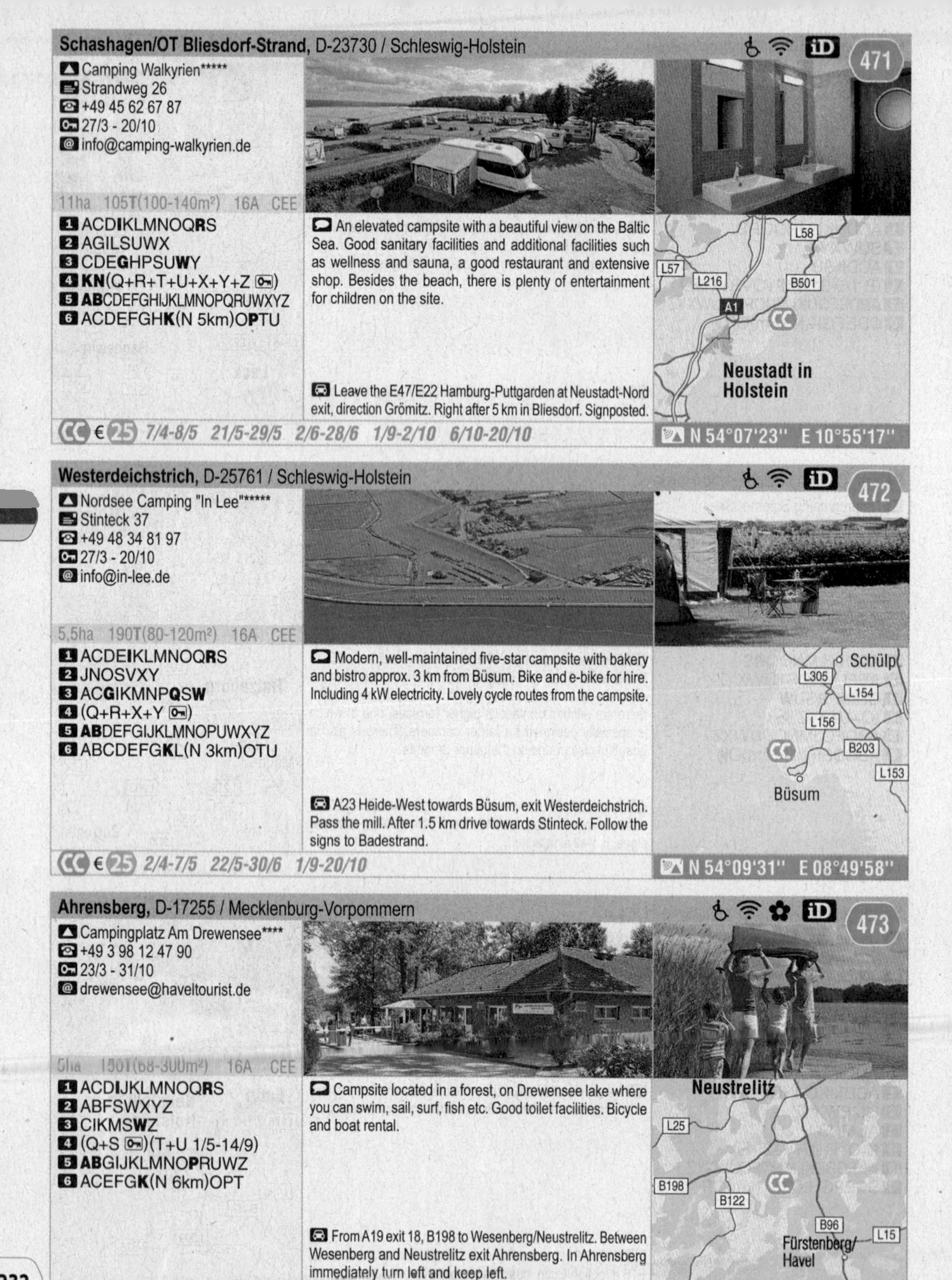

Schashagen/OT Bliesdorf-Strand, D-23730 / Schleswig-Holstein

471

Camping Walkyrien*****
Strandweg 26
+49 45 62 67 87
27/3 - 20/10
info@camping-walkyrien.de

11ha 105T(100-140m²) 16A CEE

1 ACD**I**KLMNOQ**RS**
2 AGILSUWX
3 CDE**G**HPSU**WY**
4 **KN**(Q+R+T+U+X+Y+Z)
5 **AB**CDEFGHIJKLMNOPQRUWXYZ
6 ACDEFGH**K**(N 5km)O**P**TU

An elevated campsite with a beautiful view on the Baltic Sea. Good sanitary facilities and additional facilities such as wellness and sauna, a good restaurant and extensive shop. Besides the beach, there is plenty of entertainment for children on the site.

Leave the E47/E22 Hamburg-Puttgarden at Neustadt-Nord exit, direction Grömitz. Right after 5 km in Bliesdorf. Signposted.

CC € 25 *7/4-8/5 21/5-29/5 2/6-28/6 1/9-2/10 6/10-20/10*

N 54°07'23'' E 10°55'17''

Westerdeichstrich, D-25761 / Schleswig-Holstein

472

Nordsee Camping "In Lee"*****
Stinteck 37
+49 48 34 81 97
27/3 - 20/10
info@in-lee.de

5,5ha 190T(80-120m²) 16A CEE

1 ACDE**I**KLMNOQ**R**S
2 JNOSVXY
3 AC**G**IKMNP**Q**S**W**
4 (Q+R+X+Y)
5 **AB**DEFGIJKLMNOPUWXYZ
6 ABCDEFG**K**L(N 3km)OTU

Modern, well-maintained five-star campsite with bakery and bistro approx. 3 km from Büsum. Bike and e-bike for hire. Including 4 kW electricity. Lovely cycle routes from the campsite.

A23 Heide-West towards Büsum, exit Westerdeichstrich. Pass the mill. After 1.5 km drive towards Stinteck. Follow the signs to Badestrand.

CC € 25 *2/4-7/5 22/5-30/6 1/9-20/10*

N 54°09'31'' E 08°49'58''

Ahrensberg, D-17255 / Mecklenburg-Vorpommern

473

Campingplatz Am Drewensee****
+49 3 98 12 47 90
23/3 - 31/10
drewensee@haveltourist.de

5ha 150T(68-300m²) 16A CEE

1 ACD**I**JKLMNOQ**R**S
2 ABFSWXYZ
3 CIKMS**W**Z
4 (Q+S)(T+U 1/5-14/9)
5 **AB**GIJKLMNO**P**RUWZ
6 ACEFG**K**(N 6km)OPT

Campsite located in a forest, on Drewensee lake where you can swim, sail, surf, fish etc. Good toilet facilities. Bicycle and boat rental.

From A19 exit 18, B198 to Wesenberg/Neustrelitz. Between Wesenberg and Neustrelitz exit Ahrensberg. In Ahrensberg immediately turn left and keep left.

CC € 21 *23/3-28/3 2/4-8/5 12/5-17/5 21/5-6/7 31/8-31/10*

N 53°15'46'' E 13°03'03''

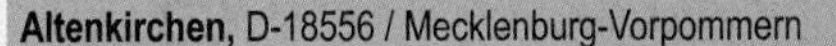

Altenkirchen, D-18556 / Mecklenburg-Vorpommern

474

Camping Drewoldke****
Zittkower Weg 27
+49 38 39 11 29 65
1/1 - 31/12
info@camping-auf-ruegen.de

9ha 340T(80m²) 16A CEE

1 ACD**I**KLMNOQ**R**S
2 ABGNPQSTXYZ
3 ACIKSWY
4 (Q 🔑)(R+T+U 1/4-30/9) (Z 1/4-1/10)
5 **AB**DEFGHIJKLMNO**PQ**RUWZ
6 ACDEFGH**K**(N 3km) OPQSTV

The campsite is located 10 metres from the Baltic Sea coast. Excellent base for cycle trips to sights such as: cape Arkena with chalk cliffs, historic fishing village Vitt, the historical town of Altenkirchen with the oldest church in Rügen and Breege harbour for boat trips. National Park Jasmund with King's Chair is 20 km away.

B96 Stralsund-Bergen dir. Sassnitz then dir. Altenkirchen. Campsite signposted.

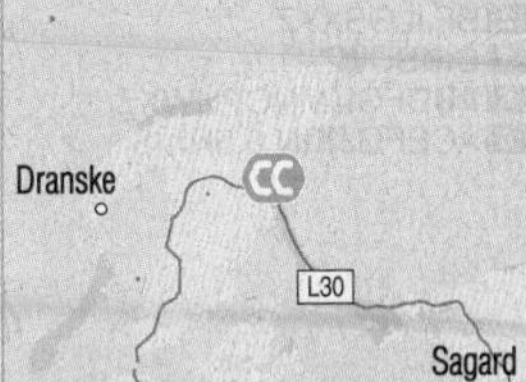

CC € 21 *1/1-6/5 23/5-20/6 1/9-31/12*

N 54°38'04'' E 13°22'24''

Altenkirchen, D-18556 / Mecklenburg-Vorpommern

475

Knaus Camping- und Ferienhauspark Rügen****
Zittkower Weg 30
+49 3 83 91 43 46 48
1/1 - 7/1, 1/3 - 31/12
ruegen@knauscamp.de

3,7ha 108T(80m²) 16A CEE

1 ACD**I**KLMNOQRS
2 GNPQSXY
3 CIKN**W**Y
4 **N**(Q 1/4-31/10)(R 🔑) (T+U+Z 1/4-31/10)
5 **AB**DFGIJKLMNOP**R**UWXYZ
6 ABCDEFG**K**(N 2km)OP

A campsite on Rügen directly by the sea with beautiful views of the peaceful, calm Baltic Sea. Ideal for surfers. 3 family baths, a sauna and even a whirlpool. A cycle and footpath goes from the campsite right along the beach to the famous chalk cliffs and the fishing village of Vitt which is a protected monument.

Coming from Sagard B96 to Altenkirchen, past Juliusruh. Turn right after 300m and the campsite is about 1200m beyond the woodland campsite.

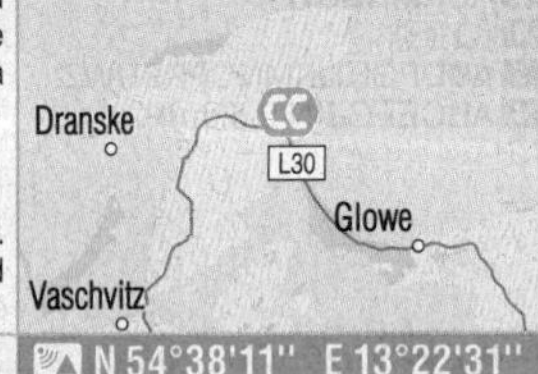

CC € 27 *1/3-8/5 12/5-17/5 22/5-28/5 3/6-21/6 3/9-30/12*

N 54°38'11'' E 13°22'31''

Dierhagen-Strand, D-18347 / Mecklenburg-Vorpommern

476

OstseeCamp Dierhagen GbR
Ernst-Moritz-Arndt Str. 1A
+49 38 22 68 07 78
15/3 - 31/10
info@ostseecamp-dierhagen.de

6ha 300T(60-125m²) 16A CEE

1 ACD**I**KLMNOQ**R**S
2 JSUVWXYZ
3 CIKMS
4 (Q+R+T 🔑)(U 25/5-30/9)
5 **AB**DFGIJKLMNOPUWZ
6 BCDEFG(N 0,7km)O**P**

Camp in the Baltic seaside resort of Dierhagen between the Baltic sea and Bodden in the heart of the Fischland-Darß-Zingst peninsula. Far from the noise and traffic you will be camping on a sunny field or in the light shade of deciduous and coniferous trees.

On B105 at Altheide take exit dir. Prerow, Ahrenshoop, then left at traffic lights dir. Dierhagen-Strand.

CC € 23 *15/3-7/5 22/5-23/6 6/9-31/10*

N 54°17'29'' E 12°20'37''

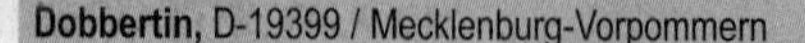

Dobbertin, D-19399 / Mecklenburg-Vorpommern

477

- Campingplatz am Dobbertiner See
- Am Zeltplatz 1
- +49 17 47 37 89 37
- 1/4 - 5/10
- dobbertincamping@aol.com

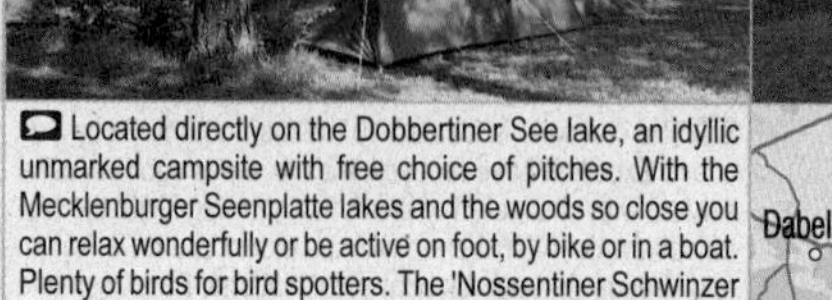

4ha 90T(100m²) 16A CEE

1 AF**I**KLMNOQRS
2 BFJLOSXYZ
3 CIKSU**W**Z
5 **AB**DFGIJMNO**P**UWXZ
6 ACEFGJ**K**(N 0,5km)S

Located directly on the Dobbertiner See lake, an idyllic unmarked campsite with free choice of pitches. With the Mecklenburger Seenplatte lakes and the woods so close you can relax wonderfully or be active on foot, by bike or in a boat. Plenty of birds for bird spotters. The 'Nossentiner Schwinzer Heide' and 'Sternberger Seenland' Nature reserves are close by.

A19 exit Malchow / A24 exit Parchim / A20 exit Bützow, continue towards Dobbertin. Follow camping signs.

€ 21 *1/4-30/6 1/9-5/10*

N 53°37'09'' E 12°03'54''

Freest, D-17440 / Mecklenburg-Vorpommern

478

- Camping Waldcamp Freest
- Dorfstrasse 75
- +49 38 37 02 05 38
- 1/4 - 1/10
- info@campingplatz-freest.de

3,5ha 80T(100-150m²) 16A CEE

1 ABC**I**JKLMNOQR
2 AGNSWXY
3 ACKMN**R**SWY
4 (Q)
5 **AB**DFGHIJKMNO**PRS**UWZ
6 ABCEFG**J**(N 2,5km)P

Space and tranquility characterise this campsite. On the edge of reedlands and with a view of the sea, 200 metres from the beach. Even, spacious pitches in the grass. Good area for cycling.

Freest is located on the L262. From Lubmin, turn left 100 m before the 'Freest' sign. This is where the built-up area begins. Campsite is signposted. Coming from the other direction, the campsite is on the right, at the end of the built-up area.

€ 23 *1/4-17/5 20/5-20/6 9/9-30/9*

N 54°08'22'' E 13°43'02''

Grambin/Ueckermünde, D-17375 / Mecklenburg-Vorpommern

479

- Campingpark Oderhaff
- Dorfstraße 66a
- +49 39 77 42 04 20
- 1/1 - 31/12
- info@campingpark-oderhaff.de

6,2ha 100T(80-100m²) 16A CEE

1 AD**I**JKLMNOPQRS
2 ABGJNOSTUXYZ
3 CKMU**W**Y
4 (Q+R+T+U+Z 1/5-30/9)
5 **AB**DFGHIJKMNPUWZ
6 ACDEFGJ(N 2,5km)OP

The Campingpark Oderhaff team welcomes you directly next to the white beach of Ueckermünde/Grambin.

B109 Anklam towards Pasewalk take exit Ducherow to Grambin.

€ 27 *1/5-18/5 21/5-4/6 31/8-1/10*

N 53°45'39'' E 14°00'39''

Groß Quassow/Userin, D-17237 / Mecklenburg-Vorpommern

480

Camping- und Ferienpark Havelberge*****
An den Havelbergen 1
+49 3 98 12 47 90
1/1 - 31/12
info@haveltourist.de

ACSI AWARDS WINNER

24ha 302T(90-287m²) 16A CEE

1 ACD**I**JKLNO**R**S
2 ABFLMOSTWXYZ
3 ACIKMNPSU**VW**Z
4 (**A** 1/7-31/8)**LN**(Q)
(R+T+U+Y 1/4-31/10)(Z)
5 **AB**DEFGIJKLMNOPQRUWXYZ
6 ACDEFG**K**(N 7km)OSTUV

For those who don't mind a big site and want to have everything: sauna, restaurant, shop, bicycle-boat rental, beach and disco.

Via the B198 from Mirow or Neustrelitz to Wesenberg. From there via Klein Quassow to Groß Quassow. It is signposted from Wesenberg.

CC € 23 *1/3-28/3 2/4-8/5 12/5-17/5 21/5-6/7 31/8-3/11*

N 53°18'32" E 13°00'08"

Jabel, D-17194 / Mecklenburg-Vorpommern

481

GenussFerien, Natur und Strandcamping
Am Heidenfriedhof 01
+49 39 92 97 67 12
1/4 - 31/10
rezeption@genuss-ferien.de

5ha 123T(80-150m²) 4-16A CEE

1 ABCD**I**KLMNQ**R**TU
2 ABFOSXYZ
3 CIKMS**WZ**
4 (Q+R+T+U+W+X+Z)
5 **AB**DGIJMNOPUWX
6 BCEFGJ(N 9,9km)OPT

Quiet campsite located by a lake amid the countryside. Good cycling options and water sports facilities. Lovely patio with views of the water.

A19 exit Malchow, drive towards Nossertin (L20), then Jabel. Campsite is signposted. The exit to the campsite is 1 km outside the village (not by the marina).

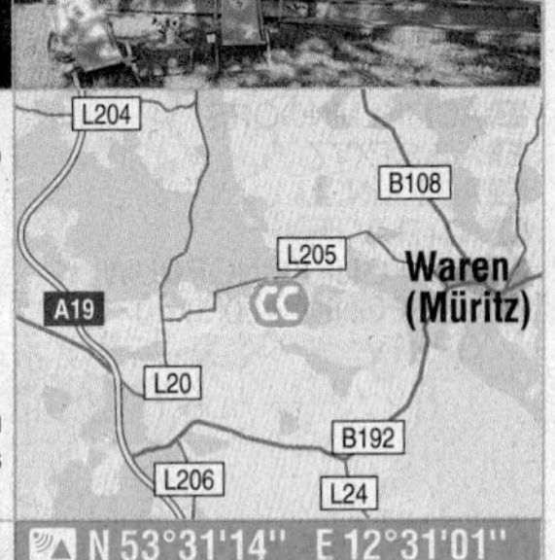

CC € 21 *2/4-8/5 27/5-5/7 1/9-31/10* ***7=6***

N 53°31'14" E 12°31'01"

Karlshagen, D-17449 / Mecklenburg-Vorpommern

482

Dünencamp Karlshagen*****
Zeltplatzstraße 11
+49 38 37 12 02 91
1/1 - 31/12
camping@karlshagen.de

5ha 265T(80-90m²) 16A CEE

1 ACD**H**JKLMNOPQ**R**S
2 ABGJMSTXYZ
3 ACIKMN**R**SU**W**Y
4 (A 15/6-15/8)
(Q+R+T+U 1/5-30/9)
(X 1/4-30/9)
5 **AB**DEFGIJKLMNOPQRUWZ
6 ACDEFGHJ(N 0,5km)
OPSTV

Family-friendly campsite right by the Baltic Sea with its own large sandy beach. Suitable for taking cycle trips.

B111 Wolgast-Ahlbeck. In Bannemin turn left towards Karlshagen. Campsite signposted.

CC € 27 *1/1-20/6 1/9-31/12*

N 54°07'04" E 13°50'42"

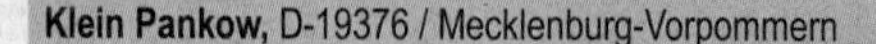

Klein Pankow, D-19376 / Mecklenburg-Vorpommern

483

Camping am Blanksee
Am Blanksee 1
+49 38 72 42 25 90
15/4 - 4/10
info@campingamblanksee.de

12ha 80**T**(100-150m²) 10-16A CEE

1 A**I**KLMNOQ**R**S
2 ABFINOSTVXYZ
3 CKMPSU**W**Z
4 (Q+R+S)
(T+U+X+Z 1/5-3/10)
5 **AB**FGIJLMNO**P**UWZ
6 ADEFG**K**(N 7km)O**P**

An idyllic campsite situated by a beautiful lake with its own beach between two protected nature reserves. Lovely cycling and walking area and a place to enjoy real relaxation. Ideal for bird spotters and game spotters. Small 'Gaststätte' and shop.

A24 Hamburg-Berlin. Exit 16 Suckow. Suckow-Siggelkow-Groß Pankow dir. Klein Pankow. Then follow camping signs.

CC € 25 *15/4-7/5 22/5-30/6 26/8-4/10*

N 53°23'13'' E 12°01'14''

Koserow, D-17459 / Mecklenburg-Vorpommern

484

Camping Am Sandfeld
Am Sandfeld 5
+49 38 37 52 07 59
6/4 - 30/9
camping@amsandfeld.de

3,7ha 150**T**(80-100m²) 16A CEE

1 AC**I**JKLMNOQ**R**S
2 AJLSTXYZ
3 ACIKMNSU
4 (Q+R+V)
5 **AB**DFGIJKLMNOP**Q**UW
6 CDEFGHKL(N 0,5km)
OPSTV

The campsite is located in quiet surroundings at the edge of a nice village, at 700 metres from the beach. The campsite is friendly and has a natural layout and spacious sunny pitches on grass or sand.

B111 Wolgast dir. Swinoujscie. Take 2nd exit Koserow, campsite indicated from here.

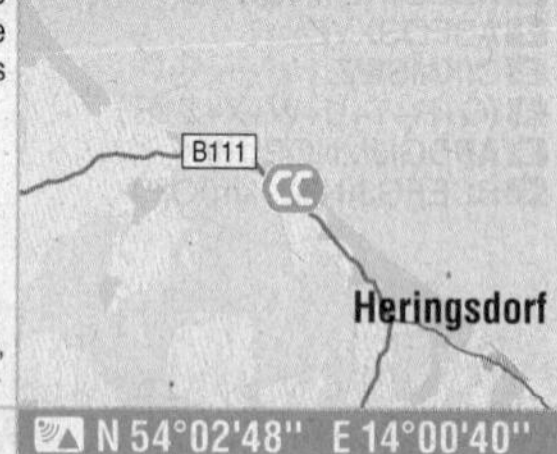

CC € 25 *6/4-17/5 20/5-16/6 1/9-30/9*

N 54°02'48'' E 14°00'40''

Lohme/Nipmerow, D-18551 / Mecklenburg-Vorpommern

485

Krüger Naturcamp
Jasmunder Straße 5
+49 3 83 02 92 44
1/4 - 3/11
info@ruegen-naturcamping.de

4ha 125T(80-100m²) 16A CEE

1 ABCDIKLMNOQRS
2 BCJNQRSTUVXYZ
3 AC**G**IKMNPRS
4 (Q+R+T+U+X+Z)
5 **AB**DFGIJKLMNO**PQ**UWYZ
6 ACEFG**J**(N 8km)OPST

A campsite in the countryside on the island of Rügen, 8 km north of Sassnitz. Ideal base for walks in the Jasmund National Park. Dogs welcome. The ideal stopover for holidaymakers en route to Northern Europe. 1.5 km from the Baltic Sea. Excursions to the cliffs with a forester are possible.

B96 Bergen-Altenkirchen, turn right after Bobbin towards Sassnitz. Campsite signposted.

CC € 25 *1/4-1/7 1/9-3/11*

N 54°34'10'' E 13°36'36''

Lütow, D-17440 / Mecklenburg-Vorpommern

486

Natur Camping Usedom
Zeltplatzstraße 20
+49 38 37 74 05 81
1/4 - 31/10
rezeption@natur-camping-usedom.de

18ha 450T(30-250m²) 16A CEE

1 ACDIKLMNOQRUV
2 ABGMSWXYZ
3 ACKMNPSUWY
4 (A+Q)(S 1/5-1/9) (T+U+Y+Z 1/6-15/9)
5 ABDEFGIJLMNOPQRUWXY
6 ACEFGJ(N 8km)OPT

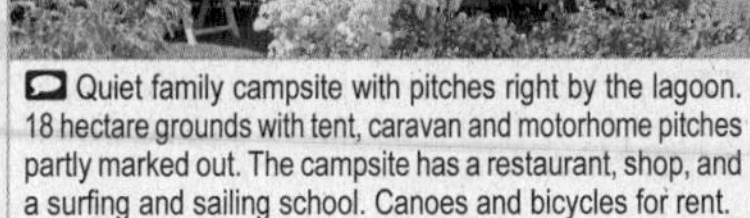

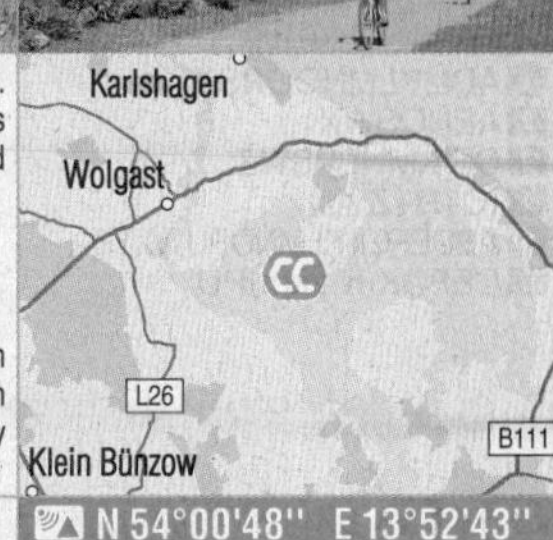

Quiet family campsite with pitches right by the lagoon. 18 hectare grounds with tent, caravan and motorhome pitches partly marked out. The campsite has a restaurant, shop, and a surfing and sailing school. Canoes and bicycles for rent.

B111 from Wolgast to Ahlbeck. Before Zinnowitz, turn right. Campsite is signposted. Take note! Some navigation systems take you through the forest, which is a very tricky forest road. A fine tarmac road leads to the campsite.

Karlshagen
Wolgast
L26
B111
Klein Bünzow

CC € 23 *1/4-8/5 13/5-16/5 21/5-16/6 6/9-31/10*

N 54°00'48'' E 13°52'43''

Markgrafenheide/Rostock, D-18146 / Mecklenburg-Vorpommern

487

Camp. & Ferienpark Markgrafenheide
Budentannenweg 2
+49 38 16 61 15 10
1/4 - 31/12
info@baltic-freizeit.de

28ha 1136T(100-140m²) 10A CEE

1 ACDIKLMNOQRS
2 ABGJSTWXYZ
3 CEIKMNOQRSWY
4 (B 1/6-30/9)(F)KLN(Q)(S 15/5-15/10)(T 1/7-31/8)(U)(V 1/7-31/8)(W 1/4-31/10)(Y+Z)
5 ABDFGJNPUWZ
6 ACEFGJM(N 0,6km)OU

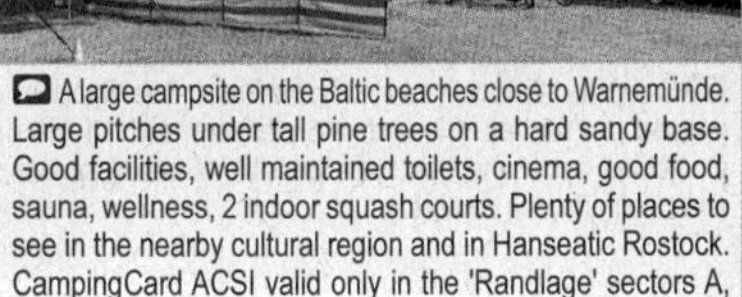

A large campsite on the Baltic beaches close to Warnemünde. Large pitches under tall pine trees on a hard sandy base. Good facilities, well maintained toilets, cinema, good food, sauna, wellness, 2 indoor squash courts. Plenty of places to see in the nearby cultural region and in Hanseatic Rostock. CampingCard ACSI valid only in the 'Randlage' sectors A, B, C, M, pitches of 100 m².

B105 Rostock-Stralsund exit Rövershagen-Hinrichshagen-Markgrafenheide.

Graal-Müritz
Markgrafenheide
Elmenhorst/Lichtenhagen
L22 B105
L182
B103

CC € 25 *1/4-8/5 20/5-30/6 31/8-3/10*

N 54°11'39'' E 12°09'20''

Ostseebad Rerik, D-18230 / Mecklenburg-Vorpommern

488

Campingpark 'Ostseebad Rerik'*****
Straße am Zeltplatz 8
+49 38 29 67 57 20
1/1 - 31/12
info@campingpark-rerik.de

5,2ha 299T(80-100m²) 16A CEE

1 ABCDEIKLMNOQRS
2 AGJQSUVWXYZ
3 ACIKMNPRSUVWY
4 N(Q+R)(S 1/4-31/10)(T+U)(Y 1/4-31/10)(Z 1/1-31/12)
5 ABCDEFGIJKLMNOPQRSUWXYZ
6 ABCDEFGKL(N 0,8km)OPQSTVX

Cosy campsite in quiet surroundings with very modern sanitary facilities. 300m from the Baltic Sea. 900m from the centre of Ostseebad Rerik. An excellent area for walking, cycling, swimming and fishing.

A20 exit 12 Kröpelin (L11). A20 Autobahnkreuz/Wismar 105 as far as Neubukow. Then direction Rerik. Follow the camping signs in Rerik.

Kühlungsborn
L11
B105
Neubukow
L12

CC € 23 *1/1-8/5 20/5-30/6 30/8-27/12*

N 54°06'47'' E 11°37'51''

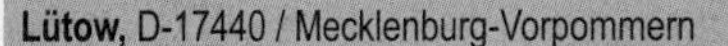

Penzlin (OT Werder), D-17217 / Mecklenburg-Vorpommern

489

Seeweide Naturcamping Penzlin
Halbinsel Werder 33
+49 3 96 22 57 82 90
1/4 - 30/10
info@seeweide.de

7,5ha 196**T**(120-150m²) 16A CEE

1 AD**I**JKLMNOQ**R**S
2 AENOSWX
3 CEIKMNP**R**S**W**Z
4 (Q+R+Z)
5 **AB**DEFGIJKLMNOPUWXYZ
6 CEFGK(N 2km)PU

Large, modern campsite by a lake. Ideal for those seeking quiet but also for families with children. Stunning views of the area from the campsite.

Via the B192 or B193 towards Penzlin. Through the centre of Penzlin towards Werder. Follow the signs to Werder. That is a tiny village. Just before the village, to the campsite.

CC € 23 *1/4-8/5 22/5-15/6 1/9-30/10*

N 53°29'19'' E 13°05'28''

Plau am See/Plötzenhöhe, D-19395 / Mecklenburg-Vorpommern

490

Campingpark Zuruf****
Seestraße 38D
+49 38 73 54 58 78
1/3 - 31/10
campingpark-zuruf@t-online.de

8ha 131**T**(70-100m²) 10-16A CEE

1 ACD**I**JKLMNOQ**R**S
2 AEOSVWXYZ
3 CKMS**W**Z
4 **N**(Q+R 1/3-31/10) (T+U+V+Z 24/4-4/10)
5 **AB**DEFGIJKLMNO**PQR**UWXYZ
6 ACDEFG**K**L(N 2,5km) OPSTV

Campsite attractively located on the Plauer See. Spacious marked out pitches. Close to the pleasant town of Plau. Combined cycle and boat trips possible. Special section and beach for dog owners.

A24/E26 Hamburg-Berlin take Meyenburg exit. Then B103 towards Plau. In Plau, at traffic lights turn right towards Plötzenhöhe. Campsite (on the lake) is signposted.

CC € 25 *1/3-26/4 20/5-21/6 1/9-31/10*

N 53°26'17'' E 12°17'13''

Rerik/Meschendorf, D-18230 / Mecklenburg-Vorpommern

491

Campingplatz Ostseecamp Seeblick
Meschendorfer Weg 3b
+49 3 82 96 71 10
16/3 - 3/11
info@ostseecamp.de

9ha 400**T**(60-150m²) 16A CEE

1 ACDE**I**KLMNOQRS
2 AHNQSUWXYZ
3 CIKMNPSUV**W**Y
4 (A 1/6-28/10)**N**(Q+S) (T+U 1/4-31/10)(V+Y)
5 **AB**DEFGJKLMNOP**QRS**UWXYZ
6 ABCEFGHKM(N 4km) OPSTUV

A beautiful, large campsite directly on the sea with a lovely beach. Spacious, sunny pitches. Campsite offers all comforts. The area is perfect for cycling and fishing. There is a diving school on the campsite called 'Ostseebasis Rerik'.

A20, exit 9, then B105 direction Neubukow. Then left towards Rerik. Follow Rerik-Meschendorf, then 2nd campsite.

CC € 25 *16/3-28/3 2/4-15/5 28/5-23/6 8/9-3/11*

N 54°07'40'' E 11°38'44''

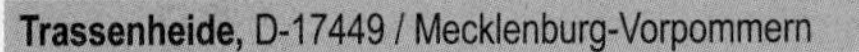

Trassenheide, D-17449 / Mecklenburg-Vorpommern

492

Camping Ostseeblick****
Zeltplatzstraße 20
+49 38 37 12 09 49
2/2 - 18/2, 1/4 - 1/11
campingplatz@trassenheide.de

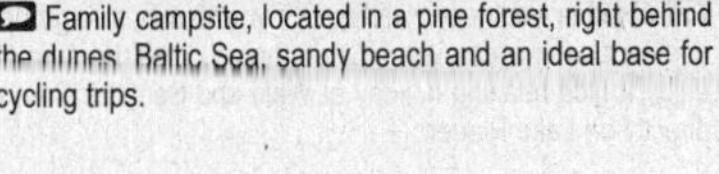

4,1ha 250**T**(65-100m²) 16A CEE

1 ACD**I**KLMNOQRUV
2 ABCOMOTWYZ
3 ACHIKMNSU**W**Y
4 (A 1/5-30/9)(Q)
(R+T+U+X+Z 15/5-15/9)
5 **AB**DEFGIJKLMNOP**QRS**UWZ
6 ABCDEFGH(N 1,5km)
O**P**QTV

Family campsite, located in a pine forest, right behind the dunes. Baltic Sea, sandy beach and an ideal base for cycling trips.

B111 Wolgast-Ahlbeck. Turn left in Bannemim to Trassenheide. Campsite well signposted.

CC € 23 *2/2-18/2 2/4-8/5 13/5-16/5 21/5-12/6 2/9-1/11*

N 54°05'25'' E 13°53'08''

Ückeritz, D-17459 / Mecklenburg-Vorpommern

493

Naturcamping Hafen Stagnieß
Stagnieß Hafenstrasse 10A
+49 38 37 52 04 23
1/4 - 31/10
info@camping-surfen-usedom.de

4ha 180**T**(80-100m²) 16A CEE

1 ACD**I**KLMNOQ**R**S
2 ENSTUXYZ
3 MZ
4 (Q+T)
5 **AB**DFGIJMNO**P**UWZ
6 EFG**J**(N 1,5km)OP

Quiet and centrally-located campsite on the island of Usedom. Pitches are not marked out and are on grass. Situated on the lake, forest edge, and harbour. Good cycle and walking routes nearby, and within cycling distance of the lovely Baltic Sea, bathing resorts and Swinemünde in Poland.

From Anklam via B110 and B111. From Wolgast on B111. Campsite clearly signposted around the village of Ückeritz.

CC € 23 *1/4-7/5 13/5-17/5 21/5-15/7 1/9-31/10*

N 54°00'08'' E 14°02'44''

Wesenberg, D-17255 / Mecklenburg-Vorpommern

494

Camping Am Weissen See****
Am Weissen See 1
+49 3 98 12 47 90
23/3 - 31/10
weissersee@haveltourist.de

3,5ha 150**T**(90-120m²) 16A CEE

1 ACD**I**JKLMNOQ**R**S
2 ABEJLMSWXY
3 AIKMSU**WZ**
4 (Q+R+U+Y+Z)
5 **AB**DEGIJKLMNO**P**UWZ
6 ACEFG**J**(N 1km)OT

A campsite set under tall pine trees on very hilly grounds with many amenities.

Campsite well signposted from the centre of Wesenberg. Follow the C63.

CC € 19 *23/3-23/3 2/4-8/5 12/5-17/5 21/5-6/7 31/8-30/10*

N 53°17'02'' E 12°56'54''

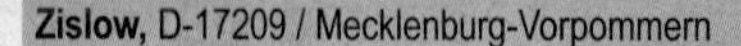

Zislow, D-17209 / Mecklenburg-Vorpommern

495

- Wald- u. Seeblick Camp GmbH
- Waldchaussee 1
- +49 3 99 24 20 02
- 1/1 - 31/12
- info@camp-zislow.de

11ha 220T(80-100m²) 16A CEE

1 ACD**I**JKLMNOQ**R**S
2 EIOSWXYZ
3 CIJKMNPU**WZ**
4 (Q 🔑)(R+T+U 15/4-15/9) (X 1/4-30/9)
5 **AB**FGIJKLMNO**P**UWXYZ
6 ACEFG**J**(N 9,8km)OSU

Whether you're on holiday with your family or a group, in a tent, with a caravan or motorhome, you'll be sure to enjoy a nice relaxing holiday at Wald-und-Seeblick Camp, directly on Lake Plauer.

From A19 (B192) at exit Waren/Petersdorf head towards Adamshoffnung/Zislow. Then follow signs.

CC € 27 *1/1-8/5 22/5-15/7 1/9-31/12*

N 53°26'32'' E 12°18'50''

Zwenzow, D-17237 / Mecklenburg-Vorpommern

496

- Camping Zwenzower Ufer****
- Am Großen Labussee (C56)
- +49 3 98 12 47 90
- 23/3 - 31/10
- gr-labussee@haveltourist.de

2,6ha 75T(80-132m²) 16A CEE

1 ACD**I**JKLMNOQ**R**S
2 FJOSTWXY
3 AIKMS**WZ**
4 **N**(Q+S+T+U+Z 🔑)
5 **AB**DEFGIJKLMNO**P**UWZ
6 ACEFG**K**(N 6km)OT

The campsite is located on the Großer Labussee lake and borders the Müritz National Park. You can easily reach various numerous forest lakes from here. The level terrain is lush with grass, shrubs, deciduous trees and conifers. Some of the sanitary facilities have been adapted for the disabled. Only 300 m from the 'Badehus' with sauna, solarium and indoor swimming pool.

B96 from Berlin via Neustrelitz towards Userin and Useriner Mühle to Zwenzow. Campsite is signposted.

CC € 21 *23/3-28/3 2/4-8/5 12/5-17/5 21/5-6/7 31/8-30/10*

N 53°19'08'' E 12°56'42''

Zwenzow, D-17237 / Mecklenburg-Vorpommern

497

- FKK-Camping Am Useriner See****
- +49 3 98 12 47 90
- 23/3 - 31/10
- info@haveltourist.de

10ha 140T(80-162m²) 6-10A CEE

1 ABCD**I**JKLMNOQ**R**UV
2 ABFLOSTWYZ
3 ACIKMPS**WZ**
4 (Q+S+Z 🔑)
5 **AB**DEFGIJKLMNO**PR**UWZ
6 AEFG**K**(N 6km)OPT

Campsite located in the forest on a lake with good toilet facilities and mini-shop. The sandy road to the campsite is unproblematic to drive on.

B198 to Mirow. On the L25 turn off towards Userin. Continue via Granzow and Roggentin to Zwenzow.

CC € 21 *23/3-28/3 2/4-8/5 12/5-17/5 21/5-6/7 31/8-30/10*

N 53°19'49'' E 12°57'19''

Bergwitz/Kemberg, D-06901 / Sachsen-Anhalt

498

Campingplatz Bergwitzsee GmbH
Strandweg 1
+49 34 92 12 82 28
1/1 - 31/12
reception@bergwitzsee.de

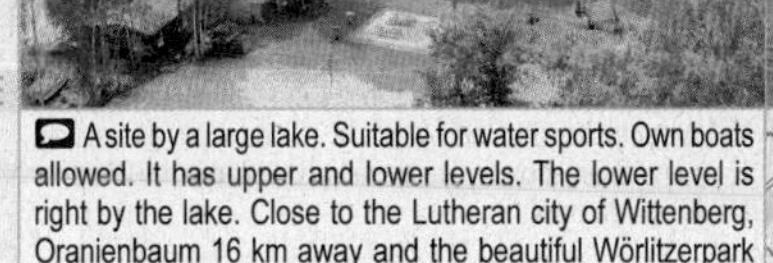

11ha 100T(70-150m²) 16A CEE

1 ACIKLNQRS
2 AFOSXYZ
3 CIKMPS**W**Z
4 M(Q+R)(T+U 1/5-2/10)
(X 30/4-30/9)(Y 1/5-2/10)
(Z 1/5-30/10)
5 **AB**DEFG**J**MNO**PQR**UWXYZ
6 CEFGK(N 1,3km)OT

A site by a large lake. Suitable for water sports. Own boats allowed. It has upper and lower levels. The lower level is right by the lake. Close to the Lutheran city of Wittenberg, Oranienbaum 16 km away and the beautiful Wörlitzerpark 16 km. Good for longer stays.

A9 Berlin-Leipzig exit 8. B187 via Wittenberg, B2 Leipzig. In Eutzsch take B100 direction Gr-Hainchen, 2nd exit behind Service Station-Bergwitz. Campsite sign at 5-way interchange in village.

CC € 21 *1/1-7/5 20/5-30/6 1/9-31/12*

N 51°47'28'' E 12°34'15''

Harzgerode/OT Neudorf, D-06493 / Sachsen-Anhalt

499

Ferienpark Birnbaumteich***
Am Birnbaumteich 1
+49 3 94 84 62 43
1/1 - 31/12
info@ferienpark-birnbaumteich.de

11,5ha 150T(50-100m²) 16A CEE

1 A**I**JKLMNOQRS
2 ABEJOSTUWXY
3 ACMPSUV**W**Z
4 **N**(Q+R)
(T+U+X+Z 1/4-30/9)
5 **AB**DEFGIJK**L**MNO**PQS**UWZ
6 CEFGK(N 9km)OPV

A very peacefully located campsite in the Harz Mountains, by a lake with a beach for swimming. Restaurant with a lovely terrace. Beautiful walking and cycling in the area. Lovely villages close by such as Stolberg, and a trip by steam train to the Brocken is a must.

B81 Magdeburg-Nordhausen, exit Hasselfelde B242 direction Halle. 1 km past Harzgerode towards Stolberg. Turn right 4.3 km further on. Left at campsite signs near bus stop.

CC € 25 *1/1-22/3 8/4-30/4 29/5-30/6 1/9-30/9 1/11-23/12*

N 51°36'30'' E 11°05'05''

Naumburg, D-06618 / Sachsen-Anhalt

500

Campingplatz Blütengrund
Blütengrund 6
+49 34 45 26 11 44
1/1 - 31/12
info@campingplatz-naumburg.de

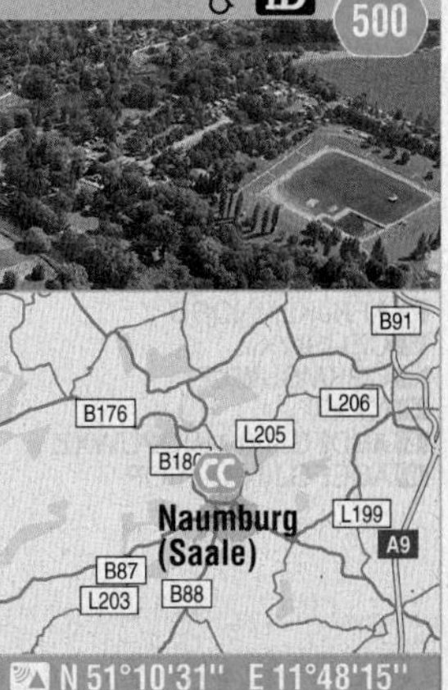

8ha 450T(50-100m²) 16A CEE

1 ACDE**I**JKLMNOQ**R**S
2 CISUVXYZ
3 CIKMS**W**
4 (Q+R+U+X+Z 1/4-31/10)
5 **AB**DFGIJKLMNO**P**UWZ
6 ABCEFG(N 4,5km)OPU

Campsite located on the Saale and Unstrut rivers with possibility of canoeing. Cycling and walking routes in the vicinity. Close to the cathedral city of Naumburg.

Signposted from B180 and B87. Campsite is situated on the river Saale (Naumburg direction Freyburg).

CC € 25 *20/5-30/6 1/9-30/9*

N 51°10'31'' E 11°48'15''

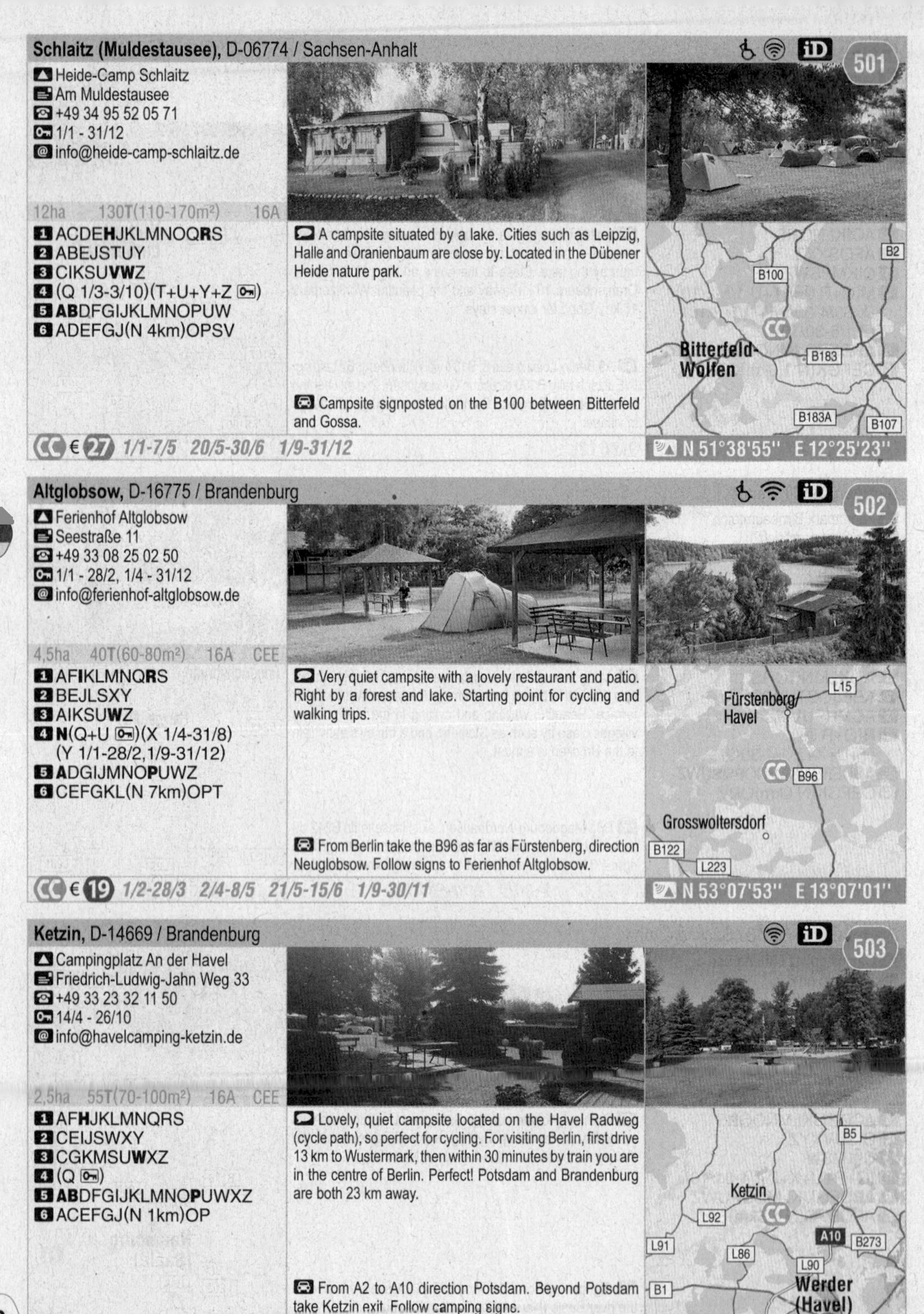

Schlaitz (Muldestausee), D-06774 / Sachsen-Anhalt

501

Heide-Camp Schlaitz
Am Muldestausee
+49 34 95 52 05 71
1/1 - 31/12
info@heide-camp-schlaitz.de

12ha 130T(110-170m²) 16A

1 ACDEHJKLMNOQRS
2 ABEJSTUY
3 CIKSUVWZ
4 (Q 1/3-3/10)(T+U+Y+Z)
5 ABDFGIJKLMNOPUW
6 ADEFGJ(N 4km)OPSV

A campsite situated by a lake. Cities such as Leipzig, Halle and Oranienbaum are close by. Located in the Dübener Heide nature park.

Campsite signposted on the B100 between Bitterfeld and Gossa.

CC € 27 *1/1-7/5 20/5-30/6 1/9-31/12*

N 51°38'55'' E 12°25'23''

Altglobsow, D-16775 / Brandenburg

502

Ferienhof Altglobsow
Seestraße 11
+49 33 08 25 02 50
1/1 - 28/2, 1/4 - 31/12
info@ferienhof-altglobsow.de

4,5ha 40T(60-80m²) 16A CEE

1 AFIKLMNQRS
2 BEJLSXY
3 AIKSUWZ
4 N(Q+U)(X 1/4-31/8)
(Y 1/1-28/2,1/9-31/12)
5 ADGIJMNOPUWZ
6 CEFGKL(N 7km)OPT

Very quiet campsite with a lovely restaurant and patio. Right by a forest and lake. Starting point for cycling and walking trips.

From Berlin take the B96 as far as Fürstenberg, direction Neuglobsow. Follow signs to Ferienhof Altglobsow.

CC € 19 *1/2-28/3 2/4-8/5 21/5-15/6 1/9-30/11*

N 53°07'53'' E 13°07'01''

Ketzin, D-14669 / Brandenburg

503

Campingplatz An der Havel
Friedrich-Ludwig-Jahn Weg 33
+49 33 23 32 11 50
14/4 - 26/10
info@havelcamping-ketzin.de

2,5ha 55T(70-100m²) 16A CEE

1 AFHJKLMNQRS
2 CEIJSWXY
3 CGKMSUWXZ
4 (Q)
5 ABDFGIJKLMNOPUWXZ
6 ACEFGJ(N 1km)OP

Lovely, quiet campsite located on the Havel Radweg (cycle path), so perfect for cycling. For visiting Berlin, first drive 13 km to Wustermark, then within 30 minutes by train you are in the centre of Berlin. Perfect! Potsdam and Brandenburg are both 23 km away.

From A2 to A10 direction Potsdam. Beyond Potsdam take Ketzin exit. Follow camping signs.

CC € 25 *14/4-7/5 26/5-20/6 1/9-26/10*

N 52°28'14'' E 12°50'54''

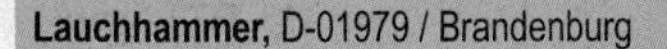

Lauchhammer, D-01979 / Brandenburg

504

Themencamping Grünewalder Lauch****
Lauchstrasse 101
+49 35 74 38 26
27/3 - 27/10
anfrage@themencamping.de

8,5ha 126**T**(100-120m²) 16A CEE

1 ACDE**I**KLMNO**R**S
2 AEIOSTUVWXYZ
3 ACM**R**SZ
4 **N**(Q+R+U+W+X+Y)
5 **AB**DEFGIJK**L**MNOPQRUWXY
6 ABCDEFG**K**L(N 3km) OPQTW

Family campsite in a quiet nature reserve on a large lake with a sandy beach, naturist beach and beach for dogs. Cafe restaurant with patio. Many walls bear fun quotes from the owner and anyone can add their contribution. Cycling and walking round the lake.

A13 exit Ruhland no. 17. Then B169 direction Lauchhammer. In Lauchhammer towards Grünewalde and follow camping signs.

L60 L62 Lauchhammer Elsterwerda B169 B101 L63 A13

CC € 27 *27/3-8/5 21/5-16/6 1/9-27/10*

N 51°30'25'' E 13°40'01''

Lübbenau/Hindenberg, D-03222 / Brandenburg

505

Spreewald-Natur Camping "Am See"****
Seestraße 1
+49 35 45 66 75 39
1/1 - 31/12
am-see@spreewaldcamping.de

15ha 85**T**(80-140m²) 16A CEE

1 ACD**I**KLMNOQ**RS**
2 ABFIJMNOPSVWXYZ
3 ACEKMNP**Q**S**T**UWZ
4 (**A** 1/7-31/8)**KMN** (Q+R+T+U+V+X+Y+Z)
5 **AB**DEFGIJKLMNO**P**TUWXYZ
6 CDEFGJ**KL**(N 7km) OPQSVW

Natural campsite with marked-out comfort pitches directly on a beautiful recreational lake, far from the hustle and bustle of the Spreewald and yet in the middle of it. Luxury toilet facilities and sauna. Attractive restaurant with good cuisine, nice bar and sunny terrace, all pleasantly staffed. In addition to a meadow with animals and a playground, there is also a bowling alley.

On A13, AS9 Spreewalddreieck, direction Luckau. After 4 km campsite is on left.

B115 Lübben (Spreewald) L71 L49 B87 Lübbenau (Spreewald) A15 Luckau B96 L52 A13 L55

CC € 27 *1/1-24/3 14/4-3/5 1/6-30/6 1/9-31/12*

N 51°51'28'' E 13°51'23''

Märkische Heide/Groß Leuthen, D-15913 / Brandenburg

506

Eurocamp Spreewaldtor*****
Neue Straße 1
+49 35 47 13 03
1/1 - 16/11, 15/12 - 31/12
info@eurocamp-spreewaldtor.de

9ha 130**T**(80-100m²) 16A CEE

1 ACDE**I**KLMNOQRS
2 AEOSUWXY
3 CIKMNPSU**W**Z
4 (**A** 1/7-31/8)(**C** 15/5-15/9) **KLN**(Q+R) (U+X 1/4-31/10)
5 **AB**DFGIJKLMNOP**R**UWX
6 ACEFG**K**LMOPSTUX

Easy-going young owner offers pitches on many small fields, near swimming lake with sandy beach. Excellent, token-free toilet facilities. Friendly staff. Amenities set on a nice square, where a shuttle bus leaves for Lübben, Poland and others. New: Spa and spacious outdoor pool.

A13 Dresden-Berlin, exit Lübben, B87 dir. Beeskow, left at intersection Birkenhainchen onto B179 dir. Königs Wusterhausen. In Gross Leuthen turn right; follow the campsite signs.

CC € 21 *1/1-27/3 2/4-8/5 20/5-8/7 25/8-16/11 15/12-31/12*

N 52°02'53'' E 14°02'08''

Ortrand, D-01990 / Brandenburg

507

- ErlebnisCamping Lausitz
- Am Bad 1
- +49 3 57 55 55 35 09
- 1/1 - 31/12
- erlebniscamping@t-online.de

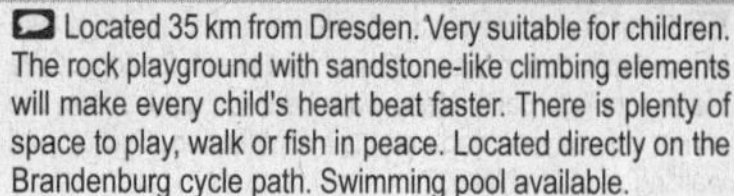

5,5ha 67**T**(100-120m²) 16A CEE

1 ABCDE**I**JKLMNOQ**R**S
2 CISUVWXYZ
3 CEIKMS**W**
4 (B 15/6-31/8)J**N**(Q+R)
(T 1/4-30/9)(U+X 1/5-30/9)
5 **AB**CDEFGHIJKLMNOPQRUWXYZ
6 AEFGHK(N 2km)OPQU

Located 35 km from Dresden. Very suitable for children. The rock playground with sandstone-like climbing elements will make every child's heart beat faster. There is plenty of space to play, walk or fish in peace. Located directly on the Brandenburg cycle path. Swimming pool available.

A13, exit 18 Ortrand, L59, then follow the L55, turn right into Walkteichstrasse, then turn left into Heinersdorferstrasse. At Am Bad, turn right where the campsite is located.

CC € 23 *1/1-7/5 21/5-30/6 1/9-31/12*

N 51°22'20'' E 13°46'45''

Prenzlau, D-17291 / Brandenburg

508

- Campingplatz Sonnenkap****
- Uckerpromenade 85
- +49 3 98 48 62 91 80
- 1/3 - 1/12
- anfrage@sonnenkap-camping.de

10,5ha 230**T**(70-150m²) 16A CEE

1 ABCDE**I**JKLMNOQRS
2 AFJOSUWXY
3 AIKMNPS**W**Z
4 **N**(Q+R+U+X)
5 **AB**FGIJMNOP**S**UWXYZ
6 CEFGKL(N 2km)OPT

Lovely landscaped, modern campsite on a spacious site by the lake. Lively bistro with patio. Large, luxury sauna. Prenzlau is an interesting town to visit. Many cycling and walking options. Water sports facilities in the direct vicinity.

A11 exit Granzow/Prenzlau, A20 exit Prenzlau, in Prenzlau follow campsite signs.

CC € 27 *1/4-8/5 27/5-20/6 30/8-31/10*

N 53°17'32'' E 13°52'18''

Bautzen, D-02625 / Sachsen

509

- Natur- und Abenteuercamping
- Nimschützer Straße 41
- +49 35 91 27 12 67
- 1/4 - 31/10
- camping-bautzen@web.de

5ha 100**T**(100-150m²) 16A CEE

1 ACDE**I**KLMNOQRS
2 AEIJLMNSTUVWY
3 ACDKMSU**W**Z
4 (Q+R)
5 **AB**DEFGHIJLMNOPQRUWXYZ
6 ACEFK(N 1,5km)OPV

Campsite laid out on terraces with spacious, marked out pitches in a park-like setting and on the outskirts of a large reservoir, with a sandy beach, sunbathing lawn and water sports opportunities. Lovely patio by the water. Very modern toilet blocks with the possibility of renting family toilet facilities.

On A4 motorway from Görlitz and Dresden, exit at Bautzen east. Then towards Weißwasser, then direction B156. Follow the campsite signs.

CC € 27 *1/5-4/5 1/6-30/6 1/9-30/9*

N 51°12'08'' E 14°27'38''

Dresden, D-01217 / Sachsen

510

Campingplatz Dresden-Mockritz
Boderitzerstr. 30
+49 35 14 71 52 50
1/1 - 31/1, 1/3 - 31/12
camping-dresden@t-online.de

0,5ha 158T(30-100m²) 6A CEE

1 ACDE**I**KLMNOQRS
2 EIJSUWXYZ
3 CIKMNPSZ
4 (C 1/5-31/8)(Q+R)
(U 1/4-31/10)(X)
5 **AB**CDEFGHIJKLMNO**P**QUWZ
6 CEFGKL(N 0,5km)OPQUX

Campsite is located in a beautiful, quiet suburb of Dresden, 1 km from the town centre. Bus stop is right by the campsite and a cycle path goes from the campsite. There is an outdoor pool, wifi, playground, volleyball field, bicycle hire and shop on the site.

A4 intersection Dresden-W direction Prag on A17. Then exit 3 Dresden-Sud, B170 direction Dresden. Turn right after about 1 km. Right again after 800m. After 1 km the campsite is on left.

CC € 25 *1/4-8/5 21/5-30/6 1/9-31/12*

N 51°00'52'' E 13°44'49''

Großschönau, D-02779 / Sachsen

511

Camping Trixi Park
Jonsdorferstraße 40
+49 3 58 41 63 14 20
1/1 - 31/12
info@trixi-ferienpark.de

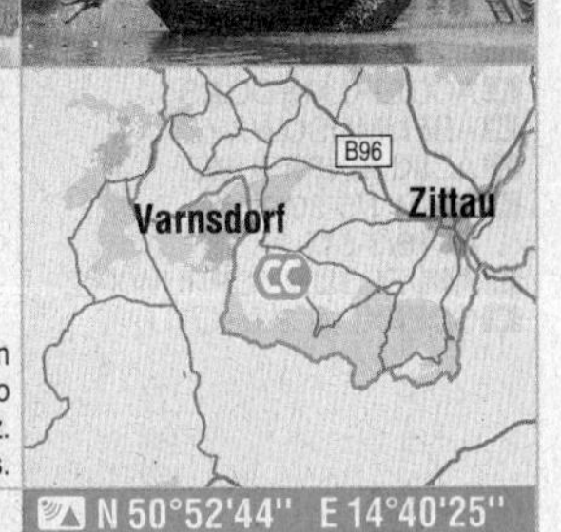

15ha 70T(72-100m²) 16A CEE

1 ACD**I**JKLMNOQRS
2 AEJOPSUWX
3 ACEHIJMNPSU
4 (**A**)(B 1/6-31/8)
(**F**+**H**)**IJKLMNP**
(Q+R+T+U+W+X+Y+Z)
5 **AB**DEFGHIJKLMNOP**QRS**UWXYZ
6 CEFGHKL(N 1km)OPUVWX

Luxurious campsite. Part of Trixi Holiday Park.

From Großschönau towards Zittau, take the first exit on the right after Trixi water park. From Bautzen, take the B6 to Löbau-Zittau. In Herrnhut, turn right towards Oberoderwitz. Then head towards Großschönau and follow campsite signs.

CC € 27 *1/1-22/3 7/4-8/5 22/5-30/6 9/9-31/10*

N 50°52'44'' E 14°40'25''

Pirna, D-01796 / Sachsen

512

Camping Pirna
Äußere Pillnitzer Straße 19
+49 35 01 52 37 73
27/3 - 3/11
info@camping-pirna.de

6ha 152T(90-116m²) 16A CEE

1 ABCD**I**JKLMNOQRTV
2 ABEJOSUVWXY
3 ACKS**W**Z
4 (A+Q+S+T+U+X)
5 **AB**DEFGHIJKLMNOPUWXYZ
6 CDEFGHKL(N 0,3km)
O**P**QSTW

The Pirna-Copitz, a parkland and wooded campsite on a natural lake is located on the outskirts of the historic town of Pirna between Sächsische Schweiz and Dresden. The pitches are marked out, about 100 m² and some of them offer lovely views of the lake. Modern clean toilet facilities.

Motorway A4 exit Prague. A17 towards Pirna via B172. In Pirna cross the Elbe bridge in the direction of Pirna/Copitz, and then take exit Graupa.

CC € 25 *14/4-7/5 2/6-27/6 1/9-3/11*

N 50°58'54'' E 13°55'30''

Pöhl, D-08543 / Sachsen

513

Talsperre Pöhl, Campingplatz Gunzenberg****
Möschwitz, Hauptstraße 38
+49 37 43 94 50 50
27/3 - 3/11
tourist-info@talsperre-poehl.de

11ha 126T(80-120m²) 16A CEE

1 ABCD**I**JKLMNOQRS
2 EIJLQSUWXY
3 ACD**G**IKMNPS**W**Z
4 (**A**+Q+R+U+X+Y)
5 **AB**CDEFGHIJKLMNOPUVWXYZ
6 ACDEFGHKM(N 6km) OPQTW

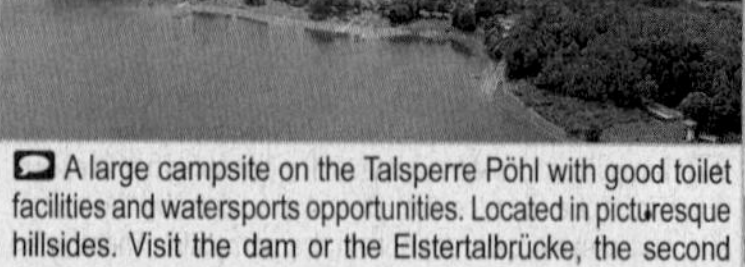

A large campsite on the Talsperre Pöhl with good toilet facilities and watersports opportunities. Located in picturesque hillsides. Visit the dam or the Elstertalbrücke, the second largest brick-built bridge in the world. The campsite has the 'Strandhaus' restaurant.

A72 exit 7 Plauen-Ost/Thalsperre Pöhl. Drive towards the city centre and then towards Talsperre Pöhl. The campsite is located on the left side of the Stausee, beyond the car park.

CC € 25 *27/3-5/5 21/5-17/6 31/8-2/11*

N 50°32'19'' E 12°11'06''

Hohenfelden, D-99448 / Thüringen

514

Camping Stausee Hohenfelden****
Am Stausee 9
+49 36 45 04 20 81
1/1 - 31/12
info@campingplatz-hohenfelden.de

22,5ha 194T(80-140m²) 16A CEE

1 ACDE**I**KLMNOQ**R**S
2 ABFIJMOSUWXYZ
3 ACIKLMNP**R**SU**W**Z
4 (Q+R 1/5-30/9) (X 16/3-31/12)
5 **AB**DEFGIJMNO**P**RUWXYZ
6 CDEFKL(N 3km)OTU

A large campsite located by a reservoir. Watersports opportunities. There is an (indoor) swimming pool with wellness facilities 700 metres from the site. The perfect base for making city trips (Erfurt, Weimar, Gera etc.). Within walking distance of the campsite is a large outdoor centre with climbing, mini golf and organized hiking tours.

A4 exit Erfurt-Ost, then direction Kranichfeld (about 6 km). Campsite on the right side. Well signposted.

CC € 23 *1/1-7/5 20/5-30/6 1/9-31/12*

N 50°52'20'' E 11°10'42''

Nöda, D-99195 / Thüringen

515

ThürKies See-Camping
Alperstedter Landstrasse 1
+49 16 23 69 09 90
1/1 - 31/12
info@thuerkies-see-camping.de

3ha 90T(50-100m²) 10A CEE

1 ABCDEIKLMNQRS
2 AEIOSUVWXY
3 CIKMWZ
4 (Q+T+U+Y+Z)
5 ADGIJKLMNOPUW
6 BCEFK(N 1,8km)O

You can relax and feel good at this idyllic campsite situated by the turquoise water of the Alperstedter See. Close to the capital of the state of Thuringia. There is a beach bar where musical events take place in summer. This creates an amazing atmosphere at the campsite. The 70 pitches and 20 tent pitches are natural and very spacious.

A4 exit 47b, 7 towards A71, exit 8, to Alperstedter See.

CC € 25 *21/5-26/5 3/6-10/7 2/9-30/9*

N 51°04'10'' E 11°02'22''

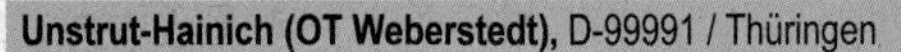

Unstrut-Hainich (OT Weberstedt), D-99991 / Thüringen

516

- Camping Am Tor zum Hainich****
- Am Hainich 22
- +49 36 02 29 86 90
- 1/3 - 1/12
- info@camping-hainich.de

3,5ha 126T(80-100m²) 16A CEE

1 ADIKLMNOQRS
2 BMNSXY
3 CIJKLU
4 (G)M(Q+R)
5 **AB**DGIJKLMNOPUWXYZ
6 ACEFGK(N 2km)OPS

Located on the border of the Hainich National Park, this quiet campsite has good walking opportunities and lovely views towards the Süd-Harz. A UNESCO heritage site since 2011 with the largest deciduous woods.

Exit A4 at Eisenach, follow B84 to Bad Langensalza. Follow signs to Weberstedt. Then turn left. Alternatively, you can take the A44 to Kassel, then the A7 and B7. Finally, the L1042 to Weberstedt.

CC € 25 *29/5-30/6 1/9-30/9*

N 51°06'10'' E 10°30'32''

Attendorn/Biggen, D-57439 / Nordrhein-Westfalen

517

- Camping Hof Biggen***
- Finnentroper Straße 131
- +49 2 72 29 55 30
- 1/1 - 31/12
- info@biggen.de

18ha 100T(80-100m²) 6A CEE

1 ACD**I**KLMNOQ**R**S
2 BJMNSUXY
3 APS**TUW**
4 (Q+S+T+U+Y+Z)
5 **AB**DFGIJKLMNO**P**UVWZ
6 ACDEFG(N 4km)OPUW

A peaceful family friendly campsite just 5 minutes by car from Bigge lake and the village of Attendorn with its medieval centre and famous stalactite caves. Free loan of car for motorhome campers.

A45 Dortmund-Frankfurt, exit 16 Meinerzhagen. After about 20 km you come to Attendorn, then take direction Finnentrop. The campsite is beyond the village opposite restaurant 'Haus am See'.

CC € 25 *7/1-22/3 7/4-8/5 20/5-29/5 2/6-5/7 22/8-11/10 27/10-20/12*

N 51°08'12'' E 07°56'23''

Barntrup, D-32683 / Nordrhein-Westfalen

518

- Ferienpark Teutoburgerwald Barntrup****
- Badeanstaltsweg 4
- +49 52 63 22 21
- 29/3 - 6/10
- info@ferienparkteutoburgerwald.de

2,5ha 103T(90-250m²) 16A CEE

1 ACD**I**KLMNORS
2 BJLSVWXYZ
3 AC**FG**HIJKLMN**O**PSU
4 (A 1/6-15/9)(C+H 1/5-15/9) (Q+U)
5 **AB**CDEFGHIJKLMNOPQR**T**UWXZ
6 ABCDEFGHK(N 0,5km) OPSTV

In woodland surroundings, 5 minute walk to the centre of Barntrup. Good starting point for cultural excursions. Excellent toilet facilities. Beautiful swimming pool next to the site. Camping guests can make free use of it. Eco supplement is 3 euros.

B66 towards Lage, Lemgo, Barntrup. In Barntrup direction swimming pool. Or A2 exit 35 Bad Eilsen, N328 direction Rinteln/Barntrup. From Paderborn B1 direction Hameln via Blomberg to Barntrup. Follow camping signs in Barntrup.

CC € 25 *29/3-7/5 13/5-16/5 21/5-5/7 26/8-5/10*

N 51°59'12'' E 09°06'30''

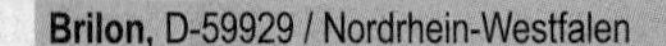

Brilon, D-59929 / Nordrhein-Westfalen

519

Camping & Ferienpark Brilon
Hoppecker-Straße 75
+49 29 61 97 74 23
1/1 - 8/10, 26/12 - 31/12
info@campingbrilon.de

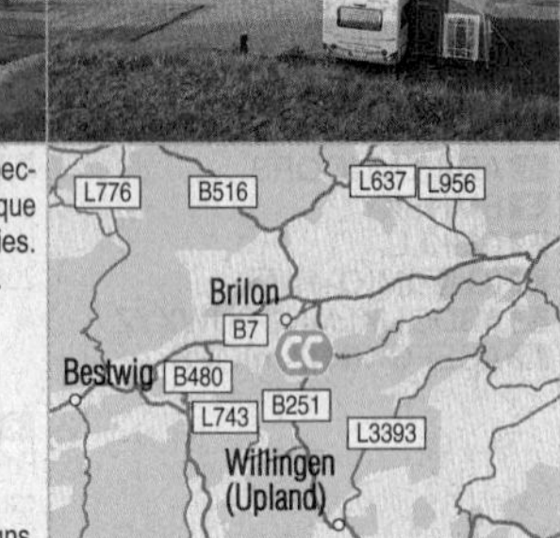

19ha 100**T**(120-160m²) 10-16A CEE

1 ADI**K**LMNOQ**R**S
2 BJLMNSUVWX
3 C**F**IJKLS
4 (A+Q+X+Y+Z)
5 **AB**DEFGIJKLMNOPUWXYZ
6 ABCDEFG**K**(N 2,5km)OS

Summer and winter campsite in the Sauerland with spectacular views. Spacious pitches right next to a wood. Its unique location makes it an ideal base for (winter) sports activities. Dutch/German management. Restaurant in 400 metres.

B251 dir. Willingen; turn right towards Brilon. Follow signs.

CC € 23 *8/1-26/3 2/4-25/4 13/5-16/5 22/5-28/5 3/6-7/7 25/8-1/10*

N 51°22'45'' E 08°35'08''

Essen-Werden, D-45239 / Nordrhein-Westfalen

520

Knaus Campingpark Essen-Werden****
Im Löwental 67
+49 2 01 49 29 78
1/1 - 31/12
essen@knauscamp.de

6ha 140**T**(80-100m²) 16A CEE

1 ACD**I**JKLMNOQRS
2 CIJLSTUVWXYZ
3 CIKSU**W**
4 (Q+R)(T 1/2-31/12) (U+X+Z)
5 **AB**DEGIJKLMNOPQRUWZ
6 BCDEFGK(N 1km)OPTU

Campsite in a quiet area. Level camping pitches situated on a river. Campsite has a small shop for necessities. Campsite is in the town of Essen.

On A52, exit 26 Essen/Kettwig/airport. Follow signs Werden (x2). Site is then signposted.

CC € 27 *1/1-8/5 12/5-17/5 22/5-28/5 3/6-21/6 3/9-30/12*

N 51°22'56'' E 06°59'44''

Extertal/Bösingfeld, D-32699 / Nordrhein-Westfalen

521

Camping Bambi****
Hölmkeweg 1
+49 52 62 43 43
31/3 - 15/10
info@camping-bambi.de

1,7ha 30**T**(100-120m²) 10A CEE

1 ABC**I**JKLMNQRS
2 BMSVWXYZ
3 AIKSU
4 (Q)
5 **AB**DGIJMNOPUWZ
6 ABCDEFGK(N 4km)PT

Small-scale campsite between Rinteln and Hameln in a rural and idyllic setting. Many towns worth visiting are within 50 km and there are plenty of possibilities for cycling and walking.

From Bösingfeld drive towards Hameln. 2 km past Bösingfeld roundabout take second exit left towards Egge. From there 2 km to campsite.

CC € 21 *1/4-9/5 21/5-1/7 1/9-15/10*

N 52°04'59'' E 09°09'31''

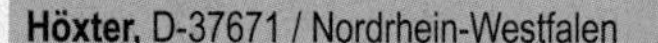

Höxter, D-37671 / Nordrhein-Westfalen

522

- Wesercamping Höxter***
- Sportzentrum 4
- +49 52 71 25 89
- 1/1 - 31/12
- info@wesercamping-hoexter.de

3ha 80**T**(80-120m²) 6-10A CEE

1. ACIKLMNOQRS
2. CJNSWY
3. CHIKMN**O**P**Q**SU**W**X
4. (**C** 11/5-30/9)J (Q+R+T+U+X 15/4-15/10) (Z 1/4-15/10)
5. **AB**DFGI**J**KMNO**P**RUWZ
6. CDEFGK(N 1km)OPV

A pleasant, child and youth friendly campsite on the Weser, you can bring your own boat. Pretty village. A good base for cycling, walking, mountain biking and fishing. Good opportunities for cultural trips out.

A44 direction Kassel, exit Bühren direction Paderborn. B64 direction Höxter. In Höxter direction Boffzen/Fürstenberg and follow campsite signs and Brückfeld. Bridge closed for cars higher than 2.10m, follow signs.

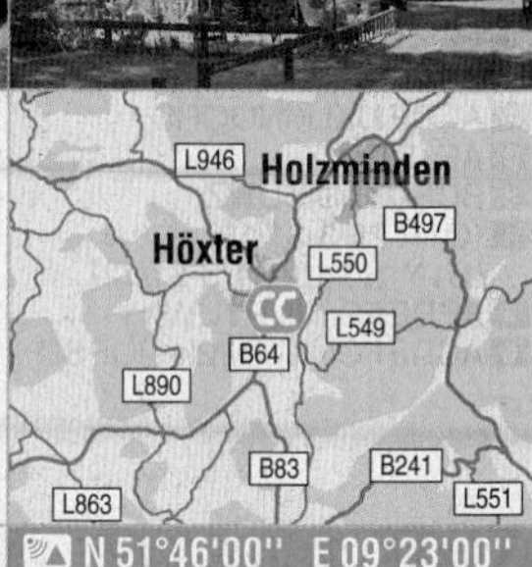

CC € 23 *1/1-5/5 21/5-29/5 2/6-21/6 1/9-31/12*

N 51°46'00'' E 09°23'00''

Lienen, D-49536 / Nordrhein-Westfalen

523

- Camping Eurocamp
- Holperdorp 44
- +49 5 48 32 90
- 1/1 - 20/12
- info@camping-lienen.de

7,8ha 60**T**(80-100m²) 10A CEE

1. ACDE**I**KLMNOQ**R**S
2. MNSTUXY
3. CIK
4. M(X 🔑)
5. **AB**DEGJLN**P**UWZ
6. EFHK(N 5km)

Tranquil (dog-friendly) campsite with well-maintained toilet facilities. You can also leave or enter the campsite between 1 and 3 pm. Many walking routes signposted in the area. Visits to Bad Iburg and Osnabrück are recommended.

B51 Osnabrück/Nahne direction Bad Iburg then direction Holperdorp. The campsite is signposted.

CC € 21 *1/2-26/3 3/4-6/5 22/5-28/6 3/9-29/11*

N 52°10'00'' E 07°58'52''

Meschede (Hennesee), D-59872 / Nordrhein-Westfalen

524

- Knaus Campingpark Hennesee****
- Mielinghausen 7
- +49 2 91 95 27 20
- 1/1 - 3/11, 20/12 - 31/12
- hennesee@knauscamp.de

12,5ha 209**T**(80-130m²) 8-16A CEE

1. ACD**I**JKLMNOQ**R**S
2. EIJMOQSUWXYZ
3. ACEHIKMNPSU**WZ**
4. (F 🔑)**N**(Q+R+T+U+Z 🔑)
5. **AB**CDEFGIJKLMNOPR**S**UWXYZ
6. ACDEFGK(N 3km)OPSUV

A terraced campsite separated by rows of trees. Peacefully located by a reservoir. CampingCard ACSI rate does not include entrance to indoor pool.

B55 from Meschede to Olpe. After 7 km, at the end of the reservoir, cross the bridge and turn left towards the campsite.

CC € 27 *7/1-8/5 12/5-17/5 22/5-28/5 3/6-21/6 3/9-2/11*

N 51°17'54'' E 08°15'51''

Sassenberg, D-48336 / Nordrhein-Westfalen

525

Camping Münsterland Eichenhof*****
Feldmark 3
+49 25 83 15 85
1/1 - 31/12
info@campmuensterland.de

18ha 95T(100-120m²) 16A CEE

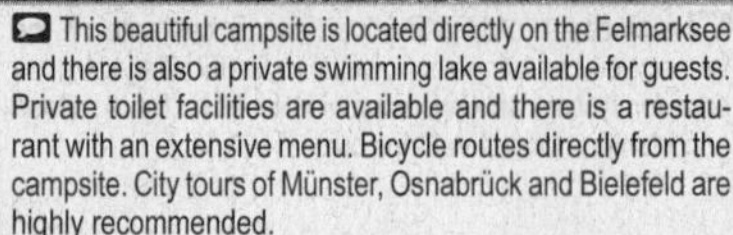

1 ACDEIJKLMNOQRS
2 AEJSTXYZ
3 BCEGKMNSUWZ
4 (Q+R 25/3-31/10)
(U+Y 1/1-15/1,1/3-31/12)
5 ABDEFGHJNPTUWXY
6 ACDEFGHKL(N 2km)OPSU

This beautiful campsite is located directly on the Felmarksee and there is also a private swimming lake available for guests. Private toilet facilities are available and there is a restaurant with an extensive menu. Bicycle routes directly from the campsite. City tours of Münster, Osnabrück and Bielefeld are highly recommended.

A30 dir. Osnabrück. Exit 18, N475 dir. Warendorf, then Sassenberg. In Sassenberg dir. Versmold. Signs to campsite outside the built-up area.

CC € 23 *5/1-15/3 1/4-7/5 20/5-29/5 2/6-5/7 22/8-11/10 26/10-20/12*

N 52°00'16'' E 08°03'51''

Wettringen, D-48493 / Nordrhein-Westfalen

526

Campingpark Haddorfer Seen****
Haddorf 59
+49 59 73 27 42
1/1 - 31/12
info@campingpark-haddorf.de

14,6ha 250T(80-200m²) 16A CEE

1 ACDEIJKLMNOQRS
2 AEOSTXYZ
3 AKRSWZ
4 M(Q+T 25/3-31/10)
(U 1/4-31/10)
(X+Z 25/3-31/10)
5 ABDEFGJLMNPQWXYZ
6 ACDEFGHJK(N 7km)OS

Campsite Haddorfer Seen is nestled in the Münsterland parklands and offers many sports and leisure activities, such as cycling, boating, miniature golf, fishing and swimming. Guests can stay at the attractive camping pitches under the trees and near the natural swimming lake.

A31 exit Schüttorf-Ost direction Wettringen. Campsite signposted north of this town.

CC € 23 *8/1-15/3 7/4-7/5 21/5-28/5 2/6-21/6 1/9-30/9 28/10-20/12*

N 52°16'25'' E 07°19'12''

Eschwege, D-37269 / Hessen

527

Knaus Campingpark Eschwege*****
Am Werratalsee 2
+49 56 51 33 88 83
1/3 - 3/11
eschwege@knauscamp.de

6,8ha 90T(80-100m²) 16A CEE

1 ACDIJKLMNOQRS
2 ADEJNOSUVWXY
3 ACHIKPSUWZ
4 (Q 1/3-30/10)(T+U+X)
5 ABDEFGIJKLMNOPQRSUWXYZ
6 ACDEFGK(N 1km)OPUV

A campsite next to a lake. Excellent toilet facilities. Good cycling opportunities, close to the lovely village of Eschwege.

A4 Kassel-Hannover, exit 74. B27 direction Bebra, exit Eschwege. Or A4 Frankfurt-Dresden, exit 32. Then B27 direction Eschwege.

CC € 27 *1/3-8/5 12/5-17/5 22/5-28/5 3/6-21/6 3/9-3/11*

N 51°11'29'' E 10°04'07''

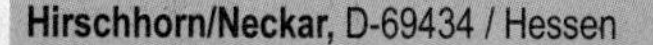

Hirschhorn/Neckar, D-69434 / Hessen

528

Odenwald Camping Park
Langenthalerstraße 80
+49 6 27 28 09
28/3 - 3/10
odenwald-camping-park@t-online.de

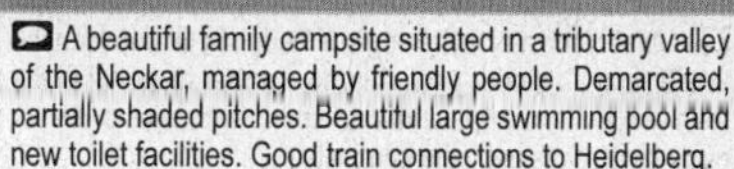

8ha 200**T**(80-150m²) 6-16A CEE

1 AF**H**JKLMNOQRS
2 DJSLUWXYZ
3 C**G**HIK**O**RSX
4 (C 21/5-12/9)
(Q+S+U+Y+Z)
5 **AB**DFGIJKLMNOPUWXY
6 ACDFGK(N 1,5km)OPSV

A beautiful family campsite situated in a tributary valley of the Neckar, managed by friendly people. Demarcated, partially shaded pitches. Beautiful large swimming pool and new toilet facilities. Good train connections to Heidelberg.

A5, exit 37 Heidelberg. On the B37 direction Eberbach/ Mosbach. Exit Hirschhorn. In Hirschhorn follow signs, direction Langenthal at the end of Hirschhorn.

CC € 27 *28/3-3/5 2/6-1/7 1/9-3/10*

N 49°27'09'' E 08°52'40''

Hünfeld, D-36088 / Hessen

529

Knaus Campingpark Hünfeld Praforst*****
Dr.-Detlev-Rudelsdorff-Allee 6
+49 66 52 74 90 90
1/1 - 31/12
huenfeld@knauscamp.de

3,5ha 135**T**(100-150m²) 16A CEE

1 ACD**I**JKLMNOQ**R**S
2 BIJSUVWXYZ
3 A**G**IKPRSU**W**
4 (Q+R)
5 **AB**DEFGIJKLMNOPUWXYZ
6 ACDEFG**K**(N 5km)OT

A short distance from the main road and located on the edge of extensive woods. Shaded and sunny pitches next to a newly laid out golf course. Easily accessible for stopover campers. Beautiful countryside, 20% discount at the golf course next door.

A7 Kassel-Frankfurt, exit 90 Hünfeld/Schlitz. Campsite then signposted. Can also be reached via B27, exit Hünfeld/Schlitz.

CC € 27 *1/1-8/5 12/5-17/5 22/5-28/5 3/6-21/6 19/7-2/8 3/9-30/12*

N 50°39'12'' E 09°43'26''

Oberweser/Gieselwerder, D-34399 / Hessen

530

Camping Gieselwerder***
In der Klappe 21
+49 55 72 76 11
25/3 - 14/10
info@camping-gieselwerder.de

2,5ha 80**T**(80-100m²) 16A CEE

1 ACD**I**JKLMNOQRS
2 CJNSWXY
3 CIKMNP**R**S**W**X
4 (C+H 14/5-3/9)
(Q+T+U+V+Y+Z)
5 **AB**DFGIJKLMNOPRUWZ
6 ACDEFG**K**(N 0,2km)OP

The campsite is located on the Weser, on an elongated piece of land, next to a (free) heated pool. The Weser cycle route is next to the campsite, the wooded hills stretch to just 1 km from the campsite. A few attractive towns are within 40 km.

A21 exit 35, B83 to Bad Karlshafen. B80, in Gieselwerder turn left at Aral, before the bridge turn right. A7: exit 75 or 76 to Hann.Münden, then via B80 direction Bad Karlshafen. In Gieselwerder to the right.

CC € 25 *25/3-5/5 27/5-24/6 26/8-14/10*

N 51°35'55'' E 09°33'18''

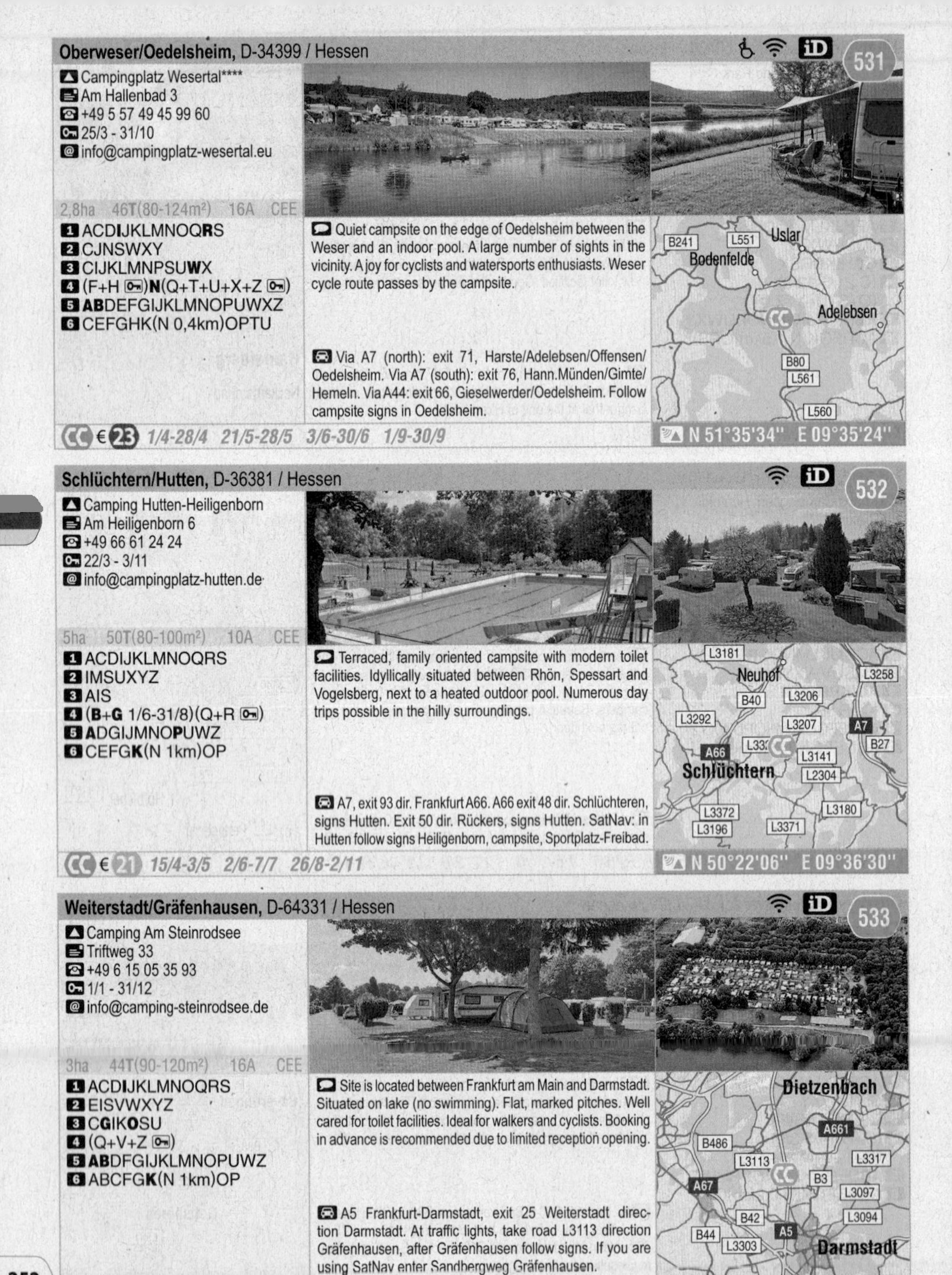

Oberweser/Oedelsheim, D-34399 / Hessen

531

- Campingplatz Wesertal****
- Am Hallenbad 3
- +49 5 57 49 45 99 60
- 25/3 - 31/10
- info@campingplatz-wesertal.eu

2,8ha 46**T**(80-124m²) 16A CEE

1 ACD**I**JKLMNOQ**R**S
2 CJNSWXY
3 CIJKLMNPSU**W**X
4 (F+H) **N**(Q+T+U+X+Z)
5 **AB**DEFGIJKLMNOPUWXZ
6 CEFGHK(N 0,4km)OPTU

Quiet campsite on the edge of Oedelsheim between the Weser and an indoor pool. A large number of sights in the vicinity. A joy for cyclists and watersports enthusiasts. Weser cycle route passes by the campsite.

Via A7 (north): exit 71, Harste/Adelebsen/Offensen/Oedelsheim. Via A7 (south): exit 76, Hann.Münden/Gimte/Hemeln. Via A44: exit 66, Gieselwerder/Oedelsheim. Follow campsite signs in Oedelsheim.

CC € 23 *1/4-28/4 21/5-28/5 3/6-30/6 1/9-30/9*

N 51°35'34" E 09°35'24"

Schlüchtern/Hutten, D-36381 / Hessen

532

- Camping Hutten-Heiligenborn
- Am Heiligenborn 6
- +49 66 61 24 24
- 22/3 - 3/11
- info@campingplatz-hutten.de

5ha 50**T**(80-100m²) 10A CEE

1 ACDIJKLMNOQRS
2 IMSUXYZ
3 AIS
4 (**B**+**G** 1/6-31/8)(Q+R)
5 **A**DGIJMNO**P**UWZ
6 CEFG**K**(N 1km)OP

Terraced, family oriented campsite with modern toilet facilities. Idyllically situated between Rhön, Spessart and Vogelsberg, next to a heated outdoor pool. Numerous day trips possible in the hilly surroundings.

A7, exit 93 dir. Frankfurt A66. A66 exit 48 dir. Schlüchteren, signs Hutten. Exit 50 dir. Rückers, signs Hutten. SatNav: in Hutten follow signs Heiligenborn, campsite, Sportplatz-Freibad.

CC € 21 *15/4-3/5 2/6-7/7 26/8-2/11*

N 50°22'06" E 09°36'30"

Weiterstadt/Gräfenhausen, D-64331 / Hessen

533

- Camping Am Steinrodsee
- Triftweg 33
- +49 6 15 05 35 93
- 1/1 - 31/12
- info@camping-steinrodsee.de

3ha 44**T**(90-120m²) 16A CEE

1 ACD**I**JKLMNOQRS
2 EISVWXYZ
3 C**G**IK**O**SU
4 (Q+V+Z)
5 **AB**DFGIJKLMNOPUWZ
6 ABCFG**K**(N 1km)OP

Site is located between Frankfurt am Main and Darmstadt. Situated on lake (no swimming). Flat, marked pitches. Well cared for toilet facilities. Ideal for walkers and cyclists. Booking in advance is recommended due to limited reception opening.

A5 Frankfurt-Darmstadt, exit 25 Weiterstadt direction Darmstadt. At traffic lights, take road L3113 direction Gräfenhausen, after Gräfenhausen follow signs. If you are using SatNav enter Sandbergweg Gräfenhausen.

CC € 23 *21/5-28/5 3/6-12/7 1/9-30/9*

N 49°56'41" E 08°36'20"

Ahrbrück, D-53506 / Rheinland-Pfalz

534

Camping Denntal****
Denntalstraße 49
+49 26 43 69 05
1/4 - 30/10
urlaub@camping-denntal.de

8,2ha 80T(100-120m²) 16A CEE

1 ADIKLMNQRS
2 DONOVWXY
3 CIKLMNSV
4 (B)**LN**(Q+R)
5 **AB**DFGIJLMNO**P**UWXY
6 ABCDEFGK(N 1,5km)OPTU

A peaceful and well-equipped campsite located by the Dennbach, a stream in a beautiful valley. Good base for walking, cycling and trips out (also by train). The site has excellent toilets, sauna and fitness.

A61 Meckenheimer Kreuz exit Altenahr. B257 direction Nürburgring/Adenau. Nearly through Ahrbrück. On Hauptstrasse turn left to Kesseling (L85). After about 800 metres turn right (Dentalstrasse) and follow camping signs.

CC €27 *1/4-28/4 11/5-16/5 20/5-28/5 2/6-15/7 1/9-2/10*

N 50°28'33'' E 06°59'11''

Bacharach, D-55422 / Rheinland-Pfalz

535

Camping Sonnenstrand
Strandbadweg 9
+49 67 43 17 52
29/3 - 3/11
info@camping-sonnenstrand.de

1,2ha 55T(100m²) 6A CEE

1 ADIKLMNOQ**R**S
2 ADIJOSTUXY
3 AKSU**WX**
4 (Q+R+U+X+Z)
5 **AB**FGIJMNO**P**UW
6 CDGK(N 0,5km)OV

Campsite with a sandy beach right by the Rhine near the city of Bacharach. Good restaurant. Great cycling and walking options. Cycle route along the Rhine. Pitches by the Rhine are Euro2 extra. Reduced rate for pitches on the motorhome site next to the campsite. Free wifi. Dutch owner.

Via the A61. Exit 44 Laudert via Oberwesel to Bacharach (B9). Turn SatNav off after Laudert. Follow signs Oberwesel-Bacharach.

CC €23 *29/3-8/5 21/5-14/7 2/9-3/11*

N 50°03'13'' E 07°46'22''

Bad Dürkheim, D-67098 / Rheinland-Pfalz

536

Knaus Campingpark Bad Dürkheim****
In den Almen 1
+49 6 32 26 13 56
1/1 - 31/12
badduerkheim@knauscamp.de

16ha 280T(80-160m²) 16A CEE

1 ACD**I**JKLMNOQ**R**S
2 AFIJOSTUWXY
3 C**G**HIKLOP**Q**S**WZ**
4 **N**(Q+R+U+Y+Z 15/3-30/11)
5 **AB**DFGIJKLMNOP**S**UWZ
6 ABCEFGHK(N 1km)OT

A very attractive campsite in the middle of the wine area with vineyards on the campsite. Located next to a small airfield but with little disturbance, and a site suitable for longer stays.

A61, exit 60 Autobahnkreuz (motorway intersection) Ludwigshafen. Then route 650 to Bad Dürkheim. At the second traffic lights turn right and then immediately turn right again at the second road.

CC €27 *1/1-8/5 12/5-17/5 22/5-28/5 3/6-21/6 3/9-30/12*

N 49°28'23'' E 08°11'29''

Bernkastel/Kues, D-54470 / Rheinland-Pfalz

537

Knaus Campingpark Bernkastel-Kues
Am Hafen 2
+49 65 31 82 00
1/3 - 3/11
bernkastelkues@knauscamp.de

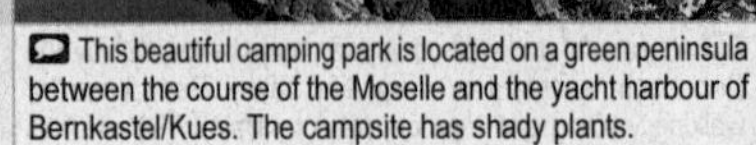
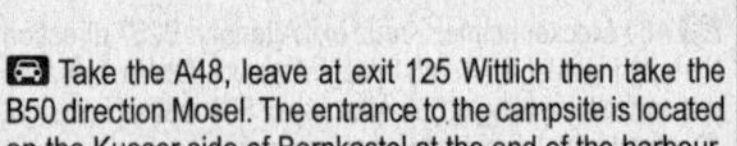
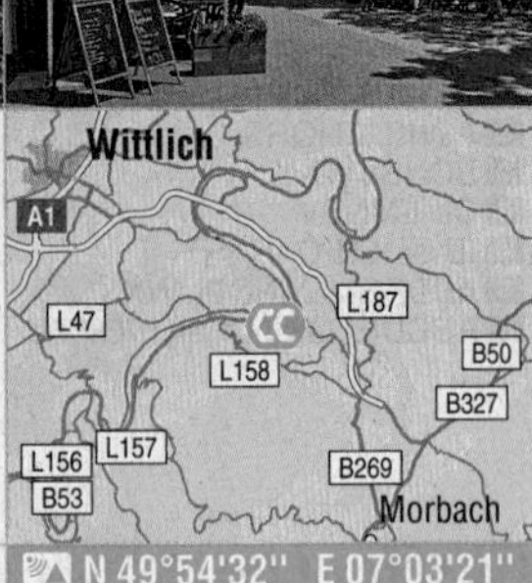

3,2ha 202T 16A CEE

1 BCDIJKLNQRUV
2 DNSXYZ
3 ACJKMNUWX
4 (Q+R+T+U+V)
5 ABDEGIJKLMNOPUWZ
6 CEFGJ(N 1km)OPTUV

This beautiful camping park is located on a green peninsula between the course of the Moselle and the yacht harbour of Bernkastel/Kues. The campsite has shady plants.

Take the A48, leave at exit 125 Wittlich then take the B50 direction Mosel. The entrance to the campsite is located on the Kueser side of Bernkastel at the end of the harbour.

CC € 27 *1/3-8/5 12/5-17/5 22/5-28/5 3/6-21/6 3/9-3/11*

N 49°54'32'' E 07°03'21''

Bockenau, D-55595 / Rheinland-Pfalz

538

Camping Bockenauerschweiz
Daubacher Brücke 3
+49 6 75 62 98
1/4 - 31/10
campingbockenauerschweiz@gmail.com

23ha 50T(tot 100m²) 16A CEE

1 AEIKLMNOQRS
2 BCJSUVY
3 CHIK
4 (Q+R+U+Y+Z)
5 ABDGIJKLMNOPU
6 EFGK(N 8km)PV

A lovely campsite but with few shaded pitches. The campsite has a speciality restaurant featuring German cuisine. Plenty of walking and cycling opportunities.

A61 exit 51 Bad Kreuznach. Follow B41 to Wald Bockelheim, then towards Bockenau/Winterburg.

CC € 23 *1/4-5/5 3/6-4/7 26/8-30/10*

N 49°51'05'' E 07°39'34''

Bollendorf, D-54669 / Rheinland-Pfalz

539

Camping Altschmiede****
Altschmiede 1
+49 6 52 63 75
28/3 - 31/10
info@camping-altschmiede.de

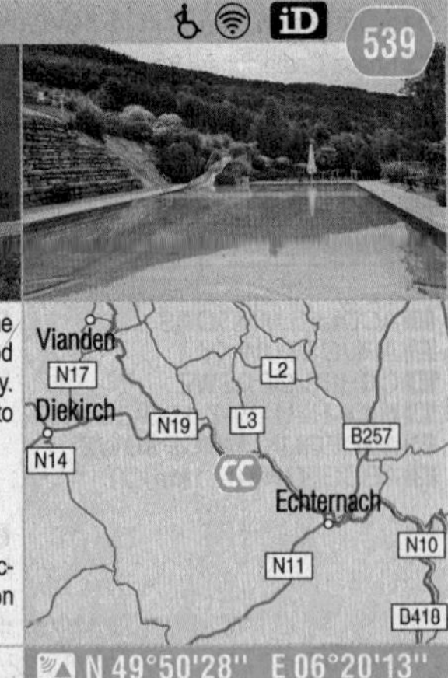

5,5ha 220T(100m²) 6A CEE

1 ADIKLMNQRS
2 DNSTWXY
3 AIKPSUVWX
4 (C 1/6-31/8)IJ(Q 1/5-21/8)
(R 1/6-21/8)(Z)

5 ABDEFGIJKLMNOPUZ
6 ACEFGJL(N 2km)PV

Hospitable and family-friendly campsite right by the German-Luxembourgian boundary river the Sauer. Good toilet and washing facilities. The farm has a gin distillery. Unique! In the summer months, you have free access to the campsite's leisure pool with three slides.

B257 from Bitburg, exit Echternacherbrück. Right direction Bollendorf before the border bridge. In village direction Körperich. It is the 2nd campsite and is signposted.

CC € 21 *1/4-7/5 3/6-30/6 27/8-31/10*

N 49°50'28'' E 06°20'13''

Bullay (Mosel), D-56859 / Rheinland-Pfalz

540

Bären-Camp****
Am Moselufer 1 + 3
+49 65 42 90 00 97
28/3 - 3/11
info@baeren-camp.de

ACSI AWARDS WINNER

1,9ha 145T(70-105m²) 16A CEE

1 ACDIJKLMNOQRS
2 DJNSWXYZ
3 IJKLPSWX
4 (Q+R+U+X) (Y 18/4-31/10)
5 ABDFGIJKLMNOPUWZ
6 ACEFGK(N 0,2km)OPT

'Bären-Camp' is surrounded by the Marien Castle, the Arras Castle and steep vineyards. There are very sunny pitches on the campsite, but also shaded pitches. The site has an attractive restaurant. The campsite is centrally located beside the Moselle on the Moselle cycle route. By bus, train, boat, car and bicycle you can easily reach the most beautiful places.

A1 exit 125 Wittlich, via B49 to Alf. Then cross the bridge to Bullay.

Cochem, L52, L106, L202, L98, L200, L103, Zell (Mosel), B49, B53, L194, L55, L189, L193

CC € 27 28/3-7/7 24/8-3/11

N 50°03'14'' E 07°07'49''

Bürder, D-56589 / Rheinland-Pfalz

541

Camping Zum stillen Winkel*****
Brunnenweg 1c
+49 1 57 77 72 22 16
29/3 - 3/11
info@camping-zumstillenwinkel.de

5ha 90T(100-150m²) 16A CEE

1 ACDIKLMNOQRTU
2 BDJSVXYZ
3 ACIKPSWX
4 (Q+U)
5 ABCDEFGHIJKLMNOPQRUWXYZ
6 AEFGK(N 4km)OPTV

A friendly, attractive campsite located by a river with pitches on the river bank. New, unique toilet facilities with comfortable full bathrooms. Fresh bread available daily. Restaurant delivery service. Beautiful hilly surroundings where peace and relaxation play an important role. Dutch manager.

A3, exit 36 Neuwied towards Neuwied, and then drive towards Kurtscheid. Continue to Niederbreitbach then turn left towards Neuwied as far as Bürder exit. Campsite sign number 2.

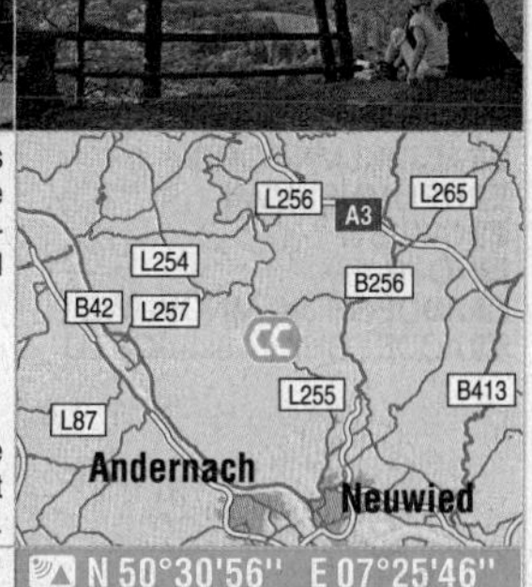

CC € 23 3/4-7/5 22/5-28/5 3/6-12/7 1/9-2/11

N 50°30'56'' E 07°25'46''

Burgen, D-56332 / Rheinland-Pfalz

542

Häppy Life Camping & Beachclub Burgen****
Am Moselufer
+49 26 05 23 96
22/3 - 10/11
burgen@haeppy-life.de

4ha 120T(60-100m²) 16A CEE

1 ACDIJKLMNOQRS
2 DJNQSUVWXYZ
3 AIJKMPSUWX
4 (B 31/5-1/9)KN (Q+S+T+U+V+X+Z)
5 ABDFGIJKLMNOPTUWZ
6 ABCDFGHK(N 9km)OPTUV

Fantastic location right by the Moselle with views of Bischofstein Castle. Friendly family campsite with new sanitary facilities and various amenities such as swimming pool, wine bar, restaurant, SUP, canoe and bike hire. Hourly bus connection to Koblenz centre. 300 m from the village. Ideal base for walking and cycling tours or visiting the castle.

Follow the A61 and take exit 39 Dieblich. Then follow the B49 towards Cochem/Trier as far as the edge of the village Burgen.

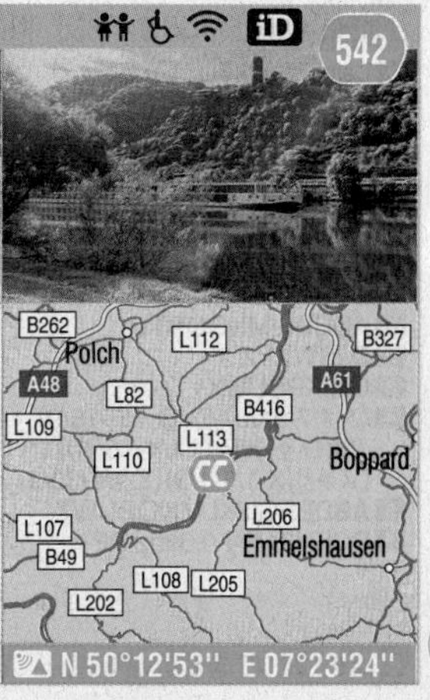

CC € 23 22/3-28/3 1/4-26/4 21/5-29/5 3/6-12/7 1/9-2/10 7/10-10/11

N 50°12'53'' E 07°23'24''

Burgen, D-56332 / Rheinland-Pfalz

543

Knaus Campingpark Burgen/ Mosel****
Am Bootshafen(B49)
+49 26 05 95 21 76
21/3 - 13/10
burgen@knauscamp.de

4ha 125**T**(80-120m²) 16A CEE

1 ACD**I**JKLMNOQRS
2 DJNSTXY
3 ACIJKLS**W**X
4 (C 15/5-15/9) (Q+R+T+U+X+Z 🔑)
5 **AB**DFGIJKLMNOPUWZ
6 ABCDFK(N 8km)OTU

A beautiful campsite located directly on the Moselle overlooking a romantic castle. Small, solar heated, swimming pool, restaurant and harbour. You can go canoeing, water skiing or fishing on the Moselle. This site is of course a good starting point in low season for visiting one of the lively wine festivals in the area.

A61 exit 39 Dieblich. Follow the B49 until past Burgen.

CC € 27 *21/3-8/5 12/5-17/5 22/5-28/5 3/6-21/6 3/9-12/10*

N 50°12'19'' E 07°22'53''

Dockweiler, D-54552 / Rheinland-Pfalz

544

Campingpark Dockweiler Mühle
Mühlenweg 1
+49 65 95 96 11 30
1/1 - 31/12
info@campingpark-dockweiler-muehle.de

10ha 100**T**(80-90m²) 16A CEE

1 ACD**I**KLMNOQRS
2 DEIJMNSUVWY
3 CIKLSW
4 (Q+R 🔑)
5 **AB**DFGHIJKLMNO**P**UWZ
6 ACDEFGHK(N 8km)OPTU

A large campsite located in a protected area with its own fishing lake. There are pitches for tourists on the terrace next to the permanent pitches, but there is also a separate field surrounded by a hedge.

A61 and A1 direction Daun. Via Hillesheim and B410 follow campsite signs.

CC € 21 *11/5-16/5 20/5-28/5 2/6-15/7 1/9-2/10*

N 50°15'20'' E 06°46'47''

Echternacherbrück, D-54668 / Rheinland-Pfalz

545

Campingpark Freibad Echternacherbrück
Mindenerstraße 18
+49 6 52 53 40
22/3 - 31/10
info@echternacherbrueck.de

8ha 400**T**(85-110m²) 12A CEE

1 ADE**I**KLMNOQ**R**TU
2 DJSWXYZ
3 CHIKPSU**W**X
4 (A 1/7-31/8)(C+G 1/5-15/9) JM(Q 🔑)(T+U 1/4-15/10) (V 🔑)(X 1/5-1/9)(Z 1/5-30/9)
5 **AB**DEFGIJKLMNOPUWZ
6 BCFHKM(N 0,3km)OPV

Plenty of trees and grass on marked out pitches. From the campsite you can walk across the bridge into Echternach in Luxembourg! (Really nice). Extra charge for pitches on the river.

From Maastricht-Verviers direction St. Vith/Bitburg. Then to Echternach direction Echternacherbrück. Campsite signposted.

CC € 21 *22/3-8/5 2/6-30/6 30/8-31/10*

N 49°48'43'' E 06°25'53''

Ediger/Eller, D-56814 / Rheinland-Pfalz

546

Camping Zum Feuerberg
Moselweinstraße
+49 2 67 57 01
29/3 - 31/10
info@zum-feuerberg.de

1,8ha 100**T**(100-150m²) 16A CEE

1 ACD**I**KLMNOQRS
2 DJNOSWXYZ
3 **FG**IJKLMNS**W**X
4 (**A**)(B 19/5-30/9)(T+Z)
5 **AB**DFGIJKLMNOPUWZ
6 CEFG**K**(N 0,3km)OPT

This campsite on the Moselle is located close to the picturesque wine village of Ediger-Eller at the foot of Europe's steepest vineyard hill, the 'Calmont'. The campsite has a 50 m2 big swimming pool. Campsite is on the "Moselle cycling route".

A48 exit 3 Laubach dir. Cochem then towards Senheim and another 4 km along the Moselle. Don't use SatNav but follow the Moselle to Cochem.

CC € 23 *29/3-8/5 13/5-18/5 21/5-29/5 3/6-30/6 16/9-31/10*

N 50°05'30" E 07°09'48"

Girod, D-56412 / Rheinland-Pfalz

547

Camping Eisenbachtal
Eisenbachtal 1
+49 6 48 57 66
1/1 - 31/12

3,5ha 30**T**(80m²) 6A CEE

1 AF**I**JKLMNOQRS
2 DILSUVWXY
3 CIKPSU
4 (A 1/7-15/9)(Y)
5 **AB**DFGIJKLMNO**P**UWXYZ
6 CDEFG(N 1,5km)OPTV

In natural countryside at the foot of an old volcano. Interesting biotopes have been laid out including a natural lake. Children are challenged to an adventure in nature and technology. Well marked out walking and cycling paths. Also suitable as a stopover campsite, being a short distance from the A3 motorway. Campsite open all year round.

A3 Köln-Frankfurt exit 41 Wallmerod/Diez. Then direction Montabaur. Campsite 5 km further (see sign).

L303 L300 L3364 B255 L316 B54 L314 A3 B8 L3462 L313 L309 Limburg an der Lahn L329 L326 B417 L327 L318

CC € 25 *1/4-15/7*

N 50°26'16" E 07°54'16"

Guldental, D-55452 / Rheinland-Pfalz

548

Campingpark Lindelgrund
Im Lindelgrund 1
+49 6 70 76 33
15/3 - 15/11
info@lindelgrund.de

8ha 60**T**(80-100m²) 10A CEE

1 ACD**I**JKLMNQRS
2 BCIMNSUVXY
3 CEHIKSU
4 M(Q+Y 15/4-15/10)
5 **AB**DFGHIJKLMNOPQRUWXZ
6 ABCDEFG**K**(N 1,5km)OPT

Terraced campsite with grass surface, some shaded pitches. Narrow gauge railway museum and sand quarry on the site. Suitable as a stopover campsite. Caravans do not have to be uncoupled. Bread service available - order and pay in the evening and collect in the morning.

A61 exit 47 Waldlaubersheim, through Windesheim/ Guldental. Follow the camping signs beyond Guldental.

A61 Bingen am Rhein Ingelheim am Rhein Bad Kreuznach B41 B48

CC € 25 *15/3-27/3 3/4-26/4 2/5-9/5 3/6-1/7 1/9-1/10 7/10-15/11*

N 49°53'03" E 07°51'25"

Hausbay/Pfalzfeld, D-56291 / Rheinland-Pfalz

549

Country Camping Schinderhannes****
Campingplatz 1
+49 6 74 63 88 97 97
1/1 - 31/12
info@countrycamping.de

20ha 200T(100-120m²) 16A CEE

1 ACDEIJKLMNOQRS
2 EIMSUXYZ
3 CIPSTUW
4 (Q+R)(U+Y 1/4-3/10)
5 **AB**DEFGHIJKLMNOP**QR**UWZ
6 CDEFGJ(N 1km)OPT

Large campsite in park-like surroundings with pitches with little to lots of shade. Passers-by campsite by the A61. Central location for longer stays near the Hunsrück, Rhine and Moselle. Great walking options. Cycle along a former railway. Renovated toilet facilities.

A61 exit 43 Pfalzfeld, then follow the camping signs (3 km). Enter: Hausbayerstraße/Pfalzfeld into your SatNav.

CC € 25 *1/1-24/6 26/8-31/12*

N 50°06'21" E 07°34'04"

Irrel, D-54666 / Rheinland-Pfalz

550

Camping Südeifel
Hofstraße 19
+49 6 52 55 10
15/3 - 1/11
info@camping-suedeifel.de

3ha 60T(50-100m²) 6A CEE

1 ADIKLMNQRTU
2 DIJSXY
3 CIKWX
4 (V+X+Z)
5 **AB**DFGIJK**L**MNOPUWXZ
6 AEFGK(N 0,5km)OP

Relax on grasslands next to a river just a few kilometres from the Luxembourg border. Friendly bar on the site, supermarket close by. Wifi at every pitch. Luxurious toilet facilities. Quiet campsite with central location and level pitches.

B257 Bitburg-Echternach. Take exit Irrel towards the village (Ortsmitte). There are signs to the campsite.

CC € 21 *15/3-27/3 1/4-8/5 12/5-17/5 20/5-29/5 1/6-30/6 1/9-31/10*

N 49°50'31" E 06°27'26"

Lahnstein, D-56112 / Rheinland-Pfalz

551

Camping Wolfsmühle
Hohenrhein 79
+49 26 21 25 89
15/3 - 1/11
info@camping-wolfsmuehle.de

3ha 150T(70-150m²) 6A CEE

1 ADEIKLMNOQ**RS**
2 DSUWXY
3 CIKSU**W**X
4 (Q+R 29/3-30/9)
(T+X+Z 22/3-15/10)
5 **AB**DGIJLMNPUW
6 ABCDGHK(N 2km)OPTV

Popular with guests for years, located directly on Lahn in romantic Lahntal valley. Many cycling and walking options. Beautiful, even grounds with heated toilet facilities and restaurant. Very centrally located, Koblenz easily accessible by bike and bus (7 km). Dutch owner.

A61 or A3 to Koblenz A48 exit Vallendar B42 to Koblenz then Rüdesheim exit Oberlahnstein. First right at roundabout. Follow signs. Put Ostallee in your SatNav. Then follow camping signs.

CC € 23 *15/3-6/7 25/8-1/11*

N 50°18'52" E 07°37'40"

Langsur/Metzdorf, D-54308 / Rheinland-Pfalz

552

Camping Alter Bahnhof***
Uferstraße 42
+49 6 50 11 26 26
1/3 - 31/10
info@camping-metzdorf.de

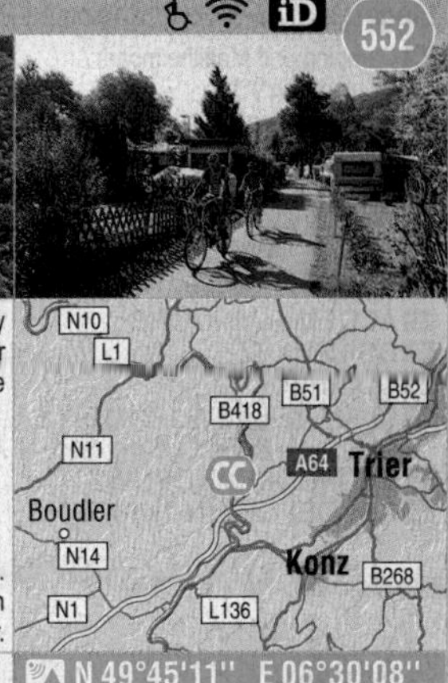

4ha 53T(50-80m²) 16A CEE

1 ACD**I**KLMNOQRS
2 BCIJSVXYZ
3 ACHIKLSWX
4 (Q+R+U+Y+Z)
5 **AB**DFGIJMNOPQRUWZ
6 ACDEFGK(N 5km)OPT

The campsite is situated on the border between Germany and Luxembourg on the banks of the River Sauer. This river offers opportunities for fishing and canoeing. Excellent cycle paths in area. Relaxed atmosphere.

E44 towards Luxembourg exit Mertert (Luxembourg). On the N1 towards Wasserbillig. In Wasserbillig turn left on B418 after the bridge over the River Sauer. Approx. 6 km further.

CC € 23 *1/3-30/6 1/9-31/10*

N 49°45'11'' E 06°30'08''

Leiwen, D-54340 / Rheinland-Pfalz

553

Camping Landal Sonnenberg*****
Sonnenberg 1
+49 6 50 74 91 39 00
8/3 - 15/11
sonnenberg@landal.com

2,5ha 130T(65-120m²) 10A CEE

1 ACD**I**KLMNOQ**R**S
2 BMSUVWXYZ
3 ACDE**G**IKLMP**R**S**T**U
4 (A+F+H)K
(Q+S+T+U+X+Y)
5 **AB**DFGIJMNOPQRUWZ
6 ABCEFGHJ**K**L(N 6km)
OPSTV

A family campsite on a wooded plateau above the Moselle vineyards. Many indoor and outdoor activities (including an indoor pool with whirlpool, indoor playground with climbing wall, 'vinotheque', bowling alley, climbing wood, large playground, animal park with deer). These good facilities make it very suitable for camping holidays outside the high season.

A1 Koblenz-Trier, exit 128 Föhren-Leiwen. Follow signs Sonnenberg.

CC € 23 *8/3-28/3 5/4-30/4 13/5-16/5 21/5-5/7 30/8-30/9 4/11-15/11*

N 49°48'12'' E 06°53'30''

Leutesdorf, D-56599 / Rheinland-Pfalz

554

Campingplatz Leutesdorf
Campingplatz 1
+49 26 31 97 87 37
1/1 - 7/1, 20/3 - 29/10, 1/12 - 31/12
info@camping-leutesdorf.de

2,2ha 80T(80-130m²) 16A CEE

1 ABCDE**I**JKLMNOQ**R**S
2 CJMNSUWXY
3 AIKN**W**
4 (Q+R+T+U+X+Z)
5 **AB**DEFGIJMNOPUWZ
6 BCEFGK(N 5km)OPTX

The campsite is by the Rhine, separated by a strip of greenery. Many birds! Also views of the vineyards. You can cycle and walk there from the campsite. Excursions to Andernach (geyser), Koblenz, a zoo. Take part in a wine tasting picnic or ride on one of the steam trains in the area.

A3 exit 36 towards Neuwied - B256 - B42 towards Linz. Turn left after Leutesdorf.

CC € 25 *20/3-29/3 1/4-27/4 13/5-16/5 3/6-1/7 1/9-1/10 7/10-29/10*

N 50°27'41'' E 07°22'03''

Lingerhahn, D-56291 / Rheinland-Pfalz

555

Camping und Mobilheimpark Am Mühlenteich****
Am Mühlenteich 1
+49 6 74 65 33
1/1 - 31/12
info@muehlenteich.de

15ha 150T 6-16A CEE

1 ACDE**I**JKLMNOQRS
2 BCILSUXYZ
3 CDIKPSU
4 (A 1/7-15/8)(B 1/1-31/12) (Q+U+Y+Z)
5 **AB**DFGIJKLMNOPUWZ
6 ABCDEFGH**K**(N 1km)OPTV

A campsite in the 'Hunsrück' between the Rhine and the Moselle. Plenty of walking and cycling opportunities. Camp in beautiful natural surroundings. Child-friendly. Lovely natural swimming pool. Great restaurant. A campsite for longer stays, but also as a stopover campsite, close to the A61.

A61 exit 44 Laudert, direction Laudert. In Laudert direction Lingerhahn. Follow the camping signs (4 km). Your navigation system may show another route; but still follow the signs.

L205, B9, Oberwesel, B42, CC, Kastellaun, L224, A61, Rheinböllen

CC € 27 *1/1-17/6 9/9-31/12*

N 50°05'58'' E 07°34'25''

Neuerburg, D-54673 / Rheinland-Pfalz

556

Camping in der Enz****
In der Enz 25
+49 65 64 26 60
1/4 - 31/10
info@camping-inderenz.com

6ha 77T(80-100m²) 16A CEE

1 ACDE**I**KLMNQ**R**S
2 CSUWXY
3 CIK**O**SU**W**
4 (C+H 15/5-1/9)J(Q)
(T+U 1/6-31/8)(X 5/4-30/9)
5 **AB**DEFGIJKLMNO**P**UWXY
6 ABCDEFGKL(N 1,5km)OP

Campsite on grassland in the woods with excellent toilet facilities. Good cycling and walking opportunities close to the historic town of Neuerburg. Campsite run by an enthusiastic Dutch couple.

From E42, in Germany A60 exit 3 direction Neuerburg. Via Arzfeld to Emmelbaum and Zweifelscheid. After 3 km turn left at Camping In der Enz. Signposted.

Heinerscheid, B410, L10, A60, L12, CC, L4, N10, Hoscheid, Mettendorf

CC € 23 *1/4-6/7 24/8-30/10*

N 50°01'40'' E 06°16'37''

Oberweis, D-54636 / Rheinland-Pfalz

557

Prümtal-Camping Oberweis*****
In der Klaus 17
+49 6 52 79 29 20
25/3 - 1/11
info@pruemtal.de

3,8ha 240T(65-101m²) 16A CEE

1 ADE**I**KLMNQRS
2 DJSVWXYZ
3 CIKLPSU**WX**
4 (A 15/5-30/8)(C+H 1/5-1/9) J(Q+R)(T 1/6-21/8) (U+V+X+Y+Z)
5 **AB**DEFGIJKLMNOPRUWXYZ
6 ABCDEFGHK(N 9km) OPSTUV

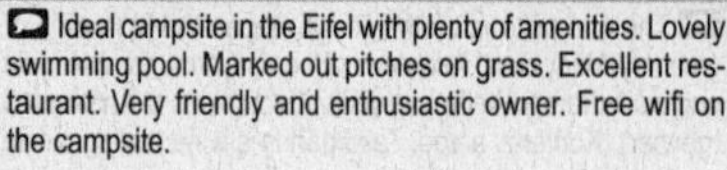

Ideal campsite in the Eifel with plenty of amenities. Lovely swimming pool. Marked out pitches on grass. Excellent restaurant. Very friendly and enthusiastic owner. Free wifi on the campsite.

B50 from Bitburg direction Vianden. Turn left in the centre of the village. Follow the signs campsite and swimming pool.

CC € 27 *25/3-6/7 25/8-1/11*

N 49°57'32'' E 06°25'28''

Pommern, D-56829 / Rheinland-Pfalz

558

Campingplatz Mosel Wunder GmbH & Co. KG
Moselweinstraße 12
+49 26 72 24 61
15/3 - 30/10
hackmann.lohne@yahoo.de

4,5ha 250T(60-100m²) 16A

1 ACDE**I**JKLMNOQ**R**S
2 DJSVWXYZ
3 ACIKSU**WX**
4 (B+G 1/5-15/9)
(Q+R+T+U)
(V+Y 15/4-15/10)(Z)
5 **AB**DGIJKLMNOPUWZ
6 ACFGK(N 4km)OTUV

Lovely family campsite right by the Moselle with a lovely swimming pool, restaurant and beer garden. You can go walking and cycling, take a boat trip on the Moselle or the train to Koblenz or Trier straight from the campsite. Visit a castle or go to a wine festival in one of the historic towns.

A61 Koblenz, exit B416 Cochem/Trier.

Kaisersesch
B416
L206
L205
L108
L98
Cochem
B49
L204
L202

CC € 21 *15/3-8/5 20/5-29/5 2/6-3/7 21/8-30/10*

N 50°10'08'' E 07°15'56''

Pünderich, D-56862 / Rheinland-Pfalz

559

Camping Moselland
Im Planters
+49 65 42 26 18
29/3 - 27/10
campingplatz.moselland@googlemail.com

3,1ha 120T 16A CEE

1 A**I**KLMNOQRS
2 DNSWXYZ
3 ACIJKPSU**WX**
4 (Q+R+T+U+V+Z)
5 **AB**DGIJKMNOPUWXZ
6 ABCDEFGJM(N 1,5km)OPV

Relaxed camping on large sunny or shaded pitches on the banks of the Moselle at Moselland Campsite. The starting point for many wonderful cycle trips along the Moselle, and on your return to enjoy the views of the hillside vineyards.

A48 exit 125 Wittlich. Via Kinderbeuern, Bengel, Reil and Pünderich.

CC € 23 *29/3-30/6 1/9-27/10*

N 50°02'16'' E 07°07'19''

Saarburg, D-54439 / Rheinland-Pfalz

560

Camping Landal Warsberg****
In den Urlaub
+49 6 58 18 35 35 00
23/3 - 4/11
warsberg@landal.de

11ha 460T(80-100m²) 16A CEE

1 ACD**I**KLMNQRS
2 LNSWXYZ
3 ACEHIJKLMNP**R**SU
4 (A 1/7-31/8)(F+H)**KL**MN
(Q+S+T+U+X+Y)
5 **AB**DFGIJLMNOPQRUWZ
6 ACFGHJ**K**L(N 3,5km) OPTUV

Wonderful views from the campsite, which is set on a plateau. You can reach the centre of Saarburg by cable car. The various camping terrains are surrounded by hedges. The campsite, which includes a bungalow park, has good sanitary facilities and a lovely swimming pool.

A60, exit Bitburg, follow B51. In Konz direction Saarburg. In Saarburg follow the Warsberg camping signs.

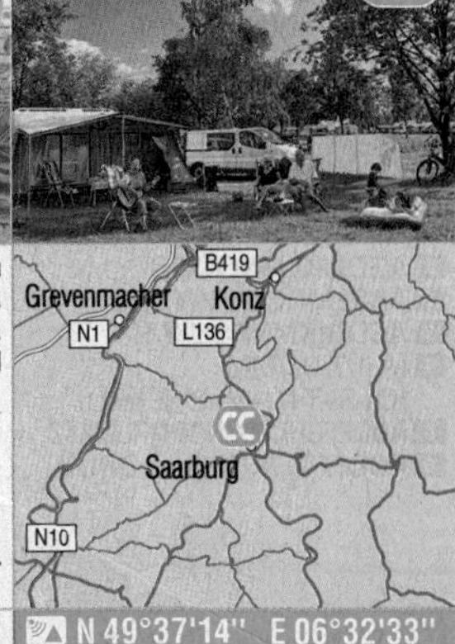

CC € 23 *23/3-29/3 5/4-26/4 24/5-5/7 30/8-4/11*

N 49°37'14'' E 06°32'33''

Saarburg, D-54439 / Rheinland-Pfalz

561

Camping Leukbachtal***
Leukbachtal 1
+49 65 81 22 28
24/3 - 2/11
info@camping-leukbachtal.de

2,5ha 80T(80-130m²) 16A CEE

1 AIKLMNOQRS
2 CSVWXYZ
3 ACHIKLMSU
5 **AB**DFGIJKLMNOPUWZ
6 ABCDEFGK(N 0,2km)PT

This agreeable campsite is located by the river at Saarburg, within walking distance of the lively centre. The parklike grounds make a good starting point for walking and cycling trips. The toilet building was fully modernised in 2017.

From Trier take the B51 towards Saarburg. Follow the signs to the hospital and then the signs to the campsite.

CC € 25 *2/4-7/5 13/5-16/5 21/5-28/5 3/6-30/6 9/9-2/10*

N 49°35'58" E 06°32'29"

Saarburg, D-54439 / Rheinland-Pfalz

562

Camping Waldfrieden****
Im Fichtenhain 4
+49 65 81 22 55
1/3 - 31/12
info@campingwaldfrieden.de

6,5ha 62T(85-120m²) 16A CEE

1 ADIKLMNOQRS
2 BJLSVWXYZ
3 CIKLSU
4 (Q+R)
5 **AB**DFGIJKLMNOPUWZ
6 ACDEFGK(N 1,5km)OPU

Lovely peaceful campsite located between woods and a town. Interesting possibilities with horses (such as therapy with Icelandic horses). Comfort pitches for a supplement.

From Trier take the B51 direction Saarburg, follow the signposts of the hospital, through the tunnel, after that follow the signposts to the campsite.

CC € 23 *1/3-28/3 2/4-30/4 3/6-30/6 2/9-31/12*

N 49°36'03" E 06°31'40"

Seck, D-56479 / Rheinland-Pfalz

563

Camping Park Weiherhof*****
Campingplatz Weiherhof
+49 26 64 85 55
1/4 - 31/10
info@camping-park-weiherhof.de

10ha 211T(100-120m²) 16A CEE

1 ACD**I**JKLMNOQRS
2 ABELMNOSUVWXYZ
3 ACD**G**IKMNPSU**W**Z
4 (A 1/7-31/8)M
(Q+S+T+U+V+Y+Z)
5 **AB**DEFGHIJKLMNO**PQ**RUWXYZ
6 ACDEFGJ**K**(N 5km)OPUV

Quiet campsite with spacious pitches on rolling meadows, partly with views of the lake. Comfortable, heated toilet facilities. Lovely walking and cycling area. Modernised restaurant (Italian menu). Afternoon break: 1-3 pm.

A3 Köln-Frankfurt, exit 40 Montabaur, then the B255 to Rennerod as far as Hellenhahn, at roundabout to Seck and immediately left again. From south: exit 42 Limburg an der Lahn N, then B49/54 to Siegen. Signposted.

CC € 25 *15/4-7/5 3/6-7/7 24/8-31/10*

N 50°35'12" E 08°02'07"

Senheim am Mosel, D-56820 / Rheinland-Pfalz

564

Camping Holländischer Hof****
Am Campingplatz 1
+49 26 73 46 60
21/4 - 27/10
info@moselcamping.com

4ha 250T(60-200m²) 10A CEE

1 ABCDEIKLMNORS
2 DJNOSVWXYZ
3 AGHIJKMNOPSUWX
4 (A+Q+S+T+U+V+X+Y+Z)
5 ABDEFGIJKLMNOPTUWZ
6 ABCEFGHKM(N 5km)OPTU VWX

Walking, cycling, good food and drink, rest and above all hospitality are the keywords for a stay on Holländischer Hof campsite.

A61/A48, exit 4 Kaisersesch towards Cochem. Cross the bridge in Cochem and then drive towards Senheim. Continue alongside the Mosel.

CC € 23 *21/4-8/5 20/5-29/5 2/6-1/7 15/9-27/10*

N 50°04'56" E 07°12'29"

Sensweiler, D-55758 / Rheinland-Pfalz

565

Camping Sensweiler Mühle-Naturlich Camping
Sensweiler Mühle 2
+49 67 86 23 95
1/1 - 31/12
campingplatz@sensweiler-muehle.de

3ha 50T(80-120m²) 16A CEE

1 AFIJKLNOQRS
2 CJMNSXYZ
3 AGIJKLPSUW
4 (Q+U+X+Z)
5 ABDGIJKMNOPUWZ
6 EFGJK(N 3km)P

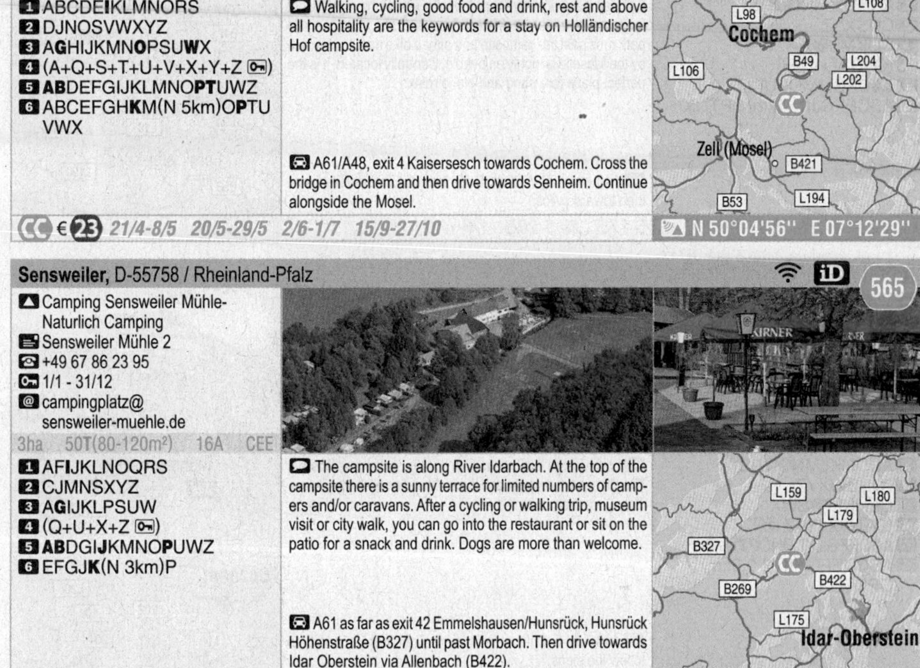

The campsite is along River Idarbach. At the top of the campsite there is a sunny terrace for limited numbers of campers and/or caravans. After a cycling or walking trip, museum visit or city walk, you can go into the restaurant or sit on the patio for a snack and drink. Dogs are more than welcome.

A61 as far as exit 42 Emmelshausen/Hunsrück, Hunsrück Höhenstraße (B327) until past Morbach. Then drive towards Idar Oberstein via Allenbach (B422).

CC € 21 *8/1-8/2 25/2-25/3 2/4-5/5 3/6-30/6 1/9-31/10 1/12-19/12*

N 49°46'09" E 07°12'18"

Stadtkyll, D-8004 DE / Rheinland-Pfalz

566

Camping Landal Wirfttal****
Wirftstraße 81
+49 6 59 75 91 35 00
29/3 - 15/11
wirfttal@landal.de

5ha 150T(75-80m²) 16A CEE

1 ACDIKLMNORS
2 BCESUWXYZ
3 ACDIKLMNOPRSW
4 (A+F+H)KN (Q+S+U+X+Y+Z)
5 ABDFGIJKLMNOPQUW
6 ABCEFGHJK(N 1km)OSTU

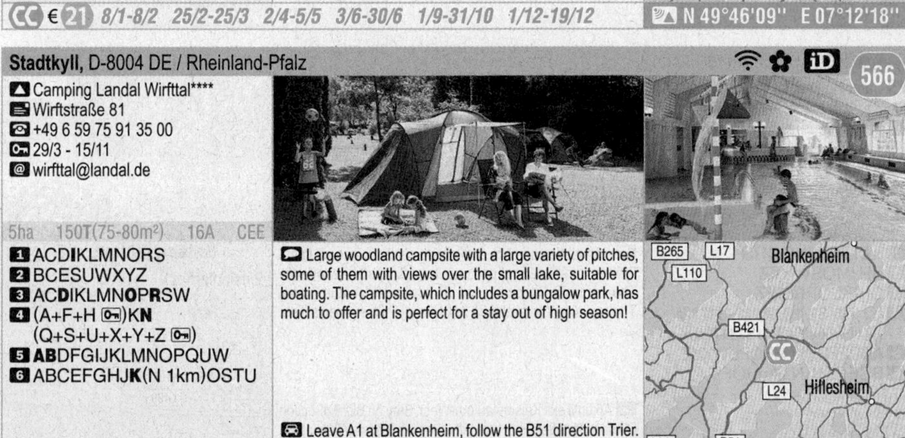

Large woodland campsite with a large variety of pitches, some of them with views over the small lake, suitable for boating. The campsite, which includes a bungalow park, has much to offer and is perfect for a stay out of high season!

Leave A1 at Blankenheim, follow the B51 direction Trier. In Stadtkyll follow signs Ferienzentrum Wirfttal.

CC € 23 *29/3-29/3 5/4-26/4 24/5-5/7 30/8-15/11*

N 50°20'18" E 06°32'21"

Traben-Trarbach, D-56841 / Rheinland-Pfalz

567

Moselcamping Wolf****
Uferstraße 16
+49 65 41 31 11
29/3 - 3/11
wolf@moselcampingplatz.de

3ha 125T(100m²) 16A CEE

1 ACDIKLMNOQRS
2 CNSXYZ
3 CIJKMUWX
4 (Q+S+T+V)
5 ABDFGIJMOPUWZ
6 ABCEFGJ(N 3km)OPTUX

Campsite right by River Moselle with stunning views of the famous Kröver Nacktarsch vineyard. The Moselle cycle path runs past the campsite and after a bike ride, the terrace by the Moselle is highly enjoyable. Centrally located, it is the perfect place for young and old to relax.

A48 exit 125 Wittlich. Drive towards Traben-Trarbach, then towards Wolf.

CC € 25 1/4-26/4 1/5-8/5 12/5-17/5 20/5-29/5 2/6-12/7 20/9-1/11

N 49°58'52'' E 07°06'14''

Treis-Karden, D-56253 / Rheinland-Pfalz

568

Mosel-Islands Camping*****
Am Werth
+49 26 72 26 13
27/3 - 27/10
campingplatz@mosel-islands.de

6ha 130T(80-120m²) 16A CEE

1 ACDIJKLMNOQRS
2 DJNSWXYZ
3 CEIJKLPRSWX
4 (Q+U+X+Y+Z)
5 ABDEFGIJKLMNOPTUWXY
6 ABCDEFGHK(N 0,5km) OPQTU

Lovely, large family campsite, directly on the river Moselle. The pitches are on grass and there are sufficient shady pitches. There is a marina by the site.

A48, exit 5 Kaifenheim towards Treis-Karden and then follow the signs.

CC € 27 8/4-28/4 3/5-7/5 3/6-1/7 1/9-1/10

N 50°10'15'' E 07°17'33''

Trippstadt, D-67705 / Rheinland-Pfalz

569

Camping Freizeitzentrum Sägmühle*****
Sägmühle
+49 6 30 69 21 90
1/1 - 1/11, 18/12 - 31/12
info@camping-saegmuehle.de

10ha 200T(100-120m²) 4-16A CEE

1 ADIJKLMNOQRS
2 BEJMOSWXYZ
3 CHIKLOPRSWZ
4 (Q 1/3-31/10,18/12-31/12) (R+U+X+Y+Z 1/3-31/10)
5 ABDEFGIJKLMNOPUWXYZ
6 BCEFGK(N 3km)OPT

Sägmühle campsite and leisure centre is located in the Pfälzer Forest natural park, south of Trippstadt spa town. The campsite is located on an idyllic and natural lake. The restaurant is famed for its regional Pfälzer specialities.

A6 until exit Kaiserslautern-West. Stay on B270 direction Pirmasens. After 9 km turn left, direction Karlstal/Trippstadt. Follow the camping signs.

CC € 23 1/1-30/4 20/5-29/5 2/6-5/7 7/9-1/11

N 49°21'06'' E 07°46'51''

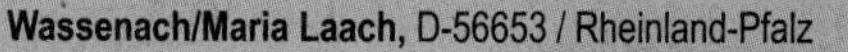

Wassenach/Maria Laach, D-56653 / Rheinland-Pfalz

570

RCN Laacher See****
Am Laacher See/ L113/ Vulkaneifel
+49 2 82 13 93 99 97
8/4 - 30/9
contact@rcn.nl

7ha 190T(80-120m²) 16A CEE

1 BCDE**H**KLMNOQ**R**S
2 BFIJLMNOSVWXYZ
3 ACIJKLRSU**W**Z
4 (**A**+Q)(R 1/5-1/9) (T+U+W+X+Y)
5 **AB**DEFGIJKLMNOPUWXYZ
6 BCEFGHK(N 6km)OTV

Campsite in an idyllic location with gastronomy in the Blockhaus restaurant, open all year round, on the northwest bank of Laacher See. The Laacher See is the largest volcanic lake in the Eifel. Suitable for cycling and walking trips, for example to Maria Laach Benedictine Abbey. Arrivals from 1 pm, departures before 12 pm. Payment possible by cash as well as debit card and credit card.

A61 exit Mendig/Maria Laach. Then approx. 5 km to the north.

L83 L86 L255 L88 L87 Andernach Neuwied A61 L10 A48

CC € 25 *8/4-16/5 22/5-25/5 30/5-6/6 13/6-6/7 28/8-30/9*

N 50°25'19'' E 07°15'54''

Waxweiler, D-54649 / Rheinland-Pfalz

571

Campingpark Eifel*****
Schwimmbadstraße 7
+49 6 55 49 20 00
23/3 - 5/11
info@ferienpark-waxweiler.de

2ha 100T(80-120m²) 16A CEE

1 ADE**H**KLMNQ**R**TU
2 CISWXY
3 CIKMSUW
4 (C 15/5-15/9)
5 **AB**DEFGIJKLMNOPUWZ
6 CEFGJ(N 1km)PV

Well organised campsite situated on grassland on level grounds. Sunny pitches are marked out with hedges. Award winning toilet facilities. Lovely area for walking and cycling along the River Prüm in Bitburger Land. Close to Belgium and Luxembourg. Large pool directly on the campsite.

On the Prüm-Bitburg road take exit Waxweiler. In the village follow the signs to 'Ferienpark Camping'.

CC € 27 *2/4-30/4 6/5-8/5 13/5-17/5 21/5-29/5 3/6-12/7 29/8-4/11*

Waxweiler/Heilhausen, D-54649 / Rheinland-Pfalz

572

Camping Heilhauser Mühle
Heilhauser Mühle 1
+49 6 55 48 05
29/3 - 31/10
walter.tautges@t-online.de

6ha 120T 10A CEE

1 AF**I**KLMNOQRS
2 CIJSYZ
3 BIKP**W**X
4 (Q 1/7-25/8)(U 1/7-31/8) (Y+Z)
5 **AB**DFGIJKLMNO**P**RUWX
6 EFGJ(N 2km)OPU

Quiet campsite on grassland positioned between the hills. This small, well maintained campsite is ideal for cyclists and walkers. Good restaurant housed in an old mill-house with a terrace.

E42 Luik (Liège)-St. Vith-Prüm to exit 3 direction Habscheid/Pronsveld. In Pronsveld direction Lünebach-Waxweiler.

CC € 19 *30/3-30/6 18/8-31/10*

N 50°06'29'' E 06°20'58''

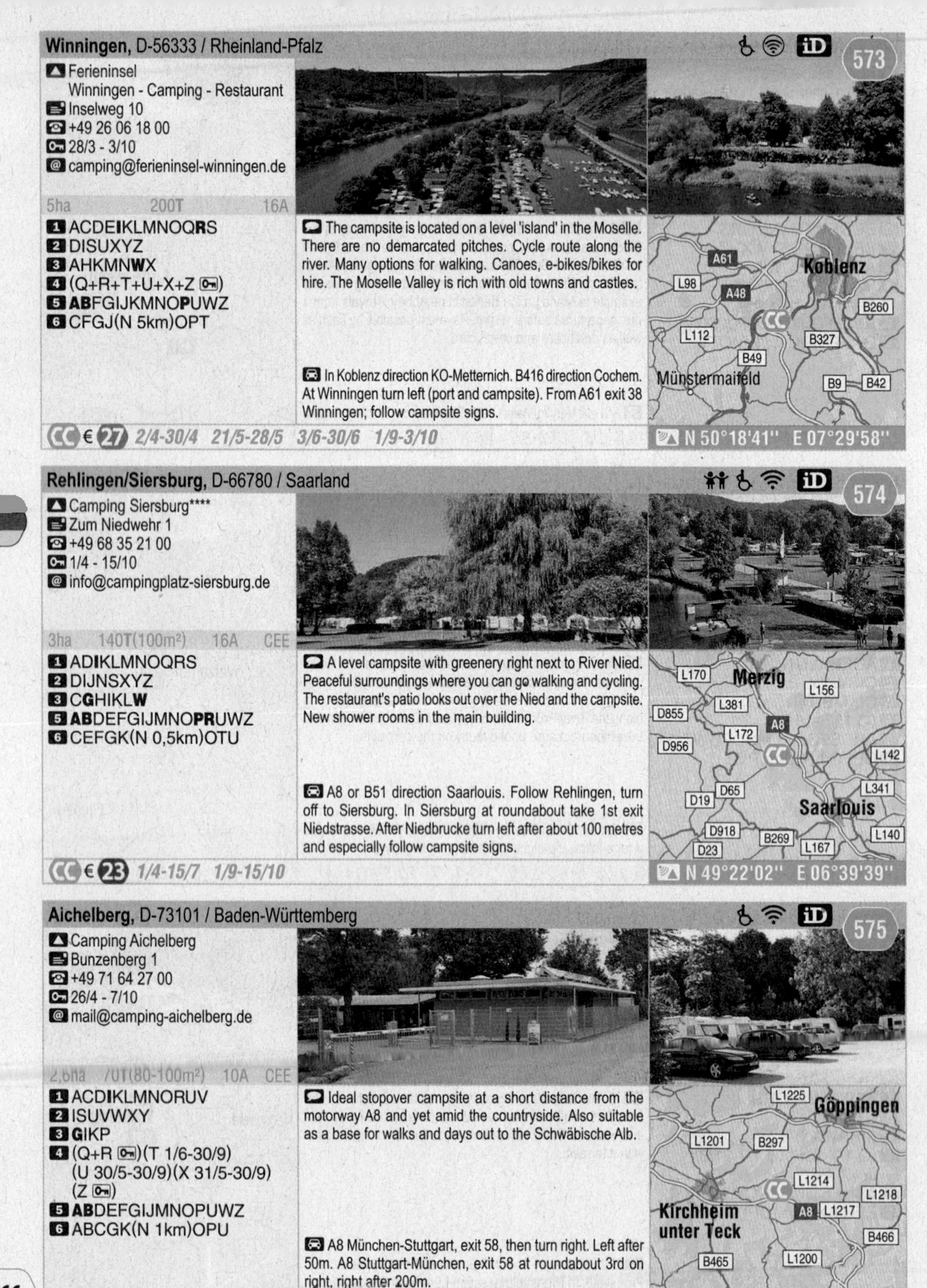

Winningen, D-56333 / Rheinland-Pfalz

573

Ferieninsel
Winningen - Camping - Restaurant
Inselweg 10
+49 26 06 18 00
28/3 - 3/10
camping@ferieninsel-winningen.de

5ha 200T 16A

1 ACDEIKLMNOQRS
2 DISUXYZ
3 AHKMNWX
4 (Q+R+T+U+X+Z)
5 ABFGIJKMNOPUWZ
6 CFGJ(N 5km)OPT

The campsite is located on a level 'island' in the Moselle. There are no demarcated pitches. Cycle route along the river. Many options for walking. Canoes, e-bikes/bikes for hire. The Moselle Valley is rich with old towns and castles.

In Koblenz direction KO-Metternich. B416 direction Cochem. At Winningen turn left (port and campsite). From A61 exit 38 Winningen; follow campsite signs.

CC € 27 *2/4-30/4 21/5-28/5 3/6-30/6 1/9-3/10*

N 50°18'41'' E 07°29'58''

Rehlingen/Siersburg, D-66780 / Saarland

574

Camping Siersburg****
Zum Niedwehr 1
+49 68 35 21 00
1/4 - 15/10
info@campingplatz-siersburg.de

3ha 140T(100m²) 16A CEE

1 ADIKLMNOQRS
2 DIJNSXYZ
3 CGHIKLW
5 ABDEFGIJMNOPRUWZ
6 CEFGK(N 0,5km)OTU

A level campsite with greenery right next to River Nied. Peaceful surroundings where you can go walking and cycling. The restaurant's patio looks out over the Nied and the campsite. New shower rooms in the main building.

A8 or B51 direction Saarlouis. Follow Rehlingen, turn off to Siersburg. In Siersburg at roundabout take 1st exit Niedstrasse. After Niedbrucke turn left after about 100 metres and especially follow campsite signs.

CC € 23 *1/4-15/7 1/9-15/10*

N 49°22'02'' E 06°39'39''

Aichelberg, D-73101 / Baden-Württemberg

575

Camping Aichelberg
Bunzenberg 1
+49 71 64 27 00
26/4 - 7/10
mail@camping-aichelberg.de

2,6ha 70T(80-100m²) 10A CEE

1 ACDIKLMNORUV
2 ISUVWXY
3 GIKP
4 (Q+R)(T 1/6-30/9)
(U 30/5-30/9)(X 31/5-30/9)
(Z)
5 ABDEFGIJMNOPUWZ
6 ABCGK(N 1km)OPU

Ideal stopover campsite at a short distance from the motorway A8 and yet amid the countryside. Also suitable as a base for walks and days out to the Schwäbische Alb.

A8 München-Stuttgart, exit 58, then turn right. Left after 50m. A8 Stuttgart-München, exit 58 at roundabout 3rd on right, right after 200m.

CC € 23 *26/4-28/6 2/9-7/10*

N 48°38'22'' E 09°33'18''

Creglingen/Münster, D-97993 / Baden-Württemberg

576

- Camping Romantische Strasse
- Münstersee Strasse 24-26
- +49 7 93 32 02 89
- 15/3 - 10/11
- camping.hausotter@web.de

6ha 100**T**(80-120m²) 6A CEE

1. ABCD**IJ**KLMNOQRS
2. DEMPSVXYZ
3. CIJP**R**SU**WZ**
4. (F)**N**(Q+R+U+Y)
5. **AB**DFGIJKLMNOPUWXYZ
6. CEFG**K**(N 4km)P

Campsite in a 'Luftkurort', a health spa, in natural surroundings. Indoor swimming pool, sauna and miniature golf. Swimming lake next to the campsite with separate dog area. Restaurant with extensive menu. Great cycling area. Close to Rothenburg ob der Tauber, Weikersheim and Schillingsfürst.

A7 exit Rothenburg. Drive in the direction of Bad-Mergentheim. In Creglingen signposted, direction Münster. The campsite is located just after Münster on the right side of the road.

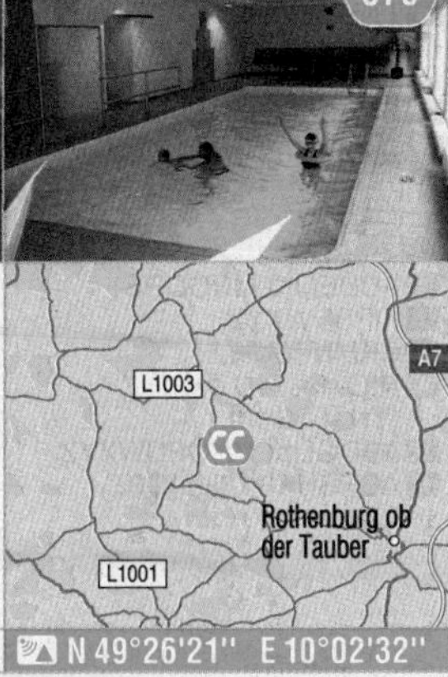

CC € 23 *15/3-8/5 2/6-7/7 1/9-10/11*

N 49°26'21'' E 10°02'32''

Eberbach, D-69412 / Baden-Württemberg

577

- Camping Eberbach
- Alte Pleutersbacherstraße 8
- +49 62 71 10 71
- 28/3 - 29/10
- info@campingpark-eberbach.de

2ha 100**T**(60-170m²) 16A CEE

1. AF**I**JKLMNOQRS
2. DJSWXY
3. C**G**IK**O**P**W**
4. (**C** 15/6-30/9)(**F**)
   (**G** 15/6-30/9)
   (Q+R+U+V+Y+Z)
5. **AB**DFGJLMNOPUW
6. BCFGJ(N 0,8km)O

Well run campsite in the town, right on the river Neckar with an extensive restaurant. Good train connections to Heidelberg. Level marked out pitches by the water. Friendly and helpful owner.

Take the A5, exit 37 Heidelberg. Follow B37 direction Eberbach. Cross over bridge.

CC € 27 *5/5-8/5 3/6-1/7 1/9-1/10*

N 49°27'38'' E 08°58'57''

Freiburg, D-79104 / Baden-Württemberg

578

- Freiburg Camping Hirzberg
- Kartäuserstraße 99
- +49 76 13 50 54
- 1/1 - 31/12
- hirzberg@freiburg-camping.de

1,2ha 88**T**(60-100m²) 10A

1. ACDE**IJ**KLNUV
2. IJMNSXYZ
3. **G**IKLMU
4. (Q 1/4-31/10)(R+U+Y+Z)
5. **AB**DGIJKLMNOPUW
6. BCDFGK(N 1,2km)O**P**ST

The campsite is located on a hillside under trees. Almost the centre of the city, 15 to 20 mins walk from the historic centre and yet family-oriented, small-scale and quiet. There is even a breakfast to prepare in the shop. Many walking and cycling opportunities from the campsite.

A5 exit Freiburg-Mitte, towards Titisee. Follow the signs, keep to the left before the tunnel and turn left towards the (Ebnet) Sporthaus Kiefer stadium. GPS: Sandfangweg.

CC € 27 *7/1-24/3 14/4-13/5 10/6-1/7 2/9-30/9 6/10-27/10 3/11-22/12*

N 47°59'34'' E 07°52'26''

Freiburg/Hochdorf, D-79108 / Baden-Württemberg

579

Tunisee Camping
Seestraße 30
+49 76 65 22 49
1/4 - 31/10
info@tunisee.de

30ha 156T(80-119m²) 16A CEE

1 ACDE**I**JKLMNOQRS
2 FIPSUWXYZ
3 CKMNPSU**W**Z
4 **N**(Q+R+T+U)
(Y 1/4-16/10)
5 **AB**DGIJKLMNOPUWXYZ
6 ACFGH**K**(N 3km)O**P**T

A large campsite on a swimming lake with a cable water-ski and iceberg raft, not far from the motorway. Pleasant ambiance. Good meals available in the restaurant. Spacious grassy pitches. Freiburg is a beautiful old university town with a historical centre.

A5 Karlsruhe-Basel, exit 61 Freiburg-Nord. Turn right at the traffic lights, then 4 times to the left. Campsite signposted.

L115 B3 L112 A5 Freiburg im Breisgau L127 B31

CC € 27 *1/4-1/7 1/9-31/10*

N 48°03'51'' E 07°48'52''

Grafenhausen/Rothaus, D-79865 / Baden-Württemberg

580

Rothaus Camping
Mettmatalstraße 2
+49 7 74 88 00
1/1 - 31/12
info@rothaus-camping.de

2,5ha 40T(80-100m²) 16A CEE

1 ACD**I**JKLMNQRS
2 CJMSVWXY
3 AIJKL
4 (Q+R+U+Y+Z)
5 **AB**DGIJKLMN**P**UW
6 ABCEFGK(N 3km)O**P**T

Terraced campsite with both sunny as well as shaded pitches. Good restaurant. A friendly atmosphere at the campsite. Plenty of walking opportunities in the vicinity, also to Heimatmuseum and Rothaus beer brewery. About 3 km from the village of Schluchsee and the largest lake of the Black Forest. Free public transport via the so-called Konus card during the agreed period of stay.

Titisee to Schluchsee, and then towards Rothaus/ Grafenhausen, turn right after approx. 4 km.

Unadingen L156 B315 L146 B500 L170 L169 Sankt Blasien L157 L159 L154 L158

CC € 25 *1/1-30/6 1/9-31/12*

N 47°47'42'' E 08°14'06''

Herbolzheim, D-79336 / Baden-Württemberg

581

Terrassencamping Herbolzheim****
Im Laue 1
+49 76 43 14 60
26/4 - 22/9
s.hugoschmidt@t-online.de

2,2ha 80T(80-120m²) 10A CEE

1 ACDE**H**JKLMNOQRS
2 MSWXYZ
3 ACIKM**O**PSU
4 (**C**+**G** 15/5-15/9)**J**(Q)
5 **AB**FGIJKLMNOPUW
6 ACDEFG**J**(N 1km)O**P**T

Modern, very clean and quiet natural campsite with excellent sanitary facilities. Located beside the swimming pool, 1 km from the city centre. A good starting point for trips to the Black Forest, Kaiserstuhl and Europapark Rust. There is an amiable atmosphere on the campsite. Excellent cycling opportunities.

Take the A5, exit 58 Herbolzheim, just before the village turn right towards the swimming pool. Campsite is clearly signposted.

CC € 27 *26/4-8/5 13/5-17/5 2/6-1/7 1/9-22/9*

N 48°12'59'' E 07°47'18''

Leibertingen/Thalheim, D-88637 / Baden-Württemberg

582

Campinggarten Leibertingen
Beim Freibad 1 - Vogelsang
+49 75 75 20 91 71
28/3 - 31/10
info@campinggarten-leibertingen.de

2ha 60T(100m²) 16A CEE

1 ABCD**I**KLMNOQRTU
2 JMNSVWX
3 ACDEISU
4 (B+G 1/5-30/9)JM**N** (Q+R+T+U+X+Z)
5 **AB**DFGJLMNOPUWXYZ
6 CEFGK(N 6km)OPUV

Beautiful new campsite with panoramic views of the Alps. Friendly and child-oriented with an active farm during the holidays. A natural swimming pool makes for many nature-based activities. Countryside, peace, hospitality and homemade soup from Grandma's kitchen. A very friendly, hospitable stress-free campsite.

B311 Freiburg-Ulm, exit Leibertingen. In Thalheim turn left into 'Schwimmbadstraße'. Follow signs. The campsite is located on the left, at the top, next to the road.

Sigmaringen L277 L196 L443 Nendingen B311 B313 B14

CC € 21 *1/5-3/5 2/6-2/7 1/9-31/10*

N 48°00'37'' E 09°01'42''

Neubulach, D-75387 / Baden-Württemberg

583

Camping Erbenwald
Erbenwald 1
+49 70 53 73 82
1/1 - 31/12
info@camping-erbenwald.de

7,9ha 75T(80-130m²) 16A CEE

1 AF**I**JKLMNOQRS
2 SWXYZ
3 AC**D**IKLP**QRST**U**W**
4 (A 1/7-31/8)(C+H 1/6-31/8) (Q+R+T+U+Y)
5 **AB**DFGIJKLMNO**P**UWXYZ
6 ABCEFG**K**(N 2,5km)OPQRT

A campsite located on the edge of the village with a new toilet block. The site is ideal for making trips out to the beautiful 'Schwarzwald' (Black Forest). Plenty of pitches with shade. Wifi.

Take the A8, exit 43 Pforzheim-West. Then the B463 to Calw. In Calw. turn right direction Neubulach/Liebelsberg and then follow the signs to the campsite.

CC € 27 *1/1-21/3 8/4-8/5 13/5-17/5 3/6-4/7 9/9-31/12*

N 48°40'39'' E 08°41'23''

Oedheim, D-74229 / Baden-Württemberg

584

Sperrfechter Freizeit-Park
Hirschfeld 3
+49 7 13 62 26 53
1/1 - 31/12
info@sperrfechter-freizeitpark.de

30ha 100T(100m²) 16A CEE

1 ACD**I**JKLMNOQRUV
2 CFISVWXYZ
3 ACHIKPS**W**XZ
4 J(Q+R)
5 **AB**DFGHIJKLMNOPQUWZ
6 CEFGH**K**(N 2km)OP

Large family campsite in natural area. Many water recreation options, such as fishing, rowing, swimming and healing sulfur baths. Renovated toilet blocks.

From A81, exit Neuenstadt to Bad Friedrichshall to Oedheim. From A6: exit Heilbronn/Neckarsulm to Bad Friedrichshall/Oedheim, then follow signs.

CC € 23 *2/4-8/5 13/5-17/5 3/6-30/6 2/9-30/9*

N 49°14'29'' E 09°13'56''

Orsingen, D-78359 / Baden-Württemberg

585

Camping und Ferienpark Orsingen****
Am Alten Sportplatz 8
+49 7 77 49 99 91 00
15/3 - 22/12
info@camping-orsingen.de

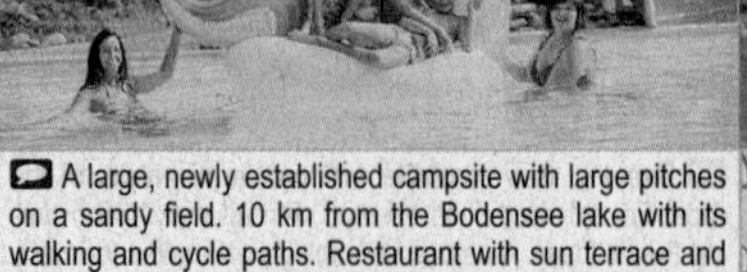

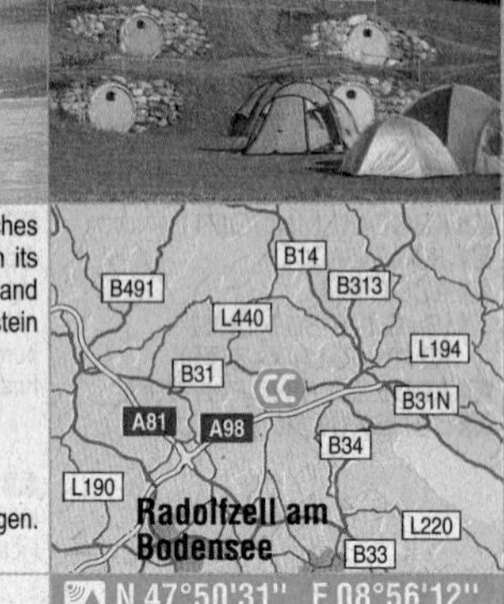

11,5ha 175T(77-136m²) 16A CEE

1 ACDIKLMNOQRUV
2 IJMNSWX
3 ACD**F**GHIKMNP**Q**RS**W**
4 (**C**+**H** 1/4-8/9)**N**(Q+S)
(T 1/4-8/9)(U+Y+Z 1/4-3/11)
5 **AB**DEFGIJKLMNOPRUWXZ
6 BCDEFGKM(N 0,05km)
OPTV

A large, newly established campsite with large pitches on a sandy field. 10 km from the Bodensee lake with its walking and cycle paths. Restaurant with sun terrace and heated swimming pool with children's pool. Near Langenstein Castle and the Fastnachtmuseum.

Stockach dir. Nenzingen, from Nenzingen on to Orsingen. Then follow signs.

CC € 27 1/5-8/5 13/5-17/5 3/6-30/6 7/9-30/9

N 47°50'31'' E 08°56'12''

Radolfzell/Markelfingen, D-78315 / Baden-Württemberg

586

Camping Willam****
Schlafbach 10, Reichenau
+49 75 33 62 11
27/3 - 6/10
info@campingplatz-willam.de

4,5ha 190T(50-110m²) 16A CEE

1 ABCDGJKLMNOQ**R**UV
2 EHIOPQSTVWXY
3 ABC**G**IKNPSU**W**Z
4 (Q+R+U+X+Y+Z)
5 **AB**FGIJKLMNO**P**UW
6 ABCDEFGHJM(N 3km)
OPRTW

Campsite located between Allensbach and Markelfingen in the wonderfully relaxing Bodensee landscape. Lovely beach with a gently sloping shore and excellent water quality. Ideal for the camper seeking relaxation. In addition to recreation on the site you can explore the versatility of the region at your leisure from Bodensee cycle path.

From Radolfzell direction Konstanz. Take Allensbach exit on the B33, follow 'Willam' signs. Campsite between Markelfingen and Allensbach.

A98 · B31N · B31 · B33 · L192 · Steckborn · Konstanz

CC € 25 27/3-17/5 2/6-14/7 1/9-6/10

N 47°43'45'' E 09°01'31''

Salem/Neufrach, D-88682 / Baden-Württemberg

587

Gern-Campinghof Salem
Weildorferstraße 46
+49 75 53 82 96 95
1/4 - 31/10
info@campinghof-salem.de

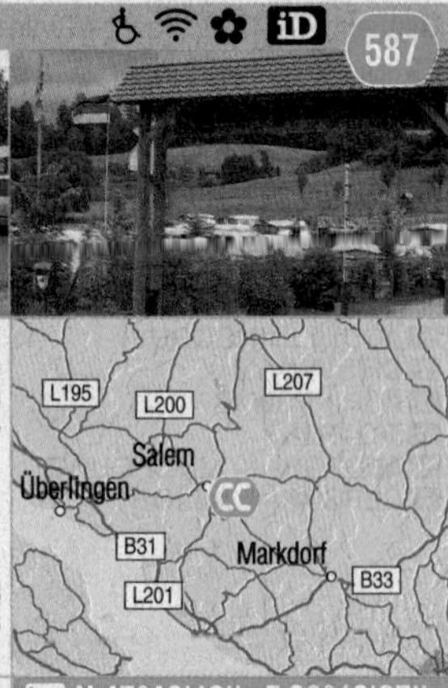

2ha 94T(80-100m²) 10-16A CEE

1 ACD**I**JKLMNOQRS
2 BGJSWXYZ
3 ACE**G**IJK**O**P**Q**SU**W**
4 **N**(Q+R+T+U+X+Z)
5 **AB**DEGIJKLMNOPUWXYZ
6 ABCEFGK(N 1km)OPQSTV

Wonderful location in Salem valley near the Bodensee. Marked walking and cycling paths at the camping. 10 minute walk to the Schloßsee, a very nice swimming lake in the region. Salem Castle close by. A small restaurant, bakery service and entertainment in the holiday period.

A81 Stuttgart-Singen, towards Lindau. Then B31 towards Überlingen-Salem. From Ulm: B30 Ulm-Ravensburg. Then B33 towards Markdorf. Then direction Salem/Neufrach.

CC € 23 1/4-5/5 12/5-17/5 1/6-15/7 8/9-31/10

N 47°46'12'' E 09°18'27''

Schömberg/Langenbrand, D-75328 / Baden-Württemberg

588

- Höhencamping-Langenbrand****
- Schömbergerstraße 32
- +49 70 84 61 31
- 1/1 - 31/12
- info@hoehencamping.de

1,6ha 39**T**(100-120m²) 16A CEE

1 ACD**H**IKLMNOQRS
2 JSWXYZ
3 AIKSU
5 **AB**FGIJK**L**MNO**P**UW
6 ABCDEFG**K**(N 1,5km)O

The campsite is located in the middle of the town with plenty of shaded pitches and excellent toilet facilities.

Take the A8, exit 43 Pforzheim-West. Left on B10 as far as the 'Bauhaus' on the right. Turn right dir. Brötzingen. Right at 4th traffic lights in Bad Büchenbronn/Schömberg. Dir. Schömberg as far as Langenbrand.

CC € 23 *10/1-30/6 1/9-22/12*

N 48°47'55'' E 08°38'08''

Staufen, D-79219 / Baden-Württemberg

589

- Camping Belchenblick
- Münstertäler Straße 43
- +49 76 33 70 45
- 1/1 - 31/12
- info@camping-belchenblick.de

2,2ha 180**T**(80-110m²) 16A

1 ADE**I**JKLMNOQRUV
2 CIJSUWXYZ
3 C**G**IKL**O**PSUV**W**X
4 (B 1/5-15/9)
(F 1/1-10/11,15/12-31/12)
(G 1/5-15/9)JP(Q)
(S+T+X+Z 1/1-7/1,1/3-5/11)
5 **AB**DFGIJKLMNOPQR**S**UWXYZ
6 ACFGK(N 2km)OPRST

The campsite is located on the edge of the forest and has demarcated and non-demarcated pitches. The campsite is surrounded by streams and has wooded surroundings and romantic walking trails. Also suitable for larger groups. Some pitches have TV reception by connecting your own coax cable. There are two charging stations for electric cars.

A5 exit Bad Krözingen towards Staufen/Münstertal. In Staufen dir. Münstertal. The campsite is located approx. 500m outside the village.

CC € 27 *8/1-21/3 7/4-8/5 13/5-19/5 3/6-1/7 11/9-20/12*

N 47°52'20'' E 07°44'09''

Stockach (Bodensee), D-78333 / Baden-Württemberg

590

- Campingpark Stockach-Bodensee
- Johann-Glatt-Straße 3
- +49 77 71 91 65 13 30
- 8/3 - 1/11
- info@camping-stockach.de

4ha 75**T**(75-120m²) 6A CEE

1 ABCDIKLMNOQRS
2 BCIJMSWXYZ
3 C**G**HIKS
4 (Q+R)
5 **AB**DGIJKLMNOPUWZ
6 CDFGK(N 1km)OPU

A lovely campsite with ancient trees situated on the edge of Stockach. Perfect starting point for exploring the Bodensee region. Directly connected to the Bodensee-Radweg cycling network. 10 minutes to Stockach train station. Good shopping options and a shop with camping supplies next to the campsite.

Follow the A81 as far as the Hegau intersection, direction Stockach. Exit Stockach-West.

CC € 25 *5/5-17/5 25/5-28/6 1/9-31/10*

N 47°50'31'' E 08°59'42''

Tengen, D-78250 / Baden-Württemberg

591

Hegi Familien Camping*****
An der Sonnenhalde 1
+49 7 73 69 24 70
15/3 - 3/11
info@hegi-camping.de

20ha 250T(100-200m²) 16A CEE

1 ABCD**I**KLMNOQRS
2 EMOSUWXY
3 ACDHIK**OQR**SUVZ
4 (B+F+H)**KL**
(Q+R)(S 22/3-3/11)
(T+U+V 15/3-3/11)(Y+Z)
5 **AB**DFGHIJKLMNOPQ**R**UWXYZ
6 ABCDEFGHK(N 0,7km)
OPTUW

Peaceful, very luxurious campsite located in a volcanic area between the Black Forest and Lake Constance. The site has both a private lake and an indoor swimming pool with sauna. Lovely walks.

Northwest of Engen. Then the A81 Singen-Stuttgart, take exit 39 Engen. Follow the camping signs.

CC € 27 *15/3-22/3 8/4-26/4 6/5-8/5 12/5-17/5 2/6-28/6 2/9-30/9*

N 47°49'26'' E 08°39'13''

Titisee, D-79822 / Baden-Württemberg

592

Camping Sandbank****
Seerundweg 9
+49 7 65 19 72 48 48
15/3 - 31/12
info@camping-sandbank.de

2ha 230T(80-115m²) 16A CEE

1 ACD**I**KLMNOQRS
2 BEMNOPSUVWXYZ
3 C**G**IJKLSZ
4 (Q+R+U+X+Y+Z)
5 **AB**DEFGIJKLMNOPUW
6 BCEFG(N 4km)OPTW

Terraced campsite located in a quiet nature reserve on the south side of the romantic Titisee lake. From each pitch there is a beautiful view over the lake and the mountains. Directly next to the campsite there is a private beach for campsite guests with a kiosk and restaurant with terrace.

A5 exit Freiburg-Mitte, follow signs till Titisee village, then direction Bruderhalde, 4th campsite from Titisee.

CC € 27 *15/3-22/3 8/4-26/4 6/5-8/5 12/5-17/5 2/6-28/6 2/9-2/11*

N 47°53'15'' E 08°08'18''

Ühlingen/Birkendorf, D-79777 / Baden-Württemberg

593

Waldcamping-Birkendorf
Im Tal 10
+49 77 43 53 73
1/1 - 31/12
info@waldcamping-birkdendorf.de

2,5ha 50T(80-120m²) 16A CEE

1 ACD**I**JKLMNOQ**R**U
2 BDESWXY
3 C**G**HIKSZ
4 (Q+R+U+X+Z)
5 **AB**DFGIJKLNPUWZ
6 CGJ(N 2km)OPQT

Quiet campsite in the Black Forest. Located behind a good restaurant and not far from a lovely natural swimming pool. Plenty of options for cycling trips and walks in the wooded area.

Take the A5 Karlsruhe-Basel, exit Freiburg-Mitte/Titisee/Schluchsee. On the bridge, turn left to Rothaus/Grafenhausen. Birkendorf is signposted, 'Im Oberholz'.

CC € 19 *2/4-8/5 21/5-29/5 3/6-30/6 8/9-31/10*

N 47°45'06'' E 08°17'35''

Wahlwies/Stockach, D-78333 / Baden-Württemberg

594

Campinggarten Wahlwies
Stahringer Straße 50
+49 77 71 35 11
1/3 - 10/11
info@camping-wahlwies.de

1,6ha 52T(70-120m²) 16A CEE

1 ACDIKLMNOQS
2 IJSUY
3 AHIJKSU
4 (Q+R+Z)
5 **AB**DFGIJKLMNOPUWXZ
6 ABCEFGKL(N 1,5km)OTU

A friendly, small campsite idyllically located between orchards in a typical Bodensee landscape. Here you can enjoy a peaceful, relaxed stay in an informal atmosphere. Wahlwies is the ideal starting point for trips out, bike and walking tours to the Bodensee, the volcanic landscape of the Hegau or to the mountain areas of the Danube and neighbouring Switzerland. New sanitary facilities.

From Stuttgart take the A81/98, exit 12 Stockach-West. Follow 'Wahlwies' camping sign.

CC € 23 *1/3-8/5 1/6-1/7 7/9-10/11*

N 47°48'31'' E 08°58'11''

Wertheim, D-97877 / Baden-Württemberg

595

Camping Wertheim-Bettingen
Furtwiesen 1
+49 93 42 70 77
22/3 - 3/11
info@campingpark-wertheim-bettingen.de

7,5ha 100T(80-100m²) 6-10A CEE

1 ADIJKLMNOQ**R**S
2 DISUXYZ
3 CKPS**W**X
4 (Q+R+U+Y)
5 **AB**DFGIJKLMNO**P**UWZ
6 CG(N 6km)OP

A campsite with a hospitable atmosphere, on the banks of the river Main in the Frankish vineyards. Perfect for water sports (harbour and boat ramp). Level terrain. Campers on the move have their own facilities; a special area where you can leave at any time day or night.

A3 Aschaffenburg-Würzburg, exit 66 Wertheim. Follow the signs to the campsite.

CC € 19 *22/3-28/3 1/4-7/5 12/5-16/5 20/5-28/5 2/6-30/6 1/9-31/10*

N 49°46'51'' E 09°34'00''

Arlaching/Chieming, D-83339 / Bayern

596

Camping Kupferschmiede
Trostbergerstraße 4
+49 8 66 74 46
1/4 - 3/10
info@campingkupferschmiede.de

2,5ha 80T(80-100m²) 16A CEE

1 ACDEIKLNQRS
2 EJOPSWXYZ
3 AC**G**IKSU**WZ**
4 (Q+R+T)(V 1/4-30/9)
(X+Y)(Z 1/4-30/9)
5 **AB**FGIJKLMNO**P**UWZ
6 ACFGK(N 1km)OPU

A campsite with grassy pitches 2 minute's walk from the Chiemsee, with a private beach on the lake. Most suitable for water sports. There are good walking and cycling routes around the Chiemsee from the campsite. Restaurants next to the campsite and restaurants and shops 6 km away in Chieming. Day trips to Kufstein, Salzburg, Passau and Munich.

A8 Salzburg-München, exit Grabenstätt. Direction Seebruck. Campsite located 1 km on the right before Seebruck.

B304
Traunreut
Traunstein
B306
A8

CC € 27 *1/4-17/5 2/6-1/7 9/9-3/10*

N 47°55'47'' E 12°29'33''

Augsburg-Ost, D-86169 / Bayern

597

Camping Bella Augusta***
Mühlhauser Straße 54b
+49 8 21 70 75 75
15/1 - 15/12
info@bella-augusta.de

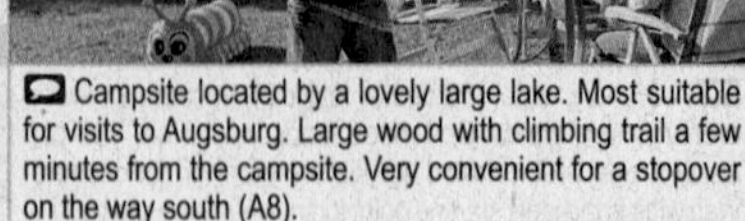

6,6ha 60T(tot 120m²) 16A CEE

1 ADIKLMNOQRS
2 EIOPSUVWXYZ
3 CGSWZ
4 (Q+R+T 1/4-31/10) (U+V+Y)
5 ABDFGIJKLMNOPUW
6 CEFGK(N 3km)OT

Campsite located by a lovely large lake. Most suitable for visits to Augsburg. Large wood with climbing trail a few minutes from the campsite. Very convenient for a stopover on the way south (A8).

A8, exit 73 Augsburg-Ost, towards Neuburg on the Donau (Danube), towards the airport. Turn right at the first traffic lights, and after 200 metres the campsite is located on the right on the Mühlhauser Straße.

CC € 25 15/1-20/5 2/6-15/7 2/9-15/12

N 48°24'44'' E 10°55'24''

Bad Abbach, D-93077 / Bayern

598

Camping Freizeitinsel
Inselstr. 1a
+49 9 40 59 57 04 01
22/3 - 27/10
info@campingplatz-freizeitinsel.de

2ha 78T(60-120m²) 16A CEE

1 ADIJKLMNOQRS
2 CIMNSVWX
3 AEGIK
4 (Q+R+X+Z)
5 ABDFGIJKLMNOPUXYZ
6 ABCEFGHK(N 3km)OPU

An idyllic and quietly located campsite on the Danube, plenty of sports such as cycling, canoeing and great for visiting Regensburg (15 km) and Kelheim, station at 800 m. Near a beautiful natural swimming pool. Stay on a comfort pitch for a €5 supplement. Reception open 8:00-12:00 and 15:00-19:00.

From the north: A93 exit Pentling (B16) dir. Kelheim. Then exit Poikam dir.Inselbad. From the south: A93 exit Bad Abbach (B16) dir. Kelheim. Then exit Poikam dir. Inselbad.

CC € 27 22/3-11/5 10/6-7/7 24/8-27/10

N 48°56'12'' E 12°01'15''

Bad Füssing/Egglfing, D-94072 / Bayern

599

Fuchs Kur-Camping****
Falkenstraße 14
+49 8 53 73 56
1/1 - 31/12
info@kurcamping-fuchs.de

1,6ha 90T(65-100m²) 16A CEE

1 ADEIJKLMNOQRS
2 JSUVWXYZ
3 ACFGIKSU
4 (A 1/5-30/9)(C 15/4-15/9) (Q)(R 1/3-1/11) (U+Y+Z 1/1-31/1,1/3-31/12)
5 ABDGHIJKLMNOPUWXYZ
6 ACDEFGK(N 0,5km)OPSV

A peaceful campsite with various amenities and a restaurant with heated terrace. Bad Füssing with its many spas, restaurants and shops is 2 km away. Beautiful cycling and walking trails in this level area. The three-river city of Passau with its many attractions is 34 km away. Free internet.

A3 Nürnberg-Passau, exit 118 Poching/Bad Füssing direction Egglfing. Follow signs.

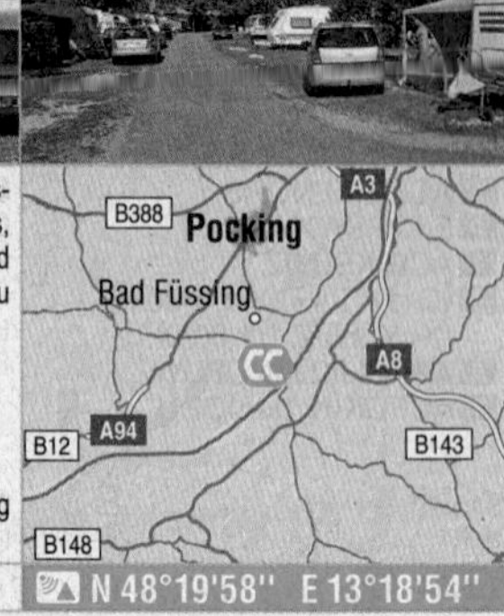

CC € 21 1/1-14/7 1/9-31/12

N 48°19'58'' E 13°18'54''

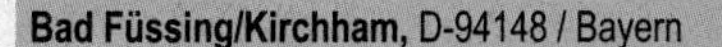

Bad Füssing/Kirchham, D-94148 / Bayern

600

ACSI AWARDS WINNER

Camping Preishof
Angloh 1
+49 85 37 91 92 00
1/1 - 31/12
info@preishof.de

6,5ha 230T(100-120m²) 16A CEE

1 ACD**I**JKLMNOQRS
2 STUWXY
3 AC**FG**IKMUV
4 **LNP**(Q)(Y 1/2-30/11)
5 **AB**DFGIJKLMNOPUWXY
6 ACEFGKL(N 1,5km)OPUVW

Quiet, family-run spa campsite on lawn with trees. Located ± 5 minutes from Bad Füssingen. Beautiful surroundings, very suitable for cycling. Very spacious pitches. Good toilet facilities. Massage and bathing possible. 18 hole golf course next to the campsite (campers get 30% discount).

A3/E56, exit 118 to the B12 direction Simbach. Exit Tutting/Kirchham, through the centre of Kirchham, direction golf course.

B388 A3 Pocking B12 Bad Füssing A8 CC B148 A94 B143 Altheim

CC € 23 *1/1-14/7 1/9-31/12*

N 48°20'17'' E 13°16'56''

Bad Kissingen, D-97688 / Bayern

601

Knaus Campingpark Bad Kissingen
Euerdorfer Str. 1
+49 9 71 78 51 39 66
1/1 - 31/12
badkissingen@knauscamp.de

2ha 123T(80-110m²) 16A CEE

1 ACD**I**JKLMNOQ**R**S
2 DIJSUVXYZ
3 AIK**W**
4 (Q+R+U+Y)
5 **AB**CDGIJMNOPUWXYZ
6 ABCGK(N 0,8km)O

Open grounds near the town's ring road and the Saale river. Adjacent to a health resort with a large park, which is accessible via its own entrance.

A7 Würzburg-Fulda, exit 96, then Bad Kissingen and signs. A71 Schweinfurt-Meiningen, exit 26, then B287 Bad Kissingen and follow signs.

CC € 27 *1/1-8/5 12/5-17/5 22/5-28/5 3/6-21/6 3/9-30/12*

Bad Neualbenreuth, D-95698 / Bayern

602

Campingplatz Platzermühle
Platzermühle 2
+49 96 38 91 22 00
1/1 - 31/12
info@camping-sibyllenbad.de

1ha 44T(100-120m²) 16A CEE

1 AC**I**KLMNOQRS
2 MSUVWXY
3 C**G**IKSU
4 (Q)
5 **AB**DGIJKLMNOPUWXY
6 CEFG(N 1km)OP

Terraced campsite, lovely toilet and washing facilities. Warm reception. Two km from Sibyllenbad wellness centre. Winter sports at 14 km when there's snow. Lovely place for walking and cycling.

A93 exit Mitterteich-Süd, then continue towards Bad Neualbenreuth.

CC € 21 *1/1-15/7*

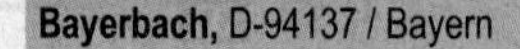

Bayerbach, D-94137 / Bayern

603

Vital CAMP Bayerbach*****
Huckenham 11
+49 8 53 29 27 80 70
1/1 - 31/12
info@vitalcamping-bayerbach.de

12ha 330T(70-130m²) 16A CEE

1 ACDIKLMNOQS
2 JMNOSUVWX
3 ACEGIJKLSU
4 (A 1/5-30/9)(F)LNO (Q+R+T+U+V+W+X+Y +Z)
5 ABDEFGIJKLMNOPQRSUWXYZ
6 BCEFGK(N 0,5km)OTUVX

Very good terraced campsite with sweeping views. Well-kept modern toilet facilities. Three naturally landscaped swimming lakes and indoor thermal bath and six saunas. Bavarian style restaurant. Large playground. Campers with CampingCard ACSI are allocated standard pitches.

A3 Regensburg-Linz. Exit 118 direction Pocking/Pfarrkirchen (388). Then exit Bayerbach. Follow camping signs.

CC € 27 *7/1-30/4 5/5-8/5 13/5-17/5 1/6-1/7 7/9-6/11*

N 48°24'55'' E 13°07'48''

Bischofsheim an der Rhön, D-97653 / Bayern

604

Rhöncamping****
Kissingerstraße 53
+49 97 72 13 50
1/1 - 25/10, 21/12 - 31/12
info@rhoencamping.de

3,8ha 80T(80-100m²) 16A CEE

1 AIJKLMNOQRS
2 JSUWXY
3 CIKRSU
4 (C+H 15/5-1/9)(Q+R)
5 ABCDGHIJKMNOPRUWZ
6 CDEFGK(N 0,5km)OP

A level campsite on the foot of the Kreuzberg mountain. Ideal base for walks. Free entrance to heated pool next door. Many options for relaxing in nature. The area is characterised by the 'Hochrhön' nature reserve with heights up to 800-900 metres.

A7 Würzburg-Fulda, exit 95 Bad Brückenau/Wildflecken direction Bischofsheim. In Bischofsheim follow the signs to the campsite.

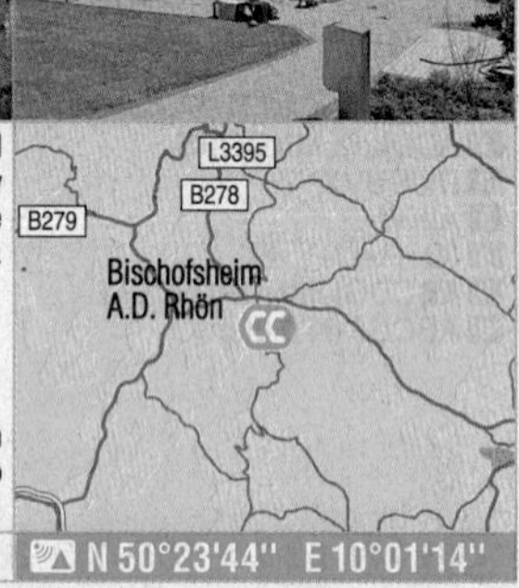

CC € 23 *8/1-22/3 7/4-8/5 2/6-1/7 6/9-25/10*

N 50°23'44'' E 10°01'14''

Bischofswiesen, D-83483 / Bayern

605

Camping Winkl-Landthal GmbH****
Klaushäuslweg 7
+49 86 52 81 64
1/4 - 30/10
info@camping-winkl.de

2,5ha 56T(80-100m²) 10A

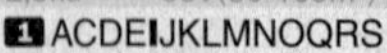

1 ACDEIJKLMNOQRS
2 CJMNSUWXYZ
3 AGIKSUWX
4 (Q+R+Z)
5 ABDFGIJKLMNOPUWXYZ
6 ABCDEFGHK(N 0,5km) OPSW

A peaceful campsite, excellent walking opportunities from the site. A good starting point for day trips to Salzburg, Berchtesgaden or Großglockner among other places. Bus stop 100 metres from the campsite. It is recommended to reserve via the contact form on campsite website.

On the A8 München-Salzburg, take exit Bad Reichenhall. Then, the B20 towards Berchtesgaden. 11 km before Berchtesgaden (Winkl).

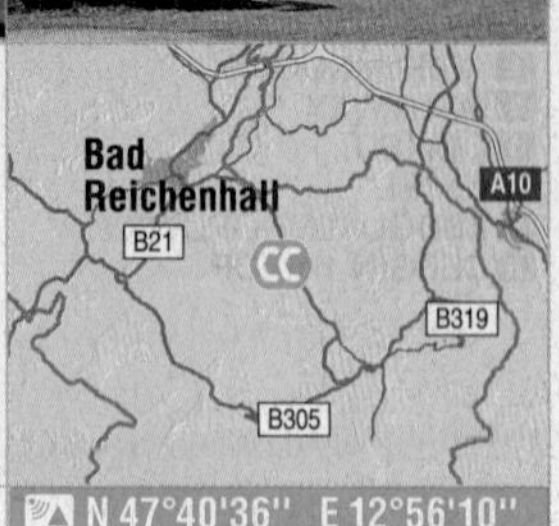

CC € 25 *1/4-17/5 2/6-7/7 1/9-25/10*

N 47°40'36'' E 12°56'10''

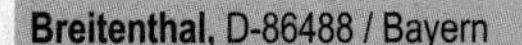

Breitenthal, D-86488 / Bayern

606

See Camping Günztal
Oberrieder Weiherstraße 5
+49 82 82 88 18 70
20/4 - 20/10
info@see-camping-guenztal.de

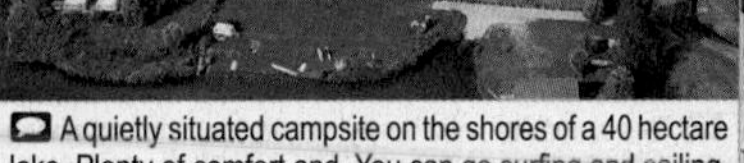

2,5ha 90T(80-100m²) 10A CEE

1 ACD**H**JKLMNOQRS
2 CENOUVWXY
3 ABCHKSU**WZ**
4 (Q+R+T+U+Z)
5 **AB**DEFGHIJKLMNOPQUWXYZ
6 ACDEFG**K**L(N 1km)OPV

A quietly situated campsite on the shores of a 40 hectare lake. Plenty of comfort and. You can go surfing and sailing, but no motor boats are allowed.

A8 Stuttgart-München, exit 67 Günzburg direction Krumbach. Straight on to Breitenthal and follow Oberrieder Weiherstraße. Look out for camping signs.

CC € 23 *20/4-16/5 3/6-27/6 2/9-20/10*

N 48°13'39'' E 10°17'32''

Chieming, D-83339 / Bayern

607

Chiemsee Strandcamping
Grabenstätter Straße
+49 8 66 45 00
28/3 - 30/9
info@chiemsee-strandcamping.de

1,5ha 135T(50-140m²) 16A CEE

1 ABCDE**I**KLMNOQRUV
2 EINPSUVWXYZ
3 AC**G**HIKS**WZ**
4 (Q+R+U+V+Z)
5 **AB**DEFGIJKLMNOPQUWXYZ
6 ABCDFGKL(N 1km)OPTV

Chiemsee Strandcamping is a well-kept site with new toilet facilities right on the lake. Motorhome service point. Table tennis, billiards, children's playground, free kayaks for children, bar/café with snacks and pizzas and small supermarket. Restaurant within 1 km. Landing stage 1200m away. Minigolf, bike hire. Free wifi on your pitch. Free bus at 200m, from Whitsun.

A8 München-Salzburg. Junction 109 direction Chieming. First campsite on the left about 5 km from the exit.

Traunreut
B304
Traunstein
A8
B305

CC € 25 *28/3-16/5 2/6-26/6 8/9-30/9*

N 47°52'35'' E 12°31'44''

Eging am See, D-94535 / Bayern

608

Bavaria Kur- und Sport Camping****
Grafenauer Str. 31
+49 85 44 80 89
1/1 - 31/12
info@bavaria-camping.de

BAVARIA SPORT CAMPING PARK

6ha 120T(120m²) 16A CEE

1 ACDE**I**JKLMNOQRS
2 CIMSTVWYZ
3 AC**G**IKLPSU
4 (Q 1/4-30/10)(R) (U+Y+Z 1/4-31/10)
5 **AB**DFGJLMNOPUWZ
6 ABCDEFG**K**(N 0,7km)OT

A lovely terraced campsite with adequate shade. All comforts, modern and well maintained toilet facilities. Health spa, swimming pool and lake all within walking distance.

A3 Motorway exit 113. Direction Eging am See. Campsite signposted before Eging am See.

B85
A3
Vilshofen an der Donau

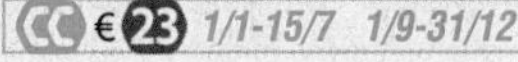

CC € 23 *1/1-15/7 1/9-31/12*

N 48°43'16'' E 13°15'55''

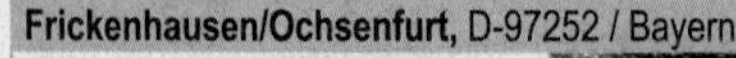

Frickenhausen/Ochsenfurt, D-97252 / Bayern

609

Knaus Campingpark Frickenhausen****
Ochsenfurterstraße 49
+49 93 31 31 71
1/3 - 3/11
frickenhausen@knauscamp.de

3,4ha 147T(80-100m²) 16A CEE

1 ACD**I**JKLMNOQ**R**UV
2 CISUWXYZ
3 CIKMSU**W**
4 (B 1/5-1/10)(Q+R+U+Y)
5 **AB**DFGIJKLMNOPQUWZ
6 ABCEFGHK(N 0,5km)OPV

This campsite with bushy vegetation and swimming pool is located on the River Main, in the middle of the idyllic Mainfranken countryside. The villages in the area, famous for their wine, are worth a visit. Prime and comfort pitches available for a supplement.

A3 Würzburg-Nürnberg, exit 71 Randersacker. B13 as far as Frickenhausen. Then follow campsings.

CC € 27 *1/3-8/5 12/5-17/5 22/5-28/5 3/6-21/6 19/7-2/8 3/9-3/11*

N 49°40'09" E 10°04'28"

Gemünden, D-97737 / Bayern

610

Camping Saaleinsel
Duivenallee 7
+49 93 51 85 74
22/3 - 15/10
poststelle@campingplatz-saaleinsel.de

5,2ha 150T(80-120m²) 16A CEE

1 ACD**I**JKLMNO**R**UV
2 DJSUXY
3 AHIKM**O**P**R**SU**W**X
4 (C+G 15/5-15/9) (T+U 1/5-15/10)
5 **AB**CDFGIJKLMNOPUWX
6 CEFGK(N 0,5km)

Campsite in an idyllic location on a peninsula in the middle of the Main Valley. Good cycling and walking paths in the area. Fishing, miniature golf, children's playground and canoe hire at the campsite. There is a heated outdoor swimming pool right next to the campsite, which campers can use for free. There are various restaurants in the nearby centre.

A3 Frankfurt-Würzburg, exit 61 Hösbach. Then B26 Lohr-Gemünden. Follow campsite signs.

CC € 25 *8/4-28/4 13/5-16/5 3/6-7/7 1/9-15/10*

N 50°03'37" E 09°41'28"

Gunzenhausen, D-91710 / Bayern

611

Campingplatz Fischer-Michl
Wald Seezentrum 4
+49 98 31 27 84
15/3 - 31/10
fischer-michl@t-online.de

4,5ha 120T(120m²) 16A CEE

1 AD**I**JLNOQ**R**S
2 AEJOSUWX
3 CHMQS**W**Z
4 M(Q+R+T+U+X+Z)
5 **AB**DEFGJMNOPUWZ
6 ACDEFGHK(N 3km)OT

Spacious campsite in rustic surroundings. Ideal operating base for cycling tours. Plenty of watersport activities.

Take the A6 Heilbronn/Nürnberg, exit 52 direction Gunzenhausen. Then direction Nördlingen/Altmühlsee Südufer-Wald.

CC € 23 *23/3-8/5 3/6-15/7 3/9-31/10*

N 49°07'32" E 10°43'00"

Illertissen, D-89257 / Bayern

612

Camping Illertissen GbR****
Dietenheimerstraße 91
+49 73 03 78 88
1/4 - 5/11
info@camping-illertissen.de

3,5ha 50T(70-100m²) 16A CEE

1 ABCDEIJKLMNOQRS
2 BCIJMSVXYZ
3 ACKL**O**S
4 (B 31/5-15/9)**I**
(Q+R+T+U+W+X+Y+Z)
5 **A**BCDFGIJKLMNOPQRUWXYZ
6 ABCEFGJ**K**M(N 1,5km)OP

An ideal long-stay or stopover campsite in peaceful surroundings. Excellent toilet facilities and electrical connections. Hot showers, free use of the swimming pool and a limited stock of provisions. Legoland can be reached in just under one hour.

Take the A7 Ulm-Memmingen. At exit 124 Illertissen, direction Dietenheim. From there on the campsite is clearly signposted.

CC € 27 *1/4-15/6 15/9-5/11*

N 48°12'44'' E 10°05'17''

Kinding/Pfraundorf, D-85125 / Bayern

613

Camping Kratzmühle****
Mühlweg 2
+49 8 46 16 41 70
1/1 - 31/12
info@kratzmuehle.de

10ha 375T(80-130m²) 16A CEE

1 ACD**I**JKLMNOQRS
2 DEIJMNSUVWXYZ
3 C**G**IKMPSU**WZ**
4 (Q+R 1/4-31/10)
(T+U+V+Y 1/4-30/9)
5 **AB**DEFGIJKLMNOPR**S**UWXY
6 ACEFGHK(N 5km)OPTV

A friendly natural campsite with excellent opportunities for cycling and walking. There is a lovely lake next to the site where you can go swimming. Also very suitable as an overnight campsite.

A9 Nürnberg-München, exit 58 Altmühltal direction Kinding. Campsite is signposted.

CC € 25 *1/1-8/5 12/5-16/5 2/6-22/6 1/9-31/12*

N 49°00'12'' E 11°27'07''

Lackenhäuser, D-94089 / Bayern

614

Knaus Campingpark Lackenhäuser****
Lackenhäuser 127
+49 8 58 33 11
1/1 - 3/11, 20/12 - 31/12
lackenhaeuser@knauscamp.de

19ha 322T(80-100m²) 16A CEE

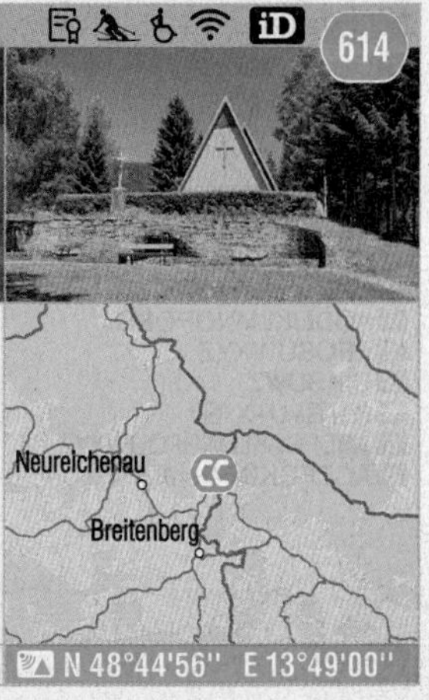

1 ACE**I**JKLMNOQ**R**S
2 BCMNOSUVWXYZ
3 CEIKLMNP**RSTUW**
4 (A 1/7-15/8)(C 15/5-15/9)
(**F**)**N**(Q+R+U+Y)
5 **AB**CDEFGIJKLMNOPUWXYZ
6 CDEFGHK(N 5km)OSVX

Lovely terraced campsite situated in woodland. Very child friendly; the various swimming pools, children's farm, entertainment clubhouse, adventure village, small lake and playgrounds are an added attraction. A relaxing or sportive holiday for young and old. CampingCard ACSI rate does not include entrance to indoor pool.

Take exit Waldkirchen on B12 between Freyung and Passau. Continue to Waldkirchen-Ost. Campsite signposted from here. Follow signs for about another 28 km.

CC € 27 *7/1-30/6 19/7-2/8 1/9-3/11*

N 48°44'56'' E 13°49'00''

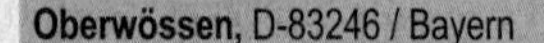

Oberwössen, D-83246 / Bayern

615

Camping Litzelau****
Litzelau 4
+49 86 40 87 04
1/1 - 31/12
camping-litzelau@t-online.de

4ha 71T(80-120m²) 16A CEE

1 AD**I**KLMNOQ**RS**
2 BCJMNSTWXYZ
3 CE**G**IKLSUX
4 **N**(Q+R+Y+Z)
5 **AB**DFGIJKLMNO**P**UWXY
6 ACEFGK(N 1km)OTV

The campsite is located in a romantic valley next to a mountain stream and is completely surrounded by woods. Many walking and cycling routes from the campsite. Plenty of sports facilities in the immediate vicinity (such as gliding and paragliding, natural toboggan run, ski lifts, ski school, inline skating, tennis and golf).

Take the A8 München-Salzburg, exit 106 Bernau and via B305 direction Reit im Winkl to Oberwössen (20 km).

CC € 23 *5/1-17/5 31/5-21/6 6/9-13/12*

N 47°43'03'' E 12°28'45''

Prien am Chiemsee, D-83209 / Bayern

616

Camping Hofbauer
Bernauerstraße 110
+49 80 51 41 36
13/4 - 19/10
info@camping-prien-chiemsee.de

1,5ha 100T(75-100m²) 16A CEE

1 AD**I**KLMNOQRS
2 IJLSVWXY
3 C**G**JKMSU
4 (C+D+H 1/5-30/9)(Q+R)
(U 30/4-3/10)(V)
(X 30/4-3/10)(Z)
5 **AB**DFGIJKLMNOPUWXYZ
6 CFGKL(N 0,6km)OPSTV

Good campsite for people passing through, but also invites you to stay. 1.5 km from Lake Chiemsee and 3 km from the motorway. The pitches are along the roads. The beautiful swimming pool can be canopied in case of bad weather. Free access to the Schöllkopf baths at Lake Chiemsee.

A8 Munich-Salzburg, exit 106 Bernau. Then approx. 3km towards Prien. Straight ahead at the roundabout, the campsite is on the left after 100m.

Prien am Chiemsee
CC
A8
B305
Unterwössen

CC € 27 *1/5-9/5 13/5-18/5 2/6-30/6 10/9-30/9*

N 47°50'20'' E 12°21'04''

Roth/Wallesau, D-91154 / Bayern

617

Camping Waldsee****
Badstraße 37
+49 91 71 55 70
1/1 - 31/12
info@camping-waldsee.de

4ha 100T(80-120m²) 16A CEE

1 ACD**I**JKLMNOPQ**R**S
2 BFOSUWXYZ
3 CIKSU**WZ**
4 (Q+R+U+X)
5 **AB**DFGIJKLMNOPQUWXYZ
6 ACEFGK(N 4km)OPT

An idyllic comfort campsite with its own lake in the woods. Ideal as a starting point for walking or cycling. Located in the Frankish lake area.

A9 Nürnberg-München, exit Allersberg towards Hilpoltstein. Turn right in Hilpoltstein towards Roth/Eckersmühlon, continue to Wallesau. On the left when entering the village.

B2
Roth
CC
Hilpoltstein
A9

CC € 25 *1/1-5/5 3/6-30/6 1/9-31/12* ***7=6, 14=12***

N 49°11'21'' E 11°07'28''

Rottenbuch, D-82401 / Bayern

618

Terrassen-Camping am Richterbichl****
Solder 1
+49 88 67 15 00
1/1 - 31/12
info@camping-rottenbuch.de

1,2ha 50T(80-100m²) 16A CEE

1 ABD**I**JKLMNOQRS
2 EJMSVWY
3 CIK**O**PSUZ
4 (Q+R+T)(U+X 1/5-30/9) (Z)
5 **AB**DFGIJKLMNOPUWZ
6 ACDEFG**K**(N 0,5km)OPTV

A slightly sloping terraced campsite with a rural character surrounded by trees and meadows. Centrally placed for trips out (Linderhof, Oberammergau, Neuschwanstein). Lovely cycle routes safe from the traffic.

From Ulm take the A7 direction Kempten. Exit 134, then the B12 until Marktoberdorf. Follow the B472 direction Schongau. Then the B23 direction Garmisch-Partenkirchen. Campsite directly at the Romantische Straße.

Schongau · Peissenberg · B472 · B17 · B23

CC € 25 *8/1-17/5 3/6-12/7 9/9-20/12*

N 47°43'39'' E 10°58'01''

Schillingsfürst, D-91583 / Bayern

619

Camping Frankenhöhe
Fischhaus 2
+49 98 68 51 11
1/1 - 31/12
info@campingplatz-frankenhoehe.de

3ha 55T(100m²) 16A CEE

1 ACD**I**JKLMNOQRS
2 BILSVXYZ
3 CGHIKSU**W**Z
4 (Q+T+U+X+Z 1/4-31/10)
5 **AB**DFGHIJKLMNOPUWZ
6 ACDEFG**K**(N 1,5km)OPV

Campsite located at an altitude of 500 m in the Frankenhöhe nature park, close to the Medieval towns of Rothenburg, Dinkelsbühl and the Rococo city of Ansbach. Many opportunities for walking and taking cycling trips in the woods. Swimming lake at 200 m. Fine restaurant with a simple menu at the campsite.

A7 exit 109 Wörnitz, direction Schillingsfürst. In Schillingsfürst direction Dombühl, campsite signposted. Turn right 100 metres after Fischhaus.

Neusitz · Leutershausen · Aurach · A6 · A7

CC € 23 *1/1-30/3 8/4-13/5 3/6-30/6 8/9-31/12*

N 49°16'25'' E 10°15'56''

Taching am See, D-83373 / Bayern

620

Seecamping Taching am See
Am Strandbad 1
+49 86 81 95 48
1/4 - 15/10
info@seecamping-taching.de

1,6ha 98T(80-100m²) 16A CEE

1 ACDE**H**JKLMNOQRS
2 AEJOPSVWXYZ
3 C**G**HIKMPS**W**Z
4 (Q 1/5-15/9)(R 15/5-15/9) (S 1/5-30/9) (U+V+X+Y 1/5-15/9)
5 **AB**DFGIJKLMNOPUWZ
6 ACEFGHK(N 0,5km)P

Family friendly site. Lovely location right on Tachinger See, one of Bavaria's warmest lakes and suitable for watersports. Good restaurant with terrace on the lake and lovely views of the mountains. Many cycling and walking opportunities into the mountains. Tourist info at the campsite. Trips to Salzburg, Passau and Munich. Free wifi on all pitches.

A8 München-Salzburg, exit Traunstein/Siegsdorf. From Waging/Tittmoning road at Taching to the lake, then another 300m.

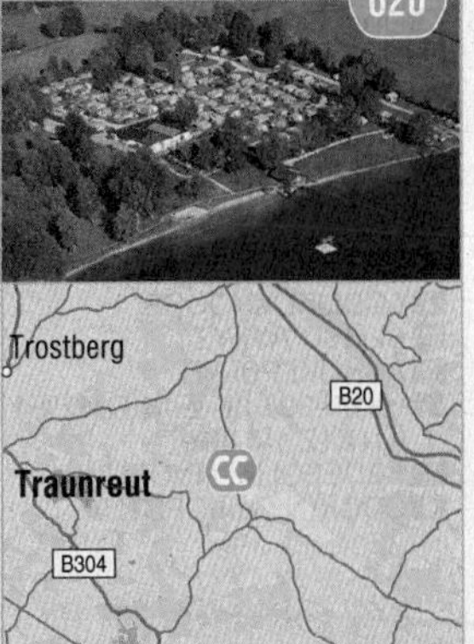

CC € 23 *1/4-1/6 1/9-15/10*

N 47°57'42'' E 12°43'54''

Triefenstein/Lengfurt, D-97855 / Bayern

621

Camping Main-Spessart-Park*****
Spessartstraße 30
+49 93 95 10 79
1/1 - 31/12
info@camping-main-spessart.de

9,5ha 180T(90-110m²) 10A CEE

1 ACD**H**JKLMNORTU
2 IMSUVWXYZ
3 CE**G**HIKNPSU
4 (Q+R 1/4-31/10)
(U+V+Y+Z)
5 **AB**DEFGIJKLMNOPUWXYZ
6 ABCDEFGK(N 2km)OPV

Well maintained campsite. Modern toilet facilities. 300 metres from swimming pool and 500 metres from River Main. Park-like landscaping between the terraces. Walking and cycling in beautiful Main Valley and Spessart Nature Park. Comfort pitches available for a supplement.

A3 Frankfurt-Würzburg, exit 65 Marktheidenfeld. Over bridge in Triefenstein/Lengfurt and follow camping signs (6 km). Or A3 exit 66 Wertheim. Along the Main dir. Lengfurt. Follow camping signs (8 km).

CC € 25 *7/4-6/5 2/6-1/7 1/9-31/10*

N 49°49'06'' E 09°35'18''

Viechtach, D-94234 / Bayern

622

Adventurecamp 'Schnitzmühle'
Schnitzmühle 1
+49 9 94 29 48 10
1/1 - 31/12
info@schnitzmuehle.de

2ha 80T(120m²) 10A CEE

1 ACDE**I**KLMNOQRS
2 CEPSTVY
3 CHIJKLNP**Q**SU**W**XZ
4 (A 1/7-31/8)**KLN**(Q+R)
(T 1/7-1/9)(U+Y+Z)
5 **AB**DFGIJKLMNOP**QR**UWZ
6 CDEFG**J**L(N 3km)OPQRUV

Idyllic location on a river and (swimming) lake for adventure and fun. Excellent wellness and a Thai and Bavarian restaurant. The Waldbahn stops at the campsite. Every hour there is a free train to various towns in the vicinity.

A3 Regensburg-Passau exit 110 direction Deggendorf. Take B11/E53 to Patersdorf. Left on B85 to Viechtach. Follow campsite signs. Attention: the access road has an incline of 12% and a bridge which is 3.20 m high.

CC € 25 *1/1-16/5 5/6-15/7 9/9-31/12*

N 49°04'10'' E 12°54'49''

Viechtach, D-94234 / Bayern

623

Knaus Campingpark Viechtach****
Waldfrieden 22
+49 99 42 10 95
1/1 - 3/11, 20/12 - 31/12
viechtach@knauscamp.de

5,7ha 134T(80-120m²) 16A CEE

1 ACD**I**JKLMNOQRS
2 BLMSUVWXYZ
3 ACHIJKLPSU**W**
4 (A 1/6-30/9)(**F**)**N**(Q+R)
(U+X+Z 1/7-30/9)
5 **AB**DEFGIJKLMNOPUW
6 CDGK(N 2km)OPSTUV

The new owners have launched a new concept of 'dog friendly campsite' with separate marked out pitches, agility training field and a dog toilet in the woods. The many footpaths and attractions in the area promise an enjoyable and active holiday. CampingCard ACSI rate does not include entrance to indoor pool.

A3 Regensburg-Passau, exit 110 direction Deggendorf. Take the B11/ E53 as far as Patersdorf. Then left onto the B85 as far as Viechtach. Follow the Knaus camping signs.

CC € 27 *7/1-8/5 12/5-17/5 22/5-28/5 3/6-21/6 3/9-3/11*

N 49°04'57'' E 12°51'12''

Waldmünchen, D-93449 / Bayern

624

Camping Ferienpark Perlsee
Alte Ziegelhütte 6
+49 99 72 14 69
1/1 - 31/12
info@campingplatz-waldmuenchen.de

5ha 250T(80-120m²) 16A CEE

1 ADE**I**JKLMNORS
2 AFLMNQSUWY
3 ACIKLMNPRSU**W**Z
4 (**A** 1/7-31/8)(Q+R 1/5-15/9)(T 1/5-1/10)(U+Y)
5 **AB**DFGIJKLMNOPUW
6 CEFG**J**(N 2,5km)OPQV

Terraced campsite with a spacious sandy beach in a beautiful mountainous area in Bavaria on the Czech border. Various options for walking and cycling. Good mountain bike routes. Swimming pool nearby for rainy days. Great area for motorcyclists. Free transport by bus and train in the Cham region.

Coming from Cham on the B22 and B85, continue to Waldmünchen. Enter the village and drive to the second roundabout, then turn 1st left (sharp bend). Follow camping signs.

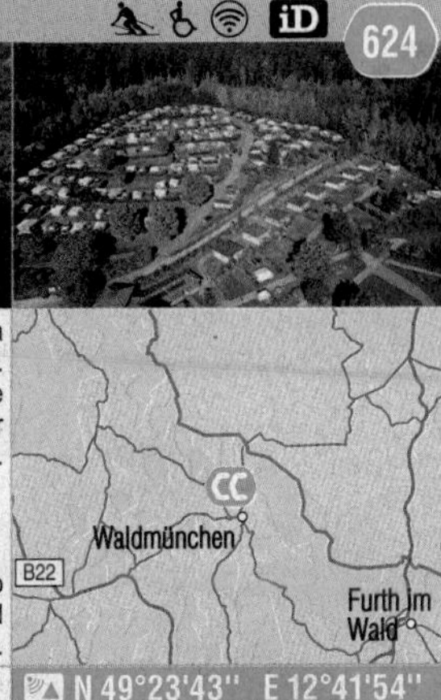

CC € 21 *1/1-16/5 10/6-27/6 2/9-31/12*

N 49°23'43'' E 12°41'54''

Zellingen am Main, D-97225 / Bayern

625

Main Camp Resort
Badstraße 7
+49 9 36 48 12 13 23
22/3 - 31/10
info@maincampresort.de

1ha 62T(80-100m²) 16A CEE

1 ACD**I**JKLMNOQRUV
2 DOUVWX
3 AIKL**OSW**
4 (**C**+**H** 15/5-15/9)J(Q+R)
5 **AB**DEGIJMNOPUWZ
6 CGK(N 0,5km)

Simple campsite by the Main with views of Benediktushöhe's chalk cliffs. The large, lovely municipal swimming pool is next to the campsite. The Main cycling route runs past the campsite.

B27 Würzburg-Zellingen. In village, follow signs for pool.

CC € 25 *8/4-28/4 13/5-16/5 3/6-7/7 1/9-31/10*

N 49°53'48'' E 09°49'36''

Switzerland

Capital: Bern
Currency: Swiss franc
Time zone: UTC +1, UTC +2 (March to October)
Language: German, French and Italian
International dialling code: +41
Alcohol limit: 0.5‰
Emergency number: general: 112, police: 117, fire brigade: 118, ambulance: 144
Tap water: safe to drink

Switzerland:
high mountains, green valleys and blue lakes

There is probably not a single European country with a landscape that is more impressive than Switzerland. The landscape will already enthrall you while on your way to your campsite in Switzerland: breath-taking and extremely varied, inaccessible or very charming, with icy peaks and frozen glaciers but also sun-drenched, green slopes and lovely lakes in the valleys.

Nature at a high level

Nature lovers can indulge in their passion in Switzerland. The Alpine landscape, perfectly accessible from campsites, is particularly interesting for those who love camping. The lower sections are perfectly fine for the inexperienced hiker, but it is also possible to get to the top in comfort by taking a mountain lift to have a look at the view. The most photogenic mountain top of Europe is located in Switzerland: the Matterhorn. Take the cable car to the top of the mountain facing it, the Klein Matterhorn (or Little Matterhorn), where the highest cable car station in the Alps is located, and admire the fantastic view of the characteristic mountain.

Camping holiday by a lake

If you prefer to camp by water, there is much to choose from in Switzerland. Along the Swiss banks of Lake Constance, it is possible to explore the beautiful city of Constance and the flower island of Mainau. Take a boat across Lake Geneva and see the Jet d'eau (Water Jet), the landmark of the city of Geneva. Follow the footsteps of William Tell at Lake Lucerne in the cities Lucerne and Küssnacht. The lake at Neuchâtel and the Walensee (Lake Walen) also offer a great deal of water fun with sailing, fishing, swimming, surfing and paddling.
A camping holiday in Switzerland becomes even more Impressive if you cross one of the elevated Alpine passes, for example, the Great St Bernard Pass, the Furka Pass or the Grimsel Pass. Much less well-known, but certainly just as beautiful, is the green and charming low mountain range in the west: the Swiss Jura Mountains. Most campsites also offer winter camping.

Switzerland for the true connoisseurs

Switzerland is famous for its cheeses, like the Emmentaler, Appenzeller or Raclette. At the Emmentaler cheese dairy, you can learn everything there is to know about the history and the production of this Swiss speciality. A good glass of wine from one of the Swiss wine regions goes well with a good piece of cheese. For those who enjoy sweets, Swiss chocolate is an absolute high point.

Winner in Switzerland

Best campsite
Camping Riarena

En route

Filling up

Petrol (Super 95 and Super Plus 98) and diesel (gazole) are widely available. LPG is reasonably available. When filling up with LPG, some fuelling stations use the European connection (acme) and other the Italian (dish) connection.
Fuelling stations are often usually open from 8:00 to 18:00. In cities and along motorways, they are often open from 7:00 to 20:00, and along motorways from 6:00 to 23:00. In addition, most fuelling stations have a night machine that allows you to fill up using a credit/debit card.

> *"Switzerland: unequalled nature in Europe, combined with charming historic cities."*
> Mr D. Kolkman, inspector 1070

Charging

There are plenty of public charging stations in Switzerland, many of which are along the motorways. In Switzerland, the rates for charging can differ significantly and can be very high at times. This has made charging for free very popular in Switzerland, and companies like IKEA and supermarkets provide the opportunity to charge for free. This means that there are, relatively speaking, many charging stations in Switzerland that are free. It is advisable to make use of these to make your holiday in Switzerland less expensive.

Traffic regulations

Low beam lights (or daytime running lamps) are mandatory during the day. At equivalent crossings, traffic from the right has right of way. Trams always have right of way. Traffic on the roundabout has right of way if so indicated by traffic signs. Uphill traffic in the mountains has priority over downhill traffic. On narrow roads, a heavier vehicle has priority over a lighter vehicle. Drivers may only call handsfree. Children younger than 12 years of age or shorter than 1.50 metres must be in a child's seat. Speed camera warnings are prohibited; if necessary, remove Swiss speed camera location from your navigation software. Winter tyres are strongly advised under winter conditions (snow chains may be made mandatory by means of a sign).

Special regulations

Switzerland has 'Bergpoststrassen' (mountain post roads, indicated by blue signs with a yellow PostBus horn), on which regular buses and the PostBus always have right of way.
If traffic jams form, keep to the right or left as far as possible so that a free lane (Rettungsgasse) is created in the middle for emergency vehicles.
Parking is prohibited at locations with yellow stripes and crosses on the road surface. A load may not stick out on the sides, and bicycles may only stick out a maximum of 20 centimetres.

Mandatory equipment

A warning triangle is mandatory in the car.

Caravan and motorhome

A motorhome or car-caravan combination may be a maximum of 4 metres high, 2.55 metres wide and 18.75 metres long (the caravan itself may be a maximum of 12 metres long).
You may not drive with your caravan (nor with a motorhome > 3.5 tonnes) in the leftmost lane on motorways with at least three lanes going in the same direction.
You are advised to take along wheel chocks to secure the wheels of your caravan when on a (minor) slant.

Cycling

A bicycle helmet is only mandatory if you cycle faster than 20 km/hour. Calling or texting while cycling is prohibited. Children up to 6 years of age may only cycle on the road if accompanied by a person at least 16 years of age. Children may be transported by someone 16 years or older on a bicycle in a child's seat with leg guards. Cyclists may only cycle side-by-side on bicycle paths or bicycle lanes.

Toll

All Swiss motorways require a vignette.
Caution! A second vignette is required for caravans and trailers. The vignette is (and costs) the same for cars, caravans, trailers and motorhomes up to a combined weight of 3.5 tonnes and is valid for one year. If the vignette is lacking, you risk a considerable fine.
Before you start your journey, it is a good idea to order the vignette online through, for example, tolltickets.com. This means less time waiting at the border.
For vehicles (including motorhomes) over 3.5 tonnes, a 'Schwerverkehrsabgabe' (lump-sum heavy vehicle charge, PSVA) must be purchased. You can report to the customs at the border for this.
For more information: ezv.admin.ch (look for 'PSVA').
You cannot pass the border post Basel-Weil (on the E35, German A5, Swiss A2) without a vignette.

> ***"High in the mountains or near a lake – everything is possible in Switzerland."***
> Mr W. Laeven, inspector 1121

Environmental zones

The Geneva canton has implemented an environmental zone for several municipalities as from January 2020. You must have an environmental sticker to enter this zone.

Tunnels

There are two tunnels for which you must pay a separate toll: the Great St. Bernard Tunnel and the Munt La Schera Tunnel. The Munt La Schera Tunnel has only one lane, so you can only go through the tunnel at fixed times. For more information: letunnel.com, livigno.eu/en/tunnel-munt-la-schera and ekwstrom.ch. You can also take the car train through several tunnels.

Breakdown and accident

Place your warning triangle on the motorway at least 100 metres (elsewhere 50 metres) behind the car if it is not properly visible to other traffic. All passengers are advised to wear a safety vest.
If you have had a breakdown, call the alarm number of your breakdown assistance insurer. You can also call a Swiss emergency breakdown service: +41 44 2833377 (ACS) or 800 140140 (TCS). On major roads and along mountain passes, you can also call breakdown assistance using an emergency telephone. Towing on the motorway is permitted up to the first exit.

Camping

Most camping sites in Switzerland are located by lakes. The campsites in mountainous areas are often small with only basic amenities for tent campers. In the west of Switzerland, campsites often have many fixed pitches.
Free camping (outside of campsites) is generally prohibited. It is only permitted with prior permission from the land owner or the local police.

Particulars

Many Swiss campsites are also open in the winter, especially in Berner Oberland and Graubünden. When camping in the mountains, it is wise to keep an eye on the weather. Swiss campsites are very strict on the use of gas. It is very possible that you will have to complete a questionnaire on the reliability of your equipment.

Staying overnight in a caravan, motorhome or car outside of pitches is only permitted for one night in parking spaces along the motorways if you are simply passing through. Apart from local exceptions, staying along the public road elsewhere overnight is prohibited.

Practical matters

Driving in the Swiss mountains demands some experience when travelling with a caravan.
The Alps have gradients of 6 to 15 percent and more.
Almost all mountain roads are secured on the side of the ravine.
Mountain passes in Switzerland, Austria and Italy can be closed temporarily, difficult to negotiate or even permanently prohibited for cars with a caravan or trailer. Check on this before you start your journey.
For more information: alpenpaesse.de (in German).
Additional costs for items such as tourist tax and environmental tax may turn out to be rather high.
If you plan to call on your mobile or use the internet, check beforehand if Switzerland is included in your EU package.

Brig, CH-3900 / Wallis

626

- Camping Geschina****
- Geschinaweg 41
- +41 2 79 23 06 88
- 3/5 - 20/10
- geschina@bluewin.ch

2ha 75T 10A CEE

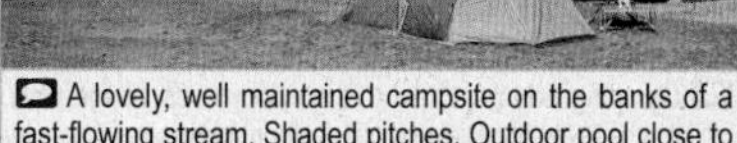

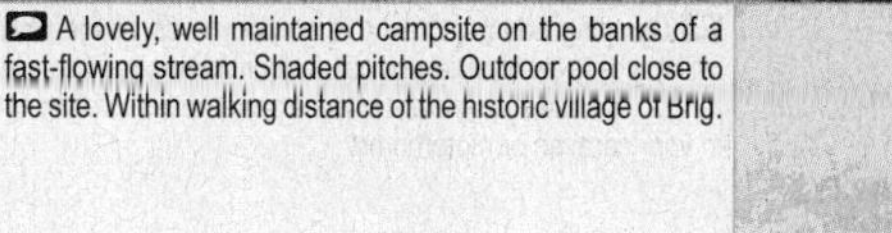

1 ACD**I**KLMNQ**R**S
2 CIJNSXY
3 ASU
4 (**C**+**H** 16/5-6/9)**J**(Q)
5 **AB**FGIJKLMNO**P**UW
6 CEFJ(N 0,6km)**P**TV

A lovely, well maintained campsite on the banks of a fast-flowing stream. Shaded pitches. Outdoor pool close to the site. Within walking distance of the historic village of Brig.

Drive to Brig, then follow Brig-Glis and 'Altstadt' (P) signs. Then follow camping signs number 9.101.

CC € 25 *3/5-30/6 25/8-20/10*

N 46°18'34'' E 07°59'36''

Chapella, CH-7526 / Graubünden

627

- Camping Chapella**
- +41 8 18 54 12 06
- 1/5 - 31/10
- info@campingchapella.ch

2ha 100T(40-100m²) 16A CEE

1 ACD**I**KLMNO**R**S
2 CMNSUXY
3 A**G**IK**W**
4 (Q+R)
5 **AB**DGIJKLMOPUWZ
6 ACFK(N 3km)OP

A romantic grassy campsite with unreserved pitches and circled by trees. Modern heated toilet block. Close to the entrance to the Swiss National Park.

Located on route 27, a few kilometres south of Cinuos-chel. Beware sharp bend and bridge!

CC € 25 *1/5-23/6 1/9-31/10*

N 46°37'57'' E 10°00'49''

Cugnasco, CH-6516 / Tessin

628

- Camping Riarena****
- Via Campeggio 1
- +41 9 18 59 16 88
- 15/3 - 20/10
- info@campingriarena.ch

3,2ha 105T(70-100m²) 16A

1 ACDGKLMNOQ**R**S
2 CIJSTXY
3 AKPSU
4 (B+G 1/5-15/9)
(Q+R+U+V+X+Y+Z)
5 **AB**FGIJKLMNOPUW
6 ABCEFGKM(N 2km)OPTV

Well-maintained, peacefully located family campsite with a swimming pool. Excellent base for cycling and walking. Lovely playground. Good facilities for the disabled. Credit cards accepted.

A2, exit Bellinzona-Süd/Locarno, direction Locarno. Continue past the airport, at roundabout take direction Gordola-Gudo. In Cugnasco follow campsite signs.

CC € 27 *15/3-29/3 2/4-9/5 13/5-18/5 21/5-8/7 26/8-20/10*

N 46°10'11'' E 08°54'51''

Erlach, CH-3235 / Bern

629

Camping Erlach****
Stadtgraben 23
+41 3 25 13 01 00
28/3 - 26/10
info@camping-erlach.ch

1,6ha 95T(70-90m²) 16A CEE

1 ACDIJKLMNOPQRS
2 FJNOPSTWY
3 ACHOPSUWZ
4 (Q+S+U+W+Y+Z)
5 ABEFGIJKLMNOPQRUWXYZ
6 CEFGHK(N 0,5km)OPT

Camping Erlach is next to the eponymous village with direct access to Lake Biel and offers stunning views of the Jura range. The site's restaurant offers an alternative to cooking in your caravan or motorhome.

From Gals direction Erlach/Täuffelen. Go left in Erlach village, 100 m past Camping Mon Plaisir.

CC € 27 2/4-8/5 21/5-29/5 3/6-1/7 1/9-26/10

N 47°02'44'' E 07°06'07''

Frutigen, CH-3714 / Bern

630

Camping Grassi****
Grassiweg 60
+41 3 36 71 11 49
1/1 - 31/12
info@camping-grassi.ch

2,6ha 68T(20-120m²) 10A CEE

1 ACDIKLMNRS
2 CJNSUXYZ
3 AHIKMNSUW
4 (Q 1/7-30/8)
5 ABDGIJKLMNOPUW
6 ACDEFGHK(N 1km)OPV

Take in the countryside and relax completely at campsite Grassi. Idyllic location on the edge of a conservation area. The view over the surrounding mountains is unique. Free wifi.

Follow the Spiez-Kandersteg road and take exit Frutigen-Dorf. Over the bridge and enter village. Turn left at Hotel Simplon. The campsite is clearly signposted.

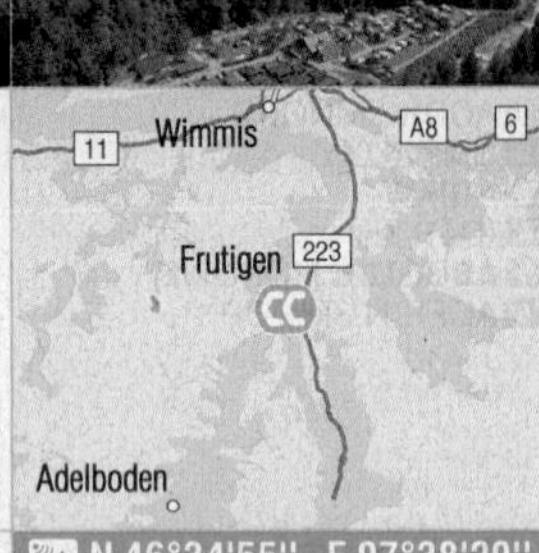

CC € 25 1/5-30/6 1/9-8/10

N 46°34'55'' E 07°38'29''

Gstaad, CH-3780 / Bern

631

Bellerive Camping***
Bellerivestraße 38
+41 3 37 44 63 30
1/1 - 31/12
info@bellerivecamping.ch

0,8ha 35T(80-100m²) 12A CEE

1 AFIKLMNQRS
2 DJNSUVWXY
3 AIKOQRUW
4 (Q)
5 ABDGIJKLMNPUW
6 CDFJ(N 1,5km)OPV

Small campsite on the edge of the village. Connected to the village by a footpath. Trains pass by occasionally. Gstaad and Saanen are easily accessible by bike via footpaths and cycle paths.

From Saanen drive in the direction of Gstaad. Follow the signs. Campsite located on the right of the road, 1.3 km past the roundabout in Saanen.

CC € 27 7/1-7/2 7/3-8/5 21/5-23/6 9/9-30/9

N 46°28'52'' E 07°16'22''

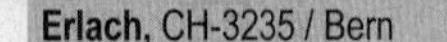

Gudo, CH-6515 / Tessin

632

Camping Isola****
Via al Gaggioletto 3
+41 9 18 59 32 44
15/1 - 15/12
isola2014@ticino.com

3ha 60**T**(40-100m²) 10A

1 ACD**I**KLMNOQ**R**S
2 CJSYZ
3 CKPSU
4 (B+G 15/5-30/9)
(Q+R 15/4-15/10)
(U+V+X+Z)
5 **AB**DGIJMNOPUWZ
6 CEFK(N 3km)V

A quietly located campsite with nice swimming pool in the Ticino valley. Bar and cocktail bar. Ideally located for walking and cycling trips. Day trips to Valle Maggia, Como and Milan for example, or the fossil museum in Meride or the Monte Generoso.

A2 exit Bellinzona-Süd/Locarno direction Locarno. After ±8 km turn right towards airport. Then towards Gordola-Gudo, then direction Gudo. Campsite is signposted between Cugnasco and Gudo. Narrow access road.

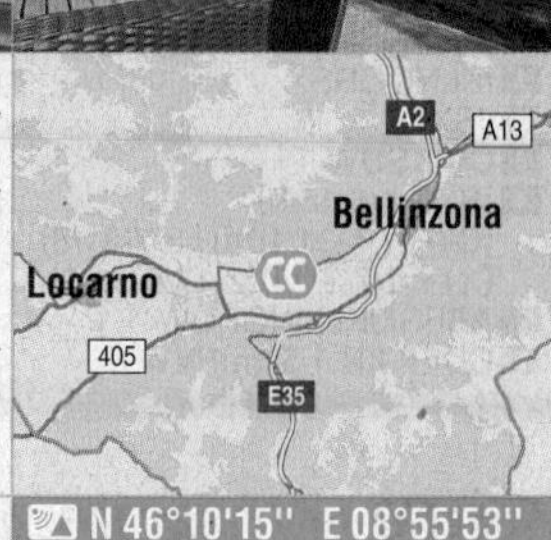

CC € 25 *15/1-27/3 8/4-30/6 2/9-15/12*

N 46°10'15'' E 08°55'53''

Innertkirchen, CH-3862 / Bern

633

Camping Aareschlucht***
Hauptstraße 34
+41 3 39 71 27 14
1/5 - 13/10
campaareschlucht@bluewin.ch

0,5ha 45**T**(50-100m²) 10A CEE

1 ACD**I**KLMNOQ**R**S
2 JLMNSXY
3 AIKLSU**W**
4 (B 15/6-15/9)(Q 1/6-15/9)
(U+Z)
5 **AB**GIJKLMNO**P**UW
6 ABCFJ(N 1km)OP

A friendly, pleasant campsite. Beautiful views of the mountain ranges. Good coin-operated showers. Located next to the impressive 'Aareschlucht' at the foot of the Susten and Grimsel passes.

Coming from Meiringen the campsite is located between Meiringen and Innertkirchen, on the left of the road, just past the entrance of Aareschlucht near Innertkirchen.

4
A8
Meiringen
11
CC
6
Grindelwald

CC € 25 *1/5-7/7 2/9-13/10*

N 46°42'34'' E 08°12'53''

Interlaken/Unterseen, CH-3800 / Bern

634

Camping Alpenblick AG****
Seestraße 130
+41 3 38 22 77 57
1/1 - 31/12
info@camping-alpenblick.ch

2,6ha 90**T**(60-100m²) 6A CEE

1 ABCD**I**KLMNOQ**R**S
2 CEIJNSVWXYZ
3 A**G**IKSUZ
4 (Q+R+T+U+X+Z)
5 **AB**DFGIJKLMNOPQRUWZ
6 ABCDFGHJL(N 3km)OPTV

Camping Alpenblick, close to Interlaken, offers views of the stunning Bernese Alps and is a stone's throw from Lake Thun. You can easily explore the Jungfrau Region from here.

Take the A8 Thun-Interlaken-Brienz. Exit 24 Interlaken-West. Follow campsite symbol 2.

CC € 27 *8/1-21/3 8/4-8/5 20/5-29/5 3/6-1/7 19/8-21/12*

N 46°40'47'' E 07°49'04''

Interlaken/Unterseen, CH-3800 / Bern

635

- JungfrauCamp 5****
- Steindlerstraße 54
- +41 7 62 95 05 11
- 28/3 - 30/9
- info@jungfraucamp.ch

2ha 90**T**(60-120m²) 10A CEE

1. IKLNOQRS
2. JSXY
3. C**G**IKSUW
4. (B+G 1/6-15/9) (Q+R 1/4-31/10)(U 3/7-31/8) (X+Y 1/7-31/8)(Z 17/6-30/9)
5. **AB**FGIJKLMNOPUW
6. CDEFJ(N 1,5km)PVW

Campsite with a friendly atmosphere, bordering a suburb of Interlaken with stunning views of the snowy mountain peaks. There is a small but lovely swimming pool. Good cycling and walking options in the vicinity. Takeaway meals and restaurant open from 19 June to 30 September.

Motorway Bern-Spiez-Interlaken. Take exit 24 Interlaken-West. Follow campsite symbol 5.

CC € 27 *1/4-9/5 12/5-17/5 20/5-30/5 2/6-13/6 15/6-6/7 24/8-30/9*

N 46°41'13'' E 07°50'03''

Le Landeron, CH-2525 / Neuchâtel

636

- Camping Des Pêches****
- rue du Port 6
- +41 3 27 51 29 00
- 1/4 - 15/10
- info@camping-lelanderon.ch

5ha 150**T**(50-100m²) 16-20A CEE

1. ABCD**I**KLMNOQ**RS**
2. ACEIJOSVWY
3. C**G**HIKLMNOS**W**Z
4. (G 15/5-31/8)M (Q+S+T+U+V+Y+Z)
5. **AB**DFGIJKLMNO**P**QUWXZ
6. ACEFGK(N 0,5km)OPV

A campsite located in an oasis of greenery with wonderful views of the Chasseral. The touring pitches are separate from the permanent pitches. There is a Euro-Relais right next to the entrance. Very good restaurant. Free pool about 800 metres away.

From La Neuville drive towards Le Landeron. In the village there are signs to the campsite. Take care: very high humps on the tourist road to the campsite; drive at walking pace.

CC € 25 *1/4-30/6 20/8-15/10*

N 47°03'11'' E 07°04'12''

Le Prese, CH-7746 / Graubünden

637

- Camping Cavresc***
- Via dal Cavresc 1
- +41 8 18 44 02 59
- 1/4 - 31/10
- camping.cavresc@bluewin.ch

1ha 50**T**(30-75m²) 13A CEE

1. ACD**I**KLMN**R**S
2. CJNSXY
3. AIKS**W**
4. (Q 1/6-1/9)
5. **AB**DFGIJKLMNO**P**UWZ
6. CEFGJ(N 0,3km)

A campsite with a lawn located in the Poschiavo valley with a southern climate. Lake Poschiavo (water sports and fishing) is close to the campsite. Rhätische Bahn station is 5 minutes from the campsite, enabling trips to Tirano (IT) or the Bernina Hospiz (2253m) of St. Moritz. Wonderful walking and cycling region.

Reaching the village Le Prese, take the side-road of the main road (29) on the eastside. Follow the signs.

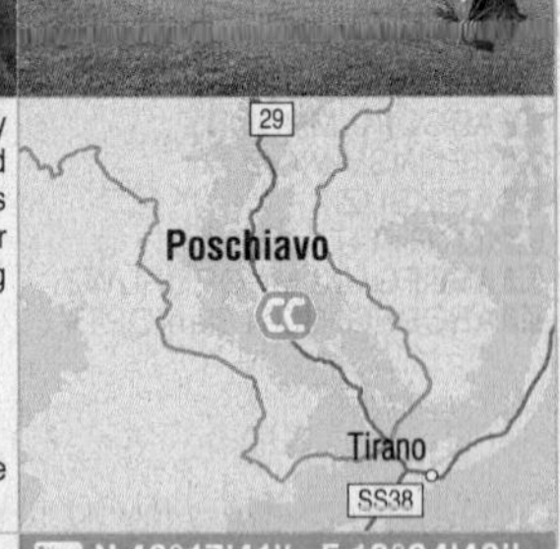

CC € 27 *1/4-15/6 15/9-31/10*

N 46°17'41'' E 10°04'49''

Lignières, CH-2523 / Neuchâtel

638

Camping Fraso Ranch****
3 ch. du Grand-Marais
+41 3 27 51 46 16
1/1 - 31/10, 23/12 - 31/12
camping.fraso-ranch@bluewin.ch

8ha 48T(50-100m²) 10A CEE

1 ACDIJKLMNOQRS
2 IJLWXYZ
3 CHIKOP**Q**S
4 (C+H 1/6-31/8)**KN**
(Q 1/4-30/10)(R 27/5-1/9)
(T+U+V)(X 1/1-31/10)
(Y 1/1-30/10)
5 **AB**DFGIJKLMNO**P**UW
6 AEFGHJ(N 1km)OPV

A sports campsite, on the sunny south slope of the Chasseral with an extensive programme of sporting options. Highly recommended for sports lovers. Children's programme once a week. Good toilet and washing facilities. Sauna and jacuzzi and a lovely heated swimming pool present.

In Le Landeron drive towards Lignières, past the Lignières village 1 km on the right side of the road.

CC € 21 *1/1-30/6 1/9-31/10*

N 47°05'10'' E 07°04'16''

Meierskappel, CH-6344 / Zentralschweiz

639

Campingplatz Gerbe
Landiswilerstrasse
+41 4 17 90 45 34
1/3 - 31/10
info@swiss-bauernhof.ch

1,6ha 60T(80m²) 16A CEE

1 ACDIKLMNOQRS
2 IJLSXY
3 AIKSU
4 (B 15/5-30/9)(Q+R+T+X)
5 **AB**GIJKLMNOPUW
6 CEFKL(N 0,5km)PV

A campsite on a traditional Swiss farm with demarcated pitches. Cuddly animals for the children. Own produce for sale. Highly suitable as a stopover campsite to and from Italy.

A4 Rotkreuz-Schwyz, exit Küssnacht. Then follow the signs 'Meierskappel'. Just before the junction turn left at the farmhouse.

CC € 27 *1/3-27/3 2/4-8/5 13/5-16/5 21/5-29/5 3/6-30/6 1/9-31/10*

N 47°07'16'' E 08°26'47''

Monteggio, CH-6998 / Tessin

640

Camping Tresiana****
Via Cantonale 21
+41 9 16 08 33 42
23/3 - 20/10
info@camping-tresiana.ch

1,5ha 67T(56-80m²) 10A

1 ABCDIKLMNOP**R**S
2 CJSUWXYZ
3 AC**G**IKPSU**W**X
4 (B+G 1/5-30/9)
(Q+R+T+U+V)
5 **AB**FGIJKLMNOPUWZ
6 CEFG**K**(N 5km)OPV

A peaceful and well maintained campsite on the River Tresa at the Italian border. Swimming pool, toddlers' pool and bistro in the grounds.

A2, exit Lugano-Nord/Ponte Tresa, towards Ponte Tresa. In Ponte Tresa drive in the direction of Luino until the border and then turn right. In Molinazzo di Monteggio there are signs to the campsite.

SS34 Luino Lugano 2 CC E35 A2 Cuveglio SS394 SS344

CC € 27 *6/4-26/4 23/5-30/6 31/8-20/10*

N 45°59'28'' E 08°49'00''

Müstair, CH-7537 / Graubünden

641

Camping Muglin
Via Muglin 21
+41 8 18 58 59 90
1/1 - 17/3, 27/4 - 27/10, 17/12 - 31/12
info@campingmuglin.ch

4,5ha 65**T**(100m²) 13A CEE

1 ACD**I**KLMNOQRS
2 CJNSWX
3 A**O**U
4 MN(Q+Z)
5 **AB**DFGIJKLMNOPWXYZ
6 ACEFK(N 1km)V

Campsite close to a village on a former farm with large open grass field. Large free sauna in the hayloft. The Convent of Saint John (UNESCO World Heritage Site) is in the village. Lovely area for walking and cycling and a trip over the Stelvio Pass. 2 km from Italian border.

On the bypass south of Mustair, follow the signs to the campsite.

Malles Venosta
SS41
SS40
Prato Allo Stelvio
28
SS38

CC € 27 *27/4-7/7 25/8-27/10*

N 46°37'26'' E 10°26'56''

Ottenbach, CH-8913 / Zürich

642

Camping Reussbrücke****
Muristrasse 34
+41 4 47 61 20 22
23/3 - 28/9
info@camping-reussbruecke.ch

1,5ha 40**T**(80-120m²) 6-13A CEE

1 CD**H**JKLMNOPQRS
2 CIJSVXY
3 CIKSUX
4 (B+G 8/5-15/9)
(Q+R+T+U+X+Z)
5 **AB**FGIJKLMNO**P**UZ
6 CDEFG**K**(N 0,5km)OTV

The campsite is by the River Reuss in a beautiful nature reserve where you can walk or cycle. Level grounds (partially) with trees. Also suitable as stopover campsite to and from Italy.

On the A4 Zürich-Gotthard take exit 31 Affoltern am Albis. Go via Obfelden to Ottenbach. Campsite is on the right before the bridge over the Reuss and is accessible via the car park; 5 km from motorway exit.

1
A3
A4
3
Affoltern am Albis
4
E41
26
25

CC € 27 *8/4-12/4 22/4-29/4 13/5-17/5 21/5-24/5 3/6-1/7 1/9-28/9*

N 47°16'47'' E 08°23'43''

Raron/Turtig, CH-3942 / Wallis

643

Camping Santa Monica****
Kantonsstrasse 56
+41 2 79 34 24 24
28/3 - 13/10
info@santa-monica.ch

6ha 134**T**(60-150m²) 16A CEE

1 ACD**I**KLMNOQ**R**S
2 BCIJNSUWXYZ
3 A**FG**IJK**O**PSU
4 (**A** 1/6-30/9)(C+H 20/5-13/9)
(Q+R+S+T+U+V+X+Y+Z)
5 **AB**DFGIJKLMNOPQR**T**UWXYZ
6 CEFGK(N 0,3km)OPV

Appealing campsite with excellent toilet facilities and friendly management. Situated next to 2 cable cars, close to a new suspension bridge (260 m long). Centrally located for various walks in sunny Valais. Excellent base for day trips to Zermatt, Saas Fee, the Aletsch Glacier and the Simplon Pass.

Campsite is located along the road Gampel-Visp. The entrance is next to the Renault Garage.

509
Raron
Brig
9
Visp

CC € 25 *28/3-30/6 26/8-13/10*

N 46°18'11'' E 07°48'08''

Unterägeri, CH-6314 / Zentralschweiz

644

Camping Unterägeri****
Wilbrunnenstraße 81
+41 4 17 50 39 28
1/1 - 31/12
info@campingunteraegeri.ch

4,8ha 150T(50-100m²) 16A CEE

1 ACDGJKLMNOQRUV
2 FNPSWXYZ
3 CHIKSUWZ
4 (Q+R 1/4-31/10)
(S 1/4-30/10)
(T+U+W+X+Y+Z 1/4-31/10)
5 ABDFGIJKLMNOPUW
6 BCDEFGHK(N 2km)OPV

Lovely campsite in a nature area with demarcated pitches, open all year. Located right on the lake, where you can go swimming, canoeing and paddleboarding. Also a nice area for walking and/or cycling. The pitches at the water and larger pitches including 'Top-Plätze' are at a surcharge. Dogs are not allowed.

A4 Luzern-Zürich, exit Baar towards Ägeri. Drive via Baar to Unterägeri. In the village follow the signs.

CC € 27 2/4-8/5 4/6-30/6 1/9-31/10

N 47°07'40'' E 08°35'31''

Zweisimmen, CH-3770 / Bern

645

Camping Vermeille****
Ey Gässli 2
+41 3 37 22 19 40
1/1 - 31/12
info@camping-vermeille.ch

1,3ha 15T(80-120m²) 10A CEE

1 ACDIKLMNOQRS
2 CJNSUXY
3 AGIKMNSUW
4 (C+G 1/6-31/8)(R+Z)
5 ABDFGIJKLMNOPUW
6 ACDEFGHKL(N 0,5km)
OPRUV

Well-placed campsite with many options for summer and winter holidays: kayaking, mountain biking, mountain walks and winter sports. Facilities for the disabled. Fitness centre in the village free for campers.

Follow road 11 from Spiez to Zweisimmen. Campsite well signposted on road 11, located just before Zweisimmen. At exit to campsite drive 200 metres further. Second campsite after railroad crossing.

189 505 Zweisimmen 11 Saanen Adelboden

CC € 27 8/1-3/2 18/3-28/4 21/5-29/5 3/6-6/7 1/9-27/9 21/10-20/12

N 46°33'46'' E 07°22'41''

Austria

Austria: camping amid nature

Capital: Vienna
Currency: euro
Time zone: UTC +1, UTC +2 (March to October)
Language: German
International dialling code: +43
Alcohol limit: 0.49%; there is complete alcohol ban for drivers who have had a driving licence for less than two years (limit of 0.1%)
Emergency number: police, fire and ambulance: 112; police: 133; fire: 122; ambulance: 144
Tap water: safe to drink

If you think of Austria, you think of the Alps. The famous mountains provide an extremely varied and unique landscape. Beautiful alpine meadows with panoramic views, stunning gorges you can walk through and deep caves you can explore; and these are just some of the things you can do in this beautiful Alpine country. You mainly find the high Alps in the south and west of Austria. In the east and north of the country it is hilly in comparison to the high Alps.

Year-round vacation

Wherever you camp in Austria, it is beautiful. And that makes perfect sense considering almost half of Austria consists of forests. It doesn't get greener than that! Throughout Austria, you will find many campsites at exceptional locations in the countryside. In Austria, you can go to many campsites in the summer as well as in winter. Many campsites in Austria are genuine winter sports campsites, complete with special amenities for skiers. In the summer, it's great for walking and cycling and visiting beautiful cities.

Active outdoors

You have a vast choice of great outings and activities in the mountains and hills of Austria. Consider the Eisriesenwelt, the World of the Ice Giants. This cave – at roughly 40 kilometres from Salzburg – has the longest and deepest ice caves in the world. If you'd prefer a warmer outing in the outside air, have a go on a real toboggan run! That's fun to do in summer as well as in winter. Or, even more spectacular, spend an afternoon doing 'via ferrata'. This is a light form of mountain climbing suitable for the whole family.

Tradition and culture in the three major cities

Austria is more than just mountains and countryside. Culture enthusiasts will enjoy themselves in big cities such as Salzburg, Innsbruck and Vienna. For example, go to the famous Spanish Riding School in Vienna, one of the oldest horse training schools in the world. And if you are in Vienna, the Schloss Schönbrunn is a must. The Baroque Salzburg is also certainly worthwhile. Here, you learn all about its most famous resident, Mozart. You could spend days wandering around the historic buildings and stunning parks in Salzburg.

En route

Filling up

Petrol (Super/Bleifrei 95 and Super Plus 98) and diesel are widely available. LPG is hardly available. For LPG, some fuelling stations use the European connector (Acme) and others use the Italian connector (Dish).
Fuelling stations on motorways and in big cities are usually open 24 hours a day, others are open between 8 am and 8 pm. There are also many that work in automatic mode at night and unmanned fuelling stations in Austria.

Winners in Austria

677	*Best campsite*	Terrassencamping Maltatal
663	*Nicest campsite for children*	Sonnencamp am Gösselsdorfersee
664	*Most dog-friendly campsite*	Camping Murinsel
661	*Best campsite swimming pool*	Tirol Camp
699	*Most sports-loving campsite*	Donaupark Camping Tulln
702	*Best campsite restaurant*	Alpencamping Mark

Winner: Tirol Camp

Charging

New charging stations are added daily. You will find most of them around the big cities and close to the main roads. There are also plenty of charging points in winter sports areas. In Austria, just like for every country, if you travel using an electric car make sure you plan your trip well!

Traffic regulations

Dipped headlights are mandatory during poor visibility, in the dark and in tunnels. At equivalent crossings, traffic from the right has priority. Traffic on a roundabout has priority if indicated with traffic signs. Trams always have priority. On narrow mountain roads, traffic that can move over the easiest must give priority.
You may not have telephone in your hand behind the wheel, not even when stopped (you can call hands free). Children up to 14 years and under 1.50 metres in height must be in a child's car seat.
You are allowed to use your navigation system to notify you of speed cameras and trajectory speed controls. Winter tyres are mandatory from 1 November to 15 April in wintry conditions (snow chains could be made mandatory by means of a sign).

Special regulations

Smoking in the car is prohibited in the presence of children under 18 years.
In traffic jams, you should stay as far to the right or left as possible to create a free lane in the centre (Rettungsgasse) for emergency service vehicles.
Parking is prohibited next to yellow lines and in zones marked with a yellow zigzag stripe, among other places. A flashing green traffic light means that the light will soon turn orange.
Emergency phones have flashing lights that warn you of, for example, cars travelling in the wrong direction, traffic accidents or traffic jams. Before driving it is mandatory to make your car snow and ice free (the roof too).
You are not allowed to leave your car running while stopped for a lengthy period, such as at a level crossing or when de-icing the car.

"Austria is a versatile holiday country with many lakes, mountains and valleys where the whole family can enjoy themselves."
Mr W. Ament, inspector 923

Mandatory equipment

It is mandatory to have a warning triangle, safety vest and first aid kit in the car.

Caravan and motorhome

A motorhome or car-caravan combination can be a maximum of 4 metres in height, 2.55 metres wide and 18.75 metres long (the caravan itself can be up to 12 metres long).
It is mandatory to have a wheel block with you for caravans with a maximum permissible mass of over 0.75 tonnes.
Outside built-up areas, a car-caravan combination must maintain a distance of at least 50 metres in relation to other combinations and lorries.

Cycling

Children up to 12 years old must wear a bicycle

helmet on a bike (also on the back). In Lower Austria, it is mandatory up to 15 years.
You may not call or text while on a bike.
Children up to 8 must be in a child's bike seat on the back with someone who is at least 16 years old. Children may not be transported in a child's seat on the handlebars.
Children up to 12 years old may cycle on the road unaccompanied. Cyclists are only allowed to cycle next to each other on bicycle paths.

Toll

In Austria, you need an 'Autobahnvignet' to use the motorways. You can buy a vignette (sticker) for 10 days, 2 months or a year. You can buy the toll vignette at fuelling stations and post offices close to the border.
For addresses: asfinag.at/maut-vignette.
It is advisable to buy the motorway vignette online in advance, for example via tolltickets.com. The vignette must be placed on the inside left of the front windscreen.
Besides the normal vignette, you can also get a 'digital toll vignette'. This digital vignette is registered by number plate and can be ordered online via shop.asfinag.at. Order this digital vignette at least 18 days before your desired starting date. The price and validity of the digital vignette are the same as the normal vignette. You do.not need an additional vignette for caravans and trailers.
Vehicles weighing over 3.5 tonnes (also motorhomes) pay a toll per kilometre via a so-called GO-Box. This box is available at the border.
More information: go-maut.at.
With the completion of the Pfänder tunnel, the 'Korridorvignette' has been discontinued. On the 23-kilometre route on the A14 Rheintal/Walgau between the German border and the Hohenems interchange in Vorarlberg, you now need an Autobahnvignet or GO-box.
Off the motorways, Austria has several so-called 'Sondermautstrecken' and mountain passes you must pay a separate toll for.
More information: https://www.asfinag.at/en/toll/section-toll/digital-section-toll/.

Environmental zones

Some regions have set up environmental zones for

vehicles weighing over 3.5 tonnes and you need an environmental sticker.
More information: green-zones.eu

Breakdown and accident

On a motorway, place your warning triangle at least 200 to 250 metres (elsewhere at 150 metres) behind the car if it is not clearly visible to other traffic. The driver must put on a safety vest.
If you breakdown, call the emergency number of your breakdown assistance insurer. You can also call the Austrian breakdown assistance service: 120 (ÖAMTC) and 123 (ARBÖ). On motorways, you can also call for breakdown assistance using an emergency phone (Notruftelefon). Towing is allowed on the motorway up to the first exit.

"In Austria, where the food and drink is good, you still breathe fresh air."
Mrs Westbroek, inspector 1079

Camping

Austrian campsites are among the best in Europe. Carinthia springs to mind for its excellent location, stable climate and beautiful lakes. Many campsites in the Tyrol specialise in wellness or focus on sportive camping guests.
Wild camping outside registered campsites is only allowed if you have permission from the local authorities or landowner.
Many Austrian campsites are also open in the winter, mainly in Vorarlberg, Tyrol and Salzburg.
Additional charges for things such as tourist taxes and environmental charges are sometimes quite high.
Overnight stays in caravans, motorhomes or cars away outside recognised campsites are permitted for one night if in transit, except in Vienna, Tyrol and national parks.

Practical

In the Alps, inclines of 6 to 15% and more are common. Most mountain roads have crash barriers on the valley side.
Please note: Mountain passes in Switzerland, Austria and Italy could be temporarily closed, difficult to access or even permanently closed off to cars with a caravan or trailer. Check this before you travel.
More information: alpenpaesse.de (in German).

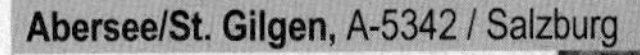

Abersee/St. Gilgen, A-5342 / Salzburg

646

Paradiescamping Wolfgangsee Birkenstrand****
Schwand 17a
+43 66 49 40 48 79
1/4 - 20/10
camp@birkenstrand.at

1,8ha 103T(80-100m²) 12A CEE

1 ACD**H**KLMNOQ**R**UV
2 FJNSUWXYZ
3 AIKMNSU**W**Z
4 **N**(Q+R+T+U+V+Z)
5 **AB**DFGIJKLMNOPUWXYZ
6 ACEFGK(N 5km)OP

Idyllic campsite with direct access to the lake and sunbathing area. The sheltered comfort pitches on the lake are also available for CampingCard ACSI. Kayak, SUP and bicycle rental. Modern toilet facilities and private Finnish sauna. Fresh bread in the mini-market. Typical Austrian restaurant on the campsite. Close to direct bus connection to Salzburg.

B158 from St. Gilgen to Strobl. 4 km past St. Gilgen in Schwand exit left. Follow signs.

CC € 25 *1/4-30/6 1/9-20/10*

N 47°44'21" E 13°24'02"

Abersee/St. Gilgen, A-5342 / Salzburg

647

Romantik Camp. Wolfgangsee Lindenstrand****
Schwand 19
+43 62 27 32 05
29/3 - 13/10
camping@lindenstrand.at

3ha 150T(80-100m²) 12A CEE

1 ACD**I**KLMNQRS
2 FJNPSUWXYZ
3 ACDIKMNPU**W**Z
4 (Q+S)(U 1/7-28/8)
5 **AB**DFGIJKLMNOPRUWXYZ
6 ACEFGK(N 4,5km)OPV

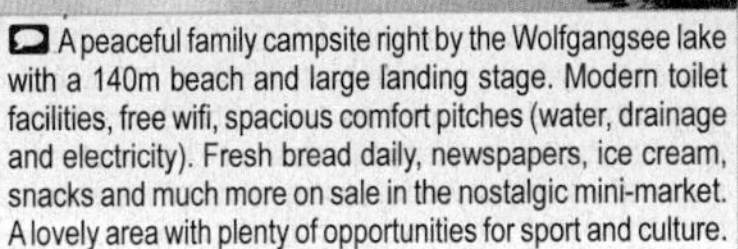

A peaceful family campsite right by the Wolfgangsee lake with a 140m beach and large landing stage. Modern toilet facilities, free wifi, spacious comfort pitches (water, drainage and electricity). Fresh bread daily, newspapers, ice cream, snacks and much more on sale in the nostalgic mini-market. A lovely area with plenty of opportunities for sport and culture.

B158 from St. Gilgen to Strobl. The exit is signposted in Schwand. Go to the left 4 km from St. Gilgen.

CC € 27 *29/3-9/5 2/6-1/7 7/9-13/10*

N 47°44'23" E 13°24'08"

Abersee/St. Gilgen, A-5342 / Salzburg

648

Seecamping Primus
Schwand 39
+43 62 27 32 28
26/4 - 30/9
info@seecamping-primus.at

2ha 75T 10-16A

1 ACD**I**KLMNOQ**R**S
2 EJNQSUWXYZ
3 CIK**W**Z
5 **AB**GIJKLMNO**P**UWXYZ
6 ACEFK(N 5km)

A peaceful campsite right on the crystal clear Wolfgangsee lake (the campsite with the second longest beach). A haven of peace in this beautiful region with plenty of opportunities for watersports (own landing stage), cycling and walking. 3 km from St. Gilgen and 40 km from Salzburg.

B158 from St. Gilgen to Strobl. The exit is signposted. Schwand 4 km after St. Gilgen. Take care: the campsite is the last but one!

CC € 27 *26/4-17/5 2/6-1/7 1/9-30/9*

N 47°44'27" E 13°24'21"

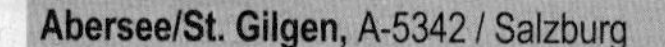

Abersee/St. Gilgen, A-5342 / Salzburg

649

Seecamping Wolfgangblick
Seestraße 115
+43 65 05 93 42 97
20/4 - 30/9
camping@wolfgangblick.at

2,2ha 80T(70-95m²) 12A

1 ACD**H**KLMNOQRS
2 FJNPQSUWXYZ
3 A**G**IK**W**Z
4 (Q+R 9/5-9/9)(T+U 9/5-31/8) (Z)
5 **AB**FGJLMNOPUW
6 EFGK(N 3km)P

Family campsite close to the lake, with level beach. With the neighbouring ferry, you'll be in St. Wolfgang in a few minutes, and at the station of the Schafberg Railway. Free wifi. Small shop with bread and pastries, newspapers and a snack bar. Ideal base for various nature reserves, and for walkers, cyclists and climbers.

Take B158 from St. Gilgen to Strobl. At the km-marker 34 exit Abersee. Signposted.

CC € 25 *20/4-30/6 1/9-30/9*

N 47°44'14" E 13°25'58"

Aigen (Ennstal), A-8943 / Steiermark

650

Camping Putterersee
Hohenberg 2A
+43 66 44 84 00 61
15/4 - 31/10
camping.putterersee@aon.at

2ha 70T(90-100m²) 13A CEE

1 ACD**I**KLMNQRUV
2 AEMNSXY
3 AIKLSU**W**Z
4 (Q+R+T+U+V+X+Z 1/5-30/9)
5 **AB**DGIJKLMNOP**S**UWZ
6 ACEFK(N 1km)OP

A beautiful campsite right next to Styria's warmest lake, peacefully located in a protected nature reserve. Lovely walks around the lake and cycle trips through the Ennstal valley. An informal camping cafe for light meals and a camp shop for supplies for breakfast. Modern, luxury toilet facilities, environmentally heated. Private toilet facilities for a fee.

A10 Salzburg, exit Radstadt direction Graz. At Wörschach continue towards Aigen/Ketten and follow signs.

CC € 23 *15/4-15/6 14/9-31/10*

N 47°31'16" E 14°07'56"

Bad Waltersdorf, A-8271 / Steiermark

651

Thermenland Camping Rath & Pichler
Campingweg 316
+43 66 43 11 70 00
1/1 - 31/12
thermenland@camping-bad-waltersdorf.at

1,6ha 73T(80-98m²) 16A CEE

1 ACDE**I**JKLMNOQRS
2 CINSUVWXY
3 A**G**IKU**W**
4 (Q+R)
5 **AB**DFGIJKLMNOPQRUWXYZ
6 ACEFGJ(N 1km)OPV

Neat, spacious family campsite. Very well-equipped toilet facilities. Suitable for visiting the thermal bath. Pool in the village is free for campsite guests. Lovely cycling and hiking routes. Special offers in July and August. Excursions from the campsite with an old-timer bus and convertible.

A2 exit 126 Sebersdorf/Bad Waltersdorf, towards Heil Therme and the city of Bad Waltersdorf. GPS: Access to campsite via Campingweg, not Muhlweg (=prohibited).

CC € 23 *1/5-8/5 12/5-17/5 21/5-29/5 2/6-14/7 18/9-30/9*

N 47°09'50" E 16°01'15"

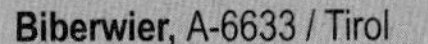

Biberwier, A-6633 / Tirol

652

- Feriencenter Camping Biberhof
- Schmitte 8
- +43 56 73 29 50
- 1/1 - 31/12
- info@biberhof.at

2,5ha 60**T**(80-100m²) 10A CEE

1. AF**H**KLMNOQ**R**S
2. CJNSUWXYZ
3. A**G**IKLS
4. (Q+Y+Z)
5. **AB**DFGIJKLMNOPUWZ
6. ACEFGK(N 0,5km)OPU

A real family campsite. Beautifully located in the Tiroler Zugspitzen area. Spacious pitches. A super trampoline for enthusiasts. A beautiful region for walking and cycling. Thanks to its location this is also a good campsite to visit during the winter.

Reutte in the direction Lermoos. In Lermoos centre take direction Biberwier. At the T-junction in Biberwier direction Ehrwald. Campsite 300 metres on the right.

CC € 23 *16/3-30/6 7/9-30/11*

N 47°22'56" E 10°54'07"

Dellach im Drautal, A-9772 / Kärnten

653

- Camping Am Waldbad
- Rassnig 8
- +43 4 71 42 88
- 15/4 - 1/10
- info@camping-waldbad.at

3ha 200**T**(70-120m²) 10-16A CEE

1. ACDE**I**KLMNOQRS
2. BCJNSUWXYZ
3. AC**G**HIKLMNPSU**W**X
4. (A 1/6-1/10)
   (C+H 21/5-11/9)IJM
   (Q+R+T+U+V+X+Y+Z)
5. **AB**CEFGHIJKLMNOPQRUWXZ
6. ACDEFGHK(N 0,5km)OTUV

Ideal campsite for a family holiday. Only 500 m from the village centre. Yet, in the heart of the countryside, very close to the Drau and the Drau cycle path. The campsite has modern toilet facilities, a lovely swimming pool and a good restaurant. Walking, cycling and other sports are possible.

2 routes: a) road B100 Spittal-Lienz; b) Mittersill-Felbertauerntunnel-Lienz-Dellach im Drautal. Site is signposted at a sharp bend in the village.

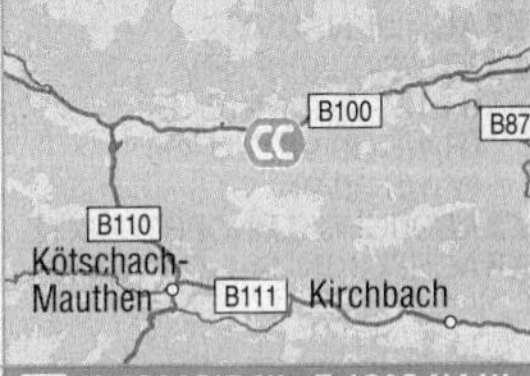

CC € 23 *15/4-29/6 1/9-30/9*

N 46°43'54" E 13°04'41"

Döbriach, A-9873 / Kärnten

654

- Camping Brunner am See
- Glanzerstraße 108
- +43 42 46 71 89
- 1/1 - 31/12
- info@camping-brunner.at

3,5ha 215**T**(60-107m²) 6-16A CEE

1. BCDGKLMNOQRTU
2. AFJNOSTUVWXY
3. CD**G**IKLMNPS
4. (S+U+V+X+Y+Z 15/5-30/9)
5. **AB**CDEFGHIJKLMNPQR**S**UWXYZ
6. ACFGHK(N 0,2km)OPT

1st class, dog free comfort site on the Millstätter See. Sunny grounds, excellent toilets. Shops, restaurants, watersports, golf, tennis, cycling, mountain biking. Guided mountain walks from Easter to autumn.

A10 Salzburg-Villach, exit 139 Millstätter See. At traffic lights left on the B98 direction Radenthein. After 12 km right towards Döbriach-See. After ca. 1.5 km right at 'ADEG-Markt'. From south: exit 178 Villach-Ossiacher See dir. Millstätter See.

CC € 27 *1/1-30/6 1/9-31/12*

N 46°46'04" E 13°38'53"

Döbriach, A-9873 / Kärnten

655

Seecamping Mössler
Seefeldstraße 1
+43 42 46 73 10
14/4 - 15/10
camping@moessler.at

1ha 72T(70-100m²) 16A

1 ACDIKLMNOQRS
2 ACENOSUWXY
3 ACGIKLQSWZ
4 (A 8/7-13/9)(C+H 20/5-23/9) (Q 15/5-30/9) (S+U+V+Y 6/5-30/9)
5 ABCDEFGIJKLMNOPUWXYZ
6 ABCEFGK(N 1,5km) OPSTVW

Small friendly site on the Millstätter See where the guests are looked after. Swimming in the heated pool or in the lake. Entertainment for all ages, including hiking. No environment surcharge.

A10 Salzburg-Villach. Exit 139 Millstätter See. Left at traffic lights on the B98 dir. Radenthein. After ± 12 km turn right towards Döbriach-See. The site is on the right about 1.5 km further on. From the south: exit 178 Villach-Ossiachersee dir. Millstätter See.

CC € 25 14/4-30/6 1/9-15/10

N 46°46'07'' E 13°38'58''

Eberndorf, A-9141 / Kärnten

656

Naturisten Feriendorf Rutar Lido
Lido 1
+43 42 36 22 62
1/1 - 31/12
fkkurlaub@rutarlido.at

15ha 218T(70-140m²) 16A CEE

1 ACDIKLMNOQRS
2 ENOSWXYZ
3 AGHIJKNSUVWZ
4 (C 1/6-30/9)(F) (H 1/7-30/9)KN(Q) (R 1/5-30/9)(T+U) (Y 1/5-30/9)
5 ABCDGHIJKLMNOPRTUWXYZ
6 ACEFGK(N 1km)OPTUVW

Naturist campsite. Spacious grounds with various outdoor pools, a small lake, indoor pool and a naturist meadow. Many pitches with privacy. Separate area for dogs, dog meadow and a separate swimming area for dogs in these large grounds. Free sauna when weather is rainy in period 1/5 - 30/9.

A2 from Klagenfurt, exit 298 Grafenstein turn left, B70 direction Graz. After 4 km turn right to Tainach, Eberndorf, Rutar Lido. From Graz A2, exit 278 Völkermarkt-Ost.

CC € 25 1/3-7/7 1/9-30/10

N 46°35'02'' E 14°37'34''

Emmersdorf, A-3644 / Niederösterreich

657

Donau Camping Emmersdorf
Donaulände 1
+43 67 66 70 66 52
1/4 - 15/10
office@ donaucamping-emmersdorf.at

1,2ha 67T(70-100m²) 16A CEE

1 ACDIKLMNOQRS
2 DIJNPSUY
3 AIKLNOWX
4 (T)
5 ABDGHIJKLMNOPQUWX
6 CDEFGKLM(N 3km)TU

A small passer-by campsite with pitches on a grass field. The campsite is located right by the Danube with small pebble and sandy beaches with swimming options. Neatly maintained toilet and washing facilities. At walking distance from the lovely town of Emmersdorf. View of Melk Abbey (Stift Melk). Stunning wine region with many apricot orchards.

The campsite is on the B3 near Melk on the Danube bridge, beside the bridge in Emmersdorf. Indicated by signs.

CC € 25 1/4-1/7

N 48°14'35'' E 15°20'25''

Faak am See, A-9583 / Kärnten

658

Camping Arneitz
Seeufer-Landesstraße 53
+43 66 45 28 75 65
26/4 - 30/9
camping@arneitz.at

6,5ha 400T(60-120m²) 16A CEE

1 ADHJKLMNORS
2 FIJNPQSTVWXYZ
3 ACDGIKLOPSUWZ
4 (A 5/7-22/8)J(Q)
(S+U+V+W+Y+Z 1/5-20/9)
5 ABCDEFGIJKLMNOPQRUWXYZ
6 CEFGHK(N 1km)PRSTUV

Pitches separated by hedges and trees with power supply, wastewater drainage and TV. (Pitches by the lake for a surcharge.) Modern toilet and washing facilities, large supermarket and self-service restaurant. Suitable as starting point for hiking, cycling and mountain bike tours and Nordic walking. Enjoy the hospitality of the Arneitz, Pressinger and Ramusch families!

A10 Salzburg-Villach, then A2 or A11, exit Villach/ Faaker See. Then first campsite on right in direction Egg.

CC € 27 26/4-30/6 9/9-30/9

N 46°34'28'' E 13°56'08''

Feistritz im Rosental, A-9181 / Kärnten

659

Camping Juritz
Campingstraße
+43 42 28 21 15
1/5 - 30/9
office@camping-juritz.com

3ha 90T 10-16A

1 ADIKLMNOPQRS
2 IJNSUXY
3 AIKLSU
4 (A 1/6-30/9)
(D+Q+U+Y+Z)
5 ABDFGIJKLNPRUW
6 ACEFK(N 0,5km)PUV

Car-free site. Sunny meadow with unreserved pitches. Several trees provide shade. Swimming pool with sliding roof which can be used from early on in the season. Excellent views of the Karawanken. Trips to Slovenia or city of Klagenfurt (15 minutes by car). A beautiful area for cycling or walking. New toilet facilities. Free wifi!

Villach, Karawankentunnel (SLO) exit St. Jakob im Rosental. Direction Feistritz (follow signs and not the SatNav).

CC € 25 1/5-30/6 1/9-30/9

N 46°31'31'' E 14°09'38''

Feistritz ob Bleiburg, A-9143 / Kärnten

660

Petzencamping Pirkdorfer See
Pirkdorf 29
+43 4 23 03 21
1/1 - 31/12
info@pirkdorfersee.at

10ha 35T(90m²) 12A CEE

1 ACDIKLMNORS
2 EJNOSWX
3 AIKNPSUWZ
4 (Q+U+Y)
5 ABCDFGHIJKLMNOPUWX
6 EFGK(N 3km)OPTV

Campsite is located at the foot of the 2114-metres high Petzen, accessible by cable car. Situated directly on Austria's warmest swimming lake, the Pirkdorfersee. Summers up to 27 degrees, but also pleasant weather in spring and autumn. Skiing and ice skating possible in winter. Fine restaurant. Good, heated toilet facilities.

From Klagenfurt B70, exit Klopeiner See. Then B82 to Eberndorf, B81 to St. Michael. Follow signs.

CC € 21 1/1-27/6 9/9-31/12

N 46°33'30'' E 14°45'05''

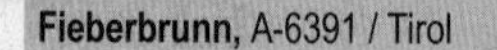

Fieberbrunn, A-6391 / Tirol

661

ACSI AWARDS WINNER

- Tirol Camp****
- Lindau 20
- +43 5 35 45 66 66
- 1/1 - 7/4, 7/5 - 3/11, 4/12 - 31/12
- office@tirol-camp.at

7ha 250**T**(100-120m²) 10A

1 ACD**I**JKLMNOQ**R**S
2 JMSUVWXY
3 AC**G**IKMPSU**V**
4 (A 19/5-1/11)(C 1/6-1/10) (F+H)J**KLNP** (Q+S+T+U+Y+Z)
5 **AB**DFGIJKLMNOPR**ST**UWXYZ
6 CEFGHKLM(N 1km)OPSV

The comfortable 4 star terraced campsite is located in the centre of the Pillerseetal holiday region, right next to the gondola to the best concealed walking and skiing area in the Alps. It has a peaceful, sunny location.

B164 St. Johann in Tirol-Saalfelden. Signposted in Fieberbrunn.

Sankt Johann in Tirol, B311, B164, Kitzbühel, B161

CC € 27 *7/5-10/7 1/9-3/11*

N 47°28'06'' E 12°33'14''

Fisching/Weißkirchen, A-8741 / Steiermark

662

- 50plus Campingpark Fisching****
- Fisching 9
- +43 3 57 78 22 84
- 1/4 - 31/10
- info@camping50plus.com

3ha 65**T**(100-130m²) 6A CEE

1 AGJKLMNOQRSW
2 EIJNSVWXY
3 **G**IJKNUZ
4 (**A**+Q+T+U+X+Z)
5 **AB**DGIJKLMNOPUWXYZ
6 ABCEFGK(N 0,6km) OPSTVW

Resplendent valley with mountains in the background. A comfortable campsite for the over fifties. Parkland setting equipped with every amenity, all pitches with cable TV. Beautiful biological swimming pool with terrace. Smaller and larger towns and countryside. 7 km from the thermal baths. Extensive cycling network from campsite with itineraries. Free wifi on entire site.

S36, exit Zeltweg-West, B78 direction Weißkirchen, direction Fisching at roundabout. Follow signs.

S36, Knittelfeld, Judenburg, B77, B78

CC € 27 *1/4-9/6 9/9-30/10*

N 47°09'47'' E 14°44'18''

Gösselsdorf, A-9141 / Kärnten

663

ACSI AWARDS WINNER

- Sonnencamp am Gösselsdorfersee
- Seestraße 21-23
- +43 42 36 21 68
- 13/4 - 28/9
- office@sonnencamp.com

7ha 211**T**(80-144m²) 13A CEE

1 AF**I**JKLMNOQRS
2 CEJSWXYZ
3 C**G**HIKLPSU**W**XZ
4 (**A**+Q+T+U+V+X+Z)
5 **AB**CGHIJKLMNOPUWXYZ
6 ACEFGK(N 2km)OPTV

A spacious, tranquil, family campsite, set on level ground. Swimming lake with lawn, and a 15-minute walk from the big lake that forms part of a nature reserve. The area offers stalactite caves, a cable car to the 2114-metre-high Petzenberg, regional museum Völkermarkt and the Eberndorf abbey with open air performances. Good possibilities to walk and cycle.

After Völkermarkt, follow the B82 2 km past Eberndorf direction Eisenkappel. Follow the camping signs in Gösselsdorf.

CC € 23 *13/4-30/6 1/9-28/9*

N 46°34'29'' E 14°37'28''

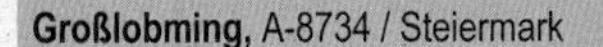

Großlobming, A-8734 / Steiermark

664

Camping Murinsel
Teichweg 1
+43 66 43 04 50 45
1/4 - 31/10
@ office@camping-murinsel.at

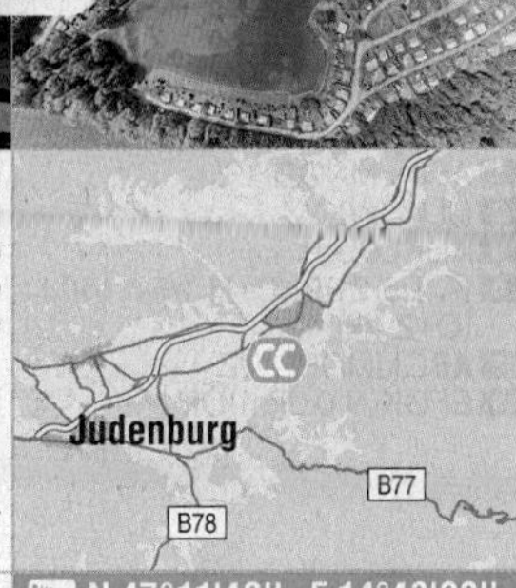

5ha 60T(100m²) 16A CEE

1 ACDIKLMNOQRS
2 CEINOSWXY
3 A**G**MN**O**U**W**Z
4 (Q)
(T+U+V+X+Z 1/5-30/9)
5 **AB**CDGHIJLMNOPUVWXYZ
6 ABCDEFGK(N 0,8km)
PTUVW

Campsite for relaxing. Excellent toilet facilities. Swimming lake in the centre of the campsite. Located on the Mur cycling route. With its flat surroundings and bicycle network, it is suitable for cycling enthusiasts. Many day trips possible to surrounding old villages and towns. Small surcharge for the camping pitches directly on the lake.

S36 Knittelfeld-Ost and follow signs. Do not go via Spielberg-Knittelfeld-West because passage is too low. Switch off SatNav.

CC € 23 *1/4-1/6 1/9-31/10*

N 47°11'40'' E 14°48'20''

Hermagor-Pressegger See, A-9620 / Kärnten

665

EuroParcs Hermagor*****
Vellach 15
+43 42 82 20 51
1/1 - 31/12
@ kcc@europarcs.nl

5,6ha 280T(80-120m²) 16A

1 CD**I**KLMNOQRS
2 AJNSUVWYZ
3 C**D**EIKM**O**PS**TUVW**
4 (A 1/6-30/9)(C 1/5-30/9)
(**F**)(**H** 1/5-30/9)**LN**(Q)
(S 15/5-15/9)(U+W+Y+Z)
5 **AB**DEFGIJKLMNOPQRUWXYZ
6 CDEFGK(N 2km)
OPQRSTUV

EuroParcs Hermagor is one of the absolute top sites in Austria. Perfect starting point for all types of holiday, active or relaxed. During the winter (from 1/11 to 30/4) you will be charged extra for electricity above 4 kWh.

A23 Villach-Italian border, exit 364 Hermagor/Gailtal. Then B111 until 2 km before Hermagor. Right at camping sign. Campsite 50m on the left. Route via 'Windische Höhen' is closed for caravans.

CC € 27 *1/1-29/3 2/4-26/4 13/5-17/5 20/5-5/7 2/9-31/12*

N 46°37'53'' E 13°23'46''

Hermagor-Pressegger See, A-9620 / Kärnten

666

Sport-Camping-Flaschberger
Obervellach 27
+43 42 82 20 20
1/1 - 1/11, 1/12 - 31/12
@ office@flaschberger.at

2ha 80T(90-120m²) 16A

1 A**I**KLMNO**R**S
2 JNSUWXYZ
3 AIKM**OPRSTU**V
4 (A 1/6-30/9)(C 1/6-10/9)**N**
(Q+T+U+X)
5 **AB**DGIJKLMNOPRUWXYZ
6 ACDEFGK(N 2km)OPSTUV

Modern, well maintained family campsite with heated sanitary facilities. An ideal base for (mountain)walks, cycle trips or for the many tourist attractions in Carinthia.

A23 Villach-Italian border, exit 364 Hermagor/Gailtal. Then B111 till ± 2 km before Hermagor and right at campsite sign. Site about 100m on right. Road via 'Windische Höhen' is closed for caravans.

CC € 19 *1/1-6/7 28/8-31/10 1/12-31/12*

N 46°37'56'' E 13°23'48''

Imst, A-6460 / Tirol

667

Aktivcamping Am Schwimmbad
Schwimmbadweg 10
+43 5 41 22 13 55
19/4 - 13/10
info@camping-imst.at

1,2ha 49T(60-100m²) 6A CEE

1 AFIKLMNOQRS
2 IJLNSWXYZ
3 AIJKLOU
4 (A 1/5-21/9)(C+H 1/5-11/9)J (Q+Z)
5 **AB**GIJMOPUWZ
6 EFGK(N 0,3km)OP

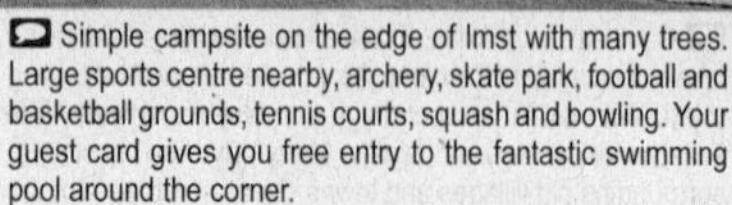

Simple campsite on the edge of Imst with many trees. Large sports centre nearby, archery, skate park, football and basketball grounds, tennis courts, squash and bowling. Your guest card gives you free entry to the fantastic swimming pool around the corner.

From roundabout Imst, exit 2. Follow signs.

CC € 19 *19/4-6/7 24/8-13/10*

N 47°14'24'' E 10°44'43''

Irschen, A-9773 / Kärnten

668

Rad-Wandercamping***
Glanz 13
+43 66 06 86 70 55
6/5 - 28/9
info@rad-wandercamping.at

0,9ha 34T(80-130m²) 6A

1 AFIKLMNOQRS
2 JMNSUXYZ
3 GIJKLU
4 (Q+R+T+U+V+X+Y+Z)
5 **AB**CDFGHIJKLMNOPQRUWXYZ
6 CEFGK(N 0,5km)PT

Lovely and quietly located family campsite bordering the herb village of Irschen and at walking distance from river Drau. The campsite can serve as a great starting point for walkers and/or cyclists. There is a 270 km cycle path along the river. Motorcyclists more than welcome.

From Lienz or Spittal follow route B100/E66, exit Glanz (municipality of Irschen). Campsite turning clearly signposted.

CC € 19 *6/5-5/7 22/8-22/9*

N 46°44'39'' E 13°02'39''

Kals am Großglockner, A-9981 / Tirol

669

Nationalpark Camping Kals****
Burg 22
+43 4 85 26 74 18
1/1 - 1/4, 18/5 - 13/10, 18/12 - 31/12
info@nationalpark-camping-kals.at

2,5ha 108T(100-120m²) 16A CEE

1 AFIKLMNOQRS
2 BCJMNSWXY
3 IKLUW
4 (Q+R)
5 **AB**DGIJKLMNOPUW
6 EFGJ(N 1km)OP

Brand-new campsite amid the countryside. Complete peace, surrounded by mountains. A truly delightful spot for walkers, winter sports fans and nature lovers! Kals is south of the Großglockner with good, accessible walks. Lovely route for motorbike riders and mountain bikers.

Kufstein-Kitzbühel-Mittersill-Felbertauern-Matrei-Huben, then turn left towards Kals. Campsite signposted from Kals.

CC € 25 *7/1-2/2 17/2-31/3 18/5-30/6 1/9-13/10*

N 47°01'18'' E 12°38'20''

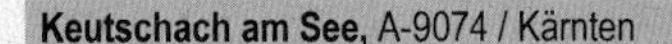

Keutschach am See, A-9074 / Kärnten

670

Strandcamping Süd
Dobeinitz 30
+43 42 73 27 73
1/5 - 30/9
info@strandcampingsued.at

2ha 155T(80-100m²) 13-14A

1 AIKLMNQRS
2 BFINPSUWXYZ
3 CGIKLSUWZ
4 (Q+R+T+U+Y+Z)
5 ABFGIJKLMNOPUW
6 ACEFGHKL(N 0,9km)PTU

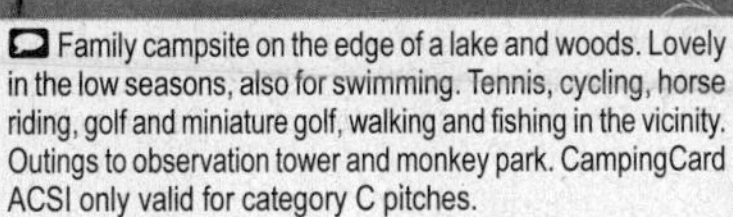

Family campsite on the edge of a lake and woods. Lovely in the low seasons, also for swimming. Tennis, cycling, horse riding, golf and miniature golf, walking and fishing in the vicinity. Outings to observation tower and monkey park. CampingCard ACSI only valid for category C pitches.

A2 exit Klagenfurt West-Süduferstraße direction Reifnitz. At Gemeindeamt Reifnitz turn left towards Keutschach. Over the roundabout and straight ahead for 1 km to the campsite.

CC € 27 1/5-4/5 12/5-16/5 21/5-28/5 2/6-24/6 5/9-30/9

N 46°35'07'' E 14°10'23''

Klosterneuburg, A-3400 / Niederösterreich

671

Donaupark Camping Klosterneuburg
In der Au 1
+43 2 24 32 58 77
13/3 - 5/11
campklosterneuburg@oeamtc.at

2,3ha 193T(60-90m²) 6A CEE

1 ACDEIJKLMNORS
2 IJSUVWXY
3 CGIKMS
4 (Q+R+U+X)
5 ABDFGIJKLMNOPUWZ
6 ABCDEFGHK(N 0,5km) OPSUV

The campsite is within walking distance of Klosterneuburg with its famous monastery. The station for bus and train services to Vienna is close by. The site is next to the Donauradweg cycle route. Vienna centre is 14 km by bike.

When approaching from the west: A1, exit Sankt Christophen B19, via Tulln and B14 to Klosterneuburg. The campsite is signposted in Klosterneuburg.

CC € 27 18/3-30/6 1/9-4/11

N 48°18'38'' E 16°19'42''

Kötschach/Mauthen, A-9640 / Kärnten

672

Alpencamp Kärnten****
Kötschach 284
+43 4 71 54 29
1/1 - 4/11, 15/12 - 31/12
info@alpencamp.at

1,6ha 80T(80-135m²) 16A CEE

1 ACDEIKLMNOQRS
2 CJNSUVWXYZ
3 ACIJKLMNQSUVWX
4 (A 1/1-31/3,1/5-15/10)LN (Q)(R 1/5-31/10)(X+Y)
5 ABCDFGHIJKLMNOPUW
6 CEFGKL(N 0,3km)OPTVW

Family campsite in a residential area. Access to the nearby leisure pool complex/aqua park at a reduced rate. Campsite is a good starting point for all kinds of trips, such as walking, cycling, canoeing, swimming, kayaking, rafting, etc. Possibility to ski in winter.

B100 Lienz-Spittal an der Drau. In Oberdrauburg take Plöckenpass/Italy exit. Campsite well signposted in Kötschach direction Lesachtal.

CC € 25 7/1-29/6 1/9-4/11

N 46°40'11'' E 12°59'30''

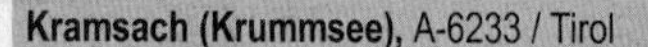

Kramsach (Krummsee), A-6233 / Tirol

673

Seencamping Stadlerhof****
Seebühel 14
+43 5 33 76 33 71
1/1 - 31/12
office@camping-stadlerhof.at

3ha 130T(70-150m²) 6-16A

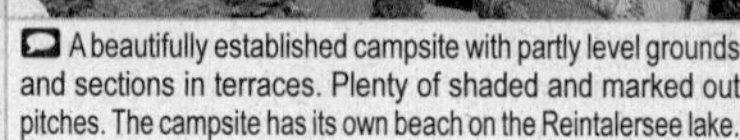

1 ADIJKLMNOQRS
2 EIJMNOPSUVWXZ
3 CDIKLNSUV
4 (C)(H 1/6-30/9)KLN (Q+R+T+U+Y)
5 ABCDEFGIJKLMNOPRSUWXYZ
6 ACDEFGK(N 1,5km)OPSU

A beautifully established campsite with partly level grounds and sections in terraces. Plenty of shaded and marked out pitches. The campsite has its own beach on the Reintalersee lake.

Inntal motorway, exit 32 Kramsach. Then follow the signs 'Zu den Seen'.

Wörgl, A12, B171, B181, Kramsach, Jenbach, B169

CC € 25 *8/5-17/6 9/9-22/10*

N 47°27'24'' E 11°52'51''

Kramsach (Reintalersee), A-6233 / Tirol

674

Camping und Appartements Seehof*****
Moosen 42
+43 5 33 76 35 41
1/1 - 31/12
info@camping-seehof.com

5ha 150T(90-120m²) 13-16A CEE

1 ACDIKLMNOQRS
2 EIJMNPSUVWXY
3 CDEIJKLMNQSUVWZ
4 (A 1/7-31/8) (Q+R+T+U+V+Y)
5 ABDEFGHIJKLMNOPRSUWXYZ
6 ABCDEFGKL(N 3km) OPQSUV

Spacious, marked-out, sunny pitches, partly in terraces. Private lawn on Reintaler See. Direct access to lake. Petting zoo. Playground. Exclusive toilet facilities, rental bathrooms. Good restaurant. Mountain lifts etc. free with Alpbachtal Seenland Card!

A12 exit 32 Kramsach. Follow green 'Zu den Seen' or 'Campingplätze' signs for about 5 km. 2nd campsite on this road. Reception on left next to entrance. If you take mountain road (not permitted) site on right.

Kirchbichl, Wörgl, A12, Kramsach, B169

CC € 25 *7/1-28/6 8/9-15/12*

N 47°27'43'' E 11°54'26''

Krems (Donau), A-3500 / Niederösterreich

675

Donau Camping Krems
Yachthafenstrasse 19
+43 2 73 28 44 55
1/4 - 31/10
office@campingkrems.at

0,8ha 60T(70-100m²) 6A CEE

1 ABCDIKLMN
2 CINSXY
3 IKLMSU
4 (Q+T+U+Z)
5 ABFGIJKLMNOPUW
6 BCEFGJ(N 0,5km)UV

Campsite right by the Danube. Wonderful view of Göttweig Abbey. 2-minute walk from the old city of Krems. Tour boats at walking distance. Cycle paths on both banks of the Danube. Around 21 June, is the 'Solsticeparty', with fireworks. Swimming pool, tennis and bowling at 500 m. Private boat jetty.

From the eastern intersection St. Pölten S33. Then B37 direction Krems. 3rd exit at roundabout in Krems, then immediately left past Schifffahrtszentrum Krems/Stein to the campsite.

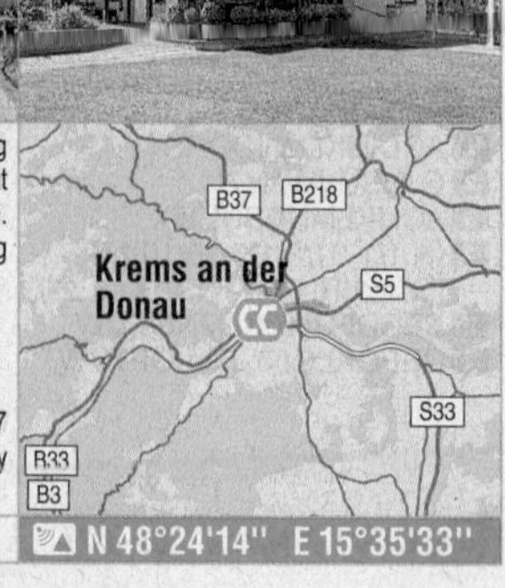

CC € 27 *1/4-30/6 1/9-31/10*

N 48°24'14'' E 15°35'33''

Lienz, A-9900 / Tirol

676

Comfort & Wellness Camping Falken****
Falkenweg 7
+43 66 44 10 79 73
1/4 - 31/10
camping.falken@gmx.at

2,5ha 132T(70-120m²) 6A CEE

1 ACDEIJKLMNOQRS
2 JNSWXYZ
3 AGIKLOSU
4 LN(Q 🔑)(R 1/6-1/10) (T+U+V+Z 🔑)
5 ABCDFGIJKLMNOPUWXYZ
6 CEFGHK(N 1km) OPQRSTVW

Quiet campsite with very luxurious toilet facilities. Only 900m from the 'Sunny town' Lienz. New wellness centre with sauna and steam bath. Ideal for shopping, walking and cycling. Special wild water canoeing and kayaking course.

Via Kufstein-Kitzbühel-Mittersil-Felbertauern tunnel towards Lienz. In Lienz direction Spittal at roundabout. Right at 2nd roundabout (ÖAMTC). Then follow signs.

CC € 25 *1/4-14/7 9/9-30/10*

N 46°49'22'' E 12°46'14''

Malta, A-9854 / Kärnten

677

Terrassencamping Maltatal*****
Malta 6
+43 47 33 23 40
22/4 - 15/10
info@maltacamp.at

3,9ha 238T(60-150m²) 6-13A CEE

1 ACDIKLMNOQRTU
2 CIJLMNSUWYZ
3 CEIKMOSU
4 (A 1/6-1/10)(C+H 1/6-15/9) LN(Q+S+T+U+V+Y+Z 🔑)
5 ABCDEFGHIJKLMNOPQRUWXYZ
6 ACEFGKM(N 6km)OPUVW

This beautiful terraced campsite has been in the family for more than 60 years and offers rest and relaxation. Restaurant and swimming pool at the campsite, toilet and washing facilities with breathtaking views. Great base for walks in Hohe Tauern National Park. There are many animals at the campsite, and you can go pony riding, etc.

A10 Salzburg-Villach, exit 130 Gmünd. Follow the signs in Gmünd in the direction of Maltatal. The campsite is located on the right 2 km past Fischerstratten.

CC € 27 *22/4-30/6 1/9-15/10*

N 46°56'58'' E 13°30'34''

Marbach an der Donau, A-3671 / Niederösterreich

678

Marbacher Freizeitzentrum
Campingweg 2
+43 7 41 32 07 33
2/4 - 26/10
gasthof@wienerin.co.at

0,4ha 35T(70-100m²) 16A CEE

1 ADIKLMNOQRUV
2 DSUWXY
3 GKLUWX
4 (Q+R 🔑)
5 ABDGIJMNOPUWXY
6 FGK(N 0,5km)

Lovely, small campsite on the bank of the Danube with partly demarcated pitches on grass. Beside a popular marina and directly on the well-known Danube cycle route along apricot orchards and vineyards. Many walking routes and fishing options in the surrounding area. Tennis and swimming pool at 1 km. Restaurant within walking distance.

A1 Linz-Wien, exit 100 Ybbs/Wieselburg. Follow road towards Ybbs/Persenbeug. Cross the Danube towards Krems. Campsite ± 7 km on the right.

CC € 25 *2/4-5/5 21/5-30/6 14/9-26/10*

N 48°12'49'' E 15°08'26''

Mauterndorf, A-5570 / Salzburg

679

Camping Mauterndorf****
Markt 145
+43 6 47 27 20 23
1/1 - 31/12
info@camping-mauterndorf.at

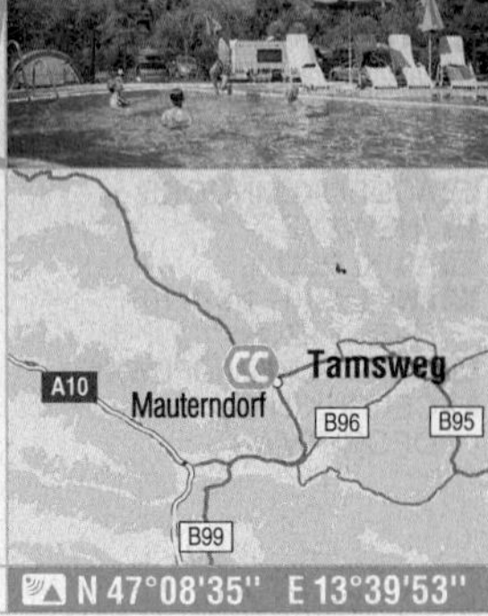

2,5ha 163**T**(65-100m²) 12A CEE

1 ACD**I**KLMNOQRS
2 CIJMNSUVWXY
3 AC**G**IKLMNUV
4 (C 1/7-31/8)**LN**(Q+R+U)
(V+Y 1/7-10/9,1/12-30/4)
(Z)
5 **AB**DEFGIJMNOPUWXYZ
6 CFGKL(N 2km)OPSV

Lovely campsite open all year in the heart of the Salzburger Lungau. Right next to the Erlebnisberg Grosseck-Speiereck cable car. Wonderful walking throughout the year. On the site: sauna, solarium, steam bath, fitness room and massage.

A10, exit St. Michael im Lungau, direction Mauterndorf. Follow B99 Erlebnisberg Grosseck-Speiereck. On B99 after 1.5 km, campsite is on the left.

CC € 27 *15/4-30/6 9/9-24/11*

N 47°08'35'' E 13°39'53''

Mayrhofen, A-6290 / Tirol

680

Camping Alpenparadies Mayrhofen****
Laubichl 125
+43 6 64 88 51 88 66
1/1 - 12/10, 13/12 - 31/12
info@campingplatz-tirol.at

2,5ha 220**T**(60-120m²) 16A CEE

1 ACD**I**KLMNOQRS
2 JMNSUVWY
3 CIKLSU**W**
4 (C+F+H)**KLN**
(Q+R+T+U+V+Y+Z)
5 **AB**CDFGIJKLMNOPQ**S**UWXYZ
6 CEFGH**K**(N 1km)OPSV

Campsite with lovely level grounds on the edge of the woods. The indoor and outdoor swimming pool offers swimming in all weather conditions. The restaurant will take care of your appetite. Infra-red cabins on the campsite. Many sports facilities in the immediate vicinity, such as cycling, walking and climbing.

Inntal motorway, exit 39 Zillertal, take the B169 to Mayrhofen.

Zell am Ziller
B165
Mayrhofen

CC € 25 *8/4-30/6 2/9-29/9 7/10-12/10*

N 47°10'34'' E 11°52'11''

Mondsee/Tiefgraben, A-5310 / Oberösterreich

681

Camp MondSeeLand*****
Punzau 21
+43 62 32 26 00
27/3 - 1/10
austria@campmondsee.at

4ha 120**T**(80-120m²) 16A CEE

1 ACD**I**KLMNOQ**R**S
2 INSWXY
3 C**G**IKPSUW
4 (**A** 1/7-31/8)(C 1/5-30/9)
(Q+S+U+V+Y+Z)
5 **AB**DFGIJKLMNOPR**S**UWXYZ
6 ABCDEFGH**K**(N 4km)
OPTUV

A peaceful luxury campsite with new toilet facilities located between the Mondsee and Irrsee lakes. Lovely cycling and walking routes from the campsite. The fortified town of Salzburg is 27 km away and is easily reached. Ideal for a breath of fresh air on the way to Vienna or further east (Hungary/Czech Republic).

A1 Salzburg-Vienna. Exit 264 Mondsee, 1st roundabout direction Straßwalchen, 3rd exit on 2nd roundabout then follow campsite signs.

CC € 27 *27/3-8/5 13/5-16/5 3/6-30/6 4/9-1/10*

N 47°52'00'' E 13°18'24''

Nassereith, A-6465 / Tirol

682

Camping Rossbach****
Rossbach 325
+43 52 65 51 54
1/3 - 31/10
camping.rossbach@hotmail.com

1ha 80T(70-80m²) 6A CEE

1 ADEIKLMNQRS
2 CJSWXYZ
3 AGIKLQSUW
4 (A 1/5-30/10)(C 1/7-31/8) (Q)(T+U+X 1/7-31/8)
5 ABDFGIJKLMNOPUWZ
6 ACEFGJ(N 1,5km)OV

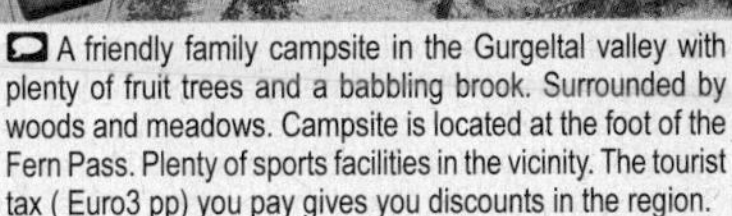

A friendly family campsite in the Gurgeltal valley with plenty of fruit trees and a babbling brook. Surrounded by woods and meadows. Campsite is located at the foot of the Fern Pass. Plenty of sports facilities in the vicinity. The tourist tax (Euro3 pp) you pay gives you discounts in the region.

Follow the B179 from Reutte to Nassereith (through the Fern pass), exit Nassereith. Direction Domitz/Rossbach in the centre. Follow the signs.

CC € 21 *1/3-30/6 1/9-31/10*

N 47°18'37'' E 10°51'20''

Neustift, A-6167 / Tirol

683

Camping Stubai****
Stubaitalstraße 94
+43 52 26 25 37
1/1 - 30/4, 18/5 - 31/12
info@campingstubai.at

2ha 110T(60-100m²) 6A CEE

1 ADEIJKLMNOQRS
2 CIJLMNSUVXY
3 AIKLSUW
4 (A 24/6-2/10)LN
5 ABDEFGIJKLMNOPQSUWYZ
6 ACGK(N 0,05km)OPV

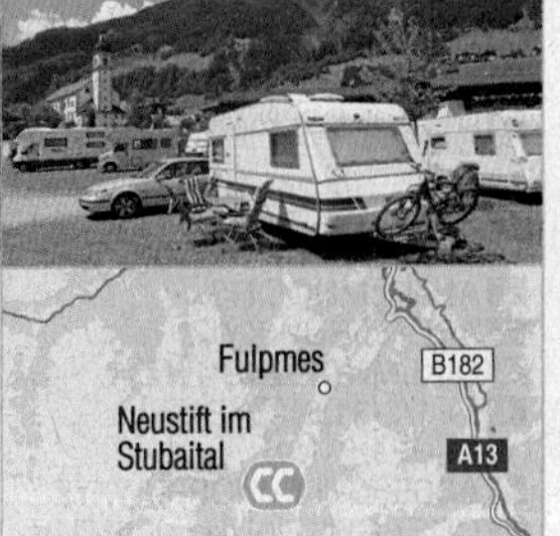

This campsite with level grounds is at the foot the mountains in the village of Neustift, right next to a supermarket. From the campsite, you have wonderful views of the mountains where paragliders engage in their sport. Tourist tax and waste charge not included. The guest card offers you many tourist options.

A13 Brenner motorway, exit Europabrücke and on the B183 to Stubaital and then to Neustift.

CC € 21 *18/5-23/6 5/9-30/9*

N 47°06'36'' E 11°18'31''

Oberdrauburg, A-9781 / Kärnten

684

Natur- & Familiencamping Oberdrauburg
Gailbergstraße
+43 47 10 22 49 22
1/5 - 30/9
tourismus@oberdrauburg.at

1,2ha 68T(80-110m²) 12A CEE

1 ACDIKLMNOQRS
2 JLMNSUWXYZ
3 ACGIKMNOPSU
4 (C+H 8/6-25/8)J(Q 8/6-31/8) (T+U)(V 8/6-31/8) (X 8/6-25/8)(Z 8/6-31/8)
5 ABCDEFGHIJKLMNOPQRUWZ
6 CEFGHK(N 0,5km)OPV

Beautifully located family campsite. Campsite can serve as starting point for walkers, canoeists, motorcyclists (Plöcken pass), nature lovers and cyclists. You can also spend a night in a mountain hut from this campsite.

Spittal dir. Lienz (B100) to Oberdrauburg, or Mittersill-Felbertauerntunnel-Lienz-Oberdrauburg. Exit Plöckenpass, site after 500 metres.

CC € 21 *1/5-3/7 20/8-29/9* ***7=6, 14=12***

N 46°44'33'' E 12°58'11''

Ossiach, A-9570 / Kärnten

685

Camping Kalkgruber
Alt-Ossiach 4
+43 65 05 17 85 07
1/5 - 1/10
office@camping-kalkgruber.at

0,9ha 30T(80-100m²) 10A CEE

1 ACD**I**KLMNQRS
2 JMNSUWXY
3 AEIKLPSU
4 (A+Q)
5 **AB**DFGIJMNO**P**UW
6 ACEFGK(N 1km)PU

A small but very well kept campsite close to the Ossiacher See lake. Here you will find peace, space and countryside. Frau Schabus will greet you with open arms. Lively recreation room. Fresh trout on sale. Good local food 1 km away. Suitable as stopover site, 12 km from the Ossiacher See exit.

A10 Salzburg-Villach, exit Ossiacher See direction Feldkirchen. In Steindorf turn right towards Ossiach. Then first campsite on the right.

CC € 21 *1/5-7/7 26/8-29/9* ***10=9, 20=18, 30=27***

N 46°41'15'' E 14°01'10''

Ossiach, A-9570 / Kärnten

686

Camping Kölbl
Ostriach 106
+43 42 43 82 23
1/5 - 10/10
info@camping-koelbl.at

17ha 140T(80-100m²) 8-10A CEE

1 A**H**JKLMNOQRS
2 AFIJNOSUWXY
3 CIKLMN**O**P**QR**SU**W**Z
4 (A 1/7-31/8)(Q+R)
(U+V 1/6-1/9)
5 **AB**DEFGIJKLMNOPRUWXYZ
6 CDEFGHKL(N 1km)OPTUV

A well maintained campsite right next to the Ossiacher See. If you like sportive holidays this is the place for you. You can walk or cycle round the lake and you will find all types of sport in the area. You will also feel at home here in spring and autumn. Dogs not allowed.

A10 Salzburg-Villach, exit Ossiacher See direction 'Südufer'. First campsite on the left past 'Heiligen Gestade'.

CC € 27 *1/5-30/6 1/9-10/10*

N 46°39'44'' E 13°58'20''

Pesenthein, A-9872 / Kärnten

687

Terrassencamping Pesenthein
Pesenthein 19
+43 47 66 26 65
30/3 - 31/10
camping@pesenthein.at

5ha 213T(70-95m²) 6A CEE

1 ACD**I**KLMNOQRTU
2 AEJLMNSUWXY
3 C**G**IKLMSUZ
4 J(Q+Y+Z)
5 **AB**CDFGIJKLMNOPUW
6 AFGK(N 2km)PTV

A terraced campsite with a private beach and stunning views of the Millstätter See lake. Both the campsite and the beach have a separate area reserved for naturists. Separate beach for dogs.

A10 Salzburg-Villach, exit 139 Millstätter See (exit on left!). Left at traffic lights B98 direction Radenthein. Campsite about 2 km past Millstatt, east of Pesenthein on the left.

CC € 23 *30/3-30/6 1/9-31/10*

N 46°47'47'' E 13°35'57''

Prutz, A-6522 / Tirol

688

Aktiv Camping Prutz****
Pontlatzstraße 22
+43 54 72 26 48
1/1 - 31/12
info@aktiv-camping.at

1,5ha 125T(60-120m²) 6-10A CEE

1 ACDE**I**KLMNOQRS
2 CIJNSUVWXY
3 CIKLMNP**Q**SU**W**
4 (A 1/5-1/10)(Q+R)
(U 15/5-15/10,23/12-31/12)
(X 15/5-15/10,20/12-31/12)
5 **AB**DFGHIJKLMNOPUWXZ
6 ABCDEFG**K**(N 0,5km)OP

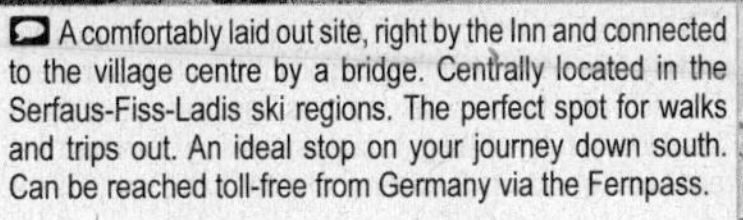

A comfortably laid out site, right by the Inn and connected to the village centre by a bridge. Centrally located in the Serfaus-Fiss-Ladis ski regions. The perfect spot for walks and trips out. An ideal stop on your journey down south. Can be reached toll-free from Germany via the Fernpass.

Via toll-free road: From Imst to Landeck, then on the B180 dir. Serfaus (Reschenpass)to Prutz. Or A12 direction Reschenpaß, through tunnel at Landeck, then on B180 (toll charges).

Landeck Fliess
Prutz
B180

CC € 23 *15/4-30/6 1/9-13/12* ***10=9, 20=18, 30=27***

N 47°04'49'' E 10°39'34''

Purbach, A-7083 / Burgenland

689

Campingplatz Storchencamp Purbach
Campingplatz 1
+43 26 83 51 70
29/3 - 26/10
office@gmeiner.co.at

10ha 58T(80-100m²) 16A CEE

1 ACDE**I**JKLMNOQ**R**S
2 EJSXY
3 AC**G**IKL**O**S**W**
4 (**C**+**H** 1/5-30/8)**J**
(Q+R+T+U+Y+Z)
5 **AB**DFGIJKLMNOPUWYZ
6 CEFG**J**(N 1km)P

The campsite is an ideal starting point for exploring the picturesque village of Purbach with its cellars. The restaurant 'Storchenbeisl' with outdoor patio provides your culinary wellbeing. Many sports and recreational activities by Lake Neusiedl. Erlebnis-Solarbad (free entry) is just past the campsite. You get the Burgenland Karte, offering many discounts.

B50 Eisenstadt-Neusiedl am See. In the village follow campsite sign or 'zum See'.

CC € 23 *1/5-17/5 3/6-19/6 1/9-30/9*

N 47°54'34'' E 16°42'20''

Rennweg am Katschberg, A-9863 / Kärnten

690

Camping Ramsbacher
Gries 53
+43 4 73 46 63
1/1 - 31/12
info@camp-ram.at

1,4ha 65T(80-100m²) 16A CEE

1 ACDIKLMNOQRTU
2 CIJNSUWXYZ
3 A**G**IJKLO**R**S**W**
4 (A 1/6-30/9)(C+G 15/6-1/9)
(Q 1/7-31/8)(U)
5 **AB**DGIJKLMNOPUW
6 CEFGK(N 2km)OP

Pleasant and sunny summer and winter campsite in the Pölltal valley on the southern slope of Katschberg mountain. Because of its location near the A10, it is also very suitable as a transit campsite. Take-away meals available in the campsite restaurant.

A10 Salzburg-Villach, exit 112 Rennweg. B99 direction Rennweg, first road on the right. Turn right at the traffic control office. Follow this main road as far as Gries. Then follow the camping signs.

CC € 23 *15/4-30/6 1/9-30/11*

N 47°01'56'' E 13°35'44''

Ried, A-6531 / Tirol

691

Camping Dreiländereck****
Ried 37
+43 54 72 60 25
1/1 - 6/11, 8/12 - 31/12
info@tirolcamping.at

1ha 60T(70-100m²) 16A CEE

1 ADIKLMNOQRS
2 EIJSUVWXY
3 IKLMNUWZ
4 (A)LNP(Q+U+V+Y+Z)
5 ABDEFGIJKMNOPUWXYZ
6 ACDEFGK(N 0,1km)OPV

Centrally located campsite guarantees both relaxation and activity. You benefit from the regional Super.Sommer.Card. Excellent toilet facilities, with wellness, sauna and steam bath. Ideal location for walking, cycling and skiing. Serfaus, Fiss and Ladis at ± 6 km. Swimming lake and cable car (300 m).

Toll-free road: via Imst on route 171 to Landeck, (direction Reschenpass) and on to Ried. Or A12 direction Meran (Reschenpass), then on B180 towards Serfaus (toll charges).

Landeck
Zams
B180

CC € 23 *6/4-5/7 1/9-6/11*

N 47°03'21'' E 10°39'24''

St. Georgen am Kreischberg, A-8861 / Steiermark

692

Camping Olachgut*****
Kaindorf 90
+43 35 32 21 62
1/1 - 1/4, 5/5 - 6/10, 6/12 - 31/12
office@olachgut.at

10ha 140T(100-140m²) 16A CEE

1 ACDIKLMNOQRS
2 CEJMNSUWXYZ
3 ACGIKPQSUWZ
4 (A 1/7-31/8)N (Q+R+U+X+Z)
5 ABCDEFGIJKLMNOPRUWXYZ
6 ACEFGKL(N 2km)OPUV

Lovely 5 star site with own lake for fishing and swimming. Our farm with its many animals and recognized riding school is popular with children. Direct, safe cycle path to the popular Mur cycle route. Wheelchair friendly amenities on the site. Good family ski area close by.

A10/E55, exit 104 St. Michael. Route 96 as far as Tamsweg, then route 97 as far as St. Georgen. The campsite is located on the right after 2 km.

Sankt Peter am Kammersberg
B96
Murau
B97

CC € 27 *6/5-16/5 2/6-28/6 6/9-6/10*

N 47°06'27'' E 14°08'22''

St. Johann im Pongau, A-5600 / Salzburg

693

Camping Kastenhof
Kastenhofweg 6
+43 64 12 54 90
1/1 - 31/12
info@kastenhof.at

2ha 40T(80m²) 15A CEE

1 ADIKLMNORS
2 CJNSUWXYZ
3 ACGHIKSUVW
4 LN(Q+R)
5 ABDFGIJKLMNOPUW
6 CDEFGJ(N 0,5km)OPSTV

Hospitable, favourable and sunny location. Beautiful views of the mountains, within walking distance of the centre of St. Johann. Modern toilet facilities and extensive wellness programme. Ideal starting point for lovely walks and car and bike trips. Located on the 'Tauernradweg' cycle route.

A10, exit 46 Bischofshofen. Dir. Zell am See B311 as far as exit St. Johann im Pongau/Grossarl/Hüttschlag. Under viaduct; cross over bridge; first road on the left. Entrance after 150m.

CC € 27 *8/1-14/1 1/2-4/2 4/3-10/3 20/5-30/6 9/9-29/9*

N 47°20'29'' E 13°11'53''

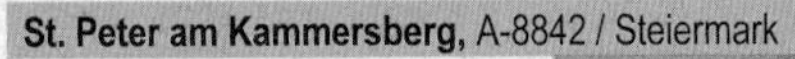

St. Peter am Kammersberg, A-8842 / Steiermark

694

Camping Bella Austria****
Peterdorf 100
+43 66 41 68 09 77
27/4 - 29/9
info@camping-bellaustria.com

5,5ha 45T(110m²) 16A CEE

1 AIKLMNOQRTU
2 CNSUWXY
3 ACEIKPSUW
4 (B+G 15/6-31/8)N
(Q+R 1/7-31/8)(U+Y+Z)
5 ABCDEFGIJKLMNOPUWXYZ
6 EFGJ(N 2km)TU

The campsite is located on the edge of the woods in the Katschtal valley in Styria, 1 km from the village of St. Peter am Kammersberg. The site has comfort pitches and a lovely swimming pool. It also has a good restaurant.

Via B99 direction Tamsweg. Take the Turracher Bundesstraße and via B95 to Ramingstein. Continue to Predlits, then from Falkendorf to Murau. Through Murau to Frojach-Katsch, then to Peterdorf and Camping Bella Austria.

Sankt Peter am Kammersberg
B75
B96
Murau
B97

N 47°10'49'' E 14°12'55''

CC € 21 *27/4-13/7 31/8-29/9*

St. Pölten, A-3100 / Niederösterreich

695

Camping am See
Bimbo Binder-Promenade 15
+43 67 68 98 79 88 98
15/4 - 15/10
office@campingamsee.at

2ha 50T(75-200m²) 16A CEE

1 BCDIJKLMNOQRS
2 FIJOPQSUWXYZ
3 ACGIKLMORSTVWZ
4 (Q)
5 ABDGIJKLMNOPUWZ
6 CEFGK(N 2km)PT

Beautifully landscaped campsite with excellent toilet facilities by a clear lake with a lovely sunbathing lawn with shade. Nearby the city of culture St. Pölten. There is a fitness centre beside the campsite. Suitable location for a visit to Vienna and for a stopover en route to Hungary. Walking and cycling in the surrounding area. Great restaurants by nearby lakes.

From A1 at St. Pölten intersection S33 towards Krems. Then St. Pölten Nord exit. West at second intersection.

N 48°13'27'' E 15°39'33''

CC € 25 *15/4-20/5 29/5-28/6 2/9-15/10*

Stams, A-6422 / Tirol

696

Camping Eichenwald
Schiesstandweg 10
+43 52 63 61 59
25/3 - 15/10
info@camping-eichenwald.at

5ha 100T(70-150m²) 13A CEE

1 AFIKLMNOQRS
2 CIJMNSUVWXYZ
3 AGIKLNSUW
4 (A 10/7-20/8)(C+H 1/5-15/9)
N(Q+R)(U+Y 1/5-30/9)
(Z)
5 ABCDGHIJKLMNOPUWXYZ
6 CEFGK(N 0,5km)OPTUV

This terraced, centrally located campsite in the Inn valley offers shaded and spacious pitches. There are many opportunities around Stams, where kings and emperors took their holiday, for an active vacation: swimming, horse riding, hiking, golf, mountain climbing (3000 routes). Eichenwald in the Oberinntal is the place for rest, relaxation and adventure.

Reutte, Fernpass, Nassereith, Mieming, direction Mötz/Stams. Campsite signposted.

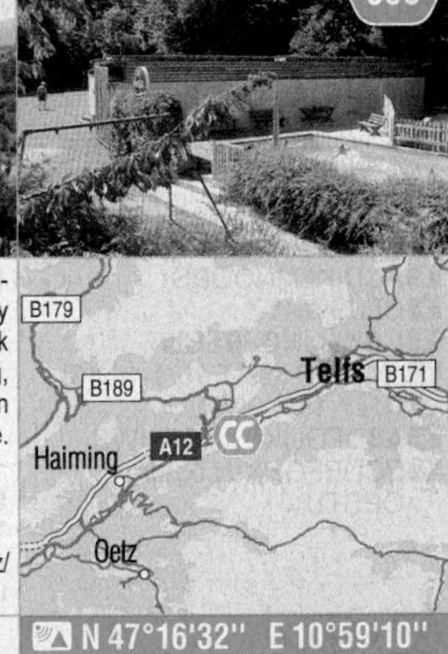

N 47°16'32'' E 10°59'10''

CC € 25 *25/3-29/6 1/9-15/10*

Steindorf, A-9552 / Kärnten

697

See-Areal Steindorf****
Seestrasse 5a
+43 6 64 73 75 66 98
15/4 - 15/10
info@seearealsteindorf.at

1ha 32**T**(25-100m²) 13A

1 AD**H**KLMNOQ**R**S
2 EIJLNOSWXYZ
3 **G**IKLMN**OW**Z
4 (A+Q+U)(Y 1/5-30/9)
(Z)
5 **AB**DFGIJKLMNOP**RS**UW
6 AEFK(N 0,2km)P

Lovely campsite with lawn. Plenty of sun and shade, located by Lake Ossiach. Incl. Wifi. Disabled sanitary facilities. Bakery. Opportunities for water sports, tennis, cycling, walking. Lovely patio, good restaurant. No play areas for children.

A10 Salzburg-Villach, ex. Ossiacher See B94 dir. Nordufer/Feldkirchen. After 15 km turn right dir. Ossiach over the railway and immediately right back dir. Steindorf. After approx. 900m turn left at the campsite sign. Enter via Dammweg!

CC € 25 *15/4-15/6 14/9-14/10*

N 46°41'40'' E 14°00'34''

Steindorf/Stiegl, A-9552 / Kärnten

698

Seecamping Hoffmann****
Uferweg 61
+43 42 43 87 04
1/5 - 15/10
info@seehotel-hoffmann.at

1ha 20**T**(50-80m²) 16A

1 AD**H**KLMNOQRS
2 FIJMNOPSUWXYZ
3 C**FG**IJKLMN**O**SW**Z**
4 (A)**N**(Q+R)(T 1/6-7/9)
(U+Y+Z)
5 **AB**EFGJLNPUW
6 AEFGKL(N 1km)**P**V

Small campsite with private beach, lovely large pitches. Amazing view of Lake Ossiach.

A10 Salzburg-Villach exit Villach/Ossiachersee, B94 direction Feldkirchen. Follow signs in Steindorf.

CC € 21 *1/5-30/6 1/9-15/10*

N 46°41'42'' E 13°59'48''

Tulln an der Donau, A-3430 / Niederösterreich

699

Donaupark Camping Tulln
Donaulände 76
+43 2 27 26 52 00
22/3 - 18/10
camptulln@oeamtc.at

10ha 120**T**(80-100m²) 6A CEE

1 ACDIKLMNOQ**R**S
2 CEJSWXYZ
3 C**G**KLMN**O**P**R**SU**W**Z
4 JM(Q+R)(T 15/4-14/10)
(U+Y 15/4-30/9)
5 **AB**DFGIJKLMNOPUWZ
6 BCDEFGHK(N 0,3km)
OPSTUV

Lovely, well maintained campsite on the Danube with spacious, partially marked out pitches on a grassy base. There is a large playpark next to the campsite with swimming facilities which are free of charge to campsite guests.

A1 Linz-Vienna, exit St. Christophen exit 41 direction Tulln (B19). At Tulln follow the signs to Klosterneuburg. Under the railway viaduct, 1st on the right. Left after 650 metres, follow 'camping' signs.

CC € 27 *22/3-30/6 1/9-17/10*

N 48°19'59'' E 16°04'08''

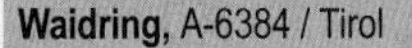

Waidring, A-6384 / Tirol

700

Camping Steinplatte*****
Unterwasser 43
+43 53 53 53 45
1/1 - 31/12
info@camping-steinplatte.at

4ha 200T 10A

1 ABCDIJKLMNOQRS
2 CFJNOPSUWXYZ
3 AGIKLRSUZ
4 (A 1/7-31/8)**N**
(Q+T+U+V+X+Y+Z)
5 **AB**DFGIJKLMNOPUWZ
6 BCEFGK(N 0,4km)OPSV

Peaceful, by small lake, beautiful views of Loferer Steinberg. Ideal for walking and cycling. Countless possibilities for sporting activities and leisure. Good, friendly eating in the restaurant.

From the north toll-free: München - exit Oberaudorf, B172 via Walchsee and Kössen far as Erpfendorf. Then direction Lofer as far as Waidring. From the west: Inntal-Autobahn - Exit Wörgl Ost as far as St. Johann, then direction Waidring.

CC € 27 *1/5-5/7 9/9-30/9*

N 47°35'00'' E 12°34'59''

Walchsee, A-6344 / Tirol

701

Ferienpark Terrassencamping Süd-See****
Seestraße 76
+43 53 74 53 39
1/1 - 31/12
info@terrassencamping.at

11ha 150T(70-150m²) 16A CEE

1 AIKLMNOQ**R**S
2 EIMNOSTUVWXYZ
3 A**G**IKMN**QW**Z
4 (A 1/6-1/10)(Q)
(R 12/4-15/10)(U+V+X
+Y 12/4-15/10,20/12-31/12)
5 **AB**DEFGIJLMNOPUWXYZ
6 CDEFGHK(N 2km)OPU

Perfect site, open all year, in walking, cycling and cross country paradise 'Kaiserwinkl'. All pitches have fantastic views of the lake. Modern toilet facilities, free hot water, private cabins. Restaurant, mini-market, lakeside lawn (24°C in summer). Peaceful location. Seasonal pitches. Toll free motorway to Walchsee.

A8 München/Salzburg direction Innsbruck. Take exit 59 to B172 from Niederndorf to Kössen. Before Walchsee, turn right. Campsite is signposted.

CC € 27 *1/4-19/6 1/9-3/11*

N 47°38'26'' E 12°19'26''

Weer, A-6116 / Tirol

702

Alpencamping Mark****
Bundesstraße 12
+43 6 99 19 99 91 09
19/4 - 30/9
info@alpencampingmark.com

2ha 95T(80-130m²) 10-16A

1 ABCD**I**KLMNOQRS
2 IJLNSVWZ
3 CIKLMN**O**P**Q**SU
4 (**A** 1/7-31/8)(C 1/5-30/9)
(Q+R)(T+U 1/5-25/9)
(V)(Y 1/5-25/9)(Z)
5 **AB**CDFGHIJKLMNOPRUWZ
6 ABCEFGHK(N 0,1km)
PUVWX

Nicely appointed family campsite on even or lightly inclined, well-maintained meadow with several trees. Many shady, spacious pitches. The campsite has an outdoor swimming pool and climbing wall. Own horse breeding (Haflinger). There is an 'Alpine and Leisure School' on the campsite.

From Innsbruck direction Kufstein, exit 61 Wattens. From Kufstein direction Innsbruck, exit 49 Schwaz or 53 Vomp, then to Weer.

CC € 23 *19/4-30/6 1/9-30/9*

N 47°18'23'' E 11°38'57''

Zell im Zillertal, A-6280 / Tirol

703

- Campingdorf Hofer
- Gerlosstraße 33
- +43 52 82 22 48
- 1/1 - 5/11, 5/12 - 31/12
- info@campingdorf.at

1,6ha 100**T**(80-100m²) 6-16A CEE

1. ACD**I**KLMNQRS
2. JNSWY
3. A**G**IKLS**W**
4. (A 1/6-15/9)
   (E 1/5-15/10)(Q)
   (T+U+Y 1/1-15/4,30/5-15/10)
5. **AB**DFGIJKLMNOPRUWZ
6. BCEFGHKLOPV

Friendly family campsite with about 100 spacious pitches. Centrally located within walking distance of the centre of Zell im Zillertal. Indoor and heated outdoor pools provide a chance to cool down. There is a 45,000 m² leisure park in Zell with countless sports and leisure facilities. Tourist and environmental taxes are not included in the CampingCard ACSI rates.

Inntal motorway, exit 39 Zillertal, take the B169 to Zell am Ziller (fourth campsite in the Zillertal).

Zell am Ziller
B165
Mayrhofen

CC € 25 *15/4-30/6 1/9-15/10*

N 47°13'44'' E 11°53'10''

Poland

Capital: Warsaw
Currency: the sloty
Time zone: UTC +1, UTC +2 (March to October)
Language: Polish
International dialling code: +48
Alcohol limit: 0.2‰
Emergency number: police 997, fire brigade: 998, ambulance: 999
Tap water: is often not safe; drink bottled or boiled water

Poland: castles, the countryside and history

Wide sandy beaches, deep gorges, the largest desert, the last primaeval forest in Europe, as well as the 'Lake District' and picturesque cities like Kraków or Warsaw. If you go camping in Poland, you can choose from many different regions that are worth seeing.

Castle route

Are you unsure of which part of Poland you want to see? Plan your holiday based on the Gothic castle route. For example, book a campsite in Malbork, Ostróda or Kętrzyn, so that you can visit one of the castles from there. The beautiful Slot Mariënburg in Malbork (or Malbork Castle) can be found along this route. This is the largest medieval castle in Europe and is listed on the UNESCO'S World Heritage List.

Going into nature

Do you feel like going into nature? Then a visit to Białowieża National Park is a must. It is home to more than 10,000 animal species. You will benefit greatly from a tour led by a guide.
Do you prefer the sun? Go on holiday along the Baltic coast. The beaches there are amazing, like

the one in Ustka. The imposing Giant Mountains along the Czech border and the High Tatra Mountains along the Slovakian border invite you to an active camping holiday in the mountains in the south of Poland.
The south also has the largest sand desert of Central Europe: the Błędów Desert. The 32-square-kilometre desert, called the 'Polish Sahara', has various hiking, cycling and riding routes as well as a viewing platform. The desert is only 45 kilometres from Kraków.

Kraków

With more than 5,000 historic buildings and monuments, Kraków is the most important cultural metropole in the country and is also referred to as 'the secret capital city of Poland'. The historic centre of Kraków has been on UNESCO's World Heritage List since 1978. Wander through the city and enjoy a typical Kraków 'Pan Kumpir' (baked potato) or 'Pieroggen' (filled dumplings).
Visit various places of interest, such as the Wawel Castle, which is certainly worth the trouble. Another tourist attraction is the Wieliczka Salt Mine. This salt mine has 287 kilometres of mine shafts, a small section of which is open for visits.

Winner in Poland

Best campsite
Camping Leśny nr 51

Impressive

From Kraków, it is possible to visit the former concentration camp Auschwitz. You can go on your own or follow a guide. A visit to this camp is an impressive experience, and you will learn a great deal about a dark period in European history.

En route

Filling up

Petrol (Benzina bezolowiowa 95 and 98) and diesel (Diesel/ON) are widely available. LPG (LPG/Autogaz) is also widely available; when filling up, the Italian connection (dish) is used.
Fuelling stations are often open from 8:00 to 19:00. In large cities and along motorways, many fuelling stations are open 24 hours.
It is prohibited to take along fuel in a reserve tank on ferries.

Charging

A limited number of charging stations can be found in Poland. Check which charging facilities are available before you leave on your trip. Plan your visit well!

Traffic regulations

Low beam lights (or daytime running lamps) are mandatory during the day. At equivalent crossings, traffic from the right has priority. Traffic on the roundabout has priority if so indicated by traffic signs. Drivers may only call handsfree. Children up to 12 years and shorter than 1.50 metres must be in a child's seat. Winter tyres are not mandatory but highly recommended in the winter (snow chains may possibly be made mandatory).

Special regulations

Loads that stick out more than 50 centimetres and bicycle carriers with bicycles must have a reflective white sign with slanted red stripes on them.
If traffic jams form, keep to the right or left as far as

ACSI Awards

Winner: Camping Leśny nr 51

possible so that a free lane is created in the middle for emergency vehicles.
On 'Mehrzweckstreifen' (the hard shoulders) along the roads outside of built-up areas, take pedestrians, cyclists and other slow traffic into account. Pedestrians walking along the road in the dark or under poor visibility conditions must wear a reflector or safety vest.
Parking by a white line, broken or not, on the side of the road is prohibited. A green arrow at a red traffic light indicates that you may turn right as long as you give right of way to other traffic, such as pedestrians. It is prohibited to transport someone who is under the influence of alcohol on the passenger seat in the front of the car.

"Once camped in Poland. You just want to go back."
Mr F. Lyskawa, inspector 1301

Mandatory equipment

A warning triangle and fire extinguisher are mandatory in the car. It is recommended that safety vests be present for all passengers. It is also recommended to have a first-aid box and replacement light bulbs.

Caravan and motorhome

A motorhome or car-caravan combination may be a maximum of 4 metres high, 2.55 metres wide and 18.75 metres long (the caravan itself may be a maximum of 12 metres long).

Cycling

A bicycle helmet is not mandatory. Calling or texting while cycling is prohibited.
Children up to 7 years must be transported in a child's bicycle seat. Cycling side-by-side is prohibited (unless accompanying a child under 10 years old).

"The people in Poland are hospitable and friendly, and the countryside and culture are fantastic."
Mr J. Hoogeboom, inspector 856

Toll

Toll must be paid on sections of the A1, A2 and A4 motorways. Payment may be cash or credit card. For more information: etoll.gov.pl, a1.com.pl and autostrada-a4.com.pl.

Environmental zones

Kraków has an environmental zone that only permits the entrance of vehicles that run on hydrogen or electricity. The zone is announced by a sign with the text 'Strefa' above the image of a green car.

Breakdown and accident

Place your warning triangle on the motorway at least 100 metres (or else 30 to 50 metres) behind the car if it is not properly visible or forms an obstacle for other traffic. All passengers must wear a safety vest. If you have had a breakdown, call the alarm number of your breakdown assistance insurer. You can also call the Polish automobile association (PZM) at +48 22 532 84 44.
You are required to phone the police with every traffic accident, even a minor collision.

Camping

Poland has a very diverse range of campsites, from small, simple campsites to large, modern sites. Polish campsites have few well-defined pitches, but they do all have electric power. Free camping (outside of campsites) is prohibited. On private property, free camping is only allowed with permission from the landowner. The campsites along the Baltic Sea and in the Carpathian Mountains are very popular. A chemical toilet is recommended in these areas.

Practical

In comparison with other European countries, there are relatively few serious traffic accidents in Poland; please drive carefully and attentively.
It is not recommended that you travel after sunset on the small, at times poorly lit, secondary roads.
Protect yourself against ticks; they can pass on diseases. Avoid contact with mammals in connection with the risk of rabies.

Chlapowo, PL-84-120 / Pomorskie

704

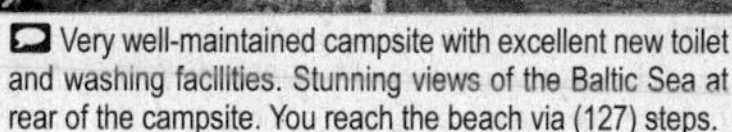

- Camping Alexa****
- Zeromskiego 44
- +48 6 06 39 74 35
- 25/3 - 31/10
- camping@alexa.gda.pl

4ha 210T(70-100m²) 10A CEE

1. ACD**I**KLMNO**R**S
2. AGJNSUXYZ
3. CDK**R**UY
4. (Q+R 1/6-31/8)(U 20/6-31/8)(Y 31/5-31/8)
5. **AB**DGIJKLMNOPQRUWXY
6. CDFGK(N 3km)PTUV

Very well-maintained campsite with excellent new toilet and washing facilities. Stunning views of the Baltic Sea at rear of the campsite. You reach the beach via (127) steps.

Road 215 from Wladyslawowo to Jastrzebia Góra. In Chlapowo centre campsite is on the right of the road.

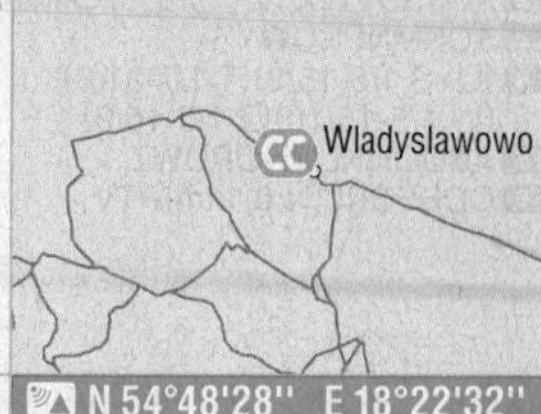

CC € 21 *25/3-16/6 25/8-31/10*

N 54°48'28'' E 18°22'32''

Chlapowo, PL-84-120 / Pomorskie

705

- Camping Pole Horyzont
- Zeromskiego 174/2
- +48 5 00 25 65 56
- 1/1 - 31/12
- polehoryzont@gmail.com

3ha 500T(70-80m²) 10A

1. ACD**I**KLMNOQRS
2. AGJNSUWXYZ
3. CPUY
5. **A**DGIJMNOPUWZ
6. EFGKM(N 0,4km)TV

Well-maintained campsite with new, clean toilet facilities. Most pitches are between tall hedges, but there are also pitches without shade. There are pitches with stunning views of the Baltic Sea at the rear of the campsite. A path to the beach runs past the campsite.

From Wladyslawowo in the direction of Jastrzebia Góra. In Chlapowo the campsite is on the right-hand side of the road.

CC € 19 *1/1-15/6 20/8-31/12*

N 54°48'20'' E 18°23'04''

Czaplinek, PL-78-550 / Zachodniopomorskie

706

- Camper Camping
- Komunalna 2a
- +48 5 37 36 38 43
- 1/1 - 31/12
- campercampingczaplinek@gmail.com

2ha 89T(25-220m²) 16-20A

1. ACDEIKLMNOQR
2. ABFMNOSXYZ
3. AKM**Q**SU**W**Z
4. **KN**(T 1/6-30/9)(Z)
5. **A**DGIJMNOPQUWX
6. DEFK(N 0,7km)ORV

Lovely campsite by the lake, where luxury and the countryside converge. Unwind in the sauna and jacuzzi. Enjoy the dishes in the restaurant. Feel the adrenaline during a boat tour on a speedboat. Enjoy the quiet of a walk on horseback. Discover relaxation and adventure today

Follow Czaplinek centre. Then follow the campsite signs.

Czaplinek
20
Zlocieniec

CC € 15 *1/1-30/6 25/8-31/12*

N 53°33'24'' E 16°13'22''

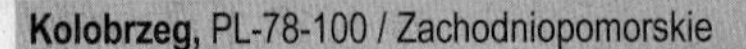

Kolobrzeg, PL-78-100 / Zachodniopomorskie

707

Camping Baltic****
ul. 4 Dywizji Wojska Polskiego 1
+48 6 06 41 19 54
29/3 - 30/10
baltic78@post.pl

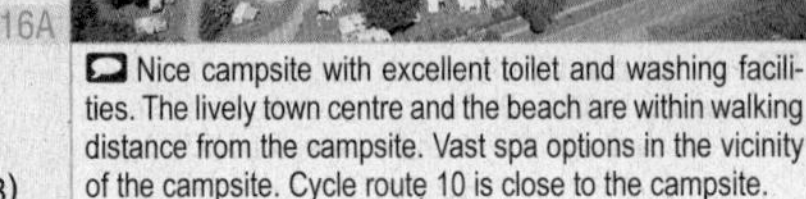

4ha 220T 16A

1 ACDIKLMNOQRS
2 AGJSUVWXYZ
3 ACKMNPSUWY
4 (Q+S 1/5-15/9)(T 1/7-31/8) (W 1/5-15/10)(Z 1/5-15/9)
5 ABDGIJKLMNOPUWZ
6 CDEFGKL(N 0,1km)PTV

Nice campsite with excellent toilet and washing facilities. The lively town centre and the beach are within walking distance from the campsite. Vast spa options in the vicinity of the campsite. Cycle route 10 is close to the campsite.

Campsite on east side of Kolobrzeg. Route 11. From Gdansk turn right at 1st roundabout. Campsite after 100 metres. From Sczecin 3rd exit on second roundabout. After 500 metres to the right, campsite is located after 100 metres.

Kolobrzeg
Grzybowo

CC € 21 *29/3-30/6 1/9-30/10*

N 54°10'53'' E 15°35'45''

Leba, PL-84-360 / Pomorskie

708

Camping Lesny Nr. 51****
Brzozowa 16A
+48 5 98 66 28 11
1/1 - 31/12
camping_51_lesny@wp.pl

ACSI AWARDS WINNER

1,2ha 150T 16A

1 ACDIKLMNOQRS
2 AGSTUXYZ
3 CKMSUVWY
4 (E 🔑)N(Q+S 10/6-30/8)
5 ABDFGIJKLMNOPUWZ
6 ACEFGK(N 0,5km)STV

Lovely campsite of the Stanuch family with attention to the planting as well as the extensive and very well-maintained toilet and washing facilities ensure a pleasant stay. Within walking distance of the beach and the centre of Leba. The campsite has a heated indoor swimming pool that stays open with good weather.

Turn right at 1st roundabout, then follow road at 2nd roundabout. First right after bridge, after 200 metres campsite is on left of road.

Sasino
Leba
Wicko

CC € 19 *1/1-30/6 1/9-31/12*

N 54°45'44'' E 17°33'58''

Leba, PL-84-360 / Pomorskie

709

Morski Nr. 21 Eurocamp***
ul. Turystyczna 3
+48 6 64 25 88 06
15/4 - 15/10
camping.morski@gmail.com

2,9ha 220T 16A

1 ACDIKLMNOQRS
2 ABGSWXYZ
3 ACKSUWY
4 (S 🔑)(T 1/6-20/9) (U 1/6-30/9)(X+Z 🔑)
5 ABDEGIJKLMNOPRUWXYZ
6 CDEFGKM(N 0,3km)OSTV

Friendly campsite with abundant plant life, close to the marina and the Baltic Sea. At walking distance from the entrance gate to the Słowiński National Park.

From Lebork-Wicko to Leba. At roundabout take 3rd exit to T-junction, turn left there. Then follow the road and follow camping signs Morski Nr. 21.

Leba
Wicko

CC € 21 *15/4-20/6 20/8-15/10*

N 54°45'43'' E 17°32'18''

Sciegny, PL-58-534 / Dolnoslaskie

710

Camp 66****
Widokowa 9
+48 7 92 56 65 69
1/1 - 31/12
biuro@camp66.pl

3ha 70T(60-200m²) 16A

1 ACDIKLMNOQRS
2 NSVWX
3 CIKLN
4 (**A** ⊶)(Q 1/1-31/12)
(T+U+V+X+Z ⊶)
5 **AB**CDEGHIJKLMNOPQRUWXYZ
6 EFGK(N 0,5km)PTV

Modern, environmentally friendly campsite close to the popular winter sports resort Karpacz with attractive restaurant and covered barbecue area. Suitable for winter sports activities, hiking and biking in the Giant Mountains.

Follow road 365 direction Karpacz. At roundabout (ignore SatNav) straight ahead. Follow signs. After 1 km turn left. Follow road with bridge ± 500 metres.

Jelenia Góra
Myslakowice
Spindleruv Mlýn
252

CC € 19 *1/1-31/3 5/5-20/6 15/9-23/12*

N 50°47'35'' E 15°46'12''

Sorkwity, PL-11-731 / Warminsko-Mazurskie

711

Camping & Glamping Szelagówka
ul. Szelagówka 4
+48 7 80 07 10 00
15/4 - 15/10
kontakt@szelagowka.pl

3ha 64T(80-120m²) 1-16A

1 ABCDIKLMNOQRS
2 BFMNSUVWX
3 ABHKM**Q**W
4 (**A**+B ⊶)**N**(Q+R+W+X+Z ⊶)
5 **AB**DEGJPQRWXZ
6 ABCDFGKL(N 3km)OPT

For a stay close to nature in comfortable surroundings. Here in Mazuria you will find unspoilt nature, meadows, lakes with crystal-clear water and hundreds of kilometres of walking, canoeing and cycling routes. Electricity and water on all pitches. Free wifi access throughout the campsite. Restaurant with local, organic products.

Road 16 Olsztyn-Mragowa. At the Sorkwity junction, follow the road to Zyndaki (along Lake Gieladzkie). You will reach the village after 5 km.

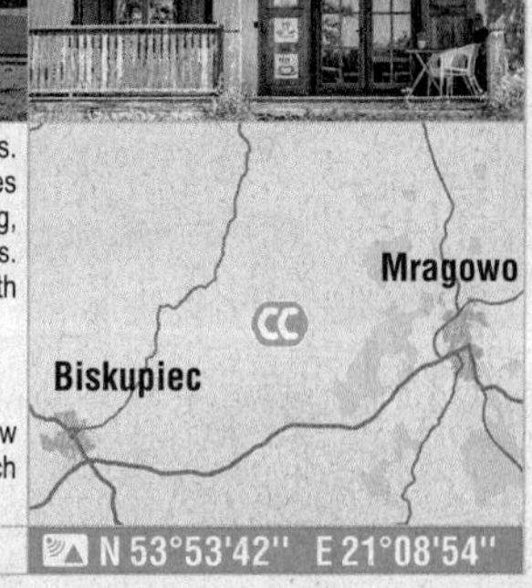

CC € 23 *15/4-7/7*

N 53°53'42'' E 21°08'54''

Czech Republic

Czech Republic: cities, history, culture and nature

In Czech Republic, as a camper, you can go anywhere. Explore culture and history in Prague and Český Krumlov or dive into the countryside. The imposing Giant Mountains and the Bohemian Forest await you. Relaxing in the sun can be done at one of the many lakes.

Capital: Prague
Currency: the Czech crown
Time zone: UTC +1, UTC +2 (March to October)
Language: Czech
International dialling code: +420
Alcohol limit: 0.0‰
Emergency number: general: 112, police: 158, fire brigade: 150, ambulance: 155
Tap water: is safe, but many people drink bottled water

Beautiful cities

Those who love city trips are in for a treat with the capital city Prague. The city was barely touched by acts of war and was able to keep its quaint streets and old buildings. The historic Charles Bridge, the huge, 9,000-m^2 Old Town Square and the Jewish Quarter Josefov should be at the top of your to-do list.
And there is much more to do in Czech Republic. The medieval Český Krumlov, located in southern Bohemia, combines the countryside and culture beautifully. Explore the city by canoe on the Vltava river or explore it by foot on the paths.
Visit the Český Krumlov castle with its beautiful gardens, wander about the centre, and explore the amazing Baroque Theatre from 1682.

Rocks and glaziers

The Giant Mountains lie on the border of the Czech Republic and Poland and live up to their name. There are great ski runs in the winter while it is a Valhalla for hikers in the summer. The rocks of Adršpach are an unusual natural phenomenon. You will be astonished by the sandstone rock formations in this city.
There are many more beautiful nature parks distributed throughout Czech Republic. Close to the German border lies the Šumava National Park, with its many woods and lakes. Plešne and Cerne are two untouched glacier lakes that simply must be seen. Would you rather relax or play and participate in sports in the water? Then the popular Lipno Reservoir is the place to go.

Spas

The Czech Republic is famous for its spas. The western Bohemian spa triangle is home to the spas Karlovy Vary, Františkovy Lázně and Mariánské Lázně. Not only can you relax in the thermal springs here, but you can also gaze at the impressive architecture of the spa buildings and the elegant parks.

En route

Filling up

Petrol (Natural 95/98/100) and diesel (Nafta) are widely available. LPG is also widely available. When filling up with LPG, the Italian connection (dish) is

Winner in Czechia

Best campsite
Camping Rožnov

Winner: Camping Rožnov

used. Fuelling stations are often open from Monday through Friday from 6:00 to 20:00 and on Saturday from 8:00 to 20:00. Along the main roads and in large cities, petrol stations are usually open 24 hours seven days a week. The Czech Republic also has a restricted number of LPG terminals available.

Charging

Most charging stations can be found in and around the large cities. Plan your visit wisely.

> *"The Czech Republic: a country of peace and quiet, nature, culture, many castles and an active camping holiday."*
> Mr F. van de Mosselaer, inspector 1171

Traffic regulations

Low beam lights (or daytime running lamps) are mandatory during the day. At equivalent crossings, traffic from the right has right of way. Traffic on the roundabout has right of way if so indicated by traffic signs; otherwise traffic from the right has right of way.
Caution! Trams always have right of way. Drivers may only call handsfree. Children shorter than 1.35 metres and lighter than 36 kg must be in a child's seat.
You may use the function of your navigation software that warns of speed cameras or average speed checks. From around 1 November through 31 March, winter tyres are mandatory under winter circumstances (snow chains may be made mandatory).

Special regulations

If traffic jams form, keep to the right or left as far as possible so that a lane that is at least 3 metres wide is created in the middle for emergency vehicles. Parking in a narrow street is prohibited unless there is still at least 6 metres left for other traffic. Parking by a yellow solid line is prohibited.

Mandatory equipment

A warning triangle, a safety vest, first-aid box and spare tyre (or tyre repair kit) are mandatory in the car. It is recommended that there be safety vests present for all passengers. Having replacement light bulbs available is also recommended.

Caravan and motorhome

A motorhome or car-caravan combination may be a maximum of 4 metres high, 2.55 metres wide and 18.75 metres long (the caravan itself may be a maximum of 12 metres long).
With a motorhome or car-caravan combination that is more than 3.5 tonnes or longer than 7 metres, you may only drive in the two right-most lanes on roads with three or more lanes going in the same direction.

Cycling

A bicycle helmet is mandatory for children under 18. Calling or texting while cycling is prohibited. Cyclists may not smoke either. Children under 7 years of age must be transported in a child's seat with footrests by someone at least 16 years old. Children who are under 10 years of age and cycling must be accompanied by someone at least 16 years old. Cycling side-by-side is prohibited.

Toll

Most Czechian motorways require a vignette. These vignettes can be purchased for ten days, for a month and for one year. Vignettes can be purchased at the border, at post offices and major petrol stations. A caravan or trailer does not require a separate vignette.
For more information: motorway.cz.
Vehicles (including motorhomes) over 3.5 tonnes pay toll per kilometre driven, using an electronic toll box. For more information: mytocz.eu/en.
Motorways without toll can be recognised by an additional sign with a vignette crossed out or with the text 'Bez poplatku' (no charge).

Breakdown and accident

Place your warning triangle on the motorway at least 100 metres (or else 50 metres) behind the car if it forms an obstacle for the other traffic. The driver must wear a safety vest. If you have had a breakdown, call the alarm number of your breakdown assistance insurer. You can also call a Czech emergency breakdown service: +420 261 104 345 or 1230 (UAMK) or +420 222 551 144 or 1214 (ACCR).
If there is an accident resulting in physical injury or material damage amounting to more than € 4,000, you are required to call the police.
If there is visible damage to the car, ask for a police report; this will be needed at the border on your way home.

Camping

In the Czech Republic, camping evokes a feeling of nostalgia because the Czechs often still camp in tents. But the amenities at campsites are becoming more extensive. More and more campsites have clearly defined pitches. Electric power is available

almost everywhere. An increasing number of campsites offer wifi for their guests.
Free camping (outside of campsites) is prohibited. Checking this can be strict, especially in the national parks.
The number of service stations for motorhomes is increasing. The number of special motorhome pitches outside of campsites is growing.

"The Czech Republic is inexpensive camping, cycling and hiking in varied, hilly landscapes, and visiting great cities and castles."
Mr N. van Gemeren, inspector 1196

Practical

In historic inner cities, you must be especially cautious when driving among the trams. Please take into account that cobblestones can be very slippery when wet. Tip! It is a handy idea to park outside of Prague's busy centre at 'transferia' (P+R, park and ride), from where it is possible to travel quickly and inexpensively to the city centre using public transportation.

Cerná v Pošumaví, CZ-38223 / Jihocesky kraj

712

Camping Olšina***
Černá v Pošumaví 200
+420 6 08 02 99 82
22/4 - 9/10
info@campingolsina.cz

5,5ha 300T 10A CEE

1 ABFIKLMNOQRS
2 ABEMNQSXYZ
3 AIKMS**WZ**
4 (R 1/7-30/8)(T)
(V 1/7-30/8)(X)
5 **AB**GIJKLMN**P**UW
6 EFG**K**(N 1,5km)OT

A friendly campsite full of character situated partly in the woods, terraced, and leading down to a quiet part of Lake Lipno with a magnificent sunset in the evening. Within walking distance of Cerná v Pošumaví and 20 km from the historic town of Ceský Krumlov. The campsite has wifi.

From Cerná v Pošumaví direction Ceský Krumlov. After about 1 km to the left. Campsite is signposted.

N 48°44'46'' E 14°07'00''

CC € 23 22/4-8/7 26/8-7/10 7=6

Decin 3, CZ-40502 / Ustecky kraj

713

Camping Kemp Decín
Polabí
+420 7 74 26 21 11
1/4 - 31/10
recepce@kempdecin.cz

12ha 55**T**(35-100m²) 16A CEE

1 ABCDIKLMNOQRS
2 DIJNSUX
3 AIJKLMNOSTU**WX**
4 (**A**+Q+T+U+Z)
5 **AB**CEFGHIJKLMNOPQUWZ
6 AFGKM(N 0,4km)OTU

Campsite close to the old town, next to the river Elbe. Very suitable for cyclists. Many facilities at 500 metres. Also suitable as a stopover site. 15 minutes from national park Bohemian Switzerland and 1 minute from aquapark. Canoeing, kayaking and rafting possible on the Elbe.

Follow route 13 from Jilové. In Decin cross River Elbe, direction E442. Campsite right next to the river and is signposted.

N 50°46'24'' E 14°12'38''

CC € 17 1/4-15/7

Horní Planá, CZ-38226 / Jihocesky kraj

714

Autocamp Jenišov***
Jenišov
+420 3 80 73 81 56
1/4 - 5/10
hajny.pa@seznam.cz

2,5ha 246T 6-10A CEE

1 ABCD**I**KLMNOQ**R**S
2 AEJLNPSXY
3 AIK**O**SWZ
4 (R+Y 1/5-5/10)(Z)
5 **AB**GIJLMN**P**UW
6 EFGK(N 1,5km)V

Lovely, quiet and welcoming family campsite right by Lake Lipno. Terraced, lightly sloping to the lake. You can hire bikes, SUP boards and go fishing. Also come and enjoy the great restaurant. A visit to the historic town of Ceský Krumlov is recommended.

Campsite is on the Lipnolake between Horní Planá and Cerná v Posumaví. Campsite is signposted.

N 48°45'04'' E 14°02'36''

CC € 23 1/4-30/6 25/8-5/10 7=6

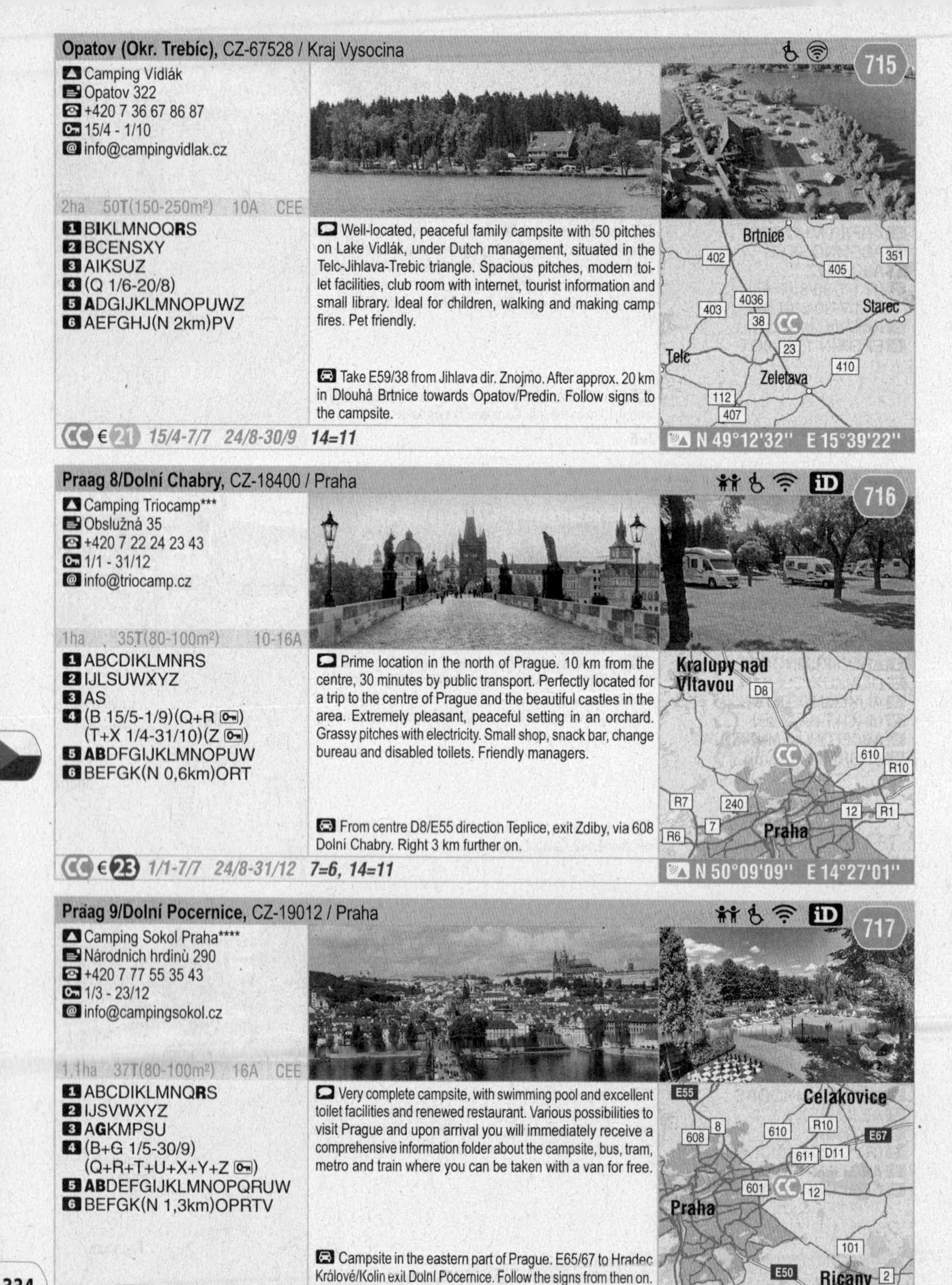

Opatov (Okr. Trebíc), CZ-67528 / Kraj Vysocina

715

Camping Vidlák
Opatov 322
+420 7 36 67 86 87
15/4 - 1/10
info@campingvidlak.cz

2ha 50T(150-250m²) 10A CEE

1 BIKLMNOQRS
2 BCENSXY
3 AIKSUZ
4 (Q 1/6-20/8)
5 ADGIJKLMNOPUWZ
6 AEFGHJ(N 2km)PV

Well-located, peaceful family campsite with 50 pitches on Lake Vidlák, under Dutch management, situated in the Telc-Jihlava-Trebic triangle. Spacious pitches, modern toilet facilities, club room with internet, tourist information and small library. Ideal for children, walking and making camp fires. Pet friendly.

Take E59/38 from Jihlava dir. Znojmo. After approx. 20 km in Dlouhá Brtnice towards Opatov/Predin. Follow signs to the campsite.

CC € 21 *15/4-7/7 24/8-30/9* **14=11**

N 49°12'32'' E 15°39'22''

Praag 8/Dolní Chabry, CZ-18400 / Praha

716

Camping Triocamp***
Obslužná 35
+420 7 22 24 23 43
1/1 - 31/12
info@triocamp.cz

1ha 35T(80-100m²) 10-16A

1 ABCDIKLMNRS
2 IJLSUWXYZ
3 AS
4 (B 15/5-1/9)(Q+R)
(T+X 1/4-31/10)(Z)
5 ABDFGIJKLMNOPUW
6 BEFGK(N 0,6km)ORT

Prime location in the north of Prague. 10 km from the centre, 30 minutes by public transport. Perfectly located for a trip to the centre of Prague and the beautiful castles in the area. Extremely pleasant, peaceful setting in an orchard. Grassy pitches with electricity. Small shop, snack bar, change bureau and disabled toilets. Friendly managers.

From centre D8/E55 direction Teplice, exit Zdiby, via 608 Dolní Chabry. Right 3 km further on.

CC € 23 *1/1-7/7 24/8-31/12* **7=6, 14=11**

N 50°09'09'' E 14°27'01''

Praag 9/Dolní Pocernice, CZ-19012 / Praha

717

Camping Sokol Praha****
Národnich hrdinù 290
+420 7 77 55 35 43
1/3 - 23/12
info@campingsokol.cz

1,1ha 37T(80-100m²) 16A CEE

1 ABCDIKLMNQRS
2 IJSVWXYZ
3 AGKMPSU
4 (B+G 1/5-30/9)
(Q+R+T+U+X+Y+Z)
5 ABDEFGIJKLMNOPQRUW
6 BEFGK(N 1,3km)OPRTV

Very complete campsite, with swimming pool and excellent toilet facilities and renewed restaurant. Various possibilities to visit Prague and upon arrival you will immediately receive a comprehensive information folder about the campsite, bus, tram, metro and train where you can be taken with a van for free.

Campsite in the eastern part of Prague. E65/67 to Hradec Králové/Kolin exit Dolní Pocernice. Follow the signs from then on.

CC € 23 *1/3-7/7 24/8-23/12* **7=6, 14=11**

N 50°05'17'' E 14°35'00''

Roznov pod Radhostem, CZ-75661 / Zlinsky kraj

718

- Camping Roznov
- Radhoštská 940
- +420 7 31 50 40 73
- 1/1 - 31/12
- info@camproznov.cz

ACSI AWARDS WINNER

4ha 150T(50-100m²) 16A CEE

1 ABCDIKLMNOQRS
2 JSUVWXY
3 ACEFIKLMNOPRSTUW
4 (B 1/6-30/9)(Q+R 1/7-31/8)
(T)(X 1/6-30/9)
(Z 1/6-31/8)
5 ABGIJKLMNOPUW
6 EFGK(N 2km)PQRTUV

A campsite located on the edge of the city of Roznov with a lovely swimming pool. Ideal area for hiking; near the Valasské open-air museum. Great winter sports options in the winter. Ski resort at 12 km. Cross-country skiing possible from the campsite.

Located close to Roznov on the E442 dir Zilina. From Roznov the campsite is located on the left of the road.

CC € 21 *1/1-30/6 1/9-31/12*

N 49°28'00'' E 18°09'50''

Sluknov, CZ-40777 / Ustecky kraj

719

- Camping De Regenboog / Kemp Sluknov
- Rumburska 718
- +31 6 83 65 54 44
- 4/5 - 15/9
- info@campingregenboog.com

8ha 148T(100-150m²) 16A CEE

1 BCDIKLMNOQRS
2 BCEJLNOSUXY
3 CEHIKLPSUZ
4 (A 8/7-25/8)(T 1/6-1/9)
(U 12/7-24/8)(Z 1/6-1/9)
5 ABCEGIJMNOPQRUWZ
6 DEFGKL(N 0,5km)T

Attractive, quiet family campsite in exceptionally beautiful surroundings. Extensive panoramas from the campsite. Good sanitary block with ample facilities and centrally located.

From Decin 253 to Ceska Kamenice. There 263 to Rumburk. Then 266 to Sluknov. The campsite is on left side of road when entering Sluknov.

CC € 21 *4/5-6/7 24/8-15/9*

N 51°00'07'' E 14°28'01''

Týn nad Vltavou, CZ-37501 / Jihocesky kraj

720

- Camping Prima
- Kolodeje nad Luznici 6
- +420 7 25 02 50 75
- 27/3 - 31/10
- info@campingprima.cz

1,5ha 50T(90-130m²) 10A

1 BCDHKLMNQRS
2 CJNOSUWXZ
3 AIKSUWX
4 (Q+T+X+Z)
5 ABFGIJMNOPQUWZ
6 EFGKPTV

Campsite located on a small river where you can swim and canoe, with a jetty. Slightly sloping grounds. Castle within walking distance.

Route 105 from Ceské Budejovice to Milevsko. Past Tyn nad Vltavou signposted.

CC € 21 *27/3-7/7 24/8-31/10* ***7=6, 14=11***

N 49°15'15'' E 14°25'12''

Vrané nad Vltavou/Praag, CZ-25246 / Stredocesky kraj — 721

Camp Matyás
U Elektrárny 840
+420 7 77 01 60 73
19/4 - 29/9
campmatyas@centrum.cz

1ha 70T(100-150m²) 10A

1 ABIKLMNOQ**R**S
2 CIJNSXYZ
3 CIKM**O**PSU**W**X
4 (Q+R+T+X)
5 **AB**CGHIJKLMNOPUWZ
6 ACEFGK(N 0,5km)PTVW

A secure, peaceful family campsite with children and senior citizens at heart, in a lovely mountain valley. On the banks of the River Vltava. Direct city train to central Prague. Station 1 km from the campsite. Also a safe, level cycle route to Prague centre. Free wifi and hot water all day. Modern facilities and warm old-fashioned hospitality.

Cross Zbraslav bridge towards Vrane nad Vltavou and follow 'Kamping Matyás' signs.

CC € 23 *19/4-30/6 1/9-29/9*

N 49°55'58'' E 14°22'20''

Hungary

Capital: Budapest
Currency: the forint
Time zone: UTC +1, UTC +2 (March to October)
Language: Hungarian
International dialling code: +36
Alcohol limit: 0.00‰
Alarm number: general: 112, police: 107, fire brigade: 105, ambulance: 104
Tap water: is safe, but many people drink bottled water

Hungary; mountains, lakes and culture

When you think of Hungary, you most likely think of Budapest. The capital city of Hungary and Lake Balaton are the biggest tourist attractions of the country. Did you know that the city actually consists of three parts that have been combined? Buda, Pest and Óbuda. Today, this cultural city is one whole and consists of 23 districts. If you only have a short time to visit the city, be sure to visit the most well-known places of interest in district 1. These include the Matthias Church, Buda Castle and Fisherman's Bastion. If you want to go to Budapest's city centre, then you should be on the 'Pest' side. This is where you will find crowd pullers such as the Széchenyi Chain Bridge and St. Stephen's Basilica.

Taking a dip in 'Balaton'

Lake Balaton: this freshwater lake should not be overlooked if you go camping in Hungary. It continues to be a huge crowd puller. Not really that surprising, once you know that the lake is beautiful and an ideal spot to take a dip on a hot day. Because the lake is at least 80 kilometres long, there will always be a good spot to settle down. The 200-kilometre cycling path that goes around the lake is definitely worth the trouble. The thermal areas are very popular in the spring and autumn.

> *"Hungary: a country with many places of interest, great swimming pools and hospitable people."*
>
> Ms T. Seijts-de Vries, inspector 850

On the steppes and through the mountains

The Hungarian countryside is special. There are mountains, low areas, the Pusztas (the steppe areas) and karst areas. Karst is limestone that has been eroded by rainwater. Hungary has various nature reserves that are open to visitors. There is the Hortobágy National Park, for example, characterised by its large steppe area. Or the Aggtelek National Park up in the north. It has dripstone caves that consist of karst. The caves are so unique they are listed on UNESCO's World Heritage List.

En route

Filling up

Petrol with octane number 95 (Szuper/Olomentes 95) is widely available; petrol with octane number 98 (Szuper Plusz 98) is more difficult to find. Make sure that you do not fill up with E85 instead by accident because that fuel will damage an ordinary engine. Diesel is widely available and LPG reasonably so. When filling up with LPG, the Italian connection (dish) is used. As a rule, fuelling stations are open from 6:00 to 20:00, however, fuelling stations in large cities and along motorways are often open 24 hours. Some fuelling stations have full service, where tipping is customary. It is prohibited to take along fuel in a reserve tank.

Charging

The majority of the charging stations are to be found in the west of Hungary and in the capital city Budapest. Plan your visit wisely.

Traffic regulations

Low beam lights (or daytime running lamps) are mandatory during the day outside of the built-up area and on all motorways. At equivalent crossings, traffic from the right has right of way. Traffic on the roundabout has right of way. Trams always have right of way.
Drivers may only call handsfree. Children shorter than 1.50 metres must be in a child's seat. Children at least 1.35 metres tall may wear a seatbelt in the back seat. Winter tyres are not mandatory. Under winter conditions, snow chains in the car are mandatory. The maximum speed with snow chains is 50 km/hour.

Special regulations

A load or bicycle carrier that sticks out more than 40 centimetres must be marked with a reflective red-and-white striped sign.
If traffic jams form, keep to the right or left as far as possible so that a free lane is created in the middle for emergency vehicles.
Parking by a yellow line is prohibited.
When crossing a street, pedestrians may not use a mobile phone or wear headphones. Pedestrians must wear a safety vest outside of the built-up area in the dark and when visibility is poor.

Mandatory equipment

A warning triangle and a first-aid box are mandatory in the car. Taking a fire extinguisher along is recommended and is mandatory for motorhomes with a maximum permissible weight of more than 3.5 tonnes. Also recommended: a spare tyre, replacement light bulbs and a towing cable. It is recommended that there be safety vests present for all passengers.

Caravan and motorhome

A motorhome or car-caravan combination may be a maximum of 4 metres high, 2.55 metres wide and 18.75 metres long (the caravan itself may be a maximum of 12 metres long).
Caravans that are towed by a passenger car may not be higher than 3 metres.

Cycling

A bicycle helmet is not mandatory. The maximum speed for cyclists outside of the built-up area is 40 km/hour. With a helmet on, the maximum is 50 km/hour. Calling or texting while cycling is prohibited. Cyclists must wear a safety vest outside of the built-up area in the dark and when visibility is poor. Only children older than 14 years of age may cycle on a carriageway.

Toll

All motorways in Hungary are toll roads. This means you need an 'e-vignette' (e-matrica). Purchase a vignette before you drive on the motorway. This can be done at border crossings, petrol stations and at the road maintenance authority's service stations. In any case, your vehicle must be registered within 60 minutes of driving on the motorway or you will receive a fine. Cameras check registration numbers. For good measure, save the receipt for a minimum of one year, in case you are wrongfully fined. An e-vignette can be purchased prior to your trip to Hungary through, for example autopalyamatrica.hu or virpay.hu.
For more information: toll-charge.hu and maut-tarife.hu (rates).

"Culture and nature are still firmly connected in Hungary."
Mr H. Willighagen, inspector 832

Environmental zones

Motorised traffic may have restricted access to the centre of Budapest and other major Hungarian cities because of the air quality.

Breakdown and accident

Place your warning triangle on the motorway at least 150 to 200 metres (or else 100 metres) behind the car. All passengers must wear a safety vest. If you have had a breakdown, call the alarm number of your breakdown assistance insurer. You can also call the Hungarian automobile association (MAK) at 188 or +36 1 345 1755.
Towing on the motorway is permitted up to the first exit. If there is visible damage to the car, ask for a

police report; this will be needed at the border on your way home.

Camping

Most campsites are located around Lake Balaton. An advantage is that Hungarian campsites are the cheapest in Europe. The toilet facilities are of a reasonable standard. Free camping (outside of campsites) is prohibited. Camping gas cylinders are often difficult to find.

Practical matters

Protect yourself against ticks; they can pass on diseases. Avoid contact with mammals in connection with the risk of rabies.

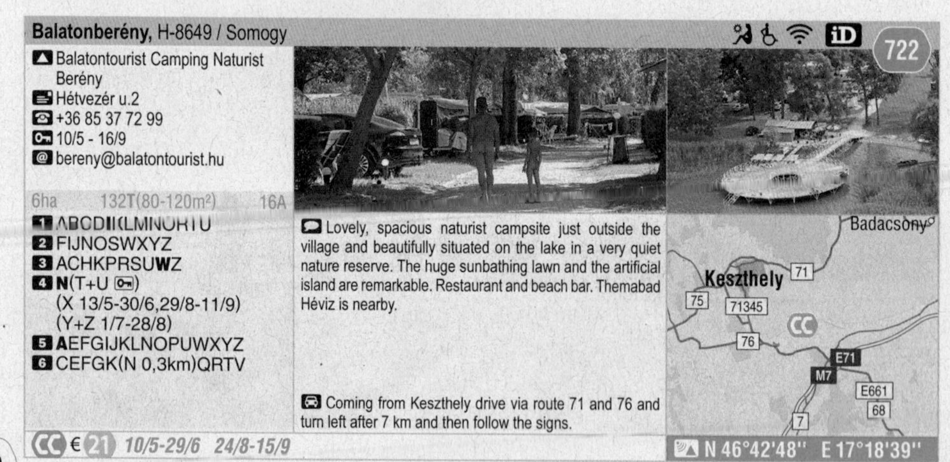

Balatonberény, H-8649 / Somogy

722

Balatontourist Camping Naturist Berény
Hétvezér u.2
+36 85 37 72 99
10/5 - 16/9
bereny@balatontourist.hu

6ha 132**T**(80-120m²) 16A

1 ABCDIJKLMNORTU
2 FIJNOSWXYZ
3 ACHKPRSU**W**Z
4 **N**(T+U)
(X 13/5-30/6,29/8-11/9)
(Y+Z 1/7-28/8)
5 **A**EFGIJKLNOPUWXYZ
6 CEFGK(N 0,3km)QRTV

Lovely, spacious naturist campsite just outside the village and beautifully situated on the lake in a very quiet nature reserve. The huge sunbathing lawn and the artificial island are remarkable. Restaurant and beach bar. Themabad Héviz is nearby.

Coming from Keszthely drive via route 71 and 76 and turn left after 7 km and then follow the signs.

CC € 21 *10/5-29/6 24/8-15/9*

N 46°42'48" E 17°18'39"

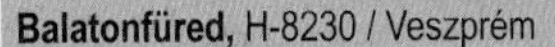

Balatonfüred, H-8230 / Veszprém

723

Balatontourist Camping & Bungalows Füred***
Széchenyi u.24
+36 87 58 02 41
26/4 - 29/9
fured@balatontourist.hu

19ha 628T(60-120m²) 6-16A CEE

1 ACD**I**KLMNOQRTU
2 AEJNOSWXYZ
3 AC**G**KLMN**O**P**R**SUZ
4 (B+G 11/6-28/8)JM**N**
(Q)(S 14/5-18/9)
(T+U+V+X+Y+Z)
5 **AB**EFGHIJKLMNOPSUW
6 ACFGHJ**K**(N 0,1km)
PQRTVX

Large campsite on the edge of Balatonfüred town centre with shaded pitches. Beautiful heated pool and a lovely beach on the lake. For a fee you can make use of the cable skiing. Recreation for the whole family. The Balaton cycle path runs right by the campsite.

Route 71 (north side of Lake Balaton), exit between km-marker 40 and 41. Directly alongside the lake. Signposted.

Balatonalmádi · 7301 · 73 · Balatonfüred · Siófok · 7117 · 71 · E71 · 7 · M7

CC € 23 *26/4-29/6 24/8-28/9*

N 46°56'45'' E 17°52'36''

Gyenesdiás, H-8315 / Zala

724

Wellness Park Camping
Napfény utca 6
+36 83 31 64 83
10/3 - 31/10
info@wellness-park.hu

4ha 80T(80m²) 16A

1 ABCD**I**KLMNOQRS
2 JSWXYZ
3 ACHKLMOPSU
4 (B 15/5-15/9)KN
(Q+T+U 1/7-31/8)
(Z 15/5-31/8)
5 **AB**GHIJMNOPQUW
6 CEFGKM(N 1km)PRV

A small, peaceful campsite situated between Lake Balaton and a hilly region. 1 km from the beach. The campsite has modern toilet facilities and various wellness possibilities.

Turn off towards the lake between 100 and 99 marker signs on road 71.

CC € 19 *10/3-27/6 1/9-31/10*

N 46°45'51'' E 17°18'09''

Révfülöp, H-8253 / Veszprém

725

Balatontourist Camping Napfény***
Halász Utca 5
+36 87 56 30 31
26/4 - 29/9
napfeny@balatontourist.hu

7,2ha 350T(60-150m²) 6-16A

1 ABCD**I**JKLMNOQRTU
2 FJNOSWXYZ
3 ACKMP**R**SU**W**Z
4 (G 1/6-24/9)(Q+R)
(T 1/6-31/8)(U+V+X+Y)
5 **AB**EFGIJKLMNOPUW
6 ACEFGHJ**K**M(N 0,6km)
PQRTV

Beautiful campsite with everything you need. Long beach. Motorboats are prohibited on Lake Balaton.

On route 71 (northside of Lake Balaton). Between km-marker 65 and 66, directly alongside the lake. Campsite is signposted.

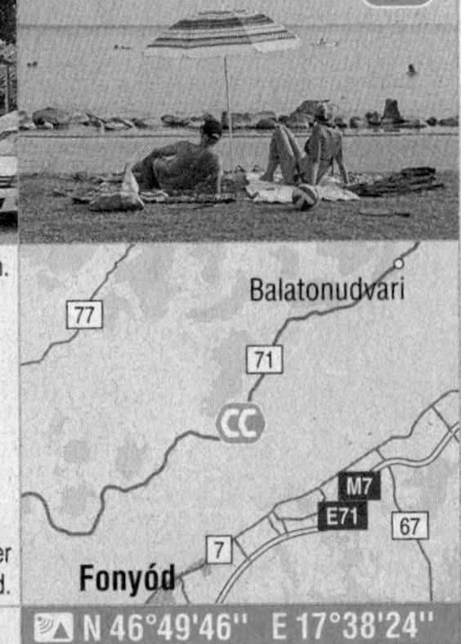

CC € 21 *26/4-29/6 24/8-28/9*

N 46°49'46'' E 17°38'24''

Slovenia

Slovenia: fabulous lakes and rugged mountains

More and more campers have discovered the magic of the versatility of Slovenia. With its fabulous lakes, rugged mountains, unspoilt woods, Mediterranean coastal strip and lovely cities, this country is certainly not inferior to its neighbours Italy, Austria and Croatia. Another advantage: your wallet will be happy with a holiday in Slovenia as well.

Capital city: Ljubljana
Currency: the euro
Time zone: UTC +1, UTC +2 (March to October)
Language: Slovenian
International dialling code: 386
Alcohol limit: 0.5‰, but 0.00‰ under 21 years of age
Emergency number: general police, fire brigade and ambulance: 112, police: 113
Tap water: the tap water is safe, but many people drink bottled water

Fairy tales do still exist

In the luscious northern part of Slovenia, fairy tales really do seem to exist. Hike, cycle or mountain bike through the Julian Alps and admire the imposing mountain tops in the distance. Explore the dense forest in Triglav National Park and see how the Sava River and the Soča River meander through the landscape to finally discharge into glassy lakes. Lake Bohinj is Slovenia's largest lake, but Lake Bled is its most famous lake. This is due to the beautiful location of a white church on an island in the middle of the lake.

White sandy beaches and healing spas

Further east and south, the landscape flattens. In the southwest, there is even a short coastal strip along the Adriatic Sea with white sandy beaches and Mediterranean seaside towns like Piran and Izola.

The famous caves of Postojna and Škocjan lie further inland. The charming capital city Ljubljana is located in the centre of the country.
Towards the east, the landscape is characterised by hills, vineyards and spas. These spas, called 'terme' in Slovenian, often have large family campsites nearby. They include swimming pools, water parks and wellness resorts. This means there is something for every family member. But do go out to cities in the area. Ptuj in particular, Slovenia's oldest city, is a cultural wonder.

Winners in Slovenia

Best location for a campsite — Kamp Danica Bohinij

Most sports-loving campsite — Camping Adria

Different climates in one country

Slovenia has different climate zones, which is rather exceptional for such a small country. The southwest borders on the Adriatic Sea and has a Mediterranean climate with dry, sunny summers and mild winters. Further inland, there is a temperate maritime climate, comparable to that of the Netherlands. In the mountainous north and northeast, you will find a continental climate, with larger differences in temperature and regular precipitation. In the winter, this usually falls in the form of snow, which means winter sports are excellent in areas such as Kranjska Gora and Mariborsko Pohorje.

En route

Filling up

Benzine (Eurosuper 95 and 98) and diesel are widely available. LPG (Avtoplin) is reasonably available. When filling up with LPG, the Italian connection (dish) is used.
Fuelling stations are often in any case open from Monday through Saturday from 7:00 to 20:00. At border crossings, along motorways and in major cities, petrol stations are usually open seven days a week and 24 hours a day.

Charging

There is a restricted number of possibilities for charging in Slovenia. Most charging stations are located around Ljubljana.

Mountain roads

Before you start your journey, check whether mountain passes are closed. For more information: alpenpaesse.de (in German).

Traffic regulations

Low beam lights (or daytime running lamps) are mandatory during the day. At equivalent crossings, traffic from the right has right of way. Traffic on the roundabout has right of way if so indicated by traffic signs. Drivers may only call handsfree. The use of earbuds or headphones are also prohibited for drivers. Children shorter than 1.50 metres must be in a child's seat. From 15 November through 15 March, winter tyres (or snow chains in the car) are mandatory.

Special regulations

If traffic jams form, keep to the right or left as far as possible so that a free lane is created in the middle for emergency vehicles. You may only enter a crossing if you are certain that you can cross and will not remain stationary on the crossing due to traffic.
Passing a stopped school bus is prohibited if children are getting in or out.
When driving in reverse, you must use your hazard lights. During the winter period, the minimum profile depth for summer and winter tyres is 3 millimetres.

Mandatory equipment

A warning triangle is mandatory in the car. Caution! Two warning triangles are mandatory for a car with a caravan or trailer. A first-aid box and spare bulbs are only mandatory in cars with a Slovenian registration number. It is recommended that safety vests be present for all passengers.

"In Slovenia, it is possible to really relax in vast wooded natural landscapes."
Mr K. Romeijnders, inspector 1355

Caravan and motorhome

A motorhome or car-caravan combination may be a maximum of 4 metres high, 2.55 metres wide and 18 metres long (the caravan itself may be a maximum of 12 metres long).

Cycling

A bicycle helmet is mandatory for children under 15 (even if they are on the back). Calling or texting

while cycling is prohibited. Nor may a cyclist wear headphones or earbuds. Children under 8 years must be transported in a child's bicycle seat. Cycling side-by-side is only allowed on bicycle paths that are wide enough.

Toll

On motorways and highways in Slovenia, a toll vignette is mandatory for vehicles under 3.5 tonnes. A caravan or trailer does not require a separate vignette. The vignette can be ordered online via evinjeta.dars.si/selfcare or at Slovenian petrol stations, supermarkets and kiosks and at major petrol stations in neighbouring countries in the border region. If you order the vignette online before you travel, it will save on waiting time at the Slovenian border.

There are other rules for vehicles (including motorhomes) over 3.5 tonnes. For more information: darsgo.si.

Use of the Karawanks Tunnel, between Austria and Slovenia, is not included in the toll vignette. Extra toll must be paid for this. For more information: asfinag.at/en/toll/section-toll/.

Breakdown and accident

Place a warning triangle at a sufficient distance behind the car if the hazard lights do not work or if the car is not clearly visible for the other traffic (place two triangles next to each other is you are pulling a trailer). All passengers must wear a safety vest. If you have had a breakdown, call the alarm number of your breakdown assistance insurer. Or call the emergency control centre of the Slovenian automobile association (AMZS) at +386 1 530 53 53 (or 1987). Towing on the motorway is permitted up

to the first exit. If there is visible damage to the car, ask for a police report (potrdilo); this will be needed at the border on your way home.

Camping

Some Slovenian campsites, located at springs with thermal water, are specialised in wellness. These campsites are at a high level. Beautifully located campsites in the Julian Alps, bordering on Austria and Italy, are somewhat simpler and more focussed on nature and families. They focus mainly on sports-loving camping guests such as hikers, mountain bikers and mountain climbers. Many campsites have playgrounds and entertainment for the little ones. Free camping (outside of campsites) is generally prohibited, only being permitted with prior permission from the local public authorities or police.

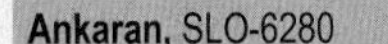

Ankaran, SLO-6280

726

Camping Adria****
Jadranska cesta 25
+386 56 63 73 50
10/4 - 1/11
camp@adria-ankaran.si

ACSI AWARDS WINNER

7ha 293T(30-100m²) 10A CEE

1 ABCD**I**KLMNOQRUV
2 HIJNOPSWYZ
3 ACIK**O**P**R**SU**VW**Y
4 (B 23/6-9/9)
(**F** 10/4-13/6,1/9-1/11)
(**G** 1/6-30/9)**KLMNP**
(Q 10/4-1/11)(R 1/5-30/9)
(T 15/4-30/9)(V 1/5-30/9)
(X 20/6-15/9)(Y+Z)
5 **AB**EFGIJKLMNOP**S**UW
6 ACEFGHIKL(N 0km)RTUV

Campsite by the sea in Mediterranean surroundings. The wellness centre is open to camping guests in the winter. Ideal for nature lovers, starting point for visits to tourist attractions in Slovenia. Bars, restaurants and free Wi-Fi point. Registration: 1.50 euros p.p. Eco tax 2.5 euros per pitch per night, hot water and swimming pool are free.

On the motorway coming from Italy or Ljubljana take the Ankaran exit. Then to Ankaran. Campsite 5 km on the left.

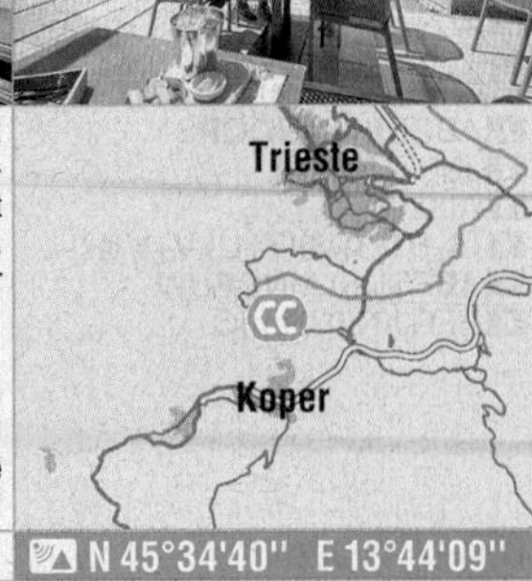

CC € 27 *10/4-14/6 6/9-1/11*

N 45°34'40'' E 13°44'09''

Bled, SLO-4260

727

Camping Bled*****
Kidriceva 10c
+386 45 75 20 00
1/4 - 15/10
info@camping-bled.com

12ha 244T(80-130m²) 16A CEE

1 ABCD**I**KLMNOQRS
2 EIJMNOPSTWXYZ
3 CD**G**IJKLMNP**Q**S**W**Z
4 **N**(Q+S+T+U+V+Y+Z)
5 **AB**DEFGIJKLMNOPQ**S**UWXY
6 ABCFGKM(N 3km)PRTVX

This well run campsite is 3 km from the centre of Bled and only separated from the lake at Bled by a road that is not very busy. The site has excellent toilet facilities, also for children. Wonderful opportunities for walking in the area.

From A2/E61 take exit 3, then drive via Bled along the lake towards Bohinjska Bistrica. Turn right after 1.5 km. You will reach the campsite after about 1 km. Route is clearly signposted.

B91
Jesenice
Radovljica

CC € 27 *1/4-1/6 1/9-15/10*

N 46°21'41'' E 14°04'51''

Bohinjska Bistrica, SLO-4264

728

Kamp Danica Bohinj****
Triglavska cesta 60
+386 45 72 17 02
1/1 - 31/12
info@camp-danica.si

ACSI AWARDS WINNER

4,5ha 250T(50-90m²) 12-16A

1 ABCD**I**KLMNOQRUV
2 DJNOPQSWXYZ
3 ADHIKLMN**O**PS**VW**X
4 (**A** 1/5-15/10)(Q 1/5-30/9)
(T)(V 1/6-1/9)(X+Y+Z)
5 **AB**EFGIJKLMNOP**S**UWZ
6 CEFGHKL(N 0,1km)RT

Quiet in low season, between small town and river. Good amenities. Starting point for mountain walks, with cable car to the Alm heights and marked out walks to various mountain cabins in Triglav National Park. Indoor leisure pool/wellness 200 metres away. CampingCard ACSI only in zone B. The Indian summer is beautiful in the autumn-coloured mountains.

Beyond Bled take dir. Bohinj. 100m past village Bohinjska Bistrica, site is to right of road.

Goreljek
Bohinj
Nemski Rovt

CC € 27 *1/4-15/6 14/9-21/12*

N 46°16'27'' E 13°56'52''

Bovec, SLO-5230

729

Camping Polovnik**
Ledina 8
+386 53 89 60 07
30/3 - 15/10
kamp.polovnik@siol.net

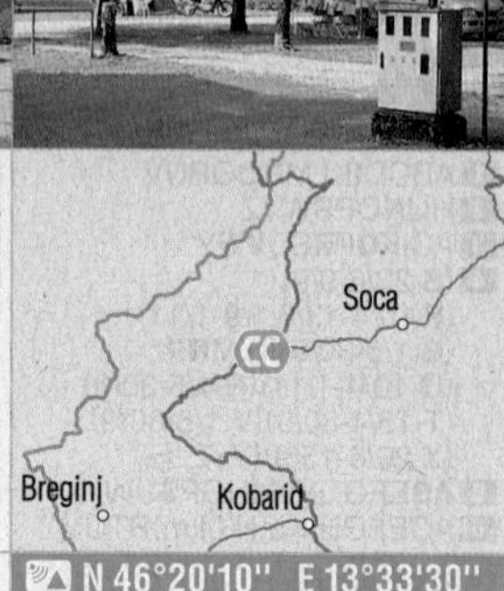

1,2ha 100T(80m²) 16A CEE

1 ABCDIKLMNOQRS
2 JNSTUWXYZ
3 AIKLW
4 (A 1/7-31/8)(T+U+V+Y)
5 ABFGIJKLMNOPUW
6 EFGJ(N 0,2km)Q

A campsite located on the edge of the Triglav National Park, walking distance to Bovec. Good starting point for excursions into this grandiose natural area. Level campsite, well shaded and with good toilet facilities. Rafting and kayaking. Good restaurant at campsite and in Bovec.

Northern side of Bovec, follow camping signs. Passo de Predil (between Tarvisio and Bovec) is not recommended for large caravans, please travel via Udine, Cividale (Italy), Kobarid, Bovec.

CC € 25 *30/3-30/6 1/9-15/10*

N 46°20'10'' E 13°33'30''

Gozd Martuljek, SLO-4282

730

Camping Spik***
Jezerci 15
+386 51 63 44 66
1/1 - 31/12
info@camp-spik.si

3ha 250T(80-100m²) 10A CEE

1 BCDIKLMNQRS
2 BJNSWXYZ
3 AGIKP
4 (F+H)N(Q)
(R 1/1-31/12)(Y)
(Z 1/7-25/8)
5 ABDEFGIJKLMNOPUW
6 EFGK(N 5km)PV

Quiet campsite with shaded and sunny pitches. Lovely view of the mountain range. Flat grounds. Good sanitary facilities. Lovely indoor swimming pool and wellness in Hotel Spik next door with discounts on the admission price for campsite guests. Restaurant in the hotel. Walking, cycling, mountain sports, skiing and cross-country skiing from easy to advanced.

Campsite located on E652/1 Podkoren-Jesenice east of Gozd Martuljek village. Arched bridge directly to the north.

CC € 27 *1/4-18/6 5/9-31/10*

N 46°29'05'' E 13°50'18''

Kobarid, SLO-5222

731

Eco-Camping & Chalets Koren****
Ladra 1B
+386 53 89 13 11
1/1 - 31/12
info@kamp-koren.si

2ha 100T(50-140m²) 16A

1 ABCDIKLMNOQRS
2 DJMNSUXYZ
3 ACEHIJKLMNSVW
4 (A)N(Q+R+T+X+Z)
5 ABCDFGHIJKLMNOPUVWYZ
6 ABEFHJL(N 0,5km)PQTUV

Kamp Koren is located by the fast flowing Soca river, 200 metres from the picturesque historic town of Kobarid with a WW1 museum and the Napoleon Bridge. There are plenty of tourist opportunities and marked out footpaths with waterfalls. Culture and sports opportunities. Bike hire.

Road Bovec-Tolmin. Take exit 'Ind. Cora' at Kobarid. Continue between the factory and the supermarket then over the bridge and turn left (40 metres). From Italy: Follow signs Dreznica in Kobarid.

CC € 27 *1/1-30/6 1/9-31/12*

N 46°15'02'' E 13°35'12''

Lendava, SLO-9220

732

Thermal Camping Lendava***
Tomsiceva 2a
+386 25 77 44 37
1/1 - 31/12
camping@thermal-lendava.com

1ha 92T(60-90m²) 16A CEE

1 ABCD**I**KLMNOQRUV
2 IJNSVWXYZ
3 AIKMNU
4 (C 1/5-15/9)(F+H)JK**NOP**
(Q)(T+U 20/6-31/8)(Y)
(Z 20/6-31/8)
5 **AB**DGIJKLMNOPUWZ
6 BEFGHK(N 0,5km)T

Easily accessible thermal campsite in a great location close to the three-country point of Slovenia, Hungary and Croatia. Lovely base for culinary events, cycling and walking trips and for visiting Vinarium. Naturist section with swimming pool from mid-September to mid-April.

A5 exit Lendava. Left at roundabout dir. Lendava, 2nd roundabout dir. Terme Lendava. Turn right before hotel, campsite 100m on the left.

CC € 27 *8/1-16/3 15/5-30/6 15/7-29/7 1/9-16/9 4/11-18/11*

N 46°33'07'' E 16°27'30''

Lesce, SLO-4248

733

River Camping Bled*****
Alpska cesta 111
+386 40 34 43 24
20/4 - 8/10
hello@rivercamping-bled.si

5,7ha 260T(80-120m²) 16A CEE

1 ABCD**I**KLMNOQRS
2 BDINPSUWXYZ
3 CD**G**IJKLMNSUV**WX**
4 (**A**)(C 1/6-15/9)
(Q+R+U+V+Y+Z)
5 **AB**DEFGIJKLMNOP**S**UWXY
6 ABEFGHK(N 1,5km)PQTUV

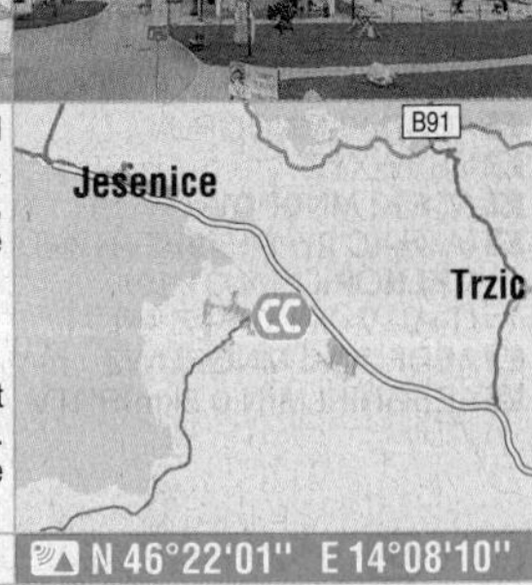

Family run modern campsite in a green oasis, surrounded by mountains and Sava River, only 2 km from Bled Lake. It offers spacious camping pitches, modern sanitary facilities, a heated outdoor swimming pool, pumptrack and adventure playground for children.

A2 Jesenice-Ljubljana exit 3 Lesce. At the roundabout continue straight on in the direction of Lesce/Bled. After approx. 1,6 km at the roundabout with the big golf ball turn to the clearly marked campsite.

CC € 27 *1/5-8/6 8/9-1/10*

N 46°22'01'' E 14°08'10''

Ljubljana, SLO-1000

734

Ljubljana Resort (hotel & camping)****
Dunajska cesta 270, Jezica
+386 70 25 38 45
1/4 - 15/10
resort@gpl.si

3ha 257T(60-90m²) 10-16A CEE

1 ABCD**I**KLMNO**R**UV
2 CIJSWXYZ
3 C**G**IKMPS**VW**
4 (**C+H** 17/6-31/8)**KP**
(Q 1/6-15/9)(T+U 1/6-1/9)
(Y 15/6-15/9)(Z)
5 **AB**EFGIJKLMNOPUW
6 CEFGHJ**K**(N 0,7km)RTUV

Located in a natural green area beside River Sava and near Ljubljana. Direct bus connection to the centre. From 15/6, swimming at a discounted rate in the resort's lovely swimming pool. Good starting point for walking and cycling in the surrounding area.

From the Karawankentunnel: A2 exit 13, Lj-Brod and follow signs. From Maribor: A1 near Ljubljana take H3 exit to Lj-Bezigrad and follow signs. Some signs still show the old name 'Jezica'.

CC € 25 *1/4-1/7 1/9-30/9* ***7=6, 14=11***

N 46°05'52'' E 14°31'08''

Maribor, SLO-2000

735

Camping Center Kekec***
Pohorska ulica 35c
+386 40 22 53 86
1/1 - 31/12
info@cck.si

2ha 100T(80-100m²) 16A CEE

1 ABFIKLMNOQRS
2 IJNSVWXY
3 CIM
5 **AB**DGIJMNOPUWXZ
6 ADEFGJ(N 0,3km)P

Small campsite on grassy field with landscaping, not far from ski resort Pohorje and sports centre. Hardened pitches for motorhomes. Views of ski slopes and hills. Perfect for visiting Maribor.

From the north on E57/A1, Maribor exit to H2, past centre of Maribor towards Ljubljana to traffic lights. Here, turn right towards Pohorje ski lift. From the south on E57/A1, Maribor exit to H2. After Bauhaus, turn left at 1st traffic light towards Pohorje ski lift.

CC € 21 *1/1-30/6 1/9-31/12*

N 46°32'10'' E 15°36'12''

Moravske Toplice, SLO-9226

736

Camping Terme 3000****
Kranjceva 12
+386 25 12 12 00
1/1 - 31/12
recepcija.camp2@terme3000.si

7ha 230T(80-100m²) 16A CEE

1 ABCD**I**KLMNOQRUV
2 IJSVWXYZ
3 AC**F**IKLMN**O**P**QV**
4 (A)(C 27/4-15/9)(F+H) IJ**KLNOP**(Q 1/4-31/10) (T+U+V+W+X+Y+Z)
5 **AB**DFGIJKLMNOPUWZ
6 AEFGHIKLM(N 0,5km)PRTV

A large campsite. Excellent toilet facilities. Leisure pool. Swimming pool not included in CampingCard ACSI rate: 7 Euros per person per day. Hiking, biking and all types of sports are possible in the area. Interesting trips out by car include the wine growing area between Ormoz and Ljutomer.

From Graz (Austria) A9/A1 dir. Maribor. Before Maribor A5 dir. Lendava till exit 7 Murska Sobota, Moravske Toplice. Campsite signposted.

CC € 27 *3/1-21/3 2/4-25/4 5/5-16/5 24/5-20/6 8/9-3/10 3/11-19/12*

N 46°41'05'' E 16°12'57''

Portoroz, SLO-6320

737

Kamp Lucija***
Seca 204
+386 56 90 60 00
29/3 - 3/11
camp.lucija@sava.si

6ha 550T(70-80m²)

1 BCDE**I**KLMNOQRS
2 HIJMNQUWXYZ
3 AIKLN
4 (Y+Z)
5 **AB**FGIJKLMNOPUWX
6 BCEGHIK(N 0,1km)R

The campsite is right by the sea in Piran and close to the nightlife in a lively area. The toilet block is fairly basic. You can swim in the sea a few steps away from your tent, caravan or motorhome.

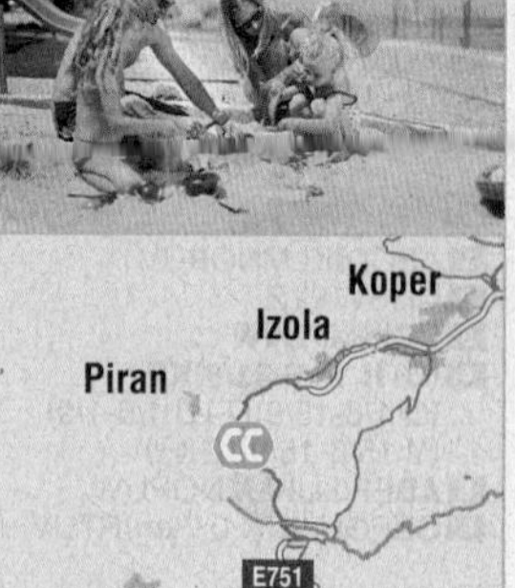

The campsite is ca 5 km south of Piran on through road 11.1

CC € 25 *1/5-1/6 1/9-3/11*

N 45°30'07'' E 13°36'02''

Ptuj, SLO-2251

738

Camping Terme Ptuj****
Pot v Toplice 9
+386 27 49 45 80
1/1 - 31/12
kamp@terme-ptuj.si

1,5ha 120T(80-100m²) 16A CEE

1 ABCDIKLMNOQRUV
2 ISWXYZ
3 CFIKLMNOPQRV
4 (A 1/1-31/12)(C 1/5-15/9)(F+H)IJ KLNOP(Q 1/7-31/8)(T+U) (V 1/7-31/8)(W+Y+Z)
5 ABDEFGIJKLMNOPUWXZ
6 ACDEFGHKLM(N 1,5km) PRTV

Level campsite divided by hedges. Close to a modern thermal centre with 12 swimming pools and many amenities. Swimming pool not included in CampingCard ACSI rate: 7 Euros per person per day. Near one of the most beautiful small Central European towns where culture and nature combine.

From route 9/E59 Zagreb-Krapina-Maribor take Hajdina/Terme Ptuj exit 4. To Ptuj/Ormoz. At the roundabout left dir. Ptuj, turn right over bridge at the south west side of the Drava. Signposted.

CC € 27 *3/1-21/3 2/4-25/4 5/5-20/6 8/9-17/10 3/11-19/12*

N 46°25'21'' E 15°51'16''

Recica ob Savinji, SLO-3332

739

Camping Menina****
Varpolje 105
+386 51 21 93 93
1/1 - 31/12
info@campingmenina.com

10ha 230T(100-200m²) 10A CEE

1 ABCDIKLMNOQRS
2 BDFPQSUWXYZ
3 ACHJKLNPQRSUWXZ
4 (A 1/6-31/8)N(T+U) (V+Y+Z 1/5-31/10)
5 ABDGIJKLMNOPQRUW
6 AFGKL(N 3km)PTV

The campsite is located in the middle of Slovenia on the River Savinja and by a small swimming lake. Excellent walking opportunities in the mountains. Perfect location for excursions into Slovenia, organised by owner. Also suitable for seniors. Campsite restaurant with local dishes.

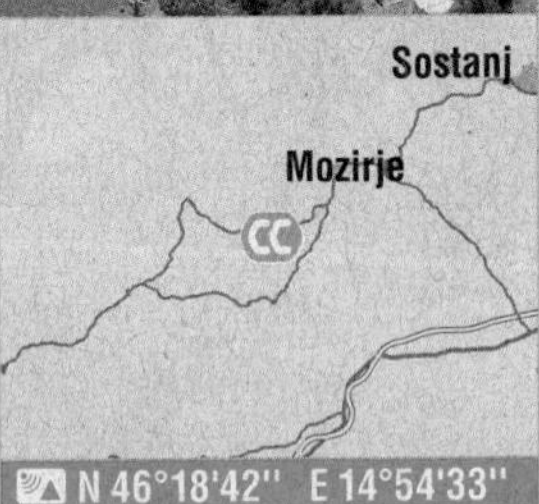

From A1 Ljubljana-Maribor, take exit Sentrupert/Mozirje (about 15 km from Celje) and continue north towards the campsite (± 20 km). Take the exit to the campsite in Nizka village.

CC € 27 *1/1-30/6 1/9-31/12 7=6*

N 46°18'42'' E 14°54'33''

Velenje, SLO-3320

740

Camp Velenje***
Cesta Simona Blatnika 27
+386 40 48 24 48
1/1 - 31/12
info@camp-velenje.com

3ha 100T(70-120m²) 10A CEE

1 ABCDIKLMNOQRS
2 FJMNOSXYZ
3 CGIKLNWZ
4 (A)M(Q)(T 15/6-15/9) (U+V+Y+Z)
5 ABDEFGHIJKLMNOPQUW
6 AGKM(N 1km)TU

The campsite is by Lake Velenje and offers stunning views of the surrounding mountains and hills. The adjacent beach and sports centre ensure a relaxing holiday.

From A1/E57 (Ljubljana-Cellje) exit 16, Velenje. Via route 4 after 14.5 km in Velenje take roundabout dir. Sostanj. Right after 450m, Cesta Talev. Left after railway crossing, Cesta Simona Blatnika. Campsite directly left after 1.8 km to the right.

CC € 25 *1/1-22/6 1/9-31/12*

N 46°22'10'' E 15°05'12''

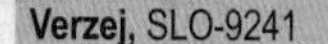

Verzej, SLO-9241 — 741

Camping Terme Banovci***
Banovci 1a
+386 25 13 14 40
1/1 - 31/12
info@terme-banovci.si

0,3ha 261T(80-100m²) 16A CEE

1 ABCD**I**KLMNOQRS
2 ISWXYZ
3 AIKMN**O**SUV
4 (**A**+C+F+H 🔑)JK**LN**O
(Q+R+T+U+V+W+Y+Z 🔑)
5 **AB**DFGIJKLMNOPUWXZ
6 EFGHKL(N 1km)PTV

Campsite with indoor and outdoor thermal baths. Has a screened naturist section with its own toilet facilities and thermal pool. CampingCard rates apply to campsite and naturist part. Access to the swimming pool is not included in CCA rate, you do get a discount.

From Graz (Austria) A9/A1 dir. Maribor. Before Maribor A5 dir. Lendava to Vucjavas exit. Turn right dir. Ljutomer to Krizevci. Left dir. Verzej. Right to Banovci after a few km. Follow signs.

Murska Sobota
Ljutomer

CC € 27 *1/1-28/3 2/4-25/4 6/5-15/7 1/9-20/12*

N 46°34'22" E 16°10'20"

Croatia

Capital city: Zagreb
Currency: the euro (as per 1 January 2023)
Time-zone: UTC +1, UTC +2 (March to October)
Language: Croatian
International dialling code: +385
Alcohol limit: 0.5‰, 0‰ for drivers under 24 years of age and drivers of a motorhome over 3.5 tonnes
Alarm number: police, fire brigade and ambulance: 112 (individual numbers as well: police 192, fire brigade 193, ambulance 194)
Tap water: safe to drink

Breath-takingly beautiful:
camping in Croatia

Heavenly beaches and an almost endless coast. That is what you find in Croatia. Unwind at the crystal clear Adriatic Sea and become familiar with its rich marine life. The nature above water is just as impressive. Journey from island to island and discover the flora and fauna in national parks like Plitvice and Paklenica. And for the lovers of culture, there are plenty of medieval cities filled with history and picturesque village to see. Camping in Croatia is adventurous, beautiful and amazingly versatile.

Enjoy the most beautiful beaches

With almost 6,000 kilometres of coast and more than a thousand islands, it is not surprising that the beaches in Croatia are so popular. They are magnificent. The unique beach Zlatni Rat is the best example, but Stiniva and Punta Rata are also very photogenic. Go swimming, snorkelling, diving or simply enjoy the peace and quiet. There are many beaches in Croatia, most of which are pebble beaches. Do you prefer sandy beaches? Then visit one of the sandy beaches on the island of Rab.

Plitvice lakes and other nature parks

At least ten percent of the Croatian land surface consists of protected nature reserves. Plitvice Lakes National Park with its azure blue lakes and large waterfalls is the example. Explore the park at your own tempo, walking on the wooden walkways, lush green pathways or with a rowboat. With a bit of luck, you will spot beautiful animals, such as wolves, otters and kingfishers.
There is much more beautiful scenery throughout Croatia. The Krka Waterfalls in Dalmatia, the gorges of Paklenica National Park and the swamps of Risnjak are certainly worth a visit. Island hopping in the Kvarner Gulf is also a great experience. The large islands Krk and Cres have a combination of beautiful landscapes and scenic villages. Losinj has an additional advantage. This quiet and beautiful island is ideally located for spotting dolphins.

Cities and villages with a history

Croatia has many wonderful cities and villages, which means there is always something to choose from. There are several places close together along the west coast of Istria that are worth a look. Poreč, Rovinj, Pula and Medulin have atmosphere and culture in abundance. From museums and old streets to Roman amphitheatres and beautiful

Winners in Croatia

820	***Best campsite***	Camping Zaton Holiday Resort
799	***Nicest campsite for children***	Camping Polari
773	***Most dog-friendly campsite***	Aminess Atea Camping Resort
818	***Best campsite swimming pool***	Falkensteiner Premium Camping Zadar
748	***Best location for a campsite***	Camping Bi-Village
766	***Most sports-loving campsite***	Camping Čikat
784	***Best campsite restaurant***	Lavanda Camping
782	***Best motorhome pitches***	Camping Omišalj
758	***Campsite with the best toilet facilities***	Krk Premium Camping Resort

Winner: Camping Zaton Holiday Resort

churches. A trip to the capital city Zagreb or amazing Split is also more than worth the trouble. Another gem requires more travel. Dubrovnik combines a historic character with an amazing location next to the sea.

En route

Filling up

Lead free petrol (Bezolovni Benzin/Eurosuper 95 of 98) and diesel (Eurodiesel) are widely available. LPG (LPG/Autoplin) is reasonably available. When filling up with LPG, the Italian connection (dish) is used. Petrol stations are open from 7:00 to 19:00 (in the summer to 22:00) and, along the major through roads, the petrol stations are usually open 24 hours. In petrol stations along smaller roads, sometimes it is only possible to pay in cash.

"Guaranteed sun in Croatia, comfortable camping along clean coasts, enjoying untouched nature and culture."

Mr H. Nibbelke, inspector 1203

Charging

The network of charging stations is not yet well-established. Plan your visit well.

Traffic regulations

Low beam lights (or daytime running lamps) are mandatory during the day from October through March. At equivalent crossings, traffic from the right has right of way. Traffic on the roundabout has right of way if so indicated by traffic signs. Uphill traffic on mountain roads has priority over downhill traffic. Drivers may only call handsfree.
Caution! Children under 12 years of age may not sit in the front; they must sit in the back in a child's seat (a child up to 2 years of age may be placed in the front seat in a seat with its back to the front.
From mid-November through mid-April, winter tyres (or snow chains in the car) are mandatory.

Special regulations

You may not pass a stationary school bus. During an overtaking manoeuvre, you must have your signal on the entire time. During the winter, you are required to clear your car of snow and ice before driving away.

Mandatory equipment

A warning triangle, safety vest, first-aid box and replacement light bulbs (with the exception of xenon, neon or LED lamps) kit) are mandatory in the car.
Caution! A car with a caravan or trailer must have two warning triangles.
During the winter, having a small snow shovel in the car is mandatory.

Caravan and motorhome

A motorhome or car-caravan combination may be a maximum of 4 metres high, 2.55 metres wide and 18.75 metres long (the caravan itself may be a maximum of 12 metres long).
With a motorhome or car-caravan combination that is longer than 7 metres, you may not drive in the leftmost lane on motorways with three or more lanes going in the same direction unless you want to turn left.

Cycling

A bicycle helmet is mandatory for children under 16 (even if they are on the back in a child's bicycle seat).
Cyclists must wear a safety vest outside of built-up areas in the dark and when visibility is poor.
Calling or texting while cycling is prohibited.
Children from 9 to 14 years of age may only cycle on the carriageway if accompanied by a person 16 years or older.
Children up to 8 years may only be transported by an adult in a child's bicycle seat.

Toll

Almost all motorways in Croatia are toll roads. You can pay cash in euros or pay with a credit card. You must also pay toll for the bridge to Krk, for the Ucka Tunnel between Rovinj and Rijeka and for the Mirna Viaduct between Rovinj and Umag.
For more information: hac.hr, azm.hr and bina-istra.com.

"Croatia is famous for its blue sea, idyllic coves and villages, but don't forget the wine and olive oil."
Ms A. Damen-Kuystermans, inspector 1024

Breakdown and accident

Outside of built-up areas, place your warning triangle at least 100 metres behind the car (2 warning triangles next to one another if a trailer is involved). All passengers must wear a safety vest.
If you have had a breakdown, call the alarm number of your breakdown assistance insurer. You can also call the Croatian automobile association (HAK) at (+385) 1 1987 (mobile).
If there is visible damage to the care, ask for a police report; you will need to show it at the border on your way home.

Camping

In July and August, there are hardly any free pitches to be found at campsites in Istria and along the northern Dalmatian coast. It would be wise to make a reservation on time if you want to go camping during the high season.
The construction of the motorway between Zagreb and Dubrovnik has made campsites in the centre and south of the Dalmatian coast increasingly popular. The often idyllically located campsites on the island are particularly suitable for campers with tents.
Campsites in Croatia can be enormous, especially on the coast. They have extensive amenities, such as shops and restaurants. Entertainment is standard at large campsites. It is prohibited to stay overnight along a public road in a caravan, motorhome or car.

Banjole/Pula, HR-52203 / Istra

742

Arena Indije Campsite**
Indije 96
+385 52 57 30 66
27/4 - 29/9
arenaindije@arenacampsites.com

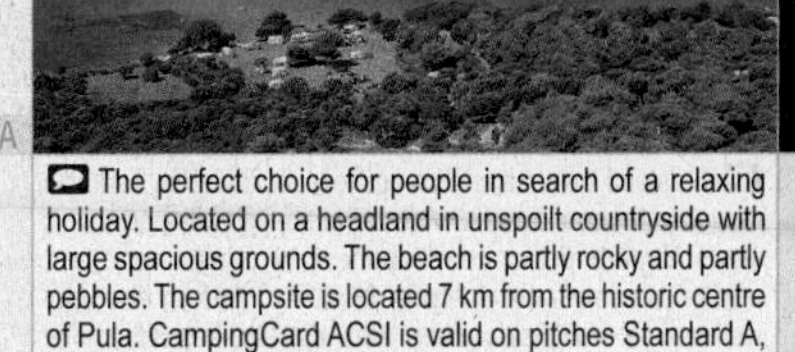

19ha 399T(60-120m²) 10A

1 ABCD**I**KLMNO**R**UV
2 HLMNOQRSUWXYZ
3 AKM**W**Y
4 (Q+S+T+U+V+Y+Z)
5 **AB**FGIJKLMNOPUW
6 AEFGKM(N 2km)PQRTV

The perfect choice for people in search of a relaxing holiday. Located on a headland in unspoilt countryside with large spacious grounds. The beach is partly rocky and partly pebbles. The campsite is located 7 km from the historic centre of Pula. CampingCard ACSI is valid on pitches Standard A, not on 'Seaside', 'Premium' and 'Superior' zones.

From the Pula ring road, drive towards Premantura, exit Banjole. Follow the camping signs.

CC € 19 *27/4-3/6 1/9-29/9*

Banjole/Pula, HR-52100 / Istra

743

Camp Peškera****
Indije 73
+385 52 57 32 09
20/4 - 29/9
info@camp-peskera.com

1,5ha 50T(75-100m²) 6A

1 ABCD**I**KLMNOQRU
2 HINQRUXYZ
3 A**W**Y
4 (B 15/5-15/9)**N**
(U+X+Z 25/5-10/9)
5 CEGHIJKMNOPUVW
6 ACEFG**J**(N 0,5km)PRT

Campsite right by the sea with a lovely pool. Touring pitches by the sea with natural rock plateaus, nice panorama, good toilets. Croatian atmosphere on a small scale.

After Pula follow motorway towards Premantura, exit Banjole and continue towards Indije. 50m before Indije campsite. Turn left, Peškera after 100m.

CC € 21 *20/4-30/6 31/8-29/9*

N 44°49'22'' E 13°51'04''

Baska (Krk), HR-51523 / Primorje-Gorski Kotar

744

Baška Beach Camping Resort****
Put Zablaca 40
+385 52 46 50 00
26/4 - 6/10
reservations@valamar.com

9ha 440T(80-120m²) 16A CEE

1 ABCDIKLMNOQRS
2 HJNPSUWXY
3 CILMN**O**P**R**S**VW**Y
4 (A 1/7-1/9)(C+F+H)**JKNP**
(Q+R+T+U+V+Y+Z)
5 **AB**EFGIJKLMNOPUWXYZ
6 ACEFGHKLM(N 0,5km)
PQRTX

The campsite is situated in the beautiful Baska Bay and positioned on level grounds. The first section, which is located on the beach, has marked out pitches with electricity and water. Section 2 also has mainly marked out pitches with electricity and water. Heated swimming pool and children's pool. CampingCard ACSI valid for comfort pitches.

Keep right before Baska. Follow 'Camp Zablace' signs.

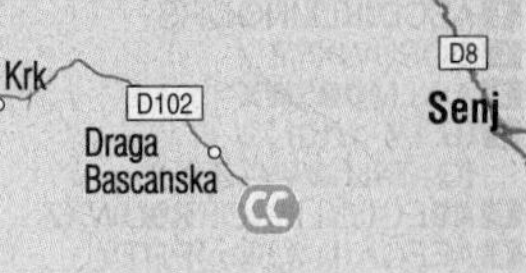

N 44°58'01'' E 14°44'43''

Baska (Krk), HR-51523 / Primorje-Gorski Kotar

745

Bunculuka Camping Resort****
Kricin 30
+385 52 46 50 00
26/4 - 6/10
reservations@valamar.com

4,7ha 400T(60-100m²) 10-16A CEE

1 ABCDIKLMNOQRUV
2 HLMNPQRSUWXYZ
3 CHILOPRSWY
4 M(Q+S+U+V+W+Y+Z)
5 ABDEFGIJKLMNOPUWXYZ
6 ACEFGHKLM(N 0,5km) PQRTV

A tasteful, quiet naturist campsite, surrounded by beautiful mountainous countryside. Wide pebble beach with panoramic views. Superb restaurant with buffet and regular menu, and adjacent terrace with designer furniture. Modern and very well-maintained toilet facilities. Wellness facilities at the hotel (2 km). CampingCard ACSI valid for comfort pitches.

Keep to the left just before Baska, in the direction of Valbiska and FKK. Then follow the signs to 'FKK Bunculuka'.

CC € 23 *26/4-6/6 6/9-6/10*

N 44°58'09" E 14°46'01"

Drage, HR-23211 / Zadar

746

Camping Oaza Mira****
Ul. Dr. Franje Tudmana 2
+385 23 63 54 19
1/4 - 31/10
info@oaza-mira.hr

4ha 192T(120-150m²) 16A

1 ABCDIKLMNOQRS
2 HMNPUVWXYZ
3 AHKLOPRVWY
4 (B 1/6-20/9)(Q+R 1/6-30/9) (T+U+V+Y+Z 1/6-20/9)
5 ABEGIJKLMNOPQRSUWXZ
6 ACEFGKLM(N 9,9km)TVW

Campsite located on a lovely bay with marked out pitches on a fine gravel base. Partially under trees, most pitches are situated on terraces with sea view. Close to Drage. Well away from the crowds. Perfect for campers with a boat. Nice starting point for many day trips, such as Korati Archipelago, Krka National Park.

A1 Karlovac-Split past Zadar, exit Biograd na Moru. Beyond Pakostane in Drage, signposted on the coastal side of the road. Follow signs to Autokamp Oaza Mira.

CC € 25 *1/4-30/6 1/9-31/10*

N 43°53'30" E 15°32'03"

Duga Resa, HR-47250 / Karlovac

747

Camp Slapic****
Mreznicki Brig 79b
+385 98 86 06 01
1/4 - 31/10
info@campslapic.hr

2,3ha 100T(100-130m²) 16A CEE

1 ABCDIKLMNOQRS
2 DOSUWXYZ
3 AIKLMOQSWX
4 (B 1/4-1/10) (Q+T+U+V+Y+Z)
5 ABEGIJKLMNOPRSUWXZ
6 AEFGK(N 3,5km)PRTV

Spacious pitches on one of Croatia's most beautiful rivers. Owner does everything to make you feel comfortable. Good toilet facilities, lively bar and a restaurant, children's playground and various sports fields. Has earned the natural campsite label. Train connections to Zagreb and trips to Plitvice possible.

From Karlovac D23 direction Duga Resa/Senj. Campsite signposted from Duga Resa.

CC € 23 *1/4-7/7 28/8-31/10*

N 45°25'11" E 15°29'01"

Fazana, HR-52212 / Istra

748

Camping Bi-Village****
Dragonja 115
+385 52 30 03 00
24/4 - 14/10
info@bivillage.com

48ha 950T(100-150m²) 10A CEE

1 ABCDIJKLMNOQRUV
2 GJNPQSWXYZ
3 A**G**KOP**R**SUVWY
4 (C+H+Q+S+T+U+V+Y+Z 🔑)
5 **AB**DEFGIJKLMNOP**R**UWXYZ
6 AEFGHIKLM(N 1km) OPQRTUVWX

ACSI AWARDS WINNER

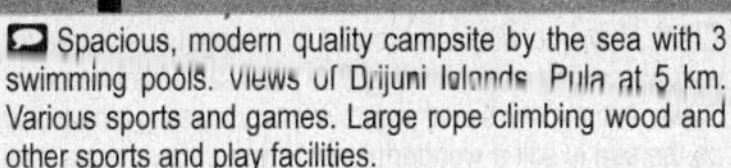

Spacious, modern quality campsite by the sea with 3 swimming pools. Views of Brijuni Islands. Pula at 5 km. Various sports and games. Large rope climbing wood and other sports and play facilities.

A9 exit Vodnjan/Fazana, direction Fazana. Follow the camping signs.

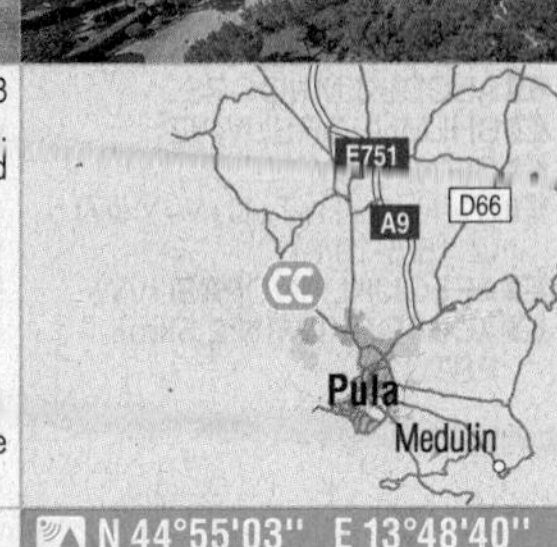

CC € 21 *24/4-22/6 31/8-14/10*

N 44°55'03'' E 13°48'40''

Funtana, HR-52452 / Istra

749

Polidor Camping Resort****
Bijela Uvala 12
+385 52 21 94 95
1/1 - 31/12
booking@campingpolidor.com

2ha 70T(80-110m²) 16A CEE

1 ABCDIKLMNOQUV
2 PUWXY
3 AIKMUV
4 (C+H 1/4-31/10)**NP**(Q 🔑) (R 1/5-1/10)(U+Y 1/4-30/9) (Z 🔑)
5 **AB**DEFGI**J**KLMNOP**S**UWXY
6 ACEFGKLM(N 1,5km)**P**QRT UVX

Polidor Camping Park is a small 4 star campsite in the vicinity of Funtana. The campsite is open the whole year and can accommodate up to 370 guests. Relax in the shade of pine trees, cooled by a fresh sea breeze, far away from the hustle and bustle of city life. Many bike routes and there are bikes for rent. Restaurant with the best traditional Istrian meals.

From Porec coastal road to Funtana/Vrsar. Campsite is located a few km north of Funtana. Campsite is signposted.

D75 · Porec · A9 · D302 · E751 · Rovinjsko Selo · Rovinj

CC € 25 *1/1-16/5 3/6-24/6 5/9-31/12*

N 45°11'27'' E 13°35'57''

Funtana/Vrsar, HR-52450 / Istra

750

Camping Valkanela***
Valkanela 6
+385 52 22 56 67
19/4 - 6/10
hello@maistra.hr

55ha 1250T(90-120m²) 10A CEE

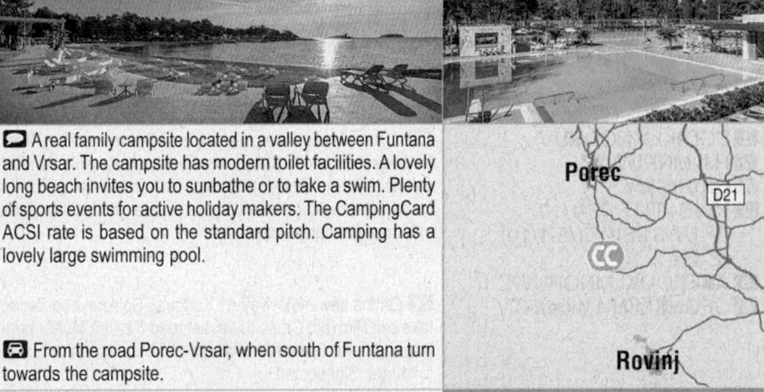

1 ABCD**I**KLMNOQ**R**UV
2 HNPQRSUWXYZ
3 ACIKM**O**P**R**SU**W**Y
4 (B+G 15/5-15/9) (Q+S+T+U+V 🔑) (W 1/5-15/9)(X+Y+Z 🔑)
5 **AB**EFGIJKLMNOP**S**UVXYZ
6 ACFGHIKLM(N 1km)RTVX

A real family campsite located in a valley between Funtana and Vrsar. The campsite has modern toilet facilities. A lovely long beach invites you to sunbathe or to take a swim. Plenty of sports events for active holiday makers. The CampingCard ACSI rate is based on the standard pitch. Camping has a lovely large swimming pool.

From the road Porec-Vrsar, when south of Funtana turn towards the campsite.

Porec · D21 · Rovinj

CC € 21 *19/4-28/6 1/9-6/10*

N 45°09'54'' E 13°36'28''

Glavotok (Krk), HR-51500 / Primorje-Gorski Kotar

751

Camping Glavotok***
Glavotok 4
+385 51 86 78 80
26/4 - 12/10
info@kamp-glavotok.hr

6ha 333T(80-120m²) 10A CEE

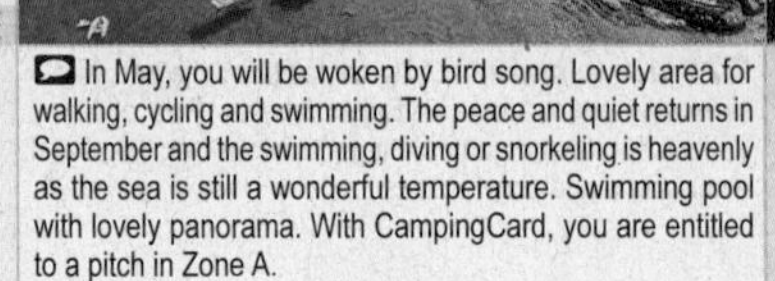

1 ABCDIKLMNOQRS
2 BHLMNPQRSUWYZ
3 CIKNPSWY
4 (C+H+Q+R+T+U+V+Y) (Z 15/5-10/9)
5 AEFGIJKLMNOPRSUVW
6 ACEFGHKLM(N 2,5km) PSTUX

In May, you will be woken by bird song. Lovely area for walking, cycling and swimming. The peace and quiet returns in September and the swimming, diving or snorkeling is heavenly as the sea is still a wonderful temperature. Swimming pool with lovely panorama. With CampingCard, you are entitled to a pitch in Zone A.

Take the main road Toll bridge/Krk. Turn right at the exit Valbiska. Then follow signs Glavotok. The last 2 km are on a narrow winding road with passing places.

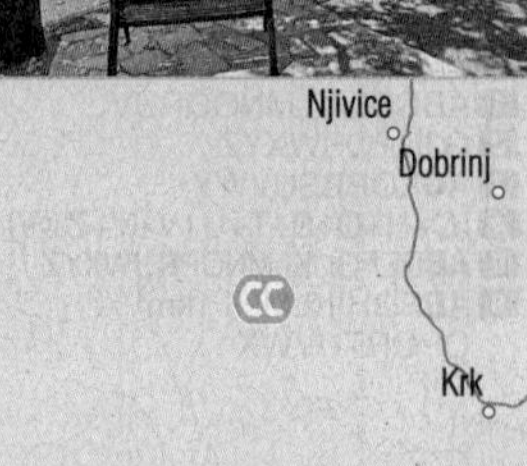

CC € 23 *26/4-19/5 10/6-29/6 7/9-12/10*

N 45°05'38'' E 14°26'25''

Grabovac/Rakovica, HR-47245 / Karlovac

752

Plitvice Holiday Resort****
Grabovac 102
+385 47 78 41 92
1/4 - 31/10
info@plitvice.com

5ha 102T(70-180m²) 16A CEE

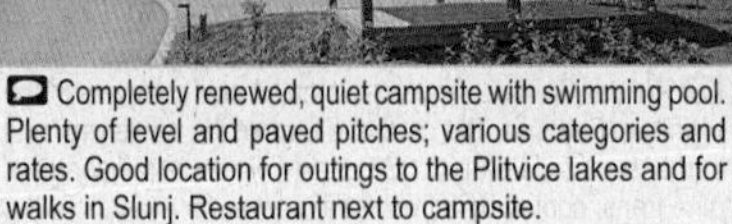

1 ABCDIKLMNOQRS
2 BJMSTUVWXYZ
3 ACHIKLNPQRS
4 (C+G 1/5-30/9)KNP (Q+R+U+V+X+Y+Z)
5 ABEFGIJKLMNOPRSUWXYZ
6 ABCEFGHKLM(N 2km) RTUV

Completely renewed, quiet campsite with swimming pool. Plenty of level and paved pitches; various categories and rates. Good location for outings to the Plitvice lakes and for walks in Slunj. Restaurant next to campsite.

D1 Karlovac-Plitvice. Located 8 km before Plitvice, in Grabovac, opposite the INA service station and next to restaurant ATG-Turist.

CC € 27 *1/4-10/6 10/9-31/10*

N 44°58'20'' E 15°38'51''

Jezera, HR-22242 / Sibenik

753

Camping Jezera Lovišća***
Uvala Lovišca 1b
+385 22 43 96 00
31/3 - 15/10
reception@jezeravillage.com

10ha 400T(100-120m²) 16A

1 BCDIKLMNOQRUV
2 HJLMNPUWYZ
3 CKORSWY
4 (Q+S+T+U 1/5-1/10) (V 1/7-31/8)(Y 1/5-1/10) (Z)
5 ABEFGIJKLMNOPUWZ
6 CFGHKM(N 1,4km)RTV

Luxury terraced campsite with beautiful views of bay. Ideal for (large) boats and water sports. Restaurant, bar, etc. An ideal campsite for real water sports enthusiasts and campers with boats. Moreover, there is the picturesque (peninsula) island of Murter for many excursions.

On the new motorway A1 Karlovac-Split beyond Zadar, take exit Pirovac. Cross the coast road 8 to the Murter peninsula. After 6.5 km in the village of Tisno cross the bridge to Murter. Signposted.

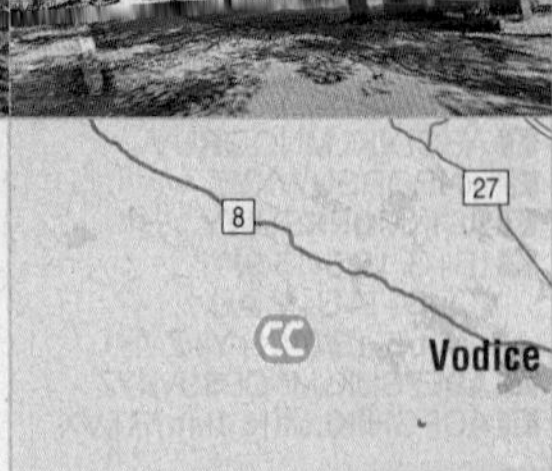

CC € 23 *31/3-15/6 9/9-15/10*

N 43°47'31'' E 15°37'39''

Klimno/Dobrinj, HR-51514 / Primorje-Gorski Kotar

754

- Camping Slamni****
- Klimno 8a
- +385 51 85 31 69
- 26/4 - 6/10
- info@kampslamni.com.hr

0,7ha 39**T**(35-80m²) 16A CEE

1. ABCDIKLMNQRS
2. HJNPVWXYZ
3. CHIKLSUVWY
4. (B+G)KM(Q+R 15/5-30/9) (U+V+Y+Z)
5. **AB**EFGIJKLMNOPUWXZ
6. ACEFGHK(N 0,3km) OPQRTV

A campsite with a lovely beach right on the Soline bay. Small campsite with wide range of modern amenities such as a fitness room, beach bar, good restaurant, pool with separate children's pool. Very suitable for families with toddlers.

Take the Krk bridge from the mainland to Krk island. Continue straight on at the next roundabout. After 1300 m, turn left towards Dobrinj (not straight on). The rest of the route to the campsite is signposted. Enter 'Klimno' as destination.

CC € 23 *26/4-18/5 25/5-8/6 1/9-6/10*

N 45°09'13" E 14°37'02"

Kolan (Pag), HR-23251 / Zadar

755

- Terra Park SpiritoS
- Sveti Duh 75
- +385 9 16 10 17 75
- 11/5 - 30/9
- info.spiritos@terrapark.hr

3ha 104**T**(75-100m²) 16A CEE

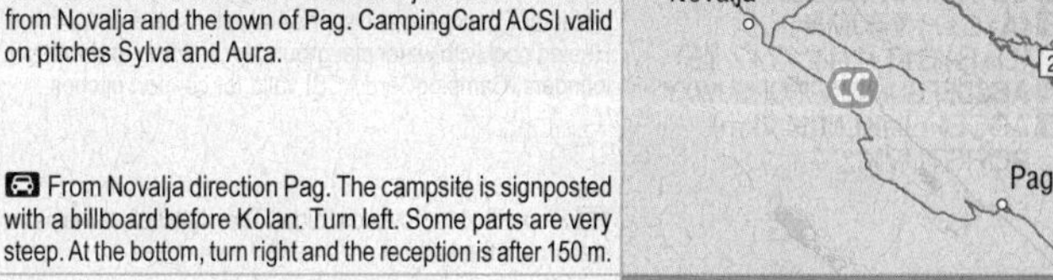

1. BCD**I**KLMNOQ**R**UV
2. HNPQTVWXY
3. ALP
4. (Q+R)(T+U+V 1/6-15/9) (Y)(Z 1/6-15/9)
5. **AB**GIJKLMNOP**QRS**UWX
6. ACEFGKM(N 7km)T

New campsite right by the sea in unspoilt nature with a view of the Velebit mountains on the island of Pag. The campsite has a beach bar and restaurant. Located just a few kilometres from Novalja and the town of Pag. CampingCard ACSI valid on pitches Sylva and Aura.

From Novalja direction Pag. The campsite is signposted with a billboard before Kolan. Turn left. Some parts are very steep. At the bottom, turn right and the reception is after 150 m.

CC € 21 *11/5-30/6 5/9-30/9*

N 44°30'48" E 14°57'39"

Krk (Krk), HR-51500 / Primorje-Gorski Kotar

756

- Camping Bor***
- Crikvenicka 10
- +385 51 22 15 81
- 1/1 - 31/12
- info@camp-bor.hr

2,2ha 201**T**(70-130m²) 10A

1. ABCD**I**KLMNOQRS
2. LMNUWXYZ
3. AIK
4. (B+G 15/5-15/9) (Q+R 15/5-30/9) (U+Y+Z 1/4-30/10)
5. **A**DEFGIJKLMNOPUWXY
6. ACEFGK(N 1km)PTV

Welcoming campsite run by the very hospitable Mrakovcic family. The campsite is on a hill, in an olive grove at walking distance from the historic centre of KrK. Panoramic views of the city and bay. Good restaurant. Possibility to visit the campsite's own wine cellar. Perfect for those seeking peace and quiet. New comfort pitches.

Before Krk follow signs to 'Centar'. Follow signs 'Autocamp Bor' from the roundabout, 1st turning right.

 € 23 *1/1-7/7 1/9-31/12* ***14=13***

N 45°01'21" E 14°33'44"

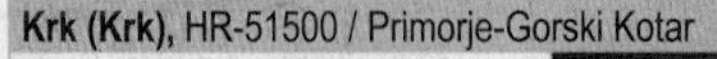

Krk (Krk), HR-51500 / Primorje-Gorski Kotar

757

Jezevac Premium Camping Resort****
Plavnicka 37
+385 52 46 50 00
22/3 - 3/11
reservations@valamar.com

11ha 459T(70-120m²) 10-16A CEE

1 ABCDEIKLMNOQRUV
2 HJLMNPRSUWXYZ
3 CHIKNOPSWY
4 (A)(C 1/4-1/11)(H)M (Q+R+S+T+U+V+Y+Z)
5 ABEFGIJKLMNOPQRSUWXY
6 ACFGHKLM(N 0,5km)PQRT UVX

A large campsite right by a lovely pebble beach with marked out pitches, 40% of which are shaded. Within walking distance of the centre of the town of Krk. Many facilities such as restaurant, beach bar, special beach for dogs, deck chairs, heated pool with special paddling pool. Extensive sports and entertainment programme. CampingCard ACSI valid for comfort pitches.

From Krk follow the Jezevac or autocamp (Jezevac) signs. Campsite is located on the west of the town.

Malinska, Vrbnik, D102, Krk

CC € 27 22/3-6/6 6/9-3/11

N 45°01'08'' E 14°34'01''

Krk (Krk), HR-51500 / Primorje-Gorski Kotar

758

Krk Premium Camping Resort*****
Narodnog Preporoda 80
+385 52 46 50 00
12/4 - 13/10
reservations@valamar.com

5,6ha 310T(80-110m²) 16A CEE

1 ABCDEIKLMNOQRUV
2 HLMNPQRSUWXY
3 CDIKMNOPRSVWY
4 (A+C+H)JMN (Q+R+S+T+U+V+Y+Z)
5 ABCDEFGIJKLMNOPQRSUWXY
6 ABCEFGHKLM(N 2km) PQRSTUVX

ACSI AWARDS WINNER

Easy-going five-star campsite on the coast, at walking distance from historical centre of Krk. Offers excellent amenities on campsite, such as wellness, a bakery, little shops, a restaurant, beach bar and sports and extensive entertainment. Heated pool with water playground for children and with sun loungers. CampingCard ACSI valid for comfort pitches.

From Krk drive towards Punat. Turn right before the petrol station (on the left).

Vrbnik, D102, Baska, Cres

CC € 27 12/4-6/6 6/9-13/10

N 45°01'28'' E 14°35'30''

Kuciste, HR-20267 / Dalmatija

759

Camping Palme
Kuciste 45
+385 98 32 83 57
20/1 - 20/12
info@kamp-palme.com

1,2ha 50T(50-100m²) 16A CEE

1 ABCDIKLMNOQR
2 GIMNPUXYZ
3 AVWY
5 AGIJKLMNOPUWY
6 FGHK(N 0,05km)QTV

Lovely campsite with sunny and shaded pitches close to the sea (50 m). Good base for visiting Korcula. There is a taxi boat.

The campsite is located on the main road through Orbic. After 3 km the campsite is clearly signposted on the right.

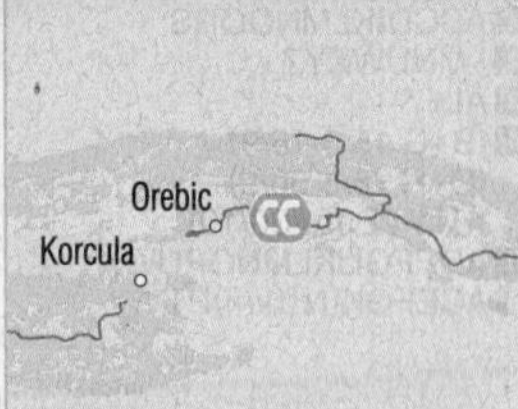

CC € 21 20/1-20/6 6/9-20/12

N 42°58'35'' E 17°07'46''

Labin, HR-52220 / Istra

760

- Marina Camping Resort****
- Sv. Marina 30 C
- +385 52 46 50 00
- 29/3 - 20/10
- reservations@valamar.com

5ha 248T(60-110m²) 16A CEE

1 ABCDIKLMNQRUV
2 HLMNPRSUWXY
3 CSWY
4 (C+H+Q+R+T+U+V+X+Z)
5 **AB**EFGIJKLMNOPUWXYZ
6 ACEFGHKM(N 0,2km) QRTUW

A campsite with a small pebble beach, ideal for people who want a good place to dive. A heated swimming pool with a fantastic panoramic view and a children's pool guarantee a relaxing holiday. Set in a peaceful bay. CampingCard ACSI rate applies to comfort pitches.

Go up the hill to the old centre of Labin. Then follow signs to Sv. Marina. The road is often narrow. Beware of cars that cut the corner off.

Labin · Rabac · D66 · Rakalj

CC € 27 *29/3-6/6 6/9-20/10*

N 45°02'00" E 14°09'29"

Lopar (Rab), HR-51280 / Primorje-Gorski Kotar

761

- San Marino Camping Resort****
- Lopar 488
- +385 52 46 50 00
- 26/4 - 1/10
- reservations@valamar.com

15ha 567T(80-120m²) 16A CEE

1 ABCDIKLMNOQ**R**S
2 AHJNSTWXYZ
3 CHILMN**O**P**R**S**VW**Y
4 **JKN**(Q+S) (T+U+V+X+Y+Z 1/5-30/9)
5 **AB**EFGIJKLMNOP**QRS**UWXY
6 ACFG**J**M(N 0,5km)OQRTV WX

Very large campsite with a real sandy beach, recommended for families with children. Many amenities such as a kids club, fitness room, wellness and restaurant. Very busy and very dry between mid-July and the end of August. Extensive entertainment programme. CampingCard ACSI valid for 'camp space with electricity'.

Clearly signposted at the fork in the road at the Lopar Tourist Office.

CC € 21 *26/4-6/6 6/9-1/10*

N 44°49'24" E 14°44'14"

Loviste, HR-20269 / Dalmatija

762

- Kamp Lupis****
- Loviste 68
- +385 20 71 80 63
- 1/1 - 31/12
- booking@camplupis.tcloud.hr

0,8ha 50T(50-100m²) 16A

1 ABCDIKLMNOQRV
2 HIJMQRUWXYZ
3 AWY
4 (R 15/6-1/10)
5 **AB**EFGIJKLMNOPRUW
6 AEFGJ(N 1km)P

Camping on the Peljesac peninsula, on one of the most beautiful bays, near the village of Loviste. The pitches are shaded by olive trees. Many water sports and (mountain) biking. Good starting point for visiting Korcula and the Miljet islands. Excellent facilities.

2022 from Orebic towards Loviste. At Loviste, th campsite is signposted. Best to take the asphalted road round the back. Suitable for large, wide motorhomes/caravans. Entrance gates open automatically.

CC € 23 *1/1-25/6 10/9-31/12*

N 43°01'41" E 17°01'48"

Lozovac, HR-22221 / Sibenik

763

Camp Krka***
Skocici 2
+385 22 77 84 95
1/3 - 30/11
goran.skocic@si.t-com.hr

1ha 40T(60-100m²) 16A

1 ABFIKLMNOQRUV
2 IJSUXYZ
3 AK
4 (**A** 15/4-15/10)(C 1/5-15/10)
(Q)(Y+Z 15/4-1/10)
5 **AB**GIJKLMNOPUWZ
6 CEFGKM(N 3,5km)V

A lovely small campsite with plenty of shaded pitches and a swimming pool. Clean toilets. Small restaurant with lovely patio and regional dishes. Well located for visiting the Krka waterfalls, Sibenik and small towns in the area such as Skradin.

From coast road south of Sibenik to Skradin/National Park Krka. From A1 motorway exit 22 Sibenik. End of exit, left on route 33. Left after petrol station. Campsite signposted. Route via A1, exit 21 less suited for caravans.

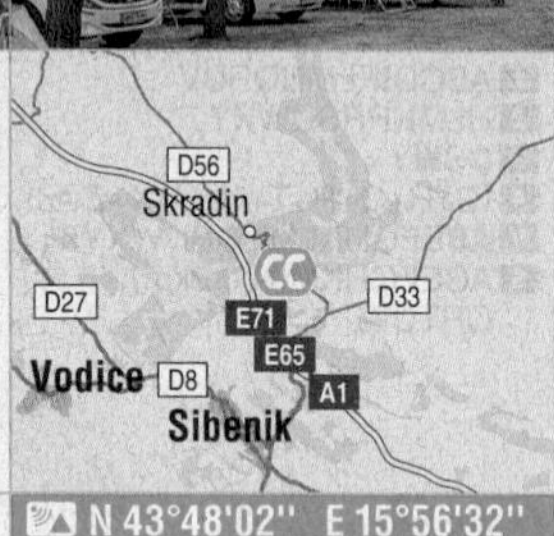

CC € 19 *1/3-30/6 26/8-30/11*

N 43°48'02'' E 15°56'32''

Lozovac, HR-22221 / Sibenik

764

Camp Marina (NP. KRKA)
Skocici 6
+385 9 13 68 33 23
1/1 - 31/12
campmarina.info@gmail.com

1ha 37T(40-100m²) 16A

1 ABCDIKLMNOQ**R**UV
2 BIJSUVWXYZ
3 AK
4 (B 1/4-1/11)(Q+X 1/3-15/11)
(Z)
5 **A**GIJKLMNOPUW
6 AEFGK(N 3km)V

Camp Marina is close to the Krka National Park (2.5 km) in Lozovac, 5 km from Skradin. A perfect location for stopover campers but also for those who want to visit the Šibenik region. Restaurant with Dalmatian dishes. Excursions to Krka National Park.

From coast road south of Sibenik to Skradin/National Park Krka. From A1, exit 22 Sibenik. End of exit, left on route 33. Left after petrol station. Campsite signposted. Via route A1, exit 21 less suited for caravans.

CC € 19 *1/1-30/6 26/8-31/12*

N 43°47'59'' E 15°56'39''

Lozovac, HR-22221 / Sibenik

765

Camping Slapovi Krke***
Lozovac 2G
+385 9 55 49 52 07
1/3 - 30/11
danijel.skocic@gmail.com

U,/ha 36T(60-100m²) 16A CEE

1 ABFIKLMNOQRUV
2 IUVXY
3 K
4 (**A** 15/4-15/10)
5 GIJKLMNOPUWXZ
6 EFKM(N 8km)U

Small enclosed campsite with trees, little shade and clean sanitary facilities. Well situated for a visit to the KrKa waterfalls (0.5 km). Close to Sibenik and smaller towns, incl. Skradin. Daytrips to National park Krka. Very suitable for campers. Excursions to National Park with owner possible.

From the coastal road south of Sibenik dir. Skradin-National Park KrKa. On the right of the road to National Park KrKa. Indicatod by sign. Last 300 m on dirt road with potholes.

CC € 17 *1/3-30/6 26/8-30/11*

N 43°47'32'' E 15°58'13''

Mali Losinj (Losinj), HR-51550 / Primorje-Gorski Kotar

766

Camping Cikat****
Cikat 6 A
+385 51 23 21 25
1/1 - 31/12
info@camp-cikat.com

6ha 1234**T**(60-120m²) 16A

1 ABCDE**I**KLMNOQRUV
2 BHJLMNPRSUWXYZ
3 AC**D**HKOPSV**W**Y
4 (A 15/5-22/9)(B 18/5-30/9) (G 18/5-22/9)**IJ**KMP (Q+S+T+U+V+X) (Y 8/4-21/10)(Z)
5 **AB**DEFGIJKLMNOPQ**RS**UWXYZ
6 ACEFGHKLM(N 2km) O**P**QRSTUV

A campsite on a pebble beach on the north-west of Mali Losinj with its large, lively marina. The campsite has three restaurants and a supermarket. Campsite open all year and has a unique Aquapark. Many lovely plateaus for sun worshipers.

Coming from the ferry, one has to cross the islands of Cres and Mali Losinj. From the 4-way intersection, just past Mali Losinj, follow signs to 'Camping Cikat'.

CC € 25 *1/5-20/5 2/6-22/6 8/9-30/9*

N 44°32'09" E 14°27'03"

Mali Losinj (Losinj), HR-51550 / Primorje-Gorski Kotar

767

Camping Village Poljana****
Rujnica 9a
+385 51 23 17 26
28/3 - 4/11
info@poljana.hr

18ha 546**T**(40-160m²) 10-16A CEE

1 ABCD**I**KLMNOQRUV
2 BHLMNPRSUWYZ
3 ACMN**O**PS**W**Y
4 (**A** 31/5-31/8) (Q+S+U+V+Y+Z)
5 **AB**FGIJKLMNOP**QRS**UVWXYZ
6 ACDEFGI**K**M(N 2km) OPQRTVWX

Luxury terraced campsite on the island of Losinj. Has the Adriatic Sea on two sides. With a bit of luck you may see some dolphins swim by. Extensive amenities: a berth for boats and a promenade to Mali Losinj with restaurants, ice-cream parlours, a marina. Excursions to nearby islands. Restaurant and supermarket at campsite.

Coming from Nerezine the campsite is on the left side of the road before Mali Losinj.

CC € 27 *28/3-17/5 2/6-25/6 9/9-5/10*

N 44°33'21" E 14°26'32"

Mareda/Novigrad, HR-52466 / Istra

768

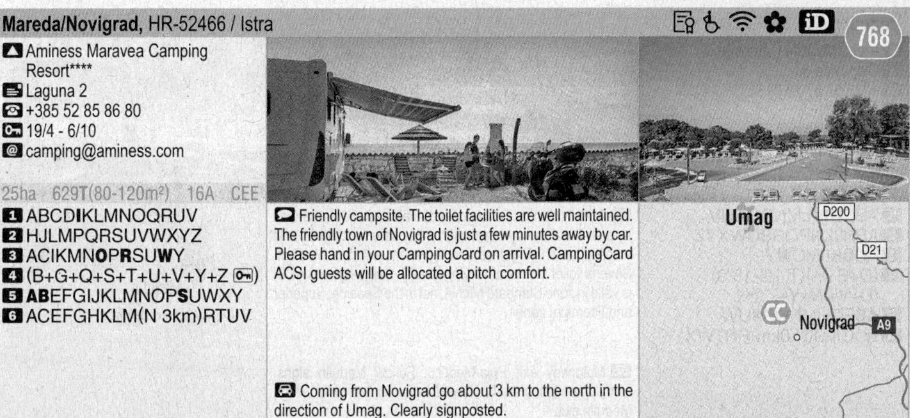

Aminess Maravea Camping Resort****
Laguna 2
+385 52 85 86 80
19/4 - 6/10
camping@aminess.com

25ha 629**T**(80-120m²) 16A CEE

1 ABCD**I**KLMNOQRUV
2 HJLMPQRSUVWXYZ
3 ACIKMN**O**P**R**SU**W**Y
4 (B+G+Q+S+T+U+V+Y+Z)
5 **AB**EFGIJKLMNOP**S**UWXY
6 ACEFGHKLM(N 3km)RTUV

Friendly campsite. The toilet facilities are well maintained. The friendly town of Novigrad is just a few minutes away by car. Please hand in your CampingCard on arrival. CampingCard ACSI guests will be allocated a pitch comfort.

Coming from Novigrad go about 3 km to the north in the direction of Umag. Clearly signposted.

CC € 25 *19/4-16/5 20/5-28/5 2/6-30/6 9/9-5/10*

N 45°20'36" E 13°32'53"

Martinšcica (Cres), HR-51556 / Primorje-Gorski Kotar

769

Camping Slatina****
Vidovici 30
+385 51 57 41 27
20/4 - 1/10
info@camp-slatina.com

15ha 463T(70-120m²) 16A CEE

1 ABCDEIKLMNOQRUV
2 HLMNPRUWXYZ
3 A**RSW**Y
4 M(Q+S)(U+V 15/6-1/9) (Y+Z)
5 **AB**EFGIJKLMNOPQ**S**UWXYZ
6 ACEFGHKM(N 1km)OPQRS TU

Terrace campsite with steep alleys leading down to the beach (20%). Pebble beach with plateaus. Beautiful spot for diving and very dog-friendly. Pitches with own water supply and electricity connection. There are sports, leisure and entertainment facilities. Clean sanitary facilities. Comfort pitches are available for CampingCard ACSI.

From Cres, drive in the direction of Osor. Turn right after about 20 km and follow the signs Slatina (8 km).

Orlec
Belej

CC € 19 *1/5-20/5 2/6-22/6 8/9-30/9*

N 44°49'16'' E 14°20'35''

Medulin, HR-52203 / Istra

770

Arena Grand Kažela Campsite****
Kapovica 350
+385 52 57 72 77
1/1 - 31/12
arenakazela@arenacampsites.com

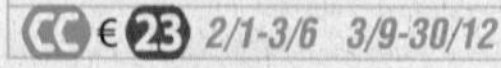
110ha 1200T(100-120m²) 10A CEE

1 ABCD**I**KLMNOQ**R**UV
2 HJNPQRSUVWXYZ
3 ABC**D**KLMN**O**PSU**W**Y
4 (**A**)(B 1/5-2/10) (G 20/6-30/9)JM (Q+S+T+U+V+Y+Z)
5 **AB**DEFGIJKLMNOPUWXYZ
6 ACEFGHIKLM(N 2km) **P**QRTUVWX

Campsite right by the sea with partially shaded pitches and two beautiful large freshwater swimming pools. CampingCard ACSI is valid in zone Superior, not in the Seaside and Premium zones.

The campsite is clearly signposted from the Pula ring road.

A9
Pula
Medulin

CC € 23 *2/1-3/6 3/9-30/12*

N 44°48'25'' E 13°57'02''

Medulin, HR-52203 / Istra

771

Arena Medulin Campsite
Osipovica 30
+385 52 57 28 01
28/3 - 6/10
arenamedulin@arenacampsites.com

30ha 932T(80-175m²) 10A CEE

1 ABCD**I**KLMNOQ**R**UV
2 ABHJLNPQRSUWXYZ
3 AC**G**KLMO**W**Y
4 (Q+S)(T 1/5-15/9) (U+V+W+Y+Z)
5 **AB**FGIJMNOP**R**UW
6 ACGKM(N 0km)PRTWX

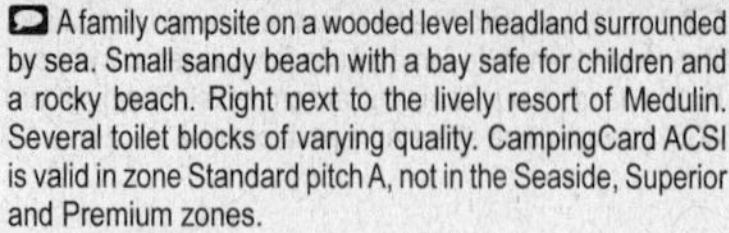

A family campsite on a wooded level headland surrounded by sea. Small sandy beach with a bay safe for children and a rocky beach. Right next to the lively resort of Medulin. Several toilet blocks of varying quality. CampingCard ACSI is valid in zone Standard pitch A, not in the Seaside, Superior and Premium zones.

Motorway exit Pula/Medulin. Follow Medulin signs, exit Camps along the boulevard as far as Camping Village Medulin exit.

CC € 21 *28/3-3/6 3/9-6/10*

N 44°48'51'' E 13°55'54''

Moscenicka Draga, HR-51417 / Primorje-Gorski Kotar

772

Autocamp Draga***
Aleja Slatina bb
+385 51 73 75 23
15/4 - 1/10
autocampdraga@gmail.com

3ha 110**T**(80-100m²) 10-16A

1 ABCD**I**KLMNOQRS
2 GJLMPSVWXY
3 AI**WY**
4 (Q+R)
5 **AB**GIJKLMNOPUWZ
6 CEFGKL(N 0,1km)PQRT

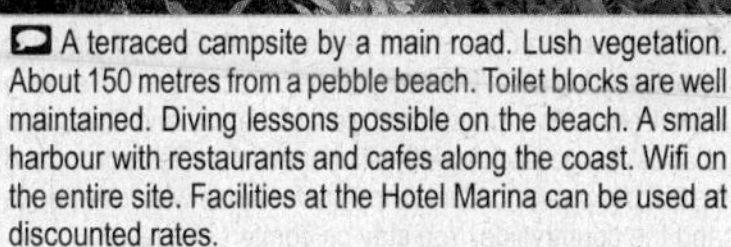

A terraced campsite by a main road. Lush vegetation. About 150 metres from a pebble beach. Toilet blocks are well maintained. Diving lessons possible on the beach. A small harbour with restaurants and cafes along the coast. Wifi on the entire site. Facilities at the Hotel Marina can be used at discounted rates.

Follow the coastal road from Opatija towards Pula. At the roundabout take the exit Moscenicka Draga and follow the signs to campsite.

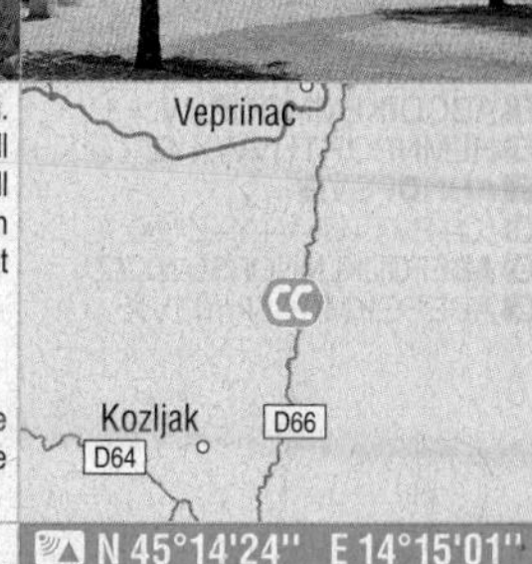

CC € 23 *15/4-7/6 1/9-1/10*

N 45°14'24" E 14°15'01"

Njivice (Krk), HR-51512 / Primorje-Gorski Kotar

773

Aminess Atea Camping Resort****
Primorska Cesta 41
+385 52 85 86 90
29/3 - 3/11
camping@aminess.com

10ha 408**T**(80-120m²) 16A CEE

1 ABCD**I**KLMNOQ**R**UV
2 HLNPQRSUWYZ
3 CHIKLMN**OQR**SV**W**Y
4 (G 1/5-15/10)M
(Q+S+U+V+X+Z)
5 **AB**DEFGIJKLMNOP**QS**UVWXY
6 ACFGKM(N 2,5km)
PQRTWX

The campsite has shaded fields with touring pitches. Wonderfully quiet in late season and you can swim to your heart's content in lovely warm water. There is an attractive town with lively restaurants and cafes nearby. CampingCard ACSI rates are based on a pitch in the comfort, standard and premium zone. New paddling pool.

Campsite is 10 km before the toll bridge to Krk. Badly signposted from the main road. Follow sign 'Hotel'.

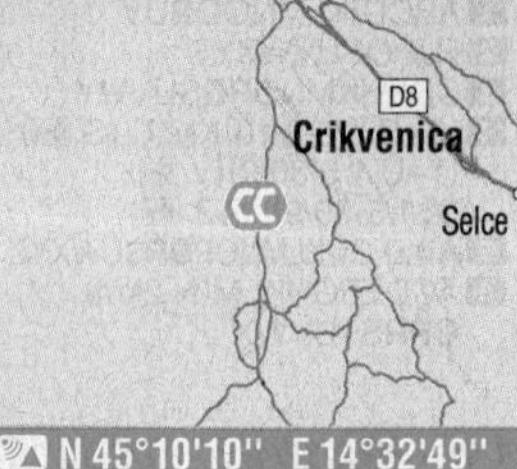

CC € 25 *29/3-16/5 20/5-28/5 2/6-30/6 9/9-2/10*

N 45°10'10" E 14°32'49"

Novalja, HR-53291 / Zadar

774

Camping Kanic
Dabovi stani 48
+385 9 81 38 01 32
15/4 - 15/10
info@campkanic.com

2ha 80**T**(30-150m²) 16A CEE

1 BCD**I**KLMNOQ**R**UV
2 AHLMNPRUVWXYZ
3 AKLNU**W**
4 (Q)
5 **A**GIJKLMNOP**S**UWX
6 ACEFGK(N 5km)PVX

Smaller campsite on the island of Pag northwest of Novalja, directly by the sea. Beautiful sea views from almost all pitches. Situated on a beautiful small bay in an olive grove. Many pitches with shade. Ideal for guests who like peace and quiet. Partly sandy beach, jetty for boats available.

After Novalja drive towards Lun. The exit for the campsite is signposted at approx. 5 km before Lun. Then follow the signs for the campsite over the rubble road.

CC € 23 *15/4-30/6 1/9-15/10*

N 44°35'48" E 14°50'03"

Novalja (Pag), HR-53291 / Zadar

775

Camping Olea
Sonjevi stani 38b
+385 21 77 00 22
24/5 - 6/10
info@oleacamping.com

6ha 250T(90-220m²) 16A CEE

1 ABCDIKLMNOQ**R**UV
2 HLMNPQRTUVWXYZ
3 AHN**O**PSV**W**
4 (Q+R+T+U+V+Y+Z 🔑)
5 **AB**EFGIJKLMNOP**S**UWXYZ
6 ABEFGKM(N 5km)TVX

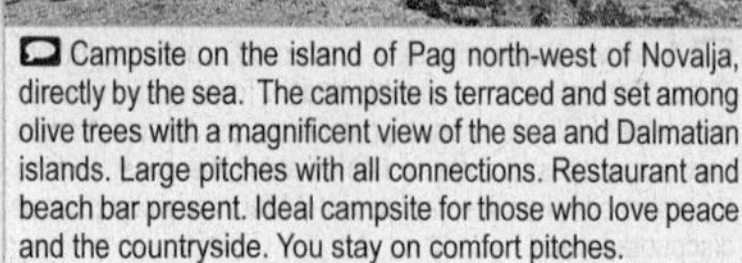

Campsite on the island of Pag north-west of Novalja, directly by the sea. The campsite is terraced and set among olive trees with a magnificent view of the sea and Dalmatian islands. Large pitches with all connections. Restaurant and beach bar present. Ideal campsite for those who love peace and the countryside. You stay on comfort pitches.

From Novalja direction Luna. After 12 km turn right. Indicated by the campsite sign. After that, approx. 1 km, follow signs.

CC € 25 *24/5-30/6 1/9-6/10*

N 44°37'41'' E 14°47'42''

Novalja (Pag), HR-53291 / Zadar

776

Camping Strasko****
Zeleni put 7
+385 53 66 12 26
12/4 - 13/10
strasko@hadria.biz

57ha 1358T(100-140m²) 10-16A CEE

1 ABCDIKLMNOQ**R**UV
2 HJPQSUVWXYZ
3 CDEHKMNOP**Q**SUV**W**Y
4 (B+G 1/5-8/10)KM(Q+S 🔑)
(T+U 1/5-30/9)(V 🔑)
(X 1/5-30/9)(Y+Z 🔑)
5 **AB**EFGIJKLMNOP**QRS**UWXYZ
6 ACDEFGHKLM(N 2km)
O**P**RSTUVWX

Large, luxury campsite under olive and oak trees with 2 km of mostly pebble beach with entertainment and sports options, clean renovated toilet facilities, restaurants, swimming pools and shops. Walking distance from Novalja. CampingCard ACSI is valid on pitches in zones Gold and Silver.

Prizna-Zigljen ferryboat is recommended. Turn left before Novalja, signposted. Or on A1 in Posedarje exit Pag (43 km), then another 32 km. Turn left before Novalja.

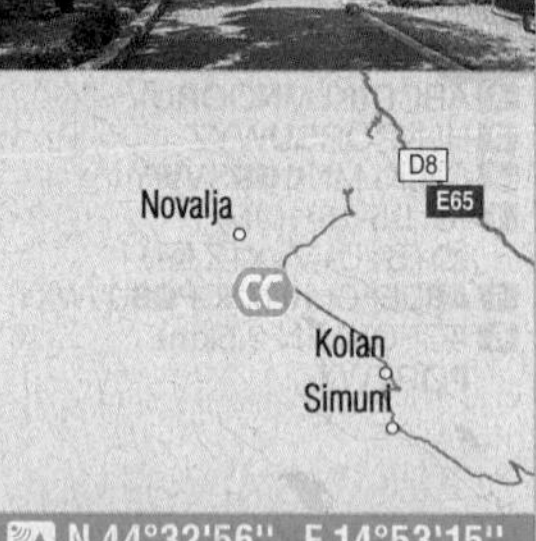

CC € 27 *12/4-1/7 1/9-13/10* ***7=6, 14=12***

N 44°32'56'' E 14°53'15''

Novalja (Pag), HR-53291 / Zadar

777

Terra Park Phalaris
Škuncini stani 100
+385 9 11 51 19 56
27/4 - 13/10
sales@terrapark.hr

1,5ha 157T(80-120m²) 16A CEE

1 ABCDIKLMNOQ**R**S
2 HNPUVWXY
3 CHKLNPSV**W**Y
4 M(Q+S 🔑)(T 15/5-30/9)
(U+V 15/5-15/9)(Y+Z 🔑)
5 **AB**FGIJKLMNOP**RS**UWX
6 AEFGKLM(N 3km)TVX

Away from the hustle and bustle, surrounding a beautiful bay with fine natural pebble beaches. Beach bar, beach showers and dog beach available. Ideal for beach and family holidays for complete relaxation. Location with nature preservation. Spacious pitches partly in the shade. CampingCard ACSI valid on pitches Tamaris and Pinus.

The campsite is on the island of Pag on the road from Novalja to Lun and is signposted. Turn left. Take care, the road is steep in places.

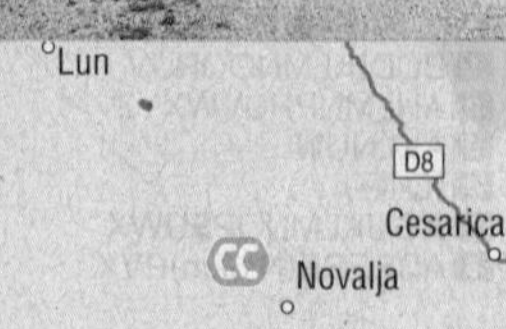

CC € 23 *27/4-30/6 5/9-13/10*

N 44°34'42'' E 14°51'18''

Novigrad, HR-52466 / Istra

778

- Aminess Sirena Campsite****
- Terre 6
- +385 52 85 86 70
- 29/3 - 3/11
- camping@aminess.com

13ha 426T(80-120m²) 10-16A CEE

1 ABCD**I**KLMNOQ**R**UV
2 HJLMNQSUWXYZ
3 ACIKMN**O**P**R**S**W**Y
4 **KN**(Q)(S 1/4-30/9) (T 1/6-31/8)(U) (V 1/6-15/9) (X+Y+Z 1/5-30/9)
5 **AB**EFGIJKLMNOPQ**S**UWXY
6 ACEFGHIKLM(N 0,8km) PQRST

The campsite is made up of a dense pine wood and a terraced section with hardly any shade. Good toilet facilities. The lively town of Novigrad is within walking distance of the campsite. Please present your CampingCard ACSI on arrival. CampingCard-users are allocated a pitch in the standard or comfort zone. CampingCard ACSI users cannot make reservations.

The campsite is located directly on the beach; 2 km from Novigrad and 16 km north of Porec.

CC € 25 *29/3-16/5 20/5-28/5 2/6-30/6 9/9-2/11*

N 45°18'54'' E 13°34'33''

Okrug Gornji, HR-21223 / Dalmatija

779

- Camping Labadusa
- Uvala Duboka bb
- +385 9 19 84 79 59
- 1/5 - 15/10
- camp@labadusa.com

0,6ha 110T(60-80m²) 16A CEE

1 A**H**KLMN**R**UV
2 GLMNPRUWXY
3 ACWY
4 (Q+X+Y+Z)
5 **A**GIJKLMNOPUW
6 AEFGKM(N 2km)PTX

A terraced campsite in an idyllic location right by the sea with sunny and shaded pitches. Good restaurant. Lovely new toilet and washing facilities. Shopping options at 2km. Access road is a challenge.

From A1 take the Trogir exit. Drive straight on towards Split. At the bottom towards Trogir. Cross new bridge, then turn right towards Okrug Gornji, 5 km. Now follow signs to Labadusa campsite, 2 km. Narrow 850 m access road, left to campsite.

CC € 27 *1/5-14/6 1/9-15/10*

N 43°28'55'' E 16°14'41''

Okrug Gornji, HR-21223 / Dalmatija

780

- Camping Rozac***
- Setaliste Stjepana Radica 56
- +385 21 80 61 05
- 29/3 - 9/11
- booking@camp-rozac.hr

2,5ha 140T(40-100m²) 16A CEE

1 AC**I**KLMNOP**R**UV
2 BHJNPQSTXYZ
3 CIKMNWY
4 (Q+U+V+X+Y) (Z 1/5-1/10)
5 **AB**EGIJKLMNOPUWXYZ
6 EFGK(N 0,2km)PTVWX

Rozac private campsite. Attractive campsite with plenty of shade, good toilet facilities. Lovely pebble and sandy beach 2 km from Trogir.

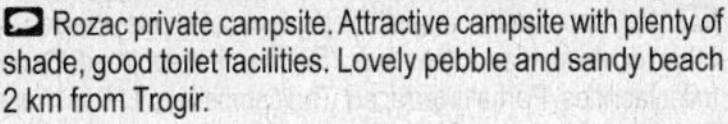

Coming from Sibenik follow D8 until 2 km past Trogir and cross new bridge. After bridge, right in direction Okrug and follow signs. From A1 exit 24A in direction Trogir, left over bridge, right direction Okrug.

CC € 27 *29/3-24/6 2/9-9/11*

N 43°30'19'' E 16°15'30''

Omis, HR-21310 / Dalmatija

781

Camping Galeb***
Vukovarska 7
+385 21 86 44 30
1/1 - 31/12
camping@galeb.hr

5ha 231T(70-100m²) 16A CEE

1 ACDIKLMNOQRV
2 AHJSTWXYZ
3 AMOPSUWY
4 (B+G 1/6-31/10)(Q 1/6-30/9) (T+U+V+X+Y+Z 1/4-1/11)
5 ABEFGIJKLMNOPRUWXY
6 EFGKM(N 0,2km)QRTUV WX

A lovely campsite by the sea with a sandy beach. The site offers plenty of shade and is equipped with every comfort. With CampingCard ACSI you can camp on zones B. Tourist tax and administration costs are not included in the rate.

From the E65 motorway take exit 25 direction Split, then follow coastal road. On the D8, after sign for Omis, on the right side before petrol station.

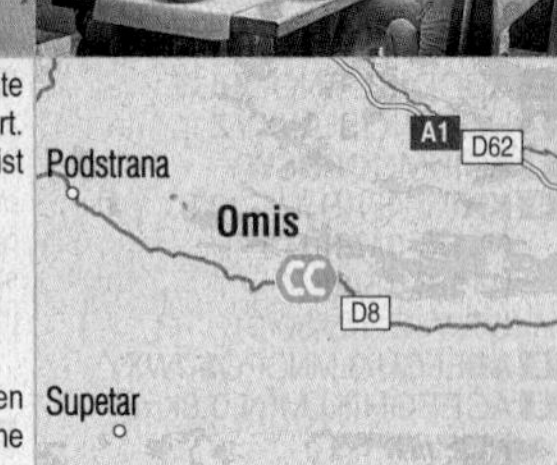

CC € 27 1/1-1/7 1/9-31/12

N 43°26'26'' E 16°40'47''

Omisalj, HR-51513 / Primorje-Gorski Kotar

782

Camping Omisalj*****
Vodotoc 1
+385 51 58 83 90
1/1 - 31/12
omisalj@hadria.biz

8ha 230T(100-140m²) 16A CEE

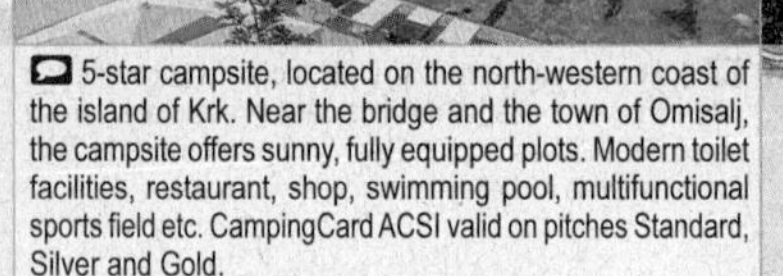

1 ABCDIKLMNOQRUV
2 HNPUVWXY
3 CEHIKLMNOPRSWY
4 (A 1/4-31/10)(B 1/4-1/10) (G 1/5-1/10)M (Q+R+S+T+U+V+Y+Z)
5 ABEFGIJKLMNOPQRSUWXY
6 ACEFGHKLM(N 2km) PQRSTUVWX

5-star campsite, located on the north-western coast of the island of Krk. Near the bridge and the town of Omisalj, the campsite offers sunny, fully equipped plots. Modern toilet facilities, restaurant, shop, swimming pool, multifunctional sports field etc. CampingCard ACSI valid on pitches Standard, Silver and Gold.

Coming from bridge on island Krk and coming from the direction Krk take exit Pusca. Follow road and after about 1 km you will see the campsite.

CC € 27 1/1-18/5 1/6-22/6 7/9-31/12 7=6, 14=12

N 45°14'06'' E 14°33'09''

Orasac, HR-20234 / Dalmatija

783

Camp Pod Maslinom
Donja banda 7c
+385 20 89 11 69
1/4 - 1/11
bozo@orasac.com

1ha 80T(50-100m²) 10A

1 ABCDIKLMNORUV
2 BGIJPTXYZ
3 AY
5 AGIJKLMNOPUWZ
6 EFGK(N 1km)RTV

Well-kept family campsite with plenty of shade, the sea is 500m down a steep footpath or 750 m via a steep road. Good toilet facilities. Partially terraced. The campsite is ±16 km from Dubrovnik. Bus stop 50 m from the campsite.

The campsite is on the E27 north of Dubrovnik. Turn right 200m past Orasac signn. Campsite clearly signposted.

CC € 21 1/4-30/6 15/9-1/11

N 42°41'57'' E 18°00'21''

Orebic, HR-20250 / Dalmatija

784

Lavanda Camping****
Dubravica 34
+385 20 45 44 84
1/1 - 31/12
info@lavanda-camping.com

ACSI AWARDS WINNER

2ha 85T(50-110m²) 16A

1 BCDIKLMNOQRUV
2 HILMNPQRUVWXY
3 AMNS**WY**
4 (Q)(T+U+ V+Y 15/4-31/10)(Z)
5 **AB**EFGIJKLMNOPQUWXY
6 ABCDEFGKM(N 0,5km) QRTVWX

The campsite is located near the picturesque village of Orebic, right by the sea. An oasis of peace and quiet. Fantastic views of the sea and the islands of Kôrcula and Mljet from the spacious pitches. All facilities available, incl. restaurant with traditional Dalmatian cuisine. Beautiful beach with free sun loungers and parasols.

On the through road head towards Orebic 2 km before the town. The campsite is on the left.

Orebic
D415
D414
Korcula
D118

CC € 23 *1/4-30/6 15/9-15/11*

N 42°58'59'' E 17°12'20''

Orebic, HR-20250 / Dalmatija

785

Nevio Camping****
Dubravica 15
+385 20 71 39 50
1/4 - 15/11
info@nevio-camping.com

1,5ha 168T(55-100m²) 16A CEE

1 BCD**I**KLMNOQ**R**UV
2 HIJMNPUWXYZ
3 CO**PR**SW**Y**
4 (B 1/5-15/10)(Q 1/6-30/9) (T)(V 1/6-30/9) (Y 1/5-15/10)(Z 15/6-15/9)
5 **AB**EFGIJKLMNOP**QRS**UWXYZ
6 ABCEFGHJM(N 0,2km)ORV

A lovely, terraced campsite with views of the sea and island of Korcula. Surrounded by olive trees. Pitches with and without shade. Right by the sea with pebble beach and 200m from supermarket. Restaurant and beach bar. Great base for visiting Korcula, Miljet islands and Dubrovnik. Beautiful pool. Limited pitches for large motorhomes.

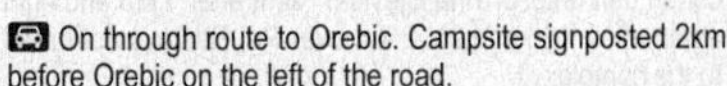

On through route to Orebic. Campsite signposted 2km before Orebic on the left of the road.

CC € 23 *1/4-15/6 15/9-15/11*

N 42°58'51'' E 17°11'55''

Pakostane, HR-23211 / Zadar

786

Camp Vransko lake - Crkvine****
Crkvine 2
+385 9 93 32 14 37
1/4 - 13/10
info@vranalake.hr

6,5ha 150T(100m²) 16A CEE

1 ABCD**I**KLMNOQR
2 BFPSXYZ
3 AHKM**O**P**R**SW**Z**
4 (Q)(S 1/5-30/9) (Y+Z 1/6-30/9)
5 **A**EFGIJKLMNOPQRUWXYZ
6 ACEFGKL(N 1,5km) **P**QTVWX

Campsite partly under trees next to an inland lake with well-maintained toilet facilities. Ideal for anglers or cyclists: route along the lake. Centrally located between Zadar and Sibenik. Renovated. Perfectly located for a visite at NP Krka and Np Kornati.

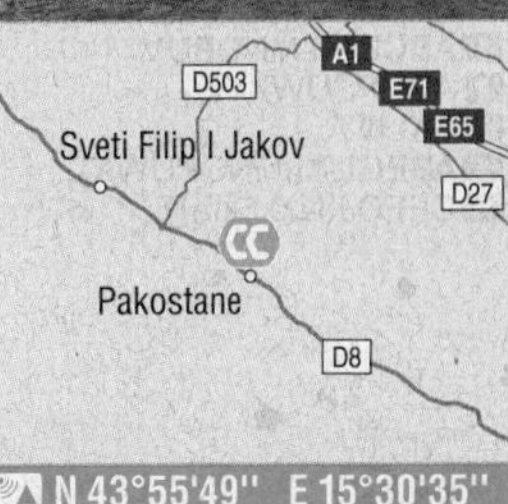

Follow coastal road no. 8 dir. Sibenik/Split. In Pakostane left to Vransko Jezero. Signposted from here.

CC € 25 *1/4-20/6 6/9-13/10*

N 43°55'49'' E 15°30'35''

Pakostane, HR-23211 / Zadar

787

Camping Kozarica****
Brune Busica 43
+385 23 38 10 70
6/4 - 31/10
kozarica@adria-more.hr

7ha 428T(80-110m²) 16A CEE

1 ABCDIKLMNOQRUV
2 HJNPQUVWXYZ
3 CHKSWY
4 (G+Q+S 1/5-30/9)
(U+V+Y 1/6-15/9)
(Z 1/5-30/9)
5 ABEFGIJKLMNOPRSUWXYZ
6 ACEFGHKLM(N 6km)
PQRTV

Large campsite under pine trees with all kinds of facilities like Supermarket, beach bar and restaurant. Ideal for water-sport fans and divers. Located between Zadar and Sibenik. A good base to visit Krka NP and for boat trips to the Kornati islands NP. With CampingCard ACSI at least a pitch in Zone B. Within walking distance of the centre.

From Zadar follow the coastal road 8 to Biograd. Between Pakostane and Biograd along the sea side of the road turn at the sign Kozarica.

CC € 23 *6/4-15/6 10/9-31/10*

N 43°54'41'' E 15°29'59''

Povljana, HR-23249 / Zadar

788

Aminess Avalona Camping Resort*****
Put Rastavca
+385 52 85 86 90
29/3 - 13/10
camping@aminess.com

3ha 323T

1 INPRS
2 HPYZ
3 CORS
4 (B+G+Q+R+T+V+Z)
5 ABFIJMNOPXYZ
6 K

Five-star holiday complex on the Pag peninsula near Povljana. You look out over an azure blue sea towards the Vir peninsula and the old royal city of Nin. CampingCard ACSI valid for comfort pitches.

On Pag dir Povljana island, left onto 108. Drive around the bay, right through town. At the end of the road in the centre, left onto Ul Tina Ujevica. Right after 1 km and right again after 1.2 km. Last 2 km over Put Rastavca dirt road to the complex.

CC € 27 *29/3-16/5 20/5-28/5 2/6-30/6 9/9-12/10*

N 44°20'05'' E 15°05'57''

Povljana, HR-23249 / Zadar

789

Camping Porat
Put Hrscice 2a
+385 23 69 29 95
19/4 - 1/10
porat@hadria.biz

1,6ha 103T(80-100m²) 16A CEE

1 ABCDIKLMNOQRUV
2 ABGPSUWXYZ
3 AKLWY
5 ABEGIJKLMNOPUWXZ
6 CEFGJ(N 0,5km)T

Simple campsite with pitches and fine gravel under the pine trees with clean sanitary facilities. Near fishing port, pebble beach and sandy beach (200m). The village of Povljana is situated in a beautiful bay and is not very touristy yet.

A1 exit 16 Posedarje dir. Pag. Left after 30 km to Povljana (6 km). Campsite signposted. From Rijeka via coast road take ferry in Prizna to Zigljen. Past Pag village 7 km on right, road 108 to Povljana.

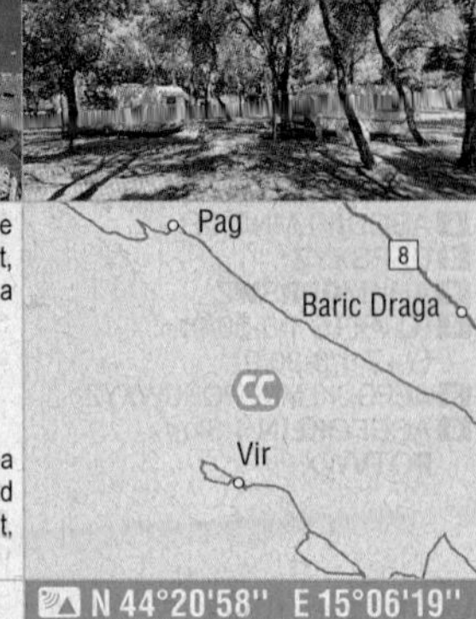

CC € 19 *19/4-1/7 1/9-1/10 7=6, 14=12*

N 44°20'58'' E 15°06'19''

Premantura, HR-52205 / Istra

790

- Arena Runke Campsite
- Runke 43
- +385 52 57 50 22
- 27/4 - 29/9
- arenarunke@arenacampsites.com

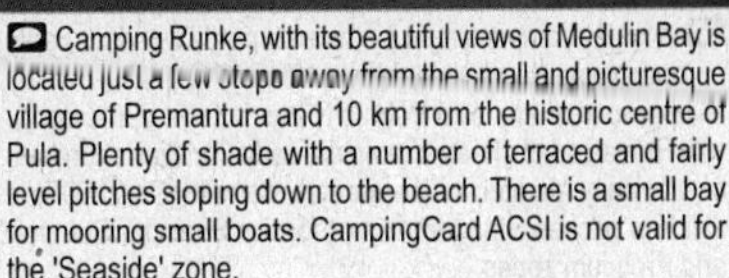

4,5ha 248T(60-120m²) 10A

1 ABCDIKLMNOQ**R**
2 HJLMNQRSUWXYZ
3 **WY**
4 (Q+R 1/5-18/9)(T+U+V)
(Y 1/5-18/9)(Z 1/7-18/9)
5 **AB**EGIJKLMNOPUWZ
6 EFGHKM(N 1km)**PT**

Camping Runke, with its beautiful views of Medulin Bay is located just a few steps away from the small and picturesque village of Premantura and 10 km from the historic centre of Pula. Plenty of shade with a number of terraced and fairly level pitches sloping down to the beach. There is a small bay for mooring small boats. CampingCard ACSI is not valid for the 'Seaside' zone.

Signposted from the ring road in Pula.

CC € 17 *27/4-3/6 1/9-29/9*

N 44°48'28'' E 13°55'00''

Premantura, HR-52203 / Istra

791

- Arena Stupice Campsite**
- Selo 250
- +385 52 57 51 11
- 28/3 - 6/10
- arenastupice@arenacampsites.com

26ha 920T(60-120m²) 10A

1 ABCDIKLMNOQ**R**UV
2 BGJLNPQRSUXYZ
3 AHMNOP**W**Y
4 (Q+R+S+T+U+V+Y+Z)
5 **AB**CEFGHIJMOP**QR**UW
6 CEFGHK(N 0,5km)PRT

In Premantura at base of Kamenjak headland, a sustainable national park where you can enjoy animals and plantlife. Located near a dense pine forest but there are also sunny pitches. Near the clear greeny-blue sea at the tip of Istria with an abundance of rocky and pebble beaches. Ideal for watersports. The historic centre of Pula is 10 km away. CampingCard ACSI not valid for the Seaside, Superior or Premium zones.

Signposted from the motorway Pula/Medulin/Premantura.

CC € 19 *28/3-3/6 3/9-6/10*

N 44°47'52'' E 13°54'50''

Premantura, HR-52100 / Istra

792

- Arena Tašalera Campsite**
- Premantura bb
- +385 52 57 55 55
- 27/4 - 29/9
- arenatasalera@arenacampsites.com

9ha 333T(80-120m²) 10A

1 ABCD**I**KLMNO**R**
2 BHLMNQSUWXYZ
3 AWY
4 (Q+S+U+Y+Z)
5 **AB**CGIJMNOPVW
6 EFKM(N 1km)**PQ**T

Partly level and open, partly sloping and wooded grounds. Right by the sea. Moderate toilet facilities. CampingCard ACSI is not valid for pitches in the 'seaside' zone. Mild climate in spring and autumn. Seawater still warm in September.

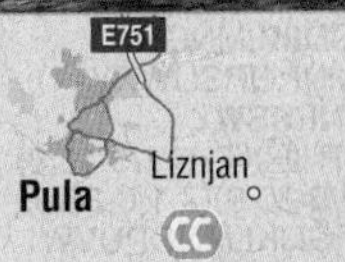

Follow Premantura signs from Pula/Medulin toll road. Follow campsite signs when entering village.

CC € 17 *27/4-3/6 1/9-29/9*

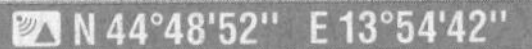
N 44°48'52'' E 13°54'42''

Pula, HR-52100 / Istra

793

Arena Stoja Campsite***
Stoja 37
+385 52 38 71 44
28/3 - 31/12
arenastoja@arenacampsites.com

16,7ha 678T(60-144m²) 10A CEE

1 ABCDIKLMNORUV
2 HIJNPQRSUWXYZ
3 AGNOPRSWY
4 (Q+S+T+U+V+Y+Z)
5 ABCDEFGHIJKLMNOPQRSUWXY
6 ACEFGK(N 3km)PQRTVWX

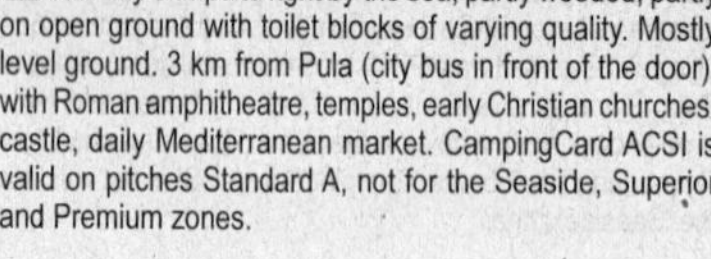

A family campsite right by the sea, partly wooded, partly on open ground with toilet blocks of varying quality. Mostly level ground. 3 km from Pula (city bus in front of the door), with Roman amphitheatre, temples, early Christian churches, castle, daily Mediterranean market. CampingCard ACSI is valid on pitches Standard A, not for the Seaside, Superior and Premium zones.

Signposted from the Pula ring road.

CC € 21 *28/3-3/6 3/9-30/12*

N 44°51'34" E 13°48'52"

Punat (Krk), HR-51521 / Primorje-Gorski Kotar

794

Camping Pila***
Setaliste i. Brusica 2
+385 51 85 40 20
19/4 - 30/9
camp.pila@falkensteiner.com

11ha 600T(80-100m²) 10A CEE

1 ABCDIKLMNOQRUV
2 HJLNQSUWY
3 CIMNPSWY
4 (Q+S+T+U+Y+Z)
5 ABEFGIJKLMNOPSUWXZ
6 CFGKM(N 0,3km)PQRTVX

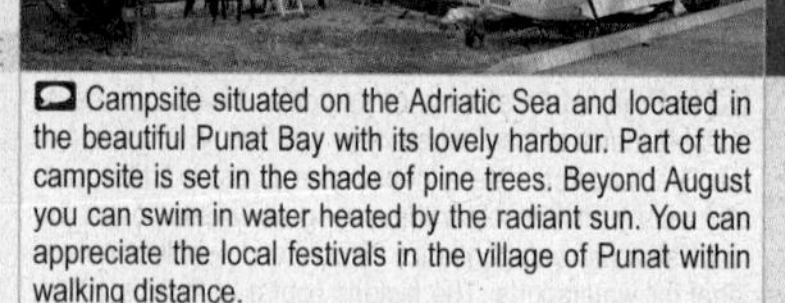

Campsite situated on the Adriatic Sea and located in the beautiful Punat Bay with its lovely harbour. Part of the campsite is set in the shade of pine trees. Beyond August you can swim in water heated by the radiant sun. You can appreciate the local festivals in the village of Punat within walking distance.

When approaching from Krk, drive past Punat in the direction of Stara Baska. The campsite is the first one located on the right. Turn right at supermarket.

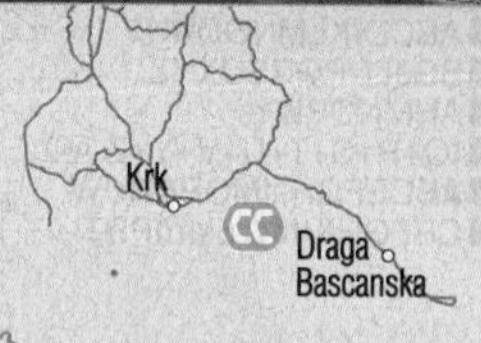

CC € 23 *19/4-14/6 2/9-30/9*

N 45°00'58" E 14°37'44"

Punat (Krk), HR-51521 / Primorje-Gorski Kotar

795

Naturist Camp Konobe***
Obala bb
+385 51 85 40 36
19/4 - 30/9
camp.konobe@falkensteiner.com

20ha 330T(60-100m²) 10A CEE

1 ABCDIKLMNQRS
2 HLMNPQRSUWXY
3 ILMNPRSWY
4 (Q+R)(T+U 1/5-15/9)
(Y 1/5-30/9)(Z 1/6-30/9)
5 ABFGIJKLMNOPUVW
6 ACDEFGJM(N 1km)PQRTX

Next to level grounds (on the left) this is a terraced site with significant differences in height (at least 20% incline). There is a pebble beach in the flat part. Lovely sea views. Very peaceful campsite, situated in the beautiful Konobe bay. The natural environment is maintained.

When approaching from Krk, drive past Punat in the direction of Stara Baska. The campsite is located to the right after about 3 km.

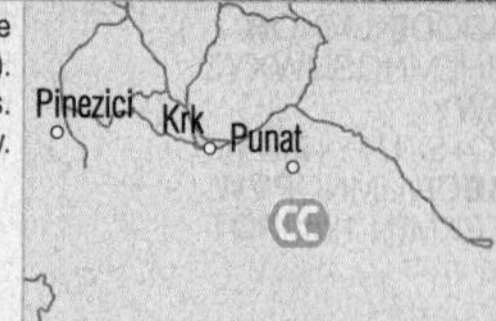

CC € 25 *19/4-14/6 2/9-30/9*

N 44°59'29" E 14°37'50"

Rab, HR-51280 / Primorje-Gorski Kotar

796

Padova Premium Camping Resort****
Banjol 496
+385 52 46 50 00
19/4 - 1/10
reservations@valamar.com

7ha 277T(80-100m²) 16A CEE

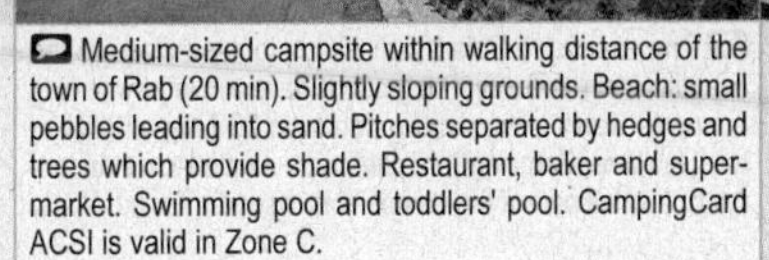

1 ABCDIKLMNOQRS
2 AHLMNPSUWXY
3 CDIKLMNSUWY
4 (C+H)M (Q+S+T+U+V+Y+Z)
5 ABEFGIJKLMNOPUVWXY
6 ACFGHKM(N 2km)OPQRT UV

Medium-sized campsite within walking distance of the town of Rab (20 min). Slightly sloping grounds. Beach: small pebbles leading into sand. Pitches separated by hedges and trees which provide shade. Restaurant, baker and supermarket. Swimming pool and toddlers' pool. CampingCard ACSI is valid in Zone C.

Drive in the direction of Rab, exit Lopar, take the first road to the left (sharp bend). The campsite is signposted to the right after about 500 metres.

CC € 23 19/4-6/6 6/9-1/10

N 44°45'10'' E 14°46'27''

Rabac, HR-52221 / Istra

797

Oliva Camp & Residence***
Maslinica 1
+385 52 87 22 58
20/4 - 19/10
olivakamp@maslinica-rabac.com

5,5ha 324T(70-100m²) 6-16A CEE

1 ABCDIKLMNOQRS
2 HPSWY
3 CILNOPRSVWY
4 (A+B+G)JLNP(Q+R) (U 1/5-1/10)(V 1/5-30/9) (Y)(Z 1/5-30/9)
5 ABFGIJKLMNOPUW
6 ACFGK(N 1km)PQRT

Campsite with many olive trees, situated on a beautiful bay with a pebble beach. Many water sports, swimming, diving and snorkelling options. Centre of Rabac is only a few minutes on foot, via the boulevard. You can bring your own boat. MTB and walking routes start at the campsite.

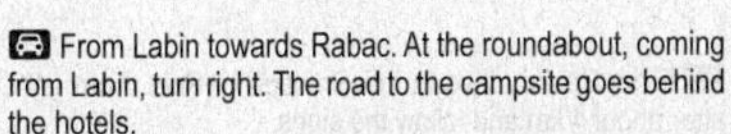

From Labin towards Rabac. At the roundabout, coming from Labin, turn right. The road to the campsite goes behind the hotels.

CC € 23 20/4-29/6 24/8-19/10

N 45°04'51'' E 14°08'45''

Rovinj, HR-52210 / Istra

798

Camping Amarin
Monsena 2
+385 52 80 22 00
26/4 - 6/10
hello@maistra.hr

12,5ha 297T(80-150m²) 16A CEE

1 ABCDIKLMNOQRS
2 HJLPQRSUWXYZ
3 ACHOPRSUWY
4 (B+G 1/5-20/9)(Q 1/6-15/9) (S)(T 18/5-20/9) (U 1/7-31/8)(V 18/5-20/9) (W+Y+Z)
5 ABFGIJKLMNOPUWXY
6 ABCEFGHIKLM(N 4km) QRTUX

Amarin campsite is located just north of Rovinj and has lovely views of the town. It is a real family campsite with a swimming pool. There are plenty of sports activities and children's playgrounds. Toilet facilities are mostly outdated but clean.

The campsite is located 3.5 km north of Rovinj, signposted.

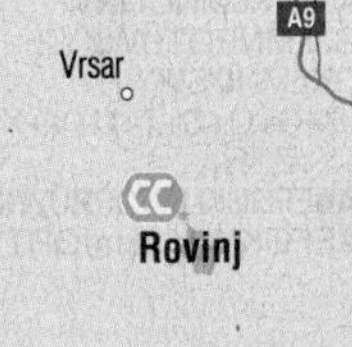

CC € 25 26/4-25/5 1/6-28/6 8/9-6/10

N 45°06'32'' E 13°37'11''

Rovinj, HR-52210 / Istra

799

Camping Polari****
Polari 1
+385 52 80 15 01
19/4 - 6/10
hello@maistra.hr

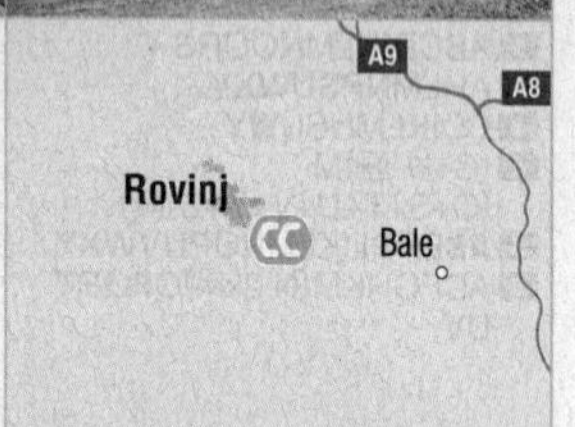

60ha 1668T(80-120m²) 10-16A CEE

1 ABCD**I**KLMNOQRUV
2 HJLMPQRSUWXYZ
3 ACHKLM**O**P**R**S**W**Y
4 (B+G 20/5-20/9)M(Q+S ⊶)
(T+U 1/5-26/9)(V+X ⊶)
(Y 1/5-26/9)(Z ⊶)
5 **AB**EFGIJKLMNOP**S**UWXY
6 ABCEFGHIKLM(N 2,5km)
QRTVX

The expansive Polari campsite is located close to the beautiful town of Rovinj. The grounds have a lovely swimming pool with water playground (open from 20 May) and good toilet facilities. CampingCard guests are entitled to a standard pitch. A small part of the campsite is reserved for naturists.

3 km south of Rovinj, follow the camping signs.

CC € 23 *19/4-28/6 8/9-6/10*

N 45°03'46'' E 13°40'30''

Rovinj, HR-52210 / Istra

800

Camping Veštar****
Veštar 1
+385 52 85 37 00
19/4 - 6/10
hello@maistra.hr

15ha 458T(60-120m²) 16A CEE

1 ABCD**I**KLMNOQRUV
2 HLNPQRSUVWXYZ
3 ACKLM**O**PRS**W**Y
4 (B+G ⊶)M(Q+S ⊶)
(T 15/6-31/8)(U+V 15/5-15/9)
(X+Y+Z ⊶)
5 **AB**EFGIJKLMNOP**S**UWXY
6 ABCEFGHKLM(N 5km)RTV

Quiet, well-maintained campsite. Lovely pebble beach and meadow. Toilet facilities are excellent and clean. The campsite has a pleasant sweet water pool with water playground.

From Rovinj, drive in the direction of Pula. Turn right after about 4 km and follow the signs.

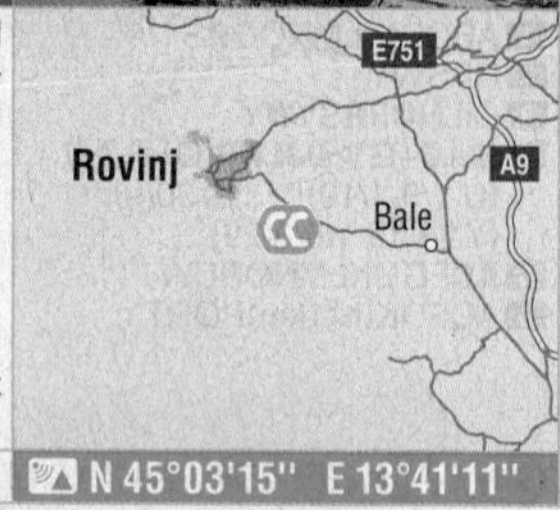

CC € 25 *19/4-25/5 1/6-28/6 8/9-6/10*

N 45°03'15'' E 13°41'11''

Seget Vranjica/Trogir, HR-21218 / Dalmatija

801

Amadria Park Camping Trogir****
Kralja Zvonimira 62
+385 21 79 82 28
1/4 - 31/10
info@amadriaparkcamping.com

15ha 329T(50-100m²) 16A

1 ACD**I**KLMNOQ**R**V
2 GJLMNPQTUWXYZ
3 CKLMN**O**S**W**Y
4 (B+G+Q+S+T+U+V+X
+Y+Z ⊶)
5 **AB**EFGIJKLMNOP**R**UWXYZ
6 AEFGKM(N 4km)QRTVW

Large terraced campsite with views of the sea and islands. Many shaded pitches and beautiful new pool, bordered by palm trees and a beautiful flower garden. Incredibly quiet due to the size of the complex. Shady beach. CampingCard ACSI is valid in zones A, B and Superior Standard.

From the motorway E65 take exit 24 direction Trogir. 5 km west of Trogir on the coastal road D8; the road from Sibenik to Split.

CC € 27 *1/4-23/6 1/9-31/10*

N 43°30'42'' E 16°11'38''

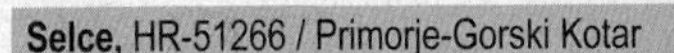

Selce, HR-51266 / Primorje-Gorski Kotar

802

Elements Camping Selce***
Jasenova 19
+385 51 76 40 38
29/3 - 1/11
kampselce@jadran-crikvenica.hr

8ha 299**T**(80-120m²) 16A CEE

1 ABCD**I**KLMNOQRUV
2 HJLMNPQSUWYZ
3 ASU**W**Y
4 (B+G 1/5-1/10)
(Q+R 15/5-15/10)
(T+U+V+X+Z 15/5-30/9)
5 **AB**EGIJKLMNOPUWXYZ
6 AFGKM(N 0,3km)PQRTVX

Campsite in terraces, located directly by the sea near the popular tourist town of Selce, which can be reached via a lovely boulevard. Large new swimming pool with very nice views over the bay and the island of Krk. Sanitary facilities have been renovated. Close to all water sports facilities. Many pitches with sea view.

The route to the campsite is clearly signposted from the coastal road near Selce. From Rijeka take the 2nd or 3rd exit to Selce.

Crikvenica Bribir D8

CC € 27 *29/3-10/6 10/9-1/11*

N 45°09'14'' E 14°43'30''

Sibenik, HR-22000 / Sibenik

803

Amadria Park Camping Šibenik****
Hoteli Solaris 86
+385 22 36 10 17
1/4 - 31/10
info@amadriaparkcamping.com

50ha 260**T**(90-140m²) 16A

1 ACD**I**KLMNOQ**R**UV
2 GJPQUVWXYZ
3 ADH**O**P**W**Y
4 (B 24/4-18/10)(**F** 24/5-18/10)
(G+Q+S+T+U+V+X
+Y+Z)
5 **AB**EFGIJKLMNOP**Q**UWXY
6 ABDFGKM(N 5km)OTVW

Large campsite by the sea with a shingle and concrete beach. Plenty of shade. The campsite offers every comfort. There is water recreation and a swimming pool for young and old. Campsite is part of resort with many amenities including a marina and an aqua park. CampingCard ACSI is valid in zone A.

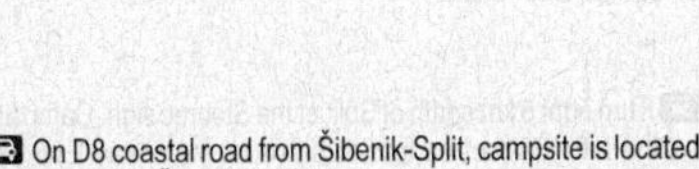

On D8 coastal road from Šibenik-Split, campsite is located 5 km south of Šibenik.

D27 D33 Vodice Šibenik A1 D58 Grebastica D8

CC € 27 *1/4-23/6 1/9-31/10*

N 43°41'57'' E 15°52'46''

Silo (Krk), HR-51515 / Primorje-Gorski Kotar

804

Autocamp Tiha Silo***
Konjska bb
+385 51 85 21 20
15/4 - 5/11
camp.silo@gppmikic.com

4ha 255**T**(60-120m²) 10A

1 BCD**I**KLMNOQRUV
2 HJNPQRVWX
3 ILN**O**Y
4 (Q+R+T+Z)
5 **AB**GIJKLMNOPQ**RS**UWX
6 CEFGKMOTWX

Campsite in the bay of Šilo on the island of Krk. New part with pitches for tents, motorhomes and caravans in the shade of a pine forest. Lovely views of the bay and mainland coast.

After bridge to island of Krk, follow signs to Šilo. Entering Šilo village, stay left until the sea, then follow signs. Camping Tiha is well signposted from village entrance.

CC € 21 *15/4-10/6 10/9-5/11*

N 45°08'56'' E 14°40'17''

Stara Baska/Punat (Krk), HR-51521 / Primorje-Gorski Kotar

805

Skrila Sunny Camping***
Stara Baska 300
+385 52 46 50 00
26/4 - 6/10
reservations@valamar.com

5,5ha 291**T**(70-100m²) 10-16A CEE

1 ABCD**I**KLMNOQRS
2 AHJLMNPRUVWXYZ
3 AI**W**Y
4 (Q+R+T+U+V+Y+Z)
5 **AB**EFGIJKLMNOPUWXZ
6 ACEFGHKM(N 9km)QRT

A terraced campsite close to Stara Baska. Attractive features are the beautiful beaches; fine shingle beaches mingling with rock formations. Part of the beach is reserved for naturists. The surrounding countryside is untouched and quite rugged. Good toilet facilities and refurbished restaurant and supermarket. CampingCard ACSI valid for standard and comfort pitches.

Coming from Krk, drive past Punat towards Stara Baska. Campsite about 9 km on the right. (Last section is 12%).

Krk
Baska

CC € 21 *26/4-6/6 6/9-6/10*

N 44°58'00" E 14°40'26"

Stobrec, HR-21311 / Dalmatija

806

Camping Stobrec Split****
Sv. Lovre 6
+385 21 32 54 26
1/1 - 31/12
camping.split@gmail.com

5ha 333**T**(70-110m²) 16A CEE

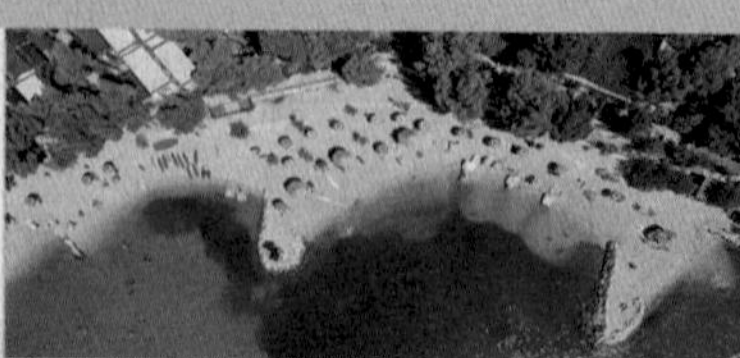

1 ACD**I**KLMNOQ**R**UV
2 GJNPRSTWXYZ
3 CPSVWY
4 (B+G 1/6-1/10)KMN
(Q+S+U+V+X+Y+Z)
5 **AB**EFGIJKLMNOPUWXYZ
6 CGHKM(N 3km)O**P**RTVX

Eco friendly family campsite with wellness and spa options. Located in a green wood by the mouth of River Žrnovnica on a headland with the sea on both sides. Only 6 km from the protected UNESCO city of Split. It is an ideal starting point for discovering the cultural and historical sights of Central Dalmatia.

Turn right 5 km south of Split at the Stobrec sign. Campsite on the left 100 metres further on (from motorway E65 exit 25 direction Split).

CC € 27 *1/1-30/6 1/9-31/12*

N 43°30'15" E 16°31'34"

Sveti Lovrec Labinski, HR-52222 / Istra

807

Tunarica Sunny Camping**
Tunarica 80
+385 52 46 50 00
26/4 - 15/9
reservations@valamar.com

3ha 160**T**(50-100m²) 6A CEE

1 ABCDE**I**KLMNOQ**R**UV
2 BHNPQRSTWYZ
3 AS
4 (Q+R+T+U+V+Y+Z)
5 ABEGIJKLMNOPUW
6 CEFJM(N 5km)PT

Campsite on the coast in an oasis of peace and quiet. Ideal location for nature lovers who want to enjoy the real camping life. Sanitary block. Excellent restaurant. Pitches under pine and oak trees. Mostly shaded pitches. CampingCard ACSI valid for standard pitches.

From Labin take direction Sveti Lovrec Labinski. At Tunarica exit, campsite is signposted (approx. 17 km from Labin).

CC € 21 *26/4-22/6 6/9-15/9*

N 44°58'09" E 14°05'50"

808 Tar, HR-52465 / Istra

Lanterna Premium Camping Resort****
Lanterna 1
+385 52 46 50 10
19/4 - 6/10
reservations@valamar.com

03ha 1372T(70-120m²) 16A CEE

1 ABCD**I**KLMNOQRUV
2 AHJLMNPQRSUVWXYZ
3 ACDHIKMN**O**P**QR**SU**W**Y
4 (C+H)IJKMP (Q+S+T+U+V+X+Y+Z)
5 **AB**EFGIJKLMNOPRUWXYZ
6 ABCDFGHIKLM(N 3km) O**P**QRTUVWX

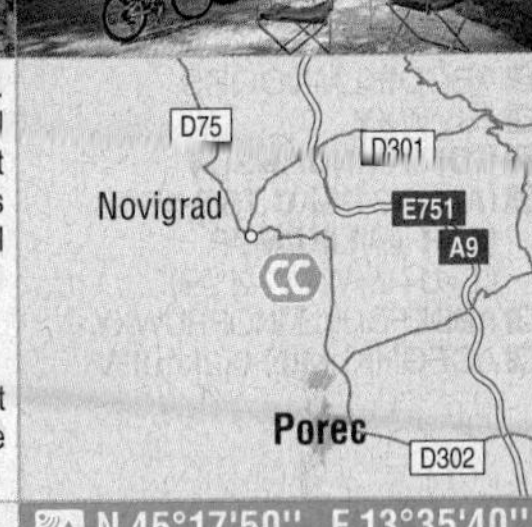

Very large, well-equipped campsite, directly on the sea. Ideal for families with children. Many sports facilities and several restaurants on the site. There are several swimming pools, at two campsite locations. Several paddling pools, water slides etc. Specially constructed sandy beach. CampingCard ACSI valid for comfort pitches.

In Istria from the motorway towards Pula, A9, take the exit 3, Nova Vas. Then via Novigrad direction Porec. The campsite exit is signposted.

Novigrad, D75, D301, E751, A9, Porec, D302

N 45°17'50'' E 13°35'40''

CC € 25 *19/4-6/6 6/9-6/10*

809 Tisno, HR-22240 / Sibenik

Olivia Green Camping****
Put Jazine 328
+385 9 16 05 66 52
28/4 - 29/10
contact@oliviagreencamping.com

3,4ha 65**T**(70-140m²) 16A CEE

1 ABCD**I**KLMNOQ**R**UV
2 HMNPQUVWXYZ
3 CKPWY
4 (C+H+Q+U+Y) (Z 1/5-18/10)
5 **A**EFGIJKLMNOPUWX
6 ABEFGKM(N 1km)STU

Terraced campsite with pitches shaded by olive trees and overlooking a beautiful bay, located on the Murter peninsula. The campsite has a bar and restaurant with beautiful sea view, nice pitches with all facilities, new swimming pool and paddling pool.

On coastal road no. 8 from Zadar to Sibenik take exit Murter. After 6.5 km before Tisno village turn again. Then follow the signs. The last part is not asphalted but easy to drive on.

Pakostane, D59, E65, D27, D8, Murter, Vodice

N 43°48'44'' E 15°37'19''

CC € 27 *28/4-10/6 10/9-29/10*

810 Tribanj, HR-23244 / Zadar

Camping Sibuljina***
Tribanj Sibuljina bb
+385 23 65 80 04
1/4 - 1/11
info@campsibuljina.com

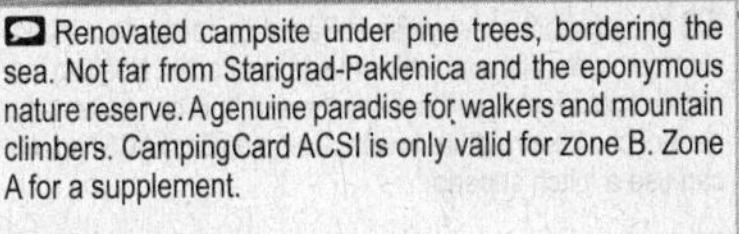

2,5ha 90**T**(50-100m²) 10-16A

1 ABCDE**I**KLMNOQ**R**UV
2 HJNPQUXYZ
3 AKWY
4 (Y+Z 1/6-1/10)
5 **A**EGIJKLMNOPUWZ
6 CEFGK(N 0,03km)T

Renovated campsite under pine trees, bordering the sea. Not far from Starigrad-Paklenica and the eponymous nature reserve. A genuine paradise for walkers and mountain climbers. CampingCard ACSI is only valid for zone B. Zone A for a supplement.

From Rijeka follow the M2/E27 coast road till 1 km north of Starigrad-Paklenica. Then signposted. Or A1 Karlovac-Split, turn off in Maslenica before Zadar towards Rijeka. Follow M2/E27 as far as Tribanj-Sibuljina.

N 44°20'16'' E 15°20'28''

CC € 21 *1/4-15/6 15/9-1/11*

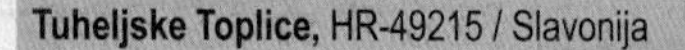

Tuheljske Toplice, HR-49215 / Slavonija

811

Camp Vita/Glamping Village Terme Tuhelj*****
Ljudevita Gaja 4
+385 49 20 37 50
1/1 - 31/12
booking@terme-tuhelj.hr

2ha 56T(100-150m²) 16A CEE

1 ABCDIKLMNOQRS
2 JSVWXY
3 CDHIKMN**O**P**R**SU**V**
4 (**A** 1/6-31/8)(**C** 15/5-15/9) (**F**+**H** key)IJK**LN**OP (T+U+V+W+Y+Z key)
5 **AB**DEFGIJKLMNOPRUWXY
6 ACFGHKLM(N 0,2km)RV

Vita Terme Tuhelj is a five-star campsite, 40 km from Zagreb. There are heated air-conditioned sanitary facilities and a large pool complex next to the campsite. It is the largest in Croatia, filled with spring water. There is also an indoor leisure pool with a large sauna complex. The area is perfect for cycling and walking.

A2/E59, Zagreb-Ptuj, exit 5 towards Zabok. Then follow the signs to Terme Tuhelj on Ljudevita Gaja. After approx. 700 metres turn left to the campsite.

CC € 27 *7/1-16/2 3/3-28/3 7/4-26/4 5/5-21/6 1/9-25/10 3/11-24/12*

N 46°03'58'' E 15°47'07''

Umag, HR-52470 / Istra

812

Camping Finida****
Krizine 55A
+385 52 71 39 50
24/4 - 29/9
finida@istracamping.com

3,3ha 282T(70-100m²) 10A CEE

1 ABCD**I**KLMNORUV
2 HJQRSTUWYZ
3 AIK**W**Y
4 (Q+S key)(Y+Z 1/5-25/9)
5 **A**EFGIJKLMNOPUWXY
6 ACEFGKM(N 5km)PQRST

The intimate atmosphere and beautiful surroundings of Camping Finida Umag make it the best choice for a quiet, relaxing holiday. This little campsite is right on the sea, featuring a natural beach lined with high trees that provide much needed shade on hot summer days. CampingCard ACSI guests can use a 'pitch superior'.

In Umag, drive in the direction of Novigrad. The campsite is located ca. 5 km from Umag, clearly signposted.

CC € 19 *2/5-17/6 14/9-29/9*

N 45°23'34'' E 13°32'30''

Umag, HR-52475 / Istra

813

Camping Savudrija****
Istarska ulica 19
+385 52 70 95 50
24/4 - 29/9
savudrija@istracamping.com

17ha 366T(80-120m²) 10A CEE

1 ABCD**I**KLMNQRUV
2 BHNQRSUWYZ
3 CMN**OR**S**W**Y
4 (B 15/6-10/9)(Q+S+T+Y key) (Z 1/6-15/9)
5 **AB**EFGIJKLMNOPUWX
6 ACEFGKM(N 8km)PQRST

The unspoilt countryside at Savudrija campsite is a constant reminder of this place's unusual character. Nestling in a fragrant pine forest and right by the sea, this campsite is the perfect choice for nature lovers. CampingCard ACSI guests can use a 'pitch superior'.

The campsite is located about 9 km northwest of Umag close to the village of Savudrija. Easy to find thanks to good signposting. It is just 800m from the village of Basanija to the campsite.

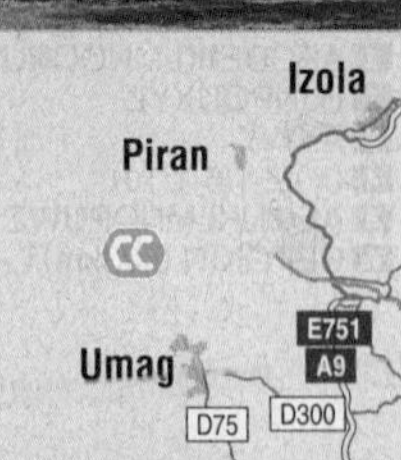

CC € 19 *2/5-17/6 14/9-29/9*

N 45°29'13'' E 13°29'32''

Umag, HR-52470 / Istra

814

Camping Stella Maris****
Stella Maris 9a
+385 52 71 09 00
24/4 - 29/9
stella.maris@istracamping.com

5ha 488**T**(80-120m²) 10A CEE

1 ABCD**I**KLMNOQ**R**UV
2 AGLPQRTUVWXYZ
3 CIKMN**O**P**RS**W**Y**
4 (B+G+Q+S+T+U+V+Y+Z)
5 **AB**DEFGIJKLMNOPRUWXY
6 ACEFGIKLM(N 2km)QRSTV

Its attractive location, modern outdoor swimming pools and sports grounds nearby make Camping Stella Maris an ideal destination for an active holiday, but it is also a nice, quiet place. The campsite was completely renovated in 2018, with a new restaurant and reception, improved and marked-out pitches and a large swimming pool complex.

From Umag, follow the signs to Stella Maris.

Piran, Izola, Umag, E751, A9, D300, D75, D301

CC € 23 *2/5-17/6 14/9-29/9*

N 45°27'14'' E 13°31'17''

Umag/Karigador, HR-52474 / Istra

815

Camping Park Umag****
Ladin Gaj 132 A
+385 52 71 37 40
24/4 - 29/9
park.umag@istracamping.com

138ha 1647**T**(80-120m²) 10A CEE

1 ABCD**I**KLMNOQRUV
2 HJNPQRSUWXYZ
3 ABCIKMN**O**P**R**SW**Y**
4 (B+G 1/5-26/9)(Q+S)
(T 1/6-27/9)(U+V+Y+Z)
5 **AB**EFGIJKLMNOPRUWX
6 ACEFGHIKM(N 5km)QRST
UVX

Camping Park Umag is one of the largest and best-equipped Mediterranean campsites. The campsite is an ideal destination for the entire family, offering something for everyone, from entertainment and activities to food and shopping. The campsite offers top-quality camping infrastructure and services, beautiful beaches, greenery and walking paths.

From Umag direction Novigrad. Campsite located 8 km further on, on the coastal side.

CC € 25 *2/5-17/6 14/9-29/9*

N 45°22'02'' E 13°32'50''

Vabriga, HR-52465 / Istra

816

Boutique Camping Santa Marina*****
Santa Marina 12
+385 9 93 59 16 69
1/5 - 1/10
info@santamarina-camping.com

4,5ha 117**T**(100-110m²) 16A CEE

1 ABCD**I**KLMNORS
2 UVWXY
3 CLPS
4 (B+G+Q+R+U+V+Y+Z)
5 **AB**EFGIJKLMNOPR**S**UWX
6 CEFGKLM(N 1,5km)QRSTV

An idyllic spot for a perfect family holiday. Spacious shaded pitches with modern toilet facilities. Watery fun is guaranteed in the large swimming pool with water park that is perfect for children. Beautifully furnished à la carte restaurant, with traditional specialities.

In Istria from motorway direction Pula A9, exit 3 Nova Vas. Then via Novigrad towards Porec. Take exit Vabriga and follow signs to campsite.

CC € 23 *1/5-1/7 1/9-1/10*

N 45°17'19'' E 13°36'31''

Vrsar, HR-52450 / Istra

817

Camping Porto Sole***
Petalon 3
+385 52 42 65 00
1/1 - 31/12
hello@maistra.hr

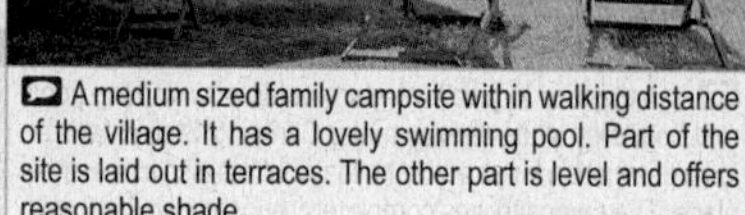

17ha 622T(100m²) 10A CEE

1 ABCDIKLMNOQRUV
2 HLMNPQRSUWXYZ
3 ACHIKMOPRSWY
4 (B+G 15/5-30/9)N(Q)
(S 1/5-30/9)(T+U)
(V+Y 1/5-30/9)(Z)
5 ABDEFGIJKLMNOPSUWXYZ
6 ACEFGHIKM(N 1km)RTV

A medium sized family campsite within walking distance of the village. It has a lovely swimming pool. Part of the site is laid out in terraces. The other part is level and offers reasonable shade.

The campsite is located 1 km south of Vrsar in the direction of Koversada.

Porec A9 E751 Rovinj

CC € 21 *1/1-28/6 8/9-31/12*

N 45°08'30'' E 13°36'08''

Zadar, HR-23000 / Zadar

818

Falkensteiner Premium Camping Zadar*****
Majstora Radovana 7
+385 23 55 56 02
1/1 - 31/12
campingzadar@reservations.falkensteiner.com

8,7ha 276T(80-140m²) 16A CEE

1 ABCDEIKLMNOQRUV
2 HJPQUVWXYZ
3 ACDKMNOPSVWY
4 (C 1/5-1/10)(G)JKLMNP
(Q+S)(T 1/5-30/9)
(U+V+Y+Z)
5 ABDEFGIJKLMNOPQRSUWXYZ
6 ABCEFGHKLM(N 3km)
PRTUVW

On the outskirst of town near Marina on flat terrain under the pine trees. Gravel beach and à la carte restaurant. Ideally located for trips to the city, Gorge Paklenica, Plitvice lakes, Krka waterfalls. CampingCard ACSI valid on standard pitch Blue.

A1 Karlovac-Split, before Zadar exit Zadar-Zapad/Nin. In Nin dir. Zadar. Right at traffic lights before Zadar to Punta Mika. Signposted. From south exit 2 Zadar. Then dir. Nin. Straight ahead at traffic lights to Punta Mika.

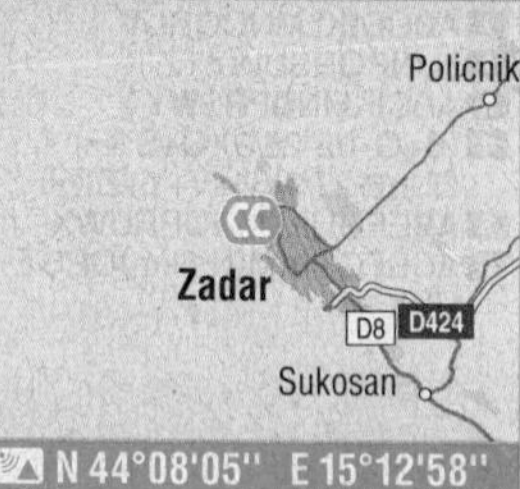

CC € 27 *1/1-14/6 9/9-31/12*

N 44°08'05'' E 15°12'58''

Zaostrog, HR-21334 / Dalmatija

819

Camping Viter
A.K. Miosica 1
+385 98 70 40 18
1/4 - 31/10
info@camp-viter.com

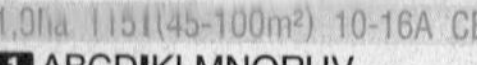

1,0ha 115T(45-100m²) 10-16A CEE

1 ABCDIKLMNQRUV
2 HIJPQUXYZ
3 AKLWY
4 (Z 1/4-15/9)
5 ABEFGIJKLMNOPUW
6 AEFGK(N 0,1km)T

Camping Viter is a friendly, family campsite directly on the shores of a beach by the Adriatic sea. It is situated between Split and Dubrovnik, 3 km from the ferry that connects the mainland with the island of Hvar. It is a one hour drive to Mostar. Various restaurants, bars and shops.

Follow Viter signs 600m on the right after the Zaostrog sign.

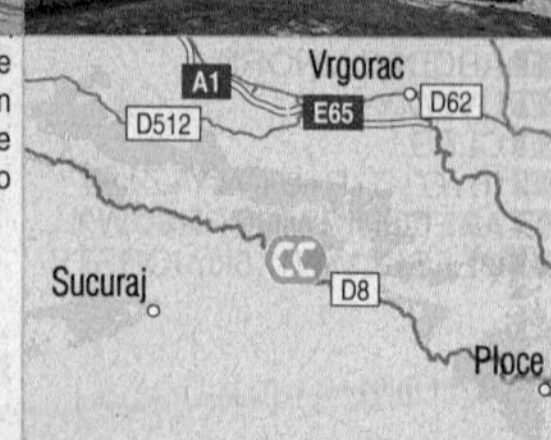

CC € 23 *1/4-1/7 1/9-31/10*

N 43°08'21'' E 17°16'50''

Zaton/Nin (Zadar), HR-23232 / Zadar

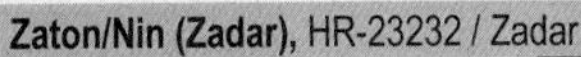

820

Camping Zaton Holiday Resort****
Draznikova 78
+385 23 28 02 15
20/4 - 5/10
camping@zaton.hr

100ha 900T(80-120m²) 16A CEE

1. ABCDE**I**KLMNOQ**R**UV
2. AHPQTUWXYZ
3. CDHKMN**OPQR**S**V**Y
4. (C+H)IM (Q+S+T+U+V+W+X +Y+Z)
5. **AB**EFGIJKLMNOP**RS**UWXYZ
6. ABCDFGHKLM(N 1km) OPQRTUVWX

A large, well-equipped luxury campsite by a sand and pebble beach with all types of accommodation. Forms part of a holiday centre. Good base for trips out to Nin and the old centre of Zadar and many old fishing villages (towards the south). Surcharge of Euro7 or Euro14 for pitches 1-631, depending on the period.

Recommended route via motorway A1 Zagreb-Zadar, before Zadar exit Nin/Zadar Zapat. In Nin left dir. Zadar. Signposted on right after 2 km.

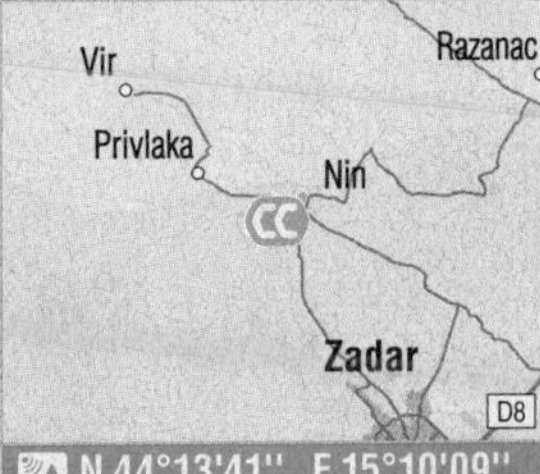

CC € 25 *20/4-21/6 7/9-5/10*

N 44°13'41'' E 15°10'09''

Albania

Capital: Tirana
Currency: Albanian lek
Time zone: UTC +1, UTC +2 (March to October)
Language: Albanian
International dialling code: +355
Alcohol limit: 0.1‰
Emergency numbers: general: 112, police: 129, ambulance: 127, fire service: 128
Tap water: often not safe, drink bottled water or boiled water

Albania: pure, unspoilt and unprecedented beautiful countryside

If you would like to camp away from the masses but would like to be surrounded by stunning countryside and beaches, Albania is the country for you! This country lies between the Adriatic Sea and the countries of Montenegro, Kosovo, Macedonia and Greece. It is a varied country with stunning nature reserves, mountains and white beaches. You sometimes feel like you are going back in time, and you will feel very welcomed by the friendly population. The campsites are extremely varied. There are large campsites with all amenities as well as smaller campsites with fewer amenities, such as those in rural areas.

Tirana

Albania's capital is Tirana. This city does not stand still, it is bustling and in full development. Skanderbeg Square is the city's central point. In the middle of this square there is a monument to General Skanderbeg (the Albanians' national hero) and it is the location of the National Historic Museum that is definitely worth visiting. You can take the cable car to Mount Dajti, where you can go on lovely walks. The Bunk'Art 1 and 2 museums are located in the former bunker complexes in a preserved nuclear fallout shelter. It is a unique place to visit. Here, you can visit many trendy restaurants, lounge bars and a range of shops.

World Heritage Cities

The city of Berat is on UNESCO's World Heritage List. It has a labyrinth of small streets. Above the city, there is a citadel with eight churches. Gjirokastër is also on UNESCO's World Heritage List. It is said to be the oldest and most charming city in the country. The narrow streets are filled with Ottoman buildings. The castle is in the mountains above the city, where you will also find a museum about the history of the city and about Albania's army. You will find many souvenirs and can have a nice drink on the narrow streets of the bazaar. Butrint, in the southernmost part of Albania, is also worth visiting. It is an archaeological site with various monuments.

Albanian Alps

You can take the ferry from Koman to Fierzë in the Albanian Alps. The ferry takes you past stunning mountains. You can take lovely walks in the Albanian Alps, and you will encounter waterfalls. Friendly residents live in the mountain villages, they will make you feel very welcome. Let the breathtaking beauty of the white mountains, beautiful lakes and green countryside astound you.

Albania's beaches

Many of the lovely beaches of the Adriatic Sea are still undiscovered and therefore not touristic. Mainly local residents go there. The well-known coastal resorts and harbour towns are Vlorë and Durrës, where there are more tourists than in other places. In Durrës, you will find Roman ruins such as an exceptional amphitheatre, a forum and thermal baths. The Byzantine castle is also highly recommended. In Himare and Sarandë, on the Albanian Riviera, you can enjoy yourself at a pavement cafe on the promenade in the evenings. There are beautiful deserted white beaches and isolated bays, but you can only get there by boat, such as at Qeparo. Ksamil is another lovely coastal resort all the way down in the south, where you can enjoy the beaches and the bright blue sea.

National parks

There are no less than 15 official national parks in Albania. Each park has its own features. In Divjakë-Karavasta, for example, you will find an enormous number of birds. In Albania's largest lagoon, you will encounter Dalmatian pelicans. In Lurë National Park, there are stunning glacial lakes surrounded by white mountains. In Theth National Park, in the north, you will spot lynxes, brown bears, wolves and can take lovely walks. Valbonëdal National Park is also in the Albanian Alps. In the summer, you can find exceptional flowers here, it is rich in flora and fauna. Albania's highest mountain is in Tomorr. The peak is covered in snow almost all year round and the route there is exceptional. There's something for everyone!

Albania's lakes

You can go to various lakes in Albania for a refreshing dip. Lake Shkodër is on the border of Montenegro and Albania. It is the largest lake in the Balkans, and you can take boat tours through the beautiful countryside. Lake Ohrid is on the border of Albania and Macedonia. It is one of the oldest and deepest lakes in the world. It is in a lovely nature reserve and surrounded by mountains. You can find rare fish here. You will feel like you are in the fjords on the reservoir on River Drin in the north of Albania.

En route

Filling up

Petrol (Euro Unleaded 95, Oktan 95, Benzinë pa plumb and Super Plus 98, Unleaded 98, Oktan 98) is readily available as is diesel (Diesel, Gazoil, Nafte).

LPG is available at a reasonable number of petrol stations. The Italian adapter (dish) is used for filling up with LPG. Petrol stations are usually open 24 hours a day. You can pay in cash everywhere, but it is not possible to pay by debit card or with a credit card at all places. There are petrol stations where the staff fill your car for you.

Charging

There are only a few charging points, and they are located around the capital of Tirana.

Roads and traffic

The roads in Albania are not the same quality as in other European countries. All sections of the main route from north to south and some large roads are in reasonable to good condition. The other roads can be narrow, and the road surface is often poorer quality. They are working hard on improving the roads, meaning you will often encounter road works. These are not always well signposted. So, you do need to pay attention and drive carefully in Albania. Also take care that your navigation system doesn't lead you away from the main roads. The Albanians don't always follow traffic rules, there could be slow-moving traffic or cattle wandering on the road.

Mountain roads

Most mountain roads are narrow, with many bends and some parts are steep. In the winter, the mountain roads in the north and southeast can be hazardous due to snow and ice.

Ferry services

You can reach Albania from Italy via various routes. Ferries often sail to Albania several times a week from Triëst, Ancona, Bari and Brindisi. Most ferries depart from Durrës, a harbour town close to Tirana.

You can also catch a boat from Brindisi to Vlorë and Sarandë in the south of Albania. A trip to Albania can easily be combined with the Greek island of Corfu. The boat departs from Sarandë.

Traffic regulations

Low beam headlights are compulsory in poor visibility, after dark and in tunnels. At a four-way intersection, traffic coming from the right has priority, unless traffic signs state otherwise. Trams and trains always have right of way. Drivers are only allowed to use mobile phones in hands-free mode. On mountain roads, uphill traffic has the right of way over downhill traffic. Children up to aged 12 must travel in a suitable child seat or booster seat, in the front seat as well as in the back. If a child is in the front seat of the car with their back facing forwards, the airbag must be deactivated.

Special regulations

We strongly advise against driving in the dark. Many of the roads are unlit. Only the important main roads have lighting. The streetlights also regularly fail. Vehicles frequently drive around without lights on.

Mandatory equipment

A warning triangle, first aid kit and safety vest are mandatory to have in your vehicle. It is advisable to take a safety vest for all occupants. Anyone walking on or along a road outside built-up areas in the dark or in poor visibility must wear a safety vest. It is also compulsory to have a set of spare lamps in the car. That does not apply to cars with xenon, neon or LED lamps. You are advised to take a fire extinguisher, spare tyre and tow rope with you.

Caravan and motorhome

A car-caravan combination can be a maximum of 4 metres high, 2.5 metres wide and 16.5 metres long (a single-axle caravan itself can be a maximum of 6.5 metres long and a twin-axle caravan can be 8 metres long). A motorhome can be a maximum of 8 metres long. Albania carries out strict checks on this and will not accept caravans or motorhomes that exceed the maximum length. Any bicycle carriers on the back are included in the length.

Cycling

Wearing a bicycle helmet is mandatory. The bike must have a bell and properly functioning brakes. You are not permitted to transport a passenger on the luggage carrier (children up to the age of 6 can be transported in a child seat). You are not permitted to cycle two abreast, but a child up to age 10 may cycle on the right next to an adult. Two people are only allowed to cycle next to each other on cycle paths.

Toll

The A1 is Albania's largest motorway. A toll is charged at the Kalimash tunnel.

Breakdown and accident

In poor visibility or when it is dark, a warning triangle is compulsory also if you are not visible in good time for other reasons such as at a bend or on a mountain. Place the warning triangle at least 50 metres behind the car. There is no roadside assistance in Albania. It can be extremely difficult to get spare parts for many car brands. Therefore, we recommend that you take some tools and spare parts with you, such as a jack, fan belt and windscreen wipers.

Call 112 in case of an accident, danger or if the car has broken down on a dangerous spot on the road. In the event of a breakdown, call the emergency number of your breakdown assistance provider.

Camping

Keep in mind that most campsites in Albania are lower quality than the European average. In most cases, the campsite will have electricity. Campsites are often near hotels and guest houses.

Free camping outside official campsites is allowed. It is always advisable to ask at the location to see whether it is allowed. Indeed, it is not permitted in national parks, on private property or in nature reserves.

Practical

Protect yourself against ticks, they can transmit diseases. Avoid contact with mammals due to the risk of rabies. You are advised to only eat fruit you have peeled yourself and well-cooked meat and fish. Euros are accepted as well but keep an eye on the exchange rate.

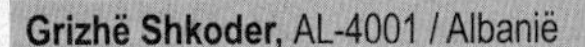

Grizhë Shkoder, AL-4001 / Albanië

821

- Hysaj Agroturizëm Camping
- Balshaj
- +355 6 96 31 77 73
- 1/1 - 31/12
- info@hysajagroturizem.al

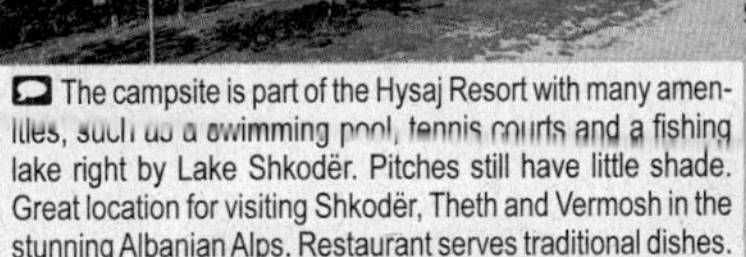

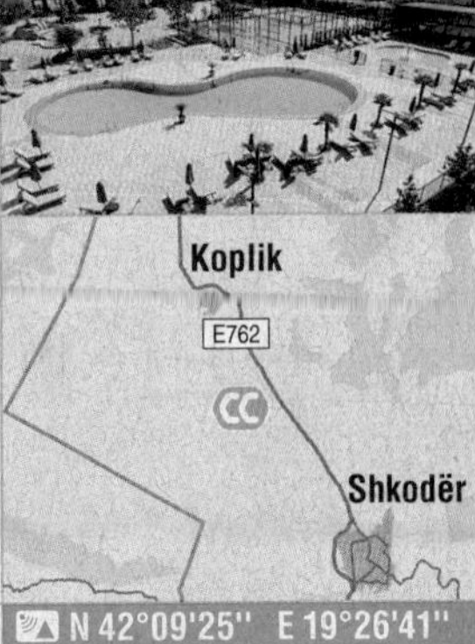

8ha 50T(40-80m²) 16A CEE

1 BCDIKLMNOQRS
2 FIOSXY
3 AMOPWZ
4 (B 1/6-15/9)(G 1/6-15/6) (Q+T+U+Y+Z)
5 ABGIJKLMNOPUWZ
6 CEFGKT

The campsite is part of the Hysaj Resort with many amenities, such as a swimming pool, tennis courts and a fishing lake right by Lake Shkodër. Pitches still have little shade. Great location for visiting Shkodër, Theth and Vermosh in the stunning Albanian Alps. Restaurant serves traditional dishes.

Coming from Montenegro (20 km) or Shkodër (8 km), the campsite and Hysaj Resort are signposted on the SH1. After the exit, follow the road for approx. 2 km.

CC € 17 *1/1-15/6 1/9-31/12*

N 42°09'25'' E 19°26'41''

Himare, AL-9425 / Albanië

822

- Moskato Camping
- Road Himare-Livadh, 2.1 km
- +355 6 74 90 55 19
- 1/1 - 31/12
- vasil_joshi@hotmail.co.uk

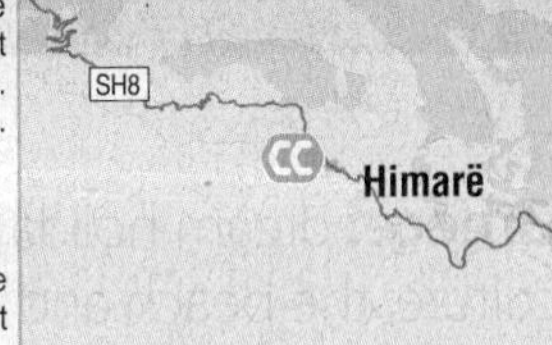

0,7ha 55T(50-70m²) 16A

1 BCIKLMNOQRS
2 HPSTXY
3 MY
4 (Q+S+T+U+Y+Z)
5 AGIJKLMNOPUWZ
6 CEFGKW

The campsite is right by the lovely beach of Livadh. Free choice of pitch and not all are completely demarcated, some with shade. Sun loungers included in the price. Renovated toilet and washing facilities. Restaurant and supermarket present. Great location for relaxing and enjoying the beach and sea.

From Vlore via SH8, take exit to Livadh about 5 km before Himare. Campsite is signposted after ca. 2.5km at the start of the promenade.

CC € 23 *1/5-30/6 1/9-1/10*

N 40°06'35'' E 19°43'22''

Omaraj, AL-4001 / Albanië

823

- Lake Shkodra Resort****
- Rruga E Liqenit
- +355 6 92 75 03 37
- 1/4 - 31/10
- faye@lakeshkodraresort.com

2,4ha 101T(80-100m²) 8-16A

1 BCDGKLMNOQRS
2 FINOSTVYZ
3 AMSWZ
4 (Q+R+T+U+V+Y+Z)
5 ABFGIJKLMNOPUWX
6 BCEFGK(N 7km)T

The campsite is by Lake Shkodra. Spacious luxury pitches with plenty of shade. Private beach with sun loungers. The restaurant by the lake serves delicious local dishes. Great starting point for visiting Vermosh and Theth in the Albanian Alps. The campsite organises excursions to there.

From Shkodra (after 7 km) or Montenegro (after 20 km), Lake Shkodra Resort campsite is signposted on the SH1. After exiting, drive for ca. 1 km.

CC € 19 *1/5-1/6 1/9-1/10*

N 42°08'18'' E 19°28'02''

Greece

Greece: dream holiday for lovers of culture, the beach and nature

Greece is located in the southeast of Europe and has been popular with holidaymakers for a long time already because of the many hours of sunshine and the expansive Mediterranean Coast. Campers are happy to make the slightly longer journey with their motorhome or caravan to spend their holiday at a campsite in Greece. With the exception of an impressive number of monuments from classical antiquity, camping in Greece has a great deal more to offer. For example: breath-takingly beautiful islands and friendly, hospitable people. And the sun shines everywhere you go!

Capital: Athens
Currency: euro
Time zone: UTC +2, UTC +3 (March to October)
Language: Greek
International dialling code: +30
Alcohol limit: 0.5‰; 0.2‰ for drivers that have had their driving licence for less than 2 years
Emergency number: police, fire brigade and ambulance: 112 (individual numbers as well: police 100, fire brigade 199, ambulance 166, tourist police 171)
Tap water: safe, but many people drink bottled water

From the Butterfly Gorge to the Greek Caribbean

Camping in Greece is not just a dream holiday for every culture enthusiast. What you find around the campsites in Greece with respect to the cultural-historic heritage is, of course, overwhelming. But the countryside in the area of your campsite is breath-taking: the famous 'Butterfly Gorge' on Crete, Mount Olympus and fields of olive trees everywhere, glowing in the soft sunlight. Lovers of sports can hike and climb in the country's many mountains and national parks – the Vikos Gorge in the Pundus Mountains in Epirus, for example. Beach lovers can sunbathe along the Mediterranean Coast. The area in West Greece around Syvota and Parga, also called the Greek Caribbean, is particularly beautiful.

"Camping in Greece means enjoying Greek hospitality to the max."

Mr N. Renes, inspector 1072

Beaches and delicious food

Most of the beaches along the thousands of kilometres of coast are in small bays and consist of fine pebbles, which means that the seawater is crystal clear. You can imagine yourself in a completely different world on the countless islands in their white cities with narrow, winding streets.

Do take the time to enjoy typical Greek street food outdoors: delicious grilled meat, fish, wine, ouzo, olives and feta.

Discovery trip

There is also much to discover on the Greek mainland. The Peloponnese peninsula in South Greece is separated from the mainland by the Corinth Canal and offers fascinating archaeological sites like Mycene. Wonderful hiking can be done in Thessaly. The Attica region is particularly famous for its capital city, Athens. Other popular holiday areas for campers are Central Macedonia and West Greece.

En route

Filling up

Unleaded petrol (Unleaded and Super plus 100) and diesel (Petroleo) are widely available. LPG is also widely available; when filling up, the Italian connection (dish) is used. In and around large cities, fuelling stations are usually open 24 hours a day, while elsewhere they are open between 7:00 and 21:00. Many manned petrol stations have full service, where tipping is customary. It is often prohibited to take along fuel in a reserve tank on ships.

Winners in Greece

836	***Best campsite***	Camping Ionion Beach
837	***Best location for a campsite***	Camping Aginara Beach
841	***Best campsite restaurant***	Camping Drepanos
844	***Campsite with the best toilet facilities***	Camping Hellas

Winner: Camping Aginara Beach

Charging

The network of charging stations is not yet well-established. Plan your visit well.

Ferries

Information about crossing times, departure times and rates can be found at ferry companies such as europeanseaways.com, grimaldi-lines.com, minoan.gr, superfast.com and ventourisferries.com. Rates depend on the season and departure time. It is recommended that you reserve on time.
Check beforehand with the ferry company whether gas bottle can be taken along on the boat. It is often prohibited to take along fuel in a reserve tank. Keep in mind that the number of places for motorhomes is limited on ferries. If you are travelling to Greece through Italy in the high season, it is wise to book early. Tickets for ferry services between the Greek islands are best purchased a day before you leave.

Traffic regulations

Low beam headlights are mandatory when visibility is poor, when it is dark and in tunnels. At equivalent crossings, traffic from the right has right of way. On a roundabout that has no right-of-way sign (or traffic light), drivers on the roundabout must give right of way to drivers coming from the right. Uphill traffic on mountain roads has priority over downhill traffic. You may only call handsfree and may not wear headphones or earbuds. Children shorter than 1.35 metres must be in a child's seat.

Special regulations

Smoking in the car is prohibited if a child under the age of 12 is present. In the countryside, you are advised to always give right of way to local traffic such as agricultural machines. Parking by a yellow line is prohibited.

Mandatory equipment

A warning triangle, first-aid box and fire extinguisher are mandatory in the car. It is also recommended to take along safety vests and a torch.

Caravan and motorhome

A motorhome or car-caravan combination may be a maximum of 4 metres high, 2.55 metres wide and 18 metres long (the caravan itself may be a maximum of 12 metres long).

Cycling

A bicycle helmet is not mandatory. Calling or texting while cycling is prohibited. You are not allowed to transport a passenger on the baggage rack (but may transport a child in a child's seat). Cycling side-by-side is prohibited.

> *"Greece has everything for an amazing holiday: culture, beautiful beaches, nature, friendly people, delicious Greek food."*
>
> Mr S. Kampherbeek, inspector 17

Toll

You must pay toll on most Greek motorways. Keep cash handy. Not all means of payments are accepted everywhere. If you are travelling with car and caravan, you must often pay a double rate. For motorhomes, the rate is often even higher. More information can be found at the websites of the road

maintenance authorities: egnatia.eu, kentrikiodos.gr, aegeanmotorway.gr, aodos.gr/en, neaodos.gr, kentrikiodos.gr, moreas.com.gr, olympiaodos.gr, gefyra.gr.

Breakdown and accident

Place your warning triangle at least 100 metres behind the car if it is not properly visible to other traffic. All passengers are advised to wear a safety vest. If you have had a breakdown, call the alarm number of your breakdown assistance insurer.

Camping

Most campsites are of a very good quality. The toilet facilities may be somewhat dated but they are usually well maintained. Campsites with clearly defined pitches can be found on the mainland and the Peloponnese peninsula. The campsites on the smaller Greek islands focus mainly on tent campers. Keep in mind that most campsites along the sea are considerably less busy during the early and late seasons than in July and August. You might not be able to make use of all amenities then. Free camping (outside of campsites) is prohibited.

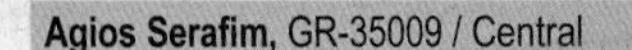

Agios Serafim, GR-35009 / Central

824

Camping Venezuela
Kamena Vourla
+30 22 35 04 16 91
1/5 - 31/10
camping@venezuela.gr

1,6ha 90T(60-80m²) 10A

1 ACDIKLMNORS
2 AHIQSTUWXYZ
3 AWY
4 (Q+R+U+Y)
5 AFGIJKLMNOPUWX
6 CEFGK(N 3km)OPTV

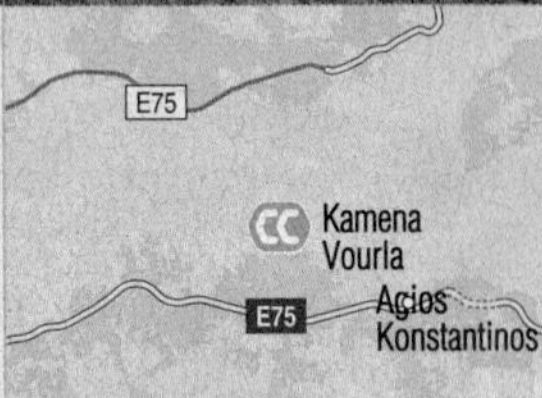

On the Maliakos Gulf, with the child-friendly beach of Agios Serafim. Quiet in a natural green area, shaded pitches and many sights in the surrounding area. An ideal destination for a longer stay. Good location for visiting Athens, 1.5 hours. Lovely restaurant with traditional Greece dishes.

From Athens-Thessaloniki E75, exit Molos. Direction Agios Serafim and follow campsite signs.

E75
Kamena Vourla
E75
Agios Konstantinos

CC € 21 *1/5-30/6 24/8-30/10*

N 38°49'23'' E 22°42'56''

Amaliada/Palouki, GR-27200 / Peloponnese

825

Camping Paradise
Palouki Ilia Peloponnese
+30 26 22 02 88 40
1/1 - 31/12
info@camping-paradise.gr

25ha 200T 10A

1 AIKLMNORS
2 AHIJSTXY
3 APWY
4 (Q+R 15/5-31/12)
(T+X+Y 15/5-30/9)
(Z 15/6-31/12)
5 AGIJKLMOPUW
6 EFGK(N 5km)PTV

A campsite located directly by the sea with unmarked pitches on grassy fields, a clean beach and sea. Many tourist sights in the immediate surroundings. The campsite has a good restaurant with traditional Greek dishes.

Located on the Patras-Pirgos road. About 70 km past Patras, turn right at exit Palouki. Follow signs (about 2 km).

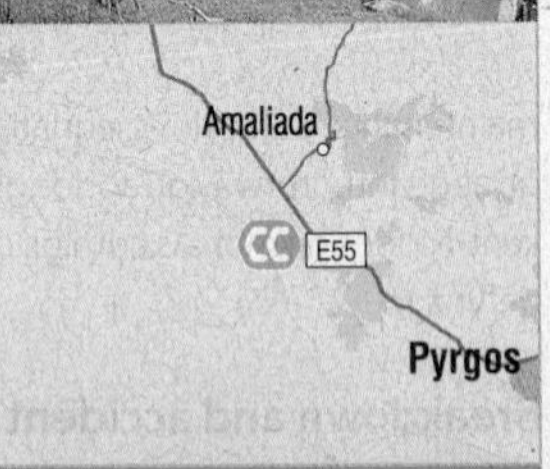

CC € 21 *1/1-20/6 1/9-31/12*

N 37°45'28'' E 21°18'17''

Ancient Epidavros, GR-21059 / Peloponnese

826

Camping Bekas
Nikolaou Pitidi
+30 2 75 30 99 93 01
25/3 - 31/10
contact@bekas.gr

2,6ha 100T(60-120m²) 16A

1 ACIKLMNORS
2 GLPTUXYZ
3 MPUWY
4 (Q+R)(Y 15/5-20/9)
5 AFGIJKLMNOPUVZ
6 ACEFGK(N 2km)OPVW

Located right by the sea with shaded pitches under tall trees. Close to Mycene, Nafplion and the most well-preserved theatre from ancient Greece: Epidaurus. Restaurant and small supermarket at the campsite. CampingCard ACSI rate does not apply for the first row by the sea.

Korinth, dir. Epidavros. Take Ancient Epidavros, Kranidi, Portocheli, Galatas, Ermioni exit. Follow road and after ±150m left under the road and left again at small roundabout. Then follow campsite signs.

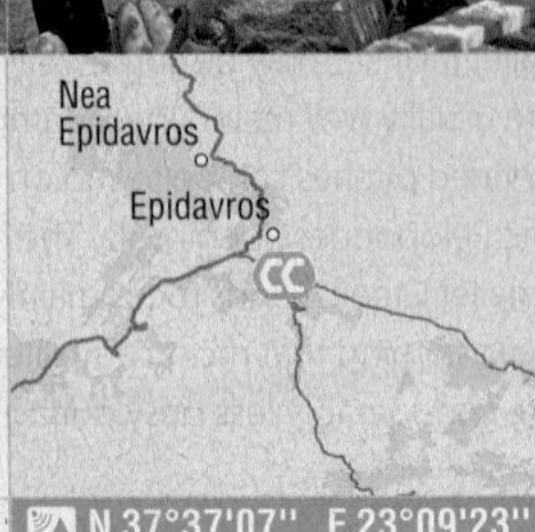

CC € 23 *25/3-30/6 11/9-31/10*

N 37°37'07'' E 23°09'23''

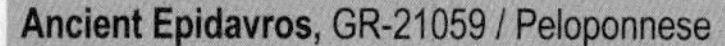

Ancient Epidavros, GR-21059 / Peloponnese

827

Camping Nicolas I
+30 27 53 04 12 97
1/4 - 31/10
info@nicolasgikas.gr

1ha 90T(20-50m²) 16A

1 ACIKLMNORS
2 GMOPQTUWYZ
3 UWY
4 (Q)(R+T 15/5-30/9) (Y 20/4-31/10)(Z 15/4-15/10)
5 **A**GIJKLMNOPUWZ
6 EFGK(N 1km)W

Plenty of space for guests and excellent communal facilities, all this in a lavishly green location directly by the sea. Convenient location near some of the most interesting sights dating back to ancient times. Campsite has a meadow with sun loungers.

Korinth direction Epidavros. Take Ancient Epidavros, Kranidi, Portocheli, Galatas, Ermioni exit. Follow road and after ±150m left under the road and left again at small roundabout. Then follow camping signs.

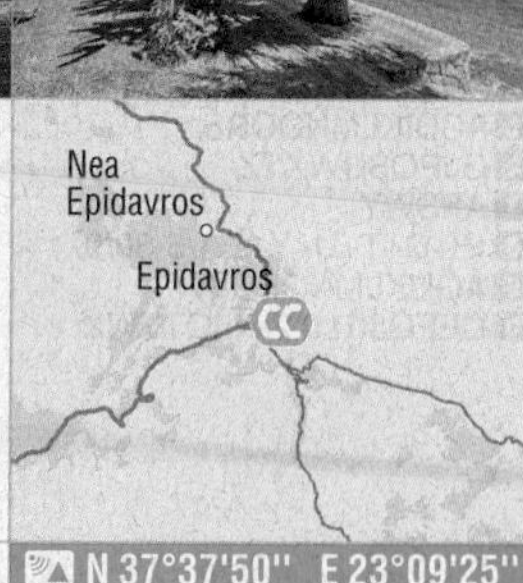

CC € 23 *1/4-20/6 1/9-31/10*

N 37°37'50'' E 23°09'25''

Ancient Epidavros, GR-21059 / Peloponnese

828

Camping Verdelis Beach
+30 27 53 04 20 05
1/4 - 31/10
campingverdelis@gmail.com

0,8ha 56T(30-70m²) 16A

1 ACIKLMNOR
2 AGPTWYZ
3 UWY
4 (Q)(R 1/4-31/10)(T) (Y 1/4-31/10)
5 **A**GIJKLMNOPUVZ
6 CFGK(N 2km)PV

Family campsite by the sea with pitches under the shade of tall trees. All facilities present for a comfortable and pleasant stay. Ideal location for visiting the archaeological sites in the area. You will receive a personal and warm welcome.

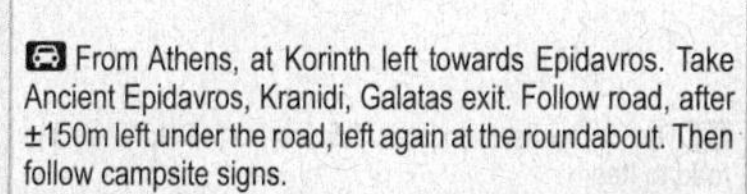

From Athens, at Korinth left towards Epidavros. Take Ancient Epidavros, Kranidi, Galatas exit. Follow road, after ±150m left under the road, left again at the roundabout. Then follow campsite signs.

CC € 21 *1/4-20/6 1/9-31/10*

N 37°37'08'' E 23°09'23''

Ancient Epidavros/Argolida, GR-21059 / Peloponnese

829

Camping Nicolas II
Nikolaou Pitidi
+30 69 73 79 28 89
22/3 - 31/10
dimitris.gikas@gmail.com

1,2ha 90T(35-50m²) 16A

1 AIKLMNORS
2 GMPSTUYZ
3 UWY
4 (Q)(R+Y 15/4-30/9) (Z 15/4-31/10)
5 **A**FGIJKLMNOPUWXZ
6 ABCEFGK(N 3km)OPW

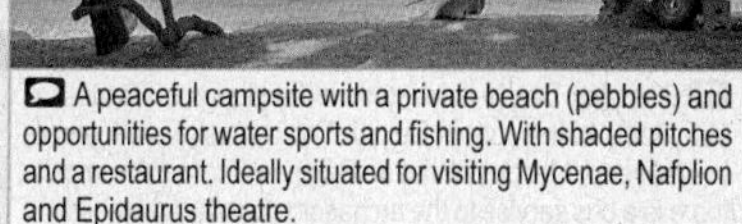

A peaceful campsite with a private beach (pebbles) and opportunities for water sports and fishing. With shaded pitches and a restaurant. Ideally situated for visiting Mycenae, Nafplion and Epidaurus theatre.

Korinth, direction Epidavros. Take Ancient Epidavros, Kranidi, Portocheli, Galatas, Ermioni exit. Follow road and after ±150m left under the road and left again at small roundabout. Then follow camping signs.

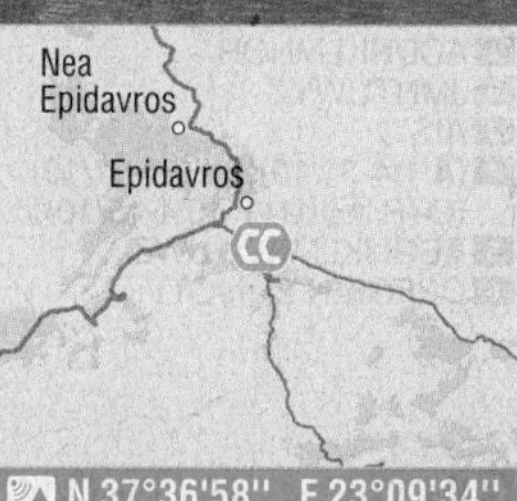

CC € 23 *22/3-30/6 1/9-31/10*

N 37°36'58'' E 23°09'34''

Dassia (Corfu), GR-49083 / Ionian Islands

830

Camping Karda Beach and Bungalows
PB 225
+30 26 61 09 35 95
27/4 - 7/10
campco@otenet.gr

2,6ha 130T(60-120m²) 16A

1 ACDIKLMNOQ**R**S
2 GJPQSUWXYZ
3 APSWY
4 (B+G+T+U+Y+Z 1/5-30/9)
5 **A**GIJKLMNOPUVW
6 CEFGJ(N 0,2km)OTVWX

Campsite by the sea 12 km from Corfu town in natural surroundings. Marked out shaded pitches on level ground with attractive landscaping. The toilet facilities are extensive and well maintained. Lovely swimming pool with nearby bar and restaurant.

From Corfu harbour take main road to Paleokastritsa. Turn right at the Dassia/Kassiopi sign after about 8.5 km. Campsite located 3.5 km further on the right. Entrance clearly signposted.

CC € 25 *27/4-30/6 1/9-7/10*

N 39°41'10'' E 19°50'19''

Delphi, GR-33054 / Central

831

Camping Apollon Cat.A
Apollonstr 70
+30 22 65 08 27 50
1/1 - 31/12
apollon4@otenet.gr

2,5ha 120T(30-70m²) 16A

1 ACDHKLMNO**R**S
2 JLMNTWYZ
3 AIMPS
4 (**A** 1/5-31/8)(B 1/4-15/10)
(Q+R+U+Y+Z 1/5-1/10)
5 **A**EGIJKLMNOPUWXZ
6 CDEFG**K**(N 1,5km)OPTV

A good campsite with all modern amenities, within walking distance of Ancient Delphi. Unforgettable views of Itea bay from the swimming pool and from the restaurant with traditional Greek cuisine. Free transfer to the archeological site and museum for CampingCard ACSI holders.

The campsite is located 1.5 km from Delphi, on the road to Itea.

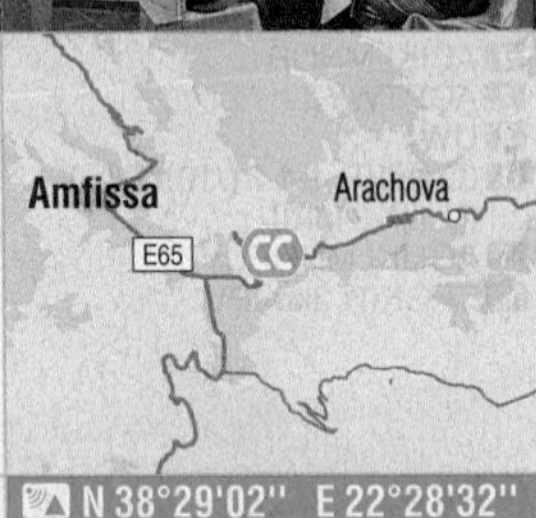

CC € 25 *1/1-7/7 24/8-31/12*

N 38°29'02'' E 22°28'32''

Delphi, GR-33054 / Central

832

Delphi Camping Cat.A
Delphi-Itea Road
+30 22 65 08 27 45
1/1 - 31/12
info@delphicamping.com

2,2ha 100T(60-80m²) 10A

1 ACD**H**KLMNOR
2 JMNTUWYZ
3 AIS
4 (**A** 1/4-31/10)(B 20/4-31/10)
(Q+R)(U+Y 15/4-15/10)
5 **A**EGIJKLMNOPUWZ
6 CEFGK(N 2km)OTV

Camping Delphi is located on the slopes of Parnassos Mountain, 4 km south of Delphi. The campsite produces its own olive oil 'Mer des olivier de Delphes'. From the campsite there is a bus service to the archaeological site and museum. From the patio and restaurant, you have magnificent views of the Gulf of Corinth. The campsite is ACSI Award 2022 winner of the 'Best location in Greece'.

Located on the Itea-Delphi road 4 km before Delphi.

Amfissa
Arachova
E65

CC € 25 *1/4-30/6 1/9-30/10*

N 38°28'42'' E 22°28'31''

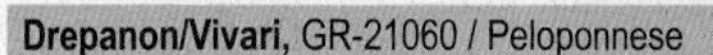

Drepanon/Vivari, GR-21060 / Peloponnese

833

Camping Lefka Beach
+30 27 52 09 23 34
1/1 - 31/12
info@camping-lefka.gr

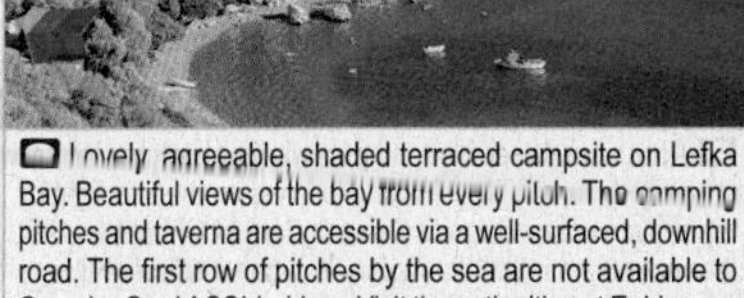

1,4ha 68T(25-60m²) 16A

1 ACDIKLMNOHUV
2 GLMPTUYZ
3 UWY
4 (Q 15/4-30/10)
(R+T+Y+Z 1/4-30/10)
5 **AB**GIJKLMNOPUZ
6 ABCEFGK(N 1km)PV

Lovely agreeable, shaded terraced campsite on Lefka Bay. Beautiful views of the bay from every pitch. The camping pitches and taverna are accessible via a well-surfaced, downhill road. The first row of pitches by the sea are not available to CampingCard ACSI-holders. Visit the antiquities at Epidavros, Ancient Korinthe, Myecne, Argos and Nafplion.

Situated on the Nafplion-Drepanon-Iria road. About 1 km to the right after village of Vivari. Campsite signposted.

CC € 21 *1/1-30/6 1/9-31/12*

N 37°32'02'' E 22°55'54''

Elafonisos, GR-23053 / Peloponnese

834

Simos Camping
+30 27 34 02 26 72
20/4 - 31/10
info@simoscamping.gr

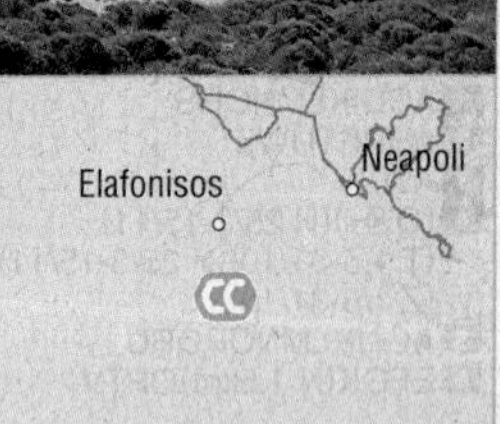

6ha 190T(35-60m²) 16A

1 ACDIKLMNOQR
2 AGNVWXYZ
3 AK**O**VY
4 (Q)
(S+T+U+V+W+Z 15/5-20/9)
5 **AB**GIJKLMNOPUWZ
6 CDGJ(N 4km)PTV

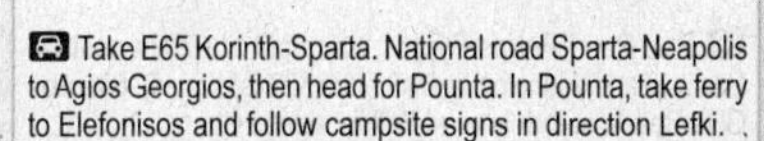

Situated on beautiful sandy beach with dunes on idyllic island of Elafonisos, a protected nature reserve. The water is crystal clear blue/green in color. Special marked out pitches for tents and caravans/motorhomes with shade nets and trees. Good facilities and self-service restaurant.

Take E65 Korinth-Sparta. National road Sparta-Neapolis to Agios Georgios, then head for Pounta. In Pounta, take ferry to Elefonisos and follow campsite signs in direction Lefki.

CC € 25 *1/5-15/6 11/9-31/10*

N 36°28'38'' E 22°58'29''

Finikounda, GR-24006 / Peloponnese

835

Camping Thines
+30 27 23 07 12 00
1/1 - 31/12
thines@otenet.gr

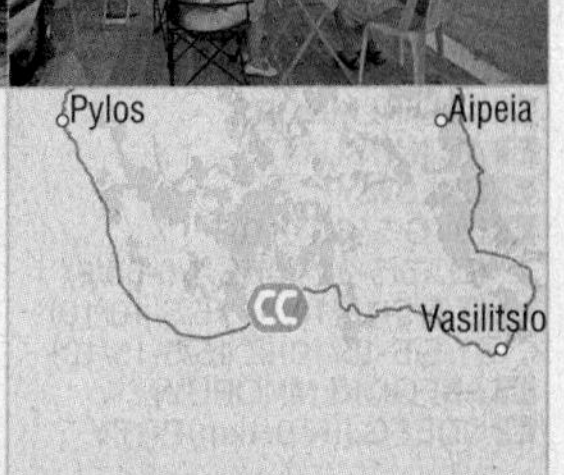

0,8ha 55T(49-56m²) 10A

1 ACDIKLMN**RS**
2 AGNUVWYZ
3 MNWY
4 (Q 1/5-31/10)
(R+T 15/5-31/10)
(U+X 1/1-31/12)
(Z 15/5-31/10)
5 **A**FGIJKLMNOPUWZ
6 CEFGK(N 0,8km)PTV

Quiet family campsite with immaculate toilet/washing facilities. Located by the wide sandy beach at Finikounda. Swimming, water sports (incl. surfing) or sunbathing. Delicious food in the restaurant, incl. locally grown produce (2-3 times a week, Tuesday and Fridays in any case).

National road Methoni-Koroni. Campsite is located 1 km west of Finikounda and is well signposted.

CC € 19 *1/1-30/6 1/9-31/12* ***30=28***

N 36°48'18'' E 21°47'43''

Glifa, GR-27050 / Peloponnese

836

Camping Ionion Beach*****
Glyfa
+30 26 23 09 68 28
1/1 - 31/12
ionionfl@otenet.gr

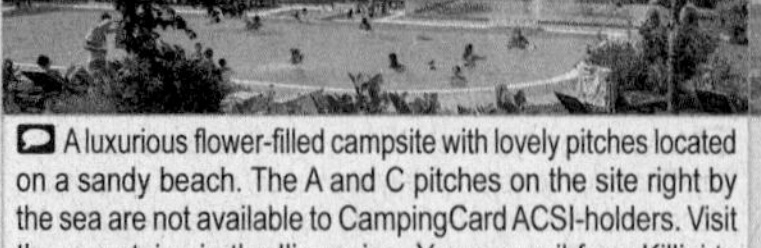

3,8ha 210T(50-120m²) 16A

1 ACDIJKLMNOQRS
2 AHPSTUWYZ
3 ACPSWY
4 (C+H 1/4-30/10)K
(Q+R+T+V+Y+Z 1/4-31/10)
5 **AB**DEGIJKLMNOPUWZ
6 ACEFGK(N 1km)OPSTV

A luxurious flower-filled campsite with lovely pitches located on a sandy beach. The A and C pitches on the site right by the sea are not available to CampingCard ACSI-holders. Visit the mountains in the Ilia region. You can sail from Killini to the beautiful island of Zakynthos.

From national road Patras-Pirgos, turn right via Gastouni and Vartalomia at km post 67 direction Loutra Killini. Left at fork in road towards Glifa Beach. Follow signs.

E55 Gastouni Vartholomio

CC € 25 *1/1-30/6 11/9-31/12*

N 37°50'11'' E 21°08'01''

Glifa/Ilias, GR-27050 / Peloponnese

837

Camping Aginara Beach***
+30 26 23 09 62 11
1/1 - 31/12

3,8ha 120T(70-100m²) 16A

1 ACDIKLMNORS
2 AHPSTUWZ
3 AWY
4 (Q)(R 25/3-15/11)
(T 1/5-31/10)(Y 25/3-15/11)
(Z 1/5-31/10)
5 **A**GIJKLMNOPQRU
6 EFGK(N 1,5km)OPTV

A campsite located on one of the most beautiful sandy beaches of the Ionian Sea with spacious, idyllic and mostly shaded pitches. Good lively restaurant. Modern, well maintained toilet facilities. Various trees, bushes and abundant plants ensure a wonderful stay.

Nat. Road Patras-Pyrgos, turn right at 67 km post via Gastouni and Vartholomio. Dir. Loutra Killinis (signed). Direction Glifa Beach at fork in road Follow signs.

E55 Gastouni Vartholomio

CC € 23 *1/1-30/6 26/8-31/12*

N 37°50'18'' E 21°07'47''

Gythion/Lakonias, GR-23200 / Peloponnese

838

Camping Gythion Bay***
Highway Gythion-Areopoli
+30 27 33 02 25 22
1/4 - 31/10
info@gythiocamping.gr

4ha 300T(30-100m²) 16A

1 ACDIKLMNO**R**S
2 AHJNPSUXYZ
3 CKLSWY
4 (B+G 5/4-31/10)
(Q 15/5-31/10)(S 1/6-30/9)
(T 5/5-15/10)(U 15/5-10/10)
(Y 5/5-15/10)(Z 15/5-15/10)
5 **AB**FGIJKLMNOPUW
6 CDEFGJ(N 0,1km)PRTV

You will always find a free, shaded pitch under the olive and orange trees. Totally renovated, modern toilet facilities. Located right by the sea with a lovely sandy beach. Also new swimming pool near the restaurant and bar.

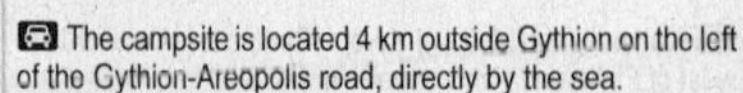

The campsite is located 4 km outside Gythion on the left of the Gythion-Areopolis road, directly by the sea.

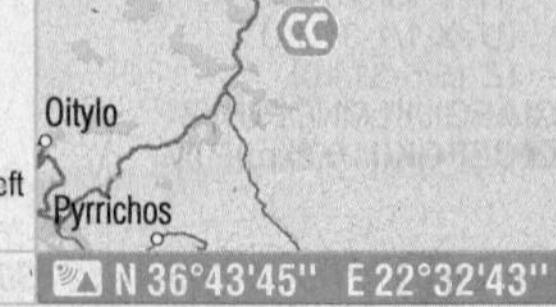

CC € 25 *1/4-30/6 16/9-31/10*

N 36°43'45'' E 22°32'43''

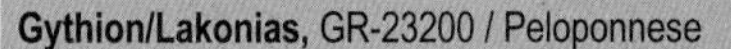

Gythion/Lakonias, GR-23200 / Peloponnese

839

- Camping Mani-Beach
- Highway Gythion-Areopoli
- +30 27 33 02 11 30
- 1/1 - 31/12
- info@mani-beach.gr

2,0ha 201T(40-100m²) 16A

1. ACDIKLMNORS
2. AHJNPSUVWXYZ
3. CSWY
4. (Q 1/4-15/10) (R+T+U+Y+Z 2/5-30/9)
5. **A**GIJKLMNOPUWZ
6. CEFGJ(N 0,2km)OPRTV

Large campsite on the coast with a wide sandy beach. Pitches in almost full shade. Ideal for all types of water sports, particularly windsurfing and kitesurfing.

The campsite is located about 4 km south of Gythion on the road to Areopolis, directly by the sea.

Prosilio, E961, Gythelo, Oitylo

CC € 21 *1/1-30/6 1/9-30/12*

N 36°43'42'' E 22°32'32''

Gythion/Lakonias, GR-23200 / Peloponnese

840

- Camping Meltemi***
- Highway Gythion-Areopoli
- +30 27 33 02 32 60
- 1/4 - 20/10
- reservations@campingmeltemi.gr

3ha 180T(40-80m²) 16A

1. ACDIKLMNORS
2. AHJNPSWYZ
3. COPSWY
4. (B 10/6-15/9)(Q)(R+S+T 1/5-15/9)(U 15/5-15/9)(W 1/5-15/9)(X 15/5-15/9)(Z 1/5-15/9)
5. **AB**EGIJKLMNOP**T**UWZ
6. CEFGJ(N 0,5km)OPRTV

The hospitable Camping Meltemi is located in a beautiful olive grove. It has spacious pitches with shade from olive and pine trees on a beautiful and clean sandy beach. The sea and the beach are a protected area for Caretta sea turtles. Well-maintained amenities. Close to the towers and Byzantine churches of Mani.

Campsite is about 3 km south of Gytheio on the left of the road to Areopoli.

E961, Gytheio, Mavrovouni

CC € 27 *1/4-30/6 1/9-20/10*

N 36°43'51'' E 22°33'12''

Igoumenitsa, GR-46100 / Epirus

841

- Camping Drepanos
- Drepanos Beach
- +30 26 65 02 69 80
- 1/1 - 31/12
- camping@drepano.gr

5ha 80T(30-100m²) 16A

1. ACDIKLMNOQRUV
2. AHJNUXYZ
3. AKWY
4. (Q)(R+U 15/5-10/10) (Y+Z 25/3-10/10)
5. **A**GIJKLMNOPUWZ
6. GK(N 4km)T

Campsite with a long, child-friendly sandy beach on a headland close to Igoumenitsa, next to an extensive nature reserve and bird sanctuary. The toilet facilities have been completely renewed, also for the disabled. Great restaurant and beach terrace. Many of the pitches are shaded under the trees. An ideal spot to relax, cycle or do watersports.

Take the coast road from Igoumenitsa northwards. After leaving the town follow Drepanos Beach signs.

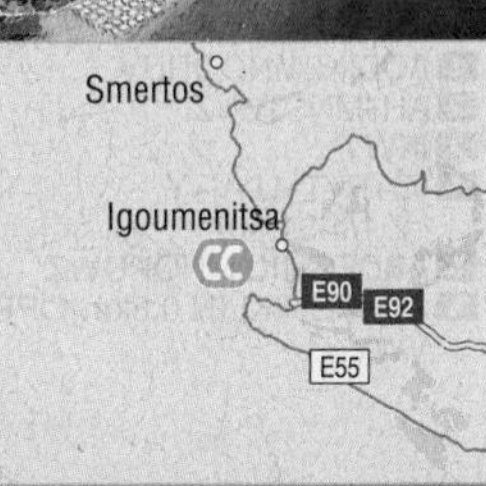

CC € 23 *1/1-30/6 1/9-31/12*

N 39°30'37'' E 20°13'16''

Kastraki/Kalambaka, GR-42200 / Thessalia Sporades

842

Camping Vrachos Kastraki
+30 24 32 02 22 93
1/1 - 31/12
tsourvaka@yahoo.gr

3,5ha 300T 16A

1 AIKLNOQRS
2 JSUYZ
3 U
4 (B 1/6-30/9)(Q+R)
(T+X+Y 1/4-30/10)
5 **A**EGIJKLMNOPUW
6 EFGJ(N 0,3km)OPTV

You can enjoy Greek hospitality at this lovely and well-run campsite at the foot of the Meteora; you will be surprised by a welcome and farewell present. Very high satisfaction ratings by camping guests for the past years. Highly recommended!

On arriving in Kalambaka take the road to Kastraki. The campsite is located 1 km further on, on the road to the Meteora abbey. The campsite is next to the bus stop.

Tymfaioi
E92
Kalampaka
Paralithaioi

CC € 25 *1/1-10/6 10/9-31/12*

N 39°42'48'' E 21°36'57''

Kato Alissos, GR-25002 / Peloponnese

843

Camping Kato Alissos**
+30 26 93 07 12 49
1/1 - 31/12
info@camping-kato-alissos.gr

1,2ha 60T(60-80m²) 6-10A

1 ACDIKLMN**R**S
2 HIJNPSUYZ
3 AWY
4 (Q+R)(U+Y+Z 1/5-30/9)
5 **A**GIJKLMNOPUWZ
6 EFGK(N 2km)OPTV

A natural rural setting. There are olive, lemon, and many other types of trees and plants on the campsite. Wonderful swimming in the sea and sunbathing on the gravel beach. Sample traditional dishes in the shade of 1000 year old olive trees with views of Patraikos Bay and the town of Patras.

New Nat. Road Patras-Pirgos. Turn right at km-marker 21, left at end of road onto Old Nat. Road; right after 700 metres, right at end of road. Follow the signs.

CC € 21 *1/1-30/6 1/9-31/12*

N 38°09'00'' E 21°34'38''

Kato Gatzea (Pilion), GR-37010 / Thessalia Sporades

844

Camping Hellas
Kato Gatzea
+30 24 23 02 22 67
15/1 - 15/12
info@campinghellas.gr

ACSI AWARDS WINNER

2ha 95T(60-100m²) 16A CEE

1 ACDIKLMNOQRUV
2 AHJMNSTUYZ
3 IKWY
4 (Q+R+T+U+V+Y
+Z 1/4-31/10)
5 **AB**DFGIJKLMNOPUWZ
6 ACEFGHIKL(N 0,8km)OPRT
VWX

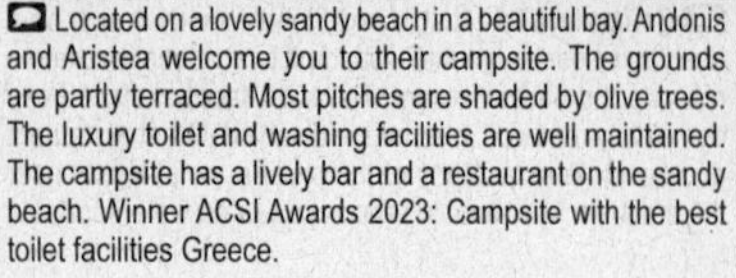

Located on a lovely sandy beach in a beautiful bay. Andonis and Aristea welcome you to their campsite. The grounds are partly terraced. Most pitches are shaded by olive trees. The luxury toilet and washing facilities are well maintained. The campsite has a lively bar and a restaurant on the sandy beach. Winner ACSI Awards 2023: Campsite with the best toilet facilities Greece.

In Volos follow Pilio/Argalasti. 18 km further on between Kato Gatzea and Kala Nera. Well signposted.

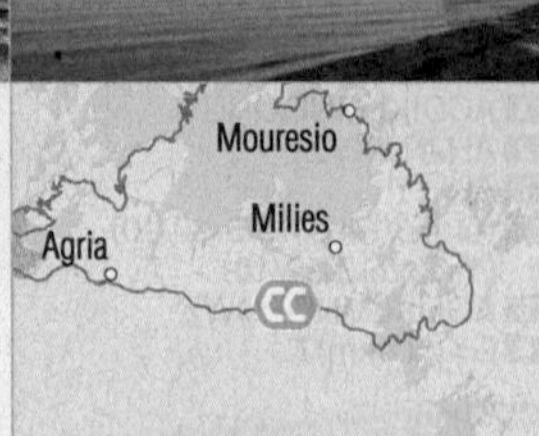

CC € 25 *1/2-23/6 16/9-14/12*

N 39°18'39'' E 23°06'33''

Kato Gatzea (Pilion), GR-37300 / Thessalia Sporades

845

- Camping Sikia
- Kato Gatzea
- +30 24 23 02 22 79
- 1/2 - 15/12
- info@camping-sikia.gr

3ha 120T 16A

1 ACDIKLMNOQRUV
2 AHJMNQSTUWXYZ
3 AIKLPWY
4 (**A** 1/5-15/9)(Q+S+T+U+V +Y+Z 1/4-15/10)
5 **A**FGIJKLMNOPQRUVWZ
6 ACEFGK(N 0,3km)OPRTV WX

A shaded campsite by a sandy beach in a beautiful bay. Many pitches with panoramic views. Well-maintained toilet and washing facilities and separate facilities for the disabled. Bar and restaurant are right on the sandy beach. The Sikia Taverne is the 2022 winner of the ACSI Awards in the category 'Best campsite restaurant in Greece'. Greek music regularly. Stunning area.

Follow Pilion/Argalasti in Volos. Campsite 18 km further in Kato Gatzea, well signposted.

CC € 25 *1/2-23/6 16/9-14/12*

N 39°18'37'' E 23°06'36''

Koroni/Messinias, GR-24004 / Peloponnese

846

- Camping Koroni
- Maizonos 27
- +30 27 25 02 21 19
- 1/1 - 31/10
- info@koronicamping.com

1,3ha 86T(25-80m²) 16A

1 ACDIKLMN**R**S
2 AGMSUWXYZ
3 SWY
4 (B+Q 1/4-31/10) (R 1/4-30/10) (T+U+Y+Z 1/4-31/10)
5 **A**GIJKLMNOPUWZ
6 ACDEFGK(N 0,2km)PV

The campsite is located near the picturesque town of Koroni. The grounds are largely shaded. There is a cozy restaurant with terrace next to the pool overlooking Koroni. Beach accessible by stairs/ path after 100 metres.

Kalamata to Pylos road, turn left at Rizomylos, continue to Koroni via Petalidi. Campsite on the left 200m before Koroni.

CC € 23 *1/1-15/6 14/9-31/10*

N 36°47'58'' E 21°57'01''

Lefkada, GR-31100 / Ionian Islands

847

- Kariotes Camping & Rooms
- Spasmeni Vrisi
- +30 26 45 07 11 03
- 15/4 - 15/10
- info@campingkariotes.gr

0,8ha 75T 16A

1 ACDIKLNOQ**R**
2 AGJPSUXYZ
3 AY
4 (B 20/5-20/9)(G 15/5-20/9) (Q+R 1/6-30/9) (T+U 15/5-30/9) (X 15/5-15/9)(Z 15/5-30/9)
5 **A**GIJKMOPUY
6 FGK(N 1,5km)RTV

The campsite is located 2 km from Lefkada town, excellent base for excursions. A small shaded campsite with a lovely swimming pool and taverna. The swimming pool, bar, restaurant and good toilet facilities, together with Greek hospitality offer an enjoyable stay. Welcome!

Campsite on the main Lefkada to Vasiliki road. Site 2 km south of Lefkada town, on the right of the road.

CC € 23 *15/4-9/7 26/8-15/10*

N 38°48'16'' E 20°42'52''

Leonidio, GR-22300 / Peloponnese

848

- Camping Semeli
- Plaka
- +30 27 57 02 29 95
- 1/1 - 31/12
- info@camping-semeli.gr

1,7ha 64T(40-70m²) 10-16A

1 ACDIKLMNOQRS
2 AHNPSTUVWXY
3 WY
4 (Q+R)(T 15/4-31/10) (Z 15/4-30/11)
5 **A**FGIJKLMNOPUVWZ
6 CDEFGK(N 4km)PV

Hospitable, friendly family campsite with floral vegetation. High quality sanitary and kitchen facilities, which are well maintained. Located at the foot of a mountain range, right by the sea/beach. A 300-metre walk to an idyllic Greek harbour.

Follow signs in Leonidio; 4 km from the centre in the direction of Leonidio harbour.

CC € 17 *1/1-30/6 30/9-31/12*

N 37°08'59'' E 22°53'31''

Nea Moudania, GR-63200 / Macedonia

849

- Oèlia Camping & Bungalows
- +30 23 73 04 29 22
- 1/5 - 30/9
- info@oelia.gr

0,8ha 60T(40-100m²) 6A

1 ACDIKLMNOQRS
2 AHIJSWXYZ
3 ASWY
4 (Q+S) (T+U+Y+Z 15/5-10/9)
5 **AB**GIJKLMNOPUVZ
6 ACEFGK(N 3,5km)OPRTV

This campsite is situated in a green surroundings for a comfortable and enjoyable stay. Luxury sanitary facilities. Shop has a very large selection of products. In the restaurant right on the beach you can enjoy your meal with a view over azure blue sea.

Nat. Road Thessaloniki-Kasandra, exit 2 km south of Nea Moudania take exit at "Local Roads". Right at end of road. Then left, follow Local Road beside motorway. Right after 1100m and take campsite on the left at end of road.

CC € 21 *1/5-30/6 20/8-29/9 7=6*

N 40°12'58'' E 23°19'06''

Nea Moudania, GR-63200 / Macedonia

850

- Ouzouni Beach Camping
- P.O Box 30
- +30 23 73 04 24 44
- 1/5 - 15/10
- info@ouzounibeach.gr

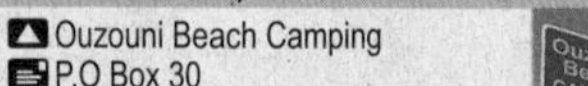

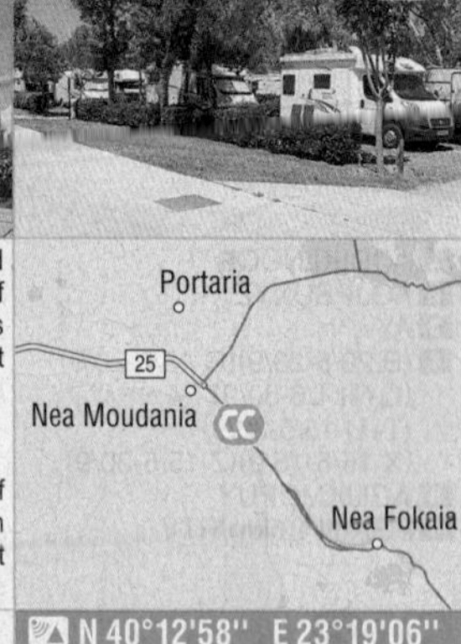

1,2ha 93T(65-85m²) 10A CEE

1 ACDIKLMNOQRS
2 AHIJSWYZ
3 WY
4 (Q+S+T+U)
5 **AB**EGIJKLMNPUVWX
6 ABCEFGK(N 3,5km)OPT

A modern campsite located by a beautiful beach. Good location for visits to Thessaloniki and the peninsulas of Kassandra, Sithonia and Athos. In 2022, this campsite was declared the Winner of the ACSI Award in the category 'Best motorhome pitches in Greece'.

Nat. Road Thessaloniki-Kasandra, exit 2 km south of Nea Moudania exit "Local Roads". Right at end of road. Then immediate left, follow Local Road parallel to motorway. Right after 1100m, right-hand campsite at end of road.

CC € 21 *1/5-30/6 26/8-14/10 7=6, 16=13*

N 40°12'58'' E 23°19'06''

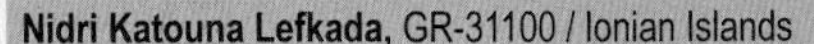

Nidri Katouna Lefkada, GR-31100 / Ionian Islands — 851

Camping Episkopos Beach
National Road Lefkas-Nidri
+30 26 45 07 13 88
15/4 - 31/10
campingvillageepiskopos@gmail.com

0,8ha 60T 10-16A

1 ACDIKLNRUV
2 GPTUZ
4 (B 1/6-30/9)(G+Q)
(T+Z 10/6-30/9)
5 AGIJKMOPUW
6 FGK(N 1km)QV

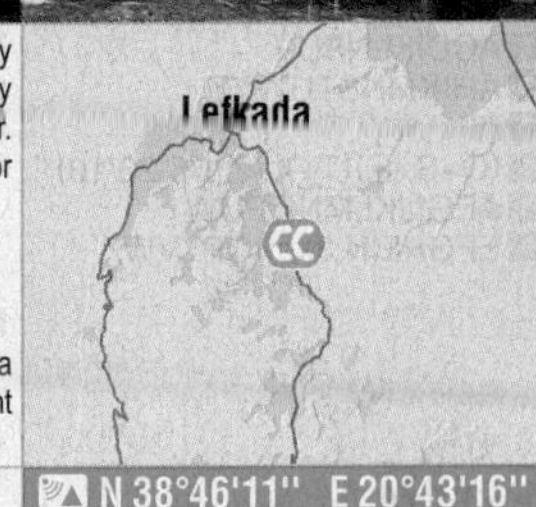

Typical Greek campsite under olive trees. Lefkada City is 8 km away, beach at 200 m and 1 km from the lovely village of Nikiana with its lovely tavernas by the small harbour. Lovely swimming pool beside the bar. Friendly welcome for a successful stay.

The campsite is situated along the main road from Lefkada to Vassiliki. The campsite is 8 km from Lefkada, on the right side of the road.

CC € 19 *15/4-9/7 26/8-31/10*

N 38°46'11'' E 20°43'16''

Nikiti, GR-63088 / Macedonia — 852

Mitari Camping & Villas
+30 23 75 07 17 75
1/5 - 30/9
mitaricamp@hotmail.com

2,5ha 70T(65-90m²) 10A

1 ACDHKLMNRS
2 AHJLMNSTUWYZ
3 WY
4 (Q+R)(Y+Z 15/5-30/9)
5 ABGIJKLMOPUVZ
6 CEFGKL(N 8km)PQTV

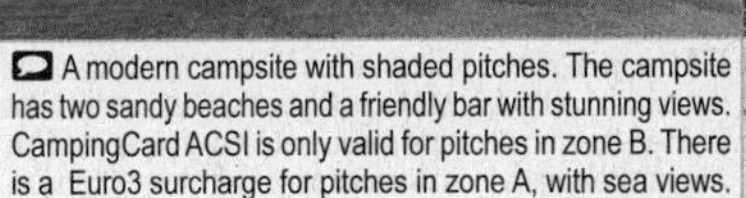

A modern campsite with shaded pitches. The campsite has two sandy beaches and a friendly bar with stunning views. CampingCard ACSI is only valid for pitches in zone B. There is a Euro3 surcharge for pitches in zone A, with sea views.

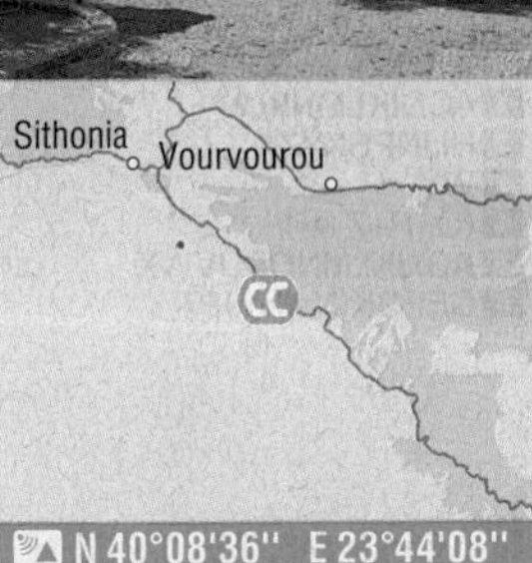

Follow the west coast of Sithonia, 12 km south of Nikiti on the right. Indicated by signs.

CC € 21 *1/5-30/6 24/8-29/9 7=6*

N 40°08'36'' E 23°44'08''

Panteleimon, GR-60065 / Macedonia — 853

Camping Poseidon Beach
Seaside Road
+30 23 52 04 16 54
1/4 - 31/10
poseidonbeach@gmail.com

1,7ha 27T(60-120m²) 6-16A

1 ACDGKLMNRS
2 AHISTWYZ
3 WY
4 (Z 1/5-10/9)
5 ABGIJKLMNOPUWZ
6 CEFGK(N 0,1km)TV

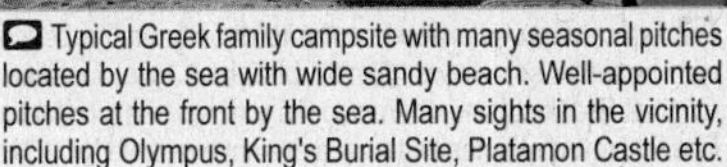

Typical Greek family campsite with many seasonal pitches located by the sea with wide sandy beach. Well-appointed pitches at the front by the sea. Many sights in the vicinity, including Olympus, King's Burial Site, Platamon Castle etc.

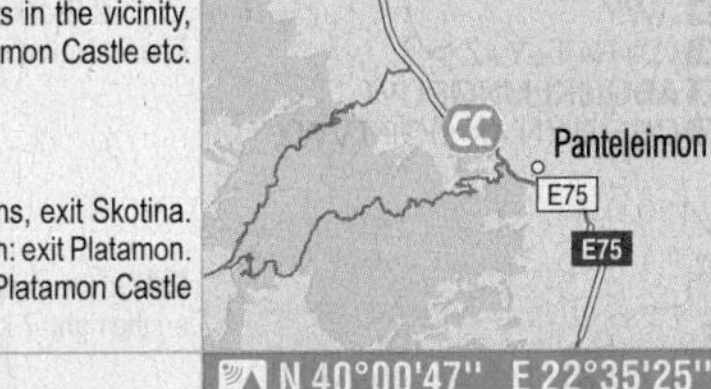

From north: A1/E75 Thessaloniki-Athens, exit Skotina. Follow Panteleimon Beach signs. From south: exit Platamon. Follow Panteleimon signs. After 3 km near Platamon Castle direction Panteleimon Beach. Follow road.

CC € 21 *1/4-15/7 1/9-30/10 7=6*

N 40°00'47'' E 22°35'25''

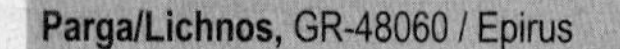

Parga/Lichnos, GR-48060 / Epirus

854

Camping Enjoy Lichnos
+30 26 84 03 13 71
1/4 - 31/10
holidays@enjoy-lichnos.net

4,8ha 134T 5-16A

1 ACDIKLNRUV
2 AHIKMNSTUWYZ
3 IY
4 (Q+S)(T+X+Z 1/5-20/10)
5 AEGIJKLMNOPUW
6 EFGKL(N 3km)OPTVW

A modern, well maintained terraced campsite with great toilet facilities, located on one of the most beautiful bays in Greece. Various watersports. Beautiful views of the Ionian Sea. Taxi boats from the campsite to Parga and back.

Take Igoumenitsa road to Parga. Exit to Parga. Or take the new Igoumenitsa road to Ioannina, exit Parga. Campsite is by the bay, on the left, 3 km before Parga, follow the signs. At end of gate, down the road on the right.

Perdika
Parga
E55
Fanari

CC € 27 *1/4-12/6 12/9-31/10*

N 39°17'01'' E 20°25'59''

Plaka Litochoro, GR-60063 / Macedonia

855

Camping Sylvia
+30 23 52 02 21 04
1/4 - 31/10
campingsylvia@gmail.com

0,8ha 45T(60-80m²) 16A CEE

1 ACDIKLMNRUV
2 HIJNPSXYZ
3 WY
4 (Q+R+Z)
5 AGIJKLMNOPUVWX
6 CEFGK(N 4km)PT

Campsite without residential seasonal pitches. Situated by the sea and at the foot of Mount Olympus. The modern toilet facilities, the site with ample shade and panoramic views of the Aegean Sea make for a pleasant stay. Visit Mount Olympus, Platamon Castle and the old village of Dion. Also possible to visit the campsite outside opening hours.

Via A1/E75, exit Plaka Litochoro. Dir. Plaka Litochoro and follow coastal road south. After 1 km campsite located between road and sea.

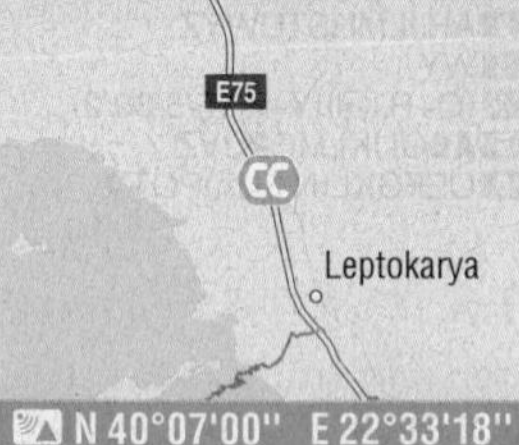

CC € 21 *1/4-30/6 1/9-30/10*

N 40°07'00'' E 22°33'18''

Plataria/Igoumenitsa, GR-46100 / Epirus

856

Camping Kalami Beach
+30 26 65 07 12 11
1/4 - 30/10
info@campingkalamibeach.gr

1,2ha 67T 4-10A

1 ACDIKLMNOQRS
2 HJLMNPUXYZ
3 AWY
4 (Q+R+T+Y+Z)
5 ABGIJKLMNOPUW
6 CEFGK(N 4km)OPTVWX

Typical Greek terraced campsite directly on the beach with beautiful sea views. Simple but clean toilet facilities. Original Greek cuisine, mama cooks with regional products. The first row of pitches by the sea are not available for CCA.

On the road from Igoumenitsa to Plataria. First campsite on the right, 7 km beyond Igoumenitsa. Clearly signposted.

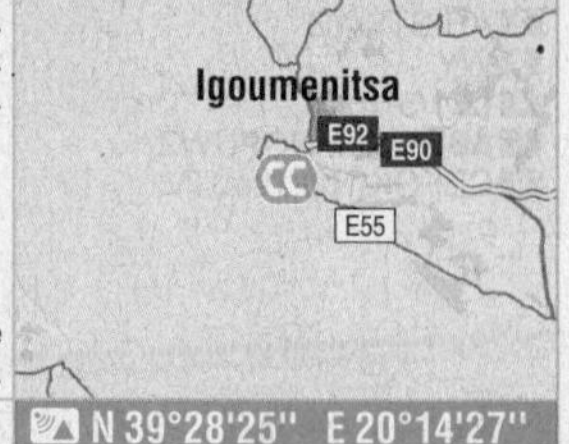

CC € 23 *1/4-3/6 1/9-30/10*

N 39°28'25'' E 20°14'27''

Sikia, GR-63072 / Macedonia

857

Camping Melissi
+30 23 75 04 16 31
1/5 - 30/9
info@camping-melissi.gr

1,5ha 70T(54-100m²) 6A

1 ACDIKLMNOQRS
2 AGNSXYZ
3 AWY
4 (Q+S 1/5-15/9)
5 AGIJKLMNOPUVWZ
6 CEFGK(N 6km)PT

In the south of the beautiful peninsula Sithonia, you'll find an endless sandy beach and bay with crystal-clear water. Quiet campsite with excellent sanitory facilities. Opposite the holy Mount Athos. Pitches with sun and shade, with sea-view.

Located to the east of Sithonia, 7 km south of Sarti. Indicated by 'Sikia Beach' signs on the coast road. Then well signposted on the asphalt road beside the beach. Follow campsite signs.

CC € 21 *1/5-30/6 1/9-29/9* ***10=9***

N 40°02'45'' E 23°59'05''

Stoupa, GR-24024 / Peloponnese

858

Camping Kalogria
Barbezea Nicos 29
+30 27 21 07 73 19
1/4 - 20/11
campingkalogria@yahoo.gr

2ha 102T(50-120m²) 16A

1 ACDIKLMNORS
2 AGJLSUWXYZ
3 WY
4 (Q)(R 1/6-31/10)
(T 15/6-25/10)(Z 1/6-15/10)
5 AGIJKLMNOPUW
6 CEFGK(N 0,25km)PV

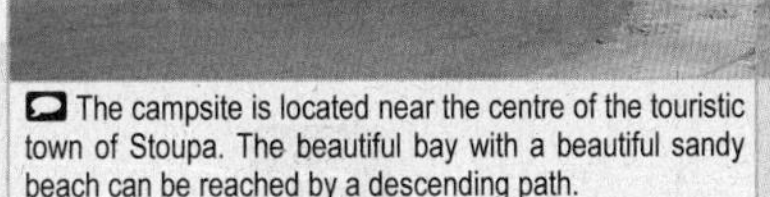

The campsite is located near the centre of the touristic town of Stoupa. The beautiful bay with a beautiful sandy beach can be reached by a descending path.

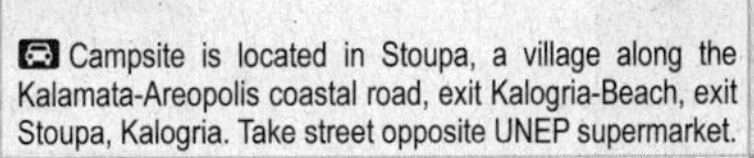

Campsite is located in Stoupa, a village along the Kalamata-Areopolis coastal road, exit Kalogria-Beach, exit Stoupa, Kalogria. Take street opposite UNEP supermarket.

CC € 21 *1/4-15/6 14/9-31/10*

N 36°50'58'' E 22°15'32''

Tiros/Arcadia, GR-22029 / Peloponnese

859

Zaritsi Camping
+30 27 57 04 14 29
1/4 - 15/11
campingzaritsi@gmail.com

3ha 120T(50-120m²) 16A

1 ACDIKLMNOPQRS
2 HJNPSUVWXYZ
3 LPWY
4 (Q+R)(T 1/5-15/11)
(U+X+Y 1/5-31/10)(Z)
5 AGIJKLMNOPUXZ
6 ACEFGJ(N 4km)PV

The campsite is located on a sun-drenched pebble beach in Zaritsi bay. The site is run by a super-friendly family that wants your stay to be great. Spacious pitches with natural and artificial shade. You can enjoy a delicious meal in the restaurant.

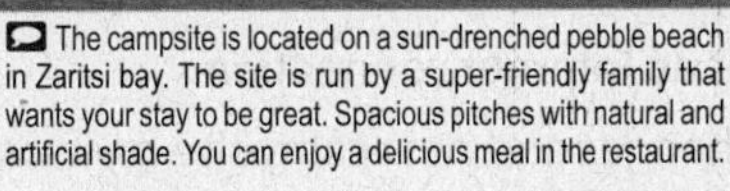

From south Gythio/Monemvasia direction Nafplion 4 km after Tiros right at campsite sign/flags. From Nafplio to Gythio/Monemvasio 4 km before Tiros left sharp bend. Attention SatNav gives detour at entrance.

CC € 21 *1/4-30/6 1/9-15/11*

N 37°16'12'' E 22°50'34''

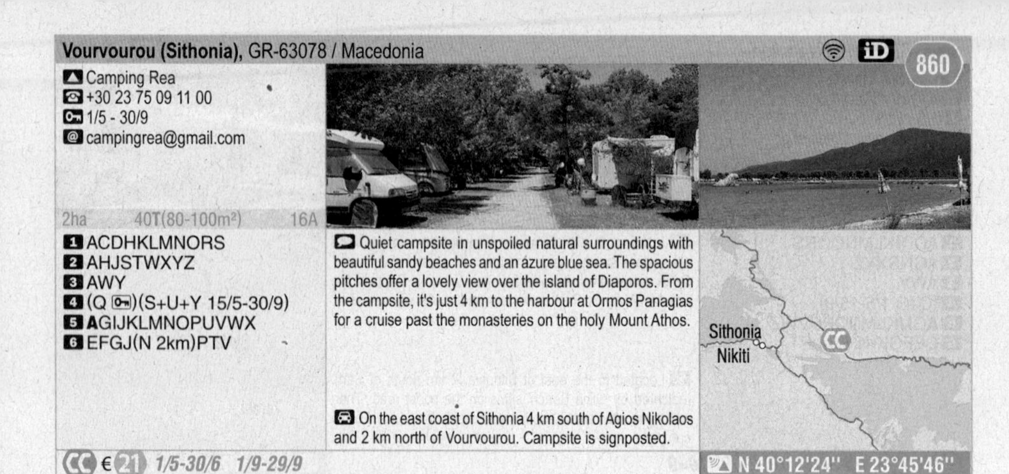

Vourvourou (Sithonia), GR-63078 / Macedonia — 860

Camping Rea
+30 23 75 09 11 00
1/5 - 30/9
campingrea@gmail.com

2ha 40T(80-100m²) 16A

1 ACDHKLMNORS
2 AHJSTWXYZ
3 AWY
4 (Q)(S+U+Y 15/5-30/9)
5 **A**GIJKLMNOPUVWX
6 EFGJ(N 2km)PTV

Quiet campsite in unspoiled natural surroundings with beautiful sandy beaches and an azure blue sea. The spacious pitches offer a lovely view over the island of Diaporos. From the campsite, it's just 4 km to the harbour at Ormos Panagias for a cruise past the monasteries on the holy Mount Athos.

On the east coast of Sithonia 4 km south of Agios Nikolaos and 2 km north of Vourvourou. Campsite is signposted.

CC € 21 *1/5-30/6 1/9-29/9*

N 40°12'24'' E 23°45'46''

CampingCard ACSI app

All CampingCard ACSI campsites in one handy app

- Can be expanded to include more than 9,000 checked motorhome pitches
- Can be used without an internet connection
- Free updates with changes and new campsite reviews
- Book quickly and easily, also when travelling

www.campingcard.com/app

United Kingdom

Capital: London
Currency: British pound
Time zone: UTC +0, UTC +1 (March to October)
Language: English
International dialling code: +44
Alcohol limit: 0.8‰, in Scotland 0.5‰
Emergency number: police, fire brigade and ambulance: 112
Tap water: safe to drink

United Kingdom: beautiful countryside, style and tradition

The campsites in the United Kingdom are spread throughout the four different sections of the United Kingdom: England, Wales, Scotland and Northern Ireland. Each of these areas has its own characteristics. A round trip is made all the more attractive by the relatively short distances to travel.

Highlands and dense forests

The various regions are very diverse, from the untouched Scottish highlands to the ancient, dense forests and swamps in protected nature reserves in the south of England. But one thing the regions all have in common: the culture and the atmosphere is unmistakeably 'different' from the continent of Europe. You will become familiar with the typical British culture and traditions at each campsite in the United Kingdom! Many of the campsites in England and Wales look like national parks, and sometimes you actually are the guest of a lord of the castle on an estate that is hundreds of years old.

To the pub

What you must not miss out on, under any circumstances, is a visit to the local pub, or an afternoon of shopping in a sleepy, mediaeval town or a fashionable warehouse in London. And then, the next day, follow a meandering country road between hedges and rock walls in search of a place to picnic in the lovely countryside or go for a walk along a steep rocky coast.

En route

Filling up

Unleaded petrol (Premium Unleaded 95 and Super Unleaded 98) and diesel are widely available. LPG is reasonably available. To fill up with LPG, the Bajonet connector is usually used, although some fuelling stations use the European connection (ACME). Fuelling stations along motorways are open 24 hours a day, and elsewhere fuelling stations are often open at least from 7:00 to 22:00. More and more unmanned petrol stations and autofuel terminals are available. A reserve can of fuel is prohibited in the Channel tunnel and on ferries.

Charging

There are plenty pf public charging stations in the United Kingdom and Northern Ireland. However, thinly populated areas do not yet have a full-service network.

"In general, tidy campsites, beautiful views and friendly staff."

Mr P. Gommers, inspector 781

Roads and traffic

England has an extensive and well-maintained road network and many motorways. Wales, Scotland and Northern Ireland do not have as many motorways, and the road network is restricted in mountainous areas and on the islands. Caution! You may encounter tractors and cyclists on dual carriageways (motorways, A-roads). Rural areas have many narrow roads bordered by hedges or walls with special passing places every few kilometres.
Keep in mind that the distances on signs are given in miles: 1 mile = approximately 1.6 km.

Ferries

Information about crossing times, departure times and rates can be found at ferry companies such as brittanyferries.com, dfds.com, poferries.com and stenaline.com. Rates depend on the season and departure time. Reserving tickets on time is recommended. Ask the ferry company beforehand if gas bottles may be transported on the boat. Taking fuel in a reserve can on the boat is prohibited.

The Channel tunnel

A good alternative to the ferry is the train via the Channel tunnel. If your car has an LPG tank, your car will not be allowed on the train through the Channel tunnel. Special requirements apply for built-in gas containers in motorhomes or caravans. Portable gas containers are usually allowed, but they must be reported. For more information: eurotunnel.com.

Traffic regulations

In the United Kingdom and Northern Ireland, you must drive on the left side of the road. Low beam headlights are mandatory when it is dark, in tunnels and when visibility is less than 100 metres. Most crossings have signs that indicate right of way ('stop' or 'give way') and/or markings indicating priority (double white line). If none of these are present, there are no general rules for priority and you must be very cautious, always giving right of way when in doubt. Traffic on the roundabout (which comes from the right!) has priority over approaching traffic unless otherwise indicated.
You may not hold a telephone while in the driver's seat, even if you are not driving at the time (handsfree calling is permitted). Children younger

than 12 years of age or shorter than 1.35 metres must be in a child's seat.
You may use the function of your navigation software that warns of speed cameras or average speed checks. Winter tyres are not mandatory.

Special regulations

If you are driving a car with the steering wheel on the left, in order not to blind oncoming traffic, the headlights of your car must be adjusted or partially taped off (with, for example, headlight stickers from visitbritainshop.com).
Smoking in a car is prohibited if a child under the age of 18 is present.
A device with a screen (other than a navigation device) may not be in the driver's field of vision. You may only enter a crossing that has a section with yellow diagonal lines (a 'box junction') if you can pass through it without stopping. Cities have 'red routes': roads with a red stripe along the side that indicates that stopping is prohibited.
You may not park on roads with a double or continuous white line in the centre.

Mandatory equipment

It is recommended that you take along a warning triangle, safety vest and first-aid box.

Caravan and motorhome

A motorhome or car-caravan combination may be a maximum of 4 metres high, 2.55 metres wide and 18.75 metres long (the caravan itself may be a maximum of 7 metres long, or 12 metres if the vehicle pulling has a maximum mass of more than 3.5 tonnes). On motorways with more than two lanes per direction, you may not drive in the rightmost lane with a caravan; the same applies for a motorhome that weighs more than 3.5 tonnes.
Driving with a caravan or motorhome can be difficult on narrow and hilly roads in some parts

of the United Kingdom. This must be taken into account when deciding on a route. Use a good road map in addition to your navigation.

> *"Friendly and helpful people, a surprising culture, island culture, beautiful landscapes and easy to communicate."*
>
> Mr H. Fennis, inspector 1091

Cycling

A bicycle helmet is not mandatory. You may not transport a passenger on the baggage rack (but may transport a child in a child's seat). Cycling on a 'dual carriageway' is permitted unless otherwise indicated.

Toll

Most motorways in the United Kingdom and Northern Ireland are toll-free. You must pay toll on the M6 north of Birmingham, on the M25 at the Dartford Crossing near London and for some bridges and tunnels. In the weekend, at night and in some sections, there is no toll. For more information: gov.uk/uk-toll-roads. At the Dartford Crossing (the London M25 ring road), it is no longer possible to pay at toll houses. You must pay beforehand or after the fact (within 24 hours) via internet. If you do not, a hefty fine will follow. For more information: gov.uk/government/collections/dart-charge.

Environmental zones

To promote the air quality, London has set up a Low Emission Zone (LEZ) and an Ultra Low Emission Zone (ULEZ). The requirements within the LEZ do not apply for standard cars, but they do apply for certain motorhomes and minibuses. The stricter requirements for the ULEZ also apply to standard cars, especially diesel-powered and older petrol vehicles. For more information: tfl.gov.uk/modes/driving If you are planning to go to London in your motorhome, you must register your vehicle with Transport for London (TfL) at tfl.gov.uk. Not registering means a fine. London also has a Congestion Charge if you drive in this zone. The rate is £ 15. It is simplest to pay online via tfl.gov.uk/modes/driving/pay-to-drive-in-london.

Breakdown and accident

It is recommended that you place your warning triangle at least 45 metres behind your car. Placing a warning triangle on the motorway itself is prohibited. All passengers are advised to wear a safety vest. If you have had a breakdown, call the alarm number of your breakdown assistance insurer. You can also call a British emergency breakdown service, such as 0800 88 77 66 (AA), or a Northern Ireland emergency breakdown service, such as +353 1 649 7460 (AA Ireland).

It is an offence to stand still on the hard shoulder because of an empty fuel tank. It is mandatory to report to the police when colliding with an animal (such as a sheep or dog).

Camping

Camping is popular in the United Kingdom and Northern Ireland and there are many campsites. The number of amenities at these sites can differ greatly.

Free camping, outside of the campsites, is permitted in Scotland. In the rest of the United Kingdom and Northern Ireland, you need consent from the land owner. Camping in the verge and in parking places are prohibited. There is often an extra charge for an extra small tent or awning.
The difference between a 'campsite' and a 'touring park' is that the former is somewhat larger and has more permanent pitches for mobile homes. 'Touring parks' are for people with their own tent or caravan. Tents are not allowed at 'Caravan Parks'. A different connecting nipple is often needed to fill gas bottles that have been taken along. In addition, an adapter is often needed for power connections.

Cullompton, GB-EX15 2DT / England (South West) — 861

Forest Glade Holiday Park****
Near Kentisbeare
+44 14 04 84 13 81
17/3 - 15/11
enquiries@forest-glade.co.uk

6ha 81T(120-140m²) 10-16A CEE

1 ACDIKLMNOQRS
2 BISUVWXYZ
3 CDILOPSU
4 (F+H)N(Q+S+U)
5 ABCDEFGHIJKLMNOPQRUWXYZ
6 ACDEFGKLM(N 9,5km)OPU

Quiet, family-run caravan park in a forest clearing with level, sheltered pitches and indoor swimming pool. Forest walks from the park, shop with off-licence and take-away food.

Do not use Satnav! Site accessible from North Honiton, direction Dunkeswell and after ±4.5 km follow brown camping signs. Cars from M5 take exit 28, A373 dir. Honiton, left just past Keepers Cottage Inn. Campsite 4 km up the hill.

CC € 23 18/3-29/3 14/4-24/5 2/6-15/7 1/9-15/11

N 50°51'31'' W 03°16'41''

Dartmouth, GB-TQ9 7DQ / England (South West) — 862

Woodlands Grove Car. & Camping*****
Blackawton
+44 18 03 71 25 98
22/3 - 3/11
holiday@woodlandsgrove.com

24ha 325T(100-120m²) 10A CEE

1 ACDIKLMNOQRS
2 JLMNSUVXYZ
3 ACDEGIKPRSU
4 (G 27/5-31/8)M (Q+R+U+V+X)
5 ABDEFGIJKLMNPQRUWXYZ
6 ACFKOPUV

Set in stunning countryside, a few minutes from picturesque Dartmouth, South Devon coastal path and National Trust properties. Hidden in the valley below is Woodlands Leisure Park with Falconry Centre and Zoo-Farm. Families, grandparents and couples love this perfect location.

Leave A38 at exit Buckfastleigh/Totnes; A384 becomes 385 past Totnes; follow brown Woodlands Leisure Park signs (not your SatNav). On the A3122 direction Dartmouth.

CC € 27 22/3-28/3 1/4-2/5 6/5-23/5 2/6-14/7 1/9-3/11

N 50°21'24'' W 03°40'19''

Dawlish (Devon), GB-EX6 8RP / England (South West) — 863

Cofton Holidays*****
Church Road
+44 16 26 89 01 11
1/1 - 31/12
info@coftonholidays.co.uk

80ha 104T(90-120m²) 10-16A CEE

1 ACDIKLMNOQRS
2 JLMNSVWXYZ
3 ACDGIKNTUVW
4 (C 19/5-17/9)(F) (H 19/5-17/9)LMN (Q+S+U+V+Y+Z)
5 ABDEFGHIJKLMNOPQRUWXYZ
6 BCEFGHJKLM(N 3km) OPSTUV

A large luxury campsite with excellent facilities, divided into several separate fields with level and sloping sections in an undulating landscape.

From Exeter, on M5 exit 30, take the A379 towards Dawlish. 2 km past Starcross service station on the right of the road. Then another 1 km. Campsite located on the left. Signposted.

CC € 23 1/3-23/5 1/6-12/7 30/8-31/10

N 50°36'46'' W 03°27'38''

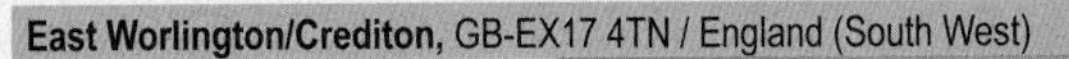

East Worlington/Crediton, GB-EX17 4TN / England (South West) — 864

Yeatheridge Farm Car. & Cp. Park****
+44 18 84 86 03 30
15/3 - 7/10
info@yeatheridge.co.uk

10ha 113T(80-200m²) 16A CEE

1 ACD**I**KLMNOQ**RS**
2 LMNSUVWXYZ
3 ADE**G**IPSUW
4 (F+H)J (Q+S+U+V+X+Y+Z)
5 **AB**DEFGHIJKLMNOPQRUWZ
6 CEFHK(N 5km)O**P**SUV

Comfortable farm campsite in undulating landscape of farmland and meadows. With a lovely indoor pool and a spacious restaurant and bar. The small town of Tiverton is nearby and so are the national parks of Devon. The stunning Arlington Court (NT) is about 35 km away.

Take exit 27 on the M5 then A361 towards Tiverton. Via A396 (south) to B3137 direction Witheridge. B3042 before Witheridge. Campsite 5 km on the left.

A361 · Witheridge · A377 · Cheriton Fitzpaine · North Tawton · A3072

CC € 21 15/3-28/3 15/4-30/4 6/5-23/5 3/6-30/6 4/9-30/9

N 50°53'12" W 03°45'04"

Ecclefechan/Lockerbie, GB-DG11 1AS / Scotland — 865

Hoddom Castle Caravan Park*****
Hoddom
+44 15 76 30 02 51
15/3 - 15/11
enquiries@hoddoMcastle.co.uk

11ha 63T(60-75m²) 16A CEE

1 ACD**I**KLMNOQS
2 CILNSUVWXY
3 C**FG**IKRSU**W**
4 (A 1/5-30/9) (Q+R+T+U+X+Z)
5 **AB**DGHIJKLMNOP**Q**RUWXYZ
6 BCEFGH(N 8km)OPTU

Wonderfully landscaped family campsite on an old castle estate. Amenities in the castle's outbuildings. Perfect stopover on the way to the north of Scotland.

M74, exit 19 to Ecclefechan. Drive through the village. Take B725 towards Dalton at the church. The entrance to the campsite is 3 km further and is signposted.

A709 · Lockerbie · A75 · Annan · Eastriggs

CC € 21 1/5-15/6 1/9-30/9

N 55°02'38" W 03°19'26"

Hayle, GB-TR27 5AW / England (South West) — 866

Beachside Holiday Park****
Lethlean Lane
+44 17 36 75 30 80
23/3 - 2/11
reception@beachside.co.uk

14,8ha 89T(110m²) 10-16A CEE

1 ACDGKLMNOQRS
2 AGJLNSTWX
3 AC**G**HIPSUY
4 (C+H+Q+S+U 29/4-29/9) (Y)(Z 29/4-29/9)
5 **AB**CDFGHIJMNOPQRUWZ
6 ACEFGHJ(N 2,5km)**P**TU

This campsite is in the dunes on the bay of St. Ives, 5 minutes from a beautiful sandy beach. With a heated outdoor pool, little shop, and bar and takeaway. No dogs allowed.

Coming from the north exit A30 in Hayle and head towards the centre. Continue straight on over two roundabouts then take the 1st road on the right. The campsite is signposted there.

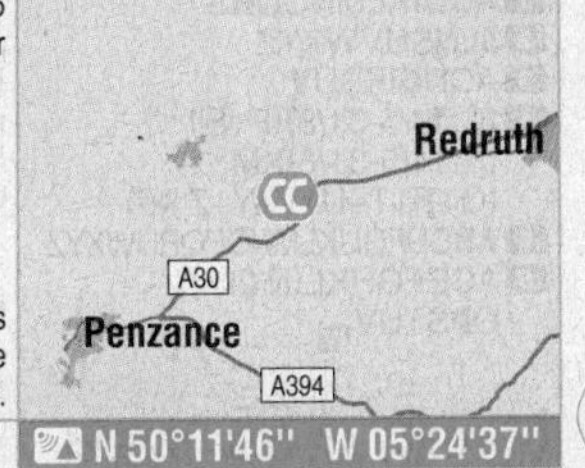

CC € 25 23/3-24/5 1/6-21/6 31/8-1/11

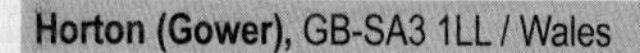

Horton (Gower), GB-SA3 1LL / Wales

867

Bank Farm Leisure, Camp. & Car. Park
+44 17 92 68 72 05
1/3 - 31/12
enquiries@bankfarmleisure.co.uk

30ha 230T(80-120m²) 10A CEE

1 ACDIKLMNQRS
2 AGJLNQRSX
3 CGIOPWY
4 (E+H+Q)(S 1/3-31/10) (T+U+V+X+Z)
5 ABDGIJMNPQUWZ
6 DEFHJK(N 2km)OPV

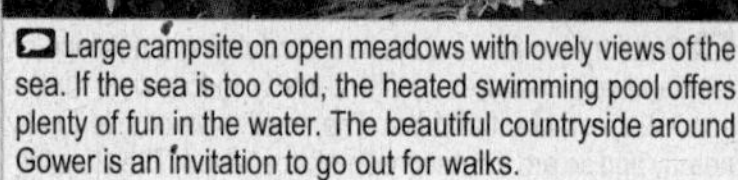

Large campsite on open meadows with lovely views of the sea. If the sea is too cold, the heated swimming pool offers plenty of fun in the water. The beautiful countryside around Gower is an invitation to go out for walks.

On the A4118 Killay-Port Eynon, just before Port Eynon, turn left towards Horton. Then follow the signs for the campsite. This is recommended over your navigation system. The roads it selects are too narrow.

Gowerton
Waunarlwydd

CC € 25 1/3-28/3 2/4-30/4 7/5-26/5 4/6-30/6 1/9-31/12

N 51°33'02'' W 04°12'15''

Looe, GB-PL13 2JR / England (South West)

868

Tencreek Holiday Park****
Polperro Road
+44 15 03 26 24 47
1/1 - 31/12
reception@tencreek.co.uk

5,5ha 250T(100-120m²) 10A CEE

1 ACDEIKLMNPQRS
2 AJLPRSVWXYZ
3 CGIKPSU
4 (F+H+R)(T+U 1/4-30/11) (V 1/4-31/10)(Y+Z 1/4-30/11)
5 ABCDFGHIJKLMNOPQRUWXYZ
6 CDEFGJKM(N 1,5km) OPTUV

Large campsite with many amenities. Beautiful surroundings, nice villages like Looe and Polperro. Many activities are organised. The campsite has plenty of indoor space, so there is always entertainment, even when the weather is bad.

A38 Plymouth-Bodmin, A390 direction St. Austell, then B3359 direction Looe/Polperro until T-junction with A387, then turn left A387 direction Looe. Signposted for the last 3 km.

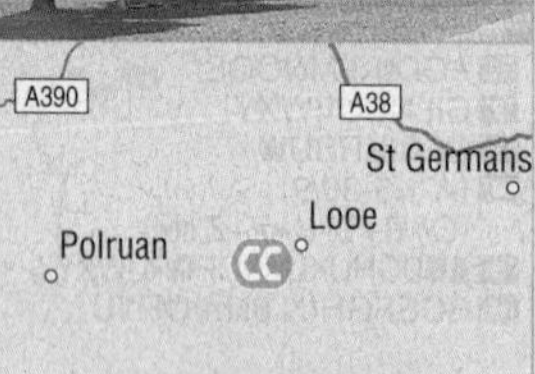

CC € 27 6/4-23/5 3/6-15/7 2/9-27/12

N 50°20'47'' W 04°29'00''

Paignton, GB-TQ4 7PF / England (South West)

869

Whitehill Country Park*****
Stoke Road
+44 18 03 78 23 38
9/2 - 13/12
info@whitehill-park.co.uk

8ha 180T(60-120m²) 16A CEE

1 ACDIKLMNOQRS
2 JLNSUVWXYZ
3 ACDGIKSUV
4 (C 14/5-31/8)(F) (H 14/5-31/8)KM (Q+R+T+U+V+Y+Z)
5 ABCDFGIJKLMNOPQRUWXYZ
6 ACEFGHKL(N 2km) OPSTUV

Well-maintained, comfortable and quiet campsite with many facilities. Panoramic views of the surrounding hills. Heated outdoor swimming pool with whirlpool and paddling pool from May to August, heated indoor swimming pool during the campsite's opening hours. Lovely restaurant with outdoor seating.

From Exeter take the M5 then A38. A380 driving south to Paignton. Then follow the A385 to 'Parkers Arms'. Stoke Road to campsite. Follow brown campsite signs.

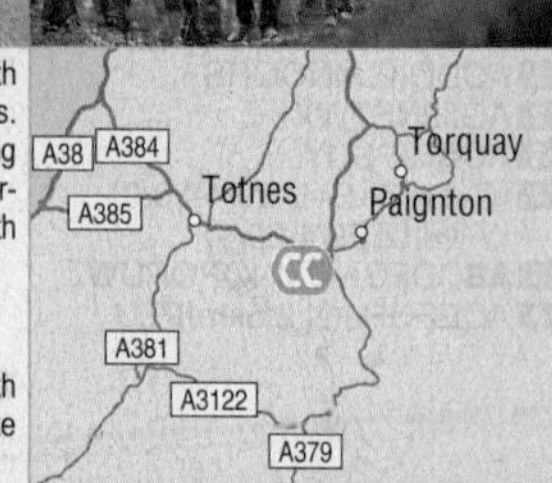

CC € 25 9/2-28/3 12/4-2/5 7/5-23/5 2/6-4/7 2/9-17/10 3/11-13/12

N 50°25'05'' W 03°36'32''

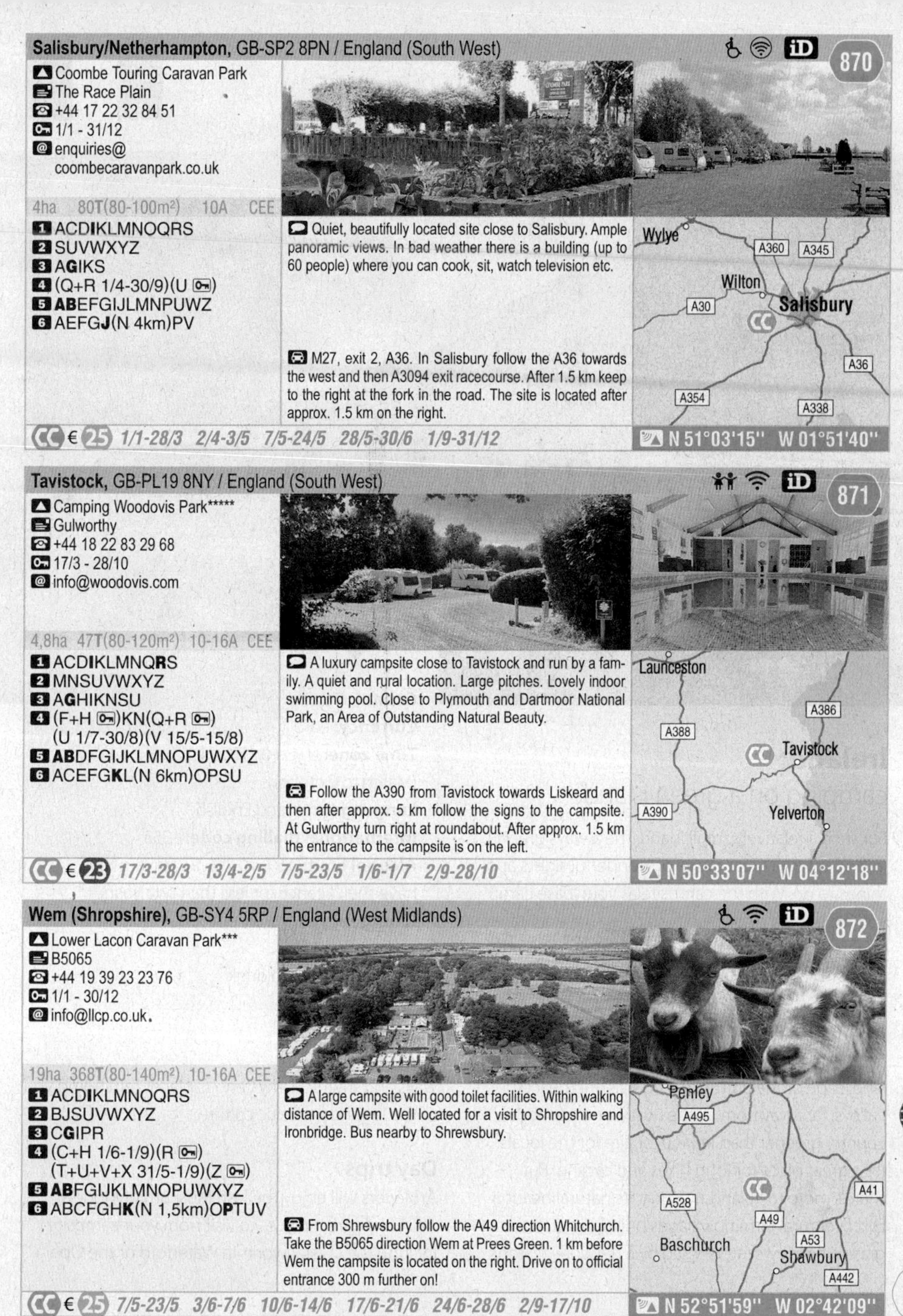

Salisbury/Netherhampton, GB-SP2 8PN / England (South West) — 870

Coombe Touring Caravan Park
The Race Plain
+44 17 22 32 84 51
1/1 - 31/12
enquiries@coombecaravanpark.co.uk

4ha 80**T**(80-100m²) 10A CEE

1 ACD**I**KLMNOQRS
2 SUVWXYZ
3 A**G**IKS
4 (Q+R 1/4-30/9)(U)
5 **AB**EFGIJLMNPUWZ
6 AEFG**J**(N 4km)PV

Quiet, beautifully located site close to Salisbury. Ample panoramic views. In bad weather there is a building (up to 60 people) where you can cook, sit, watch television etc.

M27, exit 2, A36. In Salisbury follow the A36 towards the west and then A3094 exit racecourse. After 1.5 km keep to the right at the fork in the road. The site is located after approx. 1.5 km on the right.

CC € 25 *1/1-28/3 2/4-3/5 7/5-24/5 28/5-30/6 1/9-31/12*

N 51°03'15'' W 01°51'40''

Tavistock, GB-PL19 8NY / England (South West) — 871

Camping Woodovis Park*****
Gulworthy
+44 18 22 83 29 68
17/3 - 28/10
info@woodovis.com

4,8ha 47**T**(80-120m²) 10-16A CEE

1 ACD**I**KLMNQ**R**S
2 MNSUVWXYZ
3 A**G**HIKNSU
4 (F+H)KN(Q+R)
(U 1/7-30/8)(V 15/5-15/8)
5 **AB**DFGIJKLMNOPUWXYZ
6 ACEFG**K**L(N 6km)OPSU

A luxury campsite close to Tavistock and run by a family. A quiet and rural location. Large pitches. Lovely indoor swimming pool. Close to Plymouth and Dartmoor National Park, an Area of Outstanding Natural Beauty.

Follow the A390 from Tavistock towards Liskeard and then after approx. 5 km follow the signs to the campsite. At Gulworthy turn right at roundabout. After approx. 1.5 km the entrance to the campsite is on the left.

CC € 23 *17/3-28/3 13/4-2/5 7/5-23/5 1/6-1/7 2/9-28/10*

N 50°33'07'' W 04°12'18''

Wem (Shropshire), GB-SY4 5RP / England (West Midlands) — 872

Lower Lacon Caravan Park***
B5065
+44 19 39 23 23 76
1/1 - 30/12
info@llcp.co.uk

19ha 368**T**(80-140m²) 10-16A CEE

1 ACD**I**KLMNOQRS
2 BJSUVWXYZ
3 C**G**IPR
4 (C+H 1/6-1/9)(R)
(T+U+V+X 31/5-1/9)(Z)
5 **AB**FGIJKLMNOPUWXYZ
6 ABCFGH**K**(N 1,5km)O**P**TUV

A large campsite with good toilet facilities. Within walking distance of Wem. Well located for a visit to Shropshire and Ironbridge. Bus nearby to Shrewsbury.

From Shrewsbury follow the A49 direction Whitchurch. Take the B5065 direction Wem at Prees Green. 1 km before Wem the campsite is located on the right. Drive on to official entrance 300 m further on!

CC € 25 *7/5-23/5 3/6-7/6 10/6-14/6 17/6-21/6 24/6-28/6 2/9-17/10*

N 52°51'59'' W 02°42'09''

Ireland

Capital: Dublin
Currency: euro
Time zone: UTC +0, UTC +1 (March to October)
Language: Irish and English
International dialling code: +353
Alcohol limit: 0.5‰; 0.2‰ for drivers who have their licence for less than two years
Emergency number: police, fire brigade and ambulance: 112
Tap water: safe to drink

Ireland:
camping on a green island

For such a relatively small island, the always green Ireland offers a great range of wonderful sights and things to do. With the campsite as your 'base camp', you have every opportunity to enjoy the beautiful countryside, explore the rugged coastline and visit the many fascinating towns and cities.

Idyllic green landscapes

Steep rocky coastal cliffs, the surreal natural landscape of the Burren, rolling hills and peaceful valleys, far away from all the hustle and bustle. No country greener than Ireland, or Éire for the locals. It's a great place for long hikes and cycling. But there's more to Ireland than just its natural beauty! Discover rural farming villages built from stone, grassy meadows intersected by a network of stone walls and mythical, mysterious places reminding you of the legendary Celtic culture.

Day trips

Art lovers will enjoy the Irish Museum of Modern Art. Other great places to visit from your campsite include the crystal works in Waterford or the Opera

House in Belfast. The cities on this beautiful isle are a reflection of Irish traditions and folklore. Dublin, the country's capital, is particularly regarded as a cultural centre and is perfect for a city trip.
St. Patrick's Cathedral, the largest church in Ireland, boasts a wonderful collection of paintings and sculptures. One of the oldest books in the world, the Book of Kells, is on display in Trinity College.

"Ireland: a wonderful diversity of nature, forests, mountains and rugged coastlines with friendly people who are always up for a chat in the pub."
Mrs M. Harmsen-Kunnen, inspector 51

Guinness and whiskey

Your Irish camping holiday wouldn't be complete without a lovely pint of Guinness in one of the many Irish pubs. There are thousands in Dublin alone and you can hear live music from almost every tavern and on every corner. After all, song and dance are deeply rooted in the Irish tradition. Whiskey is another drink the Irish are famous for. Why not visit a whiskey distillery to see with your own eyes how the different types are made?

En route

Filling up

In Ireland you can only get unleaded petrol with octane number 95 (Regular/Premium Unleaded); there is no Super Plus 98. Diesel is widely available and LPG is only available to a limited extent. To fill up your LPG tank, you use a Europa connection (ACME). Fuelling stations are open from 7:30 am to 8:00 pm. In larger cities and along motorways they are usually open all day and night. Make sure you have enough fuel in your tank when driving on the motorways, as the fuelling stations can be quite far apart.
If your car has an LPG tank, you will not be allowed to drive your car through the Channel Tunnel. Special requirements apply to built-in gas containers in motorhomes and caravans. Portable gas containers are allowed but must be reported. More information: eurotunnel.com.

Charging

The network of charging points doesn't cover the entire island yet, so remember to plan your journey well.

Ferry services

Information on ferry times, departures and fares are available from ferry service companies such as brittanyferries.com, irishferries.com, poferries.com and stenaline.com. Fares vary according to season and the departure time. We advise booking early to guarantee a spot.
Check with the operator whether gas bottles can be taken on board.
It is prohibited to take fuel in a reserve tank on the ferry.

Traffic regulations

In Ireland you drive on the left-hand side of the road. Low beam headlights are mandatory in poor visibility, after dark and in tunnels. Traffic coming from the right has the right of way at an equal intersection. When approaching a T-junction, traffic on the main road always has the right of way. Vehicles on roundabouts (coming from the right!) have the right of way over approaching traffic, unless otherwise indicated.
It is prohibited to hold a telephone while behind the wheel, not even when standing still at the lights (hands-free calling is permitted). Children who are under 1.50 metres and weigh less than 36 kilos must sit in a child seat. Winter tyres are not mandatory.

Roads and traffic

National roads (indicated by the letter 'N') and secondary roads ('R') generally have a good road surface, but are narrower than most of our roads. The countryside has many narrow roads and lanes lined with hedges or stone walls with special passing places every few kilometres. You have to drive in a counter-clockwise direction on the Ring of Kerry tourist route with its narrow roads. Please note that even though Ireland uses kilometres, distances on signposts are still often given in miles: 1 mile = about 1.6 kilometres.

Special regulations

If you're driving a left-hand drive car, i.e. your steering on the left, you need to adjust the headlights so that they don't shine up at oncoming traffic, or cover them partially (e.g. with headlight stickers from visitbritainshop.com).
You may only drive onto an intersection with a box junction (diagonal stripes) if you can pass it without stopping. Smoking inside vehicles with passengers under the age of 18 is prohibited. Parking is forbidden along a yellow line, among other things.

There are level train crossings in Ireland with a gate, which you need to open and close yourself (read the instructions carefully and keep paying attention).

Mandatory equipment

You are advised to carry a reflecting warning triangle, at least two high-vis vests, a first-aid kit, a fire extinguisher, a torch and spare bulbs for your vehicle.

Caravan and motorhome

A motorhome or car-caravan combination may not be higher than 4.65 metres, more than 2.55 metres wide and over 18.75 metres long (the caravan itself may not be longer than 12 metres).

Cycling

Wearing a bicycle helmet is not mandatory.

Toll

Toll is payable on a number of bridges and roads. You can pay in cash on most toll roads. On the M50 around Dublin, you can only pay the toll electronically (cameras register your licence plate). You are required to pay the M50 toll at a service station (Payzone) or online at eflow.ie by 8:00 pm the following day. More information: tii.ie, payzone.ie.

Breakdown and accidents

You are advised to place your warning triangle at a safe distance behind the car. All passengers should wear hi-visibility safety vests for extra safety. Don't set up a warning triangle on motorways. If your car or motorhome breaks down, call the emergency number of your breakdown service provider. Alternatively, you can call the Irish roadside assistance (AA Ireland) on +353 1 649 7460. You can also call for roadside assistance on motorways using an orange emergency phone on your side of the carriageway. It is illegal to repair your car on the hard shoulder.

Camping

Most campsites are in the countryside and in coastal areas. Most of the campgrounds are small, straightforward and relatively cheap. Irish campsites often have well-maintained grassy areas and hard-surfaced pitches for caravans, campervans and motorhomes. Camping for free outside campsites is in most cases prohibited in Ireland, except when a landowner specifically grants permission to camp on his or her private property.

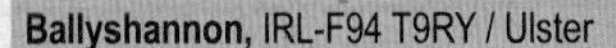

Ballyshannon, IRL-F94 T9RY / Ulster

873

Lakeside Caravan & Camping****
Belleek Road
+353 7 19 85 28 22
1/4 - 1/10
lakesidecentre@eircom.net

2,5ha 98T(30-80m²) 16A CEE

1 ACDIKLMNOQRS
2 AEIJNSVWX
3 CD**G**IKPU
4 (R+T+U+Z)
5 **AB**FGIJKLMNOPUWYZ
6 CEFGHJM(N 0,5km)PTUV

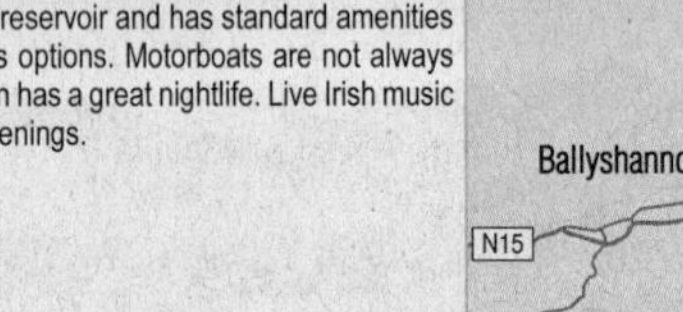

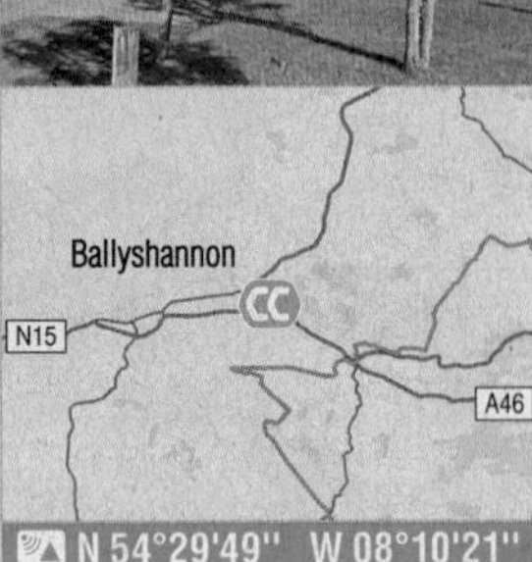

Campsite is by a reservoir and has standard amenities including water sports options. Motorboats are not always allowed. Ballyshannon has a great nightlife. Live Irish music on some Saturday evenings.

On N15 turn onto N3. Follow camping signs on Belleek Rd.

CC € 25 *1/4-1/7*

N 54°29'49'' W 08°10'21''

Tagoat, IRL-Y35 RH76 / Leinster

874

IOAC & Camping Grounds
Sixacre
+353 5 39 18 90 22
20/3 - 31/10
info@ioac.ie

6ha 84T(50-100m²) 10A CEE

1 ACDIKLMNORS
2 SUVWYZ
3 KPU
4 (Q+R)
(T+U 29/3-14/4,3/5-6/10)
5 **AB**DFGHIJMNO**P**UW
6 ACDFGJL(N 3km)P

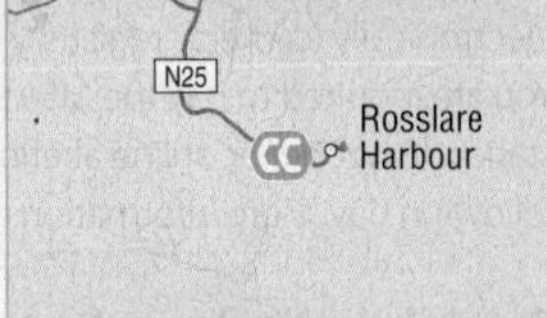

Campsite 3 minutes by car from the ferry in Rosslare. Ideal starting point for exploring the south-east of Ireland, with its famous golden arts and all that Wexford has to offer. Large pitches with separate motorhome pitches. Outdoor opportunities.

From the north N11 to Wexford, then N25 towards Rosslare to Tagoat left of the road. From Rosslare harbour N25 towards Wexford, after 3.4 km turn right.

CC € 27 *29/3-14/4 3/5-7/6 1/9-6/10*

N 52°14'37'' W 06°22'52''

Wicklow, IRL-A67 PK31 / Leinster

875

Wolohan Silver Strand Caravan Park
Dunbur Upper
+353 40 46 94 04
19/4 - 30/9
info@silverstrand.ie

7ha 75T(100-120m²) 10A CEE

1 ACDILMNOQRS
2 AGILNRSUWXY
3 **FG**WY
4 (R 1/6-31/8)
5 **AB**GIJMNO**P**UW
6 EFMOPT

A campsite on a large green field with beautiful views of the Irish Sea. Its own beach, Silver Strand is below. Plenty of peace and space. Close to the town of Wicklow. Rural setting. Less than an hour from Dublin. Rural location.

Via the N11 to Dublin-Wexford, take Wicklow exit. Through Wicklow towards the Coast Road. The campsite is located on the left after about 3 km and is the 2nd campsite on this road. Both sites are called Silverstrand.

CC € 25 *19/4-2/5 6/5-30/5 3/6-3/7 26/8-29/9*

N 52°57'17'' W 06°01'00''

Place name index

A

B

C

D

E

F

G

H

I

J

K

L

M

N

O

P

R

S

T

U

V

W

Z

Naturist camp sites

In this CampingCard guide you will find the following naturist camp sites or camp sites with a naturist section. Be aware that on most of these sites you will need to be a member of a naturist association.

Naturist camp sites

Germany	Mecklenburg-Vorpommern	**Zwenzow** / FKK-Camping Am Useriner See	240
Austria		**Eberndorf** / Naturisten Feriendorf Rutar Lido	304
Hungary		**Balatonberény** / Balatontourist Cp. Naturist Berény	340
Slovenia		**Portoroz** / Kamp Lucija	350
Croatia		**Baska (Krk)** / Bunculuka Camping Resort	358
Croatia		**Punat (Krk)** / Naturist Camp Konobe	374

Partially naturist camp sites

Denmark	**Ejstrup Strand/Brovst** / Tranum Klit Camping	72
Austria	**Pesenthein** / Terrassencamping Pesenthein	314
Slovenia	**Lendava** / Thermal Camping Lendava	349
Slovenia	**Verzej** / Camping Terme Banovci	352

Acknowledgements

2024 • 21th edition
CampingCard ACSI is an ACSI initiative.
This CampingCard ACSI guide is a publication of ACSI Publishing BV
PO Box 34, 6670 AA Zetten, the Netherlands
Telephone +31 (0)488 - 471434
Fax +31 (0)488 - 454210

Printing
westermann druck GmbH
Braunschweig, Germany

Maps
MapCreator BV, 5628 WB Eindhoven
mapcreator.eu/©Here/©Andes

ISBN: 9789493182608

Editor-in-chief
Willeke Verbeek

Editorial staff
Mariska Adriaans, Esther Baks, Gery Boerboom, Judith Brasser, Sophie Conradi, Peter Dellepoort, Rein Driessens, Dianne Hendriks, Sharon Jansen, Maurice van Meteren, Ria Neutel, Irene van der Peijl, Marloes van der Plaats, Mariëlle Rouwenhorst-Küper, Thijs Saat, Ingrid Sevenster, Erik Spikmans, Daniël Uleman, Mandy Wagener

Questions or comments?
For campers:
www.campingcard.com/customerservice
For campsites:
www.campingcard.com/sales

Each year, ACSI inspects almost 10,000 European campsites. Moreover, we stand for quality and that is one of the reasons our logo has become a quality mark as it were. Therefore, at ACSI we would like to hear if a campsite does not meet the description stated in our guide. Or indeed, if the campsite exceeds your expectations.
However, ACSI is in no way involved in the implementation of policy at the inspected campsites. Our strength is our independence above all. Campsite owners themselves decide how things are arranged at their campsite. Consider things such as the hospitality they provide, the quality of the amenities or who your neighbours will be at the campsite. This is beyond ACSI's influence.
If you have suggestions, points for improvement or complaints about a campsite, please first raise the issue at the campsite itself. They usually do all they can to ensure their guests have an enjoyable time, so they deserve the chance to resolve any issues. We cannot handle suggestions or complaints if they have not been discussed with the campsite first.

Translation
Interlingo, Eindhoven
www.interlingo.nl

The information in this guide is based on the situation on October 1st 2023.